THE PAPERS OF DANIEL WEBSTER

CHARLES M. WILTSE, EDITOR-IN-CHIEF

SERIES ONE: CORRESPONDENCE

THE UNIVERSITY PRESS

OF NEW ENGLAND

Sponsoring Institutions

BRANDEIS UNIVERSITY

BROWN UNIVERSITY

CLARK UNIVERSITY

UNIVERSITY OF CONNECTICUT

DARTMOUTH COLLEGE

UNIVERSITY OF NEW HAMPSHIRE

UNIVERSITY OF RHODE ISLAND

TUFTS UNIVERSITY

UNIVERSITY OF VERMONT

The Papers of
Daniel Webster

Correspondence, Volume 7

1850–1852

CHARLES M. WILTSE AND

MICHAEL J. BIRKNER, EDITORS

PUBLISHED FOR

DARTMOUTH COLLEGE BY THE

UNIVERSITY PRESS OF NEW ENGLAND

HANOVER, NEW HAMPSHIRE AND

LONDON, ENGLAND 1986

Library of Congress Catalog Card Number 73-92705

International Standard Book Number 0-87451-323-5

Printed in the United States of America

Library of Congress Cataloging in Publication data
will be found on the last printed page of this book.

The edition of the Papers of Daniel Webster, of which this is volume seven in the Correspondence series, has been made possible through grants from the Program for Editions and Publications of the National Endowment for the Humanities, an independent federal agency, and through the continuing support, both administrative and financial, of the National Historical Publications and Records Commission. The edition is sponsored and published by Dartmouth College.

Contents

For the page number on which each document of the Papers begins, see the Calendar.

A section of illustrations follows page 198

Acknowledgments

The deep indebtedness of the editors to libraries, archives, historical societies, and individual collectors has been many times acknowledged as new volumes of Webster Papers have appeared. As in earlier volumes, the source of each individual letter printed or calendared is indicated by the standard location symbol; to each of these depositories, and the patient men and women who administer them, our most sincere thanks are once again extended.

A number of institutions have continued to supply documents and to answer questions as we have called upon them. Chief among these are the Library of Congress, where manuscript historian John McDonough has been consistently helpful; the Massachusetts Historical Society, especially its director emeritus Stephen T. Riley, librarian John D. Cushing, and senior assistant librarian Robert V. Sparks, who has uncovered a substantial amount of new material for us; the New Hampshire Historical Society: R. Stuart Wallace, director, and William Copely, associate librarian; Phillips Exeter Academy: Edouard L. Desrochers, archivist; the Historical Society of Pennsylvania, for answering many research questions and providing new manuscripts; the New-York Historical Society: Thomas Dunnings, curator of manuscripts; the New York Public Library: John D. Stinson, manuscripts specialist, and Gunther Pohl, division chief, who has been kind enough to provide identifications and sources of information on various residents of New York state in Webster's time; the Buffalo and Erie County Historical Society, where the Fillmore Papers are housed.

For their help with portraits for the entire Correspondence series, we thank the National Portrait Gallery: Mona Dearborn, keeper of the catalog of American portraits; and the National Museum of Art, Inventory of American Paintings: Martha Shipman Andrews, coordinator.

And most of all we are under obligation to Dartmouth's Baker Library, where the project has been housed since its inception. We extend particular thanks to all the reference services staff, especially Patricia A. Carter, in charge of interlibrary loans; Virginia L. Close, Marilyn G. Curphey, Robert D. Jaccaud, Lois A. Krieger, Francis X. Oscadal, Cynthia F. Pawlek, and Robin Wagner-Birkner; to L. Sue Marcoulier, supervisor of circulation services; special collections librarian Stanley W.

Brown, archivist Kenneth C. Cramer, and curator of manuscripts Philip N. Cronenwett.

Among individuals who have aided the project, we are especially grateful to Stephen R. Parkhurst, senior vice president and cashier of the Barnstable County National Bank, for his initiative in securing for us copies of papers in the vaults of the New England Merchants National Bank, Boston, documenting Webster's ties with Franklin Haven, president of the Merchants' Bank, as it was then called; to Dr. George Hamilton, of West Hartford, Connecticut, for providing papers of his ancestor Henry Sargent, who was Webster's secretary at the State Department in 1850–1851; and John R. Morison, of Peterborough, New Hampshire, descendant of George Jacob Abbot, Sargent's successor, whose letters written from Marshfield in October 1852 give a daily account of Webster's last days.

Our debt is equally great to those who have supplied the generous financial support that has kept the project going: the National Endowment for the Humanities, the National Historical Publications and Records Commission, Dartmouth College, and individual donors who have put up matching funds when such were needed.

We wish to express particular appreciation to Helen Augera, program officer, and Kathy Fuller, program specialist in the Endowment's division of research programs; James B. Rhoads, retired archivist of the United States, and Robert M. Warner, who succeeded him; Frank G. Burke, executive director of the National Historical Publications and Records Commission, and Richard N. Sheldon, his assistant; Roger Bruns, director of the publications program, and the research staff: Mary A. Giunta, Sara Dunlap Jackson, and Anne Harris Henry, who over the years have provided us with countless needed documents from the National Archives.

Among those at Dartmouth who have contributed in ways tangible and intangible, we may single out for special mention Leonard M. Rieser, former provost, and Agnar Pytte, his successor in that exacting office; William B. Durant, faculty executive officer emeritus; the associate dean for academic planning and resource development, Gregory M. Prince, who in his former capacity as vice provost added the administration of the Webster Papers to an already overwhelming schedule; and Barbara D. Klunder, assistant to the provost.

Finally we must acknowledge the substantial contribution to this volume of past and present members of the Webster Papers staff, including student research assistants: William A. Cole, Robert Conley, Bruce Martin, Robin Shaffert, and Scott Simmons; assistant editors Rexford D. Sherman and Alan R. Berolzheimer for their compilation and review of the calendar; Wendy B. Tilghman, assistant editor for volume six, and Kenneth R. Stevens, co-editor of the Diplomatic Papers. The labors of Mary V. Anstruther, special assistant to the editor in chief, have been extraordinary. Her commitment to excellence at the Webster Papers has been both a prod and an inspiration. Most of all, for seventeen years, she has been there when it counted.

Introduction

By 1850 sectional tensions, built up over half a century, seemed close to splitting the nation apart. Webster's own perception of the basic differences—social economic and political—between North and South went back at least as far as 1804 [*Correspondence*, 1: 59–60]. He went on record against the extension of slavery in 1819 when he drafted the Boston memorial against the Missouri Compromise [*Speeches and Formal Writings*, 1]; and his justly famous Reply to Hayne of 1830 was a painstaking refutation of the Southern doctrine of state sovereignty. Yet when he reached Washington a few days before Christmas 1849 to take his customary seat in the Senate, Webster seemed almost indifferent to the powerful crosscurrents swirling about the capital. He appeared utterly engrossed in his pursuit of a patronage job for his son Fletcher, and only peripherally aware that the perennial question of slavery was about to engulf the Congress.

Should the territory acquired from Mexico be open to settlement by slaveholders? or should the Wilmot Proviso govern? Should the South be appeased by genuine enforcement of the fugitive slave law that had been on the books since 1793? Should slavery be abolished in the District of Columbia? Should the slave trade between the states be abolished, or restricted? These and similar questions had been before Congress and the country since the close of the Mexican war, but there was an urgency about them now. California, following the discovery of gold early in 1848, had achieved a quick maturity. Her emissaries—two senators and three representatives-elect—were understood to be on the way to Washington, carrying an antislavery constitution and a petition for admission to the Union as a free state. The even balance between North and South that had kept the Senate neutral since the Missouri Compromise would thus be destroyed. Southern leaders, in Congress and out, talked openely of secession should this be allowed to happen. A convention of the slaveholding states had already been called to meet in Nashville in June, perhaps to take the South out of the Union.

Webster was still uncommitted when the aging but still persuasive Henry Clay approached him late in January with the basic elements of the legislation that would set in motion the Compromise of 1850. The Massachusetts senator agreed in principle, but he was not yet convinced that the Union was in danger. Before the end of February, however, his

Southern colleagues had persuaded him that this time they were not bluffing. He entered the debate on March 7 with what he came ultimately to regard as his greatest speech. Somberly he appealed to both sections to accept a compromise solution of the most divisive issue ever faced by the American people. To the extent that he went into detail, he followed Clay's proposals, including the enactment of a new, more rigorous fugitive slave law.

In the Senate the Seventh of March speech [*Speeches and Formal Writings*, 2] was a triumph and may well have been decisive in the ultimate success of the compromise. In the South Webster was lionized for his broad view; but among Free Soilers, and especially the abolitionists of New England, his speech was little less than treason—a sellout to the South for the presidency in 1852. The criticisms stung but did not deter him. Convinced that his truth-telling approach was essential to a settlement of the crisis and a return to normalcy, Webster plunged ahead with increased resolve and vigor. He was active on various fronts. In the Senate he continued his efforts to pass Clay's compromise, either as a package, or, preferably, seriatim in separate bills. At home in Massachusetts he wrote and planted newspaper pieces favorable to compromise, responded to public letters endorsing his speech, and debated in the press with critics.

This phase of the compromise battle ended in July with the death of President Zachary Taylor and the accession of Millard Fillmore, a procompromise Whig from New York. Webster accepted Fillmore's invitation to head a revamped cabinet, and continued from his new position his lifelong fight to strengthen the bonds of union.

Webster reentered the State Department in 1850 as he had returned to the Senate in 1845, with a private "Webster fund" contributed by friends and supporters to supplement his official salary. He was then, as he had been throughout most of his adult life, deeply in debt yet enjoying a lifestyle far beyond his visible means. Even the rather substantial sum raised for him in New York and Boston was not enough to keep him from accepting the most lucrative legal case of his career as counsel for Charles Goodyear in the India rubber patent infringement suit early in 1852 [*Legal Papers*, 3]. The fund was sufficient, however, to enable one hostile congressman to brand him the hireling of private interests. Though immediately denied, the suspicion of improper influence remained with him for the rest of his life—and remains with him still.

Extradition between states was at that time a responsibility of the secretary of state. The fugitive slave law, enacted in September 1850, fell within that category. Webster was soon deeply involved in the return of runaways, especially in his rebellious home state of Massachusetts, where public opinion and many of the local authorities favored the slaves. Ellen and William Craft were spirited away to England; "Shadrach" was snatched from a Boston courtroom and carried to Canada; and those involved in the bloody slave rescue at Christiana, Pennsylvania, could not be convicted. Only in the case of Thomas Sims, arraigned in Boston before Webster's handpicked commissioner, George Ticknor Curtis, was the fugitive actually returned—at a cost to the taxpayers of $20,000.

Webster's unwavering determination to enforce the law seemed, in the eyes of his detractors to be no more than a callous bid for Southern votes. It was, however, completely consistent with his appeal of March 7 for mutual concessions by North and South to save the Union they had jointly created. He was equally adamant in enforcing the terms of the compromise where Southern interests were in jeopardly. The boundary between Texas and New Mexico, for example, was drawn to favor the New Mexican claim, despite Texan threats to send an army into the disputed area.

Although his second term as secretary of state was no less exacting than the first, Webster yet found time and energy for domestic politics. Indeed, upon occasion he adroitly used foreign affairs as an instrument of domestic policy, as he did with the Hülsemann letter and the Thrasher incident [*Diplomatic Papers*, 2]. The compromise little influenced partisan conflict, save perhaps in its tendency to strengthen the opposition. The stern measures taken to enforce the fugitive slave law only increased the strength of the Free Soil party in Massachusetts, where abolitionist Charles Sumner, despite Webster's active opposition, was elected to fill the vacant Senate seat. Fillmore, who favored the compromise, lost control of New York to the rival Seward faction. At the same time, in the more radical states of the South, notably Georgia, South Carolina, and Mississippi, a frankly disunion splinter showed for a time an ominous strength.

Webster continued to urge upon both sides the necessity of compromise, and to deny emphatically that there was or could be any right of peaceable secession. A presidential campaign was meanwhile getting under way. Early moves were made by the secretary's friends about the middle of 1851, and by the end of the year he was unreservedly working for the Whig nomination. President Fillmore had indicated that he would not seek another term, and although his support had not been promised, Webster believed he would have it when the time came. With Fillmore thus sidetracked, only General Winfield Scott stood in the way. But Fillmore's supporters had not given up. The president was popular in the South, and as the Whig convention approached he was persuaded, if not to run, at least not to declare that he was unavailable. Fillmore himself was ambivalent about standing for reelection, but Webster chose to interpret the president's position as favorable to a Webster nomination.

The final result was a comedy of errors. The first ballot in Baltimore gave the combined Webster-Fillmore delegates a clear majority, but no one withdrew, and for another 48 ballots the relative strength of the candidates changed little. On the first ballot Fillmore had 133 votes, Scott 131, and Webster was far behind with 29. Had he asked his delegates early in the balloting to support Fillmore, the president would have been chosen; but he did not yield, and neither did Fillmore. When at last each man offered his delegates to the other, it was too late. Scott's strength began to rise on the 50th ballot and he won the nomination on the 53rd. Webster thus saw his last chance for the coveted office pass by. Scott he believed unfit for the presidency, and he never came out in favor of the Whig ticket. Webster was urged to run as an independent, but he never took the option seriously or encouraged a draft. It is unlikely however, that the outcome would have been different, even if he had. The Democrats named likeable and uncommitted Franklin Pierce of New Hampshire—the northern man with southern principles—who with veteran senator William R. King of Alabama as his running mate overwhelmed the Whig ticket of Scott and navy secretary William A. Graham of North Carolina.

Webster's refusal to support the Whig ticket was not typical, and there may indeed have been some deeply buried physical reason for it. On May 8, 1852, a month before the convention, he was thrown heavily from his carriage, injuring both wrists, but as he assured the president, otherwise unharmed. Between this fall, however, and his death on October 24, his actions were by spells erratic. His aggressive and unwise approach to the Lobos Islands controversy with Peru, and the fisheries dispute with Canada [*Diplomatic Papers*, 2] may have been manifestations of a deeper hurt than anyone perceived at the time.

Webster's last days were marred both by financial troubles and physical debility. A dependable salary combined with substantial earnings as a lawyer and the continuing largesse of friends and associates failed to clear his many debts. Meanwhile he continued to face a heavy diplomatic docket, including delicate negotiations on fisheries with Canada, the Lobos Islands, and efforts to win Mexico's support for a railroad across the Isthmus. He spent most of the summer of 1852 not in Washington but at his beloved Marshfield. He conducted business there, but increasingly his thoughts focused less on statecraft than on personal affairs. As the gravity of his condition became apparent, in early October, he began to put his house in order. He met his end surrounded by family and friends on the morning of October 24, 1852.

PLAN OF WORK

From its inception the Papers of Daniel Webster was planned as an integrated project, using both microfilm and letterpress publication. The persistent pressure of time and the steadily rising cost of book publication were important factors in the choice of the dual media, but the overriding consideration was the desire to bring all of Webster together, without abridgment or gloss, for those who were equipped to use it that way, while providing the less dedicated scholar and the general reader with the essential Webster in convenient annotated form. The microfilm edition, in four different groupings, is as complete as the surviving records permit. Webster's correspondence, including letters received as well as letters sent, together with miscellaneous notes, memoranda, briefs, drafts, formal writings, reports, petitions, and business papers, has been issued with printed guide and index as *The Papers of Daniel Webster* by University Microfilms, Ann Arbor, Michigan. *The Legal Papers of Daniel Webster*, also to be issued with guide and alphabetical list of cases by University Microfilms, consists of records drawn primarily from the county courts of New Hampshire and Massachusetts and from the state and lower federal courts in New England. Records of the Department of State and of the Supreme Court are available on film from the National Archives and Records Service of the General Services Administration, but the user must select for himself the reels that may contain Webster material.

The value of this film, including as it does virtually all known Webster papers, cannot be overstated, but its very magnitude makes it unmanageable. It is relatively expensive, requires special equipment to use, is hard on the eyes, and effectively buries the grains of wheat by mixing them unevenly with an enormous amount of chaff. The user of the film, moreover, must decipher for himself often difficult or faded handwriting. He must search out the identity of persons and the nature of events alluded to, and finally he must rely upon his own judgment as to the significance of the given document. In the letterpress edition all this has been done for him, even to the selection of documents in terms of their significance, by editors totally immersed in the time and place and almost as familiar with the central characters as was Webster himself.

The letterpress edition in effect complements and renders more useful these various microfilm collections, whose very existence has made it possible to select more rigorously the documents important enough to be offered to the larger audience reached by the printed book. Each volume of correspondence, moreover, includes a calendar of letters written in the same time period but not selected for publication. For each of these the microfilm frame number is cited, as is volume and page citation for any document now available only in a printed version. Footnote references are also made to the film wherever appropriate. Undated items spanning the entire *Correspondence* series are for convenience included in *Correspondence* 6, following the regular calendar. Items found subsequent to publication of the appropriate volume are calendared at the end of the *Correspondence* series. For the general reader and for the student of the period rather than of the man, the editors believe the selections will be ample. The biographer, and the scholar pursuing an in-depth study of some segment of the times, will need the film, to which he will find the printed volumes an indispensable annotated guide.

The letterpress edition is being published in four different series, overlapping in time but not in content, in order to make maximum use of subject matter specialists as technical editors. The edition has been planned to fill a total of fourteen volumes, of which seven are correspondence, three are legal papers, two are diplomatic papers, and two are speeches and formal writings.

The present volume, including the period 1850–1852, is the seventh in the *Correspondence* series.

EDITORIAL METHOD

Letters and other documents included in this volume are arranged in chronological sequence, irrespective of whether Webster was the writer or the recipient. The only exception is for letters that were sent as enclosures in later correspondence. These have been placed immediately after the document that they accompanied. Date and point of origin have been placed at the upper right of each letter. If all or part of this information has been supplied by the editors, it appears in square brackets, with a question mark if conjecture. The complimentary close, which in the original manuscripts often takes up three or four lines, has been run continuously with the last line of the text.

All letters are reproduced in full except in rare instances where the only surviving text is incomplete or is from a printed source that did not reproduce it in its entirety. Needless to say, texts from printed sources are used only when the original manuscript has not been found but the letter is of sufficient importance to warrant its inclusion.

The letters themselves have been reproduced in type as nearly as possible the way they were written. Misspellings have been retained without the annoyingly obtrusive "(sic)"; and abbreviations and contractions have been allowed to stand unless the editor feels they will not be readily understood by a present-day reader. In such cases the abbreviation has been expanded, with square brackets enclosing the letters supplied. Punctuation, too, has been left as Webster and his correspondents used it, save only that dashes clearly intended as periods are so written. Superscript letters in abbreviations or contractions have been brought down, but a period is supplied only if the last letter of the abbreviation is not the last letter of the word abbreviated. In all other cases, periods, apostrophes, dashes, and other forms of punctuation have been left as Webster and his contemporaries used them. The ampersand, far more frequently used than the spelled out *and*, has been retained, but diacritical marks over contractions have been omitted even where the contraction itself is retained.

Canceled words or passages that are obvious slips, immediately corrected, have been left out altogether; those that show some change of thought or attitude or have stylistic or psychological implications have been included between angled brackets. Interlineations by the author have been incorporated into the text, but marginal passages, again if by the author, have been treated as postscripts and placed below the signature.

In order to keep explanatory footnotes to a minimum, general notes have been interspersed from time to time with the letters that constitute the text of the volume. These serve to indicate what Webster was doing at a particular time or to explain a sequence of events that may help to clarify subsequent correspondence. Footnotes are used to identify persons, places, events, situations, problems, or other matters that help to understand the context of a particular reference.

Individuals are identified only once, generally the first time they are mentioned. For the convenience of the reader who may have missed this first reference, the appropriate index entry is printed in boldface type. Well-known individuals—those in the *Dictionary of American Biography* or the *Biographical Directory of the American Congress*—have not been identified at all unless the context seems to require it. For those in the *DAB*, the index entry is marked with an asterisk, and with a dagger for those in the *BDAC*. The extent of footnoting has been reduced by adding given names and initials in square brackets where text references are to surnames only.

Immediately following each document is an unnumbered note indicating the provenance of the document and, if appropriate, giving some information about the writer or recipient. Symbols used in these provenance notes are the standard descriptive symbols and the location symbols developed by the Union Catalog Division of the Library of Congress. Those appearing in the present volume have been listed under Abbreviations and Symbols, below.

Webster Chronology, 1850–1852

1850

January 21 Henry Clay seeks Webster's support for a broad-based compromise on sectional issues.

January 29 Clay introduces eight resolutions embodying his compromise proposals.

March 4 Mason reads the dying Calhoun's speech against the compromise.

March 7 Webster argues eloquently for the compromise, including concessions to the South.

March 11 Seward opposes the compromise in terms of a "higher law" than the Constitution.

March 16 Nathaniel Hawthorne's *Scarlet Letter* published.

April 19 Webster named to "Committee of 13," chaired by Clay, to draft compromise measures.

April 19 U.S. and Great Britain agree by Clayton-Bulwer Treaty that neither power will seek exclusive control over an interocean canal.

April 27 The American Collins Line of steamships goes into operation, in competition with the British Cunard Line.

May 8 The Committee of Thirteen reports an omnibus bill admitting California without slavery, providing territorial governments for New Mexico and Utah, resolving the territorial dispute between Texas and New Mexico, and strengthening the fugitive slave act of 1793; a separate bill prohibited the slave trade in the District of Columbia.

May 19 Narciso Lopez leads an abortive invasion of Cuba; withdraws to Key West.

June 3	Southern Convention assembles in Nashville, in response to invitation of October 1849.
June 3	Webster introduces a substitute fugitive slave bill, providing among other things for trial by jury in the community where captured, if the fugitive denies he owes service.
June 10	Nashville Convention rejects measures pending in Congress; asks extension of Missouri Compromise line to the Pacific; adjourns until November.
July 1	Texas governor calls legislature to consider military action against New Mexico.
July 2	British Prime Minister Sir Robert Peel dies.
July 9	Zachary Taylor dies.
July 10	Millard Fillmore sworn in as President of the United States.
July 17	Webster informs the president that the Senate would agree to consider the various compromise proposals separately.
July 23	Webster becomes secretary of state in Fillmore's reconstituted cabinet.
July 31	Omnibus bill abandoned, paving way for eventual piecemeal passage of compromise measures, under leadership of Stephen A. Douglas.
August 6	Webster drafts proclamation for Fillmore, writes to Texas governor, in boundary dispute with New Mexico: asserts national supremacy.
September 9	California admitted as a free state; New Mexico and Utah Territories organized without reference to slavery; Texas given $10 million to give up her claims against New Mexico.
September 18	Fugitive slave act becomes law.
September 20	Slave trade banned in the District of Columbia.
September 24/ October 1	New York State Whig Convention, meeting at Syracuse, splits into Fillmore (pro-compromise) and Seward (anti-compromise) factions.

October 16   Agents from Georgia, arriving in Boston to pick up runaway slaves Ellen and William Craft, are detained in jail while the Crafts escape to England.

October 23   Women's rights convention meets in Worcester, Massachusetts.

November 11–18   Nashville Convention reassembles but few attend; compromise is denounced and right of secession affirmed.

December 13   Fillmore issues proclamation, drafted by Webster, warning Texas not to interfere with boundary established by compromise.

December 13–14   Georgia convention sets tone for South: accepts compromise so long as fugitive slave law is enforced.

December 21   Webster, in letter to Chevalier Hülsemann, the Austrian chargé in Washington, extols American democracy.

1851

January 17   List of subscribers to the "Webster Fund" sent to Webster.

January   Edward Everett and George Jacob Abbot begin editing Webster's *Works*.

February 15   Shadrach, a fugitive slave, arrested in Boston, but rescued from the courthouse by a mob.

February 18   President issues strongly worded proclamation, drafted by Webster, calling upon citizens to aid in quelling riots and in capturing fugitives.

February 25   Charles Allen, Free Soil congressman from Worcester, Massachusetts, charges Webster with corruption in connection with payments to Mexico; House refuses to investigate.

March 1   Hamilton Fish of the Seward-Weed faction elected Senator from New York against Fillmore's wishes.

March   Webster receives a fine carriage, horses, and harness from a group of New York City businessmen for his contributions to sectional peace.

April 11	Fugitive slave Thomas Simms remanded to his Georgia owner at cost of $20,000.
April 23	Charles Sumner, an abolitionist, sent to U.S. Senate from Massachusetts, despite Webster's opposition.
May 1	Queen Victoria opens the first world's fair at Crystal Palace, London.
May 8/June 3	Webster accompanies Fillmore and other cabinet members to Dunkirk, New York, to celebrate completion of Erie Railroad; returns by way of Buffalo, Rochester, Syracuse, Albany.
June 5	Webster's partisans meet in Boston to organize for his 1852 presidential campaign.
June 5	"Uncle Tom's Cabin" begins serial publication in the *National Era* of Washington, D.C.
July 3	Despite large expectations, Webster receives virtually nothing from the Mexican Claims Commission for his Union Land Company and Trinity Land Company scrip.
July 10	Treaty of Friendship, Commerce, and Navigation signed with Costa Rica.
July 26	Similar treaty signed with Peru.
August 11	Narciso Lopez again invades Cuba, but is captured and executed, along with 50 of his men; U.S. makes reparation.
September 4	Supreme Court Justice Levi Woodbury dies; to succeed him Webster recommends Benjamin Robbins Curtis of Massachusetts, who is appointed.
September 11	Arrest of fugitive slaves successfully resisted at Christiana, Pennsylvania, at cost of three lives. Leader of the mob tried for treason, but acquitted; all charges then dropped.
September 18	The *New York Times* begins publication, edited by Henry J. Raymond.
October 1	Fugitive slave, Jerry, picked up in Syracuse, New York; rescued by a mob before court action could be taken, and sent to Canada.

October 22 Fillmore issues proclamation against a military expedition believed outfitting for an invasion of Mexico.

November 14 Herman Melville's *Moby Dick* published.

November 25 Webster's presidential campaign formally launched with a mass rally at Faneuil Hall.

December 30–31 Louis Kossuth, Hungarian rebel leader, welcomed in Washington, entertained by Webster in defiance of protocol.

1852

January 10 Britain disavows naval interference with the American merchant vessel *Prometheus* in the harbor of San Juan, Costa Rica.

February 23 Webster lectures before the New York Historical Society on "The Dignity and Importance of History."

March 20 *Uncle Tom's Cabin* published in book form.

March/20 April 2 Webster successfully upholds Charles Goodyear's patent in *Goodyear* v. *Day* before the U.S. Circuit Court for the District of New Jersey.

March Webster's *Works* published in six volumes, carrying an 1851 copyright date.

May 8 Webster is shaken and bruised in a carriage accident near Plymouth, Massachusetts.

June 5 Democrats nominate Franklin Pierce of New Hampshire for president.

June 21 Winfield Scott nominated for president by the Whigs; Webster a poor third behind Fillmore.

June 29 Henry Clay dies.

July 9 Webster receives a tumultuous reception in Boston.

July 25 After toying for a month with the thought of going as minister to England; Webster refuses the post when Fillmore offers it.

August 17–18 Webster declines to seek a third-party nomination, but is nevertheless put up by a splinter group in Georgia.

September [2–3?] Webster discusses the Japan expedition with Commodore Matthew Calbraith Perry; Perry's instructions issued after Webster's death.

October 24 Webster dies at Marshfield in his 71st year.

October 29 Webster buried at Marshfield.

Abbreviations and Symbols

CaOOA	Public Archives of Canada, Ottawa
CoDu	Durango Public Library, Durango, Colo.
CoHi	Colorado State Historical Society, Denver
Ct	Connecticut State Library, Hartford
CtHi	Connecticut Historical Society, Hartford
CtWat	Watertown Library, Watertown, Conn.
CtY	Yale University
CtY–M	Yale University, Medical School
DHU	Howard University, Washington, D.C.
DLC	Library of Congress
DNA	National Archives
DSI	Smithsonian Institution
DeHi	Historical Society of Delaware, Wilmington
GEU	Emory University, Atlanta
H–Ar	Hawaii Public Archives, Honolulu
HuOSzK	Orszagos Szechenyi Konyvtar (National Szechenyi Library), Budapest, Hungary
ICHi	Chicago Historical Society
ICN	Newberry Library, Chicago
IGK	Knox College, Galesburg, Ill.
IHi	Illinois State Historical Library, Springfield
Ia–HA	Iowa State Department of History and Archives, Des Moines
IaDaM	Davenport Public Museum, Davenport, Ia.
InHi	Indiana Historical Society, Indianapolis
InU	Indiana University, Bloomington
InU–Li	Indiana University, Lilly Library, Bloomington
KU–M	University of Kansas, School of Medicine, Kansas City
KyU	University of Kentucky, Lexington
LU–Ar	Louisiana State University, Department of Archives and Manuscripts, Baton Rouge
MAnP	Phillips Academy, Andover, Mass.
MB	Boston Public Library
MBAt	Boston Athenaeum
MBBS	Bostonian Society
MBCo	Countway Library of Medicine, Boston
MBSpnea	Society for the Preservation of New England Antiquities, Boston
MBU	Boston University
MCo	Concord Free Public Library, Concord, Mass.
MDeeP	Pocumtuck Valley Memorial Association, Deerfield, Mass.
MDuHi	Duxbury Rural and Historical Society, Duxbury, Mass.
MGlHi	Cape Ann Historical Association, Gloucester, Mass.

MH	Harvard University
MH–AH	Harvard University, Andover-Harvard Theological Library
MH–Ar	Harvard University Archives
MH BA	Harvard University, Graduate School of Business Administration
MH–H	Harvard University, Houghton Library
MH–L	Harvard University, Law School
MHi	Masachusetts Historical Society, Boston
MLen	Lenox Library, Lenox, Mass.
MNS	Smith College, Northampton, Mass.
MNS–S	Smith College, Sophia Smith Collection
MPlPS	Pilgrim Society, Plymouth, Mass.
MS	Springfield City Library, Springfield, Mass.
MSaE	Essex Institute, Salem, Mass.
MWA	American Antiquarian Society, Worcester, Mass.
MWalB	Brandeis University, Waltham, Mass.
MWiW	Williams College, Williamstown, Mass.
MdBJ	Johns Hopkins University, Baltimore
MdBP	Enoch Pratt Free Library, George Peabody Branch, Baltimore
MdHi	Maryland Historical Society, Baltimore
MeB	Bowdoin College, Brunswick, Me.
MeHi	Maine Historical Society, Portland
MeWC	Colby College, Waterville, Me.
MiD	Detroit Public Library
MiU	University of Michigan, Ann Arbor
MiU-C	University of Michigan, William L. Clements Library, Ann Arbor
MnHi	Minnesota Historical Society
MoHi	Missouri State Historical Society, Columbia
MoLiWJ	William Jewell College, Liberty, Mo.
MoSHi	Missouri Historical Society, St. Louis
MsBB	Beauvoir–Jefferson Davis Shrine, Biloxi, Miss.
N	New York State Library, Albany
NAurW	Wells College, Aurora, N.Y.
NBLiHi	Long Island Historical Society, Brooklyn, N.Y.
NBu	Buffalo and Erie County Public Library, Buffalo, N.Y.
NBuHi	Buffalo and Erie County Historical Society, Buffalo, N.Y.
NCH	Hamilton College, Clinton, N.Y.
NCooHi	New York State Historical Association, Cooperstown, N.Y.
NHC	Colgate University, Hamilton, N.Y.
NHi	New-York Historical Society, New York
NIC	Cornell University, Ithaca, N.Y.

NN	New York Public Library
NNC	Columbia University
NNMus	Museum of the City of New York
NNPM	Pierpont Morgan Library, New York
NOsU	State University of New York, Oswego
NRU	University of Rochester, Rochester, N.Y.
NSchU	Union College, Schenectady, N.Y.
NSyU	Syracuse University, Syracuse, N.Y.
NbO	Omaha Public Library, Omaha, Neb.
Nc–Ar	North Carolina State Department of Archives and History, Raleigh
NcD	Duke University, Durham, N.C.
NcU	University of North Carolina, Chapel Hill
Nh	New Hampshire State Library, Concord
NhCla	Fiske Free Library, Claremont, N.H.
NhD	Dartmouth College, Hanover, N.H.
NhExP	Phillips Exeter Academy, Exeter, N.H.
NhHi	New Hampshire Historical Society, Concord
NjHi	New Jersey Historical Society, Newark
NjMD	Drew University, Madison, N.J.
NjMoHP	Morristown National Historical Park, Morristown, N.J.
NjP	Princeton University
NjPHi	Historical Society of Princeton, Princeton, N.J.
NjR	Rutgers–The State University, New Brunswick, N.J.
NmU	Universiy of New Mexico, Albuquerque
OCAJ	American Jewish Periodical Center, Cincinnati, Ohio
OCAJA	American Jewish Archives, Cincinnati, Ohio
OCHP	Cincinnati Historical Society
OClW	Case Western Reserve University, Cleveland
OClWHi	Western Reserve Historical Society, Cleveland
OGK	Kenyon College, Gambier, Ohio
OHi	Ohio Historical Society, Columbus
Or–Ar	Oregon State Archives, Salem
OrHi	Oregon Historical Society, Portland
PHC	Haverford College, Haverford, Pa.
PHi	Historical Society of Pennsylvania, Philadlephia
PP	Free Library of Philadelphia
PPAmP	American Philosophical Society, Philadelphia
RP	Providence Public Library, Providence, R.I.
RPB	Brown University
RPB–JCB	Brown University, John Carter Brown Library
RPB–JH	Brown University, John Hay Library
ScU	University of South Carolina, Columbia

T	Tennessee State Library and Archives, Nashville
TNJ	Joint University Libraries, Nashville
TxSjM	San Jacinto Museum of History Association
TxU	University of Texas, Austin
UPB	Brigham Young University, Provo, Utah
Uk	British Library
UkENL	National Library of Scotland, Edinburgh
UkLPR	Public Record Office, London
UkLiU	University of Liverpool
ViHi	Virginia Historical Society, Richmond, Va.
ViU	University of Virginia, Charlottesville
ViW	College of William and Mary, Williamsburg, Va.
VtU	University of Vermont, Burlington
WHi	State Historical Society of Wisconsin, Madison
WMUW	University of Wisconsin, Milwaukee
WaHi	Washington State Historical Society, Tacoma
WaU	University of Washington, Seattle

SHORT TITLES

Adams, *Diary*	Charles Francis Adams, ed., *Memoirs of John Quincy Adams, Comprising Portions of his Diary from 1795 to 1848.* (12 vols. Philadelphia, 1874–1877).
Cong. Globe	*The Congressional Globe* (46 vols., Washington, D.C., 1833–1873).
Correspondence	Charles M. Wiltse and others, eds., *The Papers of Daniel Webster, Correspondence* (7 vols., Hanover, N.H., and London, 1974–1985).
Curtis	George Ticknor Curtis, *Life of Daniel Webster* (2 vols., New York, 1870).
DNB	*Dictionary of National Biography.*
Diplomatic Papers	Kenneth E. Shewmaker and Kenneth R. Stevens, eds., *The Papers of Daniel Webster, Diplomatic Papers* (2 vols., Hanover, N.H. and London, 1983–).
Frothingham, *Everett*	Paul Revere Frothingham, *Edward Everett: Orator and Statesman* (Boston and New York, 1925).
Fuess, *Cushing*	Claude Moore Fuess, *The Life of Caleb Cushing* (2 vols., New York, 1923).
Fuess, *DW*	Claude Moore Fuess, *Daniel Webster* (2 vols., Boston, 1930).
Hamilton, *Graham*	J. G. de Roulhac Hamilton and others, eds., *The Papers of William Alexander Graham* (8 vols., Raleigh, N.C., 1957–).
Harvey, *Reminiscences*	Peter Harvey, *Reminiscences and Anecdotes of Daniel Webster* (Boston, 1877).
Hill, *Lawrence*	Hamilton Andrews Hill, *Memoir of Abbott Lawrence* (Boston, 1883).
Lanman	Charles Lanman, *The Private Life of Daniel Webster* (New York, 1852).
Legal Papers	Alfred S. Konefsky and Andrew J. King, eds., *The Papers of Daniel Webster, Legal Papers* (3 vols., Hanover, N.H., and London, 1982–).
Lyman, *DW*	Samuel P. Lyman, *Life and Memorials of Daniel Webster* (New York, 1853).
mDW	Microfilm Edition of the Papers of Daniel Webster (41 reels, Ann Arbor, 1971). References are followed by frame numbers.

mDWs	Microfilm Edition of the Papers of Daniel Webster, Supplementary Reel.
MHi Proc.	*Proceedings of the Massachusetts Historical Society.*
Messages and Papers	James D. Richardson, ed., A *Compilation of the Messages and Papers of the Presidents . . . 1789–1897* (10 vols., Washington, D.C., 1896–1899).
Moore, *Arbitrations*	John Bassett Moore, *History and Digest of the International Arbitrations to which the United States has been a Party* (6 vols., Washington, D.C., 1898).
PC	Fletcher Webster, ed., *The Private Correspondence of Daniel Webster* (2 vols., Boston, 1856).
Rayback, *Fillmore*	Robert J. Rayback, *Millard Fillmore: Biography of a President* (Buffalo, N.Y., 1959).
Seaton, *WWS*	Josephine Seaton, *William Winston Seaton of the National Intelligencer* (Boston, 1871).
Severance, *Fillmore Papers*	Frank H. Severance, ed.,*Millard Fillmore Papers* (2 vols., Publications of the Buffalo Historical Society, 10, 11, Buffalo, N.Y., 1907).
Speeches and Formal Writings	Charles M. Wiltse, ed., *The Papers of Daniel Webster, Speeches and Formal Writings* (2 vols., Hanover, N.H. and London, 1986–).
Van Tyne	Claude H. Van Tyne, ed., *The Letters of Daniel Webster* (New York, 1902).
W & S	James W. McIntyre, ed., *The Writings and Speeches of Daniel Webster* (National Edition, 18 vols., New York, 1903).
Works	Edward Everett, ed., *The Works of Daniel Webster* (6 vols., Boston, 1851).

SERIES ONE: CORRESPONDENCE

VOLUME SEVEN: 1850–1852

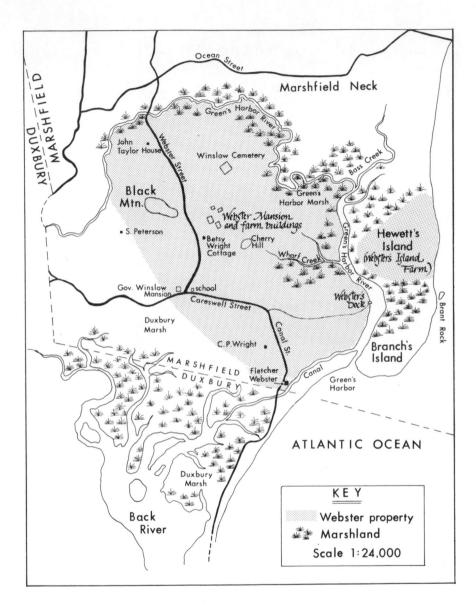

Webster's Marshfield Farm

The Papers, 1850–1852

FROM EDWARD EVERETT

Cambridge 3 Jan. 1850

Dear Sir,

I received a day or two ago—under your frank—a letter from Mr [Charles Wainwright] March,¹ to which accordingly I take the liberty to put the answer under cover to you. I believe nothing said by me on the subject alluded to was ever reported; but I have quite a distinct recollection of many things connected with your reply, and should probably be able to answer almost any question, which Mr March might put to me.²

Is there not a great constitutional objection to the admission into the Union of a Mormon state?³ It is passing a law granting the highest privilege, in the power of Congress to bestow, upon a band of fanatics and adventurers, who have made trouble wherever they have set themselves down. If admitted they must be, I trust it will not be by the ridiculous name⁴ which they give themselves; which belongs to no known human language; but is taken from the wretched farrago of lies & non-sense, which constitutes the Revelation of Jo[seph] Smith in the fundamental law of this hopeful new State. If they must come into the Union, I would make them take some Indian name from the map of the Country. The name of the great salt lake (Timpanagos) would hardly do, but *Salina* would not be bad. Lake *Utah* is put down on the maps as connected with the great Salt Lake. Anything would be better than talking Mormon. Yours ever Sincerely,   Edward Everett.

ALS. MHi.

1. March (1815–1864; Harvard 1837) was a lawyer and New York journalist. The nephew of Webster's boyhood friend Charles March (1781–1855), he was author of *Daniel Webster and His Contemporaries* (New York, 1852). Letter not found.

2. March had written Everett on December 26, 1849, seeking information about remarks Everett had made regarding Webster's preparation for

his famous "Reply" to Senator Robert Y. Hayne in 1830. See Everett to C. W. March, January 3, 1850, Everett Papers, MHi, microfilm reel 29.

3. Members of the Church of Latter-Day Saints, or Mormons, then settled around the Great Salt Lake, had drafted a petition to Congress in 1849, seeking either territorial status or statehood.

4. The new state was to be named Deseret.

FROM EDWARD EVERETT

Cambridge 9 Jan. 1850

Dear Sir,

Mr [Charles Wainwright] March informs me, in a letter received from him yesterday, that a new Edition of your speeches & public addresses, with explanatory & historical notes, has been thought of.[1] I sincerely wish you would execute the project. You would produce a work of great & permanent value in reference to the politics of the country, & in the highest degree creditable to its literature. But what I write chiefly to say, at present, is, that it ought to be published in such a way, as to afford a permanent income to you & those who come after you; which if the proper arrangements for publication are made, would be sure to accrue from the sales of the work.

It should be stereotyped at your own expense, and when ready for printing, your agent should write proposals for an edition from the principal publishing houses, & give the preference to the party which makes the best bid. This is the way in which the works of Judge [Joseph] Story were published; & in which Mr [William Hickling] Prescott & Mr [George] Ticknor have managed.

You could easily arrange the affair so, as not to be obliged to advance anything for the stereotyping.

So many copies of your volumes already published have been sold, that you could not expect the same demand for a new Edition, as would otherwise exist. But, if you could find time for a good deal of new matter in the shape of notes, it would give a degree of originality to the edition (which would at any rate contain several things not in the former Editions) & create a desire to possess it even on the part of those who possess a former edition.

Then it is to be considered that in 1875 there will be 48,000,000 instead of 24,000,000 who will be the better for reading your speeches. Ever Yours Sincerely,   Edward Everett.

ALS. MHi.

1. Three volumes of Webster's *Speeches and Forensic Arguments* (1830, 1835, 1843) and one volume of *Diplomatic and Official Papers* (1848) had already been published. *The Works of Daniel Webster*, a six-volume set edited by Everett and published by Little, Brown of Boston in 1851, consisted of papers from the earlier volumes, additional materials approved by Webster, and a long biographical sketch written by Everett.

During the long interregnum between President Zachary Taylor's inauguration in March 1849 and the convening of the Thirty-First Congress in December, California had adopted by an overwhelming margin a constitution prohibiting slavery and formally sought admission to the

*Union. President Taylor, who had encouraged this step, endorsed the
Californians' petition in his first annual message, December 4, 1849,
adding that once New Mexico followed the same procedures, he would
favor its admission to the Union also.*

*It was evident that Congress would not act swiftly or amicably on the
California statehood petition. Previous efforts to resolve the issue of
slavery in the territories, including Senator John M. Clayton's 1848 proposal to let the courts decide, had failed to muster the necessary majorities. The same sectional antagonisms that had destroyed the Clayton
compromise were increasingly intrusive in all facets of congressional
operations. It took three weeks, and sixty-two angry ballots, for the
House to elect a Speaker—Georgia Democrat Howell Cobb, who defeated
Massachusetts Whig Robert C. Winthrop by a single vote. The session
opened with fiery speeches by southern militants, which drew equally
bellicose retorts from their northern counterparts. Although moderates
like Webster discounted the heated rhetoric and the veiled threats from
both sides, the temper of the Congress appeared little conducive to a
calm and constructive legislative session.*

TO FRANKLIN HAVEN

Washington, Jan. 13. 1850

My Dear Sir,

The Senate has made no progress, or very little, with appointments.[1]
Where a vacancy happens, & a nomination is made to fill it, the nomination is considered at once. But in cases in which offices are filled, by
temporary appointments, and the public service, therefore, does not
suffer, the Senate seems not to hasten itself. The Debate springing up
from Genl [Lewis] Cass['] Resolution,[2] and from the Vermont Resolutions,[3] engrosses the attention of members, and may continue to do so
for some days.

The House will probably complete its organization tomorrow, having
already consumed six weeks, in labors for that end.

I fear the prospect of a useful session, is not encouraging. There is
so much excitement & inflammation on the subjects of Slavery, Dissolution, &c, as that it overwhelms, or threatens to overwhelm, all really
important measures. All this agitation, I think, will subside, without
serious result, but still it is mischievous, and creates heart burnings. But
the Union is not in danger.

I do not propose to take part, at present, in the fiery discussion of
these topics; but if any thing is proposed to *be done*, by way of attempting to carry evil purposes into effect, I shall have something to say.

Are you not coming this way? I am sorry our friend [Peter] Harvey[4] is not here, at this time, as some N.Y. friends are here, whom he wd. be glad to meet, on some affairs of mine. Mrs W[ebster][5] is still in N.Y. Please remember [me] to Mrs Haven[6] and your daughters. Yrs always truly   Danl Webster

ALS. MH. Published in *W & S*, 16: 529–530. Haven (1804–1893) was president of the Merchants' Bank of Boston, a friend and financial backer of Webster since the mid-1830s. DW was able to bring government business and an occasional appointment Haven's way.

1. Webster here refers to recent appointments by President Zachary Taylor that needed Senate approval. Among these appointments was Haven's as assistant United States treasurer at Boston. See *Correspondence*, 6: 341–342, and *Journal* of the *Executive Proceedings of the Senate* (Washington, 1887), 8: 217.

2. Lewis Cass, reelected to the Senate following his narrow defeat for the Presidency in 1848, introduced a resolution on December 24, 1849, instructing the Senate Committee on Foreign Relations to explore "the expediency of suspending diplomatic relations with Austria" because of its oppression of Hungary. The motion was brought up on January 4, 1850.

Congressional Globe, 31st Cong., 1st sess., pp. 75, 103–107, 113–117. See also DW to Peter Harvey, January 9, 1850, mDW 29713.

3. The General Assembly of Vermont had passed resolutions requesting its representatives and instructing its senators to oppose the extension of slavery to the new territories and to work for the abolition of slavery in the District of Columbia. A vigorous debate broke out January 8 in the Senate over whether to print the resolutions, since southern senators found them offensive. *Congressional Globe*, 31st Cong., 1st sess., pp. 119–123, 133–137.

4. Harvey (1810?–1877) was a prominent Massachusetts businessman and legislator and one of Webster's closest friends.

5. Caroline Le Roy Webster, whom DW had married December 12, 1829.

6. Sarah Ann Curtis had married Haven in 1828. They had three daughters and two sons.

FROM WILLIAM O. BARTLETT

Worcester, Jan. 16, 1850

My Dear Sir:

Sickness in my family has interrupted my attention to my ordinary duties, and will, I trust, be deemed a sufficient apology for the delay which has occurred in answering your very acceptable favor of the 11th ult.[1]

The ploughs[2] of which you speak for your New Hampshire farm shall be furnished, of the best workmanship. It would afford me much pleasure to see your farm; and a visit in company with yourself to the spot which, to me, is full of interest as your birthplace and the home of your boyhood, would afford me peculiar gratification. I should, therefore, be most happy to accept your invitation, and take a trip to Franklin at the time that the ploughs are put in operation, in the Spring, should you be in Boston.

The South Downs have arrived, in good condition and apparent health. There are six Ewes and a buck.

The Mackey boar gained 34 lbs. in the first 30 days.

The fine wild turkeys saved for you I fear will be lost, so that we shall not bc able to supply you before another year. A notorious thief in the neighborhood, was bound over on Saturday, to answer at our criminal court for taking three of them.

We have never before had such beef as we have made this year on *turneps* and corn; the quality is so superior as to attract the attention of all who partake of it and to excite inquiry as to the cause. The striking peculiarity is the tenderness of the lean meat; and I suppose that if we can apply, with any safety, chemical principles to the subject, an explanation is at once found in the effect of the *turneps* upon this part of the meat.

Certainly, it seems to me, with the facilities which we possess for producing turneps, equal, or nearly equal, to those of the English, with the great advantage over them in a climate adapted to the raising of Indian corn, we ought to produce beef and mutton of a quality even superior to theirs.

I differ widely from the common opinion in my estimate of the value of such land as constitutes a principal part of your Marshfield estate. It is not without experience that I have come to the conclusion that by an expensive system of cultivation, in which the largest possible portion of the labor is done by horse power, instead of manual, it may be made to yield a handsome annual profit; and, the crops being consumed on the land, its productiveness and consequent value, are constantly augmented.

You recollect that I handed you a Daily Spy,[3] at the Revere House, containing some comments on a letter said to have been written by your colleague.[4] The Secretary of the Ins. Co.[5] of which Gov. [John] D[avis] is President, called at the Spy office, in the absence of the editor,[6] and induced the printer to leave it out of the weekly paper! But— should there ever be occasion we will speak again. Very Sincerely Yrs.

W. O. Bartlett

ALS. NhHi. A native of Smithfield, Rhode Island, Bartlett was admitted to the Suffolk County bar in 1843, practiced law in Worcester for several years, and later moved to New York.

1. Letter not found.

2. Bartlett had developed a double plough that had been used with great success to cultivate turnips at Marshfield. See DW to Bartlett, December 8, 1849, published in *New England*

Farmer, 2 (February 2, 1850): 54.

3. The Worcester, Massachusetts, *Daily Spy.*

4. Former governor John Davis, then United States senator.

5. Clarendon Harris was then secretary of the State Mutual Life Assurance Company.

6. John Milton Earle (1794–1874), an antislavery Whig journalist and politician, served terms in both the

Massachusetts House and Senate.   Mutual Life Assurance Company.
Earle was also a director of the State

TO FRANKLIN HAVEN
Private

Washington, January 24, 1850

My Dear Sir

I think I may say that there is no manner of doubt about your confirmation.[1] Having some leisure, yesterday, I made use of it to see a good many gentlemen on the other side, not so much about any particular case, as about the general disposition of gentlemen of that party, as to the manner of treating the President's nominations. Our comee. on Foreign Relations also met, and I had then an opportunity of learning something of the general feeling, & general purposes. I am quite sure, that, at present, there is no general idea of acting an illiberal or proscriptive part. Some obnoxious individuals are nominated like Col [James Watson] Webb;[2] & probably, therefore, there will be some objections. There are, also, sundry nominations, especially in Pa,[3] which are not acceptable to all Whigs; and in these cases there may also be rejections. Any leading Whig Senator, who should be so inclined, might produce rejections, in plenty. But I suppose, in general, the nominations will be acquiesced in, though they be not very satisfactory. In regard to the highest Diplomatic appointments, there is a strong feeling that they are such as were "not fit to be made."[4] It would be the easiest thing in the world to upset them; but I think they will be allowed to pass.

You have observed the Resolutions[5] offered by Mr [James Ware] Bradbury. I believe the party intend to pass them, in substance; & I believe, also, that it is intended to defer acting, in general, in cases, where persons are in office under appointments made in the recess, until the President's answer shall come. But I am not sure that there is any settled purpose of this kind. It is a thing talked about.

Whenever it is convenient for you to come here with your Daughter, I think you should come, whatever may then be the state of your nomination. It would hardly be noticed, that your nomination was pending, or supposed that you were here, on that account.

You may expect to hear from me again in three or four days. Yours, always truly,   Danl Webster
I expect Mrs. W. this Eve'. She has been detained in N.Y. by the rains.

ALS. MH. Published in *PC*, 2: 350–351.

1. See above, DW to Haven, January 13, 1850, n. 1.

2. Named chargé d'affaires at Vienna in November 1849, Webb left for his post on December 1, but his nomination was rejected by the Senate on February 11, 1850, by a 34–7 vote. *Journal of the Executive Pro-*

ceedings of the Senate (Washington, 1887), 8: 115–116. 137. It is not clear which other nominees Webster considered objectionable.

3. Appointments for Pennsylvania included Alexander Irwin to be marshal of the Western District; William M. Gallagher to be collector of customs at the Port of Presque Isle, William D. Lewis to be collector of customs at Philadelphia, and Peter C. Ellmaker to be naval officer at Philadelphia. All of these appointments were confirmed. Journal of the Executive Proceedings of the Senate, 98–254 passim.

4. It is not clear to which diplomatic appointments Webster was objecting.

5. Bradbury, a Vermont Democrat, had submitted a resolution on December 24, 1849, that would require the President to lay before the Senate all charges against individuals in the executive departments resulting in their removal since March 4, 1849, and an accounting of the number of removals made in each department. The resolution, designed to embarrass the administration, was debated intermittently until January 7, 1851, but never came to a vote. See Congressional Globe, 31st Cong., 1st sess., pp. 74–75, 110, 160, 1081–1083, 1113, 1125–1126, 1130–1131, and 31st Cong., 2d sess., pp. 36–42, 190.

TO SAMUEL KIRKLAND LOTHROP

Washington
feb: 12. 1850

My Dear Sir

I am obliged to you for a Copy of the "Report," of which your contribution certainly forms the most practical part.[1]

I never thought that Slavery could be so strongly assailed on Scriptural authority. The Jews practiced it, like other oriental nations. And as to the New Testament, & the teachings of Jesus Christ, it seems to me, always, that the object of that teaching is to inculcate personal holiness, & to purify the heart, & regulate the life, of every individual. It enjoins the duties, belonging to the several relations of life, without prescribing those relations. But its general tendency cannot be doubted. As the Christian religion is a religion of love, kindness, & mercy, it discountenances slavery, as it discountenances every thing else which is oppressive, or unjust. The true objection to slavery is its injustice. It is opposed to the natural equality of mankind. It is founded only in the power of the strong, over the weak. Superior force is its origin, & its only origin. And, therefore, even if it were a useful social institution, it could not be defended. But, in other cases, so in this, that which is unjust cannot, on the whole, be useful. Slavery has proved itself, every where, a great social & political evil. Its influence is as bad on the master, as on the slave; and often worse. It blunts the moral feelings, inspires a false sense of superiority, & insensibly hardens the heart.

But when it has become an element of the social & political system, there are few cases, in which it can be got rid of, by violent eradication. At least, there are some, in which it cannot. In these, we must wait for events, & the orderings of Providence, who often "shapes our ends, rough hew them how we will.["]

I pray you, give my love & Mrs W's to Mrs Lothrop Yrs   D. W.

ALS. DLC. Lothrop (1804–1886; Harvard 1825) was Unitarian minister of the Church in Brattle Square, Boston from 1834 to 1876, when he resigned the pastorate and the church was dissolved.

1. The report in question has not been identified.

TO PETER HARVEY

Washington Feb:14. '50

My Dear Sir

I do not partake, in any degree, in those apprehensions, which you say some of our friends entertain of the dissolution of the Union, or the breaking up of the Government. I am mortified, it is true, at the violent tone assumed here, by many persons, because such violence in debate only leads to irritation, & is, moreover, discreditable to the Govt & the Country. But there is no serious danger, be assured; & so assure our friends.

My own opinion is, that California will be admitted, by a large majority of the House of Representatives, & by two thirds of the Senate. I take it all the Northern members in this House will vote for her admission; together with both the Kentucky Senators,[1] both the Maryland members,[2] one or both of the N. Carolina members,[3] I hope both, or perhaps only one, of the Louisiana members;[4] one Tennessee member,[5] & one Missouri member.[6]

I have, thus far, upon a good deal of reflection, thought it advisable for me to hold my peace. If a moment should come, when it shall appear, that any temperate, *national*, & practical speech which I can make, would be useful, I shall do the best I can. One purpose I wish to execute—& that is to call on Mr [John Macpherson] Berrien,[7] & other Southern Gentlemen, to state, distinctly, what are the acts of the North, which, it is said, constitute a series of aggression[s], by the North on the South. This matter <has> ought to be looked into, a little more carefully than it has been. Let the North keep cool. I hope Mass. will send us *no* resolutions, at present. They can do no good. This is a most important matter, & I hope our friends will understand it so. Yrs truly   Danl Webster

ALS. MWalB. Published in Curtis, 2: 398–399.

1. Henry Clay and Joseph Rogers Underwood.

2. James Alfred Pearce and Thomas George Pratt.

3. George Edmund Badger and Willie Person Mangum.

4. Solomon Weathersbee Downs and Pierre S. Soule; of the two, DW was probably more hopeful of winning the support of Downs for the admission of California.

5. John Bell.

6. Thomas Hart Benton.

7. Berrien had delivered a speech

on February 11 and 12 in which he argued that the Constitution followed the flag, hence slavery was protected in the new American territories of the Southwest. He also charged a "united North" with "systematic and extended" aggression against southern interests. *Congressional Globe*, 31st Cong., 1st sess., *Appendix*, pp. 202–211.

TO WILLIAM HENRY FURNESS

Washington Feby 15. 1850

My Dear Sir,

I was a good deal moved, I confess, by reading your letter of the 9th January.[1] Having great regard for your talents & character, I could not feel indifferent to what you said, when you intimated that there was, or might be, in me, a power to do good, not yet exercised or developed. It may be so; but I fear my Dear Sir, that you overrate, not my desire, but my power to be useful in my day & generation. From my earliest youth, I have regarded slavery as a great moral & political evil. I think it unjust, repugnant to the natural equality of mankind, founded only in superior power, a standing & permanent conquest by the stronger over the weaker. All pretence of defending it, on the ground of difference of races, I have ever contemned. I have ever said that if the black race is weaker, that is a reason against, not for, its subjection & oppression. In a religious point of view, I have ever regarded it, & ever spoken of it, not as subject to any express denunciation, either in the old Testament or the new, but as opposed to the whole spirit of the Gospel & to the teachings of Jesus Christ. The religion of Jesus Christ, is a religion of kindness, justice & brotherly love.

But slavery is not kindly affectioned, it does not seek another's, & not its own, it does not let the oppressed go free. It is, as I have said, but a continued act of oppression; but then such is the influence of a habit of thinking among men, & such the effect of what has been long established that even minds religious, & tenderly consciencious, such as would be shocked by any single act of oppression, or any single exercise of violence, & unjust power, are not always moved, by the reflection that slavery is a continued & permanent violation of human rights.

But now My Dear Sir, what can be done by me, who act only a part in political life, & who have no power over the subject of slavery, as it exists in the States of the Union? I do what I can to restrain it, to prevent its spread, & diffusion. But I cannot disregard the oracles, which instruct me not to do evil that good may come; I cannot co-operate in breaking up social & political systems, on the warmth, (rather than the strength) of a hope that in such convulsion, the cause of emancipation may be promoted. And even if the end would justify the means, I confess I do not see the relevancy of such means, to such an end. I confess,

My Dear Sir, that in my judgment, confusion, conflict, and embittered controversy, violence, bloodshed, & civil war, would only rivet the chains of slavery the more strongly. In my opinion, it is the mild influences of Christianity, the softening & melting power of the Sun of Righteousness, & not the storms, & tempests of heated controversy, that are in the course of those events which an all-wise Providence overrules, to dissolve the iron fetters by which man is made the slave of man. The effect of moral causes, though sure, is slow. In two thousand years, the Doctrines & the miracles of Jesus Christ have converted but a very small portion of the human race; and among Christian nations, even, many gross & obvious errors like that of the lawfulness of slavery, have still held their ground

But what are two thousand years, in the great work of the progress of the regeneration & redemption of mankind. If we see that the course is onward, & forward, as it certainly is, in regard to the final abolition of human slavery, while we give to it our fervent prayers, and aid it by all the justifiable influences which we can exercise, it seems to me, we must leave both the progress & the result in His hands who sees the end from the beginning, & in whose sight a thousand years are but a single day. I pray you, my Dear Sir, accept this, the product of half an hour of the evening, & unread by the writer, as a respectful & grateful acknowledgment, of your very kind & friendly letter.   Danl Webster

LS. NhHi. Published in *PC*, 2: 353–355.

1. Furness to DW, January 9, 1850, mDW 29725, was an impassioned appeal to the senator to join forces with the abolitionists.

TO JAMES WILLIAM PAIGE, WITH ENCLOSURE

Washington Feb. 17. 1850

My Dear Sir

You will perceive that Mr [William Morris] Meredith[1] has written, already, to the Comee. of Commerce in the House, on the subject mentioned in your letter.[2] I shall take your letter to the Senate tomorrow, & place it in the hands of our Committee, with a view to greater expedition.

I believe we shall not break up, or break down, or overset the Union at present; though, when California comes in, it may be tipped, a little; as a cart is liable to tip up when a heavy weight is put in to the hind end.

You may go on, buying & selling, & getting gain. Yrs always truly

Danl Webster

ALS. Mrs. Irvin McD. Garfield, Southboro, Massachusetts. Paige (1792–1868), Grace Fletcher Webster's half brother, was a prosperous Boston merchant and one of DW's most reliable financial backers.

1. Then secretary of the Treasury.
2. See enclosure. Letter not found.

ENCLOSURE: FROM WILLIAM MORRIS MEREDITH

16 Feby 1850

My Dear Sir

The Law limits the amount to be applied in exchanging coin for the bullion to $1,000,000. This sum is in existing circumstances too small, & I have already written to the Chmn. of the Commee of Commerce[1] in the House, asking that it should be doubled. Always respectfully ys

W. M. Meredith

ALS. Mrs. Irvin McD. Garfield, South-boro, Massachusetts.

1. Robert M. McLane of Maryland.

TO JAMES WILLIAM PAIGE

Washington Feb: 18. 50

Dear Mr Paige,

The Chairman of Comee. of Commerce in H.R.[1] says he will report a Coinage Bill,[2] &c, tomorrow mor[n]i[n]g, & put it, immediately on its passage. If any thing should occur, to cause delay, in H.R. I shall move for leave to bring in [a] similar bill, in the Senate.

So you see, Col Paige, how promptly your *hints* are obeyed. Yrs

D. Webster

ALS. Mrs. Irvin McD. Garfield, South-boro, Massachusetts.
1. Robert M. McLane of Maryland.
2. On February 20, 1850, McLane introduced a bill doubling the amount of coin to be kept on deposit in the mint from one million to two million dollars. Following its approval by the House, the bill passed the Senate in a slightly amended form on April 30 and returned to the House, which accepted the revised bill on May 16. *Congressional Globe*, 31st Cong., 1st sess., pp. 393–394, 416, 864, 1011.

FROM EDWARD EVERETT

Cambridge 18 Feb. 1850

My dear Sir,

Before this letter reaches you, my daughter[1] will I trust have arrived safe in Washington, & have placed herself under the kind protection and government of yourself and Mrs. Webster. I had hoped, at one time, to accompany her; but besides some engagements that keep me at home, I do not like to leave Mrs Everett[2] alone, her health being quite indifferent.

If the letter writers of the newspapers are correctly informed that the President has of late consulted you confidentially, I cannot but congratulate him on recovering from the extraordinary delusion under which he entered office, that these were times, when the government of the Country could be administered with the assistance of second rate men. I believe his intentions to be excellent and his judgment sound, on questions within the range of his experience. But he was of necessity wholly ignorant of many things necessary for a President to know; & in putting himself into the hands of newspaper editors & local electioneerers, he laid the foundation of some of the mortifications he has had to submit to.

A public meeting in Faneuil Hall has been proposed for the purpose of making a very imposing demonstration in favor of preserving the Union.[3] I have been asked if I would attend to speak, which I am not averse to. It appears to me, however, that the time is not quite come. The South has not yet shewn her hand, (her foot I had almost said and that not solidungulous), nor do we know the precise issue which will be joined at Washington. As one great end of the meeting would be to strengthen the hands of our Senators and representatives at Washington, it strikes me that the meeting had better be delayed, till we know more definitely what ground they will be called to take. It seems to me that events are impending of the most momentous character, & that if we wait till they are more distinctly foreshown, we shall speak with greater effect. Please let me know what you think on these points vizt. whether it is best to have a meeting at all, & if so whether you would have it quite soon;— or after some time.

Remember me most kindly to Mrs W. and believe me as ever, with sincere attachment, faithfully Yours, Edward Everett.

ALS. MHi.

1. Charlotte Brooks Everett (1825–1879).

2. Everett married Charlotte Gray Brooks (1800–1859) in 1822. They had six children.

3. No record of the proposed meeting has been found.

Webster viewed the increasingly acrimonious congressional debate in January and early February 1850 as a regrettable but not necessarily ominous development. He had heard all of the words before, including southern threats of disunion in the absence of an acceptable territorial settlement, and abolitionist encouragement for such a move. But he did not believe that a true secession crisis lay in prospect.

Although he had little regard for the abilities of President Zachary Taylor, who reinforced the Massachusetts senator's opinions by failing to consult him on policy or patronage matters, Webster nonetheless privately supported Taylor's plan for the immediate admission of California as a free state. An hour-long meeting in his Washington boardinghouse with Henry Clay on January 21, persuaded Webster that the President's plan would never pass the Congress and that a more comprehensive agenda for sectional conciliation was essential to preserve the Union. Webster endorsed the general principles of Clay's six-point compromise, which the Kentuckian introduced to the Senate on January 29.

In the wake of Clay's initial presentation, and his subsequent im-

passioned Union speech before the Senate on February 5 and 6, Webster
felt more confident that the current controversy could be contained and
resolved. In letters to Peter Harvey on February 12, 13, and 14, he assured his friend that there was no need to be "frightened" and that
California would enter the Union in due course without any sectional
"disruption." He offered a similar optimistic assessment to Edward
Everett on February 16, observing that "if, on our side, we keep cool,
things will come to no dangerous pass."

In the week between the letter to Everett and the letter of February 24
to his son, Fletcher, printed below, Webster's assessment of the sectional
crisis shifted substantially. No longer did he dismiss southern talk of
secession; no longer did he think that simply remaining "cool" would
dissolve sectional antagonisms. By the third week of February, Webster
had ceased to believe that his quiet, behind-the-scenes support for compromise would suffice to carry it. Anxious, but also more energized by
public affairs than he had been for several years, Webster resolved to
speak out forcefully in the Senate for sectional comity. The specific approach that he would take was still to be drawn.

Events in and outside Washington contributed to Webster's determination to do what he could to alleviate what he now perceived as a
genuine secession crisis. On February 16, the day Webster wrote opti-
mistically to Everett, the House of Representatives extended an olive
branch, voting to table a resolution endorsing the Wilmot Proviso. Two
days later, however, Georgia Congressman Alexander H. Stephens led a
successful southern filibuster in the House obstructing the admission of
California without a decision regarding the status of New Mexico and
Utah. On February 23 Stephens joined his Georgia colleague Robert
Toombs in a visit to the White House, where a highly charged interview
with President Taylor took place. When Stephens and Toombs warned
that the South would secede if its concerns were not addressed, the
President responded with a Jacksonian-like dictum that any secessionist
act would be crushed. Reports of the exchange spread rapidly through
Washington, dashing any lingering hopes that the President would support a compromise acceptable to his native region.

Events beyond Washington also shaped Webster's outlook. As February progressed, the movement for a southern convention in Nashville,
planned for June 1850, with secession as a possible option, was proceeding apace. Five states went on record endorsing Mississippi's call
for the Nashville conference, and several other southern states, although
declining at this juncture to appoint delegates, expressed their strong
determination to reject any congressional prohibition of slavery in the
new territories. That the Nashville convention enjoyed widespread support in the South was made evident to Webster when, in a meeting with

southern congressional leaders on February 23, he was shown letters demonstrating the strong views of their constituents. The tenor of editorial comment in the South and North further served to bury doubts on Webster's part that the two sides were in earnest.

In this context Webster began work on the last great speech of his Senatorial career.

TO DANIEL FLETCHER WEBSTER

Sunday Feb. 24, '50.

My Dear Son,

I received your two despatches yesterday, in answer to mine.¹ I shall see Mr. [William Morris] Meredith, this Evening, or early tomorrow. There will be no difficulty in getting delay, if that is desirable. Mr. [George] A<shmun> is most anxious that his brother² should have the office. I am nearly broken down with labor and anxiety. I know not how to meet the present emergency, or with what weapons to beat down the Northern and the Southern follies, now raging in equal extremes. If you can possibly leave home, I want you to be here, a day or two before I speak. As soon as I can guess the time, I will telegraph you. I have poor spirits, and little courage, "non sum, qualis eram." Your affectionate father   Danl Webster.

Copy. MHi. Published in *W & S*, 16: 533–534. Daniel Fletcher Webster (1813–1862; Harvard 1833), DW's only surviving son, was living in Boston and awaiting nomination as surveyor of the port of Boston.

1. Letters not found.
2. Lewis Ashmun (d. 1852), active for many years in the India trade. The post went to Fletcher; see DW to Peter Harvey, March 1, 1850.

FROM WILLIAM HENRY FURNESS

[February 1850]

My dear Sir,

Allow me in acknowledgt. of your letter of the 15th,¹ for which I thank you, to ask your indulgent attention to that view of the Abolition of Slavery which most deeply interests me. But let me first say that, altho' the friendly reception, which my letter met with, emboldens me to address you again. I have no wish to draw you into an irksome correspondence, or into any correspondence at all. I do not consider you as bound even in courtesy to answer me, unless indeed, to use a phrase befitting the city of Wm. Penn, the spirit should move you so to do.

In this matter of getting rid of Slavery, it is not the object aimed at, magnificent as it is, the emancipation of some millions of human beings —it is not this alone or chiefly that interests me; but it is the ennobling regenerating, saving influence which blesses those who labor for this end. There is under heaven, I solemnly believe, no mightier means of grace, to the greatest as well as to the least, than working for justice & man, than speaking for them, especially at a period like the present, when words are works & when he, who speaks, acts. Into the inmost life of him who takes hold of the chains of the slaves to unloose them, there flashes a divine virtue with a more than electric facility & illumination; & words now-a-days, make those chains crack again, if we may judge from the excitement of the slave holders.

It is, my dear Sir, a part of my philosophy, if I may presume to have any, that we must *do* before we can *know*. "He that doeth truth cometh to the light," in the very act of doing it. "If any man will do His will, he will know what is of Heaven & what of earth, what is true & what is false. Dr [William Ellery] Channing once said to me in a letter, "I have been trying all my life to find some means of Virtue besides Virtue." The knowledge we get of what is just, humane & free by being ourselves just, humane & free is the only knowledge that enlightens & saves us. It does more than save us. It makes us over again & we enter into a new life.

May I say it? I say it with all respect when I wrote you the other day,[2] I was not more moved, I was not so much moved by a concern for the slaves or for the country as for yourself personally. Mr Benton's statue of Columbus[3] or the highest peak of the Rocky Mountains dwindles in comparison with the idea I have of Mr Webster speaking out, as he alone can, for the Eternal law of God, pouring out his great nature in the burning words of Liberty. You question whether you can do anything. May I answer you in your own words[:] "all the justifiable influences which we can exercise." Heaven forbid that I should be supposed to wish you to do anything unjustifiable. May you not, nay, should you not avail yourself of one of the fundamental principles of American liberty, the principle of free thought & free speech? Is it loyal to the country to doubt the safety of that? Ought we to fear that social order will be broken up by fidelity to one of the very principles upon which our social order rests, & which make that order valuable? There are thousands & tens of thousands in the land thirsting for the words which you alone can speak, & whom those words would crystallize into adamant to resist & break down the slave power. Freedom of thought & speech cannot get into full play without commotion, but it is worth the cost; besides disturbance is temporary & will cure itself. It seems to me the country is making progress every day in its appreciation of the principle of free speech. We still have violent passions & they get very hot, but they burn nothing. The resistance to slavery is not a matter of private opinion & self-will; & Southern men cannot be so blind as not to see that fact. As the note of remonstrance grows deeper, & when our ruling men, like yourself, help to increase it, it will be seen & felt to be, not the whim of individual caprice, but the mighty protest of nature, the living voice of God, not to be resisted without madness & folly.

Slavery is a great evil, but great as it is, such a mighty people as this, bursting all over into life & energy, might abolish it in a day, were our will only good. Is there anything the North would not do to help in the good work, if the South would only profess itself ready to be helped? See how the tide of immigration sweeps by the rich lands of the South, & all because of Slavery. Let all at the South who have slaves & no land, be paid, if they are willing to be paid, fourfold for every slave. Let those who have slaves and land, remove the curse of Slavery & the land will compensate them tenfold. But I want no interference with the South. It is the interference with northern freedom that must be got rid of, interference with our freedom of thought & speech & with much more. Mr [Henry] Clay tells us we should all consider ourselves bound to help slave catchers. May our right hands fester first!

Praying your allowance for thus intruding on you again, I remain with fervent good wishes very truly & respectfully yr friend

W. H. Furness

ALS. NhHi.   2. Furness to DW, January 9, 1850,
  1. See above, DW to Furness,   mDW 29725.
February 15, 1850.   3. Not identified.

Committed by February 22 to make a formal speech on the sectional controversy, Webster did not advertise the views he intended to express in it. He had spoken infrequently during January and February and, aside from his private endorsement of Clay's compromise efforts, offered little counsel to political friends or acquaintances during these increasingly tense weeks. His public silence contributed to the growing interest in and uncertainty regarding the stand he would take. As late as March 3, Massachusetts Congressman Robert C. Winthrop, who knew the senator well, though they were no longer intimate, speculated that Webster would sustain President Taylor's position in favor of the immediate admission of California, without conditions and without concessions to the South on related issues. Others felt Webster would take a more conciliatory approach but could not predict the particulars of it.

During the two-week period between Webster's announcement to his son, Fletcher, on February 24 that he would speak and delivery of the Seventh of March speech, Webster consulted with close friends and also with his old adversary John C. Calhoun at the latter's rooms in Washington. There the two Senate giants discussed the current crisis at length; each man expressing respect for, if not full agreement with, the other's position.

Calhoun's speech of March 4 before the Senate emphasized the need to restore an equality between the North and South that he believed had been dissolving slowly for a generation. Although it was the equal of his previous great speeches in its piercing realism, the substance of Calhoun's anticompromise position was not embraced by key southern senators thus leaving an important opening for Webster to reach out to the South.

Webster intended to make a "Union" speech, as he explained to Peter Harvey and to Charles Henry Warren on March 1 (see below). Although he told friends that he felt unequal to the task before him, that his spirits were low, and that his speech would be little remembered, good or bad, a month hence, he was nonetheless preparing intensely for it. Moreover, he did nothing to discourage the heightened drama surrounding the speech, which may well have surpassed public anticipation of the second reply to Hayne. His correspondence in the days immediately preceding the Seventh of March speech would have dispelled any doubts Webster entertained that, indeed, the speech would be a "turning point" for him, and perhaps for the nation as well.

TO PETER HARVEY

> In the Senate.
> Friday 2 o'clock.
> [March 1, 1850]

My Dear Sir,

Fletcher's nomination[1] was concurred in this morning, under the most pleasant circumstances. His conduct in relation to Gen. [John] McNeil's[2] re-nomination was stated, and every body seemed disposed to compliment him, for his honorable conduct towards an old soldier; and all concurred in immediate confirmation without delay.

I wish it had been a different office; but under all the circumstances it is right for him to take it. He will have left Boston probably before you receive this. I mean to speak on Wednesday or as soon after as I can get a chance. I fear it will be later than Wednesday.

As yet, no nominations for Assistant Treasurers have been sent in.[3] Unless in case of actual vacancies, there seems at present no disposition to act upon nominations.

As time goes on, I will keep you advised by Telegraph as well as I can on what day I shall speak.

As to what I shall say, you can guess nearly as well as I can. I mean to make a *Union* Speech, and discharge a clear conscience.

I hope you will be here and give good advice. Yrs   D. W.

Copy. NhHi. Published in *PC*, 2: 356, misdated February 22.

1. Fletcher Webster had formally been nominated for the post of Surveyor of the Port of Boston on February 27. *Journal of the Executive*

Proceedings of the Senate (Washington, 1887), 8: 145–146.

2. McNeil (1784–1850), an officer in the War of 1812, had been the surveyor for Boston since 1830. He died on February 23, leaving open the post to which Fletcher was nominated four days later.

3. Webster's close friend Franklin Haven was awaiting formal nomination as assistant United States treasurer at Boston. See above, DW to Haven, January 13, 1850, and DW to Harvey, January 9, 1850, mDW 29713.

TO [CHARLES HENRY WARREN]

Washington <Feb: 28> Mar: 1.
1850

My Dear Sir:

Your friendly letter of the 6th <instant> ultimo[1] has lain open on my table, from the day of its receipt, & I have intended, from hour to hour, to give it answer. Two things have prevented; one, that I have happened to be all the time much engaged; the other, that I have hoped, every day, to have something to say the next day.

Probably the best return I can now make, is to tell you, as far as I can, how things stand here on this 1st day of March.

Imprimis. There is a little lull, in the storm of angry words, reproaches & threats. Southern Gentlemen are a little less violent, & I think abolitionists find themselves a good deal rebuked, by public opinion. The Debate[2] goes on, in both Houses, but not with quite so much heat & fury, as were manifested a fortnight ago. Mr [John Caldwell] Calhoun's speech[3] will be read in the Senate on Monday. It will be in his usual [vein] of dogmatical assertion, & violent denunciations of the North. Alas! poor man he will speak in the Senate, I fear no more.[4] Seldom agreeing with him, for the last 20 yrs, I yet feel touched, <by> at the prospect of his death. I am near his own age, & it is now more than thirty years since we met in Congress. Personally, good feelings have always subsisted between us, & I shall most sincerely lament his death, if that should be his immediate destiny.

After Mr Calhoun Govr. Seaward [William Henry Seward] wishes to speak—& so does Mr. [George Edmund] Badger—& these having spoken, I shall get the floor if I can on Wednesday, but fear it will be later. You may wish to know the substance of what I propose to say; but as my budget will soon be out, I think I shall give you no abstract of contents in advance. I mean to make an honest, truth telling speech; & a Union Speech;[5] but I have no hope of acquitting myself with more than merely tolerable ability. But we shall soon know, & I neither despond, nor enjoy a premature exultation at success. Whether the speech be good or bad, nobody will [care] a fig about it, a month hence, if any thing occurs, mean time, to give quiet to the Country. Yrs   D. W.

ALS. NN. Published in *W & S*, 16: 534–535. Warren (1798–1874; Harvard 1817), a prominent Massachusetts attorney and jurist, was at this time president of the Boston and Providence Railroad.

1. Letter not found.

2. The Senate was then debating a series of resolutions introduced by Henry Clay on January 29 as the basis for sectional compromise.

3. Because he was too weak to present it, by unanimous consent Calhoun's speech of March 4 was read by Senator James Murray Mason of Virginia. To ensure that Mason would read the speech accurately, Calhoun had it printed prior to March 4; it is likely that Webster saw a copy of it before he wrote this letter to Warren.

4. Calhoun made his last comments in the Senate on March 13; he died in Washington on March 31.

5. The speech we have come to know by its date of delivery was called by Webster "The Constitution and the Union." See *Speeches and Formal Writings*, 2.

FROM WADDY THOMPSON

Washington March 2, 1850

My dear Sir,

Our mutual friend Genl. James Hamilton repeated to me in confidence a conversation which he had yesterday with Mr. [John Caldwell] Calhoun with permission to me to communicate it to you.

It is so honorable both to Mr. Calhoun & yourself that I desire to place it in a more permanent form than our conversation this morning.

Genl. H. said to Mr. Calhoun suppose that Mr. Webster does interpose and succeed in adjusting the question which is now agitating the country. What shall we of the South do for him. Mr. Calhoun instantly replied make him President Sir—for he will deserve it for that single act. Besides his eloquence genius and great public services Mr. Webster possesses many noble qualities. I shall most probably never recover my health but if I do I would not only not allow my name used against him but would regard it as a sacred duty to support him.

None but high natures can feel or inspire such sentiments and I regard this little incident as more honorable to both of you than all the intellectual triumphs which have illustrated your brilliant public lives.

If it would add any value to the sentiments expressed by Mr. Calhoun allow me to express my entire concurrence in them. Faithfully yr friend

Waddy Thompson

ALS. DLC.

FROM R[ICHARD?] B. BARKER

Beaver Mar 4th. 1850

Sir

Do it, Mr. Webster; as you can do it, like a bold and gifted Statesman and Patriot reconcile the North and South, and *preserve the Union*.

Blessings will attend you, if you succeed, and your name will be embalmed in the hearts of your Countrymen.

You will be greater than he whom we call the Father of his country. He achieved its Independence, through the valor of our Countrymen and the aid of France. I venerate Washington!! but now the aspect is changed. He secured the Liberty of the Colonies. *Whoever preserves the Union, secures the Liberties of the world.*

Allow me in times like these to address you in a familiar style. Offer Mr. Webster, a liberal compromise to the South, and my word for it the North will sustain you.

Pardon the freedom I use in addressing you. I am an humble practitioner of Medicine—a democrat—but I go for the "Constitution as it is, and the Union as it is." I am, very humbly, your servant,   R. B. Barker

ALS. NhHi. Probably Richard B. Barker, for many years a resident of Borough Township in Beaver County, Pennsylvania. Barker had published a pro-Jackson newspaper, the *Beaver River Gazette*, for several months in 1834.

FROM BENJAMIN DOUGLAS SILLIMAN

New York March 5. 1850

My dear Sir

I pray you to pardon my intruding on you for a moment at a time when your whole mind is so much engrossed by the important events which call for all your thoughts & powers. Let me however tell you in a few words that the hopes of this community never before so hung on the wisdom, eloquence & power of one man as it does at this moment on yours. Your speech on "[Samuel Augustus] Foot's resolution"[1] was a turning point in your own life. Your speech this week may be the turning point in the life of this nation. God knows I mean no empty flattery when I say that I believe you, & you only, adequate to "set right" the mind of the whole country North & South on the great question which so agitates it. The same intellect, the same wisdom, the same power of demonstration & force of thought & of language which turned back the Niagara torrent of public sentiment & opinion in the former case can now shew to the South itself where right & reason lie. The "equilibrium" plan[2] by which slavery is to repress & keep back the institutions of freedom is a *confession* of the weakness of slavery. It shews what must be its own destiny in case of Disunion & if left to itself. Why is it that the slave states need new "guards"? Simply because free institutions are outstripping them. In this age can it be *dreamed* of that Freedom shall be kept back because slavery cannot go forward? I cannot now name one mortal man in the whole circle of my acquaintance who would now, or who ever heretofore would meddle with slavery in the slave states. Why should the slave states meddle with my rights by insisting on an extension of the inequality of representation by which one man owning five slaves has as much power as *four* northern farmers, lawyers, mechanics or merchants?[3] This is the point which galls me. I am sadly deficient in philanthropy, & don't know that I should object to own slaves if I lived in a slave state, but it is this political preponderance which gives to one man[']s property so much power over me that I rather fight than submit to any further increase of it. How would it do to suggest the idea that if they wish to carry slaves with them into new states & territories, such slave[s] shall not form a basis of representation? I take the liberty of sending to you a number of the "L[ong] Island Star"[4] which paper I think contains some just views on the subject of the *"exclusion of the entire South["]* from *any* participation in the new territories. I am not sure that the writer's statistics are accurate, but his general proposition seems to me to be a most important one which is quite overlooked in the storm of opinions at Washington.

I was struck this morning with a remark of young Mr. Rives[5] that no man's position in the land was equal to yours for so displaying & putting the whole case as to satisfy even the reasonable & reasoning portion of the Southern people as to what is the enlarged & right view of the whole question—because your position has always been strictly *national* while Mr. [John Caldwell] Calhoun's has been strictly *sectional*. He added that he looked for the greatest argument now that this country had ever produced. I need not repeat to you the ardent expressions which he used as to your ability to give it.

Again I pray you excuse this trespass on your time. With warmest wishes & *prayers* for your victory & honor as you go forth to this great battle believe me Dear Sir Your Sincere friend   Benj. D. Silliman

ALS. NhHi. Silliman (1805–1901; Yale, 1824), a Rhode Island native, was a prominent attorney active in New York Whig politics.

1. Webster's second reply to Hayne. See *Correspondence*, 3: 15–31; *Speeches and Formal Writings*, 1.

2. In his last formal speech before the Senate on March 4, 1850, John C. Calhoun had argued that the gradual demise of political "equilibrium" between North and South was the underlying cause of sectional controversy. *Congressional Globe*, 31st Cong., 1st sess., pp. 451–455; Richard K. Crallé, ed., *Works of John C. Calhoun* (New York, 1854–1857), 4: 542–573.

3. Under the constitution each slave counted as three fifths of a free man for the purposes of determining both taxation and representation in the House of Representatives.

4. The *Long Island Star* was a Whig weekly published in Brooklyn, New York, for Long Island subscribers to the *Brooklyn Evening Star*. Silliman's enclosure has not been found, but some of his arguments and language follow that in a *Star* editorial, "Mr. [Willie Person] Mangum and Slavery," February 21, 1850.

5. Probably Francis R. Rives (1822–1891; Virginia 1840), son of the then minister to France William Cabell Rives.

TO EDWARD EVERETT

Mar: 10. '50

My Dear Sir

If you can conscientiously defend my Speech, I beg of you to go to Faneuil Hall,[1] & do so.

Charlotte [Brooks Everett][2] is very well. She is giving us a great deal of daily pleasure.

Look to the [Boston] Atlas for the most correct copy of my Speech.[3] Yrs truly   Danl Webster

ALS. MHi.

1. A mass meeting was being organized by Webster men in Boston to endorse his conciliatory posture toward the South. "This project," Everett later recalled, "was abandoned as hazardous, & likely to disclose a formidable amount of dissent." See Everett to Abbott Lawrence, April 29, 1850, Everett Papers, microfilm reel 29.

2. Everett's daughter, who was staying with the Websters.

3. Summary versions of Webster's Seventh of March speech were telegraphed to Boston the morning following its delivery. The first complete text of the speech appeared on March 9 in the Washington National Intelligencer. A few days later Webster expressed dissatisfaction with the accuracy of the Atlas's account. See DW to Redding & Company, March 15, 1850, mDW 29998. For the text, consult Speeches and Formal Writings, 2.

Although Webster's Seventh of March speech contained no dramatic new initiatives for compromising sectional differences—he stood, on specifics, with Henry Clay—the speech nonetheless was recognized immediately as one of the most formidable public addresses in the American experience. In both spoken form and the carefully edited pamphlet version that soon circulated in the scores of thousands, its power was acknowledged by everyone who discussed it.

Concerned as it was to assuage the deep sense of grievance felt in the South, the speech struck a responsive chord there, as Webster had hoped it would. Editorials hailed it, and, as the sampling of letters below suggests, so did individuals, prominent and obscure. By contrast, the speech sparked bitter controversy in the North. Free Soilers denounced Webster for betraying both morality and the true interests of his section. In communities from Maine to Illinois meetings were called to condemn the speech. Much of the northern Whig press questioned both Webster's motives and his reasoning, and in one telling salvo, the poet Whittier stigmatized Webster as a "fallen angel" whose soul had "fled." Many of his closest political friends, such as Edward Everett (see below), declined to endorse the speech in all particulars.

In this context, the words of support that Webster received in letters from friends, acquaintances, and individuals previously unknown to him provided a special sustenance, and an incentive to battle on in what would be a bruising and complex struggle for sectional conciliation.

FROM HENRY ALEXANDER SCAMMELL DEARBORN

Hawthorn Cottage
Roxbury, March 11, 1850

My Dear Sir,

I was highly gratified in reading your admirable, patriotic & powerful speech, in relation to the new territories. It was a bold, independent & dignified discharge of the high duties devolved upon you. The *Crisis* required, that the ablest men should come forth, in the majesty of their strength, & rebuke the fanatics & demagogues throughout the land, who, by their mad & treasonable efforts, have basely attempted to shatter the massive pillars of the UNION.

The abstractionists, the impracticable, the unprincipled, & the ignorant will evince their wrath, at the signal defeat, which they must perceive awaits them; but you are protected against their vindictive assaults by the holy buckler of Patriotism; & all honest men *now*, & for all coming time, will be grateful for such a fearless & noble illustration of devotion, to the stability, prosperity & glory of the Republic.

It is on such momentous occasions that the really great men of a nation can show how immensely important are the services they can render. Thus far we have had only three before this, when such aid was so imperiously required: —the contest for national independence, the Establishment of the Constitution & the suppression of Nullification. Equally fearful perils have been again bravely met, & so triumphantly encountered, that the foundations of the Union have been consolidated forever.

The North & the South will again be reconciled, by a magnanimous adjustment, based upon the rights, the interests, & sectional opinions of all parts of the country. Wisdom will restore harmony, & the criminal conduct of those factionists, who have disgracefully & rebelliously urged Cecession & encouraged *Civil War*, will be consigned to oblivion, or a dishonored immortality.

As a humble American Citizen, I offer my sincere thanks, for the distinguished manner, in which you have performed the responsible duties of a *NATIONAL* Senator. Would to God, that every member of that august body had sufficient scope of mind, to forget his *state* prejudices, & at all times *feel* & *act* as *one* of the *sixty* legislators of *all the United States*. With assurances of the highest respect, I have the honor to be your most Obt. St.   H. A. S. Dearborn

ALS. NhHi.

FROM JOHN TAYLOR

Franklin March the 11. 1850

Mr Webster Dear Sir

I receivd your letter of the 8.th, to day.[1] Encloesed Was a check on Merchants' Bank, Boston for $50-00 to pay for the Stear, & take care of the rest.—You say you are a fraid I have paid $5.00 to much, for the Stear—Last Saturday, I was offerd $50-00 for the stear, by Mr Sawyer[2] of Salsbury N.H. To mate one, which his Brother[3] had. I shal be sure to take good care of the Great Stears, I will give you next November, for the Great Stears, $125.-00 & take my own resk.

I think it best to fat the Stevens oxen, as they are fat now, & I wish you to have the best Beef, that you Ever salted in your Marshfield seller, I can work them a little this spring, you say that I may by a pare of Cheap oxen, if I cant git along with out, about that I can tell better when the Spring opens, if we have an erly spring I can do a good deal of work, with the team which I have, you say money is not plenty with you. I think there is not $100. in all the Town of Franklin, I mean in mony, Mr Webster you say you forget some things, Which we agreed upon about farming this year, you wish me to stait how we fixt it, as we had no ritings I will state what you & I talked, over,

First. 1. the 15 acre piece, which was to be plowed & sowed in oats, as the grass seed did not cetch last year, there is on 15 acer peice know, 300 loads of mud & manure, which was to be spread over the whole piece & plowed in, & then sowed in oats & grass, that will make 15 acers of oats, /2nd Next my last year potater ground, was to be sowed in oats, 8 acers, which makes 23 acers,—3d, is where my corn grew last year, that was to be one half planted with potaters, & the other half, with Turnips. 4th—the ground which was plowd last faul, 7 acers join-in Berrinyground, was to be corn.—5th, potaters, this year, 8 acers, or 9, to be south of my potater piece last year, which will, run from the Railroad & strike south End of corn field, near Old fort, that will make an Ell,—I mean the corn peice, & potater peice, makes the Ell, 6th you ask me if I could turn Gra back, the Morrison Horse, for a good work horse, so that you can have the horse which went To the White Hills, he is as good a horse as there is in NewHamps[hire].—you must have the Horse which Went to the White Hills,—I think Gra Back, will traid of well, If your people hav not worked him to hard this winter, If you think Best, you can scend him up. I think he would work well, with Old Eagle. I am, you most obdt. Servent,   John Taylor

ALS. NhHi. John Taylor, Jr. (1801–1869), had managed Webster's farm at Franklin since 1835.

1. See DW to John Taylor, March 8, 1850, mDW 29922.

2. Probably Stephen Sawyer, from

whom Webster purchased a farm in
Franklin later in the year. See agreement dated November 2, 1850, mDW

40435.
   3. Not identified.

TO FRANKLIN HAVEN

Washington, Mar. 12, '50

My Dear Sir,

   Three or four years ago, there was a talk, among friends in Boston, of taking some measures to arrange those old debts which were hanging over me, at that time. Some schemes were suggested; among which one was, to interest me in some shares in the Phila. & Baltimore R.R. in the hope that a rise in those shares would make a profit. Unhappily, I believe, there has been little or no rise. Meantime, the burden falls on Mr. [James Kellogg] Mills.[1] Now the question is, whether any thing can be done, by means of my Mexican scrip,[2] or otherwise. I would not trouble you too much about my affairs; but I cannot well stay here, unless I get into a condition in which I can "breathe more freely." Think of these things at a leisure moment. Yrs,   D. W.

   Mar. 13 P.S. I thank you for the letter,[3] rec'd this morning. We shall have a fight, with abolitionists, under the lead I fear of Mr. [William Henry] Seward; and a fight, too, with the violent party of the South under the lead of Mr. [John Caldwell] Calhoun. But I shall stand on the principles of my speech, to the end; & we shall beat them, & the Union party will triumph. Tell Peter Harvey not to despond. If necessary, I will take the stump in every village in New England. We will put the disorganizers down, *if we can.* Yrs   D. W.

Text from *W & S*, 16: 536–537. Original not found.

   1. Mills (1799–1863), an influential Boston merchant and banker, frequently provided Webster with financial aid and advice.

   2. Webster's "Mexican scrip"— actually certificates of ownership in Texas properties issued through the Union and Trinity Land companies— became the subject of increased sale, transfer, and speculation as a United States government commission con-

vened in 1849 to weigh the claims of land company scrip holders. DW's hopes of a large windfall from his holdings (see, e.g., DW to Haven, April 25, 1850, pp. 74–75, below, December 7, 1850, mDW 31784; to Samuel P. Lyman, April 21, 1851, mDWs) dissolved in the spring of 1851 when awards were announced. See DW to Caleb Cushing, June 6, 1851, mDW 33780, and pp. 264–265, below, DW to Haven, July 3, 1851.

   3. Not found.

FROM EDWARD EVERETT

Cambridge 12 March 1850

Dear Sir,

   Yesterday we got your speech—the speech—in extenso.[1] I need not tell you with what satisfaction I read it. A wretched telegraphic abstract had reached us last week. Every point likely to discontent the north had been prominently stated, without any of the qualifications & preliminaries with which it was conditioned by you. As disapproval is always more active than approval, a good deal of dissatisfaction was expressed at the ground you had taken.[2] I have not conversed with any one since we have the speech itself; but I take it for granted that reasonable men will be satisfied. The very circumstance however that your speech has been to some extent satisfactory at the South will lead our ultraists to dislike it. They do not wish for an adjustment; & to confess the truth, I suspect there are those at the South who wish it as little.

There is one idea which I will take the liberty to suggest to you, which I think is entitled to more weight than has been allowed it. When slavery is prohibited in a territory there is, of course, *in terms* no favor granted to the north; no disability imposed on the South. It applies equally to both, so that *prima facie* neither party has lost or gained. But to this the Southerner replies "this equality of treatment is delusive, because the northern emigrant does not wish to go with slaves, nor the Southern emigrant without them, so that, under a show of equality, in point of fact the north monopolizes & the South is excluded." Now this is wrong both ways. Many northern men invest their funds in slave property. There are a great many plantations in the Southern states & in Cuba owned by northern men, and a vast number as I am told mortgaged at the North, the slaves being the only valuable part of the security. On the other hand, a great many Southern men have at all times emigrated to the country North West of the Ohio, some expressly to get away from slavery, others, without caring much about it one way or the other—because they saw the country N.W. of the Ohio to be a very prosperous one. I was told in Ohio that when that state was filling up with emigrants after the treaty of Greenville,[3] they always reported themselves at the land office there as coming either from Massachusetts or Virginia. If pains were taken to illustrate that point, I think it would appear that there was a very strong emigration from Slaveholding states into the non-slaveholding territory, & I have no doubt in many cases for the very reason that it was non-slaveholding. I am not sure that the case is not similar in California. Although, as the South alledges & complains, the agitation of the territorial question has had the effect of keeping away slaves, it has not had the effect of keeping away Southern emigrants. The South is, I believe, very fairly represented in their elections; & though their convention has unanimously voted that there shall be no slavery, there were in that convention many slaveholders.[4] In fact the idea that a Southerner, as such, is one half of a pair of Siamesse twins of which the other half is a negro slave, so that to prohibit the latter is to prohibit the former, is as unfounded as it is derogatory. Neither is there anything so anti-Slavery at the north, as would prevent a great deal of northern capital from being invested in slave property in any new country into which circumstances favored its introduction. So that not only nominally but really the exclusion of slavery from the N.W. Territory & from California is a measure bearing equally upon North & South. It was unanimously voted by the congress of 1787 & unanimously voted by the California Convention of 1849, in both of which the South was fully represented.

You mention having "heard it said," that Mr [John] Jay was not aware in 1774 [1794], that cotton was an article grown in the United States for exportation. That statement I have frequently made in Congress & elsewhere. I send you a pamphlet[5] where you will find it on page 26 (By the way how like an old almanac, these things of twenty years standing read!) Whether I had any positive authority for saying that Mr Jay was ignorant of this fact, I do not now recollect; but it is matter of safe inference from the twelfth article of his treaty, which, on this very account, was rejected by the senate. That article contained the following proviso intended to have the effect of preventing the U.S. from participating in the carrying trade from the British W. Indies to the mother country: "It being expressly agreed & declared that during the continuance of this article, the U.S. will prohibit & restrain the carrying any molasses, sugar, Coffee, Cocoa, or *Cotton*, in American vessels, either from his majesty's islands *or from the United States to any part of the world*, reasonable sea stores excepted."[6] If you have occasion to revert to this topic, as very likely you may, it might be as well to remind our Southern brethren that the proximate cause of the extension of the culture of cotton was [Eli] Whitney's saw gin;*[7] & that all ingenious machinery is by a law of our nature the indigenous growth of free-soil. But you will be disposed to think on reading these suggestions, that among the prohibitions of Mr Jay's treaty, it would have been well if he had included carrying coals to New Castle.

But as that is not the case I will give you one more bushel. Mr [John Caldwell] Calhoun is (unintentionally) unjust to Lord Aberdeen[8] & the British government, in saying that "the British government had given encouragement to the abolitionists of the U. States who were represented at the world's convention.[9] The question of the abolition of slavery in the U.S. was agitated in that convention. One gentleman stated that Mr [Charles Francis] Adams informed him, that if the British government wished to abolish slavery in the U.S. they must begin with Texas. A commission was sent from this world's convention to the British Secretary of state Lord Aberdeen, and it so happened that a gentleman was present when the interview took place between Lord A, & the committee, who gave me a full account of it shortly after it occurred. Lord Aberdeen fell into the project, & gave full encouragement to the Abolitionists."

All this is so contrary not only to the cautious & highly conservative character of Lord Aberdeen, but to the general tone of the conservative party in England, on the subject of slavery, that I am a little surprized Mr Calhoun did not himself mistrust his information. It is intrinsically as impossible, as that you, while Secretary of state, should have received a deputation from the northern Abolitionists on the subject of abolishing slavery in Texas, & should have fallen fully into the project.

My despatches to Mr [Abel Parker] Upshur No 62 and No 64[10] have been published at Washington & contain a full & authentic account of Lord Aberdeens interview with the deputation of the world's convention. I took the precaution to send to Lord A. my written report of our conversation, that he might correct it if I had not remembered it accurately. My despatch No 62 (3 Nov 1843) was written with his corrections, they were immaterial, before me. Lord Aberdeen told the deputation in general terms that the British government would use their legitimate influence in every quarter to promote the abolition of slavery. But so far from falling into the project of the deputation, which was that Great Britain should guarantee a loan to be applied to promote the abolition of slavery in Texas, Lord A. expressly assured me that "he gave them no countenance whatever." If you think it likely that the debate will get back to that topic, it would be worth your while to refresh your memory with those despatches, though I cannot refer you to the volume of Congressional Documents that contains them. General [William] Hick[e]y[11] will no doubt find them for you.

In the despatch No 64 there is a slight mistake at the beginning of the second Paragraph. Mr Ashbel Smith was not present at the interview with Lord Aberdeen.[12] He received his information from some one who was present; perhaps the same individual from whom Mr Calhoun derived *his* information. But whoever was the author of the statement, it was most certainly entirely incorrect. In fact it appears from Mr Ashbel Smith's statement to me, that his informant gave it only as matter of inference, that Lord Aberdeen would favor their project. All this appears from my published despatches. No. 64 was written on the 16th of November. On the same day I wrote a confidential letter to Mr Upshur containing the following passage "In speaking in my interview with Lord Aberdeen of the 6th inst. of the uneasiness which had been excited in the United States in reference to the measures supposed to be pursued by Great Britain to effect the abolition of slavery in Texas, I told him that there were persons in the United States, who firmly believed, that Great Britain was pursuing this object and resolved if possible to accomplish it, with a view to aggrandize herself & colonies, at the expense of the United States in particular & I sketched to him briefly the plan of policy in this respect, which is ascribed to great Britain in a letter recently addressed by General Duff Green to the editor of the Boston Post.¹³ Lord Aberdeen treated it as a notion too absurd and unfounded to need serious contradiction. He said, however, that bearing in mind the sensibilities that existed on this subject, he would endeavor hereafter to express himself with great caution, when it became necessary to speak of slavery."

I am aware that such disclaimers would not be credited by the ordinary run of politicians, who give no faith to diplomatists, & especially by those in our own country, who as a matter of course distrust a British minister. Lord Aberdeen however is in the opinion of Mr Calhoun a direct, worthy & honest man. I agree with Mr C. in this opinion; and I think his repeated assurance that he gave no countenance to the project of the committee who waited upon him ought to be believed in opposition to the inferences of Mr Calhoun's anonymous informant.

Pardon the unreasonable length of this letter, & believe me with sincere attachment ever yours.

P.S. *Query* whether General [Zachary] Taylor remains of opinion if he ever entertained it, that those of his northern friends who counselled him against your influence & persuaded him to give another direction to his confidence gave him good advice.

LC. MHi. Published in part in Frothingham, *Everett*, p. 319.

1. See *Boston Semi-Weekly Atlas*, March 11, 1850.

2. The same issue of the *Atlas* that printed DW's March 7 speech included an editorial bluntly dissociating the paper from Webster's arguments. DW's sentiments, editor William Schouler wrote, "are not our sentiments. They are not, we venture to say, the sentiments of the Whigs of New England."

3. The Treaty of Greenville of 1795 required the Indians to leave most of Ohio and thus spurred immigration from Eastern states into the region.

4. At their constitutional convention in September 1849, Californians adopted antislavery provisions without dissent from the fifteen representatives who had emigrated from the South.

5. Not found.

6. For greater perspective on Jay's Treaty, see Samuel Flagg Bemis, *Jay's Treaty* (New York, 1923), and Jerald A. Combs, *The Jay Treaty: Political Battleground of the Founding Fathers* (Berkeley, Calif., 1970).

7. Added in the margin for insertion here are the words "See note B. to the Pamphlet."

8. George Gordon Hamilton, fourth earl of Aberdeen (1784–1860), served as foreign secretary under Robert Peel, 1841–1846. *DNB*.

9. The World Convention of Abolitionists met in London during the summer of 1843 with a large American representation. Everett was at that time United States minister to England. For Calhoun's perspective on the British government's relations with the abolitionists, see Charles M. Wiltse, *John C. Calhoun: Sectionalist* (Indianapolis, 1951), pp. 153–155, 167–170.

10. Everett to Upshur, November 3, 1843, No. 62; November 16, 1843, No. 64, DNA, RG 59 (Despatches, Britain), published in *Senate Documents*, 28th Cong., 1st sess., Serial 435, Doc. No. 341, pp. 38–42. Upshur had succeeded DW as secretary of state.

11. Hickey was clerk of the Senate.

12. Ashbel Smith was chargé d'affaires of the Texas Republic in London and Paris.

13. Duff Green's long letter from London, dated September 18, 1843, appeared in the *Boston Post* on October 10 of that year.

FROM JOHN STROTHER PENDLETON

Redwood Va
March 12th 1850

My Dear Sir

The first mail since my return home, brings this. On my way I passd through three or four villages—three of them county-seats where one meets the active and leading county politicians. Your late speech was the topic of conversation on all hands, and it affords me great pleasure to say to you, that it recieves, without distinction of party, unanimous & ardent approbation. The Loco Focos will of course presently begin to differ about it—for their leaders will find there is too much approbation, but still the impression on even that party is deep and will last. For the Whigs it is the best event for a long time—Falsifying the declarations of our Southern agitators—less respectable than your fanatics of the North and having much less sense—it at the same time gives great increase of strength to our honest and reasonable men in their position, and takes from the disunionists three fourths of their entire Capital. The other fourth will follow instantly upon the actual settlement of the question. I have thought and said for several years past that the slave subject so settled as to leave the public mind quiet & easy and Southern democracy was ready for the benefit of a general Bankrupt law. It has nothing left to keep it together & it dissolves at once—for of all the old issues on which it has heretofore maintained its organisation nothing is left. The ultraisms &c of the more progressive school have as yet found but little favor in the South.

I will send you in due time a list of names for this county and some others. At Warrenton (Fauquier C[ount]y) a gentleman told me that he and some others should order a thousand copies of your speech for that county—And Sam[ue]l Chilton (my immediate predecessor in Congress) will send you a list for that county of prominent gentlemen of both parties. I requested him to send about fifty names for your own frank. Very respectfully & truly Your friend & obt St   Jno Pendleton

P.S. I shall write a note to the Whig (Richmond) today   J S P

ALS. NhD.

FROM WILLIAM H. WINDER

Philadelphia 12 March 1850

Sir,

It may be great presumption in me to address this letter to Mr. Webster, but humble as I am, I value my intelligence & good opinion too high to waste their expression upon ordinary occasions.

I have read carefully & with reflection your late speech of Thursday last. It appears to me if Washington had arisen from his tomb, & had addressed the Senate on that day, he would have uttered the words of your speech.

It bears throughout the impress of one lifted up above the mists of passion, prejudice & faction, surveying with a clear vision all that is passing below, & truthfully stating it. Divested of sectional feeling, forgetful of the character of a special representative, the words of truth & soberness fell from the lips of one impelled by a sense of the general good.

That a class of persons, blinded to every sense of duty, heedless of every thing except the liberation of *Negroes*, per fas aut nefas should disregard your patriotic admonitions & exhortations, is not strange. We have seen they act upon the principle that no faith is to be kept with Heretics: & they constitute themselves the infallible tribunal of determining what is heresy. They have avowed that Orthodoxy means a flagrant & declared disregard of the requisitions of the constitution, & their purpose unscrupulously & unhesitatingly to violate its provisions whenever & wherever it shall interfere with their purposes of emancipating, of letting loose those facsimiles of the imps of darkness upon their Brethren.

I have ever noticed that the agitation of this Negro question invariably & disastrously reacts upon the labor & the interests of the North. That being an absorbing question at the South swallows up all other issues. To strengthen themselves on this point the friends of the Tariff at the South are compelled to abandon it, to secure themselves against attacks upon a sensitive interest at Home. Every practical man at the North, every one connected with manufacturing interests must *feel* constantly that as often as this question is agitated the knife is driven into him. He must feel also that the tendency of your speech is to bring about a right spirit & to mitigate that feeling at the South which in retort for such attacks on their sensibilities & interest would strike down these great interests of the North. As pugilists express it, when the North makes an abolition blow at the South, it counters with an Anti-Tariff blow; & unfortunately the counter is usually "planted" in professional parlance, the more effectually of the two. Indeed I look upon those parties at the North as the worst & most dangerous enemies to the working classes &

to all manufacturing interests. The justice & propriety of a tariff discriminating in favor of American industry would of necessity recommend itself to the intelligence of the South, if the matter were not poisoned with the stream of bitterness which flows so constantly from that quarter. Practical men partake comparatively little of it, but like leaven it renders the mass offensive to the sufferers at the South.

An invincible hostility to Slavery, & an unwavering conviction of its injury & its wrong, are perfectly consistent with a faithful adherence to the requisitions of the constitution; & the North by so doing is exempt from responsibility for the existence of slavery in the Southern States. Raw & festered indeed must be that conscience that feels itself impelled to disregard all moral restraints in the pursuit of an object, to attain which, the barriers of the constitution must be broken through; while at home admitted evils, within their acknowledged reach are permitted to run riot undisturbed.

Your speech so far as I glean opinions meets with a hearty approval, except with politicians having an aim, in not approving it. The more it is considered, the deeper will be the convictions of its justice & fitness. Wise as a serpent & harmless as a dove, is a motto which might not inappropriately precede it.

I have read many of your great speeches with the admiration which must have warmed all who did so, but I never before felt myself so strongly impelled to express to you directly, how greatly, *as a citizen of the Republic*, I feel indebted to you for these timely words of wisdom & conciliation. I am with profound respect your most obt. Servt

W. H. Winder

ALS.NhHi. A prominent Philadelphia merchant with real estate interests in the District of Columbia, Winder underwrote construction of a number of prominent Washington buildings, including rebuilding the National Theater in 1851.

FROM SIDNEY BREESE

Carlisle, Illinois
March 16, 1850

My Dear Sir.

The whole Country looks to you to settle the great question now threatening to divide our glorious & heretofore happy Union. Throw off, I beg of you, the trammels of section and of party, & be, what your talents & position indicate you should be, the "Savior of your Country." Be firm & bold. You have nothing to fear—nothing to lose, but every thing to gain. How unfortunate for the Country that you adopted opinions adverse to the democracy! Had you not, you would have been President. As it is, propose a proper compromise, & you cannot fail to attain that high place. As, by our Treaty with Mexico,[1] we *cannot* attach, or annex any Mexican territory without the consent of Mexico (which will never be given) propose the Missouri Compromise line of 36, 30′ or 34° (which will suit the South[)]—or [John Middleton] Claytons Compromise bill.[2] The last is the best, for every body knows that the Supreme Court would *never* decide that the Slaveholders could take their slaves, to California or N. Mexico. The great error of the Southern gentlemen consists in this, that they say, *by the Constitution*, Slaves are *property*, but it is not so. They are alluded to in but *three* places & in every one, are considered as *Persons*. See [Thomas] Jefferson's letter to John Holmes in which he speaks of slaves as *miscalled* property.[3] Do my D[ea]r Sir, arouse yourself & propose the Missouri Compromise. Do not let the Union fall to pieces, & "drenched it may be, with fraternal blood." Your position is an excellent one. I hope you will avail of it. Though we differ politically— are antipodes on general questions—yet on this of the Union I cannot think we differ. Throw yourself into the breach and save the Union & the Country. Your talents, fair fame, high and distinguished character, justify you in taking the lead. [John Caldwell] Calhoun & his friends are for disunion "for the sake of Disunion." With the highest regard, yr. friend   S. Breese late U.S. Senator

ALS.NhD.

1. The Treaty of Guadalupe Hidalgo ending the Mexican War was signed on February 2, 1848.

2. Some congressmen, including such southern rights proponents as Armistead Burt, had proposed an extension of the Missouri Compromise line to the Pacific as a means of resolving the territorial question. The Clayton Compromise of 1848 would have permitted the extension of slavery to the territories acquired from Mexico with the proviso that the courts must ultimately decide whether the institution was legal in those territories. The bill passed the Senate by a 2-1 majority but was tabled in the House by a combination of southern slaveholders and northern abolitionists.

3. See Jefferson to John Holmes, April 22, 1820, in Paul Leicester Ford, ed., *The Writings of Thomas Jefferson* (New York, 1899), 10: 157–158.

FROM WILLIAM GILES JONES

Greensboro Alabama
March 17th. 1850

Dear Sir,

I take pleasure as a Southern man in tendering to you my most heartfelt thanks for the noble firm & patriotic stand you have lately taken in the U.S. Senate in behalf of our common Country. It is a source of much consolation to every honest man & sincere friend of freedom to know that we yet have statesmen like yourself whose souls are expansive enough to feel themselves American citizens & to look far above the little local jealousies so common with the most of our underling politicians of the day whose great & sole object seems to be to foster unpleasant sentiments between the North & South. What are we but brothers of the same great confederacy closely united by ties of blood & interest? The good of one section like the members of the human system is necessarily felt by the whole body & our intercourse & commerce is constant & reciprocal that the prosperity of one section cannot fail to extend its influence to all. Before this event you had many devoted admirers in the South but Sir the man who does not now [k]now the name of Daniel Webster living South of Pennsylvania deserves not the name of an American & allow me to say that it is my ardent hope & opinion that the people of this Country will do that justice to you which you so highly deserve of electing you to the Presidency of the U. States. There is one only reason why you have not been already elevated to that office & that is simply that others aspiring to that place & their expectants have from the dread of your talents labored constantly to impress our people that you were a Northern man a federalist &c and have prevented your nomination thereby. I know well that many of the Whigs here popular as Mr [Henry] Clay has been would have preferred your nomination to his. But if you are never called to fill that place rest assured (& it should be a proud consolation to you) that if it were left to the intelligence & worth of the people to decide you would be chosen by acclamation.

A peaceable seperation of the States is too great an absurdity for a sane mind to embrace. Where could we make a line of division. How could we divide the Navy & Army. How apportion the public property at Washington & elsewhere. It does seem to me when Mr. [John Caldwell] Calhoun talks of peaceable secession he is either (mad) deranged or wishes to be President of the South. But let us once seperate & never will such another Government be organised in this World. I sincerely trust your life may be long spared & your future days be prosperous & happy as they have been usefull.

In June 1841 while on my way to Europe I stopped at Washington & then in company with Mr. [Kenneth] Rayner of N Carolina & Mr. [Caleb] Cushing of your State while you were Secretary of State was made acquainted with you in your office. I never shall forget the easy & agreeable manner I was received & noticed by you nor the warmth & cordiality with which you insisted on my calling again to see you on leaving you to go into Mr. [Horatio?] Jones'[1] room to get my Passport a pleasure I did not again allow myself because I knew too well the value of time to men of business to make myself obtrusive.

Col W[illia]m R[ufus de Vane] King our Senator is the only member of Congress with whom I am well acquainted. He can tell you who I am

as you most likely have forgotten our short interview. With sentiments
of the highest regard I am sir Your obedt Humble Sert   William Jones

ALS. DLC. Jones (1808–1883), an
Alabama lawyer and Democratic politician, was then representing Mobile

County in the state senate.
    1. Horatio Jones was a clerk in the
State Department.

FROM JOHN OVERTON CHOULES

Newport R I
18 March 1850

Dr Sir

Dining on Saturday with your Son [Fletcher] in Boston he wished me
to write you, or I would not venture to task your time at such a moment. I named to Fletcher a conversation which Gov[erno]r Isaac Hill
had at the Tremont on Saturday morn[in]g wh[ich] he Fletcher wished
me to name. Mr Hill spoke in the very widest terms of admiration of
your Speech,[1] & said he regarded your effort as the crowning act of your
Life, he said it placed you in his esteem immeasurably before any man
who had acted in public life since [George] Washington—& that it was
20 years in advance of any other public man. Gov[erno]r [Henry] Hubbard said pretty much the same. In Boston I found the best men delighted. Dr [Daniel] Sharp said he had read it 3 times & was satisfied
that the sober thought of N England would come to it. I met Col: [Mar-
shall Pinckney] Wilder the Pres[iden]t of the Senate. He goes against it
& intimated at the Horticultural Club Dinner that Gov[erno]r [George
Nixon] Briggs & the Legislature would head it. Mr [Nathaniel Briggs]
Borden late M[ember of] C[ongress] from Fall River was bitter. Mr
[Joseph Henry] Billings[2] member of the House of Repres[entative]s for
Roxbury said he had that day read a Letter[3] from Horace Mann stating
that the Northern Members would follow [Orin] Fowler & endeavor to
undo the influence of the Speech. I am more <than ever> & more convinced that with the best people of N.E. your position is highly acceptable—& however it may be now assailed yet they will come round to it.
Gov[erno]r [William Henry] Seward has made a capital mistake—& will
feel it yet.[4] Mr H[enry] Y[oung] Cranston (ex. Mem.) is producing a
deep impression here with our citizens in favor of the Speech. I am Dr
Sir Yours with great respect faith[full]y   J. O. Choules

P S
Dear Sir
    Your favor of the 17th[5] is recd. I will forward a carefully made *list of
Names*[6] in a day or two as you desire. resp[ectfull]y   J.O.C.

ALS. ViU. Choules (1801–1856) was
a prominent New England minister,

writer, and editor of Christian publications.

1. Although Hill and Webster had been bitter adversaries dating back to the latter's activity in New Hampshire politics, the sectional crisis and the Seventh of March speech seeking to contain it spurred a rapprochement. See below, Hill to DW, April 17, 1850, and DW to Hill, April 20, 1850.

2. A Roxbury farmer, Billings (1809–1874) served in the Massachusetts House of Representatives in 1845–1846 and 1849–1850.

3. Strongly committed to a free-soil position regarding the western territories, Mann made no secret of his opposition to Webster's efforts at sectional conciliation. See Jonathan Messerli, *Horace Mann: A Biography*

(New York, 1972), pp. 512–514.

4. Seward had delivered a strong "no compromise" speech in the Senate on March 11, insisting on California's admission to the Union as a free state without concessions to the South. *Congressional Globe*, 31st Cong., 1st sess., *Appendix*, pp. 260–269.

5. Not found.

6. Webster was planning to distribute copies of his Seventh of March speech to influential individuals in the respective New England states and had probably requested a list from Choules for Rhode Island. See below, DW to Fletcher Webster, March 31, 1850.

TO THOMAS BUCKMINSTER CURTIS

Washington, Mar. 21, 1850

My Dear Sir,

Except a letter from Mr. [James Kellogg] Mills, yours[1] was the first to let me know that there were some things in my Speech that Boston people, or some of them could approve. But it informed me, also, much to my regret, that Mr. [Joshua Thomas] Stevenson[2] was dissatisfied. There is hardly any one I like better, or whom I should be more glad to please; and I hope, still, that upon reflection, he will modify his feeling.

It is a speech containing two or three propositions, of fact, and law. Mr. Stevenson is a very good judge to decide, whether all or any of these are without foundation. That the speech presents not an agreeable state of things, respecting the slavery question, is plain enough; the question is, does it present the *true* state of things?

I hope to be able to send you, today, a copy of a corrected Edition.[3] I shall send another to Mr. Stevenson; and perhaps he will look the Speech over again. One thing appears to me to be certain, and that is, that if we would avoid rebellion, out-breaks, and civil war, we must let Southern Slavery alone. Another is, that the keeping up of this Slavery agitation, useless as it is, in Massachusetts, disaffects the whole South, Whig and democrat, to all our Massachusetts interests.

But it is enough that you have had to read a Speech. I will not "superinduce," as they say here, the infliction of a political letter. I have been a sufferer from colds, and a sore throat; but am better, and hope to get to the Senate today. Yours, truly, always,   Danl Webster

I have much occasion to go home, to see to my own affairs; but I cannot leave my place, pending this California question.[4] California will come in, in due time, exactly as she is.

Text from MHi *Proceedings*, 3d Series, 45 (November 1911): 164. Original not found. Curtis (1795–1871), a Boston merchant and banker, was one of DW's most reliable allies during the spring of 1850.
    1. Letters not found.
    2. Stevenson (1807–1876; Harvard 1826) was a Massachusetts businessman and sometime politician who had represented Boston in the legislature.
    3. Webster was then sending out copies of a pamphlet edition of his speech. See below, DW to Daniel Fletcher Webster, March 31, 1850.
    4. The issue of California's admission to the Union had sparked the current crisis and remained a centerpiece of the ongoing congressional debate.

FROM NATHANIEL GREENE PENDLETON

Cincinnati March 21. 1850

My dear Sir

Upon the slavery question, your position local & political, gives you a decisive influence; and I am happy to say to you, that in the opinion of all reflecting men hereabout, that influence has been most happily exerted in the grounds so independently assumed, & nobly vindicated in your late speech. Hitherto, the discussion in the Senate has done nothing but good. It has ascertained the precise points of difference—what may be conceded, and what will be maintained. It has designated the Ultras on both sides, & broken up the unity between them and their respective parties—so that Mr [John Caldwell] Calhoun will find he cannot rally the South; and Mr [William Henry] Seward (in whom I have not the slightest confidence) that he cannot manage the North.

Notwithstanding the good I think the discussion has done, I doubt very much whether the continuance of the debate will add to that good.

This question is to be settled by action, not by words. Is there any risk in the prediction that the following measures can be adopted, & if adopted will be generally acquiesced in North & South.

    1. A sufficient law to be executed independent of State legislation for the surrender of fugitive slaves.

    2. The admission of California *as it is*.

    3. Governments for the territories, without any proviso upon the subject slavery.

    4. The abolition of the *Slave trade* in the district of Columbia according to Mr [Henry] Clay's plan. Leave the question of new States out of Texas[1] to be determined when application shall be made for their admission. Indeed I do not see how any thing else can be done at present— new resolutions will add nothing to their *right* under the annexation resolutions.

The law for the surrender of fugitives you have now before you.[2] Make it sufficient for its purpose without wounding the pride of the North, and tender it to the South as a peace offering. Mr [James Murray] Mason ought to be told distinctly that if the law shall give authority to U S officers to break open our houses upon suspicion they conceal runaway Slaves, the law will never be permitted to be executed. These Southern gentlemen are so eternally & offensively blustering about their pride, they forget that Northern men have their pride as well as they; which if not quite so inflammable as theirs, if once ignited, will burn quite as fiercely.

If the measures referred [to], or any other be just, pass them, & leave just & conciliatory measures to their just influence with the American people.

The object of this letter was to give you the pleasure which all right minded men receive from a general appreciation of their good deeds. Excuse all the rest and believe me with great respect Yr obt Sv

N. G. Pendleton

ALS. NhD.

1. Various proposals had been offered regarding a Texas boundary, ranging from Texas's own boundary claims west to Santa Fe to partition of Texas into as many as five new states. See *Diplomatic Papers*, 2.

2. On January 4, 1850, Senator Mason introduced a fugitive slave bill providing for a thousand-dollar fine as punishment for obstruction of the rendition of runaways. Subsequently he modified the bill in an effort to win northern support. Other senators, including Clay and William Seward, offered their own formulas for a fugitive slave law, and the issue remained to be settled.

FROM EDWARD EVERETT

Cambridge 22 March 1850.

My dear Sir,

I read your speech with so much admiration of its power and so much sympathy in its great object,—the rescue of the Union from the great impending danger, and I have been so long accustomed to say "ditto to Mr. Burke", that I did not stop to scrutinize details. It was not till I began to examine the separate propositions, in order to prepare myself for a public meeting in Faneuil Hall,[1] if one should be called to respond to it, that I found on looking back to papers & documents, that I was pretty strongly committed on the subject of Texas.

During the elections of 1837 & 1838 & 1839, when I was a candidate for Governor, questions were proposed by the abolitionists to all the candidates for State Offices. My answers were written on consultation with friends, and expressed the opinions by which they were willing to abide. The Correspondence of 1839 I enclose you.[2]

Among the resolves of 1838 was one relative to Texas, which if I mistake not was *unanimously* adopted by both houses of the general Court, in the following terms:

"Resolved that we, the Senate and House of Representatives in General Court assembled, do, in the name of the People of Massachusetts, earnestly & solemnly protest against the incorporation of Texas into the Union, & declare that no act done or compact made for such purpose by the government of the United States, will be binding on the United States or the People."[3]

In a letter[4] afterwards published by me, I said that these resolutions not only received my official signature, but my personal concurrence. Such a committal seems to me to put it out of my power, with any credit or to any good purpose, to hold an opposite language at this time. The only friend to whom I have named the matter,—Mr George T[icknor] Curtis,—fully concurs with me in this opinion.

On the extradition of fugitives I had misgivings from the first, not at all of the Constitutional right; every word you say on that point I agree with, & it is argued with much power in a very able article of this day, in the Daily Advertiser.[5] It is however the incident of Slavery,— itself an anomaly in a free government,—which is most repugnant to the Public Sentiment of the Free States. It was under this sentiment, that the law of 1793[6] broke down. I much fear that legislation by Congress will inflame instead of subduing this feeling. Cannot the real patriotic men of the South be made to see this & to extend to the North, on this point, the same toleration which they require us to exercise toward them, when they violate, as they do each day, the first clause of the very same section of the Constitution, which, in the third clause, gives the right of extradition. It strikes me that some provisions of Mr. [James Murray] Mason's bill,[7] are unnecessarily stringent and otherwise ill-advised;[8] such as the creation of a board of Commissioners expressly for the arrest of fugitives *in every County* of the free States. I think such a step would give a vast impulse to anti-slavery agitation.

Pardon the freedom with which I express my dissent from you on this point (Mr Mason's bill) & believe me as ever Sincerely Yours,

Edward Everett.

ALS. MHi. Published in Frothingham, *Everett*, pp. 318–319.

1. See above, DW to Edward Everett, March 10, 1850, n. 1.

2. Everett enclosed a newspaper clipping (mDW 30068) of an open letter addressed to him by Nathaniel B. Borden, October 18, 1839, and his reply of October 24 (see also Everett

Papers, MHi. microfilm reel 26). Borden asked if Everett was in favor of the abolition of slavery in the District of Columbia and the slave trade between the states, and if he opposed the admission of new slave states. Everett's answers to both questions were affirmative.

3. See "Resolves against the an-

nexation of Texas to the United States," March 16, 1838, in *Resolves of the General Court of the Commonwealth of Massachusetts . . .* (Boston, 1838), pp. 665–666.

4. See above, n. 2.

5. "Mr. Webster as a Senator," anonymously written for the *Boston Daily Advertiser* by George Ticknor. See below, pp. 105–107, DW to Ticknor, June 1, 1850.

6. Northern hostility to the Fugitive Slave Act of 1793 was reflected in the 1830s and 1840s in the passage of "personal liberty laws," which hampered the rendition of fugitives and infuriated southerners.

7. See above, Nathaniel Greene Pendleton to DW, March 21, 1850, n. 2.

8. At this point Everett inserted in the margin the following: "In this opinion, Mr. Curtis expressed his concurrence; but thinks if Senators from the North and South would take counsel together, they could frame a bill, that would be received."

TO FRANKLIN HAVEN

Washington Mar: 23. 1850

My Dear Sir

Last Summer you were kind enough to allow me, on the security of the deposite of Scrip in the Unity Land Co,[1] to draw checks on the Bank to an amount not exceeding, at any time, $3000. This limit I have endeavored to preserve, & am, at present, within it.

When I came from home last autumn, in the autumn, I gave you an order, or Dr[a]ft, on Mr [Asbury] Dickens,[2] for $800. Whether this amount was to be applied when recd to the credit of my account in the Bank, or whether a distinct advance was made to me for it, I do not remember. The Books will of course show.

I have now the happiness to say, that within two or three days I expect to see in the papers an official announcement that the claim of the Unity Land Co. *is admitted;* amount of damages &c to be assessed hereafter.[3]

Now it occurs to me to inquire of you, whether it would not be better, at this time, to make up the interest account, on this over-draft, or the amount which has thus been standing on the books charged to me, & take my note for it, so as to place the matter in proper shape. If the note should be taken at 7 months, one renewal, at six months, would reach to the period when the awards are to be paid; by the 12 of April of next [year.] All this, however, I leave to be arranged as you may think best. If you think it as well, that the amount should stand as it has done, then I shall regard the limit, & endeavor to keep within it, as heretofore.

I have been Counsel for Mr John Baldwin,[4] a claimant before the Board, whose claim has been allowed. My commissions amounted to a considerable, tho' no very large sum. My friends Mr [Richard Milford] Blatchford & Mr [Samuel] Jaudon,[5] in order to help me to the means of making some payments, which will be coming along, have been kind enough to take an assignment of my amount of Commissions, & therefrom to give me their respective acceptances for $1200 each, at 7 ms. They were put at this length of time, for the reason stated above; viz, that one renewal for 6 months would bring them to April 1851, when the awards will be paid. These acceptances I now enclose, & shall be glad to have their amounts placed to my credit.

It is the opinion of the Commissioners that the Three & a quarter millions appropriated by Congress will be sufficient to pay all the awards, in full; tho this opinion is not to be quoted.

So then, my Dear Sir, after much toil, Mexican claims seem now about to result in something "available"; & I hope you will not suffer from your kindness, exerted in my behalf, always so usefully & efficiently. Yours very truly, always,   Danl Webster

ALS. MH-H.

1. DW here conflates the names of the Union and Trinity Land companies. No "Unity" Land Company had claims against Mexico.

2. Dickens (1773–1861) was secretary of the United States Senate from 1836 to 1861.

3. Webster was overoptimistic. Awards were not announced until April 1851, and even then DW had to await a further court test before finding that he would realize only a fraction of his imagined windfall from the Mexican claims. See DW to Franklin Haven March 28, 1850,

mDW 30130, and July 3, 1851, pp. 264–265, below.

4. Dr. John Baldwin of Pennsylvania, an early and persistent claimant against the Mexican government. See Baldwin et al. to DW, December 15, 1841, mDW 20832.

5. Jaudon (1796–1874, Princeton 1813), a prominent Wall Street banker, had long been associated with Webster's financial activities and was familiar with his Mexican scrip. See headnote preceding DW to Jaudon, April 15, 1848, *Correspondence*, 6: 282–283.

During the spring of 1850 Webster's attention focused on two distinct though related concerns. As he pressed his campaign in Massachusetts to win public support for a compromise with the South—an enterprise that gained momentum with the publication of supportive letters by prominent citizens in New York, Boston, and Newburyport (see below)— he was also deeply engaged in the task of finding a majority in Congress for a solution to the sectional crisis.

Although he had endorsed a compromise along the broad lines laid down by Henry Clay on January 29, Webster preferred to pursue the admission of California to the Union as prelude to a more general legislative settlement. He spoke and voted against Senator Henry Foote's motion to establish a special committee of thirteen senators to devise an omnibus bill treating all facets of the sectional controversy, on the ground that such a bill could never pass a Congress so divided in its interests and priorities. As Webster put it in debate on April 12, "nothing

can come of it but a fresh series of instructions and amendments, bring-
ing on debates and discussions of which no one can see the end." (Con-
gressional Globe, 31st Cong., 1st sess., pp. 721–722.)

Despite Webster's opposition, and a series of controversial amend-
ments offered by Thomas Hart Benton between April 11 and April 17 to
separate California from other issues on the special committee's pro-
posed agenda—each of which was defeated after long and often acri-
monious debate—the Foote resolutions carried. Webster was appointed
to the special committee of thirteen, but his disappointment with the
course of events was reflected in his unwillingness to participate in its
deliberations. He left Washington in late April for Boston, where he
remained until May 10. During his absence the committee wrote a com-
prehensive bill that Webster supported in principle but recognized could
not pass the current Congress. With President Taylor unbending in his
own no-compromise position, and extremists in both sections continuing
to agitate against sectional conciliation, the state of the Union remained
perilous.

FROM THOMAS HANDASYD PERKINS ET AL.

[Boston, March 25, 1850]

Sir,

Impressed with the magnitude and importance of the service to the
Constitution and the Union, which you have rendered by your recent
Speech in the Senate of the United States on the subject of Slavery, we
desire to express to you, our deep obligations for what this speech has
done and is doing to enlighten the public mind and to bring the present
crisis in our national affairs to a fortunate and peaceful termination.

As Citizens of the United States, we wish to thank you for recalling
us to our duties under the Constitution, and for the broad, national and
patriotic views which you have sent, with the weight of your great
authority and with the power of your unanswerable reasoning, into
every corner of the Union.

It is, permit us to say, Sir, no common good, which you have thus
done for the country. In a time of almost unprecedented excitement,
when the minds of men have been bewildered by an apparent conflict of
duties, and when multitudes have been unable to find solid ground on
which to rest with security and peace, you have pointed out to a whole
people the path of duty, have convinced the understanding and touched
the conscience of a nation. You have met this great exigency, as a
patriot and a statesman; and although the debt of gratitude which the
people of this country owe to you was large before, you have increased

it, by a peculiar service, which is felt throughout the land. We desire, therefore, to express to you our entire concurrence in the sentiments of your Speech, and our heartfelt thanks for the inestimable aid it has afforded towards the preservation and perpetuation of the Union. For this purpose we respectfully present to you this our Address of thanks and congratulation in reference to this most interesting and important occasion in your public life. We have the honor to be with the highest respect, Your obedient Servants   T H Perkins [et al.][1]

LS. NhHi. Published initially in *Boston Courier*, April 3, 1850 (and again on April 15, with many added signatures), and Washington *National Intelligencer*, April 6, 1850; reprinted in Van Tyne, pp. 406–407. Evidence suggests that George Ticknor Curtis composed the "Boston letter," as it came to be called. Peter Harvey, perhaps at Webster's instigation, was instrumental in collecting signatures for it and circulating the letter once published. See Charles Pelham Curtis to DW, April 5, 1850, mDW 30179,

and below, Edward Curtis to Peter Harvey, March 28, 1850. For DW's carefully crafted public response, see DW to Thomas Handasyd Perkins et al., April 9, 1850, below.

1. The letter was appended by more than 700 signatures, representing every major segment of the Boston community and its environs. Benjamin Robbins Curtis, George Ticknor, Nathan Hale, Jr., Rufus Choate, John Eliot Thayer, Albert Fearing, and Moses Stuart were included among their number.

EDWARD CURTIS TO PETER HARVEY

Washington
28. March [1850]

My dear friend—

We are getting along here pretty well with distributing the Speech. More than one hundred thousand copies have been published & sold in Washington. Our chief anxiety is to see your letter & its signatures.[1] at the earliest possible day. How shall we get the speech extensively circulated in Mass[achusetts], since your Whig Committee is Atlas?[2] So far as I can [ascertain] the most vindictive of all opponents are in Mass. Cannot something be done to distribute to all the towns of Mass *some copies* of the Speech? If Redding[']s Edition[3] be too good & too dear, then a cheaper edition might be gotten up. In New York, I will be responsible for a most thorough circulation. The money to do it with, is now, chiefly, subscribed, & the showering of the interior of New York with that speech will begin next week.

This letter is written at the dictation, & in the presence of Mr. Webster, in his office. Truly your's   E. Curtis

ALS by Curtis, from dictation by DW. NhHi. Published in Van Tyne, p. 407.

1. See above, Thomas Handasyd Perkins et al. to DW, [March 25,

1850]. Webster's "anxiety" was doubtless occasioned by a desire to counteract the criticisms of his speech expressed in the *Boston Atlas* and to demonstrate the strength of procompromise sentiment in the North.

2.The Massachusetts Whig central committee was at that time domi-nated by anticompromise men, who shared the *Atlas*'s dissatisfaction with Webster's conciliatory posture toward the South.

3. Redding & Company, a Boston publishing house, had just brought out a revised pamphlet version of Webster's Seventh of March speech.

FROM JAMES BANKHEAD THORNTON

Memphis, March 28th 1850

Sir,

I once had the gratification of a personal introduction to you. It was in the city of Richmond, on the occasion of your visit to my native State to aid in the strenuous effort then made to prevent the re-election of President [Martin] Van Buren.[1] Subsequent events connected with my course have allowed me no opportunity of a further cultivation of your acquaintance and that incident, I have no doubt, passed from your remembrance in the course of the hour succeeding its occurrence. It is with no expectation of a recognition from you, for that reason, and with no claim for any other that I address you this letter—but should you wish to know any thing of me, I refer you to the hon. R[obert] M[ercer] T[aliaferro] Hunter and Mr. [John Caldwell] Calhoun of your body—to most of the Virginia Delegation and Mr. [Frederick Perry] Stanton from this State in the House of Representatives.

The object of this communication is, to acknowledge an obligation, and to discharge the correlative duty, by a due expression of my thanks. As a Southerner, with all the sensibilities (prejudices if you please) which are entertained by those thus designated in the political language of the day—and more especially as an ardent admirer and sincere votary of this, our Union, I acknowledge the profound obligation under which your speech, delivered in the Senate on the 7th inst. has placed me, and tender you my sincere thanks for it.

It is almost impossible for any individual however well informed generally, who may not be in immediate intercourse with the great body of the Southern people at this time, duly to appreciate and fully comprehend, the state of sentiment which now exists among them, upon the subject of slavery, as it has been agitated in the Free States and in Congress for some years past. I do not believe that the Newspapers furnish a fair indication of it, and I regret to express the deliberate conviction, that the impression very generally prevails among them, that this odious subject is to issue in the odious result of an entire dissolution of the Union. Every man of observation and reflection knows, when the mind settles down on the necessary occurrence of any future event, as an inevitable fact, however calamitous and abhored, that the effort to prevent ceases, and cautionary measures to provide for lightening its evils, commence. I regard the course at present being pursued by the Southern people in reference to this subject as belonging to the latter stage.

I allude not to the proceedings of public, or rather political meetings— they are always more or less tinged with individual selfishness and party feeling—but no thoughtful man acquainted with what is going on here, can fail to perceive that in all the various connexions of society, the people are shaping & preparing their concerns, to the end, of an existence seperate, as to any legal bond, from the North.

I do not mean Sir, to trouble you with a reference to the various indications of this condition of the public mind; the question is how came this opinion to be thus generally entertained? Without attempting any examination into more remote causes for it, I am satisfied it is immediately prompted, by the settled conviction on the part of the South, that the North is determined at every risk, to use the authority of Congress, <or the general government, whether directly and immediately applied to the end, or indirectly and gradually exerted> for the destruction of slavery in the United States. This settled, the subject admits of no further debate. It is understood to be conceded here, that such an exercise of power, on behalf of Congress, or the general Government at all, whether directly and immediately applied to the end, or indirectly and gradually exerted, is utterly incompatible with the safety or just rights of the South, and therefore not admissable in any contingency.

Scarcely a reasonable hope seems to have been retained for some time past by the people of this section, that the North would forbear in this particular. Hence the state of feeling here. Now your speech Sir, has created new hopes. I mean no idle, far less deceitful complement, (self respect as well as respect for your elevated position would forbid such,) in saying, that there is not now one public man, whose course on this exciting subject, is esteemed here as capable of creating a more salutary and conservative influence than yours. Least this remark may, by possibility, be misunderstood, I wish to be regarded as not expressing my own opinion, (which would be of comparatively little worth) but as presenting that which I believe to be generally entertained here.

It is thought you may save the country—you may keep us still united. Your speech bids us hope, you will apply your powerful assistance in the only direction, in which it can be available in bringing about that happy result. To effect this, in the present crisis would seem to me to be an attainment worthy the ambition of any man.

But I will trouble you no further—in delivering my thanks I have accomplished the object with which I commenced.

In conclusion, I am requested by the Rev. and venerable Dr. John Finley[2] to express to you his high admiration of your speech, and thanks for so disinterested and opportune an effort to extricate the country from impending difficulties. Dr. F. is an esteemed acquaintance of the Hon. Mr. [Thomas] Corwin, of the Senate. I remain Sir Very respectfully your obdt Servt   Jas B. Thornton

ALS. DLC. Thornton (1806–1867), a native Virginian who had moved to Memphis in 1847, was best known for his *Digest of the Conveyancing, Testamentary & Registry Laws of all the States of the Union* . . . (Philadelphia, 1847), a text used at Harvard Law School.

1. On October 5, 1840, DW had addressed an estimated 15,000 cheering partisans at the Virginia Whig convention in Richmond. His speech was carried in *Niles' National Register*, 59 (October 17, 1840): 107–111; it is reprinted in *W & S*, 3: 83–102.

2. Pastor of the First Baptist Church in Memphis, 1849–1852, Finley has not been further identified.

TO DANIEL FLETCHER WEBSTER

Washington Mar: 31. 50
Sunday two oclock

My Dear Son

Mr [John Caldwell] Calhoun died this morning at 7 oclock. It is remarkable, that his body servant, who has waited upon him for thirty years, died also last night.

Mr Calhoun was just about my own age, born in the same year. I found him a prominent member of the House of Representatives, when I first took a seat in that body, in May 1813, the year of your birth.

The Secretary of the Senate[1] has come to signify Mr [Thomas Hart] Benton's wish, that I should say something in the Senate tomorrow, which I shall try to do.[2]

I have your letter[3] of friday, which Mr Curtis[4] likes very much. He is anxious to know—a great deal more than I am—how things move in your quarter.

The "Speech" continues in demand. One hundred & twenty thousand have gone off. I am sending a handsome copy to each member of the Legislature, & shall send the Speech also pretty general[ly] to the Clergy of Mass. But the great mass, throughout the State, ought to be supplied, freely. Every man that reads the [Boston] Atlas ought to have a copy.

I am pretty well, tho a little rheumatic. Yrs   D W.

ALS. NhHi. Published in *PC*, 2: 363–364.

1. Asbury Dickens.

2. Webster spoke on April 2, paying eloquent tribute to his departed colleague's talents and character.

Congressional Globe, 31st Cong., 1st sess., p. 625. See also Charles M. Wiltse, *John C. Calhoun: Sectionalist*

(Indianapolis, 1951), pp. 476–477.
3. Letter not found.
4. Probably Edward Curtis.

FROM LINUS CHILD

Lowell April 1 1850

Dear Sir

You may perhaps deem it presumptuous in me to thrust upon your attention my views upon your late speech in the Senate upon the Slavery question. But as you have dedicated your speech, to the people of Massachusetts I trust that you will pardon me for troubling you with an expression of my entire approbation of the speech and the sentiments contained in it.

I feel a stronger inclination to make to you this declaration, because a very careful perusal of your speech has to some extent modified opinions which I had previously entertained, and I now thank you for having made the speech & take this form to assure you, that I have not the slightest doubt that very shortly if not at this moment, it will be approved by a large majority of the people of Massachusetts. As you are well aware I am now entirely retired from any active participation in the politics of the day, and therefore feel myself as well qualified to form a cool & dispassionate judgement as are those who have personal interests to subserve by fanning the flames of popular excitement. I have no hesitation in expressing it as my belief that your speech has already had a powerful influence upon the public mind through out the New England states.

So much has the Slavery question been agitated in this portion of the country and so fruitful a theme has it been made, of popular excitement in our popular elections that even the wise and conservative portion of our citizens have been led to adopt to some extent extreme opinions and advocate extreme measures. It is therefore well that the whole subject has been so fully calmly and ably discussed by yourself as the effect will be to produce a more quiet & moderate state of feeling upon the most difficult question which now agitates the public mind. I have regretted the course which some portion of the press of Massachusetts have taken upon the subject. I cannot doubt that such of the conservative portion of the community as have taken exceptions to your course will very speedily be compelled to retrace their steps. They will find I apprehend that there is less disposition among the people to push antislavery doctrines & measures to extremes than they now imagine. If I am not greatly mistaken in public sentiment, the people are becoming heartily sick of this constant agitation of the slavery question especially when that agitation leads to no practical result. Any fair adjustment of the matter which will occasion the agitation and discussion of the subject to cease for a time at least will be satisfactory to the people. There are factions it is true which nothing but a continued agitation contention & confusion can satisfy. These are the elements in which they live. Their object is to keep up the strife that they may be borne upon its billows unto places of power & influence to which their merit or talents would never elevate them.

But with these factions the great mass of the people have no sympathy. Should Congress at its present session pass a judicious fugitive slave bill & abolish the Slave trade in the District of Columbia admit California with her present constitution & boundaries and organize a territorial government for New Mexico *without* the Wilmot Proviso I have no doubt that such a course would be satisfactory to the people of Massachusetts. It would be satisfactory because it would tend to restore quiet and peace to the country. I think that members of Congress very much mistake the sentiments of the people of the North if they expect that their constituents should wish them to press an abstract principle if not to the dismemberment of the Union, at least to the entire neglect of all the other great interests of the country. Will the great West and North West be willing that the improvement of their rivers & harbors shall be utterly neglected by their members of Congress and their whole time be spent in discussing abstract propositions pertaining to slavery? Will it satisfy the free laborers of the North that all the time and attention of their representatives are exhausted in keeping out slavery from a region of Country where Providence has ordained that it cannot go, & nothing be done by Congress to protect free labor from the ruinous effects of foreign competition? I think not. Let the slavery question be settled and substantially upon the basis indicated in your speech and then let Congress set about the consideration of some of the other great questions now waiting their action; let appropriations be made for the Rivers & Harbors; let the Tariff of 1846 be amended so as to get rid of the odious advalorem principle let the rate of postage be reduced and other kindred measures receive the sanction of Congress, and Northern representatives will not fear to meet their constituents even if they have voted to adjust the slavery question upon your basis.

But let the North pass extreme measures on the slavery question and as a consequence let nothing be done upon any of the other important subjects alluded to, I am greatly mistaken if the people do not send to the next Congress men who are *a little more practical* than those who now represent them. I cannot say that I am one of those whose fears are much awakened lest the Union should be speedily dissolved. I doubt not that the strongest feeling prevails among the people in favor of the

Union. But if the attention of Congress is to be exclusively occupied in wrangling upon sectional questions to the neglect of all the great interests of the nation I cannot see how an attachment by the people can long be preserved for a government which entirely fails to protect & subserve their interests, I am therefore for a settlement of the Slavery question, so that other important subjects may be considered & measures adopted for the best interests of the people. Again permit me to apologize for troubling you with this communication. I have written far more than I intended. I should be pleased to hear from you. Very truly & Respectfully your friend & Obedt servant   Linus Child

ALS. DLC. Child (1803–1870; Yale 1824), a Southbridge, Massachusetts, attorney who served for six years as state senator from Worcester County, had moved to Lowell in 1845 to become an agent of several large manufacturing corporations there.

FROM EDWARD EVERETT

Cambridge 3 April 1850.

Dear Sir,

I was much gratified by your remembering me in the distribution of the corrected edition of your great speech,—as important a speech probably as you have ever made. I have sent copies of it this morning to Mr [John Evelyn] Denison, Mr. [Henry] Hallam, Lord Ashburton, Mr [Nassau William] Senior, and some other English friends.[1] Its effect at the South, as far as I can judge from the newspapers, appears to be entirely satisfactory. It was almost a necessary consequence of this circumstance, that the North should receive it with some misgiving. The open attacks upon your positions are however made by those whose support you could not expect, avowed abolitionists and free soilers, & whose denunciations will rather aid than impair the effect of the speech with the Conservative portion of the Community. A good many of that class (the conservatives) are individually too much pledged, on some points, to avow their specific concurrence with you, in all respects;—but they are too well satisfied with the great object of the Speech, not to wish it to have its full effect in allaying the irritation of the South & promoting an amicable adjustment.

I wish it were possible to arrange some extradition bill that would be less likely to excite the North, than that which Mr [James Murray] Mason has reported.[2] Southern gentlemen, who wish the Union preserved, must make that allowance for Northern feeling, which they claim for Southern feeling. Mr. [Andrew Pickens] Butler did not scruple the other day to defend the conduct of the Charlestonians, in driving

Mr [Samuel] Hoar & his daughter from their city,[3] on the ground that, if he had staid, he would have been mobbed, and that the mob once roused could not be controlled. But Mr Hoar's errand was merely to argue the 1st clause of the 2d section of the 4th article of the Constitution in the Circuit Court of Carolina, the same article & section by the way which give the right to claim extradition. If such a cause is enough to rouse a mob in Charleston, how can Southern gentlemen expect our mob to assist in arresting their fugitives? A great deal of good would be done, if the Southern states would have the considerateness to give up this practice of imprisoning black cooks & stewards, which I imagine had its origin in the alarm produced by the plot in Charleston in 1822,[4] & not in any real danger to the South from the presence in their waters of two or three hundred negro scullions, scattered about in Northern vessels, arriving in the course of the year in twenty different ports, without the possibility of concert with each other.

Nothing could be happier than the passage from the third book of Livy, which you have adopted for your motto.[5] It is a speech of itself. Will not Mr [John Caldwell] Calhoun's decease have some effect on the great questions at issue? I have always found, in reference to small troublesome men, that when one disappears another takes his place. The individual changes but the pest remains. But it is not so with men of Mr C's depth & Courage. One such man makes a state of things, which ceases (Or at any rate may cease) with its author.

Our daughter[6] returned to us last Evening, full of grateful recollections of the kindness of yourself and Mrs Webster. I remain, Dear Sir, as ever with sincere attachment Yours,   Edward Everett

ALS. MHi.

1. Denison (1800–1873), member of Parliament and later Speaker of the House of Commons, had enjoyed a close friendship with DW since 1824–1825. Hallam (1777–1859) was an English barrister and author. William Bingham Baring, second Lord Ashburton (1799–1864), the son of Britain's chief negotiator in the Webster-Ashburton Treaty of 1842, served in Parliament for many years. Senior (1790–1864) was an economist and author. *DNB*.

2. See above, Nathanial Greene Pendleton to DW, March 21, 1850, n. 2.

3. On Hoar's visit to Charleston in 1844, see *Correspondence*, 6: 67, 69–70; *Samuel Hoar's Expulsion from Charleston: Old South Leaflets No. 140*, a Reprint of Senate Document No. 4 (Commonwealth of Massachusetts, 1845), pp. 313–332; and Alan F. January, "The First Nullification: The Negro Seamen Acts Controversy in South Carolina, 1822–1860" (Ph.D. diss., University of Iowa, 1976), pp. 298–318.

4. As a consequence of the abortive slave insurrection in Charleston led by free black Denmark Vesey in 1822, the South Carolina legislature passed a law, which it then strengthened in 1823, requiring free black seamen on any vessel entering a South Carolina

port to be confined in jail until the vessel prepared to depart. Subsequently, six other southern states enacted similar laws, all of which were strongly criticized by antislavery men. See January, "First Nullification," chaps. 1–4.

5. Webster's motto was *vera pro gratis*. The latin passage in question—taken from a speech by the Roman Consul Titus Quinctius Capitolinus, in the third book of Livy,

chapter 68—translates as follows: "I know that there are other things more pleasant to hear; but even if my character did not prompt me to say what is true in preference to what is agreeable, necessity compels me. I could wish to give you pleasure, Quirites, but I had far sooner you should be saved, no matter what your feeling towards me is going to be."

6. Charlotte Brooks Everett, who had been visiting the Websters.

TO DANIEL FLETCHER WEBSTER

In Court. Wednesday 1/2 past 2
[April 3, 1850]

Private

My Dear Son

I have recd yrs,[1] & will send 1000 speeches by Express tomorrow.

The Senate has voted to send a Comee. with [John Caldwell] Calhoun's remains to Charleston.[2] Of course, I shall be much pressed to be one. *Should I go?* Think of it, *two days,*—& say little to anybody—& then send me a Telegraphic Despatch—saying "Aye" or "No." But think deep. Yrs   D. W.

ALS.NhHi. Published in Van Tyne, p. 409.

1. Letter not found.
2. Webster was named to the committee on April 4, and, because of his deep respect for Calhoun, he gave serious consideration to serving on it. On April 9, however, he declined the appointment on the ground that personal business required his return to Massachusetts. He was replaced by John Hopkins Clarke of Rhode Island. *Congressional Globe*, 31st Cong., 1st sess., pp. 631, 637, 670; and see below, DW to Daniel Fletcher Webster, April 8, 1850.

TO PETER HARVEY

Baltimore, Sunday morn'g.
April 7, 50

My Dear Sir

I came from Washington yesterday morn'g, to pass the day here, & dine with the Historical Society of Maryland; I shall return tomorrow morning. The "Letter"[1] was published in the [Washington Daily] Republic of Friday, & the [Daily National] Intelligencer of yesterday. It really produced much surprise. It was supposed, before the letter came, that I might, perhaps, weather the storm in Massachusetts, but it was still expected that there would be a storm, & a violent one. The Short Article in the Boston [Semi-Weekly] Courier[2] was very well written; & this, & the letter itself will go through the whole Country, and be read every where. The demand for "Speeches" still continues; & I suppose that by the first day of May 200,000 will have been distributed from Washington. So you see, My Dear Sir, that among us, we have made some stir. I remember how Mr. Edward Curtis & yourself & Fletcher & I, held counsel the evening before the speech was made, questioning and doubting how it would go.

I am happy that Mr. [George] Ashmun took the same ground that I did, in some important particulars;[3] but I doubt whether any of the rest of our members will follow the example. They are timid; I think they are sent here for little else than to keep up the quarrel on the Slavery Subject.

There is a strong majority in both Houses for bringing in California, & it could be done in ten days if it were not the notion which is entertained, by some, of uniting several measures in one Bill. In the end, it will be done. And Bills for the Govt. of the Territories will pass the Senate, without the [Wilmot] *Proviso.* I propose to go to Boston, when the Committee[4] leaves Washington with Mr. [John Caldwell] Calhouns remains; as it is not likely any important questions will be taken in the Senate, during their absence.

I shall have but a very few days to pass in Massachusetts, & they must be mainly spent at Marshfield. Yr friend always,   Dan'l Webster

P.S.

I have just recd yours[5] of yesterday, sent down from Washington. All seems well.

This business of the State Committee is of great importance.[6] I had already, this very morning, written to Honble Myron Laurence [Lawrence], & now enclose the letter,[7] for you to deliver if you see fit.

Text from typed copy. DLC. Postscript from MS copy. MHi. Original not found. Variant texts published in PC, 2: 364–365, and W & S, 18: 364.

1. See above, Thomas Handasyd Perkins et al. to DW, [March 25, 1850].

2. The editorial introduction to Perkins's letter, published in the Courier on April 3, emphasized the eminence of the letter's signers and suggested that the contents reflected Boston opinion on DW's course in Congress.

3. Ashmun's speech in the House of Representatives on March 27 followed in all essentials the line of DW's March 7 oration. See *Congressional Globe*, 31 Cong., 1st sess., *Appendix*, pp. 396–401.

4. See above, DW to Daniel Fletcher Webster, [April 3, 1850].

5. Not found.

6. DW's friends in Massachusetts

hoped that the recently reconstituted Whig State Central Committee would actively advocate compromise with the South on slavery-related issues. They were to be disappointed.

7. Lawrence (1799–1852; Middle-bury 1820), Boston lawyer, served many years in the Massachusetts legislature and as chairman of the Whig State Central Committee. Letter not found.

FROM H. J. ANDERSON

Toulon, Haywood County Tenn.
April 8th. 1850

D. Sir,

One who has been politically opposed, ah! almost hostile to you ever since the War of 1812, presumes to address you a few lines and to thank you in all sincerity and from the very bottom of a heart overflowing with *"love of Country"* for your Great Speech, recently delivered in the U.S. Senate.

When I recur to my impressions touching your past political history, I involuntarily exclaim QUANTUM MUTATUS AB ILLO,[1] tho. I must now confess, prejudice may have had undue sway. *Certainly*, no man who has so nobly—so patriotically *"lifted"* himself above sectional influence and stepped forth, at this dangerous crisis, to vindicate the Constitution of his country and assert the *rights* and *privileges* of her Citizens, *could* have been the man, once regarded as the *enemy* of the South, if not, the *enemy* of his Country. I need not tell you, how your speech has gladdened—has *rejoiced* the Patriot hearts of the South—of the whole Union.

I recd it, the last mail, through my personal and political friend, the Honr. F[rederick] P[erry] Stanton and must beg to be excused for relating a family incident of rare occurrence. I commenced reading it and became, at once, so delighted, that I read it aloud to my family, without interruption—& regret that it was not, four times as long.

You recollect a noble Roman once *rounded* every period of a famous speech—with the exclamation "Sed Carthago delenda est." I must confess, that I mentally "rounded" the periods of your speech with Respublica salva est.

You have been long regarded the ATLAS of the North—*you* standing erect, on the Constitutional platform, each State will revolve in its respective orbit and the UNION is safe.

I am an old man and well recollect the events of 1832[2] which you so truly represent, I was then residing near Richmond, Va. and attended that memorable Convention of which you speak, as a Spectator. How changed, the tone of southern men since! As you truly say, the Abolitionists—the worst enemys of the negro race, have done this, yes! have caused the South to look upon the North, as their worst enemy. They have told the South, not *what,* they would wish us to do, but *what* you *shall* do, such language has caused a burst of indignation, mingled with defiance, to pervade the whole South, and it is too true, one step more, and the Rubicon is passed. We are no Disunionists. The South loves the Union and will die by the Union; but it is the Union of Justice & Equal rights—The Union, as our Ancestors understood it—yes! Sir, as you understand it. We ask for nothing more, we will have nothing less— and Genl. [Zachary] Taylor with his legions of bristling bayonets would not find a Buena Vista in the South. I think every Statesman in the land, must envy your elevated—your proud position.

How little, I ever thought "Daniel Webster" would be associated with the kindest and best of feelings, where "[Martin] Van Buren & [Thomas Hart] Benton" once claimed and enjoyed preeminence. Van Buren and Benton!! Now sunk in utter disgrace, to rise no more! I pray that I may be pardoned for all that I have said and done to promote their political preferment.

I expect to attend the Nashville Convention.[3] Had you spoken out before this, I truly believe the Nashville Convention had not been thought of. Your speech has disarmed—has quieted the South—we have nothing more to ask and will pledge unbroken fraternity—everlasting fellowship and ceaseless efforts to preserve "the Union of our Ancestors."

I have never thought California & N. Mexico would be "Slave states" that is not the question. There lies an apple to which, *I* have an equal right with *you,* pick it up and eat it, I have *nothing* to say, *tell* me, I shant have *any part* of it, I will fight you for it, immediately. This is human nature.

This letter will be enclosed to my friend Mr. Stanton—who will forward it to you after reading it. Yo. Obt. Svt   H. J. Anderson

ALS. DLC. Anderson, a lifelong Democrat, had served as postmaster in Toulon, 1833–1840. In his response to this "remarkable" letter, as he characterized it to Frederick Perry Stanton, Webster assured Anderson that he would "stand by the principles" of his Seventh of March speech "so long as I stand at all." See DW to Stanton, May 14, 1850, mDW 30415, and DW to H. J. Anderson, May 14, 1850, mDW 30412.

1. Virgil's *Aeneid,* Book 2, line 274, "how changed from that man [his former self]."

2. A major theme of DW's Seventh of March speech had been that antislavery agitation was useless and often counterproductive. In making this point, he contrasted the month-long debate over slavery in the Virginia House of Delegates in 1832 with the abrupt termination of such exchanges in the wake of intensified abolitionist efforts dating from 1833.

3. Mississippi fire-eaters had called for a meeting of slave-state representatives in Nashville, Tennessee, for June 1850 to "devise and adopt some mode of resistance" to northern "aggressions." See Thelma Jennings, *The Nashville Convention: Southern*

Movement for Unity, 1848–1851 (Memphis, 1980), p. 36. There is no record indicating that Anderson at- tended the Nashville convention in June or its November sequel.

FROM EDWARD SPRAGUE RAND, WILLIAM BOSTWICK BANISTER, AND OTHER CITIZENS OF NEWBURYPORT

April 8, 1850

Sir:

We address you to make known the satisfaction we have derived from the perusal of the speech recently delivered by you in the Senate of the United States, on the great topic of the day.

We admire its manly temper, the liberal and conciliatory sentiments it expresses; and the unanswerable power of analysis and exposition with which it develops and maintains the true principles of the con- stitution.

We honor, especially, the courageous patriotism which pervades it, recalling to a due sense of their constitutional obligations the North as well as the South.

We therefore beg you to accept our heartfelt thanks for the pre- eminent service you have now again performed, towards preserving and strengthening our National Union.

We have the honor to subscribe ourselves, with pride and pleasure, your friends and constituents. Edward S. Rand, W. B. Banister [and 367 others]

Text from pamphlet *Letter from the Citizens of Newburyport, Mass., to Mr. Webster, in Relation to His Speech Delivered in the Senate of the United States on the 7th March, 1850, And Mr. Webster's Reply* (Wash- ington, 1850), p. 3. Original not found. A draft of the Rand letter, in Caleb Cushing's hand, is in DLC (mDW 30358). Cushing asserted au- thorship in a letter to Charles W. March, June 5, 1850, Charles March Stephens Collection, NmU. Webster may have suggested writing and publishing the letter to provide him with a platform to defend his views on the controversial fugitive slave bill then before Congress. See below, DW to Edward Sprague Rand et al., May 15, 1850. Rand (1782–1863) and Banister (1773–1853; Dart- mouth 1797) were reliable supporters of DW's activities; each had been active for many years in various manufacturing, business, financial, and civic enterprises.

TO DANIEL FLETCHER WEBSTER

Washington April 8. '50

Dear F.

I shall not go [to] the South, on the whole.[1] First, because it might be thought I was carrying my Southern courtesy too far, considering my age & status: Second, because I should hear a great deal of commendation of Mr [John Caldwell] Calhouns particular opinions, in which I could not concur, & to which I could not, decently reply: Third, because I have no better time to go home.

If I am well, & nothing happens, I shall be with you, sooner than you expect. I shall go right down to Marshfield, & if I stay at all in Boston, shall stay on my return. Yrs   DW

Is there any objection to my coming now? Or soon? I mean to get the answer off, tomorrow.

Private & confidential. There are rumors, rather serious, of a change in the Cabinet—quoad [John Middleton] Clayton & [George Walker] Crawford.[2] *Silence!*

ALS. NhHi. Published in *W & S*, 16: 538.
  1. See above, DW to Daniel Fletcher Webster, [April 3, 1850], n. 2.
  2. Criticism of Taylor's cabinet and suggestions about specific changes in it had been circulating in Washington virtually from the outset of his administration. Al-

though reluctant to make removals, the President was preparing a cabinet shake-up just prior to his death in July. Holman Hamilton, *Zachary Taylor: Soldier in the White House* (Indianapolis, 1951), pp. 355–356, 382, and passim. See also below, DW to Jonathan Prescott Hall, May 18, 1850.

TO THOMAS HANDASYD PERKINS ET AL.

Washington, April 9. 1850

Gentlemen

It would be in vain, that I should attempt to express the gratification, which I have derived from your letter of the   instant.[1] That gratification arises, not only from its manifestation of personal regard & confidence, but <also> especially from the evidence which it affords, that my public conduct, in regard to important pending questions, is not altogether disapproved by the people of Massachusetts. Such a letter, with such names, assures me, that I have not <entirely> erred in judging of the causes of existing discontents, <&> or their proper remedy; and encourages me to persevere in that course, which my deepest convictions of duty have led me to adopt. The Country needs pacification; it needs the restoration of mutual respect & harmony, between the People in one part of the Union, and those in another. And, in my judgment, there is no sufficient cause for the continuance of the existing alienation between the North & the South. <Still less is there any cause for the increase of that alienation, until it shall threaten to overthrow the Govt.> <And yet> If we will look at things justly & calmly, there are [no] essential differences, either of interest or opinion, which are irrecon-[cilable] or incapable of adjustment. So far as the question of Slavery, or no Slavery, applies to the newly acquired Territories, there is, in my judgment, no real & practical point of importance, in dispute. There is not, & there cannot be Slavery, as I firmly believe either in California, New Mexico, or Deseret. And if this be so, why continue the controversy on a mere abstraction? The other disturbing question[s] respect the restoration of fugitive Slaves, & Slavery in the District of Columbia; & I know no reasons, why just & fair, <& reasonable> measures, all within the undoubted limits & requisitions of the Constitution, might not be adopted, which should give, on these subjects, general satisfaction. At any rate we should make the attempt; because so long as these dissention[s] continue, they embarrass the Government, interrupt the quiet of the People, & alarm their fears; & render it highly improbable that important acts of <any> legislation, affecting great objects, & in which the whole Country is deeply interested, can be <effected> accomplished. Indeed the ordinary operations, essential to the existence of the Government, & its daily administration, meet with checks & hindrances, hitherto altogether unprecedented. We must return to <the cup of conciliation> our old feelings of mutual consideration & regard: we must refresh ourselves at those pure fountains of mutual <regard> esteem, common patriotism, & fraternal confidence, whose beneficent & healing waters so copiously overflowed the land, through the <period> struggle of the Revolution, & in the early years <history> of the Govt. The day has come, when we should open our ears, & our hearts, to the advice of the great Father of his Country. "It is of infinite [moment," said he, "that you should properly estimate the immense value of your national Union, to your collective and individual happiness—that you should cherish a cordial, habitual, and immovable attachment to it; accustoming yourselves to think and speak of it, as of the palladium of your political safety and prosperity; watching for its preservation with jealous anxiety; discountenancing whatever may suggest even a suspicion that it can, in any event, be abandoned; and indignantly frowning upon the first dawning of every attempt to alienate any portion of our country from the rest, or to enfeeble the sacred ties which now link together the various parts."][2]

Notwithstanding what may occasionally appear on the surface, the American mind is deeply imbued with the spirit of this advice. The People, when serious danger threatens, will, in my opinion, stand fast by their Government. They will suffer no impairing of its foundation, no overthrow of its columns, no disorganization of its structure. The Union and the Constitution are to stand; and what we have to do, is, so to administer the Government, that all men shall be made more & more sensible of its beneficent operations, and its inestimable value.

It is not inappropriate, that I should accompany this answer to your letter by the <correspon> copy of a <corresp> recent correspondence between the Honble Hugh N[elson] Smith, Delegate from New Mexico, now in this City, & myself.[3]

I have the honor to be, Gentlemen, with profound regard, your obliged Fellow Citizen, and obet humble servt

AL draft. MWalB. Published in *Boston Semi-Weekly Courier*, April 15, 1850, and *Works*, 6: 546–548.

1. See above, Thomas Handasyd Perkins et al. to DW, [March 25, 1850]. In his draft response DW left the date blank and wrote "instant." The published versions read "25th ultimo."

2. The bracketed section of the letter is not present in the draft copy at MWalB and is transcribed from the *Boston Courier*, April 15, 1850.

3. See below, Hugh Nelson Smith to DW, April 9, 1850.

FROM RICHARD B. JONES

Burlington New Jersey
April 9th 1850

Dear Sir

In acknowledging the receipt of your patriotic speech on Mr [Henry] Clay's resolutions delivered in the U.S. Senate; replete with the profound views of a statesman, inculcating the soundest republican doctrine, displaying a full knowledge of the institutions of the country, and fearlessly pointing out to sovereign states and american citizens their respective duties. I cannot forbear expressing personally my thanks as a citizen of the Union, nor my admiration at the seasonable display of talents so long and usefully employed in the service of our country. Never, perhaps, has your voice sounded more auspiciously than in the moment you selected to silence the half smothered notes, that were swelling into loud discord, if not sedition. The designing politician has quailed before the statesman, the clap-trap orator, is silenced by the eloquence of the master spirit; the troubled are calm, and order is come forth from chaos. Few persons possessed better opportunities of knowing the merits of the present excitement. Tho reared at the North, a large proportion of my nearest relatives and friends are of the South, among whom I sometimes dwelt and always in constant intercourse. You have noticed all the real or imaginary grievances which either section of the Union complained of—the remedy is within the scope of constitutional law. The celebrated English abolitionist [Sir Thomas Fowell] Buxton,[1] who by his unremitted exertions brought about the emancipation in the British West Indies, innoculated this country with his pernicious doctrines: what has been the result? one third of the sugar & coffee plantations are no longer cultivated: valuable estates sunk to a mere nominal value: the untutored mind of the negro, freed from restraint, sinking into barbarism! Look at St. Domingo, and behold worse than Algerine tyranny exercised by an ignorant & ferocious negro. Can any enlightened mind, with more than a single idea, wish to perpetrate the same scenes on our fellow citizens of the South, can any statesman wish to be made responsible for such a convulsion, as must follow the sudden bursting of the bonds of the blacks? Are the whites prepared to labour, or the indolent negro to receive and enjoy freedom? His Heaven is exemption from labour & the gratification of his grovling passions. If suddenly cut lo[o]se, five hundred thousand, would wend their way to our large cities, to gratify their evil propensities, thieves would prowl at every hour and at every corner murder and rapine & lust would follow in the train. Had the abolitionists refrained, the fate of the blacks, would have been materially improved. It would have now been lawful to instruct in literature, to teach them piety. There would have been laws to prevent separation of families, except for crimes. There would have been laws to liberate the slave, with whom the master had carnal knowledge. Thousands would have been prepared for freedom and liberated, that now remain in bondage, many would have embarked for Liberia, had not the abolitionists deterred them by ill founded & mendacious statements. In vain did the Powers of Europe activated by cupidity attempt to force settlements in western Africa—a few Philanthropic individuals in this country, actuated by the noblest principles, seized upon the only practicable plan of colonizing. The tree of Liberty is planted, the roots have taken to the soil, it cannot fail to flourish, and benighted he[a]then or mohameden Africa, will rise regenerated, commerce will flourish, agriculture be extended. The mild precepts of the Gospel be preached to the worshiper of idols, and Christ our redeemer bless the land, unborn millions will bow to the Throne of grace & mercy! It is now time, that our Government extend their fostering hand and more liberal aid; and soon will they amply repay the debt, by the extension of our commerce over a regenerated continent, instead of keeping an expensive squadron to suppress the slave trade, let a portion of our public vessels be employed in transporting those who are destined to emigrate; furnish them with additional aid to the amount $500000 annually. I have not yet found a single individual who dreams, or speaks or thinks of a dissolution of this Union, many unite with me in opinion that the representatives of the people misrepresent their constituents. Nor do I believe it possible to produce either North or South an excitement among the masses on that subject.

I pray you Sir to excuse this long letter, in returning my thanks for your obliging attention. I here availed myself of the occasion to express my views on matters that you have so ably portrayed, my peculiar position has induced me long since to reflect deeply and feel sensibly their importance. With sentiments of highest respect & esteem I am your obdnt. Servt. Richd. B. Jones

ALS. NhHi. Jones, a veteran of the consular service in Tripoli, 1812–1819, had recently moved to Burlington from Philadelphia. An active Whig, he was a candidate for several diplomatic posts in the Taylor and Fillmore administrations, including consul at Alexandria, Egypt, to which he was appointed late in 1852.

1. Buxton (1786–1845), British philanthropist and member of Parliament for two decades, succeeded William Wilberforce as the foremost spokesman in the House of Commons against slavery and the African slave trade. *DNB*.

FROM HUGH NELSON SMITH

Washington April 9, 1850

Dear Sir

I have the honor to acknowledge the receipt of your letter of the 8th instant,[1] & reply to it with great pleasure. New Mexico is an exceedingly mountainous country, Santa Fe itself being twice as high as the highest point of the Alleghanys; and nearly all the lands, capable of cultivation, are of equal hight, tho some of the vallies have less altitude, above the Sea. The country is cold. Its general agricultural products are wheat & corn, & such vegetables as grow in the Northern States of this Union. It is entirely unsuited for Slave labor. <Free> Labor is exceedingly abundant & cheap. It may be hired for three or four dollars a month, in quantity quite sufficient for carrying on <the> all the agriculture of the Territory. There is no cultivation except by irrigation, & there is not a sufficiency of water to irrigate all the land.

As to the existence, at present, of Slavery in New Mexico, it is the general understanding that it has been altogether abolished, by the laws of Mexico;[2] but we have no established tribunals, which have pronounced as yet what the law of the land in this respect is.[3] It is universally considered, however, that the Territory is al[t]ogether a free Territory. I know of no persons in the Country, who are treated as Slaves, except <persons who> such as may be servants to Gentlemen visiting, or passing thro the Country. I may add, that the strongest feeling against Slavery universally prevails, <in> thro the whole Territory, & I suppose it is quite impossible to carry it there, & maintain it, by any means whatever. I have the honor to be, with regard, your Ob. Sert   Hugh N Smith

Draft in DW's hand, signed by Smith. NhHi. Published in *Works*, 6: 549. Smith (1820–1859), New Mexico's elected—and unrecognized—delegate to Congress in 1850, held strong anti-slavery views.

1. See DW to Hugh Nelson Smith, April 8, 1850, mDW 30194. This letter, together with the letter dated April 9, signed by Smith, was pub-

lished in the *Boston Courier* April 13, 1850, as an addendum to Webster's reply to Thomas Handasyd Perkins et al. to DW, [March 25, 1850].

2. Spain had abolished chattel slavery early in the colonial period; when Mexico achieved independence in 1821 it reaffirmed this policy.

3. A number of conferences and conventions had been held in connection with New Mexico's status in the Union, but none had spoken definitively about slavery. See Robert W. Larson, *New Mexico's Quest for Statehood, 1846–1912* (n.p., 1968), pp. 18–19.

FROM SAMUEL SUMNER WILDE

Boston April 9th '50

Dear Sir,

I wrote you a hasty note a few days since thanking you for your excellent speech, in which I remarked that I was not displeased with Mr. [John Caldwell] Calhoun's speech.[1] I should have added a word or two of qualification. I am entirely opposed to the extension of Slavery to the newly acquired territories, although I agree with you that the Wilmot proviso[2] is entirely uncalled for & useless, & ought not to be adopted because its adoption would tend to irritate the slave holding states already sufficiently irritated.

As to Mr. Calhoun's remarks on the dissolution of the Union, the peaceable secession of the Southern States, much as I should deprecate such a disastrous event, I thought on the whole that the remarks might perhaps do more good than evil, by increasing the apprehension of such a ruinous attempt, & so might lead to healing measures & conciliating counsels to <such> the adoption of such views as are contained in your admirable speech. In other respects I think there is much truth in Mr. C's remarks. I think, & I have long thought, that the South, on the subject of slavery, has been more sinned against than sinning. The persevering attacks of the abolitionists have been most outrageous, & sometimes alarming; & they have not been rebuffed as they ought to have been. The South too has a right to complain of the action & the non-action of the North in respect to the recapture of fugitive slaves.

In this respect, as you justly remark, Legislatures & individuals have evaded their constitutional obligation. All you have uttered on this & every other topic is the truth, & nothing but the truth. The historical truth, you state in respect to Texas who can deny? & your remarks thereon who can confute? I am not surprised that abolitionists, free soilers, & the Northern democracy should not be pleased, but of what can the Whigs complain? This however is not the first time that some ultra Whigs have refused to do you justice when you had performed a very great service to your Country. But as on that occasion you vanquished all opposition, so I hope & trust you will on the present occasion. But whether you do or not, I am quite sure that you will never have cause to regret a speech which will ever remain a monument to your fame as a statesman, an orator, & a lover of your Country. With great respect I am truly Yr friend & servt   S. S. Wilde

ALS. DLC. Wilde (1771–1855; Dartmouth 1789) was then at the end of a long career as associate justice of the Massachusetts Supreme Court.

1. Letter not found. Calhoun's speech was reported in *Congressional Globe*, 31st Cong., 1st sess., pp. 451–455.

2. Drafted in 1846 as an amendment to a Polk administration bill authorizing $2 million to finance the war against Mexico, Congressman David Wilmot's proviso provided for the exclusion of slavery in any territories acquired as a result of the conflict. The proviso sparked an acrimonious debate in Congress. Never enacted, it nonetheless served as a rallying point for antislavery forces in the country during the war and beyond. See *Correspondence*, 6: 209–210.

FROM THE CITIZENS OF NEW YORK

New York, April 10th, 1850

Sir,

The citizens of this commercial capital have watched with deep solicitude the progress of social and political movements tending to estrangement of feeling between the Northern and Southern sections of our country, and threatening, if unchecked, to corrode and weaken the bonds of the Union, which has created and maintained our power, prosperity, and happiness as a nation. Connected by most important and intimate relations with all parts of our wide territory, and seated at the confluence of all streams which, from so diverse and distant sources combine to swell the tide of our national wealth, the citizens of New York have felt that, as they had ever before them the most signal and imposing evidences of the magnificent results of our political system, so had they the nearest interest in its permanence and security.

Upon this whole community, imbued with these feelings as to the value of the Union, and touched with this solicitude for its preservation, your recent speech in the Senate of the United States, has produced a profound impression. The wisdom of the statesman which could discern the middle path of safety, the power of the intellect which could draw from the very elements of strife the arguments of peace and concord, and the eloquence which could bend opposing minds and wills in obedience to reason have all attracted our admiration; yet, we give our highest and sincerest homage to the devoted patriotism of the SENATOR which preferred to consult the general and permanent welfare of the nation, rather than become the strenuous advocate of a section or a party. You have foreborne, Sir, to yield to the service of a political party, or, to the purposes of a geographical section, those powers which were large enough for the whole country; and, speaking from the great centre of public opinion, we feel justified in saying that the country honors you for it.

The state of Massachusetts has, in a noble expression of public sentiment from its capital, approved your course as its Senator;[1] we, sir, hold no other relation to you than that of fellow citizens of the United States, yet, we trust this testimony of our joy and pride in the new benefits you have conferred upon our beloved country, may not be unwelcome to you. The fame of its public men is the best property of a people, and should be cordially cherished; and, in this spirit, we deem it our duty, as it is our privilege, to acknowledge that to your former honor, as the Interpreter and Defender of the Constitution, is now added a further title to the respect and gratitude of our countrymen as the Advocate and Preserver of the Union. We have the honor to be, sir, Your grateful friends and fellow-citizens

Text from *Boston Semi-Weekly Courier*, April 15, 1850. Original not found. The text, as printed, contained no signatures.

    1. The reference is to Thomas

Handasyd Perkins et al. to DW, [March 25, 1850], above, which was published in many of the major eastern newspapers early in April.

FROM WILLIE PERSON MANGUM

Thursday evening. 11th Apl. '50

My dear Sir,

I see *now*, much more plainly, than I saw *today*, the purpose to embarrass certain Gentlemen, in the amendments offerred by the Hon. Mr. [Thomas Hart] Benton.[1]

If you will permit it—I say it as one of your friends & admirers, *Vote as is best*, unless the question be got rid of,—& any thing will be done to effect that.

A caucus, I think, *may reject the whole*, and *to do that*, will commit no one that votes ag[ains]t it. My dear Sir, Suffer me to say—& one says it that knows better than the Country believes, or you or your Compeers believe—& yet I think it true—*Upon you*, the *safety* of the Country depends. You may think this extravagance, I know it *to be sense*. I understand it (pardon me for saying so) better than *you*, or *Mr.* [Henry] *Clay*, or least of all—Gen. [Zachary] Taylor & his Cabinet.

Pardon this egotism, in consideration of its truth.

I do not wish you embarrassed. You *will not be*, as you must not be— instead—there is nothing in *honor* or elevation the old North State, would not do for you, in preference to any other, as I believe.

If you choose, suggest to me any thing in the morning.

This on my part, is written in great haste, & I shall speak of it[—] no part of it—to any one. You have a right to speak of it, shew it & do what you please with it. (Never to print it, unless you make good english of it). Yrs truly & sincerely   W. P. Mangum

ALS. MHi.

1. On April 11 and again on April 12 Benton introduced a series of amendments designed to ensure separate consideration of California's admission to the Union. Webster and other senators protested that Benton's amendments were unnecessary and unproductive, and in a series of votes on April 17 and 18 they were defeated, setting the stage for passage of Henry Foote's motion to establish a special committee to consider the full range of compromise measures—a plan that Webster also opposed, although in this case fruitlessly. See *Congressional Globe*, 31st Cong., 1st sess., pp. 656–665, 701–714, 721–722, 747–748, 751–764, 769–775. The "gentlemen" whom Benton allegedly intended to embarrass by his amendments were probably Senators Clay and Foote.

FROM JOHN CANFIELD SPENCER

Albany, April 11. 1850

Dear Sir,

I return you my thanks for the handsomely printed copy of your great speech on the admission of California and the Slavery question generally, which you were so kind as to send me under your frank. I ought long since to have expressed my gratitude as one of the citizens of the United States, to you for this noble and fearless vindication of truth and right, for this appeal to our consciences and this call to a return to duty. Your exposition of the Texas compact[1] is undeniable and if repudiation is not to be our governing principle, you will have compelled men to be honest.

All sensible and sound men here, are disgusted at the course of Mr. [William Henry] Seward.[2] But I am not at all disappointed at the exhibition of his radicalism. He has no fixed principles, and is ready to embrace any extreme that promises aid to his ambition. His free-soilism is inveterate as a passion, not as a principle. And it is lamentable that the Cabinet, particularly Mr [John Middleton] Clayton and Mr [Thomas] Ewing have allowed him to fill our State with officers of his own complexion. How can we hope to maintain the views of the administration, or rather of the President, when all their mouth-pieces are speaking a different language? That patriotism must be made of stern stuff which resists all the allurements of patronage wielded by Mr. Seward and his confrere [Thurlow] Weed. Let it be once understood among the waiters on Providence that the friends of the Union, the opponents of agitation and abolitionism have some chance of being heard and recognised at

Washington, and a great change would come over the surface. Indeed I do not hesitate to say that we shall be utterly unable to make a stand against the fanatacism of zealots aided by the trickery of Weed and the patronage of the government. Some signal evidence of the disapprobation of the President of the course of Seward and Weed is most urgently demanded.[3] Weed gives out publicly that his course is approved by the Cabinet and the President, and that the latter has said to Seward & W. "take care of your own State by your own means,—we will not enquire into it;—we will take care of ourselves at Washington." And this has paralysed all our efforts. A resolution introduced into the assembly, at my suggestion and prepared by me, simply approving the President's <Californ> message in relation to California and the Territories, was cut off by the previous question moved by one of Weed's instruments and sustained by the whole force of his adherents. You and your great speech have been the theme of his incessant attack, while Seward's treasonable doctrines have been constantly defended and justified. How can there be peace with such men and on such terms?

I would advise the withdrawal of the nominations of some of the known leading partisans of Sewards such as the Postmasters in this city and Troy—the marshal of the Northern District &c. It is more than probable that the very nominations that should be rejected, will be confirmed by the Senate. [Edwin] Croswell has been very active with his democratic friends to produce this result.[4] He owes his being outside of the penitentiary to Weed's exertions with Genl [Samuel] Jones, and other officers of justice. Besides; [Daniel Stevens] Dickinson understands very well how to keep up a division between Whigs in this state and exasperate the real friends of the President. How can this be done more effectually than by keeping in office the firebrands of faction whom the President has nominated and thus making him responsible for them?

But I will not tire you by a political homily. I only say that never was decided action more necessary to avert the utter distruction of the Whig party. Look at the disastrous results of this years elections.[5] The Whigs have lost their strongest counties, even Washington county, the Gibraltar of the party for twelve years,—which was always good for 2000 majority, has gone over to the Democrats,[6]—from utter disgust with the dynasty that controls the State, and from a belief that the Democrats are friends of the Union. I have done my duty as a look-out, in giving warning. Our generals and high officers must do theirs. Most respectfully & truly yours   J. C. Spencer

ALS. NjMoHP.

1. In his Seventh of March speech DW had argued that under the agree- ment by which Texas entered the Union in 1845 it could at some future time be subdivided into four addi-

tional states, each permitting slavery. Although northern men might now deprecate the "contract," it was their obligation, DW said, to honor it. See W & S, 10: 73.

2. On March 11 Seward delivered a major speech in which he insisted on California's immediate admission as a free state, rejected DW's contention that climate prohibited slavery's successful extension to the new territories, and opposed any compromise with the South. His enunciation of "higher law" doctrine in this speech infuriated southerners and many northern conservatives. *Congressional Globe*, 31st Cong., 1st sess., *Appendix*, pp. 260–269.

3. On New York conservatives' frustration with Sewardite control of federal patronage for New York, see

Glyndon G. Van Deusen, *William Henry Seward* (New York, 1967), pp. 114–115, 119–125.

4. Spencer was displeased that some New York Democrats, including Croswell and Dickinson, were enticed by Weed to back Seward-Weed favorites for federal offices.

5. The Whig hammerlock on major New York offices, abetted for several years by divisions within Democratic ranks, had been broken in 1849, with Democratic victories in four of the eight state posts contested that year.

6. Although the Whig state ticket carried its traditional stronghold, Washington County, by a comfortable margin, the Whig candidate for county clerk was defeated. *Albany Argus*, November 9, 13, 17, 1849.

TO WILLIE PERSON MANGUM

Friday morning
[April 12, 1850]

My Dear Sir

I am greatly obliged to you for your friendly note of last Evening;[1] & hope you may find it convenient to be in the Senate Chamber by 1/2 past 11 oclock this morning.

I do not think it would be useful to me, that I should pursue this project for a Committee,[2] further; nor perhaps, for the good of the whole. I have an idea, that Mr [Andrew Pickens] Butler, Mr [Jeremiah] Clemens, & others really wish the whole subject laid upon the table. There will be one eminent advantage, in proceeding at once with the *Bill* for the admission of California. It will cause the question which is most important to the South to be first decided. Thus; the Bill will be called; then some one will move to amend, by attaching the Territorial Bill; then a motion will be made to amend<ment> this amendment, by inserting in that Bill the [Wilmot] Proviso. And this amendment to the amendment will then be the first question to be decided. And if we can reject it, by a pretty strong vote, it will, at least, satisfy the South that no Bill with a Wilmot [Proviso] in it will pass the Senate. There are a great many traps set, all round, & some spring guns; & perhaps the course above suggested may be as safe as any.

If you are at the Capitol early you can consult friends. I will be there by half past eleven. Truly, Yrs,   Danl Webster

ALS. DLC. Published, without exact date, in Henry Thomas Shanks, ed., *The Papers of Willie Person Mangum* (Raleigh, N.C., 1956), 5: 456–457.

1. See above, Mangum to DW, April 11, 1850.

2. DW is referring to Henry Foote's proposal for a special committee of thirteen to study all facets of the sectional controversy and devise an omnibus bill to resolve them.

TO PETER HARVEY

Washington April 15. '50

My Dear Sir

Your letter[1] & the [Boston] Courier of Saturday came together this morning. I am infinitely obliged to you for the pains you take to keep all things in order which respect me, & my speech. The Editorial in the Courier[2] is excellent. It is exactly in the right spirit. It *convinces* People. As to the [Boston] Atlas, I do not regard its course as important.

Public opinion will either control it, or go on independent of it.

I am very glad you inserted Mr [William] Sturgis name, & Mr. William Appletons.

From the South, the West, & some parts of the Middle, addresses, letters, & calls for speeches, continue to come in without number. It is evident that there is a milder feeling in the Country, tho I cannot yet say what will come of it. I meant to intimate, in my answer to the Boston Letter, that nothing could be done with the *Tariff* till this slavery question should be adjusted. You may depend upon it, things are yet ticklish. Our good friends from the North seem to come here with no other notion than that they are to make speeches, in daily succession, ag[ains]t Slavery. I am sorry to say, no one seems to take any comprehensive view of things, or labors for adjustment.

As to the time of my going home, my present hope is to reach N.Y. next Saturday Eve'. It depends on the time when the Com[mitt]ee[3] goes South. I will keep you well informed. Yrs ever truly Danl Webster

ALS. NhHi. Published in *PC*, 2: 365–366.

1. Not found.

2. On April 13 the *Courier* published Webster's April 9 reply to Thomas Handasyd Perkins et al. (see above). An accompanying editorial reaffirmed the validity of DW's argument, both in the Seventh of March speech and in his reply to signers of the so-called Boston letter that slavery could not survive in the new territories and that further contention on this subject was useless and wasteful.

3. See above, DW to Daniel Fletcher Webster, [April 3, 1850], n. 2.

FROM ISAAC HILL

Concord N.H. April 17. 1850

Dear Sir,

For the last eight years, partially in ill health, I have been more a looker on than an active participator in the political movements of the day.

I have at all times seen with keen regrets the Slavery agitations in the Halls of Congress, marring and mutilating, as they have, much of the legitimate and proper action of that Body. With the power of prophecy the pres[c]ience of Washington fastened in letters of adamant a rebuke on the spirit of disunion which time can never obliterate. With this early impression fixed on my mind, I hardly need say that I have been gratified beyond measure with the course taken by the great Statesmen of the Senate thus far in the present Session.

In relation to your Senior in that Body, (Mr. [Henry] Clay) during the days I was at Washington, I was struck with admiration at the temper which would not be provoked into controversy when taunts were thrown as to the maintainance of favorite theories and opinions.

The death of Mr [John Caldwell] Calhoun has proved that a great man may be wrong in many things and yet pass off as in a sea of glory.

I was in the Senate Chamber on the exciting occasion of the reading of the last effort of that truly great, but as I have believed, long mistaken & now deeply lamented man. My old resentments in opposition to nullification were revived & so expressed in the progress of that hearing; and I should on the impulse of the moment, have answered him in a different temper, from that which you displayed in your great speech afterwards. On reading the first imperfect report of it, I saw at once how much better to the dying, nervous man, was your kindly answer than might have been my own.

During the four weeks which I passed at Washington last winter, I will confess to you, that at first my concern on account of an anticipated alienation and disruption of our glorious Union threw all party differences into the back ground—it exceeded if possible the anxiety I felt, when there seemed to be no chance of escaping a conflict of blood between one of the noble old thirteen, and the confederation of which she was a part, some seventeen years previous. In the progress of these four weeks I was pleased to perceive new evidences of attachment to the Union; no less on the part of nearly every man coming from a Slaveholding State, than on the part of those coming from States claiming to be free.

I came to the conclusion that not a man in a thousand wished a disruption, and I lost no opportunity in thus assuring my most alarmed friends.

But my only purpose in writing you this letter, is to say that in defiance of what the press of either party may bear upon the surface, all that is of value in the sound discrimination, and good sense of the people, will declare in favor of the great principles of your late Union Speech in the Senate.

Its author may stand upon that alone & he will best stand by disregarding any and every imputation of alledged inconsistency or discrepancy of opinion or practice in a public career of nearly half a century. I am with great respect Your Obdt Servt Isaac Hill

Copy. MdHi. Together with Webster's appreciative response of April 20 to his old political adversary (see below, pp. 72–73), this letter was published in the *Boston Daily Advertiser*, October 22, 1850.

FROM JOHN TYLER

Sherwood Forest,
April 17, 1850.

My Dear Sir,

My thanks are due to you for the pamphlet copy of your speech on the slavery question which, before it reached me, I had read in the newspapers, but which now comes to me in a form better suited to find its place in my library. I have read it with deep interest. To say that it is what I had expected of your well known attachment to all and every part of the Union, is nothing more than what is due to it. Such so far as I have been <made acquainted with it> informed is the sentiment of the whole South. I hope it is the same everywhere. The plotters of mischief have been for years busily at work to set by the ears those who shd. acknowledge no other than feelings <than those> of brotherhood. You have exposed the results of their machinations to the good sense of the country, and their day for evil, I trust, has passed away. I doubt not but that you will persevere in your work of conciliation until all that now destracts shall be "in the deep bosom of the Ocean buried" and a new era of good feeling happily restor'd.

There is one part of your speech as to which I desire to say a single word. It is that part which refers to the motives which prompted the annexation of Texas. I say nothing of your comment on Mr [Abel Parker] Upshur's letters to Mr [Edward] Everett or Mr [John Caldwell] Calhoun's to Mr [William Sumter] Murphy.[1] You are aware that in conducting a correspondence, the President is compelld to leave much, both in language and opinion to the Secretary of State; and it moreover often happens that it will not answer to disclose the whole policy of the govt in such correspondence. This last was precisely the case <with all> in most that related to Texas. Hence the importance, after much correspondence has ended of looking to the Executive communications to Congress for true motives, objects and designs. To them I ask to be permitted to refer you. I considerd the measure as vitally important not only to the leading interests of the Union and every part of it, but as giving to the govt. by securing the virtual monopoly of the cotton plant, a greater influence over the affairs of the world than would be found in armies however strong, or navies however numerous. If the South found security in the measure, the Commercial and Manufacturing States had an immense addition made to the coastwise, and eventually the foreign trade, while <in the end> new and in the end valuable home markets were open'd to their industry. At the same time the Govt. by its controul over the cotton trade might be considerd as holding the recognizance of foreign nations to keep the peace. These were the motives in which the measure originated and which, I believe, secured its consummation.

I could not forego the opportunity of saying so much to you, and with assurances of my unfeign'd regard. I am Dr Sir Cordially Yrs   J. Tyler

ALS. DLC.

1. In his Seventh of March speech Webster said that the Tyler administration intended to annex Texas to bolster the South. He further suggested that Tyler's secretaries of state, Upshur and Calhoun, had instructed Edward Everett, then minister to England, and William Sumter Murphy (1796?–1844), interim chargé in Austin, discreetly to compile evidence of British designs on Texas. Such evidence presumably was to be presented when the administration's plans to annex Texas were made public. See Upshur to Everett, September 28, 1843 (two letters), *Senate Documents*, 28th Cong., 1st sess., Serial 435, Document No. 341, pp. 27–37. Calhoun's letter to Murphy has not been found, but DW doubtless had in mind the sentiments expressed in Calhoun's "Pakenham letter," April 18, 1843, ibid., pp. 50–53. See also Charles M. Wiltse, *John C. Calhoun: Sectionalist* (Indianapolis, 1951), pp. 165–171.

TO ISAAC HILL

Washington April 20. 1850

Dear Sir;

I regard such a letter from you, as that of the 17th of this month[1] as rather a gratifying incident, in the history of my life. And it is a gratifying incident.

For a long course of years, we have belonged to opposing Parties, espoused opposite measures, & supported, for high office, men of very different political opinions. We have not, however, taken different views of duty, in respect to the maintenance of the Constitution of the United States. From your voice, or your pen, any more than from mine, there never has proceeded a sentiment "hostile to that Unity of Government which constitutes us one People."

And now, when we are no longer young, a state of things has arisen, seriously interrupting the harmony and mutual good will, which have hitherto existed between different parts of the Country, exciting violent local animosities, impeding the regular and ordinary progress of the Government, & fraught with mischiefs of every description. And all this has its origin, in certain branches of the Slavery question, which, as it appears to me, are either quite unimportant, in themselves, or clearly settled & determined by the Constitution.

All this, I have seen with that keen regret, which you have experienced yourself, & which cannot but be a common feeling with all reflecting men, who are lovers of their country.

To this unhappy state of the public mind, I have felt it my duty to address myself, not in language of irritation, crimination, or menace, but in words of peace, patriotic sympathy, & fraternal regard. My effort has been, & will be, to the full extent of my power, to cause the billows of useless & dangerous domestic controversy to sleep, & be still.

I am as fully aware as other men, of what is to be expected from such attempts. In highly excited times, it is far easier to fan & feed the flames of passion & discord, than to subdue them. And, in such times he who counsels moderation, is in danger of being regarded as failing in his duty to Party.

These consequences I willingly meet, these dangers I encounter, without hesitation; being resolved to throw myself, with whatever weight may belong to me, unreservedly into the scale of UNION. Where Washington has led, I am willing to follow, at a vast distance, indeed, & with unequal, but not faltering steps. The Speech, which you commend so much above its merits, I submit to the Political Party, to which I belong, & to the wise & patriotic men, of all parties, in the generation in which I live; & cheerfully leave it, with the principles & sentiments which it avows, to the judgment of posterity, if I may flatter myself that any thing spoken or written by me will be remembered long enough to come before that impartial & august tribunal. I am, with regard, Your Ob. Servt   Danl Webster

ALS. NhD. Published in *Works*, 6: 550–551.

1. See above, Isaac Hill to DW, April 17, 1850.

FROM RALPH EMERSON

Theol. Sem. Andover, April 24—50

Dear Sir;

Accept my thanks for the copy of your speech just received.

Perhaps I need not tell you that Dr. [Leonard] Woods, Prof. [Moses] Stuart, & myself are now suffering our full share of the abuse so lovingly poured on you, in this region, & on all who ventured to sign the Boston letter[1] approving the speech. For myself I can say I expected it, & can therefore bear the blows without winking.

If you have not seen Judge [William] Jay's scurrillous pamphlet[2] on your speech, perhaps you will have the curiosity just to look at a brief notice of it which I wrote for the New York Observer of last week, (April 20),[3] from which you will perceive the spirit of the whole, & especially his false quotation of a sentence in the speech, p. 2, where he omits the clause, "as it (slavery) exists at the present moment in the States;"— thus perverting the whole sense of the passage, & thereby belying all you have elsewhere said on the point.[4]

I have thought it my duty, to take some notice of this pamphlet, emanating from so high a source & now diffused so widely over New England & New York. If you have seen any report of your speech which omitted the clause he has left out, I should be glad to know it, as such a fact may, in some degree, exculpate Mr Jay.

Allow me to add the hope, entertained by your friends, here, that you will be successful in your endeavors to prevent the incorporation of other matters offensive to the free States, with the bill for the admission of California. You cannot overrate our sensitiveness on this point. Yours most truly,   Ralph Emerson

ALS. NhHi. Emerson (1787–1863; Yale 1811), a clergyman and author, was for many years professor of ecclesiastical history at Andover.

1. See above, pp. 44–45, Thomas Handasyd Perkins et al. to DW, [March 25, 1850].

2. Jay's harsh assessment of DW's Seventh of March speech, which included charges that the Massachusetts senator had forfeited his credentials as an an antislavery man, appeared in the New York Evening Post on March 20, 1850, and was reprinted in two inexpensive pamphlet editions as Letter to Hon. William Nelson on Mr. Webster's Speech (New York, 1850), and A Reply to Webster, in a Letter from Hon. William Jay to Hon. Wm. Nelson, M.C. (Boston, 1850).

3. Emerson's commentary, "Mr. Jay vs. Mr. Webster," appeared under the byline, "A Bay State Man."

4. The clause to which Emerson refers is in fact omitted from the Washington National Intelligencer's March 8 report of DW's speech.

TO FRANKLIN HAVEN

Washington April 25. '50

Private

My Dear Sir,

I expect to leave Washington tomorrow Eve', & to be in Boston on Monday Eve'. I shall take with me some *Union Land Scrip*.[1] It is now understood to be certain, that the fund appropriated by Congress will be enough, & more than enough, to pay all the awards. There may be some, but it is not supposed there will be a very great deduction from the amount. I shall wish, probably, to leave this in some hands, from which an advance upon it may be had.

I do not know the State of my account, with you, as I expected some deposites to be made, about this time, but do not know if that has been done.

I shall give a check tomorrow, for $1000—which please honor, till I come. Yrs truly   Danl Webster

ALS. MH-H.   to Haven, March 12 and March 23,
    1. See above, pp. 27, 42–43, DW   1850.

FROM WILLIAM PLUMER, JR.

Epping April 25th 1850

Dear sir,

I should make, perhaps, an apology for writing you, at all, rather than one for not writing you sooner; considering the nature of your engagements & the little I can say of any interest to you. I intended, however, immediately on my return home, to have renewed to you the expression of my sense of obligation for your kind attentions, & those of Mrs Webster, to me & my daughter,[1] on our late visit to Washington. The arrival of a copy of your late speech with the tender of your "regards," increases the obligation, & reminds me that it is unfulfilled. I have re-read the speech, with great interest throughout, & with a ready acquiescence in much which it contains. But I must confess that my anti-slavery feelings are so strong, that I should much rather have heard you speak, on this occasion, as "a Massachusetts man," than as "an American." The latter character may indeed become you, but for my part, I am content, on this subject, at least, to be a New Englander. "Liberty, equality, & the rights of man"—when I once read this expression, in debate, [Henry] Clay told me, with some harshness, in reply, "not to obtrude upon him with our foolish New England notions."[2] The labor of thirty years has not made those notions less dear to me than they then were.

If the fact, which you assume, be indeed a fact, that slavery cannot, & will not, go into New Mexico, there is of course, no need of the [Wilmot] proviso. But in the uncertainty that has seemed to hang over this subject, I have, I confess, been inclined to "make assurance doubly sure, & take a bond of fate." There is no harm in writing a little in this case.

As to fugitive slaves, let them, by all means, be delivered up—for such is the constitutional provision. But in doing this, it is your business to take care that the persons delivered *are* slaves, & not freemen. Let the slave holder take his "pound of flesh," but let the judge see to it that he take "no jot of blood."

As to Texas, it is a bad affair from beginning to end. She has our bond, & I would construe it, if not strictly, at least not liberally—justly, in reference to all the circumstances of the case, but not rashly, in reference to ourselves. "Thou shalt have nothing but the forfeiture." What that is, time must show. I trust it will not show, in our day, at least, four new slave states.

I observe that you speak, in the speech (p 20)[3] with some doubt as to whether there were any persons, who were, at the same time, Members of Congress & Members of the Convention, which formed the Constitution. I think that the Journals show that [John] Langdon & [Nicholas] Gilman of N.H. [Nathaniel] Gorham & [Rufus] King of M[as]s. [William Samuel] Johnson of Ct. Yates of N.Y. [James] Madison of Va. [William] Bl[o]unt of N.C. [Pierce] Butler of S.C. & [William] Few of Ga. were members of both bodies.[4] I remember having received from Govr Langdon an interesting account of their coming on from Philadelphia to New York with the Constitution which they had formed, & of the effect which it produced in Congress, when presented to that body. Though the Journal shows that they were unanimous in referring it to the people, they were by no means unanimous in their approval of all its provisions.

In my late visit to Washington, after an interval of twenty five years, I was equally surprised at the great changes which had taken place in many things there, & the little change which had taken place in others. Society seems to me to be on a different, & in many respects, better footing than formerly. There is less talent, & more disorder in the House; & more talent, & less dignity & decorum in the Senate. As to the Executive Department, the President has more talent probably than [James] Monroe, but certainly less experience in public affairs. But where is Monroe's cabinet—or men of their talent or standing? I was sorry to see so little concerted party action among the Whigs. In this respect [Zachary] Taylor's situation is not unlike that of Monroe, who had no great united party ready to support his administration. But unlike Monroe, Taylor has a great united & busy party opposed to him. So it seemed, at least, to me, who, as an outside observer, & the visitor of a day, have perhaps no right to an opinion on this subject. You, who looks so much deeper, may see better signs for the future.

I beg you to make my best respects, with those of my daughter, to Mrs Webster. I was struck with a remark which she made on the subject of the portraits, which we have of you. They were, she said, all caricatures. It seemed to be thought that a high forehead, large eyes, &

dark eyebrows made a likeness; but those who thought so quite mistook the true character of the man. It was evident from her remarks, that the mildness & swavity of your manners had impressed her more strongly than even their force & dignity; & that, while to the world you wore "the front of Jove, an eye, like Mars, to threaten, or command," she saw in you chiefly the milder attributes of the benign power, whose smile "impugns May flowers." The compliment, implied in this remark, seemed to me equally unconscious, on her part, & appropriate to the matron & the wife. If I have found more meaning in a casual remark, than it was intended to convey, it may, at least, be taken as soon proof that the good seed was not thrown, in this case, on a barren soil. Excuse this long letter, & believe Yours truly & respectfully, W Plumer Jr

ALS. NhD.

1. Mary Elizabeth Plumer (b. 1822), eldest of Plumer's three children, lived unmarried in Epping, New Hampshire.

2. *Annals of Congress*, 16th Cong., 1st sess., p. 1426.

3. Plumer is quoting from the edition of DW's speech publishd by Gideon & Company.

4. Robert Yates was a delegate to the Constitutional Convention; Abraham Yates and Peter W. Yates were members of the Continental Congress. With this exception, Plumer's recollections are accurate.

FROM JOHN HENRY HOPKINS

Burlington Vt. April 30. 1850

My Dear Sir,

I beg you to accept my cordial thanks for the copy of your admirable speech, delivered in the Senate on the 7th. Ulto. and rendered especially acceptable by your kind superscription. For the fourth time, I have now perused this important and most timely production, first in the National Intelligencer, next in the ordinary form of Congressional pamphlet, thirdly in the fair type of the last issue, of which Mr. Morse[1] was so good as to send me a copy, & fourthly in that with which you have favored me; and it gives me pleasure to say that it has commanded my entire assent to its soundness & truth, and much more—my warm approval of the high principle of pure patriotism which, under God, enabled you to discharge so difficult a duty, in the face of popular prejudice and at the hazard of alienating a large portion of your former friends. It is one thing to exhibit the skill of a consummate orator in favour of the prevailing notions of our district or our party, when the immediate return of praise & honor is sure to attend the effort. And it is quite another matter to resolve, deliberately, to sacrifice ones self, if need be, for the public safety. I trust, however, that the wise, the intelligent & the impartial advocates of truth will succeed in directing the general sentiments of the community, and then, in a little while, the Address of your Boston friends[2] will only express the universal feeling of our Country.

You will pardon me, I am sure, if I add a brief statement which is personal to myself in relation to the exciting topic of Slavery. My own views have been long settled in precise accordance with those which you have so well expressed. Being invited, by the Rochester Athenaeum, to lecture before them on 7th. of February last, and having my thoughts much occupied by the threatening aspect of the Senatorial contest,[3] I prepared an Address on the very subject, in which I combatted the false theology which is relied on by the Abolitionists, and supported, along with this, the course which might lead to a final disposition of the existing evils of Slavery, on the grounds of its being, not a *sin*, but a *political evil*.[4] My object was to prove that Slavery was *lawful*, but *not expedient*, even for our Southern brethren themselves, and that the whole nation should unite in the effort to get rid of it, by devoting the public lands, and even (if necessary) by imposing a direct tax, to *emancipate the slaves, & colonize them on the coast of Africa, in connexion with Liberia*. I calculated that the probable value of the whole was about 900 millions, and that the expenditure of $12,000,000. per ann[um], for 50 to 75 years, would accomplish the work, at the rate of 40 to 50,000 expatriated & settled each year. I based my argument on the act of Great Britain in purchasing the freedom of the slaves in Jamaica at the cost of 20 millions sterling, = $100,000,000. and insisted that double that sum would be a light price to pay, for a result of such incalculable importance to the prosperity of the Union. Twelve millions per ann. being the interest of 200 millions, and being scattered through the Southern States, would remunerate, as I endeavored to shew, the slave owners for their loss, and enable them to employ free labour to advantage; While the expatriation of the emancipated Slaves would relieve their former masters from all fear, and the hope of their own freedom in due time, would furnish the best motive for good behavior &c. to the others. But I cannot give you more than a very rude outline of the idea in a letter. The Address was not delivered, because I doubted <of> the expediency of a man occupying my official station, going out of his professional track, and incurring the imputation of meddling with the work of Statesmen, without necessity, and without qualification. Nevertheless, so far as it respected *myself*, I was ready then, and shall be ready always, I trust, to run the risk of personal abuse, if there were any reasonable likelihood of doing any real service to the interests of truth & peace. Nor should I pause to count the cost to my own estimation, if I could see a probability of aiding, however humbly, the efforts of patriots like yourself, in a cause of such vast importance to the interests of our Country & of the world.

I fear, however, that I have intruded too long on your valuable time, and therefore close my letter with the expression of my earnest hope & prayer, that the favour of the Most High may guide & strengthen you in all your future course, and enable you to accomplish the largest measure of success, not only in the lofty career which His Providence has allotted to you in this life, but in the far more exalted glory of the life to come. With the most sincere esteem & regard, yr faithful friend & servant in Christ,   John H. Hopkins Bishop of the Diocese of Vermont.

ALS. NhHi.

1. Probably Sidney Edwards Morse (1794–1871; Yale 1811), a prolific writer on both geography and religion who lived in Boston and later in New York City, where he edited a religious paper, the *New York Observer*, 1823–1858.

2. See above, pp. 44–45, Thomas Handasyd Perkins et al. to DW, [March 25, 1850].

3. On February 6, 1849, William

H. Seward was elected to the United States Senate from New York following a complicated and at times angry contest with fellow Whig John Collier of Binghamton, who was supported by incoming vice president Millard Fillmore and his political friends.

4. Hopkins elaborated on this argument in his pamphlet, *Slavery: Its Religious Sanction, Its Political Dangers, and the Best Mode of Doing It Away* (Buffalo, 1851).

TO MOSES STUART

Boston, April 31 [May 1], 1850

My Dear Sir,

I cannot well say how much pleasure it gave me to see a name, so much venerated and beloved by me as yours is, on the letter recently received by me from friends in Boston and its vicinity, approving the general object and character of my speech in the Senate, of the seventh of March.[1] I know the conscientiousness with which you act on such occasions, and therefore value your favorable sentiments the more highly.

Is it not time, my dear Sir, that the path of Christian duty, in relation to great and permanent questions of government, and to the obligations which men are under to support the constitution and the fundamental principles of the government under which they live, should be clearly pointed out? I am afraid we are falling into loose habits of thinking upon such subjects; and I could wish that your health and strength would allow you to communicate your own thoughts to the public.[2]

We have established over us a much better form of government than may ordinarily be expected in the allotments of Providence to men; and it appears to me that the consciences of all well-meaning and enlightened individuals, should rather be called upon to uphold this form of government, than to weaken and undermine it by imputing to it objections, ill considered and ill founded, dangerous to the stability of all government, and not unfrequently the offspring of overheated imaginations.

Allow me to conclude, my dear Sir, by offering you my highest respects, and my affectionate good wishes for your health and happiness.

D. Webster

Text from *PC*, 2: 367. Original not found.

1. Stuart was among the more than 700 prominent citizens who had signed the so-called Boston letter of March 25. See above, pp. 44–45, Thomas Handasyd Perkins to DW,

[March 25, 1850].

2. Stuart had been working for some weeks on a defense of Webster's Seventh of March speech, which he published in May 1850 as *Conscience and the Constitution*. See below, Moses Stuart to DW, May 2, 1850.

TO WILLIE PERSON MANGUM

Boston May 1. '50

Private

My Dear Sir

Things are pretty well here, & are getting better fast. It is lucky I came, before the [Massachusetts] Legislature broke up. The two Houses passed some flat & foolish Resolutions, mainly thro. fear of their Constituents, but showed their real feelings, on the direct motion to instruct me.[1] They are coming to see me, all of them, some Evening this week. A little time is quite important to me, here, just now. I have not yet been to Marshfield.

If it could be done without inconvenience, I should be glad the Report of the Com[mitt]ee of 13.[2] might await my arrival. Inform me, if necessary, by Telegraph, of your progress.

I should be glad, also, if it should so happen that the vote on Mr [James Ware] Bradbury['s] Resolutions[3] should be deferred.

We have very fine weather at last. Yrs very truly   Danl Webster

ALS. NN. Published in *W & S*, 16: 538.

1. Both houses of the Massachusetts legislature passed resolutions in mid-April condemning slavery and demanding its exclusion from the new territories. The Senate, however, decisively rejected motions repudiating DW's arguments in his Seventh of March speech and instructing him to vote for the Wilmot Proviso and to oppose Senator James M. Mason's fugitive slave bill.

2. The special Senate committee of

thirteen, of which Webster was nominally a member, was at this time writing an omnibus bill treating the main issues of the sectional controversy. Henry Clay presented the committee's recommendations to the Senate on May 8, several days before Webster returned to the capital from Massachusetts. *Congressional Globe*, 31st Cong., 1st sess., pp. 944–948, and see below, DW to Willie Person Mangum, May 5, 1850.

3. See above, p. 9, DW to Franklin Haven, January 24, 1850, n. 5.

FROM MOSES STUART

Andover, 2. May. 1850

My dear Sir,

I did not get yours[1] until it was too late to answer it yesterday. I enclose this to your Son, & have requested him not to lose a moment in forwarding it.

It strikes me that I can make good use of your No. II.[2] I have an *ideal* in my mind. My *title* will be, as I now think: "*Conscience & the Constitution* with remarks on t[he] recent Speech of the Hon. D. W. in t[he] Senate of t[he] U.S." My motto (on title page) will be 1 Cor. 7. 21:

Δοῦλος ἐκλήϑης, μή σοι μελέτω, κ.τ.λ. [3]

of wh[ich] I shall make careful usage; but it is a terrible text for those who wd. fill heaven & earth with commotion about the slavery-question. In plain vulgar English the second clause means: *Do not make a fuss about it.* Pretty seriously are they beating in the face of Paul, who make all this fuss: Paul sent back to Philemon his runaway Servant Onesimus—to be *his* forever; & all this after he was a *Christian.*[4] Does our Constitution do anything more? And is *conscience* to be appealed to, in justification of breaking t[he] Constitution, & flouting at t[he] great apostle of t[he] Gentiles?

Sed verbum sat. Let me come to the point. Such is my present state as to health (& engagements too), that if it shd. be stormy on Monday, it would not be feasible for me safely to go to Boston. The most certain way to *ensure a meeting* will be for you to come up on Monday. You can get here at some 1/4 past 11, or 1/4 past 12, or (as I believe) half past 3. You can return *five* times, in the afternoon & evening, of course can choose your own hour. If you can tell me at what hour you will come, I will see that you are conveyed to my house. If you cannot, there is an *Omnibus* that will bring you direct.

Of course you will *dine* with me, unless you take the train that arrives here at 3 1/2 P.M. That will be rather too late; or at least it may be so. We may—nay shall—need some "more last words." Let us have time to speak them, if it become necessary.

In the meantime the matter has begun to concoct in my brain; & I am mounting this eminence & that, to get some proper views of the "land to be possessed." You are passing through Jordan in its flood time to get there—but never mind, you will get safe over, & stand on *terra firma.* Truly yours, M Stuart

ALS. NhHi.

1. See above, DW to Moses Stuart, April 31 [May 1], 1850.

2. Stuart is probably referring to paragraph 2 of DW's letter, above, in which he suggested that Stuart should publish an article or essay on the responsibilities of Christians to obey the Constitution and the laws.

3. "Art thou called *being* a ser-

vant? Care not for it: but if thou mayest be made free, use it rather." Stuart's point, in the motto from Corinthians and in his book, was that individuals in any civilized community must accept the legal obli-gations imposed on them, whether they agree with those obligations or not.

4. For elaboration, see Stuart, *Conscience and the Constitution* (Boston, 1850), pp. 60–61.

FROM EDWARD BISHOP DUDLEY

Jacksonville Onslow County
May 4. 1850

Dear Sir

Allow me [to] thank you very truly for your pamphlet speech on Mr. [Henry] Clay's Resolutions, & what is yet of much greater consequence to assure you of the high appreciation your just & liberal views are held by our people. They have had a great tendency to allay the feverish irritation of their minds which had been roused almost beyond controul by a few demagogues & designing men who had more regard for their own popularity than good of the country. I have had some cause of irritation, which the passing by Congress some law to surrender fugitives would very much quiet. I have lost 5 Negro fellows: detected two attempting to get away on board of vessels where free Negroes acted as cooks & no doubt were concerned in the Act, but in consequence of the severity of our law, I would not prosecute them & consequently a second attempt succeeded & they are now about New York the most worthless part of the population. One other left me on the Rail Road & who has written me since that he regretted having done so, that he found it more difficult to earn a living than he supposed. Many negroes have run away from prisons in & about Wilmington & hence the necessity of making stringent laws to prevent the free Negroes coming there in vessels from associating with our slaves, who compare very well with white as well as black sailors.[1] It would be some consolation to us to learn that their condition was improved when they escape North, but not so. They generally become the greatest of all possible vagabonds. I hope you will pardon me for making these few observations on this subject of which you have had so much <of this matter> as to disgust you I fear. I am with the highest regard & respect Your Obt. Servant

E. B. Dudley

ALS. NhD.

1. Dudley evidently hoped North Carolina would adopt a law similar to South Carolina's 1822 statute requiring free black seamen in any vessel entering the state's ports to be confined in jail until the vessel prepared for departure. A bill sharply limiting the movement of free blacks arriving in North Carolina by ship (whether as servants, crew, or passengers) was introduced in the legis-

lative session of 1850 and passed the Senate after first reading, but it was not ultimately enacted. See "A Bill Concerning Free Negroes in North Carolina," [Senate Document No. 60] (Raleigh, 1850).

TO WILLIE PERSON MANGUM

Marshfield, May 5. 50

My Dear Sir

I may be delayed, as to my return, by the weather, or other causes, & think that, upon the whole, the Com[mitt]ee should not wait for me.[1] I hope the Report will state how the members stood, on the several questions; or that Mr [Henry] Clay will be kind enough to state those particulars, when he makes the Report. I shall be in Washington before the Report, & the accompanying papers can be printed.

You will see something, written [in] the right spirit, in the Boston Daily Advertiser, & Boston Courier. The Atlas is rather growing more furious.[2] Yrs always, with entire regard   Danl Webster

ALS photocopy. NhD. Original not found.

1. See above, DW to Mangum, May 1, 1850, n. 2.

2. On May 3 the *Boston Daily Atlas* had initiated a series of essays by "An Old Whig" condemning Webster's acceptance of a strengthened fugitive slave law as part of a compromise with the South. DW was probably alluding to this piece, and to articles then in preparation rebutting "An Old Whig," which were published in the *Courier* on May 6 and May 8 and the *Advertiser* on May 7 and May 8.

TO PETER HARVEY

Astor House
Saturday morning
May 11 6 o'clock

My Dear Sir,

I had a fine passage yesterday, and was in Canal Street at 4 o'clock. I hope to reach Baltimore this evening, and Washington tomorrow morning. All in time.

The New Yorkers have sent Mr. [Thomas Buckminster] Curtis seven hundred dollars for the distribution of the Speech, all of which, and a good deal more has been expended, and the demand is far from being satisfied. If our Boston friends feel like doing something in the same way, it would like keeping up. It might be best to send whatever might be collected to Mr Curtis, who, I doubt not, is already a good deal in arrears with the Printers.

We had a fine time on Thursday evening.[1] It was particularly gratifying to me, as it furnished an opportunity of meeting many respectable and spirited men, of a younger generation, whose acquaintance I have not had heretofore the means of cultivating.

For a *crushed* man, I enjoyed the occasion remarkably well. If others felt as much pleasure, innocent enjoyment was extensively experienced. Yrs truly   Danl Webster

Copy. NhHi. Published, each in part, in *PC*, 2: 368, and Van Tyne, p. 412.

1. Webster attended a dinner in his honor at the Revere House in Boston on May 9, attended by "about fifty gentlemen," according to the Boston *Transcript*, May 10, 1850.

FROM A NEW YORKER

N.Y. May 14th 1850

My dear Sir—

I have always entertained the most profound respect for your talents as the champion of the Constitution, your integrity as a politician, & that noblest attribute of man, fearlesness and independence of character. I believe you will do me the justice to think my professions sincere. But to the point. Among the number of your political persecutors, Mr. [William Henry] Seward is the most unscrupulous. He has aimed by his speech in the Senate,[1] to put into the mouths of his friends, sentiments that have been designedly used to injure you, and which have been seized with avidity not only by editors [Horace Greeley's New York] (Tribune) but individuals of such stamp as Mr. [William] Jay &c. A clique with which he is connected in this city are deadly opposed to you—& some of them exult at the triumphant vindication as they call it, of Mr. Seward, in rescuing the Constitution from the false construction Mr. Webster has given it respecting fugitive slaves. As a Northern man they deemed your cause impolitic & radically wrong.

Now my dear Sir—Your friends in this quarter look with deep solicitude to the time when you shall analyse that speech and show the danger which such men are to the Country, when they are moved only from private views & selfish ambition. Mr. Seward is not an honest advocate—he does not practice what he preaches, & he studies only to reach the Presidential Chair, no matter what the sacrifice may cost him. But my dear Sir, you ought not to be injured & misrepresented by his friends. Do rebuke this contemptible & "toadyizing" spirit & teach him that he has much yet to learn, & study of the Constitution, before he can, by any of his own interpretations, prove your position a wrong one, or that the sacrifice of duty & principle, is not at all times & under all circumstances, unworthy of a man or Senator of the U.S. Senate. Deem these few lines not the less worthy of your notice because they reach you ano[n]ymously. I am one of your friends, & would in person talk with you on the subject, but prudence suggests the withholding my name from paper. I have heard many of your best friends in this city speak of the contemptible course of Mr Seward & of his presumption in striving to weaken your opinions, in takeing the stand he did as a Northern man. Please excuse the length of this letter, & after reading it commit it to the flames, but let the recollection of it be in your memory, as coming from one who speaks the honest sentiment of his heart, (if he knows it) that he believes himself to be one of your most sincere friends & well wishers.   A New Yorker

ALS. NhHi.   see above, John Canfield Spencer to
    1. *Congressional Globe*, 31st Cong.,   DW, April 11, 1850, n. 2.
1st Sess., *Appendix*, pp. 260–269, and

Webster's forceful appeal for sectional conciliation had two desired results: it lent a new impetus to the procompromise position in the North, and it made its author a remarkably popular figure in the South. Other consequences of the Seventh of March speech were, from his perspective, less pleasant. Public opinion in the northern states, including Webster's own Massachusetts, failed to shift noticeably in favor of a compromise. In many localities, moreover, Webster was bitterly assailed at public meetings and in the press for retreating from his earlier acceptance of the Wilmot Proviso. Particularly biting were editorials in the newly radicalized Boston Atlas, *which identified Webster as a spokesman for southern interests rather than for the interests of his own section. No attack, however, had a greater circulation, or irritated Webster more, than Horace Mann's long public letter to his constituents dated May 3, which focused much of its analysis on Webster and the fugitive slave issue.*

In the course of a wide-ranging discussion of the imperatives of antislavery, Mann castigated Webster for his failure to endorse Senator William H. Seward's version of a fugitive slave bill providing for jury trial of accused runaways in the states where they were claimed.

Provoked though he was by Mann's public letter, which appeared in the Atlas *on May 3, Webster chose not to reply directly. He responded instead to a complimentary letter, now more than a month old, from citizens of Newburyport. In the letter below he once more articulates his views on the fugitive slave bill. Having joined the debate in this fashion, Webster remained active as both public controversialist and a behind-the-scenes manipulator for the next several months.*

TO EDWARD SPRAGUE RAND ET AL.

Washington, May 15, 1850.

Gentlemen,
    I have the honor to acknowledge the receipt of your letter of the 8th

of April,[1] approving the sentiments of my speech delivered in the Senate on the 7th of March last. As considerable differences of opinion prevail, in Massachusetts, on the subject of that speech, it is grateful to receive, in a letter so respectably and numerously signed, opinions so decidedly concurring with my own.

Circumstances have occurred, within the last twenty years, to create a new degree of feeling, at the North, on the subject of slavery; and from being considered, as it was at the adoption of the Constitution, mainly as a political question, it has come to be regarded, with unusual warmth, as a question of religion and humanity.

It is obvious enough, that the government of the United States has no control over slavery, as it exists in the several States. Its proper jurisdiction, in this respect, is confined to its own territories, except so far as it is its duty to see that that part of the Constitution which respects the surrender of fugitive slaves be carried fairly and honestly into execution.

The Constitution of the United States, in the second section of the fourth article, declares: —

"A person charged in any State with treason, felony or other crime, who shall flee from justice, and be found in another State, shall, on demand of the executive authority of the State from which he fled, be delivered up, to be removed to the State having jurisdiction of the crime.

"No person held to service or labor in one State, under the laws thereof, escaping into another, in consequence of any law or regulation therein, be discharged from such service or labor, but shall be delivered up on claim of the party to whom such service or labor may be due."

This provision of the Constitution seems to have met with little exception or opposition, or none at all, so far as I know, in Massachusetts. Every body seems to have regarded it as necessary and proper. The members of the convention of that State for adopting the Constitution were particularly jealous of every article and section which might in any degree intrench on personal liberty. Every page of their debates evinces this spirit. And yet I do not remember that any one of them found the least fault with this provision. The opponents and deriders of the Constitution, of this day, have sharper eyes in discerning dangers to liberty than General [Samuel] Thompson, Holder Slocum, and Major [Samuel] Nason had, in 1788;[2] to say nothing of John Hancock, Samuel Adams, and others, friends of the Constitution, and among them the very eminent men who were delegates in that convention from Newburyport: Rufus King, Benjamin Greenleaf, Theophilus Parsons, and Jonathan Titcomb.[3]

The latter clause, quoted above, it may be worth while to remark, was borrowed, in substance, from the celebrated Ordinance of 1787, which was drawn up by that great man of your own county, and a contemporary of your fathers, Nathan Dane.[4]

Mr. Dane had very venerable New England authority for the insertion of this provision in the Ordinance which he prepared. In the year 1643, there was formed a confederation between the four New England Colonies, Massachusetts Bay, Plymouth, Connecticut, and New Haven; and in the eighth article of that confederation it is stipulated as follows: "It is also agreed, if any servant run away from his master into any other of these confederated jurisdictions, that, in such cases, upon the certificate of one magistrate in the jurisdiction out of which the said servant fled, or upon other due proof, the said servant shall be delivered, either to his master, or any other that pursues, and brings such certificate or proof." And in the "Articles of Agreement," entered into in 1650, between the New England Colonies and "the delegates of Peter Stuyvesant, Governor of New Netherland," it was stipulated that "the same way and course" concerning fugitives should be observed between the English Colonies and New Netherland, as had been established in the "Articles of Confederation" between the English Colonies themselves.

On the 12th of February, 1793, under the administration of General Washington, Congress passed an act for carrying into effect both these clauses of the Constitution. It is entitled, "An Act respecting fugitives from justice, and persons escaping from the service of their masters."[5]

The first two sections of this law provide for the case of fugitives from justice; and they declare, that whenever the executive authority of any State or Territory shall demand any person, as a fugitive from justice, of the executive authority of any State or Territory to which such person shall have fled, and shall produce the copy of an indictment, or an affidavit made before a magistrate, charging the persons so demanded with having committed treason, felony, or other crime, certified as authentic by the governor or chief magistrate of the State or Territory whence the person so charged fled, it shall be the duty of the executive authority of the State or Territory to which such person shall have fled, to cause him or her to be arrested or secured, and notice of the arrest to be given to the executive authority making such demand, or to the agent of such authority appointed to receive the fugitive, and to cause the fugitive to be delivered to such agent when he shall appear; but if no such agent shall appear within six months, the prisoner may be discharged; and all cost or expenses incurred by arresting, securing, or transmitting the fugitive shall be paid by the State or Territory making the demand; and that any agent who shall receive such fugitive into his custody shall be authorized to transport him to the State or Territory from which he fled; and any person rescuing or setting such person at liberty shall, on conviction, be fined not exceeding five hundred dollars, and be imprisoned not exceeding one year.

The last two sections of the act respect persons held to labor in any of the United States or Territories, escaping into any other State or Territory; and are in these words: —

"Sect. 3. *And be it further enacted,* That when a person held to labor in any of the United States, or in either of the Territories on the northwest or south of the River Ohio, under the laws thereof, shall escape into any other of the said States or Territories, the person to whom such labor or service may be due, his agent or attorney, is hereby empowered to seize or arrest such fugitive from labor, and to take him or her before any judge of the Circuit or District Courts of the United States, residing or being within the State, or before any magistrate of a county, city, or town corporate, wherein such seizure or arrest shall be made; and upon proof, to the satisfaction of such judge or magistrate, either by oral testimony or affidavit taken before and certified by a magistrate of any such State or Territory, that the person so seized or arrested doth, under the laws of the State or Territory from which he or she fled, owe service or labor to the person claiming him or her, it shall be the duty of such judge or magistrate to give a certificate thereof to such claimant, his agent or attorney, which shall be sufficient warrant for removing the said fugitive from labor to the State or Territory from which he or she fled..

"Sect. 4. *And be it further enacted,* That any person who shall knowingly and willingly obstruct or hinder such claimant, his agent or attorney, in so seizing or arresting such fugitive from labor, or shall rescue such fugitive from such claimant, his agent or attorney, when so arrested pursuant to the authority herein given or declared, or shall harbor or conceal such person, after notice that he or she was a fugitive from labor, as aforesaid, shall, for either of the said offences, forfeit and pay the sum of five hundred dollars; which penalty may be recovered by and for the benefit of such claimant, by action of debt, in any court proper to try the same; saving, moreover, to the person claiming such labor or service, his right of action for, or on account of, the said injuries, or either of them."

It will be observed, that in neither of the two cases does the law provide for the trial of any question whatever by jury, in the State in which the arrest is made. The fugitive from justice is to be delivered, on the production of an indictment, or a regular affidavit, charging the party with having committed the crime; and the fugitive from service is to be removed to the State from which he fled, upon proof, before any authorized magistrate, in the State where he may be found, either by witnesses or affidavit, that the person claimed doth owe service to the party claiming him, under the laws of the State from which he fled. In both cases, the proceeding is to be preliminary and summary; in both cases, the party is to be removed to the State from which he fled, that his liabilities, and his rights, may be there regularly tried and adjudged by the tribunals of that State, according to its laws. In the case of an alleged fugitive from justice, charged with crime, it is not to be taken for granted, in the State to which he had fled, that he is guilty; nor in that State is he to be tried, or punished. He is only to be remitted for trial to the place from which he came. In the case of the alleged fugitive from service, the courts of the State in which he is arrested are not to decide that, in fact or in law, he does owe service to any body. He, too, is only to be remitted, for an inquiry into his rights and the proper adjudication of them, to the State from which he fled; the tribunals of which understand its laws, and are in the constant habit of trying the question of slavery or no slavery, on the application of individuals, as an ordinary act of judicial authority. There is not a slave State in the Union, in which independent judicial tribunals are not always open to receive and decide upon petitions, or applications for freedom; nor do I know, nor have I heard it alleged, that the decisions of these tribunals are not fair and upright. Such of them as I have seen evince, certainly, these qualities in the judges.

This act of Congress of the 12th of February, 1793, appears to have been well considered, and to have passed with little opposition. There is no evidence known to me that any body at the time regarded any of its provisions as repugnant to religion, liberty, the Constitution, or humanity. The two Senators of Massachusetts at that time were that distinguished legislator and patriot of your own county, George Cabot; and that other citizen of Massachusetts, among the most eminent of his day for talent, purity of character, and every virtue, Caleb Strong. Mr. Cabot, indeed, was one of the committee for preparing the bill. It appears to have passed the Senate without a division. In the House of Representatives it was supported by Mr. [Benjamin] Goodhue, Mr. [Elbridge] Gerry, both then, I believe, of your county of Essex, (Mr. Goodhue afterwards a Senator of the United States, and Mr. Gerry afterwards Vice-President of the United States,) Mr. [Fisher] Ames, Mr. [Shearjashub] Bourne, Mr. [George] Leonard, and Mr. [Theodore] Sedgwick, members from Massachusetts, and was passed by a vote of *forty-eight* to *seven*; of these seven, one being from Virginia, one from Maryland, one from New York, and four from the New England States; and of these four, one, Mr. [George] Thatcher [Thacher], from Massachusetts.[6]

I am not aware that there exists any published account of the debates on the passage of this act. I have been able to find none. I have searched the original files, however, and I find among the papers several propositions for modifications and amendments, of various kinds; but none suggesting the propriety of any jury trial in the State where the party should be arrested.

For many years, little or no complaint was made against this law, nor was it supposed to be guilty of the offences and enormities which have since been charged upon it. It was passed for the purpose of complying with a direct and solemn injunction of the Constitution; it did no more than was believed to be necessary to accomplish that single purpose; and it did that in a cautious, mild manner, to be everywhere conducted according to judicial proceedings.

I confess I see no more objection to the provisions of this law than was seen by Mr. Cabot and Mr. Strong, Mr. Goodhue and Mr. Gerry; and such provisions appear to me, as they appeared to them, to be absolutely necessary, if we mean to fulfil the duties positively and peremptorily enjoined upon us by the Constitution of the country. But since the agitation caused by Abolition societies and Abolition presses has to such an extent excited the public mind, these provisions have been rendered obnoxious and odious. Unwearied endeavors have been made, and but too successfully, to rouse the passions of the people against them; and under the cry of universal freedom, and under that other cry, that there is a rule for the government of public men and private men which is of superior obligation to the Constitution of the country, several of the States have enacted laws to hinder, obstruct, and defeat the enactments in this act of Congress, to the utmost of their power. The Supreme Court of the United States has solemnly decided, that it is lawful for State officers and State magistrates to fulfill the duties enjoined upon them by the act of Congress of 1793, unless prohibited by State laws; and thereupon prohibitory State laws have been immediately passed, inflicting fine and imprisonment on all State officers and magistrates who shall presume to conform to these requisitions of the act of Congress.[7] And these prohibitory and penal laws of the States have rendered it imperative on Congress to make further and other provisions for carrying into effect the substantial intention of the act of 1793. This is the cause of the introduction into the Senate of a bill on the subject, recently, by the Committee on the Judiciary.[8] Notwithstanding all that may be said by shallow men, ignorant men, and factious men, men whose only hope of making or of keeping themselves conspicuous is by incessant agitation and the most reckless efforts to alarm and misguide the people, I know of no persons, in or out of Congress, who wish any thing more to be done on the subject of fugitives from service, than what is essentially necessary in order to meet the requirements of the Constitution, and accomplish the object of the act of Congress of 1793. Whatever enactments may be deemed essential to this purpose, I, for one, shall certainly support, as I feel bound to do by my oath of office, and by every consideration of duty and propriety.

As I have already said, the act of Congress of 1793 made no provision for any trial by jury in the State where the arrest of a fugitive is made. I have considered the subject with a conscientious desire to provide for such jury trial, if possible, in order to allay excitement and remove objections. There are many difficulties, however, attending any such provision; and a main one, and perhaps the only insuperable one, has been created by the States themselves, by making it a penal offence in their own officers to render any aid in apprehending or securing such fugitives, and absolutely refusing the use of their jails for keeping them in custody till a jury could be called together, witnesses summoned, and a regular trial had. It is not too much to say, that to these State laws is to be attributed the actual and practical denial of trial by jury in these cases. These ill-considered State laws it is which have absolutely deprived the alleged fugitive, as the case now stands, of any trial by jury, by refusing those aids and facilities without which a jury trial is impossible.

But at the same time, nothing is more false than that such jury trial is demanded in cases of this kind by the Constitution, either in its letter or in its spirit. The Constitution declares, that in all criminal prosecutions there shall be a trial by jury; the reclaiming of a fugitive slave is not a criminal prosecution. The Constitution also declares, that in suits at common law the trial by jury shall be preserved; the reclaiming of a fugitive slave is not a suit at the common law. And there is no other clause or sentence in the Constttution having the least bearing on the subject.

I have seen a publication by Mr. Horace Mann,[9] a member of Congress from Massachusetts, in which I find this sentence. Speaking of the bill before the Senate, he says: "This bill derides the trial by jury secured by the Constitution. A man may not lose his horse without a right to this trial, but he may his freedom. Mr. Webster speaks for the South and for slavery, not for the North and for freedom, when he abandons this right." This personal vituperation does not annoy me, but I lament to see a public man of Massachusetts so crude and confused in his legal apprehensions, and so little acquainted with the Constitution of his country, as these opinions evince Mr. Mann to be. His citation of a supposed case, as in point, if it have any analogy to the matter, would prove, that, if Mr. Mann's horse stray into his neighbor's field, *he cannot lead him back without a previous trial by jury to ascertain the right.* Truly, if what Mr. Mann says of the provisions of the Constitution, in this publication, be a test of his accuracy in the understanding of that instrument, he would do well not to seek to protect his peculiar notions under its sanction, but to appeal at once, as others do, to that higher authority which sits enthroned above the Constitution and above the law.[10]

Gentlemen, I am extending these remarks, I fear, to quite too great a length; but there is still one characteristic of this "agitation" too remarkable to be omitted.

A member of Congress from Illinois, of talent and rapidly increasing distinction, in a speech delivered in the House of Representatives on the 21st day of February, made these very true and pertinent remarks: —

"I am not so unmindful of truth as to deny that, in respect to the subject now under consideration, some of our Southern friends have good cause to complain. But it must have been remarked by all of us, that the Representatives from those States which have really been aggrieved in this respect are not those who have threatened us with disunion. These threats have come from the Representatives of States, from which, I venture to say, on an average not one slave escapes in five years. Who ever heard of a slave escaping from Mississippi or Alabama? Where does he go to? Who helps him away? Certainly not the people of the North. Kentucky, Virginia, Maryland, and Missouri, the only States that are really sufferers by the escape of slaves, do not seem to have dreamed of dissolution as a remedy; while the Representatives from a few of the extreme Southern States, whence slaves could no more escape than from the island of Cuba, see ample cause and imperious necessity for dissolving the Union, and establishing a 'Southern Confederacy,' in the alleged fact that their slaves are enticed away by the citizens of the North."[11]

Now, the counterpart of the "agitation" presents an equally singular and striking aspect, in the fact, that the greatest clamor and outcry have been raised against the cruelty and enormity of the reclamation of slaves in quarters where no such reclamation has ever been made, or if ever made, where the instances are so exceedingly few and far between as to have escaped general knowledge. What, and how many, are the instances of the seizure of fugitive slaves which have happened in New England? And what have been the circumstances of injustice, cruelty, and atrocity attending them? To ascertain the truth in this respect, I have made diligent inquiry of members of Congress from the six New England States. On a subject so general, I cannot be sure, of course, that the information received is entirely accurate; and therefore I do not say that the statement which I am about to present may be relied on as altogether correct; but I suppose it cannot be materially erroneous. The result, then, of all I can learn is this. No seizure of an alleged fugitive slave has ever been made in Maine. No seizure of an alleged fugitive slave has ever been made in New Hampshire. No seizure of an alleged fugitive slave has ever been made in Vermont. No seizure of an alleged fugitive slave has been made in Rhode Island within the last thirty years. No seizure of an alleged fugitive slave is known to have been made in Connecticut, except one, about twenty-five years ago; and in that case the negro was immediately discharged for want of proof of identity. Some instances of the seizure of alleged fugitive slaves are known to have occurred, in this generation, in Massachusetts; but, except one, their number and their history are uncertain. That one took place in Boston twelve or fifteen years ago; and in that case some charitably disposed persons offered the owner a sum of money which he regarded as less than half the value of the slave, but which he agreed to accept, and the negro was discharged. A few cases, I suppose, may have occurred in New Bedford, but they attracted little notice, and, so far as I can learn, caused no complaint. Indeed, I do not know that there ever was more than a single case or two arising in that place. Be it remembered, that I am speaking of reclamations of slaves made by their masters under the law of Congress. I am not speaking of instances of violent abduction, and kidnapping, made by persons not professing to be reclaiming their own slaves.

If this be a true account of all that has happened in New England within the last thirty years, respecting the arrest of fugitive slaves, and I believe it substantially is so, what is there to justify the passionate appeals, the vehement and empty declamations, the wild and and fanatical conduct, of both men and women, which have so long disturbed, and so much disgraced, the commonwealth and the country? What is there, especially, that should induce public men to break loose from all just restraint, fall themselves into the merest vagaries, and fan, with what they call eloquence, the fires, ever ready to kindle, of popular prejudice and popular excitement? I suspect all this to be the effect of that wandering and vagrant philanthropy which disturbs and annoys all that is present, in time or place, by heating the imagination on subjects distant, remote, and uncertain.

It is admitted on all hands, that the necessity for any legal provision for the reclaiming of fugitive slaves is a misfortune and an evil; as it is admitted by nearly all, that slavery itself is a misfortune and an evil. And there are States in which the evil attending these reclamations is practically felt. But where the evil really exists, there is comparatively little complaint, and no excitement. Maryland and Pennsylvania, for example, lie, the one on the slave side of the line, the other on the free side. Slaves escape from Maryland, flee into Pennsylvania, and are arrested. These instances are not unfrequent, and usually create no disturbance and excite no exasperated feeling. In one instance, indeed, a mob assembled to rescue the fugitive, violence ensued, and a life was lost. This of course created popular resentment, and for a considerable time agitated the neighborhood. But in general the people of Pennsylvania understand their neighbors' rights, and are willing that they should be secured and enjoyed. Massachusetts grows fervid on Pennsylvania wrongs; while Pennsylvania herself is not excited by any sense of such wrongs, and complains of no injustice. The Abolitionists of Massachusetts, both the out-and-out and the *quasi*, rend the welkin with sympathies for Pennsylvania, while Pennsylvania would quite as willingly be left to her own care of herself. Massachusetts tears fall abundantly for Pennsylvania sufferings, of which sufferings Pennsylvania herself knows little or nothing. No people are more opposed to slavery than the people of Pennsylvania. We know, especially, that that great and respectable part of her population, the Friends, have borne their testimony against it from the first. Yet they create no excitement; they seek not to overthrow or undermine the Constitution of their country. They know that firmness, steadiness of principle, a just moderation, and unconquerable perseverance, are the virtues the practice of which is most likely to correct whatever is wrong in the constitution of the social system. No doubt there are sometimes to be found Friends subject to the frailty of desiring to become conspicuous, or to the influence of a false sentimentality, or borne away, by the puffs of a transcendental philosophy, into an atmosphere flickering between light and darkness. But that is not a malady of the great body. They remain of sound and disposing minds and memories. I am misled by authority which ought not to mislead, if it be not true that that great body approves the sentiments to which I have given utterance on the floor of the Senate.

Between Kentucky and Ohio complaints have arisen, occasionally, on the subject of fugitive slaves; but by no means to the extent which has been represented by the Abolition societies. Slaveholders in Kentucky complain of the difficulties which they encounter in reclaiming fugitives; and the people of Ohio complain, not of the execution of the act of Congress, and reclamations under it, but of the conduct of slaveholders, in coming into the State and taking and carrying back their slaves by force, and without legal process. The State of Ohio has had the discretion not to prohibit her officers and magistrates from performing the duties enjoined on them by the act of Congress. Such duties they perform when occasion requires; yet as they may be prohibited by the legislature, and as the Supreme Court has decided that it is in the power of Congress to make complete provision, by law, for the whole subject, and to give the power of executing such law to officers of the United States; and as the prohibitory acts of some of the States make an appropriate and suitable law of the United States indispensable, such law, if passed, would of course be general, and would comprehend Ohio with other States.

The act of 1793 gives a right of action to the owner of a fugitive slave against any person who shall harbor or conceal him. Such actions have been brought in Ohio, and I have heard an eminent judicial authority say, that he has found no more obstruction to the course of judicial proceedings in these cases than in others. Ohio juries try them with as much impartiality and calmness as they try other causes.

Gentlemen, from what I know of the subject, and of the public men and the people of those two States, I fully believe, that, if left entirely to them, a law might be passed perfectly satisfactory to every body except those whose business is agitation, and whose objects are any thing but the promotion of peace, harmony, patriotic good-will, and the love of UNION among the people of the United States.

And now, Gentlemen, does not every sober-minded and patriotic man see the necessity, and feel the duty, of rebuking that spirit of faction and disunion, that spirit of discord and of crimination and recrimination, that spirit that loves angry controversy, and loves it, most especially, when evils are imaginary and dangers unreal, which has been so actively employed in doing mischief, and which, it is to be lamented, has received countenance and encouragement in quarters whence better things were looked for?

We are now near the close of the sixth month of the session of Congress. What important measure has been adopted for the advancement of the great interests of the country? For one, I hardly dare expect any progress in useful legislation, until a spirit shall prevail, both in Congress and the country, which shall look more to things important and real, and less to things ideal and abstract. That there are serious difficulties in our present condition, growing out of the acquisition of new territories, is certainly true. These difficulties were foreseen and foretold. An honest and earnest effort was made to avoid and avert them. They are now upon us. But WE CAN overcome them, and still remain a prosperous, happy, and UNITED PEOPLE, if prudence and conciliation shall animate our public counsels, and a spirit of forbearance, moderation, and harmony spread over the land. I am, Gentlemen, with entire regard, your obliged fellow-citizen, and obedient servant,

Daniel Webster

Text from *W & S*, 12: 225–236. Original not found. First published in *Boston Daily Advertiser*, May 31, 1850.

1. See above, p. 57, Edward Sprague Rand et al. to DW, April 8, 1850.

2. Thompson, a veteran of the Revolution, was a resident of Topsham, Maine, which he represented for many years in the General Court. Slocum (1748–1827) was a Dartmouth Township farmer and a frequent participant in public affairs. Nason, of Sanford, Maine, was a storekeeper who served one term in the General Court. For their arguments against the Constitution in

1788, see Jonathan Elliott, ed., *Debates in the Several State Conventions on the Adoption of the Federal Constitution* . . . , (2d ed.; Philadelphia, 1888), 2: 61, 79–81, 133.

3. Greenleaf (1732–1799; Harvard 1751), was a Newburyport merchant and jurist. Titcomb (1727–1817), Newburyport blacksmith and merchant, was a naval officer at the local customhouse during much of the 1780s.

4. As early as his Second Reply to Hayne (1830) DW had attributed the Northwest Ordinance, barring slavery from territories north of the Ohio River, to the work of Nathan Dane. Subsequently, Manassah Cutler's role came to his attention (see Ephraim Cutler to DW, February 1847, *Correspondence*, 6: 212–214), but it proved convenient here to credit Dane, whose contribution to the ordinance proved relevant to DW's purposes in this letter.

5. 1 U.S. Stats. 302.

6. See *Annals of Congress*, 2d Cong., p. 861.

7. *Prigg* v. *Pennsylvania*, 16 Peters 558. On northern resistance to the Fugitive Slave Law, consult Thomas D. Morris, *Free Men All: The Personal Liberty Laws of the North, 1780–1861* (Baltimore, 1974).

8. On January 16, 1850, Senator Andrew P. Butler of South Carolina, chairman of the Judiciary Committee, reported favorably on Senator James M. Mason's bill to strengthen the Fugitive Slave Act of 1793. The proposed bill, and Butler's remarks on it January 24 in debate, are in *Congressional Globe*, 31st Cong., 1st sess., *Appendix*, pp. 79–83.

9. Originally published May 3 in the *Atlas*, Mann's letter to his constituents was republished in pamphlet form as *Horace Mann's Letters on the Extension of Slavery Into California and New Mexico and on the Duty of Congress to Provide Trial by Jury for Alleged Fugitive Slaves* (Washington, 1850); also in Horace Mann, *Slavery: Letters and Speeches* (Boston, 1851), pp. 263–281.

10. At this point in both the text published in the press and that republished in DW's *Works* (6: 551–563), DW included the following footnote: "I may be permitted to add, in a note, an extract from a private letter from one of the most distinguished men in England, dated as late as the 29th of January: 'Religion is an excellent thing in every matter except in politics. There, it seems to make men mad; and I do not know of any people more mad than the antislavery people, on your side of the water and ours. Up to the present time, I have no doubt they have aggravated every evil they have endeavored to mitigate or prevent. If you tell one of them what has been the result of his officiousness, he answers, "*Liberavi animam meam.* I may have done wrong, but I shall go to heaven for it." So I believe that your Abolitionists have made the state of the slave, and still more that of the free black, much worse than it would have been; and probably in many States, that of Virginia, for instance, have retarded his enfranchisement. But they care little, if they save their own souls. On the other hand, the Southerners seem as unreasonable. To require California to accept slavery seems both wicked and unjust.'

In these sentences my friend means, undoubtedly, to ascribe the evils which he so truly states not true and genuine religion, not to the religion of the Gospel, but to that fanatical notion of religion which sometimes possesses men's imaginations. The religion of the New Testament, that religion which is founded on the teachings of Jesus Christ and his Apostles, is as sure a guide to duty in politics as in any other concern of life."

The "distinguished" Englishman quoted here is Nassau William Senior, whose words are extracted from his letter to Edward Everett, January 29, 1850, mDW 30441, a copy of which is enclosed in DW to Everett, [May 19, 1850], mDW 30440. In his brief note to Everett

DW indicated that he was using the extract for his response to Rand et al.

11. DW is quoting from a speech by William H. Bissell. See *Congressional Globe*, 31st Cong., 1st sess., *Appendix*, pp. 225–228. Quote is on p. 227.

FROM ELISHA MILLS HUNTINGTON

Misletoe Lodge
May 15th 1850.

My dear Sir.

I am just starting for Indianapolis where I shall be detained some five weeks in holding our Federal court. Having a moment of leisure before the Steamer reaches my landing (near Cannelton Ind) I gladly employ it to assure you of the pleasure which the perusal of your Speech in the Senate on the Slavery question has given me. As may have been expected, your views have been the subject of universal comment in the country, and it is not a matter of surprise that they have been attacked in the North by those who have been so long and so violently committed to different opinions. Those whose political lives depend on keeping up a spirit of discontent by an appeal to bad passions and false sympathies, will of course make the most they can out of long cultivated prejudices, and can only do this by assailing those who have the independence and the honesty to rebuke those unworthy prejudices.

From a pretty general and accurate knowledge of the real sentiments of the people of Indiana, I feel warranted in saying, that of the one million of souls in our state, there are not two thousand who if calmly consulted on this agitating question and left free from the influence of demagogues who would not fully concur with you. Each of the great political parties have been struggling to get the votes of this miserable free soil party, & thus have given that party a consequence it is not entitled to, but I believe that lately both of the great parties are determined to throw them off. I am sure that the judgment and the morality of the country is with you, and I am in hopes that there will be enough men found in Congress to indorse them by their votes.

I can see no great objection to the measures reported by the committee of thirteen[1]—I fear however that they may be defeated by a union of the extreme men. I have no doubt that the time will come when these factionists will be overwhelmed by the force of a sound public sentiment, but in the mean time they will do all the harm they can. You have bearded the Lion in his den, and I hope and believe that in doing so you have rendered a service to the country which the country can and will appreciate. I need not assure you sir of my undiminished personal and political attachment to you, or my lively remembrance of your many kindnesses to me. <The time may come when> Western political senti- ment has always been corrupted by demagogues, but I have a hope that it may not always be so.

I shall write you again in a few days in regard to a matter of some public interest here, and in which there is a very general desire for your aid.

We want you to come out and lay the cornerstone of a monument to [Robert] Fulton[2] sometime this fall. The occasion will draw together an immense concourse of people, and especially if you will consent to come. Upon this subject I will however write you again. In the meantime I remain Your friend   EMH

ALS. InU-Li. Huntington (1806–1862), attorney and Whig politician, was then serving as a federal judge for the Indiana District.

1. The committee's proposals, lumped together in one "omnibus" bill, provided for the immediate ad- mission of California, establishment of territorial governments in New Mexico and Utah without stipulations regarding slavery, settlement of the Texas–New Mexico boundary con- troversy, passage of a new fugitive slave law, and abolition of the slave trade in the District of Columbia. The recommendations were nearly identi- cal to those Henry Clay had made on January 29, which Webster had endorsed in his Seventh of March speech.

2. Huntington was serving on a committee planning construction of a monument to Fulton on land the inventor had owned in Troy, Indiana. The enterprise began with fanfare but did not achieve its goal. See Thomas James de la Hunt, *Perry County: A History* (Indianapolis, 1916), pp. 126–127, and Elisha Mills Huntington to DW, June 10, 1850, mDW 30551.

TO WILLIAM WHITWELL GREENOUGH

Washington,
May 18. '50

Dear Sir

As to what I said of the sympathies of California, at the dinners at the Revere,[1] I suppose I was referring to the Gentlemen[2] sent here to represent her, in the Senate, who are both, you know, Southern men.

But, nevertheless, I confess I am a little fearful that when California becomes one of the family of the U.S. her position, & her pursuits, will be likely to lead her to adopt broader notions of *Free Trade* than may comport with the prosperity of New England. Yrs truly   Danl Webster

ALS. DLC. Published in *W & S*, 16:
540. Greenough (1818–1899; Harvard 1837), Boston merchant, was
active for many years in civic affairs.
1. During his sojourn in Boston,
DW had attended two dinners in his
honor at the Revere House on Bowdoin Square, where he made some
informal, unrecorded remarks about

the prospects for compromise.
2. William McKendree Gwin, born
in Tennessee, and John Charles Frémont, a native of Georgia, had been
elected in December 1849 by the
California legislature to serve as
the state's first senators in Washington once California was admitted to
the Union.

TO [JONATHAN PRESCOTT HALL]

Washington May 18. '50

My Dear Sir

I love you sincerely, & always receive what you say, not only kindly
but thankfully.[1] I feel neither indifferent, or distant towards our good
President. He is an honest man, & a good Whig, & I wish well to his
administration, for his sake, & the Countrys. But what can I do? He
never consults me, nor asks my advice; nor does any one of his Cabinet,
except Mr [William Morris] Meredith. His Cabinet was wholly formed,
originally, without asking any opinion of mine, & while some are friendly
eno. others are cross-grained towards me, & excessively jealous. I shall
support, cordially, the President's measures whenever I can; but I have
been in Public life some time longer than the President, or any of his
advisors, & suppose I shall not be much blamed, if on great public questions, I feel as much confidence in my own judgment as I do in theirs.
Personally I esteem the President, & like him very well. But I cannot,
like Mr Truman Smith, and Mr [William Henry] Seward, swing my arms
in the Senate, & proclaim myself a Champion for the Administration,
in regard to all it has done, does now, or hereafter may, could, should or
would do.

The truth is, My Dear Sir, that with a good deal of regard for some
members of the Cabinet, the Country has not confidence in it, as a
whole, nor has the Whig party. Hence I fear, that the Administration is
doomed, & the Whig Party doomed with it. Nevertheless, I shall do all
I can to avert the catastrophe.

My Dear Sir—You have sometimes very hot fires at the Astor.[2] Throw
this letter, immediately, into the very hottest of them. Yrs   D.W.

ALS. DLC. Published in *W & S*, 16:
539–540. Hall (1796–1862; Yale
1817), a New York City lawyer, had
served as United States district attorney for southern New York under
President Tyler and, with an assist

from DW, won a reappointment to
the same post under President
Fillmore.
1. Letter not found.
2. The Astor House, a leading New
York City hotel.

TO FRANKLIN HAVEN

Washington May 18. 50

My Dear Sir

The success of the "Compromise Bill," as it is called, depends on the No. of Southern Senators who may fall off, from its support. It is said Va. & South Carolina, & one member from Alabama will vote against it.[1] If more than *six* Southern Senators refuse their support, the Bill will fail, in the Senate. In my opinion, it is unfortunate that the measures were all put together. When I left the Com[mitt]ee to go home, it was agreed they should not be; but that vote was rescinded, in my absence. The situation of things is singular. There is an unquestionable majority of votes in the Senate, in favor *of every one of the propositions contained* in the Bill perhaps with some amendments; & yet I have fears that no majority will be found for them, all together. The policy of putting all in one Bill was founded in calculations respecting the best chances of votes in the H. of R.

I believe it is time, that many leading persons, of all parties, in the South & west, out of Congress, urge the passage of the Bill as it is. I shall, of course, vote for it, & for all measures, & almost any measure, intended to settle these questions; but am sorry to say, I fear our Eastern members will hardly go the same way. It is a strange, & a melancholy fact, that not one single *National* speech has been made in the H. of R. this session. Every man speaks to defend himself, & to gratify his own Constituents. That is all. No one inquires how the Union is to be preserved, & the peace of the Country restored. Mean time, all important public measures *are worse than stationary*. The tariff, for instance, is losing important friends, thro the irritation produced by these Slavery Debates. I suppose no history shows a case of such mischiefs, arising from angry debates, & disputes, both in the Govt. & the Country, on questions of so very little real importance. But we must persevere. The peace-makers are to inherit the earth; & our part of the inheritance would be a very good one, if peace could really be made. Yrs always truly   Danl Webster

ALS. MH-H. Published in *PC*, 2: 369–370.

1. Senators James M. Mason and Robert M.T. Hunter of Virginia, Andrew P. Butler of South Carolina, and Jeremiah Clemens of Alabama opposed the compromise. One South Carolina seat was still vacant following John C. Calhoun's death. William R. King, who held the other Alabama seat, was not viewed as steadfast against compromise.

FROM [?]

Charleston S C May 20th—50

Dear Sir

This letter although anonymous is addressed to you by one who knows

you well, and who was in early life one of your pupils, myself a native
of M[assachuset]ts. Although I left the land of my birth and parentage
at an early period and settled here, where I found fortune more propitious than at home, I still feel a deep interest in and strong attachment
for my native home, emotions of pride and exultation arise within me
at being able to point to a Senator from Mts., who is confessedly and
deservedly considered one of the two very great men now left to our
distracted country. You, Sir, possess moral courage of which you have
given unquestionable evidence during your recent visit to Boston, the
period has now arrived when in all human probability you can become
the master spirit that will still the storm which threatens our beloved
country. You may perhaps think it presumptuous in an obscure individual like myself (who thinks himself too insignificant to disclose even
his name) to obtrude his crude remarks upon one of the most profound statesmen and accomplished diplomatists of the age, but bear
with me whilst I say in plain truth, that some of the features of Mr
Clay's compromise can in their present shape never be accepted by the
South, nay will always encounter the most determined opposition; I allude, as you may suppose, to the proposed mode of trying by Jury in a
slave-holding state by virtue of *An Act of Congress* the masters title to
his slave,[1] or in other words the identification of the property, this is
wholly inadmissible, and any law of Congress which in the slightest
degree encroaches upon the *exclusive* right of such state to legislate
upon the subject of its own slaves within its own limits will ever prove
fatal to compromise, this I mention as one of the most prominent barriers to an adjustment of existing difficulties, there are others which
are obvious to you which it is unnecessary to mention, a meeting of the
Citizens of Charleston is called for this very evening for the purpose of
repudiating Mr Clay's compromise, you will doubtless see those proceedings, let me implore you to weigh well the substance of them, your
judgment as a *statesman* will, I am persuaded, approve of the resolutions—if so—stand, I conjure you, by the South, once more in the U S
Senate give to the subject that energy, earnestness, and eloquence demanded by the occasion, the result will be, that not only New England
but the whole North will be brought over and swayed by your counsels.
The late Dr. Cyrus Perkins of N Y,[2] whom you and I well remember,
whom it was my lot to have seen but once since we were all together in
early days, said to me on that occasion (when you and Ld. Ashburton[3]
were negotiating) "Danl Webster can bring the people of New England
to do what he pleases"—I believe it implicitly—prove to our New England brothers, what is undeniably true, that to agitate and perhaps
dissever the Union is equally inconsistent with *their* interest and prosperity, as with that of the South, and the voice of opposition will cease,

tell them what is equally true, that however divided the South may be at this moment, the moment is rapidly approaching when every Southerner will speak as one man; you are the person and the only person who can pour oil on the troubled waters. Considerations merely political and sectional must be laid aside, the preservation of the Union is our only safety-valve, and for that grand object sacrifices must be made, the South has been wronged grievously wronged by the North, t'is high time the North were roused *by you* to a sense of justice and of their own interest.

Sir I conscientiously believe you can effect all that is to be desired, and I feel persuaded you will not withhold your powerful services at this important crisis.

I have by long residence here, by inter marriage, by means of children born & educated here, and by various other ties become in my political views to all intents and purposes a Southerner, I am still proud of being from the same region that gave birth to Webster, and I can not but believe that on him now depends, and by him will be effected the tranquility of our common country, which will, when the occasion occurs, shew herself grateful to her patriot Son, who saved her in the hour of peril—I remain, Dr Sir, with feelings of friendship, and the most profound respect Yr well-wisher

AL. NhHi. Neither the identity of the writer nor the circumstance in which he was DW's pupil have been established.

1. The writer is referring to an amendment presented to the Senate on May 8 by Henry Clay, as part of his "Committee of 13" report. It provided that a remanded fugitive slave should have the right to a jury trial in the "county, parish, or district thereof, from whence he or she may have fled." This was a modification of both the law of 1793, and Senator James M. Mason's bill of January 3, 1850, neither of which made such a provision. See *Congressional Globe,*

31st Cong., 1st sess., pp. 948–949, and Stanley W. Campbell, *The Slave Catchers: Enforcement of the Fugitive Slave Law, 1850–1860* (Chapel Hill, N.C., 1968), pp. 15–20.

2. Perkins (1778–1849; Dartmouth 1800), a classmate and lifelong friend of DW, was professor of anatomy and surgery at Dartmouth, 1810–1819. Thereafter until his death he practiced medicine in New York.

3. Alexander Baring, first baron Ashburton (1774–1848), financier and statesman, in 1842 was commissioner at Washington for the settlement of the Maine boundary dispute. See *Diplomatic Papers,* 1: 483–704.

TO PETER HARVEY

Washington May 29. 1850.

My Dear Sir,

The Courier, and the Daily Advertiser, should lose no time in coming out decidedly, in favor of *some* plan of adjustment and settlement. They should, at first, take strong ground against carrying on the foolish controversy about Slavery in New Mexico further, and should rebuke such politicians as Mr [Horace] Mann and Mr [John P.] Hale, with emphasis.[1] They may be assured that the side of Union and conciliation is getting to be the strong side. Mr Linus Childs[2] of Lowell, is here, and he is as strong as a lion in favor of a compromise. He talks to the Massachusetts members strong; and has written for other Massachusetts men to come on, and join him.

It is just as I knew it would be, with the Whig Senators of the South. They will not give a single vote for the Tariff until this Slavery business is settled. A very leading individual among them, told Mr Childs yesterday, that so far as depended on him, and his friends, the Lowell mills might and should all stop, unless the North quit this violence of abuse— and showed a disposition to be reasonable in the present exciting questions. I believe I told you this a month ago.[3]

Depend upon it our Northern members are getting into a tight place. If they defeat a compromise, their responsibility will be great. If they oppose it and it still should succeed they will not belong to the class of Peace makers.

I believe Mr. Childs tells them some plain truths. I write again soon. We have no Boston Mail this morning. Yrs truly   Danl Webster

Copy. NhHi. Published in *W & S*, 16: 541–542.
 1. Cf. "The Necessities of the Present Crisis," *Boston Courier*, June 3, 1850.

2. Linus Child's name was frequently spelled "Childs" by his acquaintances.
 3. See above, p. 69, DW to Peter Harvey, April 15, 1850.

FROM MOSES STUART

Andover, 30 May 1850.

My dear Sir,

I have just sent from my study, the last proof of *said Pamphlet*,[1] about 20 pages 8vo, all written & printed, i.e. set up, & now ready to be printed (being stereotyped), since I saw you. Why I am not dead I know not; for besides all this, I have had 12 pages a day, & sometimes more, to correct, of my *Commentary on Daniel*.[2] The excitement of writing, & of the subject, has kept me up; & although very tired, I think I am in better health, than when I began my labour. But I could not stand another such a bout.

As the pamphlet will be in your hands, in some 2 or 3 days, I will not undertake a view of the contents. Your Son, perhaps, has told you a part of the story—& I requested C[rocker] & Brewster,[3] to send [it] to you, when they had got 48 pages in a state to send. I hope you have them ere this.

I have nearly satisfied myself in the writing; but perhaps this is egotism. It is for you & others to say, whether I have good grounds of satisfaction.

Your *long Tom* to the good people of N[ewbury]Port⁴ has hit the mark, & made a large breach in the wall of the *Red Cap agitators*. I have amply discussed the same subject, but have presented it in another attitude. Between us both, I think the view is somewhat complete.

But *Mr* [Horace] *Mann*! I have not had such a laugh since I began to write as when I read your *exposé* of his *profound* knowledge of law & the Constitution. The *jury for the run-away horse* is *ad unguem*.⁵ All our common people here—even our mechanics—are laughing, at his expense. You will see that I have not been lacking in putting some of his positions to the test, and administering a temperate, but still a cutting rebuke.⁶ Well does he deserve it. I predict he will have the "Irishman's hoist."

As to [William Lloyd] Garrison, Judge [William] Jay, L[ewis] Tappan, *et id genus omne*, you will see that I have given to "each his meat in due season."⁷ An odious job—but one necessary to be done. Why need I fear to tell the truth, and shame them? I have nothing to lose by telling it, nor to gain by suppressing it.

If my view of the *Bible doctrine* does not lower some peaks, I shall think it strange. The thing has never been effectually done; & I feel no scruples about battling for the truth, on *exegetical* ground. Some precious specimens of our antagonists' exegesis you will see, in my little Pamphlet. It were easy to multiply them; but I think you will say: Jam satis!⁸

One word as to *copy-right*. Neither the printers nor myself w[oul]d get any remuneration otherwise. They c[oul]d do without it. Not so with me. After 40 years service here, & being sick so long that I thought it my duty to resign my office, I am, with a family on my hands, & with wretched health, doomed to an annuity of $400 *per annum*. All I have will not yield me $300 more. The expenses of living here are greater than in Boston; & I have to forego many of the comforts of life in order to keep from running into debt. From my little capital, I have been compelled to subtract $400, the past year, in order to live, even at the very humble style in which I & my family live.

I hope this will apologise for taking out a copy right.⁹ I have never complained to or of anybody; & sh[oul]d not say what I have to you, but for the sake of vindicating the matter of copy-right.

Let me hear from you, when you have read; & let me know *what is going to be done.* I think Mr [Henry] Clay is in danger of eclipsing his glory. Why attack the President?[10]

I am writing where I have not a scrap of larger paper, so must say Vale! Si valeas, Bene sum!   M. Stuart

ALS. NhHi.

1. *Conscience and the Constitution* (Boston, 1850). See above, Moses Stuart to DW, May 2, 1850.

2. *Commentary on the Book of Daniel* (Boston, 1850).

3. Boston printers.

4. See above, DW to Edward Sprague Rand et al., May 15, 1850. A Long Tom represented a gun of large size and long range.

5. "to the nail," i.e., "to perfection"; see above, p. 91.

6. See *Conscience and the Constitution*, pp. 78–80, 82–83.

7. Ibid., esp. pp. 62–65.

8. "Enough already!" a common interjection in the comedies of Titus Maccius Plautus, Roman comic dramatist.

9. Stuart effectively made his point. On June 2, DW wrote to Peter Harvey that Stuart "must get a copy-right, and the book ought to be published, in thousands and hundreds of thousands." DW to Harvey, June 2, 1850, mDW 30502. See also DW to Harvey, June 4, 1850, mDW 30522a.

10. Angered by criticisms of the omnibus compromise bill made by newspapers associated with the Taylor administration, Clay spoke out strongly on May 21 against the President's position, which he charged addressed only "one wound" then festering in the nation. *Congressional Globe*, 31st Cong., 1st sess., *Appendix*, pp. 612–616.

TO [GEORGE TICKNOR]

Washington, June 1, 1850.

My Dear Sir:

The effusion of the *Atlas*,[1] of which you sent me a slip, may receive an effectual reply.

The *Atlas* complains that I speak derogatorily of Massachusetts, and deride her for shedding tears over Pennsylvania wrongs, etc., etc.

Now two things:

1. My remarks, from their nature, were applicable to the abolitionists and fanatics of Massachusetts, and were so intended.

2. But Massachusetts, as a State, is answerable for what she does as a State. And what has she done? Let us see. The act of Congress for the reclamation of slaves was passed in 1793. All her eminent men in Congress at that day cordially concurred in it.[2] For forty years and more they obeyed its injunctions, without complaint.

At last, in 1843, she passed a law, making it penal in her officers and magistrates to obey the commands of this act of Congress;[3] and thus deprived the owners of all remedy whatever, for the recovery of their fugitive slaves. By this penal act of the State, the Constitution and the law of Congress both became, in Massachusetts, a dead letter. Massachusetts, then, herself, disturbed a state of things which had continued for half a century, nearly, without complaint. And what led her to do this? No case of illegality, inhumanity, or cruelty, had occurred. No. slave had been unjustly reclaimed. No actual injury or oppression had taken place.

But agitation had arisen—theoretic, fanatical, and fantastical agitation—and under a loud cry of antislavery led away silly women and sillier men, who formed a considerable party, and both the great parties strove to see which could win this third party[4] by the greatest yielding to its clamor and its nonsense. This ought to be presented as the real *causa causans* of the Massachusetts act of 1843.

Now it should be put strongly to the *Atlas* to say why this law was passed? What new grievance had sprung up under the act of Congress? If the Massachusetts law had not been passed, there would have been no occasion, so far as she was concerned, of any further legislation by Congress. *It was her own legislation which made further legislation by Congress indispensable.*

If this be put home to the *Atlas*, it can make no decent answer. You know, it never attempted any answer to your former article,[5] respecting this State law, and its effects upon the act of 1793.

The *Atlas* asks, if the cases of reclamation be so few, where is the necessity for a new law? The answer is *because Massachusetts has done away with the old law altogether, and left the case wholly without any provision at all.*

But now, let me say something, which is true, and perhaps the *Atlas*, if it replies, will let out, but which it may not be expedient for you, in your article, to bring out. John Davis told me, the other day, *that this act of Massachusetts was passed to retaliate on South Carolina for her law for the imprisonment of free blacks.*[6] I think the law was passed *tempore* Marcus Morton; but that it had been talked of, and perhaps recommended, the year before, *regnante* John Davis. This should be looked into. The debates in the Legislature, and the party votes, etc., etc., should be hunted up. I have no doubt that the *Atlas* has now given you an opportunity for two columns of pretty conclusive matter; and much better than Mr. Webster's letter to the people at Newburyport. Pray lay out your strength upon it.[7]

Mr. [Edward] Curtis and I, and our wives, taking advantage of a recess in the Senate for three or four days, are going to Harper's Ferry, Winchester, and return, perhaps by Charlottesville. Give our love to the ladies. I suppose you will soon be by the sea-side. Yours truly,

D. Webster

P.S.—If the *Atlas* shall answer, setting forth the real cause of passing the Massachusetts act, then this defender of Massachusetts will place her in a remarkable attitude.

Text from Curtis, 2: 426–427. Original not found. No recipient named, but correctly attributed in W & S, 16: 542, n. 2 (where the first reference to a letter of "June 3" should read "June 13").

1. See the extended editorial, "Mr. Webster's Letter," *Boston Daily Atlas*, May 30, 1850.

2. Webster emphasized this point in his "Newburyport letter," above, DW to Edward Sprague Rand et al., May 15, 1850.

3. *Mass. Session Laws*, 1843, 33. The measure, a response to the Supreme Court's ruling in *Prigg* v. *Pennsylvania* upholding the Fugitive Slave Act of 1793, was one of many "personal liberty laws" passed in the North in this era. See Thomas D. Morris, *Free Men All: The Personal Liberty Laws of the North, 1780–1861* (Baltimore, 1974), chap. 7.

4. This coalition of antislavery Democrats, Whigs, and Liberty party men formed the nucleus of Massachusetts's Free Soil party, which organized formally in 1848. See *Correspondence*, 6: 285–286.

5. "Mr. Webster as a Senator," *Boston Daily Advertiser*, March 22, 1850.

6. See above, pp. 52–53, Edward Everett to DW, April 3, 1850, n. 4.

7. See "Mr. Webster and the Atlas," *Boston Daily Advertiser*, June 7, 1850.

TO PETER HARVEY

Washington June 2. '50

My Dear Sir;

I recd yours[1] yesterday. The [Boston] Atlas continues in its malicious humor, I perceive, & will no doubt, keep on, recklessly. It is both abusive, & stupid. It is doing infinite mischief to every interest of the State, with which Congress has any concern. Mr Linus Child has been here several days, & has now gone home. He will be in Boston about the time you receive this letter. I wish you, by all means, to see him. He will tell you the truth about the state of things here.

I wish you would get some of our friends—Mr [James Kellogg] Mills, Mr [Albert] Fearing, Mr Sam[ue]l Lawrence, Mr [Thomas] Lamb, Mr Skinner,[2] &c. &c. &c. together, & give Mr Child an opportunity of stating what he has seen & heard here.

He proposes to return; & other good men ought to return with him. The *crisis* is important. All the Whigs of Massachusetts should open their eyes to it.

The question is exactly this: Will Massachusetts shut herself out from all the benefits she might receive from wise legis[l]ation in Congress, for the mere purpose of keeping up a senseless strife about such miserable abstract questions, as slavery in New Mexico, or the law for redeeming fugitive slaves?

I say, & am willing it should be known as my opinion, that if the other <Delegates> members from Massachusetts would lay aside abstractions, & go for *conciliation*, these controversies would be settled, & we should have a good Tariff, this Congress.

I by no means say this, however, by way of disparagement to the other members. They undoubtedly act conscientiously, & according to their best judgment. But I greatly lament that they do not see, as yet, that the line of duty, at least in my opinion leads the other way.

Be sure to see Mr Childs   Yrs   Danl Webster

ALS. MWalB.
1. Letter not found.
2. Fearing (1798–1875) was a ship chandler, active in Massachusetts Whig politics. Lamb (1796–1887) was president of the New England Bank. Mills and Lawrence (1801–1880) were influential Boston capitalists. Skinner is probably Francis Skinner, Boston commodity merchant.

TO DUDLEY COTTON HALL, ET AL.

Washington, June 3, 1850.

Gentlemen,

I thank you for your letter of the 3d of May last,[1] expressing satisfaction with the sentiments of my speech in the Senate on the great question which now divides the nation, and tendering your thanks for my services in strengthening and preserving our glorious Union.

Gentlemen, we have a country which we love, and of which we are proud. We have a government under which that country has prospered, for sixty years, in a degree surpassing every thing which has been known in the history of mankind. And this government is founded on the union of the States; which union is established, defined, and sanctioned by the Constitution of the United States. And, Gentlemen, I can conceive no rashness or folly greater than that which would either seek to overturn this Constitution, or, by unprincipled agitation, by heated local controversies, or angry mutual criminations and recriminations between different parts of the country, would effectually weaken the bonds which hold the Union together. It has been, it is, and it will be, my great object to preserve and strengthen the Union, to establish it deeper and stronger in the regard and affections of the people. I wish to see all the powers vested in the government by the Constitution administered with so much prudence, impartiality, and patriotism, that every State, and all the people of every State, should feel profoundly that the union of the States, as now existing, is honorable, useful, and indispensable to the prosperity of every part of the country. And with this purpose always uppermost in my mind and always filling my heart, I studiously avoid useless local controversies, useless abstract questions, and every thing else which unnecessarily exasperates, embitters, or wounds the feelings of any portion of the United States. I have no doubt, Gentlemen, that you and the great body of your fellow-citizens of Massachusetts approve these sentiments and opinions, and will sustain those who honestly act upon them. I have no fear that that great State, which has been among the first and foremost for UNION, from early Colonial times down to the present moment; I have no fear that that great State, which poured out her blood and her treasure like water in the Revolutionary struggle, and afterwards strained every nerve and every muscle for the establishment of the present Constitution; that State, which has enjoyed so fully and felt so sensibly the benefits derived from this united government; I have no fear, not the least, not a particle, that the Commonwealth of Massachusetts will ever expect from those with whom she has intrusted her interests in Congress any thing but uprightness and fairness, impartiality and justice, and a spirit that seeks rather to reconcile opposing interests and allay irritated feelings, than to foment discord, or to sow or to cultivate the seeds of jealousy and disunion. I am, Gentlemen, with entire regard, your obliged fellow-citizen and obedient servant,

Daniel Webster

Text from *Works*, 6: 563–565. Original not found. Hall (b.1818), successful businessman and banker in both Medford and Boston, was active for many years in Medford civic affairs.

1. Dudley Cotton Hall et al. to DW, May 3, 1850, mDW 30392.

TO [PETER HARVEY?]

In the Senate,
Monday June 3. '50

My Dear Sir;

The [Boston] Courier article of Saturday is admirable, indeed.[1] I have already heard it spoken of highly, here. Let the Editor follow up his hand.

The [Boston] Atlas whines, & growles, & abuses people. It reasons nothing, it argues nothing. It only rails at Mr Webster. It denies no fact, it controverts no matter of law. "An Old Whig" is dead & buried.[2] There is no discussion, in its columns, no information communicated to its readers, no fair opposition to other mens opinions. But it rails, & rails. Its present topic seems to be, that Mr Webster's Newburyport letter[3] <is> contains matters derogatory to the Commonwealth of Massachusetts. He derides the State, & holds her up to the reproach of other states; & she must be defended.

God keep the poor old Commonwealth, if the defense of her character & conduct is to rest on the Atlas!

Mr Webster assaulting the honor of Massachusetts, & the Atlas defending her! Who would not hasten to the scene, & look on, to see the end of such a Contest.

Now, according to our apprehension, Mr Webster has never said one word, derogatory to the character of Massachusetts. He has too much respect for himself, if not for the State, to do any such thing. The State has honored Mr Webster. It is generally thought, we believe, that he has not dishonored her. <When she complains, th[en] she will elect her own or> It is not likely that the efforts of the Atlas will shake the confidence of either of them, for the other.

(If you use these foregoing paragraphs, or any of them, please copy, first)

AL. MWalB. Published in Van Tyne, p. 416 and W & S, 16: 544–546 (in probable error as to recipient), from a copy at NhHi, bearing DW's signature, in which the final admonition is not included.

1. See "Attacks of the Atlas on Webster," June 1, 1850, which chastised the Atlas writers for misrepresenting DW's views on the fugitive slave bill before Congress.

2. "An Old Whig" had written a series of letters for the Daily Atlas in May critical of DW's position on the sectional controversy, particularly his support for a strengthened fugitive slave law.

3. See above, DW to Edward Sprague Rand el al., May 15, 1850.

FUGITIVE SLAVE BILL

June 3, 1850

MR. WEBSTER. Mr. President, at an early period of the session I turned my attention to the subject of preparing a bill respecting the reclamation of fugitive slaves, or of preparing certain amendments to the existing law on that subject. In pursuance of this purpose, I conferred with some of the most eminent members of the profession, and especially with a high judicial authority, who has had more to do with questions of this kind, I presume, than any other judge in the United States. After these consultations and conferences, as early as in February I prepared a bill amendatory of the act of 1793, intending, when a proper time came, to lay it before the Senate for its consideration. I now wish to present the bill to the Senate unaltered and precisely as it was when prepared in February last.

MR. [WILLIAM LEWIS] DAYTON. I hope that the paper will be printed.

The bill was then laid on the table and ordered to be printed as follows:

A BILL amendatory of "An act respecting fugitives from justice and persons escaping from the service of their masters," approved February 12, 1793.

Be it enacted by the Senate and House of Representatives of the Unit-ed States of America in Congress assembled, That the provisions of the said act shall extend to the territories of the United States; and that the commissioners who now are, or who may hereafter be appointed by the circuit courts of the United States, or the district courts where circuit courts are not established, or by the territorial courts of the United States, all of which courts are authorized and required to appoint one or more commissioners in each county to take acknowledgements of bail and affidavits, and also to take depositions of witnesses in civil causes, and who shall each, or any judge of the United States, on complaint being made on oath to him that a fugitive from labor is believed to be within the State or territory in which he lives, issue his warrant to the marshal of the United States, or to any other person who shall be willing to serve it, authorizing an arrest of the fugitive, if within the State or territory, to be brought before him or some other commissioner or judge of the United States court within the State or territory, that the right of the person claiming the services of such fugitive may be examined. And the hearing, deposition duly authenticated, and parol proof, shall be heard to establish the identity of the fugitive and the right of the claim-ant, and also to show that slavery is established in the State from which the fugitive absconded. And if on such hearing the commissioner or judge shall find the claim to the services of the fugitive, as asserted, sus-tained by the evidence, he shall make out a certificate of the material facts proved and of his judgment thereon, which he shall sign, and which shall be conclusive of the right of the claimant or his agent to take the fugitive back to the State from whence he fled. *Provided,* that if the fugi-tive shall deny that he owes service to the claimant under the laws of the State where he was held, and after being duly cautioned as to the so-lemnities and consequences of an oath, shall swear to the same, the commissioner or judge shall forthwith summon a jury of twelve men to try the right of the claimant, who shall be sworn to try the cause ac-cording to the evidence, and the commissioner or judge shall preside at the trial, and determine the competency of the proof.

Sec. 2. *And be it further enacted,* That the commissioner shall re-ceive ten dollars in each case tried by him, as aforesaid, the jurors fifty cents each, and the marshal or other person serving the process shall receive five dollars for serving the warrant on each fugitive, and for mileage and other services the same as are allowed to the marshal for similar services, to be examined and allowed by the commissioner or judge, and paid by the claimant.

Text from *Congressional Globe,* 31st Cong., 1st sess., p. 1111. The bill may also be read on mDW 51163.

FROM HENRY WHITING WARNER

Constitution Island, near
West Point 5th June 1850

Dear Sir,

I thank you very sincerely for a copy of your speech in the great debate of the session; and should have done so at an earlier day, but for a severe indisposition that for a time unfitted me for duty. I had supplied myself already with a pamphlet copy of the speech, but was particularly gratified by such a token of remembrance at your hands.

There are men of extreme opinions both north & south, whom you have failed to please. This was to be expected. It was even to be desired; for it was the indispensable condition of a successful effort to serve the country effectually in existing circumstances. The best patriots and the soundest thinkers are, I trust, with you in the main scope of the views you have expressed. If not, God help us, for I see no other medium of a general settlement.

In matter of form, indeed, I would have preferred to act upon one subject at a time. I do not like 'omnibus' legislation.

Nor am I satisfied altogether with that part of the 'omnibus' bill, which relates to fugitive slaves. What possible need of such an army of petty magistrates of arrest?—and are the country postmasters, one and all, fit for the office? The arresting men in a free state, in order to carry them away by force, is a grave business.

I am afraid too that the suddenness of these movements may often disappoint the right of *habeas corpus* in the party seized. Admitting the jury trial is to be postponed, this right ought surely to be held sacred.

Will you pardon me a further suggestion? The rule of presumptive evidence is in favor of the freedom of all men, white or black, in a free state; for it conforms to the general fact. But at the south, the law presumes a colored man to be a slave, till proof made to the contrary; and this, by a like conformity to what is there the general fact. If then the arrested negro is not to have the benefit of a jury trial till he gets into a slave country, is there not some danger that he will be condemned to servitude *as of course*, unless he is prepared *to prove a negative*, namely, that he is *not* what the law there takes him for, a slave? And if so, the act, I think, ought specially to provide for putting the burden of proof on him who shall have caused the arrest to be made.

But I am too ignorant of the actual state of the business before the Senate, to be justified in these remarks; especially as I know well how superfluous any thoughts of mine may be on such a subject in your charge. I beg pardon therefore, and subscribe myself With great respect, Dear Sir, Your obt. servt.   H W Warner

ALS. DLC. Warner (c. 1788–1875; Union 1809), for many years a New York City lawyer, was then semiretired.

FROM FRANCIS LIEBER

Columbia S.C.
6 June 1850

My dear Sir

I received last night the three pamphlets which you have had the kindness of sending to me, and for which I beg you to accept my thanks. I had read—and read with deep interest, your *Letter*[1] before, but I am glad I now possess that masculine and substantial paper in pamphlet form, and feel proud to have a copy of it with your name inscribed. Sir, I trust in God, that all these papers may not receive an additional and most melancholy interest by being looked upon, a few years hence, as belonging to the closed period of the once existing Union. I confess, I do not believe in an immediate dissolution of the Union—though every thing is possible with reckless fanatics, and the power of mischief is incalculable in every being, even in the mouse which perforates a dyke— but this shaking and rude handling—this *labefacere* may make our Union so rickety a thing that we may suffer nearly all the misery and disgrace under which Germany has staggered for centuries in consequence of her wretched federal constitution and of her "particularism," as the body of those tendencies is there called which tears that unhappy country—destined for great things but cheated out of her history. I find that I feel far deeper upon this subject of the Union than <much> very many of the native citizens, perhaps *because* I am not a native American, and therefor naturally and necessarily a *Pan-American*, and *because* I am a native German, who knews by heart the commentary which his country has furnished and is furnishing <upon> for the text of querulous, angry, self-seaking, unpatriotic confederacies, and who finds in <his own> the history of his native country the key clearly and plainly to decypher every line of Grecian decay. While I am writing these sad lines to you, they may be engaged at Nashville[2] in a "torch-dance" which—God avert it—may end as that which <ended> concluded with the end of Persepolis and the glory of Alexander—with a conflagration.

But all this is very sad; for, as the weeping Persian said, "the saddest of all things is to see the ruin of your country and to see how it ought to be averted, but to have no power." I am with the highest regard My dear Sir Your very obdt   Francis Lieber *Pan-American*

ALS. DLC.
 1. See above, DW to Edward Sprague Rand et al., May 15, 1850, commonly called the "Newburyport letter."
 2. Supporters of "southern rights"

from nine slave states convened at Nashville on June 3, with various options for action—including a call for secession if certain concessions to southern opinion were not made by the North. For Lieber's opposition to extreme demands by the South, see Thelma Jennings, *The Nashville Convention: Southern Movement for Unity 1848–1851* (Memphis 1980), p. 100.

TO SAMUEL LAWRENCE

Monday June 10. '50
In the Senate. 11 o'clock

My Dear Sir,

I thank you kindly & heartily, for your encouraging letters.[1] I do hope you will go straight a-head. It is certain—quite certain—that if Massachusetts members would cooperate, the Compromise Bill *would pass*— and I fully believe, that with their concurrence, we put down abolitionism effectually. Thus far I have not one concurring vote from Massachusetts. I regret this much, but hope I may be able to stand, though I stand alone. At any rate, I shall stand till I fall. I shall not sit down.

The prospect has much improved, within the last 8 days. I am glad to hear that Mr. [Linus] Child is moving.[2] He is a strong man. I shall write you daily. Yours truly   (signed) Danl Webster

Copy. NhHi. Published in *W & S*, 16: 548. Lawrence (1801–1880), brother of Abbott Lawrence and Amos Lawrence, was a founder of the Lowell Mills and first president of the Boston Board of Trade.

1. Not found. DW is probably referring to Lawrence's role in collecting signatures for an appeal by the business community to Massachusetts congressmen on behalf of sectional conciliation. The appeal was published on June 12 in the *Boston Courier* and the *Boston Daily Advertiser*.

2. See above, DW to Peter Harvey, May 29 and June 2, 1850.

Waging his campaign to encourage public acceptance in the North for sectional compromise, Webster counted heavily on moral, political, and financial succor from the business community. He was not disappointed; response in leading commercial cities to his Seventh of March speech was overwhelmingly favorable. Still, Webster lacked the unanimous backing in conservative Massachusetts circles that he needed, a problem stemming at least in part from his recurrent rivalry with Abbott Lawrence of Lowell, who classed Webster with those who had denied him the Whig party's vice presidential nomination in 1848.

Lawrence had been rewarded for his early support of Zachary Taylor's presidential candidacy with the London mission and assumed his duties there in October 1849. Nearly nine months later, however, his appointment remained unconfirmed by the Senate. Rumors arose that Webster was responsible for the delay for various reasons, including Lawrence's association with the Boston Atlas, *which had been publishing anti-Webster, anticompromise articles all spring.*

Aware that Lawrence could not, from London, have directed the Atlas *campaign against him, and sensing an opportunity to heal an old rift at a propitious moment, Webster expressed his unqualified support for the nomination, as the letters below suggest. Lawrence's appointment was confirmed in the Senate on June 19, by a 34–5 vote* (Journal of the Executive Proceedings of the Senate [*Washington, 1887*], *8: 196*).

FROM SAMUEL ATKINS ELIOT

Boston, June 12. 1850.

Dear Sir,

The time has arrived when the effect of your speech of the 7th of March is beginning to be felt, in the way in which I presume you expected it to operate. The spirit with which it was imbued took strong hold of the minds of the better part of the population of New England, the independent, reflecting men, of whom you know there are so many. A man who is supported by them, & by facts, need have few misgivings as to his ultimate success in any position he may assume. Every week of cool consideration has increased the number of those who took sides with you, & it was a pretty respectable number who did that as long ago as when the public letter of your constituents was sent to you.[1] The publication of your bill respecting "fugitives from labor"[2] removed the only real impediment to a cordial support of the doctrines of the speech. At the very moment when opposition was thus giving way, when those who were lukewarm were becoming ardent, & those who were decided before, were firmer than ever, we were told by Mr. [Linus] Child that that letter was set aside & disregarded by members of Congress as a commonplace affair, hastily signed, from which many would like to withdraw their names; in short, that it was treated like a common recommendation to office. This started the gentle indignation of some of us, & we determined that something should be done to show that there was no such change of the wind in Massachusetts; & after sundry discussions as to the best form & mode of attaining the object, the address to the entire delegation was resolved on,[3] as tending to show that there was nothing personal in our motives, but that we regarded the discussion in Congress, & out of it, in a national point of view; that we adopted your spirit of honest conciliation, & that we desired to see controversy ended, friendship restored, & the business of the nation set free from the evils of fear. You will see the language of the address in the papers of today, & I hope it will be found to meet the wants of the case, & to coincide with the views of yourself, & other members who are desirous of peace rather than war. I have no doubt it will be extensively signed,— probably, I think, more extensively than the letter to yourself. The urgency of the crisis is felt to be stronger now than then. The only objection made to it by opponents, which I have heard of, is that it does not mean any thing. But the mere existence of such a paper means something, & every signature put to it will make it mean more. We could not refer to precise measures, but we do refer to almost every thing else having a bearing upon the controversy, which could be alluded to with propriety.

Another thing we were told by Mr. Child which we esteem singularly unfortunate. He said the Atlas of this city was regarded by Southern gentlemen as the organ of our minister in London[4] & so long as it printed such bitter things about the South, the nomination of that gentleman would not be confirmed. I have no interest to contradict that assertion, as you know; but I am in a position which, I think, *enables* me to do it. And as I believe that the long delay of his confirmation is beginning to produce that feeling of alienation which is now the thing most to be apprehended in a national point of view, I should be glad if any thing I could say or do, should tend to put an end to it. My relations with Mr. L[awrence] have been more intimate within three years than before, in consequence of his extraordinary liberality to Harvard College, though I have always been on familiar terms with him. And I have no hesitation in expressing my conviction that he has nothing to do with the Atlas, that it is no organ of his, that he makes, & has made no communications to it directly or indirectly, in relation to the discussions now before the public. Indeed they have arisen since his departure from the country. At least the bitterness of them has grown up within that time; & the bitterness of the Atlas has appeared principally since your speech of the 7th of March. The known spirit of the editor [William Schouler], from the positions he has heretofore occupied, is abundantly sufficient to account for the whole of it, without attributing any part to Mr. L. It seems to me, therefore, knowing as well as I do, his characteristic qualities, unwise to charge upon him that for which he is not responsible. I suspect, if the truth were known, it would be found that he is not as grateful as the editor of the Atlas probably thinks he should be, for the gratuitous efforts it has made with so little adroitness, in his behalf. Under these circumstances, it seems to me, I confess, though I say it with diffidence, that some effort should be made in support of him;—not for his sake, but for that of the public feeling, which I have referred to. The present state of things is doing harm; his confirmation will do good, & will promote that reconciliation which is the true object of all our efforts. You may think it very strange that I should undertake to write to you, on such matters, with so much frankness; but having made my mind up to write at all, it would be quite impossible for me to do it in any other way; & as it seemed desirable that you should have direct testimony upon these matters, I have ventured to present it to you, & hope that you will regard it as designed as a contribution to your own means of usefulness, & as not inconsistent with the entire respect, & high consideration with which I am your friend & servt.   Saml. A. Eliot.

ALS. NhHi.
1. See above, pp. 44–45, Thomas Handasyd Perkins et al. to DW, [March 25, 1850].
2. See above, June 3, 1850.

3. "Appeal from Mass. to its Representatives," published in the *Boston Courier* and the *Boston Daily Advertiser*, June 12, 1850.
4. Abbott Lawrence.

TO DANIEL FLETCHER WEBSTER

In the Senate Wednesday 2 o'clock
[June 12, 1850]

My Dear Son,

Mr [Horace] Mann's second letter is weak, though malignant; and so is the Article in the [Boston] Atlas.[1] These people you must take care of, some of you, at home. I cannot take any considerable notice of Mr Mann, tho' I have some idea of saying a word about him, in a letter which I am preparing for Kennebeck.[2]

We shall have a warm summer. The political atmosphere will be hot, however the natural may be. I am in for it, & shall fight it out. Marshfield, I must think nothing of. My health is good, & my purpose pretty well fixed.

Tell Mr. [Peter] Harvey I have his letter,[3] and expect that Boston will be heard from, ere long. Yrs truly & affectionately   Danl Webster

ALS. NhD.
1. Horace Mann's reply to DW's Newburyport letter was published, with an appreciative editorial, in the *Boston Daily Atlas*, June 10, 1850. Along with Mann's earlier letter to his constituents on May 3, it was reprinted (with additional commentary) in a widely circulated pamphlet, *Horace Mann's Letters on the Exten-*

sion of Slavery into California and New Mexico (Washington, 1850).
2. See DW to Robert H. Gardiner et al., June 17, 1850, mDW 30585, the so-called Kennebec letter, in which DW did indeed rebut Mann on the viability of slavery in New Mexico.
3. Not found.

TO GEORGE TICKNOR

In the Senate, June 13, 1850

My Dear Sir,

Mr. [Horace] Mann's second letter[1] is sufficiently disingenuous, and remarkably feeble. The [Boston] *Atlas*, I see, regards it as "conclusive." It will be "conclusive," I think, with sensible men, on the fairness and ability of the writer.

I am writing a letter to the good people on the Kennebec, in answer to one from them.[2] In this I may bestow three words on Mr. Mann, or I may not. I must leave him, in effect, to friends in Massachusetts. I would be glad you would pay your respects to him, if you can find a place in his letter solid enough to strike. It seems to me, however, that any blows upon it would be like attempting to knock a feather-bed out of the way by a sledge-hammer . . . . Puff him off, by a breath, if you can bestow a few idle hours upon such a person.[3]

The letter, now in circulation in Massachusetts, will undoubtedly produce a good impression here.[4] How far it may affect votes, we shall see. Certainly, no such paper was expected here.

Nobody from New England, so far, has given me the succor of his vote. No matter. Sometimes a single man may do something. Do you remember a rather laughable argument, used by President [John] Wheelock, to prove that the trustees of the college ought to have no power, and that the president should have all—all great things, he insisted, had been done always by a single mind. "It was Jason," said he, "who stole the Golden Fleece, it was Hercules who slew the Lernaean tiger, and the Erymanthian boar!" But as for me, I shall seize on no golden fleece, though I may be obliged to encounter some Lernaean and some Erymanthian animals.

I write this while General [Samuel] Houston is speaking loud, in answer to Mr. [Thomas Hart] Benton, who spoke louder, on the Texas part of the Compromise Bill. I made a short speech, this morning—look for it in the *National Intelligencer*.[5] If correctly reported, you will see in it a matter stated that a little chokes some people. Yours,

Daniel Webster

Text from Curtis, 2: 428. Original not found. Correctly attributed in *W & S*, 16: 545–546 (see also 542 n. 2, where the first reference to a letter of "June 3" should read "June 13").

1. See above, DW to Fletcher Webster, [June 12 1850], n. 1, and DW to George Ticknor, June 14, 1850, mDW 30573.

2. DW to Robert H. Gardiner et al., June 17, 1850, mDW 30585, in response to Gardiner et al. to DW, April 1850, mDW 30362.

3. See above, DW to [Ticknor],

June 1, 1850.

4. See above, Samuel Atkins Eliot to DW, June 12, 1850.

5. *Congressional Globe*, 31st Cong., 1st sess., *Appendix*, pp. 859–860, published in Washington, D.C., *National Intelligencer*, June 15, 1850, and reprinted in *W & S*, 10: 107–112. In his remarks Webster argued forcefully that Congress should quickly adjudicate the New Mexico–Texas boundary dispute, preserving the territorial integrity of New Mexico against Texas's claims.

TO SAMUEL ATKINS ELIOT

Washington June 14. '50

My Dear Sir,

I have recd your letter of the 12th,[1] & am much obliged to you, not only for the information which it communicates, but also for the frankness with which you express your own opinions.

In regard to the confirmation of Mr [Abbott] Lawrence's nomination, your suggestions quite concur with my own opinions. I have already repeatedly spoken of the matter, to leading Gentlemen in the Senate, & you may be assured the matter shall not be delayed, for the want of any attention on my part. No doubt there has been a suspicion here, either that the [Boston] Atlas represents Mr Lawrence's opinions, in its recent publications, or, (which is the more general notion) that the Editor [William Schouler] took it for granted that he should not offend Mr Lawrence by attacking me. The Senate would be very likely to be slow, in confirming the nomination of any Gentlemen, who should be of the Atlas association. Your letter will be useful, in refuting any imputation on Mr Lawrence, in that respect. I am, Dear Sir, with very true regard, Yours   Danl Webster

ALS. NhD.
1. See above, Eliot to DW, June 12, 1850.

TO SAMUEL LAWRENCE

June 18 [1850]

My Dear Sir,

It is the opinion of the *White House*, today, that the Compromise Bill *will become a law*. I cannot say myself what the result may be. The Mass. Delegation could settle the whole question, *this day*.

I have read the letter from Lawrence, signed by 300 good men.[1] I hope, (with Mr. Hudson's[2] permission) that the business will go on, as fast as may be convenient; *for this is the very moment*.

Should not the papers be sent to others of the Delegation, and not to me? Do not mention what I have said about the White House. Yrs
D.W.

Copy. NhHi. Published in *W & S*, 16: 548.
1. See above, DW to Samuel Lawrence, June 10, 1850, n. 1, and Samuel Atkins Eliot to DW, June 12, 1850, pp. 114, 115–117.
2. Probably Charles Hudson, a staunch Taylor-for-president advocate in 1848, then serving as naval officer at Boston.

FROM SAMUEL LAWRENCE, WITH ENCLOSURE

Boston June 19th 1850.

My Dear Sir

I have read the within,[1] & parts of it I know, & all I believe to be true. It is not for me to proclaim the character of my brother [Abbott Lawrence], but I confess it would strike me as a little ludicrous, if it were not a rather serious matter, to hear him accused of unfriendliness to the South whether in the Atlas or any where else. At all events it is something new, as it is not a great while since he was accused here of the very reverse. You may be sure he has nothing to do with the Atlas *directly or indirectly*. As to Mr [Charles] Hudson, I think it would be both proper & expedient for the President to dismiss him at once. I remain mo[st] respectfully yr. obt sert.   Saml Lawrence

ALS. NhHi.
    1. See enclosure.

ENCLOSURE: FROM SAMUEL ATKINS ELIOT

Boston, June 18 1850

My Dear Sir,

I have recently learnt that one reason for the unusual delay in the confirmation of the nomination of Mr. Abbott Lawrence, as minister to London, is the belief entertained that the Atlas of this city is the exponent of his views & feelings. This is particularly unfortunate, as I have reason to believe it is an entire mistake. My relations with Mr. Lawrence have for many years been familiar, & for the last three years quite intimate. I have conversed with him on all subjects, political as well as others, but I never heard a word fall from him, by accident or design, which looked as if he had any connexion with the Atlas whatever. I should have been likely to know something about it for another reason. I had assisted the former editor of the Atlas (Mr. [William] Hayden)[1] to make the purchase of the paper, & when he sold out he repaid, me & told me how Mr. [William] Schouler obtained the means to purchase. I forget now who it was that advanced him some money, but it certainly was not Mr. Lawrence.

The course of the Atlas was not particularly obnoxious till about the time the present session of Congress began, if I recollect right; & then Mr. L. was out of the country, & of course, could not personally direct in the matter; while the known disposition of the editor, manifested in other positions, is quite enough to account for the tone of the paper, without supposing any influence from Mr. L. Besides, I can scarcely conceive of his influence being exerted to taunt & provoke the South.

I never heard him utter a word which had the slightest unfriendly bearing upon Southern gentlemen, & I know of no man among us who takes wider, more national, or more liberal views upon political subjects generally. Certainly he has no sectional narrowness.

I shall be glad if any obstacle in the way of the confirmation can be removed, for the long delay is producing some degree of feeling here that is not desirable, at a moment when every thing likely to produce alienation should be carefully avoided. I am, Dear Sir, very truly & respectfully Yours,   Saml. A. Eliot

ALS. NhHi.

1. Hayden (1795–1880) edited the *Atlas* from 1841 through April 1847, when he sold out his interest in the paper to William Schouler.

TO FRANKLIN HAVEN

Washington July 4. 1850

My Dear Sir

We are worrying along here, as well as we can, under a hot sun, & with difficult work on hand. The vote in the Senate[1] will be close, & I hardly dare say which way I think it will turn. In the Senate yesterday, it was rather thought we had a majority. Mr [James Ware] Bradbury has returned from Maine. He is strongly in favor of the Bill, & would gladly have voted for it, but for the ridiculous resolutions passed by the Legislature of Maine,[2] last week. He says nobody approved them; but that they were passed to catch a few abolition votes. I am afraid we shall need Mr Bradbury's aid, & not receive it. Mr John Davis & Mr [William] Upham have made the most bitter speeches,[3] against the whole South, & have very much exasperated the feelings of those who wish to act with us.

I expect Mr. Trueman [Truman] Smith will sing the same tune.

We labor under two great disadvantages. The first is, that many many members do not wish to vote against the Presidents Plan.[4] He seems to have more feeling on the subject than I can well account for, & I believe some members of his Administration take a good deal of pains to defeat the compromise.

In the next place, Mr [Henry] Clay with all his talents, is not a good leader, for want of temper. He is irritable, impatient, & occasionally over-bearing; & drives people off.

We shall now not get the question this week. Before the vote on the ingrossment is taken, I propose to make a few remarks. The Mass. members in the House feel badly; but I doubt if any one of them will throw of[f] the shackles, & give an independent vote.[5]

The [Boston] Atlas seems incapable of stating any thing truly. Its falsehoods respecting Mr [Abbott] Lawrence's nomination[6] may make it necessary to give particulars; which I regret, as I should be sorry to see any thing published, which should not be agreeable to Mr. L. or his friends. Yrs Truly   Danl Webster

I hope our friend [Peter] Harvey is well.

ALS. MH-H. Published in W & S, 16: 549.

1. The Senate was nearing votes on the respective components of the omnibus bill reported on May 8 by the special committee of thirteen.

2. On June 26 the Maine legislature had instructed its senators to "vote for no territorial bills without a proviso against slavery" and further resolved that it was Congress's obligation to admit California, without qualifications, as a free state. Washington, D.C., National Intelligencer, July 1, 1850.

3. See Congressional Globe, 31st Cong., 1st sess., Appendix, pp. 879–886, 1014–1021. Davis spoke on June 28 and 29, Upham on July 1.

4. President Taylor had proposed in his annual message of December 24, 1849, that California and New Mexico be permitted to apply directly for statehood, thus bypassing territorial status and avoiding controversy over the Wilmot Proviso. Taylor was firmly opposed to the broad approach favored by Clay, DW, and other congressional leaders.

5. Only George Ashmun from Springfield supported compromise.

6. DW is referring to articles denying that his support influenced the Senate vote on June 24 confirming Lawrence as minister to England. See Boston Daily Atlas, June 26, 29, and July 3, 1850.

Through the spring of 1850 rumors, not entirely unfounded, circulated in Washington that President Taylor intended to reshuffle his cabinet. Taylor's death on July 9 provided the basis for a change of personnel, as well as an opportunity for reorientation of the administration's position on the omnibus bill.

President Fillmore was receptive to recommendations that Webster be invited to join his administration as secretary of state. Ambivalent about the prospect of returning to his old post, Webster refused to press for the job. To friends he suggested that Edward Everett would be an appropriate selection (see below, DW to Franklin Haven, July 12, 1850), though there is no evidence he passed this recommendation on to Fillmore. Moreover, he did nothing to discourage Haven and other business friends from raising a fund to make his acceptance of the State Department financially feasible.

Following a week of consultations, the President invited Webster into the cabinet, assuring the Massachusetts senator that he would sign any reasonable compromise measures that crossed his desk. Webster immediately accepted, resigned his seat in the Senate on July 22, and, a day later, was sworn for his second tour as secretary of state.

FROM WILLIAM S. MILLER

New York 10th July /50

My Dear Sir,

A great calamity is upon the Nation! President Taylor is dead![1] And in view of this fact, & without other apology, I have been desired by those of your friends, whom I have met this morn'g, to address you a word on this subject.

We believe the peace & general welfare of the country at a crisis never before realised, & we know no other Councillor whose ability & wisdom is equal to the task of commanding order from the chaos which exists: —and we therefore most earnestly and respectfully pray you to take Office, (which it is presumed will be tendered you)[2] to aid directly in the future Administration of your country's welfare. I sincerely believe, such an event would give great & general satisfaction throughout the land. I remain with profound respect your very obdt   Wm. S. Miller

ALS. DLC.
1. Taylor died late in the evening on July 9.
2. Millard Fillmore was expected to make significant changes in the cabinet, with Webster first choice for secretary of state.

TO FRANKLIN HAVEN

Washington July 11. '50
Thursday morng
8 oclock

My Dear Sir

It is not to[o] easy [to say] what will be the extent of the changes, in consequence of Genl. [Zachary] Taylor's death, & Mr [Millard] Fillmore's accession. It is at this moment supposed that there will be an entirely new Cabinet. Certainly not more than one or two can remain. Who will succeed to the vacant places I have [no] means of saying, with any certainty. One thing I feel sure of, & that [is that they] will be sound men. The President is a sensible man, & a conservative Whig, & is not likely to be in favor of any *isms*, such as have votaries at the present day. His coming to power is a heavy blow to Gov [William Henry] Seward, & Mr [Horace] Mann, & all such half abolition Gentlemen.

I believe Mr Fillmore favors the compromise, & there is no doubt that recent events have increased the probability of the passage of that measure. Nothing will be done in Congress this week. The funeral ceremonies[1] will take all that remains of it.

P.S. 2 oclock

I am rather confirmed in the expectation of total change. Beyond this I know little, & nothing which I can communicate.

The idea is now general that the compromise will go thro. I have a few words to say, on Monday or Tuesday. Yrs truly   Danl Webster

ALS. MH-H. Published in *PC*, 2: 376.

1. Taylor's funeral, conducted with great ceremony at the White House on July 13, was followed by interment in Washington. Webster represented the Senate on the funeral committee and served as a pallbearer along with Henry Clay and other congressional leaders.

FROM DANIEL DEWEY BARNARD

Albany July 11. 1850

My dear Sir,

In the changes which must occur in the Cabinet, if not immediately, certainly before long, I cannot doubt that you will be solicited to take your appropriate place at the head of it. I think Mr. Fillmore will naturally—necessarily almost—turn at once to you in the trying position in which, he is so suddenly placed. I wrote to him to say so, and to commend that course to him, within the hour in which the news of Genl. [Zachary] Taylor's death reached us. It is not too much to say that the country instinctively looks to you in this crisis. I believe that from one end of it to the other, an expectation and an earnest desire exist with singular unanimity, among disinterested & patriotic men, that you will take your place at the right hand of President Fillmore. You, more than any man of the North, have the confidence of the South, while, at the same time, in my judgment, you stand stronger today in the confidence & affection of the North than ever before.[1] If you will take your place at the right hand of the President, and as the right arm of his Administration, that Administration will at once be understood to be, and will be in fact, eminently national, constitutional & conservative in its character, and as such will command the harmonious support of the Whig party, and the confidence of the Country. Faction in the Whig party, sectionalism, & every other "ism" will be rebuked; we shall be strengthened every where by settling down on our old principles, & our nationality will be revived. In this state of things, too, it being once known in Congress, and in the country, that the President, and Mr. Webster, and Mr. [Henry] Clay, think alike, and are acting, & mean to act in harmony, there cannot be a doubt that the chances of bringing the distracting and disastrous issues between North & South, now pending in Congress, to a satisfactory adjustment, are greatly increased—nay, the adjustment seems to me to be rendered almost certain.

Nothing is clearer to my mind than that our people are ready, with great unanimity, to adopt & assume precisely the ground you have advocated for the settlement of the Slavery question. Mr. Fillmore, I believe, agrees with you in your opinions on this subject, fully—though he is probably not so clear about the state of public opinion in this quarter. I have endeavored to satisfy him, on this point—at least in regard to New York. Beyond a doubt, or a shadow of doubt, he will be sustained here, if he will take, as I am sure he is disposed to do, *National* ground along with you.

But I write to you now, with one subject only, and this is to beg of you that you will not, for any reason short of an imperious necessity (and I trust no such reason will be found to exist) decline accepting the call that I am sure will be made upon you by the President. Of course the effect of your withdrawal from the Senate just at present, must be considered; but all that can be, and no doubt will be taken care of on the spot. At the proper time I trust in God you will not refuse—great as the sacrifice may be—to take your place as the Chief constitutional adviser of the President. I am, my dear Sir, most faithfully, yr. friend

D. D. Barnard

ALS. DLG.

1. Four months after the Seventh of March speech, Webster's standing in his home section had substantially revived. See also below, Edward Everett to DW, July 16, 1850, n. 2.

TO FRANKLIN HAVEN

Washington, friday morng,
July 12. '50

My Dear Sir

You will hear various rumours, respecting appointments to the Cabinet, but none of them will deserve credit, any further than they rest on general probability. Nothing is decided, as yet. The Present Cabinet have all tendered their resignations, but they will not be answered till after the funeral.[1]

The three important Departments are State, Treasury, Interior. I have no doubt some man known to be thoroughly sound on Revenue matters will be appointed to the Treasury. As to the State Dept, I have no idea who will have it, altho. if the power were with me, I think I could find a man, without going out of Massachusetts, who has talent eno. & knowledge enough, but whether he is, at this moment, so fresh in the minds of the People, that his appointment would strike the public mind favorably, may be a doubt.[2] Nobody can well be Secretary of State, who has not a fortune, unless he be a Bachelor. The Secretary of State is the head of the Administration, & he must have a house, sometimes to receive guests in. He is of course necessarily in daily communication with the Diplomatic corps, which I believe is twice as numerous now, as it was twenty years ago.

My Dear Sir, you see the spirit of good will, which is manifesting itself here. This is the golden hour of opportunity, be assured. The opposition Gentlemen are determined, all the conservative part of them at least, to give the Administration fair play. Mr Fillmore is well intentioned, & discreet. He will meet with annoyances, from the rather overbearing spirit *of a certain quarter*; but I hope he will stand stiff.[3] If he is successful in forming his Administration, I verily believe a prospect is before us for a better state of things than we have enjoyed for twenty years. Yrs truly   Danl Webster

ALS. MH. Published in *PC*, 2: 376–377, and *Diplomatic Papers*, 2.
   1. Fillmore took the oath of office on July 10, and the cabinet submitted their resignations, effective July 20, that evening.

2. Edward Everett, to whom DW is likely referring, had not held public office since resigning as minister to Great Britain in August 1845.
   3. Probably a reference to Senator William H. Seward of New York.

TO FRANKLIN HAVEN

July 16. 50
Tuesday morning

My Dear Sir
   The President goes slow, but I trust will come out well. He will undoubtedly have a *sound* Cabinet, & accessible to all good Whigs. How *able*, he may make it, I cannot say. As yet, I believe he has not committed himself.
   I hope we shall, at last, finish this so long protracted measure, in the Senate. The story yesterday was, that the extreme South would join the extreme North & lay the Bill[1] on the Table; preferring, as the less evil in their opinion, to let California come in, at once—& the Territorial Bills go over. Yrs truly   Danl Webster

ALS. MH-H. Published in *PC*, 2: 377.
   1. A coalition of senators opposed to compromise commenced parliamentary maneuvers on July 1 to block passage of the committee of thirteen's omnibus bill. By July 31,

when the bill came to a vote, only one piece of the omnibus had survived—the organization of Utah. See *Congressional Globe*, 31st Cong., 1st sess., pp. 1376–1382, 1489–1491, and passim.

FROM EDWARD EVERETT

Cambridge 16 July 1850.

Dear Sir,
   I have been truly rejoiced to learn from Mr Hale,[1] that he has reason to think that the department of State will be placed in your hands by Mr

Fillmore. Such an arrangement would go far to make up for the loss of the President; for though there were some things in his position & character, which made his continuance of the highest importance, & his loss apparently irreparable; yet it has always seemed to me, that his cabinet operated as a complete non-conductor between him & the Country. Individually he commanded entire confidence. Whatever he could do & say, in his own person, was received by the mass of the people with great favor. But almost every thing, of course, must be done through the medium of the departments;—& beyond those who are in the enjoyment or the hope of favors, no one of the Secretaries seems to enjoy even an average popularity; the Secretary of State perhaps less than any of them. You see the language held by the [Boston Daily] Advertiser² yesterday on the subject of your expected nomination;—and <I> this I have no doubt will be the tone of most of the Whig papers.

My more immediate object in writing at this moment,—after expressing my extreme gratification at the prospect of your taking the helm,—is to speak about a little matter of business. Our daughter will probably be married next month.³ Mr [Henry Augustus] Wise owns a house in Washington, which is at present in the occupation of his brother;⁴ who he thinks will not be prepared to vacate it, quite as soon as our young folks wish it. It has occurred to me as possible, that you might be obliged to change your residence, & that in that case you would like to have your present house taken off your hands. I write this without any consultation with Mr Wise, who is on duty on Nantucket Shoals. It may be that since I have seen him, he has made arrangements with his brother, which will put his own house at his disposition, as soon as he will need it. But as this may be other wise, I should like to have you, in case you are to leave your house, & have no other use for it, give him the refusal of it, till we can hear from him.⁵ Yours ever, dear Sir, with sincere attachment,

ALS. MHi.

1. Probably Nathan Hale, editor of the *Boston Daily Advertiser*, who was Everett's brother-in-law.

2. On July 15 an editorial in the *Advertiser* urged Webster's appointment as secretary of state, on the ground that his current popularity, no less than his "eminent" qualifications for the post, made him "the man of all others the most able to render effective aid to the Executive, in extricating it from the difficulties [with] which it is in danger of being

surrounded."

3. Everett's daughter Charlotte, a favorite of the Websters, married navy lieutenant Henry Augustus Wise, kinsman and ward of Henry Alexander Wise, on August 20.

4. George Douglas Wise (1817–1881) was the only brother of Henry Augustus Wise.

5. The Websters chose to retain their residence on Louisiana Avenue. See DW to Edward Everett, July 22, 1850, mDW 30728, and Fuess, *Webster*, 2: 249.

DANIEL FLETCHER WEBSTER TO PETER HARVEY

New York, July 16, 1850

For P. Harvey

Not a word of truth in it.[1] The offer will be made to another.[2]

Fletcher Webster

Printed telegraph form with manuscript insertions. NhHi.

1. Fletcher is probably referring to an article in the *New York Tribune* on July 15 reporting that "it is quite probable that the charge of our Foreign Affairs *will* be formally tendered to Mr. Webster, and that it will be accepted."

2. Fletcher is referring to Robert C. Winthrop, whose name was frequently bruited as a possible secretary of state in the new administration. His conviction that an offer would be made to Winthrop was based on his conversation at the White House with President Fillmore on July 15. See Daniel Fletcher Webster to Peter Harvey, July 15, 1850, in Van Tyne, pp. 419–420.

FROM JAMES KELLOGG MILLS

Swamscot July 17. 1850

My dear Sir

I have been for three or four days pretty much confined here by illness, & have had very little opportunity to see the few friends who I have wished to consult on a matter of great interest to us & to the whole country. I have however seen a few choice spirits, and find their views to correspond so completely with my own, that I venture to write to you.

Every body here is looking with anxiety to Washington and in the hope & belief that you will accept the vacant office of Secretary of State. It is very plain, that the salary is altogether insufficient for the expenses of the place. It is right & proper that any obstacle in your mind, to the acceptance of the office on this ground should be removed. You may be assured My dear Sir, that such of your friends here as you would be willing should stand in that relation with you, will readily do whatever may be necessary to this end.[1]

You may also assure yourself that whatever is done, will be done by the persons, and in the mode & to the extent which will be most agreeable to your wishes.

Pray let me hear from you & believe me Most truly your friend

J K Mills

ALS. DLC. Published in *Diplomatic Papers*, 2.

1. By way of inducement forty New York businessmen subscribed $20,000 for DW's use. See below, pp. 194–195, George Griswold to DW, January 17, 1851.

TO [MILLARD FILLMORE]

[c. July 18, 1850]

For the Presidents consideration, merely

Sec of State	* *
Do. Treasury	Mr [Samuel Finley] Vinton
Do Interior	Mr [William Alexander] Graham—[James Alfred] Pierce
#Do. War,	Mr Edward Bates—<Conrad>
Do. Navy,	Mr [Charles Mynn] Conrad—Graham
P.M. Genl.	Mr. [William] Pennington—[William Lewis] Dayton
Atty Genl	Mr [John Jordan Crittenden][1]

#. This will come near being a *North Western* appointment, & is better I think on that account. Mr Bates is well known, not only to the People of Missouri, but also to those of Illinois, Wisconsin, & Iowa—& I believe highly respected by the Whigs, in those States. This point, I think, is better than one further South, especially if there shall be a member from Louisiana.

I will call, between 1. and 2 oclock.   D.W.

ALS. NBuHi. Misdated July 11, and published in Van Tyne, 420–421. The names Pierce, Conrad, Graham, and Dayton are in another hand. Pierce is a misspelling of Pearce.

1. Of Webster's suggested nominees, Conrad, Crittenden, and Graham were named and accepted, Crittenden as attorney general, Graham as secretary of the navy, and Conrad as secretary of war. Edward Bates was offered the Interior Department but declined. Vinton and Pennington were considered for the appointments that ultimately went to Thomas Corwin and Nathan K. Hall.

TO [PETER HARVEY?]

Washington friday 3 oclock
[July 19, 1850]

My Dear Sir

We have no news today. We are upon the Texan Boundary,[1] which is a very difficult question. I fear its influence on the general question.

On the whole, the progress of things for the week has been such as *to encrease the hope of carrying the present measure*[2] thro. We expect to hear *an important voice from Pa.*[3] I begin to think the Mass. Reps *must* come in, & go for reconciliation, in the end. Yrs   D.W.

I shall not leave, for an hour, till this business is finished in the Senate.

ALS. NhHi. Published in *W & S*, 16: 558, misdated August 9, 1850.

1. Texas's hotly disputed territorial claim to the eastern side of the upper

Rio Grande Valley, a leading topic of the Senate's debate over the "omnibus" compromise package during the week of July 15, eluded a settlement during Webster's tenure in the upper chamber.

2. The omnibus compromise bill.

3. Not further identified.

TO FRANKLIN HAVEN

Washington July 21. 1850
Sunday morng. 6 oclock

Private

My Dear Sir

You probably recd, a Telegraphic despatch from me yesterday.[1] In the morng, I recd your letter, & one from Mr [James Kellogg] Mills, & one from Mr [Peter] Harvey;[2] & I thought it better to decide, at once, as affairs are pressing, & as the President, who had agreed that I might have time to go home, before deciding whether I would take the office or not, felt some anxiety, nevertheless, about the delay, & was desirous, that, if possible, I should accept, at once. He behaved in the most handsome manner, in all respects; & when the proper time came, sent me word, by a member of the Senate, offering me the Dept of State, & desiring me to come to his House, at once, & confer on other appointments. I am quite satisfied with the Cabinet, in all respects. Mr Fillmore is exceedingly cautious, & takes time for consideration; but he is not wanting in firmness, I think, & is a thorough conservative Whig.

I never did any thing more reluctantly, than taking the office, which I have taken. From the time of Genl. [Zachary] Taylor's death, I supposed it might be offered, & pressed hard upon me, by members of Congress. The fear rendered my nights sleepless. And the truth is, I was so much urged, on all hands, that resistance was out of the case, except upon the grounds, which the letters recd yesterday removed.[3]

The old Cabinet quits tomorrow, & I suppose the new will be sworn in, on Tuesday. It is likely enough that Mr. [Thomas] Ewing will be immediately appointed to the Senate, by the Govr. of Ohio,[4] in Mr [Thomas] Corwin's place. Unfortunately, the Govr of Maryland[5] is not of our politics. I write, of course, to Govr [George Nixon] Briggs, & shall look with interest to see whom he may send. You will smile, on being informed, that there were *some* N.E. Whigs who expressed a wish to the President, that I might not be appointed, as my appointment would appear to be an approval of my recent course in Congress, &, of course, more or less of a censure on theirs. But you will be glad to know that Mr [Robert Charles] Winthrop acted in the most friendly, open, & decided manner.[6] He behaved like a man, throughout. I am, Dear Sir, yours truly

Danl Webster

F[letcher] W[ebster] left Washington last Eve', & will probably be in Boston when you receive this.

ALS. MH-H. Published in Curtis, 2: 465.

1. Not found. Curtis says that on July 20 DW sent a telegram to Haven, reporting that Fillmore had offered him the State Department and that he had accepted. (2: 464–465)

2. See above, Mills to DW, July 17, 1850. Harvey's and Haven's letters not found.

3. Mills's letter of July 17, above, eased DW's expressed fears that he could not afford to serve as secretary of state.

4. Seabury Ford (1801–1855; Yale 1825) was the last Whig governor of Ohio.

5. Phillip F. Thomas (1810–1890; Dickinson 1830) was a Democrat.

6. See above, p. 128, Fletcher Webster to Peter Harvey, July 16, 1850, n. 2.

In the week following Webster's assumption of duties at the State Department, the new administration faced its first major test, stemming from a long festering boundary dispute between New Mexico and Texas. Throughout the spring of 1850 the issue had been building to a direct confrontation between the Texans and the federal government. President Taylor's consistent support for New Mexican statehood implicitly recognized an eastern boundary for New Mexico that the Texans steadfastly rejected. Nonetheless, encouraged by the President and his military emissaries, Governor John Munroe and Colonel George A. McCall, New Mexicans wrote a constitution, elected representatives, and petitioned for statehood. In response, Texas governor Peter H. Bell called a special legislative session for August 12. By that date, he said, unless Congress returned the disputed territory north and east of the Rio Grande to Texas jurisdiction, he would ask for—and expected to receive—a mandate to send an army to Santa Fe. Further, on June 14, Bell wrote to President Taylor, bluntly asking whether the President had authorized New Mexico's assertions of jurisdiction over the disputed territory, hinting broadly that if this were the case, a direct federal-Texas clash was inevitable.

Webster viewed Bell's letter, which reached Washington following Zachary Taylor's death on July 9, as an opportunity for the new President to assert federal authority in the entire region, while urging calm and moderation in keeping with his announced concern to soothe sectional feelings. With Fillmore's consent, Webster wrote a special message to Congress to this effect (transmitted August 6) as well as a formal letter under his own name to Governor Bell emphasizing that Congress, not President Taylor's representatives, had the responsibility to adjudicate the territorial dispute. Both letters were designed (see below, DW to Franklin Haven, August 10, 1850) to encourage congressional support

for a Texas boundary bill drawn by Maryland senator James A. Pearce,
which was introduced on August 5 and passed the Senate four days later.

TO MILLARD FILLMORE

Department of State,
July 30. [1850]

To the President:

Is it not time that the answer to the Governor of Texas was prepared, considered, and despatched?[1] The Legislature of Texas meets at Austin on the 12th. prox. I shall, in the course of the day, send a draft for your examination. It will be well, I think, to put in as many soft words as we can to soothe the irritation of Texas, which seems to have taken offence at the military aspect of the proceedings at Santa Fe.[2] I doubt whether the late President expected Col. [George A.] McCall to take the lead in forming a Constitution for New Mexico,[3] or to act in that respect in his military character. Nevertheless, it is desirable that we should avoid every thing which might look like a reprimand to him. I think it will be necessary to send this answer by express. Yours truly,   Danl Webster

LS. NBuHi. Published in *W & S*, 16: 554–555.

1. Governor Peter H. Bell's letter, dated June 14 and addressed to President Taylor, was published, with the President's and Webster's responses, in *Congressional Globe*, 31st Cong., 1st sess., pp. 1525–1527.

2. On April 13, 1850, Taylor's representatives, Colonels George A. McCall and John Munroe (the latter then serving as territorial governor), called New Mexicans to meet preparatory to convening at Santa Fe to write a state constitution.

3. Contrary to Webster's supposition, President Taylor had been consistent to the point of inflexibility in sustaining New Mexico's claims to the disputed territory and its ambitions for statehood.

TO PETER HARVEY

Washington Wednesday
Aug. 7. '50

My Dear Sir

I recd your letter this morning. I do most fervently hope that Mr [Albert] Fearing will come to Congress.[1] We need him. I am tired of standing up here, almost alone from Massachusetts, contending for practical measures, absolutely essential to the good of the country. All must see, that it cannot but be disagreeable to me to struggle, day after day, & waste my health, in the Senate, or in the Department, to bring about a settlement of National difficulties, & yet have *no Massachusetts following*. I will not say I am altogether alone. Mr [George] Ashmun is acting a very proper, & a vigorous part. I rely on him entirely. And I hope that a better feeling is beginning to inspire others of the members, but there has not been one of these, as yet, who has ventured to stand up, & say, that he would stand by me, or my principles, or my views of policy. This is disagreeable & mortifying; altho. instead of discouraging me, it only puts me up to greater efforts to maintain myself, & to defend my position. I *feel* that something has been accomplished, by my feeble efforts, aided or unaided, & if, even, Massachusetts should leave me altogether without succour or encouragement, from her, there will be no fainting, in my heart, & no slackening of my exertions. But if Mr Fearing would come here, I should feel that I had a friend near me, free & independent, above all pledges & commitments, & having a single eye to the great good of the Country. Coming fresh from Boston, since these great measures have been under discussion, he wd. have great weight, & with Mr Ashmuns assistance, might exercise a salutary influence with our other Representatives. He will be able to speak for Boston, & her voice is wont to be respected.

I thank you for the kindness expressed in other parts of your letter. I am busy, enough, but my health is good, & I hope I may yet live to see the return of a better state of things. I am, Dear Sir, with regard, always truly yrs   Danl Webster

ALS. MWalB. Published in *PC*, 2: 382–383.

1. Harvey's letter not found. The evening before Webster wrote this letter, the Suffolk County Whig committee had nominated another pro-compromise man, Samuel A. Eliot, a former mayor of Boston, for the congressional seat vacated when Robert C. Winthrop replaced DW in the Senate. See *Boston Semi-Weekly Atlas*, August 7, 1850.

FROM CHARLES AUGUSTUS DAVIS

New York 9 Augt. 1850

My Dr Sir

I have been for the last two weeks jaunting about among our watering places—and have met a great variety of folks—at Saratoga and elsewhere—drawn together from all quarters of the Country, and I can say that I have not met a single individual who has not directly or indirectly expressed a kind of feeling of security that the President has you along side of him.

I was once at sea with the late Comdr. [Thomas] MacDonough as passenger in his Cabin with him—and Lieut. Jos. Smith (now at head of one of the Bureaux at Washing[to]n) was 1st Lieut. Whenever there was a blow or any trouble or noise on deck at night, the Commodore wd call a midshipman of the deck to him and enquire who had command on deck—and altho' he had great confidence in all his Lieuts—I generally found he wd get up and go & take a look for himself unless he was told that "Mr Smith" was there then he would turn over & go to sleep.

Among the younger officers this same Smith was generally spoken of as "old Joe"—but not so spoken to—to me he seem'd just as old then as he is now—tho' a qr. of a Century ago. I always have had a high regard for that officer ever since, and mainly because I found that when he was on deck the Commodore wd sleep soundly—and I also—and so I find public sentiment now, in regard to the Comdr. and 1st Lieut. at Washington—at any rate *we* the passengers feel easy.

I met Mr [Martin] Van Buren at Saratoga & found him very sociable—he seem'd particularly struck with the difference between the present period and that when he was President. "*Now* the masses are all busy with their own affairs—and dont trouble Govt.—when on the contrary in his time it was exactly the reverse." I found some Southern gentlemen there exceedingly bitter toward him—but he has a quick eye & can see as well at a right angle as on a straight line—and guided his walks accordingly, so there were no unnecessary "*cuts.*" I am either obtuse or I am right in asserting that all this *new platform* work of "free soil"—and "Wilmotism"—has got into a somewhat similar *twist* or difficulty which befel old Federalism when it was charged with having turn'd *blue*—very good to talk about among friends—but making sad work when it came to the ballot boxes, showing to my mind pretty conclusively that like all other *ultraisms* it wont work far into the masses. The whole negro question in my judgment is as firmly decided upon in the public mind as Christianity—and no power or party or any new platform can alter it. A man may be a good Christian altho he may oppose an "awakening" or a "love feast"—and still be a humane man altho he may turn away from these new fancies of "free soilery."

If I could only find a solitary individual owning what he calls "free soil"—willing to share it with a *free negro* I might regard the doctrine with less animosity—but when I see even Gerrit Smith the "quinine" of anti slavery taking care to measure off surpluss acres which are worthless even on the tax books—& when a Slave under the lash could not earn his salt—much less a free and independent negro—I can see nothing but gross humbug in it—and nothing practical in it, but humbug—and *that* is a quality not destined to longevity.

We want now, in my judgment, a new name for party. A "union party"—there is some *meaning* in this *name*—and as for "Whig" or "Democrat"—both seem possessed of this "potatoe rot" of negroism and I dont see any way of ridding ourselves of it in the Whig party—for one I feel that the bugs have got into my bed, and I have the choice of getting into a clean new bed to finish my nap—or spend the whole night in hunting out the bugs. I think the new bed preferable.

I am not quite gratified with the course pursued toward Portugal[1]— as the matter is reported to the public—it looks a little too short and sharp—too much like the Greek matter of England. I advised the Portu guese minister here three months ago that he had better advise his Govt to offer to leave the matter to a decision of our US Court, on the ground that it was on old matter which the Queen had no personal knowledge of—but wd rely on a fair decision & abide it—by this course she wd be regarded by our people as a high minded Lady &c. Otherwise we might be constrained to visit Mafra or Cintra as we did Mexico. It does not seem to molest our Stock credit in London—neither does the death of the President—and Mr [Joshua] Bates writes me (recd today) that the only anxiety felt in London is in regard to the new Cabinet. They will be well satisfied when they hear what has been done[2]—and like my old friend MacDonough finish their nap after hearing who is on deck. Very truly your friend   Ch: Augt. Davis

ALS. DLC. Davis (1795–1867), a New York City businessman, occasionally contributed political commentaries to the press.

1. See *Diplomatic Papers*, 2.

2. On July 24 the London *Times* mentioned Webster's probable appointment to the State Department and commented that "we could desire no stronger guarantee for the prudent and energetic direction of the affairs of the Union both at home and abroad." For the *Times*'s expressed satisfaction with Fillmore's other cabinet choices, see issues of July 30 and August 6, 1850.

TO FRANKLIN HAVEN

Washington Aug. 10. 1850
6 oclock

Private
My Dear Sir

You see that we are going ahead; & I am indebted to you for so much kindness, & so many evidences of good will, that I have thought I would occupy half an hour, in the cool of the morning, by letting you see the inside of things, a little. I had been much urged to find an opportunity for the President to send a message to Congress, especially by Mr [William D.] Merrick, a shrewd man, formerly a member of the Senate from Maryland, & a friend of mine. He said, "Mr [Henry] Clay has failed, in his project; let us hear from you, or the President.["] I s[ai]d I would do so, if an occasion could be found. Two or three days afterwards the President sent me Govr [Peter Hansborough] Bell's letter,[1] saying it must be respectfully acknowledged, &c. I was writing a formal letter of acknowledgement, when a thought struck me like a shot, that here was a case for a message. I went immediately to the President, & proposed it. He acquiesced at once, & requested me to prepare both an answer to the Govr. & a draft for a message. It cost me one day, (Sunday) & two nights. I called in two of the best men in Washington, Mr [George] Ashmun, & Mr Edward Curtis. We got the draft ready, & Mr Ashmun went with it to three or four or half a dozen Senators, & twice as many members of the H. R. He travelled over the whole City in the burning heat on Sunday to *consult* with these Gentlemen. This gratified them. Some of them suggested amendments, & all took an interest in the *measure*. On Monday morng it was read to the President, & altered, where necessary, till it was approved by him, & the other members of the Cabinet. Monday night I kept the Clerks up, to make out the necessary number of copies, &c. Tuesday morng, between 5. & 7. I went over every paper again, & saw that all was right. The papers were all read again to the President, at 9 oclock, & before eleven he signed them & sent them off. He is a man of business, & a man of intelligence, & wide awake.

The effect of this previous consultation was excellent. Friends understood the subject, & were ready to act their part. Among others Mr [Christopher H.] Williams of Tennessee was consulted, & yesterday he made a capital speech on the subject, in the H. of R.[2] Mr. [Robert Charles] Winthrop was consulted, & we had his vote. We had also Mr [John] Davis' vote, which I did not expect. A friend asked me, two days ago, to see Mr Davis, & urge him to come in for the measure. I said, no; let circumstances crowd him in. Mr [James Alfred] Pearce, of course, consulted me on his bill,[3] on Sunday; & it was arranged that he should introduce it on Monday, & that it should be immediately followed by the message. Finally—if it be not too slight a circumstance to be mentioned—I gave ten minutes to the preparation of an Editorial for the Intellegencer,[4] which you will see in the paper of this morning. Excuse this unimportant chit-chat. I thought it might amuse you. Yrs always

D. Webster

ALS. MH-H. Published in *W & S*, 16: 558–559.

1. See above, DW to Fillmore, July 30, [1850], n. 1.

2. Williams's speech strongly endorsed Fillmore's message to Congress on August 6 and rebuked Texas for rejecting federal authority in resolving its boundary dispute with New Mexico. *Congressional Globe*, 31st Cong., 1st sess., *Appendix*, pp. 1051–1054.

3. With the advice and encouragement of DW and Stephen A. Douglas, Pearce introduced a new bill on August 5 revising the Texas boundary mandated in his earlier measure, which had failed in the Senate on July 31. The new bill, like its predecessor, provided for a $10 million payment to Texas as part of the boundary settlement. With minor revisions, the bill passed on August 9 by a 30–20 vote. *Congressional Globe*,

31st Cong., 1st Sess., pp. 1520–1521, 1554–1556.

4. DW's commentary in the Washington *National Intelligencer* of August 10, titled "The Question Settled," referred to Pearce's bill as "a healing measure" and "the first step in the restoration of national harmony." It praised the bill's backers and predicted that the House would quickly follow the Senate's lead.

FROM JOHN MCLEAN

Cincinnati.
16 Aug 1850

My Dear Sir,

I cannot refrain from expressing to you the gratification I feel, at the position taken by the administration in the controversy with Gov [Peter Hansborough] Bell of Texas. It was the true ground and it sustained, in a fit and proper manner, the dignity and character of the government. I think it will lead to an adjustment of this controversy. I am reconciled to the payment of the ten millions on the ground, that, under any circumstances, the general government would have to pay the debt of Texas, and under the proposed arrangement we shall pay a less sum, than we should otherwise have to pay.

In establishing the legal boundaries of Texas must we not look to the territory over which her sovereignty was exercised at the time of annexation. Her sovereignty was not acknowledged by Mexico, consequently, she could only claim a jurisdiction as far as it had been maintained by force. This, I understand to be a well established principle of public law. The late acquisition of New Mexico by the United States, cannot affect the question of boundary. It is the mere substitution of one sovereignty for another. We represent the rights of Mexico. Texas in strict law, can only claim the territory subject to her, when she became one of the states of the Union. The friends of annexation disclaimed any act which would afford any just ground of war by Mexico. Now this could not have been contended, if the boundaries of Texas extended beyond the limits over which she exercised an unobstructed jurisdiction.

Pardon these crude suggestions and believe me to be most truly and sincerely yours   John McLean.

ALS. DLC.

FROM ALPHONSO TAFT

Cincinnati Aug. 23. 1850.

My Dear Sir,

Without being certain that I have any thing to say, worth writing, I have determined to write you a letter. When President Taylor died the Whigs of Ohio felt peculiar concern. The Freesoilers, who hold all important influence in a portion of our state, had gone against General

Taylor's election. But they regarded his position on the Slavery question as so near their own, that they could find no room or excuse for a separate organization. The consequence was that the freesoilers (who were generally original Whigs) were about to co-operate again with the Whig party. This, I take it, was anything but satisfactory to the political champions of the freesoil faith. They wanted nothing so much as a separate platform. But so strong was the current of freesoil opinion in Ohio, that General Taylor was with them, that these politicians gave up the idea of opposing him; and things looked favorable to Whig supremacy here.

On the death of Genl Taylor, it was seen that these freesoil politicians began to rustle, and say that they must have a candidate of their own, especially when they found that Mr Webster, in abusing whom they had spent so much strength, was to be a member of the new cabinet. Judge [William] Johnston our Whig candidate for Governor was a good deal alarmed by the known perversity of the Western Reserve in the Slavery questions.[1] He had been among them and had made successful use of General Taylor's position, to hush the ravings of Freesoilism.

But the change has come; the message and the correspondence on the Texas & New Mexico questions have been published,[2] and my belief is that the present administration have more entirely the confidence of our State Whigs & freesoilers, than General Taylor's administration ever had, and the prospect is that the Whigs will carry the state at the next election, Governor, Legislature, Congress & all. Mr [Thomas] Corwin's appointment was a fortunate one for Ohio.[3]

We shall gain more than we shall lose, in Ohio, by the change. The Whigs, will have more courage, regarding this Administration as more decidedly Whig, than the former. Everybody feels that the State Department is safe, and will be well administered, whatever may befal us.

As to the measures now pending in Congress, for the settlement of the consequences of the Mexican War, the California Bill, the Texas Boundary Bill, the New Mexico Territory Bill, and the Utah Bill, Everybody desires them to pass except the restless Freesoil agitators, whose reliance is upon the disquiet and political embarrassments of the country. The Compromise Bill, if it had passed would have been popular undoubtedly among our people. But the passage of these Bills separately will generally suit the popular mind better than the Compromise or Omnibus. The truth is that the press here at the North had incautiously and without much examination, committed themselves against the Compromise Bill, <without> not very well knowing what it contained. The Omnibus was supposed to carry a good many passengers, that were not on board. All the sins and claims of the wicked South, were thought to be seated somewhere in that omnibus; and the newspapers having committed themselves against it, did not take any pains to correct the popular ideas on the subject. What shows, that the measures actually contained in the Omnibus Bill, were not unacceptable to the people of this part of the Country and the Editors themselves, is, that they all now regard the Texas Boundary as the most objectionable thing in it, and they regard the boundary drawn by the general bill, as decidedly better for the North than that of Mr [James Alfred] Pearce's Bill;[4] but nevertheless they desire the passage of the Pearce bill, rather than the delay or defeat of the measures before Congress. If the vote could be taken of the people by a show of hands, there would be four fifths in favor of the adoption of all of these measures, without one moment's delay. The Ten Millions given to Texas, is on all hands regarded as no more than a mess of potage, from which the South derive no substantial advantage over the North.

Our agricultural anniversary, or fair, has been postponed to the first days of October. I hope it may be so, that you can be present on that occasion. Yours very truly   Alphonso Taft

Alphonso Taft is a highly respectable person. A Gentleman from Michigan has just been here, who says, that he never knew so much pleasure produced by a Public Doc: as the Message[5] has caused throughout the South.   D. W.

ALS with ANS by DW. OHi.

1. Johnston (1804–1891), a Carrollton lawyer, was then serving a term on the Ohio superior court. He lost the gubernatorial election by 11,000 largely Free Soil votes.

2. See above, DW to Millard Fillmore, July 30, [1850], and DW to Franklin Haven, August 10, 1850.

3. Corwin was installed in the new cabinet as secretary of the Treasury.

4. See above, DW to Franklin Haven, August 10, 1850, n. 3. Pearce's new bill added some 33,333 square miles more to Texas than the omnibus bill had allowed.

5. Fillmore's August 6 message to Congress.

The logjam blocking compromise finally broke on August 9, with Senate passage of James A. Pearce's revised Texas boundary bill. Following this initial success, other elements of the original compromise package carried as separate bills, thanks in large measure to the shrewd and persistent lobbying of Senator Stephen A. Douglas. By the end of the third week of August, when Webster penned the following anonymous editorial for the National Intelligencer, *the Senate had assented to the admission of California, the establishment of territorial government in New Mexico, and a strengthened fugitive slave law. Only the District of Columbia bill was held over until the House could act. Webster's editorial was designed to encourage quick and decisive movement in the House on all compromise-related measures.*

EDITORIAL ON THE COMPROMISE MEASURES

[August 26, 1850]

The Important Week

Congress has now commenced the Week which is to witness the fate of those vastly interesting measures which have engrossed its attention for nine months. The Senate, after a series of Debates, never surpassed in that body, or elsewhere, for ability, earnestness & patriotism, has presented the glorious results of its labors to the other Branch of the National Legislature. *The Peace of the Country is now in the hands of the House of Representatives*; And if it be found not to be safe, in those hands, <an irreparable> a blow, irreparable in its consequences, will be struck, not only on the prosperity & happiness of the People of the United States, but upon the great cause of popular Freedom throughout the world; for if this Union cannot be preserved, & the Government established under it maintained, it will be demonstrated that there cannot exist among men, a free powerful, Representative Government, over a Country of large extent. Petty Republics there may be; small States may continue to exist, & to enjoy free institutions by the permission of their neighbors; but the experiment of a great Republican Government, formed by the Union of Independent States, & clothed only with such powers as concern the common defence & general welfare, & leaving all local legislation to the States themselves, will have failed, & failed under such circumstances, as will forbid all idea of its repetition.

That the House of Representatives will rightfully discharge the momentous duties, which it has now to perform, we confidently believe. Recent <events> occurrences have been calculated to dispel doubts, & to reassure the best hope of the friends of the Union. In the first place, the example of the *Senate* is a bright & shining light, upon which members of the other House are not likely to turn their backs. In the next place, the recommendation of measures of conciliation & peace, by an Administration which possesses, at the present moment, <a respectable portion of> the public confidence, will not pass altogether unheeded. But the influence of these external considerations needs not to be relied on. The power which is to carry the pending measures through the House of Representatives is their own propriety, their own justice, their own necessity. They move by a force inherent in themselves. Their objects every man sees, & every patriotic man loves. Those objects are peace, harmony, & the security of the Union, & in the march of measures, having such ends in view, & suitable to the attainment of such ends, not only will all small <objects> obstacles be crushed, but mountains will give way, the North will give up, & the South will not <hold> keep back. There will be a surrender of individual preferences, & personal opinions, & the flocking together of patriotic purposes <& firm Am> and true

American feelings, such as shall render this *last week of August 1850,* ever memorable in the Annals of the Country.

These are our hopes; & this our belief, as to the issue of these questions. We have faith, full faith, in the intelligence & integrity of the House of Representatives. <Individuals may waver.>

But this is not all. "There is a power behind the throne," exclaimed Lord Chatham "greater than the throne itself." In a Constitutional monarchy, this is an *omen* of ill. But in a popular, representative Government, it is no omen of ill, that there is behind Legislative bodies & Executive bodies, a power greater than those bodies themselves; & that power is the known will of the People. What that will is, in the present crisis, is not doubtful. No jarring or discordant sounds reach the ear. There is an imperative unity in the public voice, such as was hardly ever known before, such as no man can mistake, & no wise man will disregard. We use terms not too strong, when we say that the cry of the Country is for the adoption by the House of the Bills of the Senate one & all. <separately or together.> In forty years experience we have not known public opinion more clear, united, & decisive. We suppose our means of knowledge, in this respect, as good as those of most others, who like ourselves are confined to one place; & we aver our conviction <that public opinion was never more> that a vast majority of the people look for the salvation of the Country to the sanction to be given by the House to the measures of the Senate. All manifestations of sentiment<s> show this. The Press, from every quarter, teems with proof, the results of public meetings on the subject, wherever holden, <prove> proclaim it, every man we see, & who has come hither, by the Rail Roads & the Steam Boats, from the extreme margins of the country, declares that he has heard the expression of but one opinon, & one hope; & that opinion not faint & hesitating, but firm & strong, & that hope earnest, anxious, & enthusiastic.

It is not, therefore, to be doubted, that if nothing occur to mar the prospect, the Bills which have passed the Senate, will pass elsewhere, & become laws. The members of the House of Representatives are servants who know their Lords will, & who mean to do it.

There is, indeed, one possible danger. The pending measures are in separate Bills, & some of these are more warmly espoused, or more cheerfully supported, by one part of <this> the Country than by others. It is possible, that on this account, a contest about priority may spring up, aided or instigated, on the one side or on the other, <in whose hear> by those few in whose hearts the root of bitterness is still so rank, as to leave place for nothing but purposes of disunion & mischief. Any such contest would be most deeply to be deprecated. If, in all humility, we might presume to address a word of advice, or, perhaps, more appropriately, of request & supplication to the friends of the measures in the House of Representatives, we should say, "have confidence in one another. Confidence! Confidence! Let no distrust disturb your counsels. If there be any controversy, let it be that controversy, so patriotic, so becoming, so graceful, in which the point shall be who shall be most ready to give confidence in advance. How cheering it would be to hear it said, on all sides, "we act upon honor, & in good faith; we know that you act upon honor, & in good faith. Let us take up the measures, then, as they arise, orderly, & in regular course of proceeding, & dispose of them. Neither our cheeks, nor yours, shall hereafter be crimsoned by blushes, caused by the recollection of faith violated or honorable understandings left unfulfilled."

We must <here> bring these remarks to a close, but as we hardly knew where to begin, so we hardly know where to end. What we have said, we trust will be regarded as written in no spirit of dictation, distrust or disrespect. Our responsibilities, in comparison with those of others, are inconsiderable. Yet we have felt that we had a duty to perform, & we have endeavored to discharge it, in a very feeble manner certainly, by giving utterance to the sentiments expressed in this Article. For ourselves, we feel that if our lives & our labors should be prolonged to a far more distant period than it is probable they will be, we shall never address our readers on a subject of more vital importance to the honor & happiness of the People of the United States.

AD. NN. Published in Washington, D.C., *National Intelligencer*, August 26, 1850, and reprinted in *W & S*, 15: 228–231.

Webster's most earnest hopes for compromise were realized in the House deliberations. Sensitive to the continuing crisis in Texas, and to the growing public clamor for compromise, leading House members devised a "little omnibus" combining the bill for the Texas boundary and payment of Texas's debts with the bill organizing the New Mexico Territory. Despite various parliamentary challenges, the little omnibus passed on September 6, by a 107–98 vote. The following day, the California and Utah bills passed the House by comfortable margins, spurring celebrations throughout the capital. Two days later, the Senate accepted the House legislation, and within that week the fugitive slave and District of Columbia slave trade bills were enacted. President Fillmore signed the various bills as he received them, and by September 20, the compromise was the law of the land. Webster's correspondence during September reflects his relief and satisfaction with the course of events — and, understandably, his sense of vindication.

TO PETER HARVEY

Tuesday, 2 oclock Sept. 10. 50

My Dear Sir,

You have heard how all things have gone, so far. I confess, I feel relieved. Since the 7th of March, there has not been an hour, in which I have not felt a "crushing" weight of anxiety, & responsibility. I have gone to sleep at night, & waked in the morning, with the same feeling of "eating care." And I have sat down to no breakfast, or dinner, to which I have brought an unconcerned & easy mind. It is over. My part is acted, & I am satisfied. The rest, I leave to stronger bodies, & fresher minds. My annual cold is now heavy upon me, weakening my body, & depressing my spirits. It has yet a fortnight to run; & perhaps will sink me lower than it did, when strong excitements enabled me to withstand it. I have lost a good deal of flesh, & you will think me thin, & haggard. I have had little sleep, not four hours a night, on an average, for the whole six months. Now, I mean to grow stupid, & lazy; & if I can get rid of my catarrh, to eat & drink like an alderman.

It is a day of rejoicing here, such as I never witnessed. The face of every thing seems changed. You would suppose nobody had ever thought of disunion. All say, they always meant to stand by the Union, to the last.

Boston, ever true & glorious Boston, has helped us, immensely. Mr [Samuel Atkins] Eliots triumphant Election[1] awakened entirely new hopes. Up to that period, they had no hopes of the North. I never knew an election, by its mere character of *an election*, on certain principles, produce half so much effect. He is quite a lion here. He is decided, straight-forward, without any shadow of turning. It ran thro the whole City, on friday, after the main vote had been taken, that Mr Eliot said, "now we have trodden Satan, & all his works, under our feet." I mention this, only to show with how much eagerness every thing is listened to, that a sound Northern man says agt. abolitionism, & all the other *isms*.

Pray remember me to Mr T[homas] B[uckminster] Curtis, Mr [James Kellogg] Mills, Mr [Franklin] Haven, & other friends. There is a host of them, I shall never cease to love. Boston, forever!

My eyes allow me to write only about one hour a day.

I hope to see the State House, & the Common, & the Steeple of the old South, two days after Congress adjourns.

Among others, remember me kindly to [Albert] Fearing. Yrs truly

D. Webster

I look to hear from you tomorrow morning

ALS. NhD. Published in *PC*, 2: 385–386.

1. In a special election held on August 20 to fill the congressional seat

vacated by Robert C. Winthrop, Eliot
decisively defeated Free Soil nominee

Charles Sumner, 2355–489. *Boston Semi-Weekly Atlas*, August 21, 1850.

TO FRANKLIN HAVEN

Washington, 12 Sept. 1850

Private.

My dear Sir,

I use the confidential hand of another to write you a short letter, my eyes holding out only to perform a small part of the duty expected from them every day. I am in the midst of my periodical catarrh, or "hay fever," or whatever you please to call it, but which you know all about. I read nothing, and hardly write any thing but signatures. The disease is depressing and discouraging; I know that there is no remedy for it and that it must have its course. It produces loss of appetite and great prostration of strength, but since the events of last week terminated, I have some little time for rest, and shutting myself up very much I keep as quiet as I can.

My dear Sir, I think the country has had a providential escape from very considerable dangers. I was not aware of the whole extent of the embarrassment likely to arise till I came here last December, and had opportunities of conversation with General [Zachary] Taylor and the gentlemen of his Administration. General Taylor was an honest and truly patriotic man; but he had quite enough of that quality which, when a man is right, we call firmness, and when he is wrong we denominate obstinacy. What has been called the president's plan was simply this, to wit: to admit California under her free constitution, and to let the territories alone, altogether, until they could come in as States. This policy, as it was thought, would avoid all discussion, and all voting on the question of the Wilmot proviso. All that matter, it was supposed, might be thus postponed and the Slavery Question staved off. The objection to this plan, was the same as that to poor King Lear's idea of shoeing a company of horse in felt, and stealing upon his enemies. It was flatly impossible—that's all, but the purpose was settled and decided. General Taylor told me, in the last conversation I had with him, that he preferred that California should not come in at all, rather than that she should come in bringing the Territories on her back. And, if he had lived, it <may be do> might have been doubtful whether any general settlement would have been made. He was a soldier, and had a little fancy, I am afraid, to see how easily any military movement by Texas could have been put down. His motto was, "vi et armis." He had a soldier's foresight, and saw quite clearly what would be the result if Texan militia should march into New Mexico and there be met by troops of the regular army of the United States. But that he had a statesman's foresight, and foresaw what consequences might happen in the existing state of men's opinions and feelings, if blood should be shed in a contest between the United States and one of the Southern States, is more than I am ready to affirm. Yet long before his death, and in the face of that observation which he made to me, as already stated, I made up my mind to risk myself on a proposition for a general pacification. I attempted to sound one or two New England friends, but found them afraid. They were [George] Ashmun and Wilson,[1] who have since acquitted themselves nobly, and deserve all thanks. I then resolved to push my skiff from the shore alone, considering that in that case, if she foundered, there would be but one life lost. Our friend [Peter] Harvey happened to be here, and with him and Mr. Edward Curtis, I held a little council the evening before the speech. What followed is known. Most persons here thought it impossible that I could maintain myself and stand by what I had declared. They wished, and hoped, and prayed, but fear prevailed. When I went to Boston, soon afterwards, and was kindly received, and intimated that I should take no march backward, they felt a little encouraged. But, truly, it was not till Mr. [Samuel Atkins] Eliot's election[2] that there was any confident assurance here that I was not a dead man. It would be of little consequence, my dear Sir, if I could only say that Boston loved me; but I can say with all sincerity, and with the fullest conviction of its truth, that Boston saved the country. From the commencement of the Government no such consequences have attended any single election as those that flowed from Mr. Eliot's. That election was a clear and convincing proof that there was breaking out a new fountain of brilliant light in the East, and men imbibed hopes in which they had never before indulged. At this moment, it is true, that Mr. Eliot is the greatest lion that exhibits himself on Pennsylvania Avenue. He is considered the personation of Boston; ever intelligent ever patriotic, ever glorious Boston; and whatever prejudices may have existed in the minds of honorable Southern men, against our good City, they are now all sunk and lost forever, in their admiration of her nationality of spirit.

But I must stop here. There is much else that I could say, and may say hereafter, of the importance of the crisis through which we have passed. I am yet not free from the excitement it has produced. I am like one who has been sea-sick, and has gone to bed. My bed rolls and tosses by the billows of that sea, over which I have passed.

My Dr Sir, This is for your own eye. You are much younger than I am, & hereafter, possibly you may recur to this hastily dictated letter, not without interest. If you think it worth reading, you may show it to

T[homas] B[uckminster] Curtis, [James Kellogg] Mills, [Albert] Fearing, & [Peter] Harvey &c. It is but half an hour's gossip, when I can do nothing but talk, & dictate, to a confidential clerk. Yrs always truly

Danl Webster

LS, with last paragraph in DW's hand. MH-H. Published in *PC*, 2: 386–388.

1. Probably James Wilson, a New Hampshire Whig, who voted for the compromise measures in the House.

2. See above, DW to Peter Harvey, September 10, 1850, n. 1.

TO PETER HARVEY

Washington, D.C.
Sept. 13./50

My dear Sir,

I have received today, your exceedingly kind letter of the 11th inst.[1] Your heart is full of joy, at recent occurrences, and your friends are apt to imbibe your own enthusiasm. I see you have a good deal of rejoicing in Boston, and I am heartily glad of it. Nothing has occurred since I wrote you last, except the passage of the Fugitive Slave Bill through the House of Rep.; this with one exception completes the circle. I am afraid it is too late to do anything with the Tariff, except to make preparation for action at the commencement of the next session—now only two months and a half off. I am considering however, whether some decided expression of opinion by the House of Representatives might not now be obtained and be useful; it is a subject upon which I have been occupied with friends all day. Possibly something stronger than a mere expression of opinion may be produced. There are several gentlemen here, interested in that subject principally from Pennsylvania.

I shall be glad to see the Boston friends who you say are coming. I wish you would come with them. Yours always truly,   Danl Webster

Typed copy (from the original, not found, at Middlesex County Historical Society, Middletown, Connecti-cut). DLC. Published in *PC*, 2: 388–389.

1. Letter not found.

FROM EDWARD EVERETT, WITH ENCLOSURE

Cambridge 13 Sept. 1850

Dear Sir,

I cannot forbear to write you a line, to congratulate you on the happy result of last week's doings in Congress,—probably as momentous a week as any in our political history. You surely have a right more than any one else to be congratulated, for it is mainly the consequence of your wisdom & courage. I trust the country will have the discernment & the gratitude to appreciate & recompense the service. We live here in an horizon so narrow and under an atmosphere so cloudy, that we know less than almost any where else what is the real state of public opinion in the United States;—but I take it to be clearly in favor of the settlement which has been made. Efforts will no doubt be made in New England, to keep up the Anti-Slavery agitation. But so much of the material of that agitation has been withdrawn, that a considerable portion of the free-soilers will, I rather think, fall back into the Whig party;—which is now somewhat paralyzed by their defection, and by the policy pursued by the most active part of the Whig press, in attempting to conciliate them.

I am quite at a loss to know how Mr. [Thomas Hart] Benton became acquainted with any portion of the contents of my private letter to you of the 31st of March 1843, relative to Oswald's map.[1] I wrote that letter and my public despatch No. 34 of the 28th of March,[2] with a good deal of care, intending to make them convey respectively what was & what was not well adapted to be communicated to Congress. The appearance of Oswald's map was one of the most extraordinary incidents in that most extraordinary negotiation. [George William] Featherstonhaugh,[3] in concealing the knowledge of it from his superiors, certainly behaved with great dishonesty;—and the only thing which I ever saw in Lord Aberdeen, that I could not reconcile with a high sense of honor, was giving a good office (the consulate at Havre) to Featherstone, for his services in reference to the boundary, & after this dishonest concealment was known.

I have some communications with the State Central Committee, whose chairman (Mr. [George] Morey)[4] is my classmate;—although I have not possessed their entire confidence, since my signing the letter addressed to the Massachusetts delegation in Congress.[5] If I can be of any use to you, by any suggestions in that quarter, I pray you to let me know it.

The proprietor [Lyman Willard] of the Brattle-house in Cambridge,—a very good hotel lately opened here—is very desirous that I should say to you, that he would deem it a great favor, if you would come to his house, were it but for a day & a night;—or even a part of a day;—and that he should be too happy to place his whole establishment at your service. I could not refuse to convey his message to you;—but I need not say that I should be grieved to have you find a home even for a part of a day at any house in Cambridge but mine.

I remain, as ever, dear Sir, with sincere attachment Yours,

Edward Everett.

P.S. I enclose an extract from a late letter from Mr. [Abbott] Lawrence, which I suppose it would be quite agreeable to him, that you should see.

ALS. MHi.

1. On September 6, 1850 Benton had communicated to the Senate a letter of August 28 from the state department transmitting "a copy of the paragraph from one of Mr. Everett's letters, requested by Mr. Benton. The paragraph has just been discovered" (*Cong. Globe*, 31st Cong., 1st sess., p. 1766). For Everett's private letter to DW of March 31, 1843. see *Diplomatic Papers*, 1: 787–793. "Oswald's Map, also known as "King George's Map," was a cardinal document in negotiations in 1782 with Great Britain regarding the Canadian-American boundary. The map, which favored American territorial claims in 1842, was hidden from the chief British and American negotiators prior to the boundary settlement in the Treaty of Washington. American opponents of the treaty, particularly Senator Benton, had made the map a central line of attack—with little success—in secret Senate debate over the treaty in 1843. For background, consult Howard Jones, *To the Webster-Ashburton Treaty: A Study in Anglo-American Relations, 1783–1843* (Chapel Hill, N.C., 1977), pp. 106–113, 161–165.

2. Everett to DW, March 28, 1843, No. 34, DNA, RG 59, (Despatches, Britain).

3. Featherstonhaugh (1786–1866), an English geologist, surveyed the northeastern boundary for the British government in 1839 and later joined with Lord Palmerston in hiding the Oswald map from the British negotiator, Lord Ashburton. In 1843 Featherstonhaugh published a pamphlet strongly critical of the Treaty of Washington. See dispatch 34, cited above; Jones, *To the Webster-Ashburton Treaty*, pp. 107–108, and *Diplomatic Papers*, 1: 776, 783–784.

4. Morey (1789–1866; Harvard 1811), a Boston lawyer, was for many years chairman of the Whig State Central Committee.

5. See above, p. 114, DW to Samuel Lawrence, June 10, 1850, n. 1.

ENCLOSURE: EXTRACT FROM ABBOTT LAWRENCE TO EDWARD EVERETT

[London, August 16, 1850]

I have an official announcement from Mr Webster of his appointment, whatever differences of opinion may have existed between us, I am free to say, that no man in the Union is more competent to discharge the duties of Secretary of State than Mr Webster. The Cabinet is a strong one—and I should think will command the confidence of the country. I have faith, that the President will adopt the policy generally of the late Executive. Mr. Webster's appointment is highly satisfactory to the British people. The death of General [Zachary] Taylor is much deplored in this country, and in fact all over Europe. He had a great name and fame in Europe.

Mr [John] Miller[1] has been restored to office by Mr Webster, which has given him and his friends much satisfaction. He should not have been superseded. I had no knowledge of it. Your letter to Lady Peel[2] has been sent to her. Parliament was prorogued yesterday, without having accomplished any thing striking, but many useful acts have been carried through which I have no doubt will be satisfactory to the great body of the people. I have heard that the compromise Bill in Congress had failed, it came by Telegraph to Halifax. If such be the case, I should suppose the plan of the late President would be adopted.

I long to hear of the disposal of that question.

Extract in a clerk's hand. MHi.

1. An English bookseller, Miller had served for many years as a London dispatch agent for the United States government. Secretary of State John M. Clayton ordered his removal in 1850, but DW reinstated Miller, on the advice of Everett and Lawrence,

shortly after returning to the State Department.

2. Everett to Lady Julia Peel, July 23, 1850, Everett Papers, MHi microfilm, reel 29, expressed condolences on the death of her husband, Sir Robert Peel, who died July 2, 1850.

FROM CALEB CUSHING

Newburyport 14 Sept. 1850

Dear Sir:

I have been daily expecting for the last month to go to Washington; otherwise I should have written to congratulate you, as I now most heartily do, on your accession to the State Department. The death of Genl. [Zachary] Taylor seems to have saved the country from civil war. To you, it must be a proud triumph to step at once over the heads of your enemies, and be giving orders to Mr [Abbott] Lawrence and the rest.

It has given me peculiar satisfaction, also, to witness the election of my classmate Samuel A[tkins] Eliot, and to note the manly & independent course he has pursued in the House. O si sic omnes!

I suppose your engagements have caused you to overlook my letter of July.[1]

I have received a proposition in regard to the Rock Island City tract,[2] which requires attention, and is the immediate occasion of my now writing to you.

Mr Wm Brackett,[3] who holds the tax titles as against you, offers to release on payment of his outlay & a bonus of $100 besides, making in all about $300.

The suit comes on in October, and therefore it is desirable to reply immediately.

Upon the fullest investigation of the subject, I find that the land has now little or no value excepting for agricultural purposes. Mr [Nathaniel] Norton, who owns 1/16th (your interest having been 1/8th), and whose 1/16th is free & clear, he having paid the taxes, offers to sell for $1000, which is at the rate of $16000 for the whole, making your interest $2000.

If you reflect that this is $26 per acre, you will conceive that Mr Norton thus far finds no purchaser; and most careful inquiries do not give any thing like this for a *cash value*.

I will, as you may think best, either trade with Mr Brackett to get a release from him & so clear up the title, or to sell to him.

Begging you to bestow a moment's attention on this subject, I am Very truly & respectfully   C Cushing

ALS. DLC.

1. Not found.

2. To meet a large indebtedness, Webster deeded to Cushing a tract of unimproved land in Rock Island, Illinois, supposedly worth $20,000. See DW to Cushing, November 30, 1849, *Correspondence*, 6: 359. DW, however, had failed to pay taxes, and without his knowledge the land was sold to one William Brackett. Apparently the arrangement suggested in this letter fell through. The land became tied up in litigation, and the case remained unsettled at DW's death.

3. Not further identified.

TO [?]

Washington D. C.
Sept 15/50

My dear Sir,

I have recv'd yours of the 13 inst.[1] this morning, and will take care of the wishes of Mr. [Francis] Tukey, and Mr. [William H.] Ropes,[2] until they or their friends arrive. I shall also take care of the private reputation of Mr. [Philip] Greely;[3] I never heard anything against him in that respect, except, his being sued for small debts, and I have already told the President, that those, were debts incurred before the failure of his mercantile House. His nomination will not be recalled, and how it will fare in the Senate, I know not.[4] I take no part in it, and have not heard a word said about it, since I wrote Mr. [Albert] Fearing.[5] Mr Greely has not acted as he should have done, as probably he is aware by this time; but I wish him no harm and will cheerfully take care that his reputation as a man shall not suffer. I never heard of any letter from Mr. [Samuel] Hooper.

My eyes are weak and painful, and I can write very little with my own hand. Twenty letters a day are hardly more, than I am called on to write, beside my official correspondence. My general health is quite good, or else I could not live under this load. Since the seventh of March, letters from every quarter of the Union, respecting my speeches, public letters &c have come in, in such numbers, that they fill up my desk, like that of a merchant; of all these I am obliged to take respectful notice, and the work is no light one.

The last of the pacification Bills, passed the Senate yesterday by a large majority, and will go through the House on a gallop. It is a Bill for the Abolition of the Slave Trade in the District of Columbia.

The[re] is, undoubtedly a great change in mens feelings here, in favor of conciliation and harmony and peace. Men are a great deal happier than they were six months ago, and crimination and recrimination, are no longer the order of the day: some things which have recently occurred in the Senate,[6] may seem to be an exception to this remark, and for their occurrence I am extremely sorry; they were unnecessary, as I think, and might well have been omitted.

Mr [Linus] Child, Mr [William W.] Stone[7] and Bartlett,[8] arrived here last evening, and I shall see them to day. I fear there is not time to do any thing to the Tariff, though the general feeling is very favorable. Yours always truly,   Danl Webster

LS. NhHi. Published in *W & S*, 16: 567.

1. Letter not found.

2. Tukey (d. 1867; Harvard 1843), marshal for Boston, 1846–1852, was then seeking the United States marshalship for California. Ropes, a Boston merchant with a substantial cotton export business to Russia, was a successful candidate for a consulship in St. Petersburg. *Journal of the Executive Proceedings of the Senate* (Washington, 1887), 8: 232, 244.

3. A Boston merchant active in Whig politics, Greely (1806–1854) had been appointed by President Taylor in January 1850 as collector of customs for Boston and Charlestown, despite DW's preference for George Ashmun, who was not running for reelection to Congress. See DW to Millard Filmore, September 11, 1850, mDW 31068.

4. Greely's nomination was confirmed on September 24, 1850. *Journal of the Executive Proceedings of the Senate*, 8: 249–250.

5. Letter not found.

6. Webster is referring to acrimonious exchanges in the Senate on September 11 and 12 between antislavery and southern rights senators, prior to the Senate's final approval of the compromise bills recently carried in the House. *Congessional Globe*, 31st Cong., 1st sess., *Appendix*, pp. 1647–1665.

7. Stone was a Boston commission merchant, partner of Samuel Lawrence in the firm Lawrence, Stone, & Co., and also an incorporator of the Middlesex Manufacturing Company.

8. Probably Sidney Bartlett (1799–1889; Harvard 1818), a Boston attorney who frequently argued before the United States Supreme Court.

FROM HENRY ALEXANDER SCAMMELL DEARBORN

Hawthorn Cottage,
Roxbury Sep 23, 1850

My Dear Sir,

I saw it intimated, in one of the morning papers,[1] that you were negociating with the Spanish government, for the purchase of Cuba, & sincerely hope it is, or will be true.

After the acquisition of Louisiana, Mr. [Thomas] Jefferson often re-

marked, That Florida & Cuba formed the MOUTH of the Mississippi,—
that they were the SITES of FORTS, for commanding the navigation of
that river,—& that no foreign power should be allowed to possess those
important positions, other than Spain,—which was not to be feared;—
& that at no distant period they would belong to the United States.

How much more momentous, are those modern Pillars of Hercules
now, to this country, since the addition of Florida & Texas—New Mexico & California, & the establishment of lines of intercommunication, between the ports of the United States, on the Atlantic & those of the
Pacific, by the isthmus of Panama & Lake Nicaragua.

Florida we have, & Cuba must & will be a portion of these United
States, either by *purchase*, or *conquest*, & the sooner it can be obtained
by *purchase* the better. It is of more value than all the other West India
islands, as it is equal to them in size; & in fertility, extent of cultivable
area & variety of the most valuable products of the vegetable realm,
there is not, a like extent of territory, on the globe, comparable to that
island. Its acquisition would render us INDEPENDENT of all other nations,
for sugar & coffee, & all the other most precious products of the tropics.

But besides all those advantages, its possession would do more to remove the *slaves* from most, if not ultimately the whole of the states,
where that population exists, than all the possible measures, which it is
in the power of the National or State Governments to adopt, for the
accomplishment of that object; for as the Slave-Trade, now clandestinely
carried on, between Cuba & Africa, would cease, the moment that island
became one of the States of this Union; & as the products of the Southern states, which are most profitably cultivated, viz. Cotton & Sugar,
can be more advantageously raised in Cuba, there will be, not only a
great emigration of the *Whites*, from this country, but all the *Blacks* of
Maryland, Virginia, Kentucky, Tennessee, Mississippi, Missouri, & North
Carolina, will rapidly be sent thither,—so great will be the demand for
them & the consequent enhanced value; & the territory of those *Slave*
states will be successively added to the domain of *Free Labor*, & the
dream of universal freedom be realized, in *Continental* North America;
& this too, without an effort for that purpose; but by a process which
God has foreordained;—& we seem to be his "CHOSEN PEOPLE." If, therefore, you can purchase Cuba, it will be the grandest act of any of our
statesmen since, since our existance as a Nation, for it is <the> indispensable to render all the other acquisitions of territory, most available,
& secure. It will be the Corinthian Capital, of our mighty Column of
Empire, & the Diplomatist who rears it, to its lofty position, will merit
a wreath more splendid, than has encircled the brows of any man, who
has held the office of State, for it will enable us to command the entrance
of the Gulf of Mexico, & thus remove all apprehensions of the difficulties

& dangers which might be encountered, if any one of the *large* European powers, was allowed to take poss[ess]ion of that DARDANELLES of the AMERICAN EUXINE,—as the immense Sea, west of Cuba & Yucatan, may be truly called.

The vast amount of American & Foreign Navigation which is destined to pass between the MORO CASTLE & KEY WEST, within the coming half century, will be more than the whole existing tonnage of the United States, &, I have no doubt, more than double,—that is, 6,000,000 tons as the whole trade, between the Western coast of North & South America, Hindooston, China & all the islands of the Pacific & Indian Oceans, with our Atlantic ports & Europe, will take the route through the channel, between Cuba & Florida. Such a commercial Defile has never been known, as that will present before the close of this century.

That is the only *island*, in the Southern cluster, which we require, for the whole of the Mexican & other possessions, to the Isthmus of Darien. will, in less than *twenty* years, be a part of this Union. It is not in the compass of the stren[g]th of nations to prevent it. Our adventurous people will march *over* & *occupy* it, as a portion of the high duties of their grand MISSION, as the *Pioneers* of *Freedom;* & within the same brief period all the British Provinces in North America from the Atlantic to the Pacific, will likewise become additional states, in this extensive Republic. "*Time,* which is the MOTHER of Truth," will, within those comparatively few years, confirm all these assertions, I am fully confident; & ever honored will be the statesman who shall *Pacifically*, thus far enlarge the boundaries of the Union.

No sum can be too great—within 100,000,000 of dollars, which we can afford to pay for Cuba, as the revenue of the ports & the sale of the public domain in the island, will be amply sufficient to meet the interest & pay the debt within twenty five years.

There will be short-sighted men, & a few mazed fanatics who will clamor about negros, but their feeble voices will be lost in the loud shout of the whole Nation, at such a glorious acquisition. It is a Decree of Omnipotence, that the CAUCASIAN PILGRIM RACE shall occupy this entire Continent, in the manner they have thus far advanced, & no earthly power can prevent it. That Race has never been *turned back* in its course, or *halted*. Westward, Southward, & Northward it moves on, & the watchword is *FORWARD*—Forward & with the Bible, the Banner of Civil & Religious Liberty & the Rifle, what have not that adventurous, indomitable, industrious & wonderful Race of men achieved, & what still greater Moral & Physical victories will they not achieve, in the next fifty years?

From these considerations, I am rejoiced to learn, that you are about to give lustre to your name & country, by cooperating in the speedy development of one of the most brilliant acts, which must be performed, in the unprecedented progress of the American people, in their sublime route, for empire, power & grandure. With assurances of the highest respect, I have the honor to be your most obt. st.   H. A. S. Dearborn

ALS. NhHi.
1. Dearborn is probably referring to an item in the September 23 *Boston Daily Advertiser*, indicating that DW had conferred in Washington with the Spanish minister about American filibustering in Cuba.

TO [EDWARD EVERETT]

Washington Sep. 26. '50

My Dear Sir

I think you might do good, if you could see your friend [George] Morey, before his Com[mitt]ee get up their Resolutions & address for the Whig Convention, next week. This Central State Com[mitt]ee for some years past has entertained very narrow notions, & pursued a miserable course. They are one half inclined to abolit[ion]ism, & when you deduct that, & also what belongs to them of other *isms*, there is very little of true, broad, just & liberal Whig principles left in them. The [Boston] Atlas has been their exponent, type, leader or interpreter; & that paper has brought the Whig party in Massachusetts to the very brink of utter separation from all other Whigs. There is no estimating the mischief produced by the Atlas, & the Albany Evening Journal, & by the insane conduct of Northern men in Congress.

Let me give you a specimen. Three days ago, certain members of the H of R came to me, desiring that I would speak to three members, Whigs, from N[orth] C[arolina][1] on the *Tariff* subject. These three members have always voted for protection, & are in all respects good men. But they have become soured. They say, the Northern men, Whigs & all, have done little else for the last nine months than to make assaults on *their* rights, their property, & their feelings; & now, they say, Northern *protection* must look out for itself. These three votes would have decided the fate of Mr [George] Ashmuns motion.[2] I have taken care to use what influence I have with these Gentlemen, & they will [do] right, but perhaps too late.

I am out of all patience with the littleness, the bigotry, the stupidity,— but as I find myself growing angry, I will stop here. Yrs truly

Danl Webster

I wish you would go to Worcester,[3] & make a Speech, & *nationalize* the Whig Party.

ALS. MHi.
1. Probably Joseph P. Caldwell,

Edmund Deberry, and David Outlaw.
2. On September 12 Ashmun had

announced his intention to introduce a tariff bill raising duties on pig, scrap, hammered, and rolled iron and all other manufactured products. Six days later he offered this bill as an amendment to a bill regulating the terms by which vessels from Canada and the British West Indies could be admitted into American ports. Following a brief debate, Ashmun's bid to attach the amendment to the bill was defeated by a 101–85 vote. There was no further action on the tariff in this session. *Congressional Globe*, 31st Cong., 1st sess., pp. 1858, 1949–1951.

3. See below, Everett to DW, October 5, 1850.

TO PETER HARVEY

Washington, Oct. 2, '50

Private

My Dear friend;

I feel well, & in good spirits. My cold is going off, & although it leaves me weak, my eye[s] and head are clear, & that awful depression, which accompanies the disease has disappeared. It will return, occasionally, for a fortnight, perhaps; but not for long visits.

My main relief, however is, that Congress got thro' so well. I can now sleep anights. We have gone thro' the most important crisis, which has occurred since the foundation of the Government; & what ever party may prevail, hereafter, the Union stands firm. Faction, Disunion, & the love of mischief are put under, at least, for the present, & I hope for a long time.

Another effect of recent occurrences is the softening of political animosities. Those who have acted together, in this great crisis, can never again feel sharp asperities towards one another. For instance, it is impossible that I should entertain hostile feelings, or political acrimony towards Gen'l [Lewis] Cass, [Daniel Stevens] Dickinson, [James] Shield[s], [Jesse David] Bright, [Thomas Jefferson] Rusk, &c. &c. in the Senate. We have agreed, that as we are never likely to be called on to act in a matter of so much moment to the Country, again, so we will not mar the joy, or the honor of the past, by any unnecessary quarrels for the future.

Another thing is not altogether improbable. And that is, a remodelling of Parties. If any considerable body of the Whigs of the North should act in the spirit of the majority of the recent Convention in N. York,[1] a new arrangement of Parties is unavoidable. There must be a Union Party, & an opposing Party under some name, I know not what, very likely the Party of Liberty. Many good men among our Whig friends of the North could not make up their minds to renounce their old ideas, & support the great measures. Very well; & if, now that the measures are adopted, & the questions settled, they will support things as they now are, & resist all further attempts at agitation & disturbance, & make no efforts for another change, they ought still to be regarded as Whigs. But those who act otherwise, or shall act otherwise, & continue to talk about Wilmot Provisos, and to resist, or seek to repeal, the Fugitive Slave Bill, or use any other means to disturb the quiet of the Country, will have no right to consider themselves either as Whigs, or as friends to this Administration. Because there is one thing that is fixed, & settled; & that is, that the present Administration will not recognize one set of Whig Principles for the North, & another for the South.

In regard to the great questions of Constitutional Law, & Public Policy, upon which the Whig Party is founded, we must all be of one faith, & that can be regarded as no Whig Party, in N. York, or Mass., which espouses doctrines, & utters sentiments, hostile to the just, & Constitutional rights of the South, and therefore such as Southern Whigs cannot agree to.

You will be glad that I have reached the bottom of the 4th page. Yrs truly   Danl Webster

Copy. MHi, Webster-Hale Papers. A second, somewhat amended, copy is in MHi, Everett Papers. Published in Van Tyne, pp. 432–434, and W & S, 16: 568–569.

1. At their state convention in Syracuse on September 26, New York Whigs attempted but failed to reach agreement on resolutions regarding the recent congressional compromises relating to slavery, the conduct of Senator William H. Seward, and the character of the Fillmore administration. Following the Seward wing's triumph in the platform contest, a group of conservatives, led by convention president Francis Granger, stalked out. See Aida DiPace Donald, "Prelude to Civil War: The Decline of the Whig Party in New York, 1848–1852" (Ph.D. diss., University of Rochester, 1961), pp. 232–246.

FROM EDWARD EVERETT

Cambridge 5 Oct 1850

My dear Sir,

I duly received yours of the 26th of September[1] & I lost no time in going to Boston to call upon Mr [George] Morey. He was too ill to see any one but he sent Mr Ezra Lincoln[2] to Cambridge in the afternoon to confer with me, he being one of the central committee. I had a long & free conversation with him which commenced in my saying that your friends thought that an influence unfriendly to you of which the [Boston] Atlas newspaper was the organ prevailed in the central committee & through that channel gave a character to the policy of the whig party. This he disclaimed in toto & with great apparent sincerity. He said that a majority of the committee were warmly & strongly your political friends, among whom he included himself; that in reference to the slavery question it had never been the opinion of the central committee, that it was a safe policy for the whig party to seek to strengthen itself by countenancing the anti-slavery agitation; but on the contrary to avoid it as far as could be done, without losing confidence of the *country whigs,* among whom anti-slavery sentiments were already widely spread & daily spreading. On these principles, at the legislative whig caucus last winter great pains were taken not to have anti-slavery resolutions passed; but to leave that subject with a reference to former resolutions. This course was advocated by [George Stillman] Hillard, by the editor of the Atlas, & by Mr Lincoln himself, but the country whigs, led by Worcester county, said they could not possibly stand their ground without distinct expressions of anti-slavery feeling. With respect to the Atlas Mr Lincoln attributed the hostile indications toward you to some misconceptions of a personal nature during the last Presidential campaign; he said that [William] Schouler had no wish at that time but to keep the Atlas in a position to support the whig nomination whatever it might be; & that his course with regard to your speech of the 7th of March had been mainly stimulated by the attacks upon him in the other papers which imputing to him a greater degree of dissent than he had at first indicated, abused him into a warmth of opposition he would not otherwise have made. He thought there was nothing on the part of the Atlas which would not yield to conciliatory sentiments on the part of your friends. With respect to the arrangements for the Worcester convention,[3] the address had been prepared by Mr [Alexander Hamilton] Bullock,[4] a warm friend of yours, & it was intended to give the greatest possible prominence to the points on which all whigs agree, and to leave those on which they now differ, as much as possible in the shade. The Central committee would willingly have introduced a highly complimentary allusion to your name; but they thought that this would be sure to draw forth some opposition from those who dissented from portions of your speech of the 7th of March, or at any rate would lead to the introduction of some similar notice of the course pursued by Senators [John] Davis & [Robert Charles] Winthrop, which would impair the value of any specific compliment to you. In a word, they considered the juncture of affairs as extremely critical, & that the only safe course was that which was most likely to prevail without discussion.

Such was the substance of Mr Lincoln's remarks which, both at that time, & in a subsequent interview he earnestly begged me to communicate to you, in the hope that your mind would be relieved from any uneasy feelings you may have entertained arising from a supposed unfriendliness on the part of the central committee. Since the late tidings from New York[5] (he thinks) the course pursued at Worcester must appear still more conclusively the true course.

I detail these observations of Mr Lincoln precisely as he made them.

A part of them refer to points of which I have no knowledge. The editor of the Atlas is unknown to me by sight. I could not myself go to Worcester. On the arrival of Dr Holland[6] from London, five weeks ago, he made an appointment with Dr [John Collins] Warren to hold a consultation on the state of my health on Tuesday Oct. 1. He made his arrangements to arrive in Boston, on his return from the great lakes, sometime in the course of Monday Sept 30th, & as he sailed for England on Wednesday, Tuesday (the day of the Worcester convention) was the only day on which the consultation could take place, & I passed the whole morning with them. They give me a good deal of encouragement as to the possibility of prolonging life, with a reasonable enjoyment of health; & I hope by prudence & care to be able eventually to resume my former activity.

The Trustees of the agricultural Society have shewn their want of discernment, in the course of the past Summer, by electing me of their board, & they are to dine with me on Saturday the 12th. I need not tell you how much it would gratify the other members of the Board, & me in particular if you would give us your company that day, at dinner.

With kindest regards to Mrs Webster, in which my wife & daughter unite with me. I remain, as ever, Sincerely yours,

P.S. Young Lafayette,[7] who has been staying with me this week, brought me a long and very interesting letter from his brother-in-law [Gustave Auguste de la Bonnière] de Beaumont,[8] who was, you know, high in the confidence of Gen. [Louis Eugène] Cavaignac's[9] administration. The letter is in French very illegibly written. As soon as I can get time to translate it, I will send it to you.

LC. MHi.

1. See above, p. 154.

2. A friend and associate of *Boston Atlas* editor William Schouler, Lincoln (1819–1863) was also secretary of the Whig State Central Committee and a member of the General Court.

3. Massachusetts Whigs met in Worcester on October 1 to choose the party's candidates for governor and lieutenant governor and to hammer out a manifesto for the fall elections, emphasizing traditional Whig economic themes and affirming the party's national character. See *Boston Daily Advertiser*, October 2 and 3, 1850; *Boston Semi-Weekly Atlas*, October 5, 1850.

4. Bullock (1816–1882; Amherst 1836), a Whig politician and legislator, was at this time editing the Worcester *Aegis*.

5. See above, DW to Peter Harvey, October 2, 1850, n. 1.

6. Sir Henry Holland (1788–1873; M. D. Edinburgh 1811), personal physician to Queen Victoria and Prince Albert. Holland and Everett had become friendly during the latter's tenure as minister to England in the Tyler administration.

7. François-Edmond Motier Lafayette (1818–1890), grandson of the Marquis de Lafayette, active for many years in French politics, was then serving in the national assembly.

8. Beaumont (1802–1866) was a lifelong friend, political associate,

and literary executor of Alexis de Tocqueville. In 1836 he married his cousin Clémentine de Lafayette, François-Edmond's sister.

9. Cavaignac (1802–1857) was a French soldier and politician. Following the revolution of 1848, he became minister of war in the provisional government, forced the government's resignation, and assumed power. In December 1848 Cavaignac stood for the presidency in national elections but was defeated by Louis Napoleon.

TO EDWARD EVERETT

Tuesday, Oct. 8. 11 o'clock [1850]

My Dear Sir

You are a man most patient of labor, or you would not have taken the trouble to recite at so much length, a conversation of Mr Ezra Lincoln jr.[1] It may be true, that a majority of the State Com[mitt]ee is friendly to me; but that majority does not include Mr Lincoln, or Mr [George] Morey, or Mr [John] Gardiner.[2] I wd. not wish either of these Gentlemen to suppose that I am misinformed, as to their real feelings. The proofs are relevant. My mind is "at ease"; but it is at ease, under the opposition of these persons, as I know it has been, & as I suppose it will continue to be. The proceedings at Worcester[3] could have been worse than they were, if these Gentlemen could have had their way. But eno. of this for the present. We must have a long talk.

I must go to Marshfield tomorrow, and unless Mrs W. has some reason for coming up herself, I very much fear I cannot return so as to have the pleasure of dining with you on Saturday. Yrs always truly

Danl Webster

ALS. MHi.

1. See above, Everett to DW, October 5, 1850.

2. Gardner, from Dedham, was treasurer of the Hamilton Woolen Company of Boston.

3. See above, Everett to DW, October 5, 1850, n. 3.

TO MILLARD FILLMORE

Marshfield Oct. 14. 1850
Monday Morning

My Dear Sir

Leaving Washington Friday, the fourth, I came that day to Phila-[delphi]a, & the next to N.Y; & staying over Sunday in that City, reached Boston, Monday Eve', the seventh, feeling tolerably well. Tuesday, the eighth, I was to have gone into State Street, to meet the People, but did not find myself well enough; the next day, Wednesday I came down to my house, a good deal sick, & have hardly been out doors from that day to this. My catarrh has held on, uncommonly, & for three or four days last week I was quite ill with it, so much so, that I called in a Physician Very sensibly, he recommended nothing but rest, patience, & herb teas. It is usual enough for the disease, in its last stages, to assume the form of a kind of Asthmatic cough. This I have had, & hope I am now nearly over it. Today, the weather is cold, the skies bright, & every thing out doors looks well. I hope to go over the farm.

Tomorrow the Turkish minister,[1] & suite are to be here, & I have asked some friends to meet them. It is difficult entertaining a guest, with whom one cannot exchange a word, & whose habits & wants are so unknown. We shall take care to keep all swine's flesh out of his sight, give him beef, poultry, & rice, & let him get on, as well as he can, having always coffee in plenty.

Of political occurrences, & the political state of things, in N. York & further South, your information is, of course, fuller & fresher than mine. In New England, affairs, & opinions, stand thus.

All true Whigs are not only satisfied, but gratified, with every thing done by you, since the commencement of your administration. Men of property, & business, feel a degree of confidence & security, which it is certain they did not feel under the late administration. Indeed I am at a loss to account for that want of confidence, which appears to have prevailed. A Gentleman of discernment said to me in Boston, that within a week after you had taken the chair, men met together, & without saying a word, sufficiently manifested to one another, that in their judgments, a highly important & conservative change had taken place.

The respectable portion of the Democratic Party incline to treat the administration with respect.

The Abolitionists, & the *quasi* Abolitionists are furious. Their only topic at present, is the Fugitive Slave law; & their conduct in this respect is wicked & abominable in the extreme. Their presses only recommend resistance, by force, & to the death, in case of any arrest. But no case of arrest has happened, & few, I think, if any, are likely to happen. But still, the noise & clamor are most violent. The Boston Atlas, which has been heretofore, in some manner, the leading Whig organ of the State, behaves but little better than the avowed abolition presses. It follows close in the track of the Albany Evening Journal. A considerable number of the Whig merchants of the City have discontinued it.

It is unfortunate, that the two leading officers in the Custom House, the Collector & the Naval officer, are not friendly. Greeley [Philip Greely], the Collector, is at best, indifferent, & I think him positively, tho secretly, inimical. Charles Hudson, the Naval Officer, is less reserved. I do not know that he speaks disrespectfully, of you, & I dare say is ready to assure you of his entire regard. I am honored by being the main object of his obloquy & abuse. "Daniel Webster," he said, not long ago, "is a nuisance to the Whig Party, & ought to be thrown over board." I believe this was said before I left the Senate, & the great cause of his indignation, was, that by [the] Speech of the 7th of March I had broken up the Whig Party. In his idea, the Whig Party ought to be one half abolition. He must be looked after. The Whig Party of Massachusetts is at this moment sorely afflicted by *three* priests, yea *four*, who embraced political life, at first as Whigs, & have gradually run, or are now running into extravagant abolitionism; viz Mr [John Gorham] Palfrey, Mr [Orin] Fowler, Mr [Charles Wentworth] Upham, Whig Candidate in the Essex District, & Charles Hudson. The politics of these persons are merely politics of opinion; their controversies, controversies of sentiment; for practical, useful, conservative measures of Government, they care [not]. "Is slavery scriptural, or antiscriptural?["]; "Does the color of the skin affect the rights of the individual enveloped in it"; is the "Wilmot proviso a matter of perpetual & universal obligation, like one of the Commandments." These are the great questions, which the aforesaid imported clergyman study, with intense industry, in order to enable themselves, as members of Congress, to assist in a just performance of the duties enjoined on that body by the 8th. Sect. of the 1st. Article of the Constitution. Yrs always truly   Danl Webster

ALS. NBuHi. Published in part in *PC*, 2: 394–395.

1. Amin Bey, a Turkish naval of-ficer, toured the United States as the representative of the sultan from September 1850 to April 1851.

Fillmore's accession to the Presidency in July only intensified the long-standing rift among New York Whigs. The transfer of patronage from the anticompromise Seward faction to Fillmore's conservative unionists, or "Silver Grays," was not enough to ensure victory in the fall elections. In the letter below the President outlines the strategy to be followed by the conservatives. They had walked out of the party convention at Syracuse on September 27 when a majority of the delegates voted to commend Seward and to reject the compromise. The conservatives, in their own convention, followed Fillmore's advice and nominated the Syracuse ticket, thus presenting a nominal united front to the electorate; but they also endorsed the compromise. The gubernatorial candidate, Washington Hunt, won by the narrow margin of 262 votes, a steep decline from Whig majorities in previous years. The Senate seat, moreover, went to anticompromise Whig Hamilton Fish after a two-month-long deadlock in the state legislature. The President was no longer in control of his party in his own state.

FROM MILLARD FILLMORE

Washington, Oct 17, 1850

My Dear Sir,

Yours of the 14th inst[1] came to hand this morning, and I regret to hear of your continued illness. We miss you much at the council board and I shall be happy to welcome you back as soon as your health will permit.

Today the *"Whigs of the Union"* meet in Convention at Utica, Mr. [Washington] Hunt who was nominated at Syracuse, has placed himself right before our country by a letter to Mr. [Francis] Granger, in which he states that the resolutions rejected by the majority of the Convention which met at Syracuse, had his approbation. Our friends will undoubtedly, pass the rejected resolutions, adopt a strong *"Union Whig address"* and then nominate the same ticket—and adjourn & it will be elected! But whether the Whigs of the Union and the Sectional Whigs will be able to act together during the next winter in our state legislature is somewhat problematical. That will be tested when they come to elect a U.S. Senator in the place of Mr. [Daniel Stevens] Dickinson.

We have succeeded very well in Ohio[2] but Pennsylvania[3] looks bad. I fear from what you say that we are to have trouble in Mass. I perceive that there is much agitation on the fugitive slave law. That many take the ground that it is unconstitutional because it suspends the writ of *Habeas Corpus*, and denies to the fugitive a trial by Jury. The first objection occurred to me on reading the bill, and I referred it to the attorney general [John Jordan Crittenden] whose opinion satisfied me that it did not affect the writ of habeas corpus. Thinking that it might be well to let the public see this opinion I permitted its publication in the [Washington] Republic of this morning.[4] The other objection did not occur to me as a constitutional one and I can not now think there is any weight in it. If the law be unconstitutional on this ground then the original act of '93 was equally so. And the law for surrendering fugitives from *justice* under another clause of the constitution must fall under the same condemnation. And our treaties with foreign nations for the extradition of criminals is also unconstitutional. I hope if you have occasion to speak you may express your views on this subject.

Whether the law was *expedient* is a very different question. But that, according to Whig doctrine was a question for Congress as the law making power, and not of the President for his veto. But I can not say more. The mail is closing.

I should like to have the chargéship at Brussells, the consulate at Paris and the judgeships in California settled with as much dispatch as possible.

The Dist. Atty. of S. C.[5] has resigned & I offerred the place to Pettigru

[James Louis Petigru], who declined it & recommended Bryant [George S. Bryan].[6] It is not yet determined.[7] I think we should interpose our good offices to save the Rep. of St. Domingo from the ferocity of Soloque.[8] But adieu. Yours Truly   Millard Fillmore

Have not time to read over.

ALS. InHi.

1. See above, DW to Fillmore, October 14, 1850.

2. In reality, aside from the reelection of one procompromise congressman from the southern part of the state, the fall elections in Ohio were a major setback for Whigs supporting the administration. Democrats captured the governorship for the first time in eight years, and the legislature, controlled by a coalition of Democrats and Free Soilers, soon thereafter elected a strong anticompromise man, Benjamin Wade, to the Senate seat vacated by Thomas Ewing.

3. Divided on the compromise issue, the Pennsylvania Whigs fared poorly in the elections of 1850 for governor, Congress, and state legislature.

4. Crittenden's opinion, dated September 18, held that nothing in the Fugitive Slave Act suspended "the privilege of the writ of habeas corpus, or is in any manner in conflict with the Constitution." Benjamin F. Hall, ed., *Official Opinions of the Attorneys General of the United States, 1791–1948* (Washington, D.C., 1852–1949); 5: 258.

5. Edward McCrady (1803–1892; Yale 1820), who had held the post since 1839, resigned to play an active role in South Carolina unionist politics.

6. Bryan (1809–1895), a Charleston lawyer, was, like Petigru, an ardent unionist.

7. For background on Fillmore's offer, Petigru's reluctance to accept, and his decision finally to accede to the appointment, see James P. Carson, *Life, Letters and Speeches of James Louis Petigru* (Washington, 1920), pp. 281–282.

8. Faustin Soulouque (1785–1867), emperor of Haiti, was thwarted in his bid for power in Santo Domingo by the joint efforts of England, France, and the United States. See *Diplomatic Papers*, 2.

FROM MILLARD FILLMORE

Washington, Oct. 23. 1850

My Dear Sir,

Your letter of the 19th[1] came to hand yesterday; and I am much gratified to hear of your improved health.

I have received a copy of Judge [Levi] Woodbury's charge[2] on the Fugitive Slave law, and the Report of Judge [Robert Cooper] Grier's opinion in a case before him,[3] all manfully sustaining the constitutionality of the law, and manifesting a determined resolution to carry it out. I have also just received a joint letter from Judge Grier and Judge Kane [John Kintzing Kane],[4] stating that a case has occurred before a commission in Pa. where the execution of a warrant under that act was "forcibly and successfully resisted; the posse summoned to aid the officer having refused to act," and "inquiring whether upon the recurrence of an obstruction to his Process he will be entitled to call for the aid of such troops of the U.S. as may be accessible."

This you perceive presents a very grave and delicate question. I have not yet had time to look into it and regret much that so many of my cabinet are absent, and especially yourself and the attorney general [John Jordan Crittenden]. These judges ask for a general order authorizing the employment of the troops in such an emergency; and I am disposed to exert whatever power I possess under the constitution and laws, in enforcing their observance. I have sworn to support the constitution. I know no higher law that <comes in> conflicts with it; and that constitution says, "the President shall take care that the laws be faithfuly executed." I mean at every sacrifice and at every hazard to perform my duty. The Union must and shall be preserved, and this can only be done, by a faithful and impartial administration of the laws. I can not doubt that in these sentiments you are with me. And if you have occasion to speak I hope you will give no encouragement, even by implication, to any resistance to the law.[5] Nullification can not and will not be tolerated.

It seems to me, with all due deference, to your superior wisdom that the true grounds for our friends to take is this; that the law, having been passed, must be executed. That so far as it provides for the surrender of fugitives from labor it is according to the requirements of the constitution and should be sustained against all attempts to its repeal, but if there be any provision in it endangering the liberty of those who are free, it should be so modified as to secure the free blacks from such an abuse of the object of the law, and that done, we at the North have no just cause of complaint.

We must abide by the Constitution. If overthrown, we can never hope for a better. God knows that I detest slavery, but it is an existing evil, for which we are not responsible, and we must endure it, and give it such protection, as is guaranteed by the constitution, till we can get rid of it without destroying the last hope of free government in the world. But pardon me for saying so much. I thought possibly you might desire to know my sentiments, and I can assure you, I am very anxious to know yours, as to the answer to be given to the Judges' letter. I will, finally, send a copy of it.

I will add something in another letter. With the highest consideration & Respect, I am in great haste Truly yours   Millard Fillmore

ALS. NhHi. Published in *W & S*, 16: 571–572.

1. DW to Fillmore, October 19/20

1850, mDW 31417.

2. Woodbury's charge has not been found, but its main thrust—affirma-

tion of the Fugitive Slave Law's constitutionality—was reiterated in a public letter to B. F. Ayer et al., November 15, 1850, published widely in New England newspapers and reprinted in Charles L. Woodbury, comp., *Writings of Levi Woodbury* (3 vols.; Boston, 1852), 1: 534–535. At this time Woodbury was presiding over the United States Circuit Court in Boston.

3. *Oliver* v. *Kauffman et al.*, 18 Federal Cases, 657, 658. Following Justice John McLean's precedent in *Jones* v. *Van Zandt*, 5 Howard 215 (1847), Grier had recently charged a jury to decide strictly on the letter of the Fugitive Slave Law a suit by a Maryland slaveowner against the man who had abetted the flight of twelve runaways. The jury failed to reach a clear verdict in the case, and it was reargued and decided in October 1852. See Paul Finkelman, *An Imperfect Union: Slavery, Federalism, and Comity* (Chapel Hill, N.C., 1981), pp. 251–255, and Robert M. Cover, *Justice Accused: Antislavery and the Judicial Process* (New Haven, 1975), p. 173.

4. Not found.

5. In his October 19 letter, cited above, which the President undoubtedly had at hand, DW had suggested that, health permitting, he would make a public defense of the Fugitive Slave Law's constitutionality.

TO MILLARD FILLMORE, WITH ENCLOSURE

Franklin N.H. Oct. 24. '50

My Dear Sir

I have been here five days, with evident improvement; but am concerned to say, I am not yet strong, nor has my cough entirely ceased. In dry weather I feel nothing of it, but it returns with rain & damp. I shall leave & go straight to Washington, as soon as I feel any way able.

The politics of Massachusetts are in a state of utter confusion. Many Whigs are *afraid* to act a manly part, lest they should lose the State Govt. They act a most mean part, in their courtship of abolitionism.

You see from Mr [Charles Wainwright] March's letter,[1] how the Whig State Com[mitt]ee is acting. With this Com[mitt]ee the [Boston] Atlas most vigorously cooperates, tho' it endeavors to save appearances; & so do Greeley [Philip Greely] & Charles Hudson,[2] especially the latter. Seven unfrocked Unitarian Priests are now candidates for public office— viz, members of Congress; beside a host of others, who offer for the Legislature. These are all free soil, or abolition men.

The Postmaster at Lowell[3] is represented to be a brawling abolitionist,—preaching, daily, the duty of resistance to the fugitive slave law. I shall inquire into this, when I return to Boston.

I have been able to make a draft of a reply to Mr [Johann Georg von] Hulseman[n],[4] which I hope you will approve. I have also made some notes, for that part of your annual message which may relate to foreign affairs. Yours always truly, whether sick or well,   Danl Webster

ALS. NBuHi. Published in Van Tyne, p. 437.

1. See enclosure.

2. Active supporters of Zachary Taylor in 1848 and beneficiaries of Taylor's patronage, Greely and Hudson were careful to avoid direct public attacks on the new administration. Despite private assurances of loyalty to Fillmore and Webster, both men acted behind the scenes against the administration on various matters, to DW's great aggravation. See above, DW to Millard Fillmore, October 14,

1850; Daniel Fletcher Webster to DW, October 26, 1850, mDW 31541; and below, DW to Millard Fillmore, November 15, 1850, and April 18, 1851, Charles Wainwright March to DW, April 8, 1852, and DW to Thomas Corwin, May 15, 1852.

3. Alfred Gilman.

4. Hülsemann, Austrian chargé d'affaires *ad interim*, was an antagonist in a controversy regarding American support for the Hungarian leader Louis Kossuth. See *Diplomatic Papers*, 2.

ENCLOSURE: FROM CHARLES WAINWRIGHT MARCH

Boston Oct. 22 [1850]

Dear Sir

The Whigs of Roxbury had a glorious caucus last night.[1] They poured in from West Roxbury and the suburbs generally in large numbers.

Eighteen delegates were chosen to the Congressional Convention, all Anti-[Horace] Mann men, and decided friends of yours.[2] Dorchester, Brookline, Quincy & other chief towns in the District have chosen delegates of a like disposition. But I learn that in the smaller towns, the enemy is sowing tares. Geo[rge] Morey, I am informed, has procured hostile delegates from Weymouth, by a packed caucus, and the State Committee are laboring in other towns, for Mann. The general opinion however is, that he will fail of the nomination.

The published correspondence between Mr. [Isaac] Hill[3] and yourself is most warmly received. The newspapers make a proper preface to it.

Mr. [Caleb] Cushing will hand you this. I think you will find his views on national policy accord with your own.

I go to New York this evening, to return the first of the week. Most respy & Truly Yrs   Chs. W. March

ALS. NBuHi.

1. For an account of the meeting, which was part of the attempt by conservative Whigs to deny reelection to the Free Soil congressman Horace Mann, see *Boston Semi-Weekly Atlas*, October 23, 1850.

2. Denied renomination at the Whig convention, Mann ran successfully as a Free Soil candidate in the November elections. Jonathan Mes-

serli, *Horace Mann: A Biography* (New York, 1972), pp. 519–521; *Boston Daily Advertiser*, October 31 and November 26, 1850.

3. See above, pp. 000–000, Isaac Hill to DW, April 17, 1850, and pp. 000–000, DW to Hill, April 20, 1850, both of which were published in the *Boston Daily Advertiser*, October 22, 1850.

TO MILLARD FILLMORE

Franklin, N. H. Oct. 25. 50

My Dear Sir:

I have recd a letter from the District Atty of U. S. for Mississippi,[1] giving an account of Governor [John Anthony] Quitmans call of the Legislature, with conjectures upon the probable course of events, in that State.

I have also recd. a letter from the District Atty in Alabama,[2] respecting possible contingencies in that quarter. Neither is very important, perhaps, but it has occurred to me that I might properly answer one of these letters, & in that answer take occasion to set forth, fully & explicitly, the duty of the Executive Government of the United States, under the Constitution & the Laws, in case of collision between the authority of a State, & that of the United States.[3] I think a paper may be drawn, quite applicable to the present state of things, & be a good *Union* paper, to send to Congress with your Annual Message. I am about it, this morning, here, on the banks of the Merrimac, with the tombs of my father & mother, & my brothers & sisters, all before me. There are cheerful recollections of the past; but they are somewhat softened, & saddened by the reflections, that I am the last of a large family. Yrs truly always   Danl Webster.

ALS. NBuHi.

1. Horatio J. Harris to DW, September 27, 1850, DNA, RG 59 (Misc. Letters). Citing the "momentous consequences" that could flow from the special session of the Mississippi legislature scheduled for November 18, Harris enclosed a copy of the governor's proclamation, which condemned the recent compromise measures in Congress and suggested that the legislature should take steps enabling Mississippi to "assert her sovereignty."

2. Peter Hamilton to DW, October 2, 1850, DNA, RG 59 (Misc. Letters). Hamilton warned of a possible invasion of Cuba from Mobile and urged the dispatch of federal vessels to the Alabama coast.

3. Webster's draft circular (no date, mDW 31580), emphasizing the need for obedience to federal laws, the President's responsibility and authority to uphold the Constitution, and the illegitimacy of nullification and secession, was neither printed nor circulated in 1850. According to a note in Fletcher Webster's hand, evidently intended for publication with the circular in *PC* (though not printed there), Webster's draft was shown to members of the cabinet, who discouraged publication. The circular was later printed in *New England Magazine*, 4 (June 1886): 511–515.

THOMAS BUCKMINSTER CURTIS TO DAVID SEARS, WITH ENCLOSURE

Mt Vernon St Oct 26th [1850]

Private

My dear Sir

You are aware that at the time of the change of the Cabinet great solicitude was felt that Mr Webster should accept the office to which he was invited by Presdt Fillmore, in fact he was urged by leading men of both parties to make the personal sacrifice. He was strenuously urged by our most worthy men here & was assured that his expences should be made up in case he should become Secy of State as it was apparent that he could not live the year round at Washington for six thousand dolls even if there was no obligation to entertain the distinguished strangers who are brought into connexion with the Government. With such an understanding Mr Webster took office; giving up some twenty important cases in the Sup[rem]e Court & other business and gave himself wholly to the conservation of the internal and external peace of the Country.

The papers herewith will shew what has been done towards making up the deficiency alluded to. Faithfully & with Respect Your Obd St

Tho. B. Curtis

ALS. MHi. Sears (1787–1871; Harvard 1807) was a prominent merchant, land speculator, and social leader in Boston and a longtime friend and financial backer of Webster.

ENCLOSURE: LIST OF SUBSCRIBERS TO A WEBSTER FUND

[October 1850]

It is evident to the friends of Mr Webster that the salary of the Secretary of State is insufficient for his support. They are desirous of relieving him from the embarrassment which this will occasion and agree to pay for that purpose the sums set against their respective names.

Thomas H[andasyd] Perkins 1000 $ not exceeding one fourth of the sum annually.

William Appleton	1000	"	do	do		
Nathan Appleton	1000	"	do	do		
Robt. G. Shaw & Sons	1000	"	do	do		
Samuel Appleton	1000	"	do	do		

July 31. 1850.

Thomas B. Wales	500.	on demand		
John A Lowell	500.	"		
John P. Cushing	1000.	"		
Saml Hooper	500.	George W Lyman	500.
C[harles] J. Hendee	500.	Wm Sturgis	500.
Thos. B. Curtis	500.	Ignatius Sargent	500.
Saml Lawrence	500.	Ozias Goodwin	500.
Thos W Ward	500.		8000
Eben Chadwick	500.	In cash—	10.000

F. Skinner & Co	500.	Annually for 4 years—	1250
Jno M Forbes	500.		
J[ames] K[ellogg] Mills & Co.	500.		
Fran[ci]s C Gray	500.		
Enoch Train	500.		
Francis C Lowell	500.		

Copy in David Sears's hand. MHi.

DAVID SEARS TO THOMAS BUCKMINSTER CURTIS

Beacon Street October 27. 1850.

Confidential
My dear Sir,

I last evening received your favor marked *Private*,[1] and I now have the pleasure to send my reply, marked as you see above, *confidential*.

I trust I have been, and am the friend of Mr Webster, <and> I hope still to continue so,—you will therefore please to understand me, that although I at present hesitate to sign <your> the subscription papers, now before me, I do not mean to say that I absolutely decline to do so.

I know nothing of the pledges offered to Mr Webster—or by whom given—I know nothing of the counsel he may have received—I am no party to the course he has pursued—nor have I been consulted in regard to it, nor on any thing <concerning> connected with it, until called upon, in my ignorance, to give pecuniary assistance.

Unity in the party to which Mr Webster claims to belong, and for which he <still> proposes to act, is, at the present juncture, highly important, yet I have reason to believe that some of Mr Webster's friends—injudicious may I call them?—in their zeal to aid the new theories of the last winter and in their opposition to those who differ from them are willing to put every thing at hazard, and risk the loss of the party in their support of the individual—with such I do not sympathise—when <it can be shown to me> I am satisfied that I am in error, I may then be better prepared to act in relation to the matter you have proposed, but until then, I must give my support <exclusively> in preference to the party.

Should this determination ever come to the knowledge of Mr Webster, which it will not, I am sure he would approve of it, and if in connexion with other measures it should contribute in the smallest degree to aid the means now in action for uniting the disaffected, he will thank me for the effort, and rejoice with us at the result. very respectfully—your obedient servant   Dd. Sears

ALS draft. MHi.
    1. See above, Curtis to Sears, October 26, [1850].

FROM MOSES STUART

Andover, 27 Oct. 1850

My dear Sir,

Understanding that you are to be in Boston on the morrow, I venture to address a few lines to you, on a subject of importance & in which I feel a deep interest.

You know all about the *Peace Society*.[1] Their aim, beyond all doubt is benevolent & Christian. But whether they manage all their matters in the best way, may be a question—one which I do not know enough about to satisfy myself. One great question they are anxious to put, & have expressed to me a strong desire that I would ask it. There can be no harm in this, & therefore I have promised to put it. This question is simply: Will it be a practicable thing, to add to all our *Treaties with foreign powers* an article, pledging mutually that the parties will submit all matters in dispute to an *arbitration*,[2] such as the parties may agree upon, instead of resorting to war? Have not the President & Secretary of State a full right to give such instructions to our ambassadors abroad as shall secure, or try to secure, this humane, this Christian, this magnanimous purpose? So it strikes me. I know the Senate can reject the article in question; but I verily believe they will not. To the title, *Defender of the Constitution*, may you not add that of *Pacificator of the Nations*; a title above that of kings or emperors.

I need not add one word to disclose to your mind the nature & importance of such a measure. It is all before you, at the bare mention of it.

If you think well of the thing, & that it is practicable, a petition for such an arrangement, addressed to the President & yourself may be got up with some million of names. But the friends of *peace* do not wish to push the matter, unless you think the way is fairly open. God grant that this laurel may be added to those that already adorn your brow! I say no more, for I can tell you nothing about the matter, which you do not already know. Should you think favourably of such a petition, or of moving without one, (which I think would be still better), please to drop me a note.

As to the TIMES—what next? You have seen what that bitter malignant, C[harles] F[rancis] Adames, has said before the county meeting, in respect to the achievements of Mr [Horace] Mann.[3] In my view, his speech, & many others, & many paragraphs in the news papers, are downright petty treason. They go directly to excite the country *forcibly* to resist the execution of the laws. And then, the injustice & folly of the whole matter! The same *fugitive* law has been in existence more than 60 years, & in a looser & more oppressive form than the present one. Under that, a master was not bound to get a certificate from a Court of

Record, that he had lost a slave, & a description of his person for the purpose of identification. Now he must do this. Of course the man who is carried back, if a freeman, has a right at home to claim his freedom & to sue for it. Where have these vigilant guardians of humanity been, for the last 60 years? No, no! It is all a sham, & got up in the way of revenge for disappointment. The poor persecuted outcast is placed at the real head of the nation. *Hinc illae lacrymae!* It is unpardonable & unendurable. And this younger *cock-a doodle* of the *Presidential* family, does not see why he may not have the place that his father had. That you occupy it—is *treason*, you are a *grand-traitor*. It is well. *Quem Deus vult perdere, prius dementat*—verified & I trust to be *fulfilled*, in the present case. How long the wild hurry of passion & envy & ambition will last I do not venture to say. But unless I am greatly mistaken, it cannot last long. People will return to their sober senses, in due time, & Mass. be herself again.

In the mean time—steady! steady! steady! Straight ahead without winking. They can not hurt you. There never was a time in which you were so deep in the hearts of your country as now. When the standard of rebellion is unfurled, & blood is [preven]ting the execution of the law, blind eyes will be opened, & the violent meet their due reward.

I am sorry that the *fugitive Bill* did not take the shape recommended by the Omnibus Bill. Then resistance would be so unreasonable, as to stand little chance of success. I am sorry such an occasion is in the hands of political desperadoes. But while the law is law, it must stand, & must go straight on. Neither you, nor the President are men to be frightened out of the sense of duty & justice, by Sans Culottes & raging Socialists and Red Caps.

Not a week passes still, without fresh abuse for my Pamphlet.[4] Poor little thing! It has been murdered 500 times—& yet, thank God, it is still alive; at least he is alive, whose aim it was to defend. So I am content; & withal your sincere friend & obedt. Sert.   Moses Stuart.

ALS. DLC.

1. Spearheaded by a Connecticut blacksmith, Elihu Burritt, the League of Universal Brotherhood was then organizing an international campaign to outlaw war.

2. In 1850 a number of congressmen, including New Hampshire's Amos Tuck, introduced memorials urging Congress to secure treaties providing for arbitration of disputes with other nations. See Merle E. Curti, *The American Peace Crusade, 1815–1860* (Durham, N.C., 1929),

p. 194.

3. President of a Free Soil convention held at Dedham on October 16, Adams strongly endorsed Mann's stern opposition to the compromise measures of 1850. See *Boston Semi-Weekly Atlas*, October 30, 1850.

4. See, for example, a sixteen-part series by Rufus Clark that appeared in the *Boston Semi-Weekly Atlas*, July–September 1850, critically appraising Stuart's *Conscience and the Constitution* (Boston, 1850).

FROM MILLARD FILLMORE

Washington, Oct. 28. 1850

My Dear Sir,

I have yours of the 24th[1] from Franklin, N.H. and am greatly gratified to hear of your improved health; and hope soon to learn that your
cough has entirely left you. I infer that you have not received my letters
of the 23d inst.[2] addressed to you at Boston. We have had two Cabinet
meetings, the last this morning, on the authority and duty of the president to use the Military force in aid of the civil officer to execute the
fugitive slave law, and have concluded when, necessary, to do it. We
were somewhat embarrassed by the legislation of Congress on the subject, in 1807,[3] and subsequent acts, which would seem to imply that
this was a power to be conferred by Congress, but after a careful examination of the subject, I came to the conclusion that it was an inherent
Executive power conferred by the constitution, when it made the President commander in chief of the Army and Navy, and required him to take
care that the laws be faithfully executed. In this, however, the whole
cabinet were not agreed, some thin[kin]g that the Marshall might summon <them as cit> the army as citizens and part of the *cometatus*, but
all agreed that the aid should be given, and the only question was when?
We concluded to give it to the Marshall whenever, he was unable to
sustain the laws by the civil authority, and to the special deputies in
the same cases when a judge of the District or Justice of the Sup[reme]
Court, should certify that in his opinion it was necessary. This direction
is given to the commanding officer of the Marines at Philadelphia.

Congress having authorized the Marshall to provide temporary jails
where the Sheriff refuses to admit U.S. prisoners, we did not think it
advisable to grant the use of the Receiving ship at Boston for that purpose. But I mean at all hazards to do my part towards executing this
law. I admit no right of *nullification* North or South. My object however,
has been to avoid the use of military force as far as possible, not doubting
that there is yet patriotism enough left in every State North of Mason's
and Dixon's line to maintain the supremacy of the laws; and being particularly anxious that no state should be disgraced, by being compelled
to resort to the army to support the laws of the Union, if it could be
avoided. I have therefore commenced mildly—authorizing this force only
in the last resort, but if necessary, I shall not hesitate to give greater
power, and finally to bring the whole force of the government to sustain
the law. But the mail is closing and I can not say more.

I have also yours of the 25th inst. and am gratified to hear that you
are preparing an answer to the Dist. Atty. of Missi[ssippi] and to the
Austrian minister.[4]

I can sympathise with you in the melancholy feelings which are inspired by looking upon the graves of your ancestors and kindred, but I hope soon to welcome you back to the busy scenes of active life, where your absence is so much deplored and your counsels so much wanted. I am truly your friend   Millard Fillmore

(Have not time to read over.)

ALS. NhHi. Published in *W & S*, 16: 573–574.

  1. See above.

  2. See above. Second letter not found.

  3. An act of February 28, 1795, authorizing the President to summon the militia in executing the laws was extended on March 3, 1807, to include the call of federal military forces. See 2 U.S. Stats. 443 and *Congressional Globe*, 31st Cong., 1st sess., *Appendix*, p. 1052.

  4. See above, DW to Fillmore, October 25, 1850.

TO MILLARD FILLMORE

Franklin, N. H. Oct. 29. 50

My Dear Sir:

I recd. yesterday your letter of the 23rd inst, accompanied by the communication addressed to you by the Judges of the Eastern District of Pa.;[1] and also your other letter of the same date,[2] on various subjects.

I see, that whether quite reestablished in health or not, I must prepare to go back to my place. It is quite wrong to leave you so much alone, & for so long a time. I shall consider this, therefore, as my last week, for remaining in these parts, & endeavor next week to reach Washington. I have been pressed to attend public meetings at Concord, at Boston, at N.Y. & at Philadelphia;[3] but I have declined them all, partly for reasons connected with the state of my health, & partly from considerations of prudence & propriety. To the Union Meeting, which is to be holden at Castle Garden tomorrow, I have addressed a letter which will show pretty clearly what I think on the subject of the Fugitive Slave <Bill> Law.[4]

The communication from the Judges in Pa. is highly important, & demands full consideration. No doubt, the law is to be executed; no doubt, it is your duty to call out the troops of the U. States to ensure that execution, if necessary.

The only questions are, first as to the course of proceeding, & second, whether any military order should be issued before a case occurs of *actual* forcible resistance.

On these questions, I wish to take one day to think, & to examine the statutes; & I will write you by next mail communicating the results of my thoughts & inquiries. I only now repeat that the Law must be executed, & on this point my opinions entirely concur with yours. There must be no flinching, nor doubt, nor hesitation. The thing should be done as mildly & quietly as possible; but it must be done.

I comply, readily & cheerfully, with your suggestion as to what shall be said to Mr [James Brown] Clay; & will see that a proper despatch, drawn up in that sense, goes to him immediately.[5]

I know not what to do, or say, about California Judges.[6] Competent men seem unwilling to go, & take the offices. I must make one more trial, when I reach Boston.

A answer to [Johann Georg von] Hülseman[n],[7] long enough, at least, whatever be its other qualities, is blocked out; & I am now preparing a answer, or sort of Circular, to the District attornies, such as I intimated to you some days ago I thought might be useful.[8] Yrs truly always

Danl Webster

ALS. NBuHi.

1. See above; the enclosed letter addressed to Fillmore by Judges Robert Cooper Grier and John Kintzing Kane has not been found.

2. Not found.

3. These were pro-Union meetings organized and attended largely by conservative merchants, at which the Compromise of 1850 was strongly endorsed as the final settlement of the slavery issue.

4. DW to F. S. Lathrop et al., October 28, 1850, widely published in the press and reprinted in W & S, 12: 251–253. The letter praised the Castle Garden meeting as certain to "give countenance and courage to the faithful friends of the Union throughout the land." Referring to the controversial Fugitive Slave Law, DW observed that he had preferred a different bill but believed the current law had been properly passed, that it was constitutional, and that resistance to it was both morally wrong and dangerous to the "foundation of all government."

5. James Brown Clay (1817–1864), son of Henry Clay, had recently arrived in Geneva from Lisbon, where he had been serving as chargé d'affaires since April 1849, engaged in negotiating American claims against the Portuguese government. Webster and President Fillmore offered Clay the choice of returning to Lisbon to conclude the negotiations, or to return home. DW's dispatch to this effect, however, failed to reach Clay in Europe, and upon his arrival in Washington late in 1850, Clay tendered his resignation as chargé. See DW to Clay, August 23 and November 5, 1850, mDW 30938, 31604, Clay to DW, September 21 and December 9, 1850, mDW 31427, 31806, and DW to Millard Fillmore, October 19, 1850, mDW 31417.

6. His first choice for United States district judge for southern California, John Plummer Healy, having declined, DW was currently trying to persuade Charles B. Goodrich of Boston to accept the post. See DW to John Plummer Healy, September 28, 1850, mDW 31253, Healy to DW, October 23, 1850, mDW 31451, and DW to Millard Fillmore, October 24, 1850, mDW 31452.

7. See above, DW to Fillmore, October 24, 1850, n. 4, and Diplomatic Papers, 2.

8. See above, DW to Fillmore, October 25, 1850, n. 3.

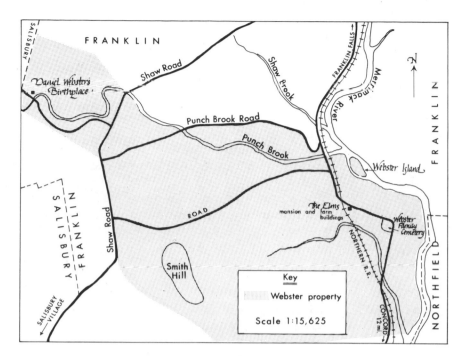

The Elms: Webster's Franklin County, New Hampshire, Farm

MEMORANDA FOR JOHN TAYLOR

Nov. 3. 1850

Things in & abt. the House—

Apples—send two barrels to Mr [Richard Milford] Blatchford—

     "   one to S[amuel] A[ppleton] Appleton[1]—Boston

     "   one in the Cellar, for myself

3 Hams to be put into ashes, nailed up, & placed in the T. chamber—

2 Dun fish—to be left in the same room—

Bottles of spirits & wine to be counted, & locked up in the wine closet —with tea, sugar, candles, coffee, &c. & 1 pr pistols, fishing rod, spy glass, &c.

    Farming———for 1851

1. continue the plowing on the Hill—

    Have the peice measured, immediately, & the acct. sent to me. I will, in season, direct about the manure, & the crops to be put in. Probably potatos, turnips, & beets——& a small patch of beans, & another of peas.

2. Break up in the Spring 12 acres, at the lower part of the field—Plant

10 acres with corn—land well manured; 2 acres, on the highest part with Potatos, without manure.

3. Sow oats & grass seed on the followings peices, viz

In the 15 acre lot, 4 1/2 acres—

Where the corn is now standing—6 3/4 acres

Where the potatos were, this year, in 2 peices, 4 acres   in all 15 1/4 acres—

4. one rye field, on the hill, already sown, say 8 1/2 acres

5. Take care of my mother's garden, & the land adjoining, & put it in good order. Do not plough up her garden— Plant the rest of the land with pumpkins—

6. Plough the Orchard, & sow it with oats—Take away the dead & useless trees, & set out a few nice young ones. In the Spring, *be sure to dig* round all the apple trees in the South pasture: —

Fill my shed—as far as necessary—with good wood—

Make 6 or 8 gates—3 of them like Mr [Horace] Noyes[2]—repair my boat, make oars &c.—

Let Charles keep over 4 or 5—or 6 turkies —

Take 2. for Thanksgiving & Christmas—get the rest fat, & send them to Revere House—Raise 100 chickens next year

Cattle

1. *My* six yr old steers to stand in the upper tie-up. To be kept very well, & used but little; & the Durgin cow—		7–<6>
2. The old oxen, the starred Steers, & the big three year old, to stand in the middle stall—		5–
3. Lower stall—9 <10> cows & the Bull, in his pen, as Mr [Samuel] George[3] was directed		9– 1
4. 11. Yearlings, steers & heifers—		11
5. 19 Calves———		19
		52.00

Steer Barn —

3 yr old Steers —	Bugles	2
	Mitchell steers	2
	Black steers	2
	Yellow steers	2
	Red steers	2
		10.00

2 yr olds. —	1 pr raised at home —	2.
	1 pr from Eben Webster[4] —	2.
	1 Stag	1
	3 bot of Mr Hastings[5]	3
		8.

Buy one pr two year olds —   2
                                                         _____
                                                          10. = 20

Sell the 6. remaining 3 yr old steers to Mr [Austin Franklin] Pike —
1 fatting ox—4 yr old
16. Sheep—on the farm
3 horses—3 Swine—2 fatting—6. pigs—young—2 older—
abt. 25 Turkies—

    Believed to be correct, & agreed to Nov. 2. 1850—
                        Danl Webster
                        John Taylor

ADS. Mrs. John W. Laverack, Center Sandwich, New Hampshire. A nearly identical copy, in John Taylor's hand, is in NhHi (mDW 31598). Published in part in Van Tyne, pp. 651–652.

1. Appleton (1811–1861), DW's son-in-law, was a business partner of James W. Paige and his uncle, Nathan Appleton.

2. DW's neighbor in Franklin, New Hampshire.

3. George was a well-known Franklin carpenter with whom DW had frequent dealings.

4. Possibly Ebenezer Webster (1787–1861), a Boscawen merchant, whose late wife, Sarah (1784–1811), was his cousin and DW's sister.

5. Hastings has not been identified.

Threatened and actual resistance to the new Fugitive Slave Law was not restricted to Pennsylvania. In Boston a "vigilance" committee led by Theodore Parker sprang to the aid of a fugitive couple, William and Ellen Craft, whose Macon, Georgia, master, Robert Collins, sought to reclaim them. Collins's two agents were harassed in Boston and briefly clapped in jail, until they left the city empty-handed. On November 7, prior to the Crafts' leavetaking for England to circumvent the law, they were married, in a highly charged ceremony conducted by Reverend Parker. See John Weiss, ed., Life and Correspondence of Theodore Parker *(New York, 1864), 2: 94–102, and below, pp. 189–190, Theodore Parker to DW, December 12, 1850.*

TO MILLARD FILLMORE

                    Boston, Nov. 5. 1850
                    Tuesday Morng
My Dear Sir,
    I left N. Hampshire yesterday, having become free of disease, & well, except so far as this protracted catarrh [h]as reduced me. I was quite

aware how inconvenient my long absence is, to you, & to the Govt; & sometimes feel, that as this illness is of annual recurrence I ought to regard it as unfitting me for an office, the duties of which require constant attention. I must now go to Marshfield, for a few days. When there a fortnight ago, I was hardly able to go out doors, & could do nothing about arranging my little affairs.

On public subjects, things are here becoming quiet. The excitement caused by the Fugitive Slave Bill is fast subsiding, & it is thought that there is now no probability of any resistance, if a fugitive should be arrested. Hundreds of young men have tendered their services to the Marshall,[1] at a moments warning. There is an evident, & a vast change of public opinion in this quarter, since the adjournment of Congress. I see the ordering of troops into this quarter, which is very well, but I have no apprehension they will [be] needed. As our people are naturally jealous of the exercise of military power, I incline to think it wise to say very little about it, before hand. Nobody doubts, that your resolution is taken, & fixed, to see the laws duly executed. The agitators themselves appear to understand that.

Warrants are out, signed by Judge [Levi] Woodbury & Judge [Peleg] Sprague;[2] but the Fugitives keep concealed. The question arises, whether, in the service of those warrants, outer doors may be broken & on this question the Marshall has requested the deliberate opinion of eminent Counsel. It is supposed that Sir Francis Bendell's case[3] is a precedent, in favor of the affirmative of the proposition.

There is much talk of a Union meeting, & a great desire to hold one. Very many persons have spoken to me on the subject, since my arrival yesterday. My opinion is, that such a meeting should be held, but that I should not attend it. My opinions are all known, & they may, perhaps, be topics of comment, before the meeting. Besides, it is, I think, expedient to bring out new men, Mr [Francis Calley] Gray, Mr B[enjamin] R[obbins] Curtis, &c.&c. & also to hear Mr [Rufus] Choates voice, once more. To avoid misconstruction, I think the meeting will not be holden till after our election, on Monday next.[4]

I look upon the result of our election, as far as respects Govr, as very doubt[ful].[5] There are many Whigs who will not vote for Mr [George Nixon] Briggs. They think him at least half an abolitionist. Yrs always truly   Danl Webster

ALS. NBuHi. Published in part in *PC*, 2: 400–401.

1. Charles Devens, United States marshall for Boston.

2. Warrants for the arrest of William and Ellen Craft were issued on

October 25, 1850. *Boston Daily Advertiser*, October 26, 1850.

3. The reference is obscure.

4. A mass meeting was being planned for Boston's Faneuil Hall on November 26, 1850. The participants

—including leaders of Boston's business community—unanimously passed resolutions calling for adherence to the Constitution and the recent congressional compromises on slavery. Mention of Webster in a speech defending the constitutionality of the Fugitive Slave Law, according to the *Daily Advertiser*, was "greeted with loud and long continued cheering." See issues of November 27 and 28, 1850, and below, DW to Peter Harvey, November 29, 1850.

5. Although far outdistancing his main opponent, Democrat George Boutwell, 56,831 to 35,871, Briggs failed to win the necessary majority. Following six weeks of complicated bargaining, a Free Soil–Democratic coalition in the legislature elected Boutwell to the governorship. *Boston Semi-Weekly Atlas*, November 16, 1850; David Donald, *Charles Sumner and the Coming of the Civil War* (New York, 1960), p. 189; and Frederick J. Blue, *The Free Soilers: Third Party Politics, 1848–1854* (Urbana, Ill., 1973), pp. 215–219.

TO ANTHONY COLBY

Marshfield, November 11, 1850

Dear Sir

I have received your letter of the 7th of this month.[1]

Experience has long since taught me how useless it is to attempt to stop the allegations of political adversaries by denials of their statements.

For your sake, however, I will say, that my public speeches show my opinion to have been decidedly in favor of a proper, efficient, and well-guarded law, for the recovery of fugitive slaves; that while I was in the Senate, I proposed a bill,[2] as is well known, with provisions different from those contained in the present law; that I was not a member of that body, when the present law passed; and that, if I had been, I should have moved, as a substitute for it, the bill proposed by myself.

I feel bound to add that, in my judgment, the present law is constitutional; and that all good citizens are bound to respect and obey it, just as freely and readily as if they had voted for it themselves. If experience shall show that, in its operation, the law inflicts wrong, or endangers the liberty of any whose liberty is secured by the Constitution, then Congress ought to be called on to amend or modify it. But, as I think, agitation on the subject ought to cease. We have had enough of strife on a single question, and that, in a great measure, merely theoretical. It is our duty, in my opinion, to attend to other great and practical questions, in which all parts of the country have an interest. Yours, very respectfully,

Daniel Webster

Text from *PC*, 2: 402. Original not found. Colby (1795–1873), a conservative New London Whig, served a term as governor of New Hampshire, 1846–1847.

1. Not found.
2. See above, pp. 110–111, June 3, 1850.

TO THOMAS CORWIN

Boston, Novr. 13th 1850

Private & Confidential

My dear Sir,

The Whigs of this State owe their recent misfortunes, especially the re-election of Mr. Horace Mann,[1] very much to the support given to him by certain Whig Papers, at the head of which is the Boston Atlas. Other causes concurred, and among these other causes, one is, the favor shown towards Mr Mann's election by certain officers of the Custom House.[2] This last subject may be attended to hereafter, but my present purpose is to request that the patronage of your Department may be altogether withdrawn from the Boston Atlas.

The reliable Union Whig Papers in this city are; the Boston Daily Advertiser; & the Boston Courier. These are large Daily Papers ably conducted & entirely sound. The Bee is a penny paper of great circulation & of good principles.

About the Country papers, I will enquire, & give you information hereafter. Meantime it is safe to say that the Springfield Republican is a highly respectable & thorough Union Paper. Yours with true regard.

Danl Webster

LS. DLC. Published in *W & S*, 16: 582–583. An AL draft, addressed to unspecified cabinet members, is in NhHi (mDW 31646).

1. See above, Charles Wainwright March to DW, October 22, [1850], enclosed in DW to Millard Fillmore, October 24, 1850, n. 2.

2. Webster's initial reluctance to oppose Philip Greely's nomination as Boston collector (see above, DW to

[?], September 15, 1850) gradually gave way to irritation, then anger, on learning the nature of Greely's political activity. See Daniel Fletcher Webster to DW, October 26, 1850, mDW 31541, and below, DW to Millard Fillmore, November 15, 1850, and April 18, 1851; Charles Wainwright March to DW, April 8, 1852, and DW to Thomas Corwin, May 14, 1852.

TO MILLARD FILLMORE, WITH ENCLOSURE

Nov. 15. 1850

Private & Confidential

My Dear Sir

For two days I have been endeavoring to do something to put this business of the attempt to arrest Crafts [William and Ellen Craft],[1] into a better shape. We are unfortunate here. The District Atty[2] has no talent, no fitness for his place, & no very good disposition. The Claimant,[3] in this Craft case, called on him for assistance, or advice which he declined to render. This claimant, or agent, has used no great discretion, but has acted clumsily. It became immediately known that a person was here, to arrest slaves; & it is supposed, I cannot say how truly, that this news spread from Mr [George] Lunt's office. Mr Lunt associates with him, in nearly all his business, a young lawyer by the name of [George Partridge] Sanger This Mr Sanger is rather clever, of much more ability, no doubt, than Mr Lunt, & is a professed & active Free Soil man; as you will see by one, out of a string of Resolutions, introduced by him into a political meeting at Charlestown.[4]

The Marshall, Mr Devans [Charles Devens, Jr.], is, as I believe, very well disposed, but I fear not entirely efficient. I sent for him yesterday & told him he must either execute his warrant, or give some good reason for not executing it; & that this reason should be made public, in order that persons interested in these matters at the South might not have it in their power to say, that U.S. officers, in the North, were not disposed to do their duty.

The Marshall has obtained the opinion of Mr B[enjamin] R[obbins] Curtis,[5] upon the subject of the Fugitive Slave Law. It is well drawn, & argues well that, which hardly seems to require any argument. The opinion, however, will do good. Mr Curtis' reputation is high, & his opinion will silence the small lawyers. It will be published in the [Boston] Courier of tomorrow, at my request.

I am sorry to be obliged to say, that the *general weight* of U.S. officers in this District is *against* the Government, & against the execution of the Fugitive Slave Law. I hear this, when I go into the Streets, from every sound Whig, & every Union man I meet. Mr Greeley [Philip Greely], the Collector, is worse than indifferent, & Mr [Charles] Hudson, without any doubt, has acted for the election of Mr [Horace] Mann, with all his power. Our Genl. State Whig Com[mitt]ee has been, & is, composed of just such men; the [Boston] Atlas has lent the aid of all its force, in the same direction; & Mr Mann's reelection is fairly enough to be attributed to the joint operation of these agencies.

I do not wish to annoy you with these local matters, in the midst of your pressure under other & greater duties; but ere long, the condition of the public offices of the U. S. in this District must be looked into. Yrs always   Danl Webster

ENCLOSURE: NEWSPAPER CLIPPING MARKED BY WEBSTER "MR SANGER'S RESOLUTION."

Resolved, That the Fugitive Slave law, in its present form, is an odious and abominable law; checking as it does, by penal enactments, some of the noblest sympathies of humanity; and that the friends of freedom throughout the Union, should unite in demanding and laboring for its immediate and unconditional repeal.

ALS. NBuHi. Published, without enclosure, in *W & S*, 16: 576–577.

1. See above, headnote preceding, DW to Millard Fillmore, November 5, 1850.

2. George Lunt, for whom Webster had a well-established distaste. See *Correspondence*, 6: 323–324.

3. John Knight, acting for the Crafts' owner, Robert Collins.

4. See enclosure.

5. Curtis's detailed opinion on the constitutionality of the law, dated November 9, rejected arguments that the law contradicted the Fourth Amendment protection against unreasonable searches and seizures and emphasized the legal precedents for the current statute. For the text, see *Boston Daily Advertiser*, November 19, 1850. Benjamin Robbins Curtis was a brother of George Ticknor Curtis, at that time Massachusetts Commissioner for the enforcement of the Fugitive Slave Law of 1850.

Turning his attention from the unhappy controversy over fugitive slaves and the continuing rift in Massachusetts Whiggery, Webster welcomed the news that Union rallies were being organized across the nation. Invariably, he was invited to participate or, at the least, send a message. Webster attended none of these rallies, but he responded to many, including the meetings in Manchester, New Hampshire, and Staunton, Virginia (see below). Carefully crafted, his themes varied according to the audience. To northerners, Webster spoke of the need for obedience to the law; to southerners, he waxed more lyrical, seeking to touch emotional chords of loyalty to the Union.

TO BENJAMIN FRANKLIN AYER

Boston, November 16, 1850

My Dear Sir—

When I received yesterday the invitation of the committee to attend the meeting at Manchester,[1] my expectation was, that I should immediately leave the city, and I contented myself, therefore, with a very brief reply. The weather having detained me for a day, I have time to write a more respectful acknowledgment of your communication, and to express more distinctly as well the gratification it would afford me to attend the meeting as my pleasure that such a convention is to be convened. A "Union meeting without distinction of party," holden in the largest town or city in the state, can hardly fail to be attended with good consequences. There is, evidently, abroad a spirit of disunion and disobedience to the laws which good men ought to meet, and to check if they can. Men are to be found who propose as their own rule of conduct, and recommend the same rule to others, "peaceable resistance to the laws"; that is to say, they propose to resist the laws of the land so far as they can do so consistently with their own personal safety. Their obligations to support the constitution go for nothing; their oaths to act, if they hold any public trust, according to law, go for nothing; it is enough that they do not, by forcible resistance, expose themselves to dangers and penalties. This is, certainly, quite a new strain of patriotism. We have never before this day known such sentiments to be circulated, commended and acted upon by any who professed love for their country or respect for its institutions. A still more extravagant notion is sometimes advanced, which is, that individuals may judge of their rights and duties, under the constitution and the laws, by some rule which, according to their idea, is above both the constitution and the laws.

You and I, sir, and our fellow citizens of New Hampshire, have not so read the books of authority, either religious or civil. We do not so understand either the institutions of Christianity or the institutions of government. And we may well value more and more highly the government which is over us, when we see that the weapons aimed against its preservation, are also, for the most part, equally directed against those great fundamental, moral and political truths upon which all good government, and the peace of society at all times, must essentially rest. I have the fullest belief, sir, that in the state of New Hampshire this disorganizing spirit will meet such a rebuke as shall put it to flight. The representation of the state in congress generally supported the peace measures of the last session, and by these measures I doubt not the state will stand. It is time that discord and animosity should cease. It is time that a better understanding and more friendly sentiments were revived between the north and the south. And I am sure that all wise and good men will see the propriety of forbearing from renewing agitation, by attempts to repeal the late measures, or any of them. I do not see that they contain unconstitutional or alarming principles, or that they forbode the infliction of wrong or injury. When real and actual evil arises, if it shall arise, the laws ought to be amended or repealed; but in the absence of imminent danger, I see no reason at present for renewed controversy or contention.

My dear sir, the Union will be preserved, and the laws will be obeyed and executed. Let us take courage, and that sort of courage which prompts men to a resolute discharge of their duties. We will save the Union for our own sake, for the sake of the country, for the honor of free governments, and even for the benefit of those who seem ready, with ruthless hands, to tear it asunder. I am, my dear sir, with true regard, your friend and obedient servant,   Daniel Webster.

Text from *Boston Daily Advertiser*, November 25, 1850. Original not found. Ayer (1825–1903; Dartmouth 1846) was a politically active Manchester attorney.

1. The Manchester meeting on No-

vember 20 was one of many Union gatherings in eastern states in the fall of 1850, called and attended by Democrats and Whigs who supported the recent congressional compromises on slavery.

TO WILLIAM KINNEY ET AL.

Washington, November 23, 1850

Gentlemen:

On my arrival in this city last evening I had the pleasure to receive your communication of the 7th instant.[1] It is a refreshing and encouraging and a patriotic letter. You speak the sentiments which become the people of the great and ancient Commonwealth of Virginia. You speak as [George] Wythe, and [Edmund] Pendleton, [Thomas] Jefferson, [John] Marshall, and [James] Madison would speak were they yet among us. You speak of the Union of these States; and what idea can suggest more lively emotion in the minds of the American people, of present prosperity, past renown, and future hopes? Gladly would I be with you, gentlemen, on the proposed occasion, and, as one of your countrymen and fellow-citizens, assure you of my hearty sympathy with you, in the opinions which you express, and my unchangeable purpose to co-operate with you and other good men in upholding the honor of the States and the Constitution of the Government. How happy should I be to present myself in Virginia, west of the Blue Ridge, and there to pledge mutual faith with the men of Augusta and Rockbridge, Bath, Alleghany, and Pocahontas, Highland, Pendleton, and Rockingham, that while we live the institutions of our wise and patriotic sires shall not want supporters, and that, as far as may depend on us, the civilized world shall never be shocked by beholding such a prodigy as the voluntary dismemberment of this glorious Republic. No, gentlemen, never, never! If it shall come to that, political martyrdom is preferable to such a sight. It is better to die while the honor of the country is untarnished, and the flag of the Union still flying over our heads, than to live to behold that honor gone forever and that flag prostrate in the dust. Gentlemen, I speak warmly, because I feel warmly, and because I know that I speak to men whose hearts I know are as warm as my own, in support of the country and the Union.

I am lately from the North, where I have mixed extensively with men of all classes and all parties, and I assure you, gentlemen, through the masses of Northern people the general feeling and the great cry is for the Union and for its preservation. There are, it is true, men to be found, some of perverse purposes, and some of bewildered imagination, who affect to suppose that some possible but undefined good would arise from a dissolution of the ties which bind these United States together, but be assured the number of these men is small, the eminent leaders of all parties rebuke them, and while there prevails a general purpose to maintain the Union as it is, that purpose embraces, as its just and necessary means, a firm resolution of supporting the rights of all the States, precisely as they stand guarantied and secured by the Constitution. And you may depend upon it that every provision in that instrument in favor of the rights of Virginia, and the other Southern States, and every constitutional act of Congress, passed to uphold and enforce those rights, will be upheld and maintained not only by the power of the law, but also by the prevailing influence of public opinion. Accidents may occur to defeat the execution of a law in a particular instance; misguided men may, it is possible, sometimes enable others to elude the claims of justice and the rights founded in solemn constitutional compact, but, on the whole, and in the end, the law will be executed and obeyed; the south will see that there is principle and patriotism, good sense and honesty, in the general minds of the North; and that among the great mass of intelligent citizens in that quarter the general disposition to ask for justice is not stronger than the dispostion to grant it to others.

Gentlemen, we are brethren; we are descendants of those who labored together with intense anxiety for the establishment of the present Federal Constitution; let me ask you, gentlemen, to teach your young men, into whose hands the power of the country must soon fall, to go back to the close of the Revolutionary war, to contemplate the feebleness and incompetency of the confederation of States then existing; and to trace the steps by which the intelligence and patriotism of the great men of that day led the country to the adoption of the existing constitution; teach them to study the proceedings, votes, and reports of committees in the old Congress; especially draw their attention to the leading part taken by the Assembly of Virginia from 1783 onward; direct their minds to the convention at Annapolis in 1786; and by the contemplation and study of these events and these efforts, let them see what a mighty thing it was to establish the Government under which we have now lived so prosperously and so gloriously for sixty years. But pardon me; I must not write an essay or make a speech. Virginia! true-hearted Virginia! stand by your country, stand by the work of your fathers, stand by the Union of the States, and may Almighty God prosper all our efforts in the cause of liberty, and in the cause of that United government which renders this people the happiest people on whom the sun ever shone! I am, gentlemen, yours truly and faithfully,   Daniel Webster

Text from Washington, D.C., *National Intelligencer*, December 5, 1850. Reprinted, with stylistic alterations, in *Works*, 6: 579–581. Original not found. Kinney (1795–1863) represented Augusta County, Virginia, for many years in the House of Delegates and the state senate.

1. See William Kinney et al. to DW, November 7, 1850, mDWs. Webster and other "friends and supporters of the Union and of the laws' supremacy" were invited to attend "a mass meeting of the friends of the Union without distinction of party" at the Augusta County Court House in Staunton on November 25 (see Boston *Evening Transcript*, December 4, 1850, and *National Intelligencer*, December 5, 1850.)

TO PETER HARVEY

Washington Nov. 29. '50

Dear Harvey;

The Resolutions, & the speeches are admirable.[1] Print 50,000 copies of the whole proceedings, speeches & all,[2] & send 20,000 here for distribution in the South. Nothing can do half so much good. The Message[3] will be delivered on Tuesday. *Fear nothing.* Where Boston leads, &c. &c. Yrs
D Webster

ALS. CSmH.

1. For an extensive account of the mass Union meeting in Boston on November 26, featuring speeches by Benjamin R. Curtis, Rufus Choate, Benjamin F. Hallett, and others, see *Boston Daily Advertiser*, November 28, 1850.

2. Published in pamphlet form as *Proceedings of the Constitutional Meeting at Faneuil Hall* (Boston, 1850).

3. Fillmore's first annual message of December 2, 1850.

TO FRANKLIN HAVEN

Washington Decr. 5. '50

My Dear Sir:

Will you be kind enough to ask Mr [J. James] May[1] to make out for me a little minute, or memorandum, of the Mexican scrip,[2] now in the Bank, deposited by me at various times. I do not know that my own memorandum is exact.

Present appearances favor the hope that this Mexican scrip will turn out to be of greater value than was expected. I incline to think it will be near par. If I should be able to furnish you evidence of that, I should the more willingly ask you to add a little latitude, or extension, to my power to draw. I will cause you to hear from me again on this subject in a day or two.

I am very glad the Message[3] is so favorably recd., in your quarter as well as elsewhere. Its various topics were all well considered, & no differences existed between members of the Cabinet. The President is a first rate business man, & the Heads of Departments, of different character & abilities, are yet agreeable, sensible, & industrious Gentlemen. So that the *inside* of the Administration is quite pleasant. Yrs always truly   Danl Webster

ALS. MH-H. Published in part in
W & S, 16: 580.

1. Clerk at the Merchants' Bank of
Boston.

2. See above, DW to Franklin
Haven, pp. 27, 42 43, March 12 and
March 23, 1850.

3. Fillmore's first annual message,
submitted December 2, 1850, was
praised in the *New York Tribune* for

its "moderation of tone and clearness
of statement," a response echoed in
much of the northern press including, perhaps to DW's surprise, the
Boston Atlas. See *New York Tribune,*
December 3, 1850; *Boston Semi-
Weekly Atlas,* December 4, 1850, and
Boston Daily Advertiser, December 4,
1850.

TO THOMAS CORWIN, WITH REPLY

Decr. 7. '50

Private & Confidential

My Dear Sir

I understand that you have recently parted with your interest in the
Union Land Co. scrip. If so, you are probably acquainted with the estimated value of the scrip, in the opinion of those who are acquainted with
the subject & who deal in such things. I would be obliged to you to say,
in a note at foot, what is probably now regarded as the sum, per cent,
on the original award, & subsequent interest included, which the scrip
is deemed worth.

Your answer will be regarded as entirely confidential. My object is only
to make it known to Mr [Franklin] Haven,[1] of Boston, who does me the
kindness, to look a little after my pecuniary concerns. Yrs truly,

Danl Webster

7th Decr 1850

The best information I have on the subject authorizes me to say that the
Stock of the U[nion] L[and] Co. will probably be worth par, but that it is
quite sure not to fall more than 20 per cent below par.   Tho Corwin

ALS. MH-H.

1. Enclosing his query and Corwin's response in a December 7 letter
to Franklin Haven (mDW 31784),

Webster observed that Corwin
"knows all about it; so you will see
that that affair looks well."

*Northern resistance to enforcement of the Fugitive Slave Law, met by
firmness in Washington, was but a part of the flammable political en-
vironment in which Fillmore and Webster were operating. Although the
Compromise of 1850 was enthusiastically embraced by southern Whigs
(William J. Cooper,* The South and the Politics of Slavery, 1828–1856
*[Baton Rouge, 1978], pp. 301–308), secessionist sentiment in the deep
South had not been quashed. Fire-eaters controlled the governments of*

South Carolina, Mississippi, and Alabama, and from the capitals of these states a steady stream of ideas and plans for another southern convention were advanced, with secession as the central theme.

TO WHITEMARSH BENJAMIN SEABROOK

Washington
Department of State
December 7th 1850

Sir,

Your letter of the 29th of November last, addressed to the President of the United States, communicating to him a Resolution,[1] which had then recently been adopted by the House of Representatives of the Legislature of South Carolina, was received by him yesterday, and has been duly considered.

That Resolution requests your Excellency "to ascertain from the Federal authorities, the purpose, for which additional troops have been sent to Charleston, and whether they are intended to remain there."[2]

The President directs me to say, in reply, that entertaining due respect, both for the House of Representatives of the Legislature of South Carolina, and for Your Excellency, as Governor of that State, he should be ready at all times to extend to both, all official courtesies, not deemed by him, inconsistent with the duties of his office. But by the Constitution, the President is Commander in Chief of the Army and Navy of the United States; and as such directs the movements and operations of both branches of the Military force, as well in time of peace as in time of war, according to his own discretion, subject only to that power which is Constitutionally competent to call him to account for alleged misdemeanors in office. Both his authority and his duty, in this respect, are clear and unqualified.

The inquiry proposed by the House of Representatives of the Legislature of South Carolina, appears to be novel and extraordinary; it is believed to have no precedent in the history of the Government. Were the President to comply with the request, it might be considered as an implied admission, that he is answerable to some other, than the Constitutional authority, for his acts as Commander in Chief of the Army and Navy of the United States; and, in his judgment, any such admission on his part, or any acts from which such admission might be inferred, would be a plain abandonment of his Constitutional duty.

The President feels bound, therefore, most respectfully to decline a compliance with the request expressed in the Resolution. I have the honor to be with due consideration Your Excellency's Most obt. Servt.

Danl Webster

LS. ScU. A draft of this letter, in DW's hand, is at NhD. Seabrook (1792–1855; Princeton 1812), planter, politician, and southern rights activist, was governor of South Carolina at this time.

1. The resolution was adopted at a special session of the House of Representatives.

2. On November 27 four companies of United States artillery dispatched from their station in Florida landed at Fort Moultrie and Castle Pinckney to reinforce the federal garrison in Charleston.

FROM THEODORE PARKER

Boston 12th. Dec. 1850

Dear Sir

Your note of Dec 1.[1] tho' received on the third did not reach me until this day. You ask about the truth of the account, from a newspaper,[2] of my marrying Mr Craft. These are the particulars: William & Ellen Craft are parishioners of mine. I have known them ever since their flight from Slavery. After the two slave hunters had gone, they wished to go to England & requested me to marry them after the legal & usual form. I told them how to get the certificate of publication, according to the new Law of Mass. It was done, & at the time appointed I went to the place appointed, a boarding-house for colored people. Before the *marriage-ceremony*, I always advise the young couple of the duties of matrimony, making such remarks as suit the peculiar *circumstances* & *character* of the parties. I told them what I usually tell *all* Bridegrooms & Brides. Then I told Mr Craft that their position demanded peculiar duties of him. He was an outlaw; there was no Law which protected his liberty in the U. S.; for that he must depend on the public opinion of Boston, & on himself. If a man attacked him, intending to return him to Slavery, he had a right, a natural right, to resist the man unto death; but he might refuse to exercise that right for himself if he saw fit, & suffer himself to be reduced to Slavery rather than kill or even hurt the Slave-hunter who should attack him. But his *wife* was dependent on him for protection; it was his duty to protect her, a duty which it seemed to me, he could not decline. So I charged him if the worst came to the worst, to defend the life, & the liberty of his wife against any Slavehunter at all hazards, tho' in doing so, he dug his own grave & the grave of a thousand men.

Then came the *marriage-ceremony*: then a *prayer* such as the occasion inspired; then I noticed a *Bible* lying on one table & a *sword* on the other; I saw them when I first came into the house & determined what use to make of them. I took the *Bible*; put it into William's right hand & told him the use of it. It contained the noblest truths in the possession of the Human race &c &c, it was an instrument he was to use to help save his own soul, & his wife's soul & [I] charged him to use it for its purpose, &c. I then took the *Sword*, it was a "California knife," (I never saw such an one before, & am not well skilled in such things;) I put that in his right hand, & told him if the worst came to the worst to use that to save his wife's life, or her liberty, if he could effect it in no other way. I told him, that I hated violence, that I reverenced the sacredness of human life, & thought there was seldom a case in which it was justifiable to <do> take it, that if he could save his wife's liberty in no other way, then this would be one of the cases, & as a *Minister of Religion* I put into his hands these two dissimilar instruments, one for the body if need were, the other for his *Soul* at all events. Then I charged him not to use it except in the last extremity, to bear no <revenge &> harsh revengeful feelings against those who once held him in bondage, or such as sought to make him & his wife slaves even now. Nay, I said; if you cannot use the sword in defence of your wife's liberty without hating the man you strike, then your action will not be without sin.

I gave the same advice I should have given to white men under the <same> like circumstances—escaping from Slavery in Algiers. I should not write you so long a reply <in> to a short note, but as you were formerly a hearer of my sermons, & still feel interest enough to inquire as to the facts, perhaps you will like the whole story. I send you a *Sermon of Conscience* & a Thanksgiving sermon[3] also, the latter in a Newspaper. Your's truly   Theo. Parker.

ALS. MH-AH.
    1. Letter not found.
    2. Newspaper account not found. Parker had described his role in marrying the Crafts in a letter to President Fillmore on November 21; it is probable that Fillmore showed this letter to Webster.

3. *The function and place of Conscience, in relation to the laws of men; a sermon for the times* ... (Boston, 1850). Delivered on November 28, Parker's Thanksgiving sermon, "The State of the Nation," was published in pamphlet form early in 1851.

FROM JOHN PLUMMER HEALY

Boston 2nd January 1851.

Private

Dear Sir,

You will perhaps remember that when you were here, the subject of an interest of yours in some East Boston lands was mentioned. I looked that matter up, & find that you were holder for Mr. Stephen White[1] for about $10,000; that Mr. White assigned some E. Boston stock as collateral for the debt he owed; & that when you were called upon, Mr.

[John Eliot] Thayer[2] paid the debt, & took the stock in his own name to be sold & accounted for with you.[3] Mr. Thayer is going to Washington in a few days, & says he will carry an account of the whole transaction to you, & show you how things stand.

At the present moment there is a speculative movement In E. B. stock & lands, which has greatly inflated the prices of both. It is not likely, it seems to me, that the prices now ruling can be long maintained.

Allow me to suggest, that when Mr. Thayer calls on you, you may do well to regard this subject worth looking fully into, though it should take an hour or two of your time; & if you have an interest there, from which anything can be realised, you may probably get more from [it] now, than at a future day. Your truly,   J P Healy.

ALS. MHi. Healy (1810–1882; Dartmouth 1835) read law with DW, 1835–1838, and remained in his office as an associate until DW's death.

1. White (1787–1841), long a close personal friend and financial supporter of Webster, was a Boston merchant who had served as a director of the East Boston Company, a speculative enterprise promoting the development of Noddle's Island. See William H. Sumner, *A History of East Boston* . . . (Boston, 1858), esp. pp. 449–547.

2. Thayer (1804–1857), a prominent Boston broker and head of the banking house John E. Thayer and Brother, frequently advised Webster on financial matters.

3. This arrangement is mentioned in DW to Franklin Haven, January 30, 1851, mDW 32335, in which Webster recalls placing "two hundred, or one hundred shares" of White's East Boston stock under Thayer's charge. Having forgotten the agreement with White until reminded by Healy, DW now pursued the matter—with what success is not known—in the hope of reaping a financial windfall on the stock. See DW to Haven, January 30, 1851, mDW 32339, and DW to John E. Thayer, January 30, 1851, mDW 32342.

In January 1851 Webster turned his attention to the publication of a new, expanded edition of his works. Original plans called for a collaborative enterprise in which Webster and various associates would edit and introduce his major writings, as well as a selection of correspondence since the publication of Speeches and Forensic Arguments *(3 vols.; Boston and New York, 1830, 1835, 1843), and in which Edward Everett would expand an introductory essay he had composed for the earlier work. By mid-January, however, Webster concluded that a single editor would expedite matters, and he turned, as he often had, to Everett (see DW to Everett, January 21, 1851, mDW 32221, and below, DW to Everett, February 3, 1851). Working closely with Webster throughout the spring and summer, Everett was assisted in the tedious process of collation and proofreading by Webster's State Department aide George J.*

Abbot. Their labors were completed in the autumn, and The Works of Daniel Webster *appeared, in six volumes, at the close of 1851 under the Little, Brown imprint.*

TO EDWARD EVERETT

Washington Jan: 8. 1851

My Dear Sir;

A new Edition of my Speeches is about to be published, probably by Little & Brown. Mr [Edward] Curtis, & another friend in N.Y., together with Mr [James William] Paige[1] and Mr G[eorge] W[illiam] Gordon,[2] have bought Mr [Eben] Tappan's[3] plates, & all his pretence of right to publish the Speeches, & these Gentlemen have undertaken to get out the new Edition.

It would gratify them much, if you should be able to add something to the Biography, which is now to be found, I think, at the beginning of the Second vol.

For my own part, I do not wish to see published with the Speeches any life, written in a very popular air, or attempted to be enlivened by variety of incident & anecdote. Your own temperate & chaste manner of composition, with your knowledge of the subject, would enable you to prepare such a notice as would be the most gratifying to me. But I am afraid, that even this, would be too much to be required of you.

We dined with Charlotte yesterday. I really like Mr Wise very much, and I think Charlotte is quite happy.[4]

I return Dr [Henry] Holland's letter. His letters are all agreeable. Yrs truly always   Danl Webster

ALS. MHi. Published in PC, 2: 411.

1. Paige (1792–1868) was half brother of Grace Fletcher Webster, DW's first wife. A prominent Boston merchant, he was one of DW's most reliable financial backers as well as a close friend.

2. Gordon was currently postmaster of Boston.

3. Tappan was a partner in Tappan Bradford, Boston engravers and lithographers.

4. Everett's daughter Charlotte had recently married Henry Augustus Wise.

FROM GEORGE WASHINGTON NESMITH

Franklin January 8. 1851

My Dear Sir.

Your favour asking my opinion &c. in relation to the use of lime, plaster &c is before me.[1]

I will give you my views on this subject, and you may endorse them, or better theories, as your own good judgment may dictate.

I have never used Guano for the reason that I have never had confidence in it as a permanent manure.

It stimulates and brings out one good crop and leaves the soil no better for the next. This has been the result of my observation, where a small quantity was used on land of one of my neighbours.

It may work differently and better on richer soils; but I prefer lime and plaster, more especially lime, for Potatoes on our Alluvial soils. I have used about 2 Thomaston hogsheads of lime and 200 lbs of plaster to an acre of tillage land, combined with clay &c in a form of compost—say 2 parts lime, 1 part Plaster, to 3 or 4 parts clay &c,—a little salt is of great value if you can afford it, and I think a bushel to an acre is profitably bestowed.

For my corn I slack my lime, and make up my compost the night before I plant. I in this way get up a warmth. And place a small handful in each hill.—then drop and cover my corn—my vegetable manures ploughed in 8 inches below. Sometimes if I have any left after planting, I place it around the stalks near the roots at weeding time, or afterwards.

I have used this compost in the same way for potatoes, with this difference—that I use but little vegetable manure.

I have never had the potatoe rot, save one year on a piece of land where my men applied too much vegetable matter, and thereby produced too much warmth or fermentation. I lost about one half of my crop on that land.

Again, we must get the earliest varieties of potatoes, and plant as early as possible to avoid the mildew, or rust. I generally succeed better in this way, in getting ripe potatoes. At all events, we must plant early.

We can now get our lime from Judge Penniman[2] of Burlington Vt. at a cheaper rate than from Boston. It comes down in the cars in Bulk. It comes in this way 1/3 cheaper than from below.

I have given you the results of my experience for the last 5 years, and if you can get any good from it, you are quite welcome to it.

We gave you some very tolerable resolutions at our Convention the other day.[3] Public opinion is getting right and more right every day. Truly Yrs   Geo. W. Nesmith

ALS. NhHi. Nesmith (1800–1890; Dartmouth 1820), a leading New Hampshire lawyer, was active for many years in civic affairs and was a longtime friend and neighbor of DW in Franklin.

1. Letter not found.
2. Probably Udney H. Penniman (1796–1862), a lime manufacturer who served as judge in Chittenden County from 1846 to 1848.
3. Nesmith had recently partici-

pated in the New Hampshire constitutional convention in Concord,
charged with revising the state constitution. Before completing its work,
the convention passed a series of
resolutions touching on national affairs, including a strong endorsement
of the Compromise of 1850 and the
unionist cast of the Fillmore administration. *New Hampshire Patriot*,
January 9, 1851.

TO MILLARD FILLMORE

[January 1851]

My Dear Sir;

I was informed by a member of Congress, yesterday, "that Mr Webster
had been with the President at least one hour, every day for the last ten
days; that their interview had no witness, & that it was well understood
that it related to the next Presidential Election, & the candidates, &c."
I replied, that all this was news to me; that I did not recollect that a word
about *candidates* at the next Election ever passed between the President
& myself; &, certainly, never a word upon the point of *our* being candidates. My "informant" was Mr [Meredith Poindexter] Gentry. He had
picked the matter up in the Hotels. Yrs always   D. W.

ALS. NBuHi.

FROM GEORGE GRISWOLD, WITH ENCLOSURE

New York 17th January 1851

Dear Sir.

Inclosed please receive a List of Subscribers to a certain Paper—referred to in my former letter.[1]

The papers are with John C[leve] Green Esq. who will, I have no
doubt, remit the amount Quarterly, as stated in the Document, on the
days payable—possibly at times a few days later. With Great Respect,
Yr. Obt. Svt.   Geo Griswold

ENCLOSURE: LIST OF SUBSCRIBERS

New York August 1. 1850.

We, whose Names are Subscribed below, will Pay each Five Hundred
Dollars, for the benefit of the Hon. Daniel Webster, the same to be paid
in Ten Quarterly Payments of Fifty Dollars each, commencing Sept. 1st
1850,[2] to John C. Green Esq. who will pay the amount over as collected.

George Griswold	M. Morgan
Robert B. Minturn	Francis Griffen
John C. Green	Edwin Bartlett
Jonathan Sturges	Gouverneur Morris
William B. Astor	Shepherd Knapp

Henry Chauncey
Paul Spofford
Morris Ketchum
Thos. Tileston
G. S. Robbins & Son
G. G. Howland
Jno. L. Aspinwall
James Foster Jr.
Sydney Brooks
Samuel S. Howland
James Brown
D. Leavitt
Wm. H. Webb
J. Prescott Hall
M. H. Grinnell

Edward Curtis
John Griswold
Warren Delano Jr.
S. Jaudon
Robt. H. McCurdy
Jacob Bell
John Bridge
Henry Grinnell
Edward King
Walter R. Jones
Stephen Whitney
A. A. Low
W. S. Wetmore
J. Boorman
Wm. H. Aspinwall

LS. MWalB. Griswold (c. 1778–1859), a prominent New York merchant, was active in banking, insurance, and civic affairs.

1. Not found.
2. If this schedule was followed, Webster should have received two quarterly payments of $2,000 each— if all the subscribers paid on schedule—by the date of Griswold's letter. No evidence has been found either way.

Disappointed by the results of the state elections of 1850, in which the Whigs failed to gain a clear majority, Webster's allies in Massachusetts faced unhappy prospects in the new legislature. By January 1851 a coalition of Democrats and Free Soilers, hungry for office, concluded an agreement by which they would divide the statewide offices elected by the legislature and shut out the Whigs. Free Soilers pledged support for Democratic gubernatorial candidate George S. Boutwell, and for Democratic aspirants for the speakership and the offices of the State House of Representatives, a majority of the governor's Council and the short-term seat in the United States Senate to replace Robert C. Winthrop, whose appointment expired with the assembling of the legislature. In return, the Free Soilers would obtain the presidency of the state senate, the remaining members of the governor's Council, and the United States Senate seat for six years, commencing March 4.

Boutwell's election was accomplished—amid charges of a "corrupt bargain" by the Whig press—on January 11, and state offices were duly divided between the coalition partners. Commitments to Charles Sumner's Senate candidacy remained fragile, however, and Webster, in a bid to thwart the Free Soilers, talked of forging an agreement of expedience with Democrats to prevent Sumner's election. Other Whigs, irritated by Webster's attempt to dictate, preferred an alliance with Free Soilers on behalf of Charles Francis Adams, an opponent of the Compromise of 1850 but nonetheless more acceptable to Whigs than Sumner was. Both strategies foundered, and after nearly four months of uncertainty Sumner achieved a bare majority on April 23. His election was a blow to the Fillmore administration and a personal setback for Webster.

TO THOMAS BUCKMINSTER CURTIS

Washington Jan: 20. 1851

My Dear Sir

I recd yrs of the 18th this morng.[1] No wonder, you decline to contribute further to Colleges, & Theological Schools, until you know whether sedition & licentiousness, or the law & the gospel are to be taught & preached in them. Religious instruction has hitherto been very well supported in this Country, under the voluntary system; but the laxity of morals, & the perverseness of sentiment, prevalent in these times casts a deep cloud over the future.

I cannot but think it to be the duty of the Whigs in the Massachusetts Legislature to join with honest conservative Democrats, & elect any good man of either party. I believe that would be much better than to let the Election go by. For one, if I had a vote, I should not hesitate to give it for a sound, sensible, Union man of the Democratic Party, if I could not elect a decided Union Whig.

I feel as if our Whig friends wanted *decision*. In my opinion, the present is the moment for the friends of the Union to *unite*, & rally in its support. Yrs truly   Danl Webster

ALS. MHi. Published in *MHi Proc.*, 45 (November 1911): 165.

1. Letter not found.

TO THOMAS BUCKMINSTER CURTIS

Washington, Jany 24th 1851

Private & Confidential

My Dear Sir,

I have received your letter of the day before yesterday.[1]

I repeat my earnest opinion, that the true course for the Whigs in the Massachusetts Legislature, is to join the Conservative Democrats, if by so doing they can elect a decided Union Man of that party.[2] I have no doubt that this is better than to put off the election.

Be assured, My Dear Sir, that there is not a syllable of truth, in all you hear about dissensions in the Cabinet, or of the President's joining new friends. The Administration will of course not refuse the support of any, in public life, or in private life, who choose to give it their support, but it will not depart a hair's breadth from the principles upon which it has acted up to this time.

I will send you the Roll of names. Yours truly,   Danl Webster

LS. MHi. Published *MHi Proc.*, 45 (November 1911): 165.
  1. Letter not found.

2. See above, headnote preceding DW to Thomas Buckminster Curtis, January 20, 1851.

TO EDWARD EVERETT

Washington Feby 3d. 1851

My dear Sir,

I sit down this evening with Fletcher & Mr. Abbott [George Jacob Abbot],[1] a friend from the Department, to state my thoughts on the order or arrangement of my works.

I incline to put as No. 1. what stands on the proposals as No. 3. Addresses, Orations & so on.

Several or many of these are contained in the three published volumes.[2]

A list of these Mr. Abbott will make out chronologically and send to you.

Then come productions of this nature since 1840 [1843], not included in the three published volumes; these will make, probably, three volumes.

Some of my productions are partly legal and partly academical, <like> as for instance the defence of the Christian Ministry, which may either go into this first part, or go among the Law arguments.

There may be others of an ambiguous nature.

Many that are in a pamphlet form have never been carefully revised by me. Many are in the form which they received from the Reporters and as they were published in newspapers. Many of these must be omitted, if all my productions are to be compressed within six volumes, and they well may be omitted, as being loose and ill considered.

Some of them if inserted in the volumes must be re-written by me.

After no little conversation this evening we have come to the following conclusion.

Mr. George J. Abbott is a graduate of Harvard of the year 1835. He has followed the business of an Instructor in this City for many years and now has a place in the Dept. of State. He has classical knowledge and is scholar-like and accurate.

I propose to put all my speeches, arguments, orations & dissertations into his hands and that he proceed to Boston and Cambridge therewith and there remain so long as may be necessary for the preparation of my works for the press. At any rate he will stay long enough to relieve you from a great portion of the hard work.

As to notes in addition to what are already prepared I must rely on you.

George Washington Warren[3] promised me a good note on the subject of the monument to accompany the Speech of 1843.

I have made a short note to the Speech in reply to Mr. [Robert Y.] Hayne; perhaps your own recollection aided by Mr. [Charles Wainwright] March's book[4] would enable you to make a *good* note to that speech, which must be regarded as No. 1. among my political efforts.

Farther to-morrow & meanwhile, I am, my dear Sir as always Yours sincerely   D. Webster

LS. MHi. Published in *PC*, 2: 414–415.

1. A native of New Hampshire and a graduate of Exeter and Harvard (1835), Abbot had originally moved to Washington to teach at a boys' academy. By 1849 he was serving as a clerk in the State Department. When DW assumed duties as secretary of state in July 1850, Abbot was retained and, in addition to his duties as a clerk, frequently traveled with DW and served as his factotum.

2. See above, headnote preceding DW to Edward Everett, January 8, 1851.

3. See DW to George Washington Warren, March 24, 1847, mDW 27744; January 7, 1850, mDWs.

Warren (1813–1883; Harvard 1830), a prominent Charlestown lawyer, was active in civic affairs. The *Works* do contain an introduction (1: 81–82) to Webster's address of June 17, 1843, "The Completion of the Bunker Hill Monument," but it may have been composed by Everett

4. March's *Reminiscences of Congress* (New York, 1850), later republished as *Daniel Webster and His Contemporaries*, included four substantial chapters on Webster's 1830 debate with the South Carolina senator. Everett did quote from March, but in his biographical introduction rather than by way of annotating the debate with Hayne.

After the Compromise of 1850 the slave states had little alternative but to accept its terms or to secede from the Union. The compromise itself was an effort to put secession talk to rest, and so for the most part it did. Only in states controlled by the radical "fire-eaters" was the compromise rejected. Immediately after the adjourned session of the Nashville convention in November failed to recommend radical action, the governor of Georgia called for a state convention to meet in December. The unionists did no more than add conditions: the compromise, and in particular the Fugitive Slave Act, must be strictly adhered to by the North. South Carolina, most radical of the southern states, was next. Governor Whitemarsh B. Seabrook called an election for early February to choose delegates to a state convention. Like that of Georgia, it was intended by its

1. Daniel Webster. Photograph. John A. Whipple Studio, c. 1847–48.
Dartmouth College Library.

2. Henry Clay. Photograph. Matthew Brady, c. 1848. National Archives.

3. John Caldwell Calhoun. Photograph. Matthew Brady, c. 1848. National Archives.

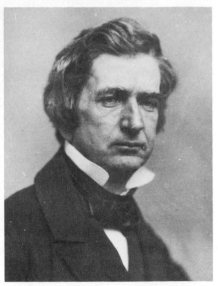

4. William Henry Seward. Photographer unknown, c. 1850. New-York Historical Society.

5. Stephen Arnold Douglas. Photograph. Possibly Brady studio or Alexander Hesler, Chicago, c. 1850–52. Library of Congress.

6. Thomas Hart Benton. Photograph. Whitehurst studio, c. 1850. Carpenter Center for the Visual Arts, Harvard University.

7. Zachary Taylor. Photographer unknown, c. 1850. Chicago Historical Society.

8. Caroline Le Roy Webster. Photographer and date unknown. New York Public Library, Division of Rare Books and Manuscripts.

9. James Louis Petigru.
Thomas Sully, 1842. Gibbes
Art Gallery, Charleston,
South Carolina.

10. Benjamin Franklin Perry. William
Garl Brown, 1853. J. Norment Baker,
Montgomery, Alabama.

11. Moses Stuart. Artist and date
unknown. Andover Newton Theological School, Newton Centre,
Massachusetts.

VIEW OF THE CARRIAGE PRESENTED TO HON. DANIEL WEBSTER BY CITIZENS OF NEW YORK.

12. "Mr Webster's State Carriage. A number of Mr Webster's particular friends and admirers in this city, have just had made by Messrs Wood & Tomlinson of Broadway, especially for presentation to him, a superb State Carriage. With this carriage it is intended to present to Mr Webster a span of horses, harness, &c., the whole costing $2500. The carriage is the most beautiful thing of the kind we have ever seen. It is built after the English style; what is called a close quarter coach, having a hammer cloth seat exquisitely fringed and resting on elliptical springs.

The color of the body is a dark green and finely varnished. The hands are pure silver. The crest of Mr Webster, a horse's head, appears on the door, with the motto *vera pro gratis*. The lamps are heavy silver plate; also, the hub plate, which contains the names of the builders. It is lined with cherry colored *broce telte*, trimmed with silk lace of the same color manufactured by the firm expressly for their own use. The Establishment is probably the most magnificent ever made in America, and will doubtless contribute its quota to the comfort of the receiver." *Boston Evening Transcript*, February 1, 1851, reprinted from the *New York Express*.

13. Horace Mann. Photograph. Southworth and Hawes studio, c. 1851. Metropolitan Museum of Art, Gift of I. N. Phelps Stokes and Hawes family, 1937.

14. George Ticknor Curtis. Engraving in Hayward and Blanche Cirker, eds., *Dictionary of American Portraits* (1967).

15. Millard Fillmore. Photographer unknown, probably c. 1850–55. Chicago Historical Society.

16. Ellen Craft. Engraving in William Still, *The Underground Railroad* (1872).

17. William Craft. Engraving in William Still, *The Underground Railroad* (1872).

18. Louis Kossuth. Photograph. Frederick De Bourg Richards, c. 1851–52. Chicago Historical Society.

19. Commodore Matthew C. Perry. Photograph. Matthew Brady, date unknown. Library of Congress.

20. Fletcher Webster. Drawn by
Homer after a photograph, engraved
by Peirce. *Ballou's Pictorial*, 16
(1859): 177.

21. Edward Everett. Photograph.
Southworth and Hawes studio,
c. 1846–50. Metropolitan Museum
of Art, Gift of I. N. Phelps Stokes
and Hawes family, 1937.

22. George Jacob Abbot. Photographer
and date unknown. Henry E. Huntington Library, San Marino,
California.

23. Charles Lanman. Engraving in
Henry Willard French, *Art and Art-
ists in Connecticut* (1879).

24. Library at Marshfield. Photograph. Dartmouth College Library.

1 Charles Henry Thomas   6 Samuel A. Appleton   12 Daniel Webster   13 Miss Caroline L. Appleton   18 Dr. J. Mason Warren
2 Jacob Le Roy   7 James W. Paige   19 Dr. John Jeffries
3 Edward Curtis   8 George Ashmun   14 Master Daniel Webster   20 Sarah Smith
4 Mrs. Daniel Webster   9 Rufus Choate   15 Master Ashburton Webster   21 John Taylor
5 Mrs. James W. Paige   10 Peter Harvey   16 Mrs. Fletcher Webster   22 Charles Porter Wright
                                  11 Fletcher Webster   17 Miss Caroline Webster

25. Last Days of Webster at Marshfield. Engraving by Charles Mottram after the painting by Joseph Ames, 1855. Dartmouth College Library.

26. General Winfield Scott. Photograph. Matthew Brady, date unknown. Library of Congress.

27. Franklin Pierce. George P. A. Healy, 1853. National Portrait Gallery.

promoters to take the state out of the Union. As Francis Lieber reports in the letter below, however, the turnout was much smaller than the radicals had anticipated. The convention duly met and chose delegates to a proposed southern convention, which Seabrook suggested should meet in Montgomery in January 1852. Mississippi followed South Carolina's lead, but the South as a whole was far from ready to leave the Union. Most were prepared to accept the compromise if all its provisions were enforced. Union sentiment rose steadily, and the Montgomery convention was never held. For this pacific response the decisive efforts of northern states to enforce the Fugitive Slave Law, including most particularly the Massachusetts trials of those involved in slave rescues, were undoubtedly partially responsible.

FROM FRANCIS LIEBER

Columbia S. C.

13 February 1851.

Dear Sir,

I own I am going to take a very great liberty in asking of you the great favour of sending the accompanying to Mr. Thayer.[1] He wrote me on the 7th instant that he was on the point of setting out for Washington, and I doubt not but that he will have called on you. I know of no one in Washington who might be likely to know where he is staying. Should he have left the city, or should you be ignorant of his whereabouts I would feel obliged if you would send the letter to Boston. Permit me to hope that you will not consider me intrusive. I do not know how to act otherwise.

You must allow me, as a citizen of the U.S. and a native German, fervently to thank you for your lionine letter to Mr [Johann Georg von] Hülseman[n].[2] I sent it to Germany to a quarter where it will warm a heart as much as it has mine.

Yester-day the election for the Convention closed, and so far as heard from the people have shown the greatest apathy. In Richland district— the district I live in—we polled 1400 votes at a late election for the legislature, and at this election, where the question is Secession or not, only about 800! My friend Mr [James Louis] Petigru sees in it a symptom of returning sense. I wish I could do the same. But to me this apathy has been fearful. To be passive when boys fire crackers near a powder magazine shows an amazing callousness, which in politics always means that the game may be taken in hand by a few trading politicians and a number of reckless editors. But one thing I must state in the spirit of truth, that I find now tens and even hundreds who frankly say that separate state secession would be folly, for one <who> a few months ago. Almost every one is for southern seperation, but we must be thankful for small favours. State Secession once given up, and we are safe, whatever account remains on the score of morality and duty. I beg to present my respects both to the president and to Mrs. Webster. Your very obedient servt. F. Lieber

ALS. DLC.
1. Enclosure not found. Thayer is probably John Eliot Thayer.

2. DW to Hülsemann, December 21, 1850, in *Diplomatic Papers*, 2.

FROM LEVI C. TURNER

Cincinnati Feby 16. 1851 —

My Dear Sir,

Your's of the 9th is received.[1] The Trinity scrip[2] you recollect I placed in Mr Kleunn's[3] hands (New Orleans) to sell at not less than 50 cts on the dollar. He could not sell it, and was directed to leave [it] in New York for me. He did not come north as he expected and still has the scrip. I have telegraphed him this day to enclose it to me by mail. I will send or bring it to you on its receipt.

I received a letter, Jan. 24th ult. from Mr. Hall[4] desiring me to return the papers to you, in relation to the Tennessee Lands.[5] You are aware that I visited these lands in 1844–5, examined into the titles, paid taxes &c. A large portion of them are embarrassed by conflicting entries, to some there are previous entries, others are entirely valueless &c. Well I gave it up as not worth looking for. But last fall a Mr H'Lommedieu[6] of this city, a man of means and in bad health, proposed to look into the matter for the benefit of his health, and see if any thing could be done with them. He visited Vermont, engaged a surveyor & others to go with him and examine the lands, ascertain to what tracts the title is good &c., and if satisfactory to the surveyor, then he has agreed to exchange Tennessee lands for Vermont Farms—paying in some cases a little money to effect the trade. H'Lommedieu & his men are going on in April, and in my opinion, if any thing can ever be realized from the Tennessee lands, it can only be effected in this wise. I have all the papers, and for years regarded them as worthless, as when I was on the lands, I could buy thousands of acres, of like kind, but with better titles, for 5 cents an acre. I am quite sure the Green Mountain Boys will be pleased with much of the land, and if a probable title can be made out of the confused entries, locations, surveys &c, something very handsome might be realized in exchanging large tracts, for small Vermont farms.

I will return to you all or such portions as you may direct, if you think you can in any wise, make them more available.

One word more, personally and privately—Mr Webster, for twenty years and more I have been your constant friend, ardent admirer, and humble but zealous and unselfish advocate and supporter. When I had money, it was subject to your call—when I had securities they were at your service, when I had lands, which I thought would realize to you large profits, I preferred that you should have them at less price and long credit than others at higher price & cash.

Well, a change came—bankruptcy and ruin prevailed everywhere—I lost money by tens of thousands by the failure of those who had my money, who owed me, & by the depreciation of the value of property. Its effects on me were disastrous, & upon yourself equally so. You have been annoyed and harrassed in consequence of our business matters, and have paid monies for which you received no returns, and I have parted with money, securities and property that was the same as cash to me to the amount of tens of thousands. For years both of us have been harrassed, and all the while have I indulged the hope that the time would come, when "circumstances," would enable me to discharge you from *certain matters*. I have spent time and money to effect it & often thought it accomplished—but still it is not done.

I suggested to you, in a letter from New York last summer,[7] how it could be done, and I really *felt*, that I was not personally & politically entitled to it, aside from our private relations. My position here is honorable, responsible, and sufficiently remunerative for individual and family purposes. I am the "writing editor" of the *Gazette*, a paper of larger circulation and patronage than any other west of New York, & my wife owns one third of the whole establishment.

But I did desire and do still desire to relieve you from *certain matters*. Now my Dear Sir, this could have been done by giving me the place vacated by *Dr.* [Thomas M.] *Foote*,[8] but I see it has been bestowed upon a gentleman from the "Old Dominion," whom I venture to say has no greater ability, experience, personal or political claims than myself; and who I do know has not contributed a tythe of the amount in personal service, in speaking and writing, for the especial benefit and popularity of yourself, as your devoted humble servant. Besides, any thing that you might have been disposed to do for me, would have been seconded or even proposed by Mr [Thomas] *Corwin*. But enough—and I beg you will excuse this freedom—it is not complaining or fault-finding—it is the expression of disappointment that an opportunity for doing what each of us so long have desired, has not been embraced.

I am editorially alone now, the Judge[9] being absent at Washington. Advise me confidentially of your wishes touching coming political events, and I will follow your instructions.

I hope to be in Washington in April, after Judge Wright's return. Most Respectfully & truly Your obt. servt.   L. C. Turner

ALS. NhHi. Turner (c. 1805–1867) was a land agent in the old Northwest for eastern speculators (including DW) in the 1830s and 1840s. A lawyer by profession, he also wrote for a Cleveland, Ohio, newspaper in the 1840s and served as co-editor and proprietor of the *Cincinnati Gazette*, while he simultaneously wrote editorials for the *New York Tribune*.

1. Letter not found.

2. See above, DW to Franklin Haven, March 12, March 23, and December 7, 1850, mDW 31784.

3. Not identified.

4. Probably David Aiken Hall (1795–1870; Middlebury 1815), a native of Grafton, Vermont, and a wealthy Washington lawyer with whom Webster had occasionally been engaged in western land speculations.

5. Webster's purchase of 250,000 acres of Alleghany pine timber lands dated back to 1836. See *Correspondence*, 4: 122–124; 5: 214–215.

6. Possibly Stephen S. L'Hommedieu (1806–1875), formerly proprietor of the *Cincinnati Gazette*, currently in semiretirement.

7. Letter not found.

8. Foote was chargé d'affaires in Bogota, New Granada, in 1849 and 1850. The appointment went to Yelverton P. King.

9. John Crafts Wright, Turner's associate on the *Cincinnati Gazette*, was then serving in Congress.

The escape of William and Ellen Craft had begun to recede in public memory when another more spectacular fugitive case aroused deep emotions in Boston and throughout the nation. On February 15 a black slave from Norfolk, Virginia, Frederick Jenkins (known as Shadrach) was arrested and carried to federal court for arraignment. Once again, however, the law was thwarted.

Immediately after his lawyers won a delay from Commissioner George Ticknor Curtis so that they might prepare a defense, a large crowd of blacks who had not been permitted into the courtroom during the hearing burst through its doors and overpowered the guards. To the equal astonishment of the fugitive and the federal marshals guarding him, they spirited Shadrach out of the courtroom and, soon thereafter, to freedom in Canada.

Shadrach's rescue was one of the most sensational events of 1851. It provoked congressional demands for investigation, southern threats against the North, and an executive proclamation, drafted by Webster and Fillmore (see below), calling for obedience to the laws and prosecution of all known to have aided or abetted the rescue.

Angry at the flouting of law in his home state, and fearful that it would further the aims of extremists in the South—emotions to which he gave expression in a public letter to a New York group celebrating Washington's birthday (February 20, 1851, mDW 32591)—Webster moved quickly to ensure that those involved in the rescue were brought to justice.

FROM CHARLES PELHAM CURTIS

Feb 17. 1851

Dear Sir

I presume you have perused Mr [Patrick] Riley's[1] statement respecting the rescue of the fugitive slave; I wrote to you yesterday to recommend Mr [Francis] Tukey[2] for the office of Marshal, in case of a vacancy. I have a note from him this morning saying that he does not want that office. This being the case, my communication touching him may be considered null & void. Mr Tukey says that the statement of Mr Riley so far as it concerns *him*, is *untrue*. This matter requires careful investigation—as to the facts—and nobody would do it with more *firmness* & accuracy than Mr G[eorge] T[icknor] Curtis.[3] I understand from what I consider good authority, that Mr Charles G. Davis,[4] a nephew of Isaac P. [Davis][5] has boasted that he assisted in this rescue; I have no personal knowledge of this. If a complaint were made ag[ains]t him I presume the truth might easily be ascertained. *If it be true*—and he were my own son or brother—I should say he ought to suffer the consequences.

It is stated by the D[eputy] Marshal that Comma[n]d[e]r [John] Downes[6] in reply to his inquiry whether he would allow the slave to be sent to the Navy Yard, answered that he could not grant his request.

If this is true, it deserves notice.

I confess that *while the U. States* have *no Prison—no safe place of detention—& the Marshal has no funds to hire assistants—*I do not wonder that Mr Tukey does not want the Office.

The conduct of our Mayor[7] has been very pusillanimous, in my opinion—but I suppose he will endeavor to justify it by the Act of Masstts. 1843 ch[apter] 69[8]—but it will not, unless *because* he is a *Justice* of the *Peace* he is prohibited from keeping the peace in his character of Mayor. Yours faithfy   C P Curtis

ALS. NhD. Curtis (1792–1864; Harvard 1811), a prominent Boston lawyer, was a member of the Common Council, 1823–1826, and state representative in 1842.

1. Riley was the deputy United States marshal who had been overpowered by Shadrach's rescuers on February 15, and who suffered the further indignity of seeing the "sword of justice" in his charge carried off by "an old negro." Robert F. Lucid., ed., *The Journal of Richard Henry Dana, Jr.* (3 vols.; Cambridge, Mass., 1968), 2: 412.

2. Letter not found. Tukey, then serving as Boston city marshal, had recently been a candidate for United States marshal in California. See above, pp. 150–151, DW to [?], September 15, 1850, n. 2. A year later, he changed his mind and applied,

unsuccessfully, for the United States marshalship in Boston. See Tukey to DW, February 14 and February 28, 1852, in DNA, RG 59 (Letters of Application and Recommendation, 1845–1853).

3. Curtis was then sitting as United States commissioner in Boston for enforcement of the Fugitive Slave Law of 1850.

4. Davis (1820–1903), a Plymouth lawyer and one of Shadrach's counsel on February 15, was arrested and indicted for aiding in his escape. He was acquitted.

5. Davis (1771–1855), Boston hemp manufacturer and businessman, a close personal friend of DW—so close that the second volume of DW's *Works* published later that year was dedicated to him.

6. Downes was commander of the Boston Navy Yard.

7. John P. Bigelow. See below, DW to Bigelow, March 10, 1851.

8. Enacted in the wake of the Supreme Court decision in *Prigg* v. *Pennsylvania* (1842) affirming the constitutionality of the federal Fugitive Slave Law, Massachusetts's "personal liberty" law of March 24, 1843, forbade judges and law enforcement officials from participating in the detention, arrest, or remander of fugitive slaves. See *Laws of Massachusetts, Supplements to the Revised Statutes, 1836 to 1849 Inclusive* (Boston, 1849), chap. 69, p. 261, and, more generally, Thomas D. Morris, *Free Men All: The Personal Liberty Laws of the North, 1780–1861* (Baltimore, 1974), pp. 112–117.

TO PETER HARVEY

Feby 17, 1851

Was it by conivence [connivance] or by absolute force? did the Marshal do his duty. Answer   D. Webster

Telegram. NhHi. Published, with addressee "Jacob Harvey," in Van Tyne, p. 457.

TO ROBERT CUMMING SCHENCK

Monday Morng
Feb. 17. 1851

My Dear Sir

I hope you will think it right to give all the aid in your power to what is proposed in favor of Collins' Line of Steam Ships.[1] I think it of great importance that England should show no superiority over us, in this Branch of the public service; and the proprietors of this line have many things to contend against, in maintaining the competition.

In the present state of the Treasury, the required aid can be rendered, without inconvenience. Yrs truly   Danl Webster

ALS. NhD. Schenck was a member of the House Committee on Naval Affairs.

1. Incorporated by Edward Knight

Collins and associates in 1847 as the New York to Liverpool U.S. Mail Steamship Company, the Collins line was contracted by Congress to carry mail between New York and Liverpool, in a concerted effort to provide competition to the well-established British Cunard line. The subsidy, represented by the mail contract, was substantially increased by Congress in 1852. See Royal Meeker, *History of Shipping Subsidies* (New York, 1905), pp. 8–9; *Congressional Globe*, 31st Cong., 2d sess., pp. 768–769, 835–837, 32d Cong., 1st sess., pp. 1146–1149, 1393, 1767.

FROM NATHANIEL GOOKIN UPHAM

Concord Feby 17th 1851.

Dear Sir,

I was in Boston on Saturday, & was greatly mortified & grieved at the utter contempt of law manifested by the rescue in open day from one of the Halls of the New Court House of a person under examination as a fugitive from slavery. The rescue was made entirely by a rush of colored people. Had the Act been carried into effect decidedly in this instance it would have settled the whole question of the enforcement of the Fugitive Slave law in New England. It will now be a precedent for other scenes of outrage, & is a public calamity.

I know nothing of the Marshall [Charles Devens, Jr.], or his assistants or whether better men could be procured. I have only to say if either of them ever expect *to die* then was the time to *have died in defence of the supremacy* of the law rather than have permitted a rescue. It seems to me, Sir, that the rescue was inexcusable, & that the only way now to give respect to the law is to dismiss these men at once for men of more judgment, efficiency, & courage.

It is the saying of some one that a good general cannot help being defeated sometimes but he may prevent being *surprised*. The Marshall & his men should be subject to the same rule.

I hope you will excuse my writing you on the subject but I was on the spot a moment after the rescue took place, & my feelings were so harrowed up on the occasion I have been unable to relieve myself except by expressing my belief that the officers of the law should immediately be held responsible. Perhaps the Marshall should be permitted to assign the causes & circumstances of the rescue, & it will be quite apparent I think on his own showing, that there is not the shadow of sufficient excuse for it. With the highest respect I am truly yours,   N. G. Upham

ALS. NhHi. Upham (1801–1860; Dartmouth 1820), lawyer and for a decade a Supreme Court justice in New Hampshire, was subsequently superintendent and president of the Concord Railroad for twenty-three years.

TO CHARLES DEVENS, JR.

Washington, Department of State
February 18, 1851

Information has reached this city, through the newspapers and private letters, that the execution of the Fugitive Slave Law has been forcibly resisted in the city of Boston by a lawless mob, which overpowered the officers of the law; and the President is surprised that no official information has been received from you respecting this occurrence.

Daniel Webster

Text from Curtis, 2: 490. Original telegram not found. Devens was United States marshal for the District of Massachusetts.

PRESIDENTIAL PROCLAMATION ON ENFORCEMENT OF FUGITIVE SLAVE LAW IN BOSTON

A PROCLAMATION
By the President of the United States

WHEREAS information has been received, that sundry lawless persons, principally persons of color, combined and confederated together, for the purpose of opposing by force, the execution of the laws of the United States, did, at Boston, in Massachusetts, on the fifteenth of this month, make a violent assault on the Marshal or Deputy Marshals of the United States, for the district of Massachusetts, in the Court-House, and did overcome the said officers, and did, by force, rescue from their custody, a person, arrested as a fugitive slave, and, then and there, a prisoner lawfully holden by the said Marshal, or Deputy Marshals of the United States, and other scandalous outrages did commit, in violation of law:

Now, therefore, to the end that the authority of the laws may be maintained, and those concerned in violating them, brought to immediate and condign punishment, I have issued this my Proclamation, calling on all well-disposed Citizens, to rally to the support of the Laws of their Country, and requiring and commanding all officers, civil and military, and all other persons, civil or military, who shall be found within the vicinity of this outrage, to be aiding and assisting, by all means in their power, in quelling this, and other such combinations, and assisting the Marshal and his Deputies in recapturing the above mentioned prisoner; and I do, especially, direct, that prosecutions be commenced against all persons who shall have made themselves aiders or abettors in or to this flagitious offence; and I do further command, that the District Attorney of the United States [George Lunt], and all other persons concerned in the administration or execution of the Laws of the United States, cause the foregoing offenders, and all such as aided, abetted, or assisted them, or shall be found to have harbored or concealed such fugitive, contrary to law, to be immediately arrested and proceeded with according to law.

Given under my hand, and the seal of the United States, this 18th day of February, 1851. MILLARD FILLMORE

Dan'l Webster,
    Secretary of State.

Printed document, DNA, RG 59 (Circulars of the Department of State). The proclamation was submitted to Congress together with the President's response to a Senate resolution of February 18 seeking information from the executive concerning the episode in Boston. Dated February 19, Fillmore's formal response deplored the rescue, offered precedents for state responsibility in safekeeping prisoners, and reiterated his determination to execute the laws "to the fullest extent." Richardson, *Messages and Papers*, 5: 101–106. A draft of the proclamation, in George J. Abbot's hand, is in Abbot Papers, CtY.

FROM HENRY ALEXANDER SCAMMELL DEARBORN

Hawthorn Cottage,
Roxbury Feby. 23. 1851

Dear Sir,

The Proclamation of the President & his message to the Senate[1] in relation to the disgraceful violations of the laws of Boston, have been universally approved,[2] & given the greatest satisfaction to all classes of the people, save the unprincipled & infamous fanatics & factionists, who have basely encouraged the ignorant blacks to put the authority of the government at defiance. The firm, independent, prompt & decisive manner in which the President evinced his determination to enforce the laws, has had a wonderful & most salutary influence. The *timid* & the *doubtful* have been brought to a just conception of the fatal consequences, which must befall the country, unless Abolitionism & Freesoilism are utterly exterminated, & the Union, Constitution & Laws maintained. Public opinion has come to the righ[t] about face as you may perceive by the *resolutions* & *orders* of the City Council of Boston, & the honorable conduct of the Civil & Military Officers of Salem,[3] since the Proclamation of the President was received. *Negroism* has been effectually prostrated in this state. Its career is, at last, ended, & it is only to be regretted, that our Senators in Congress & most of our members had not sufficient patriotism, firmness, independence & honesty to have cooperated with the ever illustrious gentlemen, who boldly united in passing the Compromise Laws. They have much to account for; to them must be attributed all the difficulty which has arisen in this state. They are men for a "summer's sea," but unfit to be in elevated positions, where the highest qualities of the *heart* & *mind* are required. Men who *dare not act* as *duty demands*, are not even proper for the *rank* & *file*, & never, by chance even, should be placed in positions, where *Death* & *Honor*, are the only alternatives. In all ages & all nations, it is a few really great, bold, able & honest men, who *save a country*, in *times* of *peril*, while in time of *peace* great men, or those who appear such, when there is no demand for a mighty & manly effort, are soon placed at the dead low water mark, from whence they never should have been elevated.

I have never known so great an effect upon public opinion, as that which has been realized by the glorious conduct of the President. He has gained a splendid victory over the demagogues & disorganizers & traitors, which is of invaluable importance to the Nation; & fortunate is it, that he has around him gentlemen, whose qualities are precisely such as the Crisis demanded. The Republic is safe. The Python of Disunion has been slain, by the arrow of indignant & omnipotent Justice. With assurances of the highest respect, Your most Obt. Servt.   H. A. S. Dearborn

ALS. NhHi.

1. See preceding document.

2. Dearborn's estimate of the popularity of Fillmore's proclamation and message was presumably based on conversations with acquaintances of like mind and the comment in the *Boston Daily Advertiser*, February 21, 1851, that the President's position was approved by the "great mass" of law-abiding Bostonians.

3. On February 18 the mayor and aldermen passed an order directing the city marshal to employ "the whole police force under his control" on behalf of the law whenever informed by state or federal authorities that "there is danger" of an obstruction of their duties by a mob. *Daily Advertiser*, February 19, 1851. In Salem on February 21 town authorities arrested a black man, Alexander P. Burton, an alleged accomplice in the Shadrach rescue six days earlier. As a large crowd gathered, the mayor "read the riot act." Boston *Daily Evening Transcript*, February 21, 1851. Burton was later released after a hearing revealed that he was not involved in the rescue.

What began as routine debate in the House of Representatives on a bill to appropriate funds to pay Mexico under the Treaty of Guadalupe Hidalgo became a question of Webster's integrity when Congressman Charles Allen of Worcester, Massachusetts, rose on the evening of February 25. In previous exchanges, several congressmen had questioned Webster's action in granting contracts to certain investment houses before Congress had passed an appropriations bill. Others criticized the granting of contracts without open bids and further suggested that the secretary of the Treasury, not the secretary of state, should handle such matters.

Allen was the dedicated Free Soiler who had pronounced the Whig Party dead and stalked out of the convention in 1848 when Taylor was nominated. (See Correspondence, 6: 285.) He now charged that Webster, before accepting the State Department, had demanded and received $50,000 from New York and Boston businessmen. The timing was wrong, but he had probably heard rumors of the "Webster Fund" then in the making. (See above, George Griswold to DW, January 17, 1851.) The arrangement, Allen charged, made Webster the "stipendiary of the bankers and brokers," who as agents stood to profit from the transfer of funds to Mexico, rather than the servant of the people (Congressional Globe, 32d Cong., 1st sess., pp. 686–687).

Allen's remarks were immediately challenged by his Massachusetts colleague, George Ashmun, who caustically suggested that if Allen had evidence of any corruption on Webster's part, he should present it, or hold his tongue. Any monies Webster had received from individuals, he explained, were voluntarily offered so that Webster might better "bear in part the expenses and burdens of office" (see Ashmun to DW, March 1, 1851, in Curtis, 2: 493). Henry W. Hilliard, an Alabama Whig who, perhaps not coincidently, was then seeking a diplomatic post, followed with a florid defense of Webster's character and, after loud calls for adjournment, the debate concluded.

On February 26 Allen renewed his attack and was again rebutted by Ashmun. The House then passed an appropriations bill without restrictive riders. Two days later, outspoken Free Soil representative George W. Julian of Indiana introduced a resolution asking for an investigation of Allen's charges. Webster had no objection, according to Ashmun, but the resolution was overwhelmingly rejected, 119–35.

As newspaper accounts indicated, the controversy over the Webster fund had its roots in hearsay testimony spread privately by Maine congressman John Otis, formerly commissioner from his state in negotiation of the Webster-Ashburton Treaty (see Diplomatic Papers, 1: 566–567 and passim). This testimony, which Allen had retailed in the congressional debates, was publicly refuted by Webster's friend Franklin Haven and, more tellingly, by Boston collector Philip Greely. Greely had been cited as Otis's source for conveying the contents of a letter Webster had allegedly written in July 1850 seeking financial support from business friends as a condition for accepting the State Department. Greely denied having seen any such letter; Haven denied such a letter had ever existed.

Like the Charles Jared Ingersoll investigation of 1846 (see Correspondence, 6: 127–128), the controversy subsided for want of evidence, but Webster's political enemies no less than his moral critics would not *let the suspicion of corruption die. It remained a shadowy presence for the rest of his life, and beyond.*

FROM ROBERT CUMMING SCHENCK

Wednes. Morning Feb. 26/51–

My dear Sir

Since the newspapers have been connecting my name with the Brazilian Mission,[1] I have been in the receipt of many letters on the subject of the Secretaryship to that legation. It has occurred to me that it may be proper that I should mention this to you as you may be considering the question of appointment. I have the names of *fourteen* applicants, the most of which are probably not on your list at the department.

You have heard of the coarse assault upon you, made last night by the Worcester man in the House of Reps.[2] His malignity was rebuked, not merely by what was said in reply by friends on the floor, but still more by the universal indignation & scorn, felt & freely expressed, all around, & on both sides of the hall. It was worth something to be attacked, to have such a triumph in the good feeling which it elicited for you in the hearts & looks & words, of all honest & honorable men who witnessed the scene. Very respectfully & truly Yours

Robt. C. Schenck

ALS. NhD. Published in part in Curtis, 2: 492.

1. Formally nominated on March 10 as "envoy extraordinary and minister plenipotentiary to the Government of Brazil," Schenck was con-

firmed, without dissent, two days later. *Journal of the Executive Proceedings of the Senate* (Washington, 1887), 8: 325, 332.

2. Charles Allen.

FROM FRANKLIN HAVEN

Boston, February 28, 1851

My Dear Sir:

The following article appeared in the papers of last evening:

The Washington correspondent of the *New-York Herald* telegraphs concerning the charge against Mr. Webster as follows:

"The facts appear to be that Mr. Webster wrote to the Sub-Treasurer, Mr. Haven, that he had been offered the State Department, but could not accept it unless his friends would make up what he would sacrifice pecuniarily by accepting. Mr. Haven showed the letter to Collector [Philip] Greely, who, at the time, told its contents to Mr. [John] Otis, a member from Maine, who was present. Mr. Otis has divulged the matter to Congressmen," etc., etc.[1]

So far as regards myself, this statement is, except in one particular, wholly untrue. You did advise me, by letter, that the President had invited you to take the State Department.[2] There was not a word in relation to the other matter set forth in the article.

Mr. Collector Greely has made a written statement that I never showed to him any such letter; that he never knew of my receiving any such letter; and that he never made any such statement to Mr. Otis or anybody else.[3]

With the request that you will excuse me for noticing an article so obviously untrue, I remain, with the highest considerations of respect and esteem, Yours always,   Franklin Haven.

Text from Curtis, 2: 493–494. Original not found.

1. For a slightly more expansive account of the same events, see George Ashmun's memorandum, March 1, 1851, in Curtis, 2: 493.

2. No such letter has been found. But see above, pp. 125–126, DW to Haven, July 12, 1850, on the subject of the new cabinet and the financial burdens of holding a cabinet post. Webster encouraged Haven to pub-

lish this letter, and it appeared in the *Boston Daily Advertiser* on March 12. See also DW to Haven, March 9, 1851, mDW 32862, and March 14, 1851, mDW 32945.

3. Greely's letter to this effect was published in the *Boston Atlas*, February 28, 1851. In remarks before the House, Otis stood by the substance of his recollections. *Congressional Globe*, 31st Cong., 2d sess., 782.

TO FRANKLIN HAVEN

Washington 2d Mar 1851

My dear Sir,

I have this morning received yours of the 28. Feby.[1]

Your previous telegraphic despatches[2] had all come safe to hand and I am quite obliged to you for the promptitude with which you have done all in your power to suppress slander and falsehood.

I suppose the fabrication began with John Otis of Maine, and that the first letter in the Atlas[3] was written with his knowledge; no human being can believe Mr. [William] Schouler[4] when he declares that he did not know to whom that letter was meant to refer. I am disposed, of course, to believe whatever Mr. [Philip] Greely distinctly states; but I should much have preferred that he had never had any conversation with John Otis on this subject, and I could wish that a question to this direct point should be put to Mr. Greely.

I have received Mr [James Kellogg] Mills' invitation to go to Boston, but on account of the inconvenience of a great dinner & the inexpediency of a small one, I have pretty much decided not to come on. I am, dear Sir, Yours very truly,   Danl Webster

Father is very well but a little tired and many things to do, and likes me as an amanuensis Yrs very truly   Fletcher Webster

LS. MH–H. In Fletcher Webster's hand.
1. See above.
2. Not found.
3. Webster is referring to a dispatch from Washington signed "Gracchus," which appeared in the *Boston Atlas* on February 15—ten days before Charles Allen's public attack—

stating that a resolution would soon be introduced in the House of Representatives condemning "a high functionary to the extent of treason, for having received a bribe of $39,000 for accepting the office which he now holds." Few readers doubted the unnamed person was Daniel Webster.
4. Editor of the *Atlas*.

TO JOHN PRESCOTT BIGELOW

Washington, March 10, 1851

Sir

The President has had the pleasure to receive your letter of the 26th February, enclosing official copies of the order and resolves lately adopted by the two branches of the Government of the City of Boston.[1]

It affords him great satisfaction to perceive that such measures have been taken by the authorities of Boston, as give assurance that no other outrage, similar to that which was, he presumes, the immediate cause of their adoption, will be permitted to take place in your city.

From his earliest youth, he has been accustomed to regard with the greatest respect and veneration the City of Boston, and the Commonwealth of Massachusetts.

He has been taught to believe that their inhabitants were, almost above all others, the friends of order and good government; intelligent enough to appreciate the advantage of free institutions of their own choice, and capable of understanding and resolving that great political problem, of the compatibility of freedom with order, of liberty distinguished from licentiousness, and of self-government the farthest removed from the dangers of anarchy; that they were especially devoted to the Union of the States, and to the Constitution which established and still maintains that Union; and that their patriotism would never fail to counsel them to fulfil all their obligations under the Constitution, justly and fully, and in the very spirit in which such obligations were entered into by their renowned ancestors.

Entertaining these sentiments, it was difficult for the President to credit the accounts which were received, of the outrage on all law, perpetrated in Boston, on the 15th of February last.

That a prisoner in lawful custody, within the wal[l]s of the Court House, in the centre of the city, and in full sight of the offices of all the municipal authorities, had been, at noonday, forcibly rescued, by a mob of one or two hundred persons, from the officers of the law, carried out of the building, and through the public streets, in a sort of triumph, and enabled to escape altogether, without an attempt on the part of any of the authorities, or any of the citizens, to preserve order and maintain the law, or to pursue and retake the fugitive, was a statement that seemed to him too improbable to be true.

It was with a feeling of great relief that he received such explanations of this strange occurrence, as showed it to have been an entire surprise upon the citizens, and upon the authorities; an act of successful temerity, on the part of a very inconsiderable number of persons, which only needed to have been apprehended the shortest time beforehand, to have been prevented.

The President is confident that the great majority of the citizens of Boston are entirely loyal to the Constitution; that they view with just indignation all such outrages, and all attempts, whether by writing or speaking, to incite the ignorant and unthinking to such acts of violence; and that they are ready to discharge the duties incumbent on them, by the Constitution and laws of the United States, faithfully and fearlessly, under all circumstances, whenever called upon by the proper authorities.

The occurrence of the 15th February is certainly greatly to be regretted, as it gives occasion to those not unwilling to seize upon it, to question the disposition of your fellow-citizens to comply with their constitutional obligations in good faith; and the history of such an outrage is spread far and wide, reaches where an explanation of it may never follow, and creates ill feelings towards those whose only connection with it is that they were residents of the place in which it was perpetrated. But if, as the President doubts not it will, this event shall arouse the attention of all good citizens to a sense of the dangers to be apprehended from the inculcation of such doctrines as have been spread abroad in the country, tending to shake the authority of a law, to unsettle society, and to absolve men from all civil and moral obligations; and shall put them on their guard against the further diffusion of such pernicious sentiments, it may, in the end, be productive of happy results; and, certainly, the almost unanimous expression of indignation which it called forth among your citizens, balances, to some extent, the ill effect flowing from it.

The President does not doubt that the people of Massachusetts perfectly well understand the difference between the freest discussion of political measures, and opposition to legal enactments already made and established. He is quite sure that they regard the law of the land not as sentiment, or an opinion; but as a rule of conduct prescribed by the general authority, and which all are bound to obey, at the risk of the penalties attached to its violation.

The President directs me to tender you his thanks for the transmission of the resolutions. I remain, Mr. Mayor, with great respect, your obedient servant,   Dan'l Webster.

Text from *Boston Daily Advertiser*, March 21, 1851. Original not found. Bigelow (1797–1872; Harvard 1815) was a successful lawyer and frequent officeholder, currently serving his last year as mayor.

1. See above, Henry Alexander Scammell Dearborn to DW, February 23, 1851, n. 3.

FROM SAMUEL PHELPS LYMAN

New York
Mar 10: 1851

My Dear Sir

I have this moment received yours of the 8th. Inst.[1]

I will set out for Albany to night at 6 oclock.

The fact cannot be concealed that the majority[2] of the Whigs in this State have made up their minds that the *minority* shall not rule—in this State at least. Hence these attacks upon every act which tends to sustain that minority.

The only question at Washington worth considering, is, which is to be sustained, the minority, or the majority? Or both?

This fact must be considered as a fact of moment—a large portion of the minority which shewed itself last fall & bolted has already gone back into the ranks of the Whig party & will not, & cannot, be separated from it. None but those clamorous for office now talk of separation or opposition, and others advise the President or Mr [Nathan Kelsey] Hall, to proscribe the [William Henry] Seward men or to do any act leading to a division—the great body of the Whigs wish to obtain a victory next fall.

The majority of the Whigs & their papers too, will support the Whig measures of this administration; and the moment it makes a move, or a demonstration favourable to the wishes of the majority on the subject of appointments, all will ground their hostile arms & thenceforth all will be harmonious between the State & the National Administrations.

The majority do not ask for the removal of one of the minority *because friendly to Mr. Fillmore*, but they ask the removal of these Custom House men,[3] because these do not belong to either—the "Fillmore men" or "The Seward men"; and they know none of them are friendly to you personally. Why retain them at such an immense sacrifice? Yrs very truly always   S. P. Lyman

ALS. DLC. Lyman (1804–1869), a Utica and Albany lawyer, was a journalist and the author of a popular series of articles on Webster's career that appeared in the *New York Commercial Advertiser* and the *Couri-*

er and Enquirer in 1849 and 1850. A friend of both DW and Albany editor Thurlow Weed, Lyman attempted unsuccessfully to mediate between the Seward and Fillmore factions of the New York Whig party. See Harriet A. Weed, ed., *Autobiography of Thurlow Weed* (2 vols.; Boston, 1884), I: 438–440; Aida DiPace Donald, "Prelude to Civil War: The Decline of the Whig Party in New York, 1848–1852" (Ph.D. diss., University of Rochester, 1961), chap. 7; and for the argument that Lyman was really a Weedite in mediator's clothing, Rayback, *Fillmore*, pp. 279–280.

1. Letter not found.

2. The "majority" referred to is the Seward wing of the party, which had demonstrated its strength at the state convention in Syracuse the previous September. The "minority" denoted conservatives identified with the administration.

3. Lyman is referring to New York collector Hugh Maxwell and subtreasurer John Young, both of whom were antagonistic to Weed and Seward, and each of whom owed his initial appointment to President Taylor. See Rayback, *Fillmore*, p. 279; Holman Hamilton, *Zachary Taylor: Soldier in the White House* (Indianapolis, 1951), pp. 208–209; and *New York Tribune*, April 3, 1851.

FROM JAMES BUTLER CAMPBELL

Charleston March 20. 1851

Confidential

My dear Sir,

I am this moment in receipt of your letter of 17th Inst.[1]

Thank you for your attention to young Edings.[2] A dinner with you will be an event he will long gratefully remember; and starting out by keeping good company I trust he will be inspired to go on with it.

The So[uth] Ca[rolina] Convention[3] will not meet till after the next Session of our Legislature. No time is fixed for its meeting in the law ordaining it. The Govr. is authorized to call it together *only in case* of a Southern Congress meeting before the meeting of the Legislature. There is not the least probability of such a contingency arising—and then the convocation of the Convention is charged upon the Legislature. You ask a question which I cannot answer even by a *guess*; and, what will appear strange to you, <in that> you are one of the very few persons who have ever asked me the *modus in quo* if Secession is to be changed from an ideality to a practical matter. I have often asked the same question but have never recieved even an intelligible answer.

The truth is, I should enjoy beyond measure a *free* conversation of a few hours with you and it would probably be useful to both [of us], but I have a great aversion to writing upon these subjects freely, because I differ so widely in my course of proceeding from those who agree with me entirely in sentiment, that I should despair of ever making myself understood. If you will pursue the course you mark out of doing nothing against *Secession* it will probably find itself in the position of the Bully who complained that none of his bystanding friends would hold his hands to prevent his fighting. The [Charleston] *"Mercury"* has very lately taken it for granted that Secession is a fixed fact. I mean *separate* State secession. Time will reveal their mistake in this. They are mistaken in the component parts of the Convention too. They are mistaken too in what will be the sentiment of the people whenever it shall develope itself. No party, deserving of the name, could be raised in this state against *"Secession"* in company with the other cotton states, and for forming a confederacy of them. This is decieving the politicians and they rely upon the same sentiment to sustain *separate* Secession.

It was my chance, and I took the whole burden of presenting a decision of parties upon this question at the late session of the Legislature. To my mind it was wise to do so and the friends who at the time reluctantly *yielded* to me now are satisfied that it is a much less[er] mischief to have called this Convention, ourselves uniting in it, than to have had it called together, against our votes and protestations. I am at this time rather inclined to urge on, and to vote for a meeting of the Convention. But there is a large chapter of events in store before I shall be called on to vote. I have less patience with some of our best and ablest friends here than I have with the *Mercury* Sett.

I may take another opportunity of writing with more care to you. At this moment, I have been driven on to write more and more carelessly than I intended. I am as ever &c   Jas. B. Campbell

ALS. DLC. Campbell (1808–1883; Brown 1826), a Massachusetts native, left for South Carolina in 1826 to teach school. Later, he studied law with Hugh S. Legaré and was active at the Charleston bar and in state politics for many years. A moderate, Campbell opposed both nullification and secession and associated politically with the prominent unionists James L. Petigru and Benjamin F. Perry. He was elected to the United States Senate in December 1866 but did not present his credentials in Washington, knowing they would not be accepted.

1. Letter not found.
2. Not identified.
3. Thwarted by opponents of separate state secession in their bid to authorize a state convention for that purpose, South Carolina radicals agreed in December 1850 to call both a southern "Congress" and a state convention, the latter to convene only after a meeting of the southern congress was assured. This "compromise" was in reality a victory for the "cooperationist" element in South Carolina, with which Campbell was identified. See Philip May Hamer, *The Secession Movement in South Carolina, 1847–1852* (Allentown, Pa., 1918), pp. 78–82; Lillian Adele Kibler, *Benjamin F. Perry, South Carolina Unionist* (Durham, N.C., 1946), pp. 246–248, 252–253; and John Barnwell, *Love of Order: South Carolina's First Secession Crisis* (Chapel Hill, N.C., 1982), pp. 138–141.

The reprobation of the antislavery men since March 1850 was rendered less painful to Webster by the outspoken approval of the northern *business community for his efforts on behalf of sectional peace. He was showered with letters of praise, toasts at dinners, and many substantial gifts. These included, as the following letter details, a magnificent carriage, harness, and horses, presented by leading New York businessmen. Custom made with silver mounting, lamps, and trim, lined with cherry-colored silk, and valued at $2,500, the carriage was a splendid tribute, and Webster did not fail to express his appreciation.*

TO WILLIAM M. RICHARDS ET AL.

Washington, 21 March, 1851

Gentlemen:

On the receipt of your letter of the 14th of February,[1] I deemed it advisable to postpone an answer until the carriage, harness and horses should arrive here. They came on, and were received, all sound and in good order, <by> in the early part of this month. Unfortunately I failed (as well at my own house as at other places) in various attempts to see Mr. [Charles B.] Wood,[2] who brought on the carriage, so that I only had one short interview with him; and the pressure of affairs at the breaking up of Congress, and until the final adjournment of the Senate, has obliged me to put off until tomorrow every thing not absolutely necessary to be done today.

And now, gentlemen, I have to thank you for your costly and handsome present. The carriage itself is thought to be as elegant as any ever seen in the country.[3] It appears to be of exquisite workmanship; and is rich, without being gaudy. It is every way commodious, and its motion pleasant and agreeable.

The horses attached to the carriage, I think, are quite worthy of it. They are certainly uncommonly handsome, and their <carriage> travelling and action, very fine. On the whole, Gentlemen! I rather fear that this equipage is too splendid and superb for a plain farmer of Marshfield; but as it has been your pleasure to make me so very valuable a gift, I accept it with all thankfulness, and shall always regard it as the measure, not of my merits, but of your bounty and munificence.

But, Gentlemen, I am more deeply your debtor for the estimation in which you are pleased to hold my public services in the counsels of the Country. If I have attempted, Gentlemen, to expound the Constitution, I have attempted to expound that which I have studied with diligence and veneration from my early manhood to the present day. If I have endeavored to defend and uphold the Union of the States, it is because my fixed judgment, and my unalterable affections, have impelled me, and still impel me, to regard that Union as the only security for general prosperity and national glory. Yes, Gentlemen! the Constitution and the Union! I place them together: If they stand, they must stand together; if they fall, they must fall together. They are the images which present to every American, his surest reliance, and his brightest hopes. If they perish in my day, or afterwards, I shall still leave, in the history of the times, my own deep, heartfelt, and engrossing conviction, that they are among the greatest political blessings ever bestowed by Providence on man; and that if, in any course of disastrous events, such as may happen to all human institutions they should become severed and broken, even their history and their memory will constitute a tract of light upon which all lovers of human liberty, in after times, may gaze with admiration. Yes, Gentlemen! Union and the Constitution!

Fortunati ambo! Si quid mea carmina possunt

Nulla dies unquam memori vos eximet aevo.

Dum domus AEneae Capitoli immobile saxum

Accolet, imperiumque pater Romanus habebit.[4]

I was not unaware, Gentlemen! on the morning of the 7th of March of last year, that I was entering upon a duty, which, as you suggest, might bring into peril that favor which had been long shown me, by that political party whose general principles I had for a long time steadily maintained. A crisis had arrived in which it did not become me, as I thought, to be indifferent, and to do nothing. Still less did it become me to act a part which should inflame sectional animosities; tend to destroy all genuine American feeling, and shake the fabric of the government to its foundation. I was willing to trust, and am still willing to trust, for the vindication of my motives, to the intelligent men of my own party, and of all parties. I should, indeed, have been wholly unworthy of that character which it is my highest ambition to maintain among my countrymen, if I had allowed any personal peril, to bear, with the weight of a feather, against my profound <and conscientious> sense of public duty. Whatever may now happen, I shall meet it with a clear conscience, and a fixed purpose; and while acting in full coöperation with the great mass of our fellow citizens, who hold the same sentiments that you hold, <and act for the good perform their duties to their coun> I shall fear nothing. I am, Gentlemen, your obliged friend, & fellow citizen

Draft. NhHi. Published in *PC*, 2: 423–425. Richards was a New York merchant and importer.

1. mDW 32542. Appended to the letter was a listing of seventy-six individuals and businesses whose contributions had made the gift possible.

2. Wood's firm, Wood, Tomlinson & Company, had manufactured the carriage.

3. A drawing of the carriage was published in *Gleason's Pictorial Drawing Room Companion*, July 5, 1851 (see illustration section ff. p. 198).

4. Ah, fortunate pair! If my poetry has any influence
Time in its passing shall never obliterate your memory,

As long as the House of Aeneas
    dwell by the Capitol's moveless
Rock, and the head of the Ro-

man family keeps his power.
(*Aeneid*, 9. 446–449)

TO WILLIAM PICKERING HILL

Sunday 1 o clock
Mar: 23. 51

My Dear Sir

After your encouraging note, rec'd by me yesterday,[1] respecting the State of your father,[2] I was shocked this morning by hearing of his sudden decease.

As I understand you proceed immediately North, with his remains, I suppose there is nothing I can do for you; if there be, please command my attention. For many years, your father & myself were attached to opposite parties, and acted, I fear, at some times, with a heated spirit of controversy. I hope we grew wiser, & better, & more candid, as we grew older. For many months, indeed for some years past, a friendly intercourse has subsisted between us; & recent events have brought us to a cordial concurrence of opinion, on questions deemed by us both to be of vital consequence to the country. If he thought of me, in his last moments, I hope he thought of me as one who had forgotten all differences, & difficulties, & who cordially wished him well.

In very early life, My Dear Sir, I had the pleasure of being acquainted with your mother,[3] & her Family. I will thank you to offer her my sincere sympathies, on this afflictive bereavement, & to accept the same sentiments for yourself. Yrs truly   Danl Webster

ALS. NhHi. Hill (1819–1901; Dartmouth 1839) was an editor and proprietor of the Portsmouth *Gazette* and later assisted his father on *Hill's New Hampshire Patriot*, which merged with the original *New Hampshire Patriot* in 1847. He later held a post in the Boston customhouse.

1. Letter not found.

2. Long in ill health, Isaac Hill died in Washington on March 22, 1851. *New Hampshire Patriot*, March 27, 1851.

3. Susanna (1789–1880), daughter of Richard Ayer (1757–1831) of Concord, N.H.; she was married to Isaac Hill on February 2, 1814.

FROM WASHINGTON HUNT

Albany March 23. 1851

Confidential
My Dear Sir,

I received your letter of the 12th instant,[1] with much pleasure. I did not fail to make its contents known, in a quiet way, to most of our

Whig friends in the Legislature. From the first, I had spared no endeavors to convince the Whig party that the Administration desired the election of Gov. [Hamilton] Fish. But my efforts were constantly counteracted by the factious opposition and violent language of certain presses and persons who identify themselves with the President by assuming a sort of special championship, and assuming to speak in his behalf. You know very well how most men form their impressions from "outward and visible" appearances; and I found it difficult to persuade many of our people that the favorites of the Executive were insubordinate to its known wishes. Your letter, therefore, was most timely and judicious.

It gives me much pleasure to congratulate you on the election of Mr. Fish.[2] You will find him sound, national and patriotic; not possessed of any shining powers of oratory, but clear in his judgment, conciliatory, full of common sense, and in short well qualified for usefulness. He is fully informed of the part you took in his favor, and I am sure he will go to Washington with the most kindly sentiments towards you, & the Administration. I remain, my dear Sir, With great regard, Yours truly

Washington Hunt

ALS. MHi.

1. Not found. DW evidently had written to dispel any doubt that the administration backed Hamilton Fish's candidacy for the United States Senate, despite his public opposition to the Fugitive Slave Law and efforts by friends of President Fillmore to block Fish's election in the absence of some public statement by him favorable to the administration. See Aida DiPace Donald, "Prelude to Civil War: The Decline of the Whig Party

in New York, 1848–1852" (Ph.D. diss., University of Rochester, 1961), esp. pp. 295–312, 321–324.

2. Fish was elected by a bare majority early on the morning on March 19. *New York Tribune*, March 19, 1851, and, for detailed inside accounts of the election, Washington Hunt to Millard Fillmore, March 23, 1851, and Jerome Fuller to Fillmore, March 19, 1851, Fillmore Papers, NBuHi.

FROM CHARLES PELHAM CURTIS

March 31. 1851

Private & Confidential

Dear Sir

What I now acquaint you of, I have learned accidentally but authentically. Mr [Rufus] Choate, who was said to be engaged to assist the D. Attorney [George Lunt] in the trial of the Indictments against the Rioters has withdrawn from those Cases.[1]

I cannot tell you his reason for doing so, for I have not spoken with him, but I can easily guess it.[2]

I think you ought to know this fact & I therefore communicate it to you. It would be highly displeasing to a *large* part of the people of Boston to have those rioters escape the punishment they so much deserve—& I fear they wi'l, if left to the D. Atty. alone.

I have no *difference* whatever with Mr [George] *Lunt*—but from what I hear—(from what Sir Wm Follet[3] in a Deposition which I caused to be taken, calls "the Atmosphere of Westminster Hall") I do not think that he has experience & vigor enough to conduct alone such a trial as the *first*[4] of those Indictments will be. Yours faithf[ull]y   C. P. Curtis

A letter from you to Mr Choate will bring you acquainted with the present state of this matter.

ALS. DLC.

1. See below, George Lunt to DW, March 31, 1851.

2. For Webster's explanations regarding Choate's action, see below, DW to Millard Fillmore, April 6 and April 9, 1851.

3. Follett (1798–1845; Cambridge 1818), one of England's leading lawyers in the 1830s and 1840s, represented Exeter in the House of Commons, 1835–1845, and was attorney general of England at the time of his death.

4. James Scott, one of four individuals indicted jointly for aiding the rescue of Shadrach, was tried before

United States District Judge Peleg Sprague. Lunt led the prosecution, and John P. Hale was senior counsel for the defense. Despite Judge Sprague's emphatic charge sustaining the constitutionality of the Fugitive Slave Law of 1850, the jury failed to reach a verdict. Scott was thereupon released. The other rescue cases were also tried with uniformly disappointing results for the prosecution. See Robert F. Lucid, ed., *The Journal of Richard Henry Dana, Jr.,* (3 vols.; Cambridge, Mass., 1968), 2: 429–431; *Boston Daily Advertiser,* May 27, June 7, 1851.

FROM GEORGE LUNT, WITH ENCLOSURE

Office U.S. Attorney
Boston March 31. 1851

Sir,

I have had the honor of your letter of the 28th inst.[1] and regret to learn, from it, that you have received no communication from Mr. [Rufus] Choate, correspondent to that despatched by me, and to which you refer. I had not learned, until the reception of your letter, that he had omitted to write, but I presume that his many engagements must be considered as his apology.

I am compelled now to inform you, that Mr. Choate, as you will perceive by the copy of the note enclosed, (which I have transcribed as nearly as I could read it), has deemed it necessary, certainly at an unlucky moment, to withdraw from the engagement into which he entered with me, to aid in the conduct of the rescue cases, of which I gave you immediate information. If needed at all it was certainly at the outset, when the fiercest battle may be expected, in the settlement of the principles pertinent to the issues involved, although I had determined to reserve until the last those cases which appeared to be subject to much conflict of testimony.

I cannot but trust, however, that this occurrence will have no embarassing effect upon the conduct of the trials, for the evidence in general is of a direct, simple & positive character, and I see nothing in the cases, as yet, presenting insuperable difficulties either upon the law or the testimony. Of course it is not very easy to try cases of such great political importance, under a new statute, but I shall endeavor to bring to them all the preparation in my power, and all the ability I may possess.

In your former letter you designated another gentleman, Mr. [Charles Greeley] Loring,[2] as one whom I was at liberty to employ.[3] But Mr. Loring, it is certain, is counted by the other side, as of their faction, and I know that he has given them assurance in writing, that he holds the law "unconstitutional, and impolitic and improper to be passed, and objectionable in various ways," or to that effect.

In this contingency I shall rely upon my own resources, in the discharge of my official duty, with the advantage of such aid, as I may be able to derive from junior counsel. And, since your suggestion of Mr. [Horace Green] Hutchins[4] is based upon the supposition that Mr. Choate was still to be with me, I shall venture to wait until I hear further from you on this subject. I think I might find, and I need, some one better qualified than I suppose Mr. Hutchins to be, to take an important part with me in the trials, though at a loss to say whom at this moment, and, perhaps, it may not prove very easy to find the exact person. If, however, the Government will allow me the usual liberty of selection, I shall, for my own sake, as well as for the honor of the Administration, endeavor to find and secure suitable aid. I feel bound also to say in regard to Mr. [George Partridge] Sanger, whom I recommended, not for services in Court, for in this respect he has not, perhaps, sufficient experience, and who has been my constant assistant, selected by me upon the highest possible legal recommendations, which could be afforded in the Commonwealth, that he has rendered me in these matters, so far, the most essential service, such as no one could render, who was not in my confidence, and that he has stood by me, in public and private, with entire fidelity, when others shrank, and when constancy to the Government was a virtue, proving a man to be made of true material.

I wish to write to you with perfect frankness, on this, as on all other subjects, because I have really nothing in the world to conceal. Mr Sanger, for ten months past has been connected in business with Mr Chs. G. Davis, who was complained of before Mr [Benjamin Franklin]

Hallet. He took an office with him, in consequence of the difficulty of procuring one near mine. For the greater part of that period he has been endeavoring to disconnect himself & to find an office near me, to his own and my convenience. Such an office, (not an easy thing to procure) I had, in fact, obtained for him, adjoining my own, six weeks ago, and he has only been delayed in moving by business arrangements. Of Mr Davis's opinions, until very lately, having had the slightest possible intercourse with him, I scarcely ever heard any thing & knew nothing whatever until the rescue occurred. I have no reason to believe that Mr Sanger has any sympathy with the views, such as they appear to have been, of Mr Davis. But immediately upon the outbreak, I inquired of Mr Sanger, who is a gentleman of entire honor and frankness, if *he was ready to sustain the law*; and learning from him opinions, on this point, entirely satisfactory, I required his aid and have received it, during the prosecutions.[5] Without this, I should not have felt justified in employing his services, nor should I have done so under any circumstances. I ought also to state, that I knew the correct opinions of Mr Sanger, on this subject, when the "Crafts' case"[6] came up. And I cannot but trust that my conduct, in this as in all other respects, during the trying events of the last six weeks has given the Government reason to feel entire confidence that I should do nothing inconsistent with its honor & my own.

Allow me, also, the liberty of saying, that, as matters are situated, in respect of these prosecutions, I am not fully persuaded that the employment of eminent leading counsel would tend to promote a favorable result. With regard to myself, of course, I have nothing to say, except that the duty officially rests upon me, and I am not disposed to shrink from it. But I do think, that the public mind might be better satisfied, if a successful issue should be secured by the ordinary and appointed means, without the employment of any of those unusual appliances and forces, which might lead to the inference of distrust in the cause at stake.

The time of trial will be fixed Tuesday, (tomorrow). The Grand Jury having, in fact, reported, and the Bills having been, in fact signed, only on Saturday last, between 2 & 3 p.m. Some little delay must take place, for there are many marine cases & quite a number of witnesses in jail, of whom it must be discharged. Besides, I ought to say, that, since the 15th of February, more than six weeks, I have been incessantly engaged upon these matters; and though I will not flinch from the discharge of any duty, yet I need some slight opportunity of rest, & time for more ample preparation. The Judge, no doubt, will fix the time, in reference to these and other considerations, at some day within the next three weeks.

I send, as you request, a copy of the Indictments,[7] they being the same. You will please perceive that the *first* is for "aiding to escape" from the master, which seems to me sufficient, as neither distance of time or place, nor can circumstances alter the original condition of *escape*; and the master was, at this moment, by his agent in the act of securing the slave. The 2d count is for "aiding &c." from the master's agent; the 3d. from the Marshal; the 4th, from the Marshal's deputy. The 5th. 6th. 7th. & 8th, are repetitions of those preceding, with the additional allegation that the slave was an *alleged* fugitive, &c. The 9th. & 10th. are narrative Counts, varied in the same manner. The 11th & 12th are counts under the rescue clause, also so varied. The 13th. 14th. & 15th. are found under the Statute of 1799, St. at L. Vol. I. p. 117. [paragraph] 22, the 13th alleging "Shadrach" to have been held under a *warrant*, &c, the 14th alleging him to have been held under an *Order* of the Com[mi]s[sione]rs, the 15th, under both *Warrant* and *Order*.

In these cases eight Bills have been found.

If you concur in my views, will you please telegraph me that I may engage some able junior counsel, subject to your approbation. I have the honor to be, Very respectfully, Your obedient servant,

George Lunt U.S. Atty.

ALS (in Lunt's hand and another). NBuHi. Forwarded, with enclosure, to President Fillmore. See DW to Fillmore, April 4, 1851, mDW 33164.

1. Not found.

2. DW to Lunt, February 25, 1851, mDW 32768. Loring (1794–1865; Harvard 1812), a leading member of the Boston bar, appeared as counsel for the accused fugitive Thomas Sims in the hearing before Commissioner George Ticknor Curtis.

3. In the margin, DW wrote: "Mr Lunt is mistaken. I designated Mr *Hutchins* & said nothing of Mr Loring. Mr Hutchins, for a subordinate, & B[enjamin] R[obbins] Curtis for leading counsel."

4. Hutchins (1811–1877; Dart-

mouth 1835), a Boston attorney, had been suggested as a possible addition to the prosecution staff by Fletcher Webster in a letter to DW, March 22, 1851, mDW 33061.

5. That DW was unconvinced by this defense of Sanger is suggested in DW to Fillmore, April 4, 1851, mDW 33164, in which he observes: "I do not think Mr Sanger is a proper person to be employed [in the prosecution of Shadrach's rescuers]. Mr. Sanger is known to have been, all along, a free soiler, or worse."

6. See above, headnote preceding DW to Fillmore, November 5, 1850, p. 177.

7. Not found.

ENCLOSURE: RUFUS CHOATE TO GEORGE LUNT

Boston 29 March 1851

Dear Sir,

I see by the evening papers, that the Grand Jury have returned their Indictments.

I should feel great pride and pleasure in assisting in these important trials in Court, but, I find, on a survey of my engagements, that it will not be practicable—certainly not so to assist in the earlier ones.

I cannot feel a doubt that you will triumphantly vindicate the law of the land and the honor of the Bar. I am most truly Your obedient servant,   R. Choate

Copy. NBuHi. Published in Van Tyne, p. 465.

FROM WILLIAM CHANNING GIBBS

Newport 4. April 1851

Dear Sir,

Mr. [Thomas Butler] King, Collector at San Francisco, is personally engaged, with the assistance of his friends to be returned to the U States Senate. If he should succeed, there will be a vacancy & I should be much gratified to obtain the appointment. I have four sons settled in San Francisco and the fifth leaves here in the Autumn to join his brothers. My oldest has lately been elected Alderman of that City at the age of 26 & carried by his personal popularity a maj. in each Ward, being the first Whig appointment. In asking for this appointment in case of a vacancy, my object is to be with my sons & believing at the same time I may be of some service to you. My sons have been brought up with such perfect respect for yourself, that no exertions on their part will be wanting to insure to you the votes of California at the next Presidential election, yet they have not the experience of old politicians & I am sensible there is something yet to be done there. In case Mr. King is not the successful candidate, I am aware, there are other appointments in the gift of the Govt. which will pay at least expences, which in fact is all I should require. The building of the New Custom House & Hospital, persons must be sent either as Com[missione]rs or in some other capacity besides many other appointments yet to be filled. I have not mentioned my wish to any one except to my friend Gen. Hamilton[1] as I did not wish to embarrass the Govt by an application to the President & I have felt I should rather be indebted to yourself. But be assured, my exertions in your cause, will not depend on office. Our Country owes you a deep debt of gratitude, which it never can repay, for years, it has been my wish to see you at the head of our Govt but it is the first time, I have felt there was a fair prospect of success; I am ready to give my whole time to this great object, but I cannot afford to do more. You will have to rely solely on the Union men for your strength with the conservative part of the Democratic party.

The free soil party have towards you & Mr. Fillmore the most deadly hostility. They never will be reconciled. No one of that class, ought to hold office for a day. If you make friends with the South & West, you will have little to fear from the New England States. For all cases, you may faithfully rely on my exertions in my own State, & elsewhere. Wherever I have influence or my voice can be heard, it will be raised in your cause. I am truly obliged to you for the two pamphlets you sent me. I sent them immediately to California. My sons there would duly appreciate any speech or address delivered by yourself & particularly so if forwarded by yourself. It will be a pleasant recollection to them in afterlife.

The election in R.I. probably has surprised some altho' it was in no way unexpected to me. The appointment of Mr. [Charles Tillinghast] James instead of your friend Mr. [John] Whipple[2] to the U[.]S. Senate has been the sole cause. It has entirely broken up the Whig party. The Whig nomination of Mr. [Josiah] Chapin[3] was not satisfactory as he was supported by the Free Soil Party. It was said he had made them some promises. Mr. [Philip] Allen on the contrary was a Gentleman & a Union man and received the support of numbers of the Whig party. It will not affect the vote of this state on the Presidential question. Dr. [John Overton] Choules left here on Monday for the World's fair,[4] he spoke with much feeling of your great kindness. I remain Dear Sir with perfect respect yours faithfully,   W. C. Gibbs

ALS. NhHi. With notation in DW's hand: "Mr Derrick: If the vacancy alluded to here, should take place before my return, show this letter to the President." William S. Derrick (c. 1802–1852) was a clerk in the State Department. Gibbs (1789–1871) had been governor of Rhode Island, 1821–1824, after representing Newport in the general assembly for several years.

1. Probably James Hamilton (1786–1857), former governor of South Carolina, whose early education is said to have been in Newport.

2. Whipple (1784–1866; Brown 1802) was a leading Rhode Island lawyer.

3. Chapin (1788–1881), a Providence merchant, was defeated for governor in 1850 by a decisive majority.

4. The great exhibition at London's "Crystal Palace" officially opened on May 1, 1851, with half of its 13,000 exhibits offered by foreign states, including the United States.

TO GEORGE LUNT

Philada: April 4th./51

Sir,

Your letter of the 31st of March[1] has been forwarded to me here, and having perused it I transmit it to the President. I quite regret Mr: [Rufus] Choate's withdrawal from the rescue causes, and am at a loss for the reason of it.

In the same letter in which I authorized you to employ Mr: Choate, I also authorized you to employ Mr. Curtis (B[enjamin] R[obbins]) if you preferred so to do.[2]

As to Mr: [Horace Green] Hutchins, I suppose him quite competent; if you think otherwise, I will hear your suggestions of some other per sons; but Mr: [George Partridge] Sanger, does not appear to me to be a proper person to be employed.

I proceed to New York, tomorrow, on my way to Boston, and shall hope to see you immediately on my arrival.

These causes are of the utmost importance. We wish them to be conducted by the best talent and experience of the Bar. Not wishing to embarrass you in the slightest degree, nor to interfere with your official responsibility, the sole responsibility, we wish you, still, to have the very first assistance which the profession can furnish. You must be fully aware of the consequence, if just decisions, should fail to be attained, thro' any want of skill, on the part of those who manage the trials. Yours respectfully,   Danl Webster

LS. NhD. Published in *W & S*, 16: 603. Copy forwarded to Fillmore is in NBuHi, along with a telegram, W. Laflin to James B. Robb, datelined Boston, April 4, 1851, mentioning the "unmitigated assault" on Fletcher Webster and the arrest of "the nigger" Thomas Sims.

1. See above, Lunt to DW, March 31, 1851.

2. See DW to Lunt, February 25, 1851, mDW 32768. DW had actually recommended Charles G. Loring, not Curtis, as a possible associate for Choate, as Lunt stated in his own letter of March 31, above.

With the prosecution of Shadrach's alleged rescuers still in preparation, under Webster's close supervision, another fugitive slave controversy erupted in Boston. Responding on April 3 to a petition by an agent of a Savannah man, Commissioner George Ticknor Curtis ordered the arrest of a young fugitive, Thomas Sims, who had been living concealed in Boston for several months. Sims was accosted by two police officers at 9:00 P.M. and, after a brief scuffle in which he stabbed one of them, was subdued and brought to the jury room at the federal courthouse. There he remained in custody for the duration of his days in Boston under the charge of United States marshal Charles Devens.

News of the arrest spread rapidly in the city, and the Court Square was soon alive with activity, as scores of Boston vigilance committee members and the simply curious milled about. The atmosphere was heavy with rumor, including talk of another rescue effort. It remained thus during the legal hearings related to Sims's rendition.

Determined to avoid any embarrassing repetition of the Crafts and Shadrach fiascoes, the authorities took every measure to ensure that

Sims would receive his lawful deserts. Boston became a veritable armed camp as all arguments by the fugitive's counsel were offered and rejected, by both Commissioner Curtis and the other jurists to whom appeals were addressed.

Public rallies assailing the Fugitive Slave Law and its chief defender, Secretary of State Daniel Webster, were ignored by the authorities, as was Theodore Parker's angry sermon at the Melodeon. Sims's appeals having been exhausted, and Curtis's judgment against him expressed, Sims was escorted out of the city shortly before daybreak on April 12, surrounded by 100 policemen and roughly an equal number of armed volunteers. A week later, at the cost of more than $20,000, Sims was returned to his master in Savannah, where he was publicly lashed. The administration had successfully upheld the law. (See Leonard W. Levy, "Sims' Case: The Fugitive Slave Law in Boston in 1851," Journal of Negro History, 35 [January 1950]: 39–74.)

FROM DANIEL FLETCHER WEBSTER

Boston April 4th 1851

For Hon Daniel Webster

You will see by the papers that I have had a difficulty with the watch.[1] Do not be troubled. I was not in the wrong and it was a gross assault on me. It originated from the arrest of a fugitive slave.   F Webster

Telegram. NBuHi. Enclosed in DW to Millard Fillmore, April 4, 1851, mDW 33164.

1. Late on the evening of April 3, as Fletcher participated in a citizens' guard at the federal court building, a fire alarm was rung. Sensitive to rumors that a rescue of Thomas Sims was being planned, Fletcher jumped to the conclusion that the fire alarm was actually a signal to would-be rescuers. Approaching the watchman who was ringing the bell, Fletcher demanded to know his intentions. According to accounts in the Boston press, a "tussle" ensued, and Fletcher was briefly jailed for assaulting the watchman. The complaint against him was soon dropped. See Boston Daily Advertiser, April 5, 1851; Boston Evening Transcript, April 11, 1851.

FROM DANIEL FLETCHER WEBSTER

Boston Apl 4th 1851
4:35 p.m.

To D Webster

On account of something with regard to Mr [George] Lunt which Mr. [Rufus] Choate will explain   F. Webster

Telegram, with AN, DW to Millard Fillmore, NBuHi. DW's note reads: "This is Fletcher's answer to my Telegraphic message, asking why Mr Choate had withdrawn from the Rescue causes."

TO MILLARD FILLMORE, WITH ENCLOSURE

Washington Sunday morng
Ap. 6. 51

My Dear Sir

I arrived here yesterday to Dinner, <pretty> well, but have seen few persons, not having felt inclined to admit many comers. My late attack was severe, & has a good deal reduced me. I propose to stay here thro tomorrow, & proceed to Boston on Tuesday, & to Marshfield just as soon as I can arrange the matter of the Rescue trials.

You doubtless have read how the Slave case stood, at the adjournment yesterday. I hardly think the Commissioner [George Ticknor Curtis] was *bound* to hear an argument [on] a law, which both the Judges of the Court appointing him have declared constitutional.[1] The Fugitive is safe enough, & I presume there will be no attempt to rescue him.

I expect trouble, in finding proper counsel to assist Mr [George] Lunt. The same reasons which induced Mr [Rufus] Choate to retire will probably induce others to be [un]willing to undertake. The truth is, Mr Lunt is not a very agreeable man to be associated with. He is not a good lawyer, theoretic or practical; and at the same time he is opinionated, self-willed, & obstinate. The members of the Bar feel that he has no right to hold the office; & as the present case is such, that a voluntary appearance in it may be viewed as in some degree odious, the leading men may not feel inclined to come to the aid of the Government for a mere fee. This, I suppose, to be the truth of the case, altho' I shall know more about it, when I reach Boston. As it might not be expedient to appoint another person Attorney, at the present moment, I have thought it best, as you will have seen by my letter to Mr Lunt,[2] to suffer him to select assistance for himself, with this limitation, only, that no known abolitionist, like Mr [George Partridge] Sanger, should be employed. This will leave the responsibility where the law leaves it; & if the trials miscarry, thro the want of skill & ability, we shall then have a plain case to deal with. I shall of course write you from Boston. Yrs always truly

Danl Webster

ENCLOSURE

[Saturday April 5]

Robert Rantoul applied for an adjournment till next Thursday in order to give him time to prepare to argue the constitutionality of the F[ugitive] S[lave] Law. Denied. Further argument will [begin] Monday at 12. This is the last proceeding   D.W.

ALS. NBuHi. Published in *W & S*, 16: 604. Enclosure in another hand, concluded and initialed by DW. Despite the dateline, Webster actually wrote the letter in New York.

1. Robert Rantoul's colleague in the defense of Thomas Sims, Samuel E. Sewall, had taken a similar tack

before the chief justice of the Massachusetts Supreme Court, Lemuel Shaw, with equal lack of success. See 7 Cushing 285 (1851) and Stanley W. Campbell, *The Slave Catchers: Enforcement of the Fugitive Slave Law, 1850–1860* (Chapel Hill, N.C., 1968), p. 118.

2. See above, DW to Lunt, April 4, 1851.

TO MILLARD FILLMORE

Boston April 9th. 1851

My Dear Sir;

I arrived here yesterday, at 5. P.M. all the way from N. Y. with less fatigue than might be expected. The road all the way is fine, & smooth.

The Commiss[ione]r [George Ticknor Curtis] has adjourned his decision till Friday, the 11th. I was quite sorry to learn this; but I suppose he wished to take pains with an opinion, & tomorrow, the 10th is Fast Day, & all business of course suspended. The fugitive is safe; the proofs are clear; & the Marshall [Charles Devens] will move South with him on friday.

Immediately on my arrival, I sent for Mr [George] Lunt. The matter of Mr [George Partridge] Sanger is just as I told you. He lives in Middlesex, & attended a meeting there last fall, at which Anti-Fugitive Slave Bill Resolutions were adopted. Mr Lunt says he did not know it, till he learned it from me. I thought it best not to dispute the point; and as Sanger has diligence & ability, & as Mr Lunt does not propose that he should appear to take a part in the trial, I told him he might employ him. As to leading, arguing counsel, the difficulty is a question of precedence.

Mr Lunt feels that holding the official station, he ought to lead; Mr [Rufus] Choate is not willing, being at the Head of the Bar here, to act a subordinate part to Mr Lunt. I think we could manage to have the aid of B[enjamin] R[obbins] Curtis' services, if his engagements allowed. But they do not. He is a member of the Legislature which is likely to sit till the middle of May; & after the Senate question[1] is over, (if it ever shall be over) he is prepared for a public discussion, upon Administration matters.

I shall make some other arrangement; probably, to suggest to Mr Lunt the employment of Mr [Otis Phillips] Lord, of Essex Co., & a very fit man, & would be quite acceptable to Mr Lunt.

The trials come on, the 28th instant. It is of great importance to convict [Elizur] Wright.[2]

In an hour, I go to Marshfield, & shall write you from that cold & bleak shore. When you write me, please address me at Boston. Yrs always truly   Danl Webster

You will see that an Anti-Fugitive Slave Law Convention was held here yesterday.³

The marvels of the moment, are; [Robert] Rantouls somerset;⁴ [William Henry] Sewards⁵ letter—

ALS. NBuHi. Published in *W & S*, 16: 604–605.

1. The protracted deadlock over the election of a United States senator for a six-year term was broken on April 24 with the triumph of Free Soiler Charles Sumner. *Boston Daily Advertiser*, April 25, 1851; David Donald, *Charles Sumner and the Coming of the Civil War* (New York, 1960), pp. 194–202.

2. Wright (1804–1885) was editor of the Boston *Commonwealth*, an antislavery, anti-Webster organ. His trial concluded, like the other rescue cases, without a conviction. Stanley W. Campbell, *The Slave Catchers: Enforcement of the Fugitive Slave Law, 1850–1860* (Chapel Hill, N.C., 1968), pp. 150–151.

3. Massachusetts opponents of the Fugitive Slave Act of 1850 met in Boston's Tremont Temple on April 8. Following a number of speeches, they passed a series of resolutions condemning the law and demanding its

repeal. *Boston Semi-Weekly Atlas*, April 9, 1851; Jonathan Messerli, *Horace Mann: A Biography* (New York, 1972), p. 528.

4. Webster is referring to Rantoul's metamorphosis to antislavery activism, after years of quiescence on this issue, and most particularly to the Democratic leader's sharp attack, in a speech in Lynn on April 3, on the Fugitive Slave Law. For the text of Rantoul's remarks, see Luther Hamilton, ed., *Memoirs Speeches and Writings of Robert Rantoul, Jr.* (Boston, 1854), pp. 729–751. Comments critical of Rantoul appeared in the Washington, D.C., *National Intelligencer*, April 8, 1851.

5. Read at the anti–Fugitive Slave Law convention in Boston on April 8, Seward's letter criticized the law as "singularly unwise" and argued further that Congress had no authority to order the return of fugitive slaves. *Boston Semi-Weekly Atlas*, April 9, 1851.

FROM MILLARD FILLMORE

Washington, April 11. 1851
3. P.M.

My Dear Sir,

I have but a moment before the mail closes to acknowledge the receipt of yours of the 9th inst.¹ This is the day appointed for the removal of the *fugitive* [Thomas Sims] & I am waiting with no little anxiety to hear the result. *I trust the law will be maintained at every hazzard and at every sacrifice.* There is a rumor in town that there has been a riot and mob, but I trust it is not so.

I hope you may succeed in obtaining the assistance of counsel of undoubted ability and loyalty to try those engaged in the recent rescue.²

There is nothing of importance here except a special dispatch from the Gov. of Calafornia [John McDougal] to protect the state from the

Indians.[3] Congress as you are aware has left us almost without means.

I hear efforts have been made by Mr. [Thurlow] Weed to induce our legislature in N.Y. to denounce the compromise measures and especially the [fugitive] slave law by resolutions, and that he has failed, and will now resort to an address for the same object.[4]

I have not time to say more than that. I am with every sentiment of respect & esteem Truly yours   Millard Fillmore

ALS. NhD.

1. See above.

2. Fillmore is referring to the prosecutions of Elizur Wright et al. in the Shadrach rescue of February 15.

3. See John McDougal to Fillmore, March 1, 1851, and Secretary of War Charles M. Conrad's response, April 30, 1851, in *Senate Documents*, 32d Cong., 1st sess., Serial 611, Document No. 1, pp. 138–142.

4. According to Robert A. Campbell, who was the apparent source of this intelligence (see Campbell to Fillmore, April 9, 1851, Fillmore Papers, NBuHi), the Sewardites' efforts to pass a resolution demanding repeal of the Fugitive Slave Law foundered on their inability to command a majority in the assembly. In lieu of this approach, an address was to be prepared denouncing the law, with signatures appended of all legislators who could be mustered. Fillmore forces in Abany thereupon prepared a counteraddress expressing support for all the 1850 compromise measures. Ultimately, the two sides called a truce on the issue, and neither address was published.

TO MILLARD FILLMORE

Marshfield, April 13. 51
Sunday P.M.

My Dear Sir

I arrived at Boston Tuesday Eve', the 8th, & came to Marshfield the next morng. The weather has been cold & cheerless; still, I have kept out doors as much as I could, & have enjoyed long walks. Nothing gives me so much health & strength as exercise in the open air.

You will have heard that the Negro Simms [Thomas Sims] left Boston yesterday morng. On this occasion all Boston people appear to have behaved well. Nothing ever exceeded the malignity, with which abolitionists & free soilers persecute all those, who endeavor to see the laws executed. They are insane, but it is an angry & vindictive insanity. Fortunately, the number is not large. They made every possible effort to protect themselves under some show of legal proceeding; but all these efforts failed. Every Judge decided against them, & these judicial opinions, taken together, make a strong exhibition of legal authority. There are, Judge [Peleg] Sprague's charge, Mr [Benjamin Robbins] Curtis' opinion, and [the] admirable judgment of the Supreme Court of Mass, not yet reported in full; & Judge [Levi] Woodbury's opinion. At the same time, also, came out Judge [Samuel] Nelson's charge. I cannot but think that these judgments will settle the question, with all sane men in Mass.

Now, we need one thing further, viz, the conviction & punishment of some of the rescuers.[1] After that shall have taken place, it will be no more difficult to arrest a fugitive slave in Boston, than to arrest any other person.

I feel much concerned about these trials, but hope for the best.

It is my purpose to go back to Boston early this week. It will so much prolong my absence to go to N. Hampshire, that I must give up that part of my purpose. I am invited to meet the People of Boston, in Faneuil Hall;[2] and as I began speaking & writing on these adjustment measures, (out of the Senate) a year ago, in Boston, & I think I shall there make a finish. If there shall be a meeting Mr [Rufus] Choate will preside, & make the Speech: I shall discuss nothing, nor speak at any length. It will [be] merely a meeting of congratulation. This over, I go South; &, indeed, will go at any time, if occasion should require. Yrs always truly

Danl Webster

ALS. NBuHi. Published in W & S, 16: 605–606.

1. Elizur Wright et al., alleged res-cuers of the fugitive Shadrach.

2. See below, headnote preceding Rufus Choate to DW [April 15, 1851].

Gratified by the successful rendition of Thomas Sims on April 12, Webster anticipated a brief, pleasant sojourn in Boston on his way from Marshfield to Washington. A meeting of his supporters was planned for April 17 at Faneuil Hall, in which Rufus Choate would deliver the main address and Webster himself would add some brief, informal comments.

On April 14, however, with the Sims case very much in the public mind, the Boston aldermen sparked a tempest by denying Webster's friends the use of Faneuil Hall on the grounds that they had recently refused a similar request from abolitionists. The rebuff was particularly mortifying because Webster was convinced that the great mass of citizens in Boston backed his stand on the Fugitive Slave Law. Moreover, all of the aldermen were Whigs and thus, in theory at least, political cohorts.

The matter became a minor cause célèbre in Boston. Pro-Webster newspapers thundered against the "contemptible insult" to Boston's leading man, and efforts to override the aldermen culminated with a formal invitation by the Common Council on April 17 inviting Webster to meet them at Faneuil Hall. Webster was not mollified. "I feel that either I am disgraced or Boston is," he told Edward Everett. "The consciousness of either makes me as unhappy, almost, as that of the other" (DW to Everett, April 23, 1851, mDW 33332). He firmly declined the council's invitation, averring that he would enter Faneuil Hall again only when its doors "were wide open . . . to let in freely and to over-

flowing . . . all men of all parties, who are true to the Union as well as to liberty" (DW to Council President Francis Brinley, April 19, 1851, mDW 33291).

When Webster finally arrived in Boston on April 21, a joint delegation of aldermen and councilmen presented themselves, "eating humble pie," according to Peter Harvey, and offering assurances that the secretary of state was an honored guest of the city with ready access to Faneuil Hall. (Peter Harvey, Reminiscences and Ancedotes of Daniel Webster [Boston, 1877], pp. 190–192). Webster, however, had no intention of making up with the officials who had slighted him. He listened patiently as the delegation's chairman read its resolutions, then dismissed his audience, promising a formal reply, which, in written form, tersely rejected the invitation (DW to Henry B. Rogers et al., April 23, 1851, mDW 33339).

TO MILLARD FILLMORE

Marshfield April 15. 51

My Dear Sir:

I was very glad to receive your letter,[1] last Eveing, & to learn that there was nothing occurring of particular urgency, at Washington. Altho the weather has been cold & wet, nearly all the time I have been here, yet I leave with regret. And I shou[l]d be tempted to prolong my stay, if there were not [to] be occasions likely to call me from Washington again, soon. About the 10th or 15th of May the important suit between the Methodist Church [North], & the Methodist Church South,[2] is to come on for argument, in the Circuit Court of U.S. in the City of New York. I have been long engaged in the cause, & drew the Original Bill, in favor of the Church South. I have been in hopes that the Parties would be satisfied that Mr [Daniel] Lord should take my place, with Mr Reverdy Johnson, but they are not so inclined. Recent occurrences, perhaps, have contributed to lead to an undue estimate of the probable value of my services, on the occasion. The division between North & South, you know, took place on the Slavery question.

A suit, equally old, & of a somewhat similar nature, is on my hands in Massachusetts, to be tried the middle of June. It is between the Old school quakers, & the Hixites, so called,[3] & the question is, which party is entitled to the funds & property. I hope nothing may occur, rendering my attention to these two things inconsistent with my public duties.

In the present state of our military means, it is to be feared we shall have trouble with Indians, in the South West; & tho' it is our duty to do all we can, with the means in our hands, yet it is necessary to remember, also, that the Govt. will be pressed to raise volunteers, mounted men,

&c &c by those who would like the employment, & the pay. I take it, that a mounted man on the frontiers is a person exceedingly well paid, for doing very little.

I go to Boston tomorrow, & expect to meet the People in F[aneuil] H[all] on Thursday.

I am not surprised at what you say about the course of Mr [Thurlow] Weed, & his friends. They will probably attempt a denunciation of the compromise measures, in some way; but I think they will find themselves less strong than they imagine themselves to be. The case is a curious one. These Gentlemen are ready & willing to express a hearty & *conscientious* approbation of, or at least acquiescence in, the compromise measures, provided only that certain office holders be not disturbed. And, on the other hand, they are equally ready & willing to denounce those measures, heartily & *conscientiously* if those officers shall be disturbed.[4]

I lament, most deeply, this schism among N. York Whigs; but I do not see how it could be avoided. At the same time, I think we have friends, who are not only not discreet, but who attempt to use their influence, whatever it is, to magnify themselves, & to gain a triumph over their enemies. They wish to be the *Administration*, at least so far as N. Y. is concerned. They require, in my opinion, sharp looking after. I am, Dear Sir, with true regard always, Yrs   Danl Webster

ALS. NBuHi. Published in *PC*, 2: 428–429.

1. See above, Fillmore to DW, April 11, 1851.

2. Initiated in 1849 by the Methodist Church South to force an equitable division of assets with the Church North in a profitable New York book publishing concern, the suit was argued—without DW's participation—between May 19 and May 29, 1851. In November the court ruled on behalf of the southern Church, and after further legal maneuvers, a settlement was reached by 1853. See R. Sutton, *The Methodist Church Property Case* (New York, 1851), and John Nelson Norwood, *The Schism in the Methodist Episcopal Church 1844: A Study in Slavery and Ecclesiastical Politics* (Alfred, N.Y., 1923), esp. pp. 162–173.

3. Similar in nature to the Methodist case, the Quaker suit was postponed until January 1852, when it was argued and decided without DW's involvement. See *Oliver Earle et al., v. William Wood et al.*, in 8 Cushing 430–471.

4. See above, pp. 214–215, Samuel P. Lyman to DW, March 10, 1851.

TO MILLARD FILLMORE

Marshfield April 15. 1851
6. P.M.

Mr Dear Sir:

I wrote you this morning; since which time I learn that the Board of Alderman have *refused* the use of F[aneuil] Hall to those who invited me. This, is doubtless, owing to the whipping they got, in my letter in answer to their Resolutions.[1] Yrs truly   Danl Webster

ALS. NBuHi.   1. Letter not found.

FROM RUFUS CHOATE

[Newburyport, Massachusetts?]
[April 15, 1851]

My dear Sir

Mr. [Peter] Harvey conveys to you the first impressions which this foolery of the Aldermen suggests. He, Mr. [Albert] Fearing, Mr. T[homas] B[uckminster] Curtis & I agree that you should not speak—subject of course to that wisdom which never deserts you. It will destroy a low clique. I think it will strike other chords & produce mighty results.

N[athan] H[ale's][1] request to you alters the invitation to the Tremont Temple—stating the refusal of Faneuil Hall—the question is if a *letter* declining it, alluding in terms of grace, dignity & feeling to the refusal & to the cause of it, to wit, your preservation of the Union—would not be a most happy idea. I dare not suggest topics, but I do think that a graceful reference to your past public relations to the State—to the duration & aims of your public life, to this last great act, the interest of Boston in the Union—to your time of life—to what *are certain* to be the Sentiments, of all good men in a few short years' time—might be brought up into a most effective delightful & reformatory paper.[2]

To tell the truth, considering the real regret which will be universally felt at not hearing you, the indignation it will excite, the impression it will any where make—that you have indeed sacrificed your State for the Nation—I am glad they have done it.

Reconsideration is all I fear. I think surely speak in no spot but Faneuil Hall. In the greatest haste, & highest affection & regard Your obedient servant   R. Choate

ALS. DLC. This letter, in Choate's inimitable scrawl, is said to have provoked the following response from DW to his son Fletcher: "Tell Mr. Choate to write better; his handwriting is barbarous. I cannot read a single word. . . . Tell Mr. Choate to go to a writing-school and take a quarter's lessons." Quoted in Claude M. Fuess, *Rufus Choate: The Wizard* *of the Law* (New York, 1928), p. 198.

1. Hale was chairman of the committee of arrangements for the Faneuil Hall meeting.

2. See DW to George G. Smith et al., April 15, 1851, mDW 33255, published in Boston *Daily Evening Transcript*, April 18, 1851, in which DW reiterated his commitment to act in the interests of "the whole country."

FROM MILLARD FILLMORE

Washington, April 16. 1851

My Dear Sir,

Yours of the 13th[1] came to hand to day, and I congratulate you and the country upon the triumph of law in Boston. She has done nobly. She has wiped out the stain of the former rescue and freed herself from the reproach of *nullification*.

I am gratified to hear that your health is improving, and we shall be happy to welcome your return to the counsel board whenever it may suit your convenience.

Movements are evidently making for another piratical descent upon Cuba.[2] Letters & telegraphic despatches speak of armed men in motion in Georgia, but as yet we can not ascertain where they are to rendezvous or whence embark. We have issued circulars to the Collectors and orders to the Army and Naval officers to arrest any movement. But unfortunately we have few vessels now at the South.

South Carolina is far from tranquil as you will see by the enclosed slip. I can not but hope that Senator [Andrew Pickens] Butler has been misrepresented.[3]

I have gone through with the voluminous testimony taken on the Charges preferred against the Collector & Surveyor of the Port of Philadelphia, and am clearly of opinion that the charges are not sustained.[4] I requested Mr. [Thomas] Corwin to send for <him> Mr [William David] Lewis and inform him of the result, but that the proof was such as to require a purgation of the weigher's office, and I suggested to him that I wished he would turn out Loco focos, and put good competent Whigs in their places, wherever it could be done without prejudice to the public service, and that in making his new appointments he would as far as practicable select from that portion of the party which complained of having been overlooked, and he promised to do so.[5]

I learn by telegraph that Pennsylvania has repealed her law which refused the use of her jails for fugitives.[6]

I understand efforts are making to induce the Whigs in the legislature of N.Y. to issue an address against the compromise measures; and especially against the Fugitive Slave law.[7] Should this be done a counter address will also be issued.

Hearing nothing from Mr. Chandler[8] as to a candidate for the consulate at Belfast, I have written him to day calling his attention to the subject.

I see by the papers that Sir Henry [Lytton Bulwer] is in Charleston. Has his visit any connexion with the movement of the British consul as to the imprisonment of black seamen?[9]

I hope you may make some satisfactory arrangement for the trial of the rescuers. It is very important that these criminals should be punished. Their crime is contagious, and they must not escape with impunity. I am truly yours   Millard Fillmore

ALS. DLC. Published in Severance, *Fillmore Papers*, 1: 341–342.

1. See above.

2. See *Diplomatic Papers*, 2.

3. Enclosure not found. On April 7 Senator Butler, widely regarded as a moderate in South Carolina politics, in a speech at Edgefield had endorsed separate state secession. Washington, D.C., *National Intelligencer*, April 14, 18, 1851.

4. Fraud charges against Collector William D. Lewis, a "Proviso" Whig identified with Zachary Taylor, who had appointed him, were rooted in political differences with the Pennsylvania Whig faction led by Senator James Cooper. Although exonerated after an extensive evaluation of the evidence, Lewis remained a friction point in Pennsylvania Whiggery. John F. Coleman, *The Disruption of the Pennsylvania Democracy, 1848–1860* (Harrisburg, 1975), pp. 34–36; Henry P. Mueller, *The Whig Party in Pennsylvania* (New York, 1922), pp. 162, 177–178.

5. Fillmore, in fact, commanded Lewis to "conciliate" Cooper's wing of the party by sharing with them appointments in the customhouse. Coleman, *Pennsylvania Democracy*, p. 36.

6. Pennsylvania legislators closed their session on April 15 by passing a bill repealing a section of the 1847 law that denied the use of jails in the state for the temporary safekeeping of fugitive slaves. Governor William F. Johnston, a Free Soil Whig, pocket-vetoed the bill. *National Intelligencer*, April 18, 1851; Thomas D. Morris, *Free Men All: The Personal Liberty Laws of the North, 1780–1861* (Baltimore, 1974), pp. 154–156.

7. See above, Fillmore to DW, April 11, 1851, n. 4.

8. Possibly Joseph Ripley Chandler, congressman from Pennsylvania.

9. During the winter of 1850–1851 the British consul in Charleston, George B. Mathew, sent several sharply worded notes to South Carolina Governor John H. Means protesting the state's 1822 law subjecting free black seamen to imprisonment while their vessels remained in South Carolina ports. South Carolinians found the notes offensive, and a major incident was avoided only through the efforts of Webster and Bulwer (then minister to the United States), who acted quickly to calm the contesting parties. See Philip M. Hamer, "British Consuls and the Negro Seaman Acts, 1850–1860," *Journal of Southern History*, 1 (May 1935): 138–168, and Alan Frank January, "The First Nullification: The Negro Seaman Acts Controversy in South Carolina, 1822–1860," (Ph.D. diss., University of Iowa, 1976), pp. 337-363 and passim.

FROM CHARLES WAINWRIGHT MARCH

Washington Ap'l 17. '51

Dear Sir

Mr. John Parrott,[1] one of your clients before the Board on Mexican claims has promised to send the amount of your fee, somewhat upwards of $3000, to you at Boston. I did not know but it could be grateful to you there.

The pertinacious and inveterate hostility of Col. [Robert T.] Paine and Mr. [Caleb Blood] Smith's timorous indecision overcame Mr. [George] Evans'[2] earnest desire and attempt to give us justice in the land claims. We get nothing in comparison with our dues. The Union [Land Company] gets but $58,000 and the Trinity about $60,000.[3] I hope, there may yet be a chance for justice.

It is said that Dr. [Thomas M.] Foote, the present editor of the Buffalo "Commercial Advertiser," and the next friend of the President is to come here, and assume the editorial management of the Republic newspaper.[4] This movement with some others seem to indicate Mr. Fillmore's willingness to be a candidate in the next canvass. I am told that Mr. Greeley [Philip Greely], the Collector at Boston, writes him often, and professes great adhesion to his views.

The refusal of the Aldermen to loan your friends Faneuil Hall excites some surprise here and more indignation. It will however not injure your cause anywhere. Ever most resp[ectfull]y & Truly yrs

Chs W. March

ALS. NhHi.

1. Parrott was a partner in Parrott, Talbot & Company, shipping merchants, and consul to Mazatlán, 1837–1850. He was awarded $63,541 by the Mexican Claims Commission. Moore, *International Arbitrations*, 2: 1284; DW to Caroline Le Roy Webster, [June 24, 1849], *Correspondence*, 6: 343–344.

2. Paine, Smith, and Evans were the Mexican claims commissioners.

3. The actual awards were $58,879.10 and $63,559.24, respectively. Moore, *International Arbitrations*, 2: 1284. See also below, pp. 264–265, DW to Franklin Haven, July 3, 1851.

4. Foote did not move to Washington to edit the *Republic*. Instead, he purchased an interest in the *Albany Register* and as its editor took a decided proadministration stance, while continuing to serve as an adviser and listening board for the President. See Rayback, *Fillmore*, pp. 333–334.

TO MILLARD FILLMORE

Marshfield, April 18. 1851

My Dear Sir

You will have seen that the Boston Board of Aldermen have been as civil to me, as they were to you.[1] They are called Whigs, but they are just such Whigs as [William] Schouler, Greeley [Philip Greely], [Charles] Hudson, &c. &c. There are nine of them, all chosen [on] one Ticket, & constituted the Whig Ticket, last fall. Among them are two or three true conservative Whigs; the rest are, in principle & feeling, all free soilers. The friends of the administration in Boston are at least 3 to 1 of these sorts of People. It is likely enough these proceedings of the Board may cause some stir.

We have had a fearful storm, along this coast, which is not over. This is the 7th day of a strong East wind; & yesterday & the day before, it raged with unusual violence, accompanied with torrents of rain. At the same time, there was a high course of tides, being at the full of the moon, & the sea broke in upon us, in [a] manner not experienced for a great many years. It broke down, or overflowed over Dykes, & sea walls, & flooded our fields, to a great extent. The water was three or four feet deep, in our garden, & washed off some of the gardener's fixtures. We have no intercourse with Boston, & apprehend great damage may have been suffered by the Rail Roads, on the low lands & marshes. Two vessels have run ashore, under our eyes. In one, all the crew lost but one; in the other, crew saved. I cannot yet stir an inch out doors. Such a sweep has been made of Bridges over the Creek, that we have to go five miles, to get to the Post office, instead of something more than one.

They send me the "Oneida Republican," & other papers of that sort, by which I see what a "John Tyler" you are represented to be.

I shall go to Boston, & thence South, as soon as fair weather appears. Yrs always truly   Danl Webster

ALS. NBuHi. Published in part in *W & S*, 16: 608–609.

1. The aldermen had recently declined to express any welcome to Fillmore on a proposed presidential visit to Boston. See DW to George G. Smith et al., April 15, 1851, mDW 33255; Henry A.S. Dearborn to DW, April 19, 1851, mDW 33298; *Boston Daily Advertiser*, April 18, 1851; and Boston *Evening Transcript*, April 16, 1851.

FROM GEORGE PETER ALEXANDER HEALY

Paris April 29th 1851.
68. Rue de L'Arcade.

Dear Sir,

I am happy to inform you that my great work[1] will be finished in time to be publicly seen in Boston about the first of September next. It has occured to me that <if> the Mayor and Corporation of that city might be induced to favor me as they did Mr. Wier [Robert Walter Weir] some years since, by lending me Fanieul Hall, it would be well that the public should first see it, where it is intended, finally, to be placed: I have just drawn up a petition to that honorable body, & as I am ignorant of the proper form of sending it, I take the liberty of begging you to forward it for me, if you do not think it an improper request. I also beg to inform you that Mr. Franklin Haven has been so good as to communicate with Mr. Curtis[2] the gilder, who is to make the frame for the picture; I have thought it would be well to have for the centre ornament at the top of the frame, the Arms of the U.S.A. with the words, The defence of the

Constitution, & for the centre of the bottom, a space for carved letters into the frame, large enough for the three or four concluding sentences of the great speech itself; perhaps you will think of some proper ornament or device for the centre of each side, and also inform Mr. Haven upon what you decide to the words etc. for the frame.

I hope My dear Sir, that you will excuse the liberty I take, in troubling you with this affair, but I am emboldened to do so, as it is a matter upon which, my reputation, and the bread of my children depends. I have the honor to remain Your Most hu[m]ble. Obt. Servant   Geo. P. A. Healy

P.S. Pray beg Mrs. Webster to be so kind as to comply with the request I made some little time since.

ALS. MHi.

1. Seven years in the making, Healy's canvas, "Webster Replying to Hayne," was completed in Paris in the summer of 1851 and exhibited at Faneuil Hall later in the year, with Webster in attendance at the initial showing. See Marie de Mare, *G.P.A. Healy: American Artist* (New York, 1954), pp. 169–171.

2. Probably Samuel Curtis of Boston.

FROM EDWARD EVERETT

Cambridge 1 May 1851

Private

Dear Sir,

In a letter received from Mr [Henry Augustus] Wise yesterday he writes me as follows:—My brother [George Douglas Wise] who is on Surveying duty at the South has returned to Washington. He has been encamped on Edisto island near Charleston. There he saw a good deal of the leading families of the State, the Seabrooks, Legares, Aikins & others, all men of talents, wealth, & influence, & of course little Kings among their friends & dependents. All to a man steeped to the brains in disunion & secession. On one occasion my brother attended a Militia drill. The companies were composed of the gentlemen of the Island; the fine for absentees being 10 pr cent on their incomes. The Governor of South Carolina, Mr [John Hugh] Means,[1] reviewed them, and when the duties of the drilling and marching were ended, he made a Speech in which he exorted "those brave sons of the Palmetto State to burnish their weapons & sharpen their swords for the battle would soon be at hand;— it would be his happiness to lead them to victory."

At a supper given later in the day, where much more of the like fanaticism prevailed they all swore to cling to one another,—to make an issue with the other States,—and to leave the Union or die. That an attempt, at least will be made by that State to secede is beyond question. They seem to be impressed with the belief, that the Union will be kneeling at the feet of S. Carolina, imploring her to return, within two years; & that England will starve without her sea-island cotton. In a word so great is their delusion, that they prefer to be vassals of a Monarchy rather than remain under republican bondage.

This much is from Mr. Wise's letter. Should you have any occasion to allude to its contents, you will have the goodness not to mention his brother's name.

I had written the foregoing when I received yours of the 29th.[2] The plates of the Wall Street Speech are cast, so that the correction you propose on p. 510 of Vol. III cannot easily be made. I had however by changing a single word, made your meaning sufficiently apparent.[3] Perhaps it was so before, though it did not happen to strike me. I missed the *apodosis* of *first*.

I will send you tomorrow the table of contents for the second volume. It does not include all your miscellaneous Speeches up to the present time; but it includes, I presume, all that you have written out yourself,— many that you have not,—& more than the volume will hold. As two volumes will be quite as much as can be spared for this class of Speeches, it will perhaps be expedient to omit some of those which are most imperfectly reported in the Campaign of 1844.

In preparing the Richmond Speech for the press I softened a passage on p. 540 of the third volume bearing very hard personally on Mr. [Joel Roberts] Poinsett.[4] I have not at all changed the opinion expressed by you of his militia bill; but have taken the personal sting out of the concluding sentence, in consideration of his present loyalty to the Union.

In preparing the Remarks made at the Pilgrim festival in Newyork 22 Decr. 1843, I was for a little while extremely perplexed with a paragraph of considerable length on the subject of the height of the Great Pyramid & other Egyptian Antiquities! It stood in the midst of some observations on American commerce as belonging not to individual States [but] to the Union. I soon perceived that the printer, in making up the column, had incorporated into your Speech a Paragraph from one of Mr. [George Robins] Gliddon's lectures,[5] of which there was a report in another part of the Paper. The like of this never befel me before.

Among the diplomatic papers the Instructions of Mr [Caleb] Cushing on his Mission to China occur to me. I do not know whether they have ever been published.[6]

☞ Please let me know whether you wish any Congressional Speeches inserted in the Collection, of earlier date than the Speech on the Bank of the United States of the 2d of Jan. 1815.

_____

You will perhaps read the piece headed "Coalition"[7] in the [Boston] Advertiser of this day. It occurs to me that before the Legislature breaks up, the whig members ought to publish a short address to the people, giving a succinct history of the coalition,—of the bargain for offices & the mode of Mr [Charles] Sumner's election. Cannot Major [Andrew Jackson] Donelson⁸ be persuaded not to exert himself so much to give a false coloring to this occurrence? I remain as ever, dear Sir, Sincerely yours, Edward Everett.

P.S. Since the foregoing was written, I have found among the papers brought up by Mr Abbott [George Jacob Abbot] a copy of the Pilgrim speech at Newyork in 1843, evidently revised by yourself, which that above referred to was not.

I enclose some notes of a speech in which Judge [John] Marshall is referred to, thinking you might like to write them out.⁹

Can you refer me to the authority for your statement in the Pilgrim speech of 1843, that James VI granted Nova Scotia seven times?¹⁰

ALS. MHi.

1. Means (1812–1862; South Carolina College 1832) succeeded Whitemarsh B. Seabrook as governor in 1850 and served for two years. Active in the secession movements of 1850–1851 and 1860–1861, he was killed at the Second Battle of Bull Run.

2. DW to Everett, April 29, 1851, mDW 33383.

3. In preparing DW's Wall Street speech, September 23, 1840, for republication in the *Works*, Everett changed the word *too* in a sentence extolling the virtues of a national circulating currency to *also*, placing the word in front of, rather than following, the word *beneficially*. See *Speeches and Forensic Arguments*, 3: 510; *Works*, 2: 57.

4. The text of DW's campaign speech in Richmond, Virginia, October 5, 1840, referring to Poinsett's militia bill suggests that Virginia had expressed oppositon "till she has made its author's heart sick; and she dont mean to pardon it even now." *Speeches and Forensic Arguments*, 3: 540. As revised by Everett, the text reads: "[Virginia] will never consent to it, by whatever weight of authority it may be urged on the country." *Works*, 2: 95.

5. See *New York Commercial Advertiser*, December 23, 1843, for the imperfect text. The problem was resolved with the procurement of a second, revised copy of the same speech. See DW to Everett, May 3, 1851, mDW 33467. Gliddon (1809–1857) was a prominent Egyptologist.

6. The instructions to Cushing had been previously published in *The Diplomatic and Official Papers of Daniel Webster* (New York, 1848), pp. 360–367—a volume Everett had edited.

7. The article had claimed that the Democratic–Free Soil coalition was based on "barter and sale of offices," most especially including the United States Senate seat to which Charles Sumner had been elected a week earlier.

8. Donelson had recently succeeded the venerable Thomas Ritchie as editor of the Washington *Union*, a Democratic paper generally sympathetic to the Fillmore administration.

9. Webster replied that Everett should omit his remarks on Marshall, "as they were imperfectly reported, and were never revised." DW to Everett, May 3, 1851, mDW 33467.

10. DW could provide no source for the remark.

FROM DANIEL FLETCHER WEBSTER

Boston May 2d. 1851.

My dear Father,

Mr. [William] Schouler is boasting among his acquaintances of having had a very pleasant correspondence with you.

As he can put his own gloss on this, which offends all your friends who know what a scamp he is, I wish you would let me have a copy of it, if you see fit, in order to put the thing right.[1]

Nothing would be more injurious than an imputation of *his* friendship.

It seems to me that if it were supposed abroad that the [Boston] Atlas were friendly it would be the very thing opponents would rejoice in. There are some men whose enmity is highly desirable, and having got the Atlas into this position I would keep it there, if the greatest contempt could affect it.

Pardon me for suggesting to you. Yr affectionate Son

Fletcher Webster

ALS. NhHi.

1. Noting that he had some months earlier made a "civil" response to Schouler's inquiry on behalf of a friend seeking a diplomatic appointment, DW promised to send copies, if they could be located, to counter Schouler's characterization of their contents. See DW to Fletcher Webster, May 4, 1851, mDW 33479; William Schouler to DW, February 5, 1851, mDW 32429; and DW to Schouler, February 7, 1851, mDW 32486.

TO PETER HARVEY

Washington May 4th '51.

Private & confidential

My Dear Sir

I wrote a short note to Mr [Albert] Fearing yesterday and have since recd yours of the 2d.[1] I have no hesitation of opinion upon the subject of which you write. I would not wish to dictate to others what course it may be proper for them to pursue, but for myself I am quite resolved not to commit any interest of mine to the management of The Whig State Com[mi]ttee of Mass. The leading object of that Com[mi]ttee will be to reestablish a Whig Government in Mass. And if we may judge by the past, we may fear that to effect this object, they will be ready to sacrifice high National Considerations, and to court as they have courted free soilers, and semi freesoilers, abolitionists, and semi abolitionists.[2] The truth is that sound Whigs and sound Union men, in other states, very strongly suspect the Whig party of Mass. of these tendencies. They are not likely therefore to be willing to cooperate wth that party in Mass. The Union Whigs, Tariff Whigs, Internal Improvement Whigs, and Constitutional Whigs are afraid, all over the South, to connect themselves with us; because they say, that on the question of all others, the most important to them, they have as little, indeed less, to expect from Mass. Whigs, than from Mass. Democrats. They think Gov. [George S.] Boutwell a better Union man, for example, than Gov [George Nixon] Briggs; they think no worse votes are to be expected from Mr [Charles] Sumner, on the point most interesting to them, than would have been to be expected from Mr. [Robert Charles] Winthrop: they think they have no more to hope from Mr Jno [John] Davis, and Mr O[rin] Fowler than from any members of the Democratic party who might succeed to their places. I speak to the fact, those sentiments may be just or unjust; but they do exist and they will influence men[']s conduct.

Besides, there is a growing opinion that the present organization of the Whig Party can not be continued throughout the United States. Georgia you perceive, has already adopted the new distinction of a Union party, and a State Rights party. Other important Southern States are on the eve of making similar demonstrations.

Under these circumstances, it appears to me that the course of the real friends of the Union in Mass. is plain enough; that is to call a meeting of Union men of all parties. Perhaps few Gentlemen of the Democratic party would attend but never mind that. If the Idea spreads and gains ground, many of that party may come in; and New Hampshire is not unlikely to follow the example.

My dear Sir, I say all these things with diffidence, and would not say them at all, if it did not seem to be necessary to let my opinion be known to my friends in Boston. Although I have marked this "private & Confidential," yet I have no wish that you should conceal its contents from Mr. [William] Appleton, Mr. [James Kellogg] Mills, Mr. [Samuel Atkins] Eliot, the Messrs. Curtis, Mr. Fearing, and other such Gentlemen as were assembled at Mr. T[homas] B[uckminster] Curtis' when I was in Boston. Mr Edward Curtis will be here from New York in three or four days, and he will communicate immediately with you and your friends. Yours always truly   Danl Webster

I have a letter from Mr [Franklin] Haven.[3] You may show him this, as I have not time to answer his.

ls. NN. Published, from a copy in the Everett Papers, MHi, in *W & S*, 16: 610–611.

1. Letters not found.

2. See also, on this, DW to Fletcher Webster, May 5, 1851, mDW 33511.

3. Letter not found.

TO ISAAC LOTHROP HEDGE

Washington May 5. 1851.

My Dear Sir;

I wished to see you, while at the North, not only for general reasons, but also in regard to an affair of business.

You remember, that in 1849 I negotiated, in behalf of the O[ld] C[olony] Rail Road Co. a contract with the Genl Post Office, for carrying the mail over the Road, for four years. I made a satisfactory bargain: Mr [Elias Hasket] Derby, then President of the Company, being willing to state, as I understand, that I saved it $44,000. The subject was first suggested by you to me, if I remember, & having expressed a willingness to undertake the business, you so stated to the Directors, & the President, by their direction, gave me instructions. I was here three weeks, or more, & went to the Department from day to day, following up the subject diligently, to its completion.

You & I had some conversation about compensation for this service. At that time I possessed, & had for some time possessed, a right of free passage over the Road, *for myself & family*. Mr. Fletcher Webster was just then establishing his family at Marshfield; and so far as I remember, our conversation was, that if I succeeded in getting the contract, my right of free passage for myself & family should be continued & confirmed, & the same right extended to Fletcher Webster & his family. Whether, in case of great success any further compensation was to be paid, I cannot say. At any rate, I was, as I supposed, to be reasonably paid, for my attention to the subject.

Now, in point of fact, instead of making any compensation, the Directors have abolished the then existing right of free passage for my family, & only allow myself to pass free. I believe, for some reason, they allow F. W. himself to pass free. I am not entirely satisfied with this treatment; & am about to commence a suit against the Corporation; & the object of this letter is, to request you to state, in a letter to me, all that you recollect on the subject. As things have turned, I get nothing; whereas I think I am justly entitled to a just remuneration.[1] Yrs truly

Danl Webster

ALS. MH. Hedge (1799–1867; Harvard 1820) was a member of the board of directors of the Old Colony Railroad, a Massachusetts line that made connections between Marshfield and Boston.

1. For indications that the railroad failed to meet Webster's demands, see below, pp. 313–314, 317, John Plummer Healy to DW, April 7, 1852, and DW to Healy, April 9, 1852. It is not clear whether DW's suit against the Old Colony Railroad brought results, in or out of court.

TO MYRON LAWRENCE

Washington May 5. 51.

Private & Confidential

I thank you cordailly my dear Sir—for the very handsome manner in which you were kind enough to speak of me, at the late Whig meeting in Boston.[1] You are a true Union man, a whole American, and have reflection and wisdom enough to judge of political objects, according to their real magnitude, respectively. And I dare say there were some ears in the crowd before you, open and ready to receive your remarks, with pleasure. But I fear there were others, which would have been better pleased with almost any other sounds.

I wish my dear Sir, that I could partake in the confidence you express, of an early return of our great and beloved commonwealth to her proper character and condition. But I confess I have deep fears. Mass. and especially our Whig party, has sustained a serious loss of confidence, in other States and with other Whigs. This cannot be concealed; and it is owing in great measure to the strong and unyielding opposition which her members of Congress manifested to the adjustment measures of the last Congress. The whole power of Massachusetts in Congress was exerted against *national settlement*, and *national harmony*; with the exception of the efforts of one individual, whom the Whigs of Massachusetts seem half disposed to repudiate, for having made those efforts. How can it be otherwise, than that the best men and best Whigs in all the south, should now think they see that on the great constitutional point, most vital to them, Massachusetts Whigs are no longer to be relied on?

My dear Sir, we must try to retrieve the character of the state from this heavy imputation. We must try to bring all Whigs to a disposition to fulfil, fully and promptly, all their constitutional duties. No one man, can do more to this end than yourself, and allow me to say, it is the path of honor and of true distinction, which now lies before you. I shall be very glad always to hear from you.[2] Yrs truly   Daniel Webster.

Copy. Everett Papers, MHi. Published in *W & S*, 16: 612–613.

1. Lawrence was one of three main speakers at the Whig state caucus in Boston on April 30. The others were Franklin Dexter of Beverly and Benjamin R. Curtis of Boston. *Boston Semi-Weekly Atlas*, May 1, 1851.

2. Expressing his gratitude for

DW's comments, Lawrence declared his loyalty to Webster and his conviction that both the Whig State Central Committee and the party at large would support Webster's "national" course in Washington. See Lawrence to DW, May 12, 1851, mDW 33601, and June 2, 1851, mDW 33715.

TO FRANKLIN HAVEN

Washington
May 9. 1851

My Dear Sir

I return you Mr [Samuel] Hooper's letter, & thank you for yours.[1] I have very high regard for Mr Hooper, & generally great confidence in his judgment. But on this occasion I think him wrong, altogether. At least, I can fall into no such policy, nor stand on any such platform, as the Whig Com[mitt]ee seem inclined to adopt.[2] I know their schemes must end in the entire rout & ruin of the Whig party of Massachusetts. I feel the more confident, in my judgment now, because I stated to the Com-[mitt]ee, in writing two years ago, what would be the result of their attempts to conciliate the free soil & abolition parties. I, for one, shall have nothing to do with the Whig party, if a part of their "platform" be, as I understand it is, to "agitate" for the modification of the Fugitive Slave law. They may just as well "agitate" for its entire repeal. An attempt at either would be certain, not only to occupy the exclusive attention of Congress for a long time, but also to break up, forever, the Whig party of the Union. Yrs truly   Danl Webster

I devoutly hope I may see some Boston friends at N. Y. Tuesday.

ALS. MH-H.

1. Letters not found.

2. Hooper, recently elected to the Whig State Central Committee, had evidently offered Haven the opinion that with some modifications of the Fugitive Slave Law, the Massachusetts Whig party could unite behind the Fillmore administration in the fall elections.

FROM HIRAM KETCHUM

New York May 10. 1851

My dear Sir

I received a letter from Mr. Williams[1] this morning intimating a wish that I should address you, and suggest my views as to your action in reference to the invitation[2] signed by a numerous body of citizens of New York. From a telegraphic dispatch sent since that letter was written, I suppose your answer to the invitation will be given before this letter shall reach you.[3]

Being therefore ignorant of your expressed views I shall forbear to say any thing more than this, that so far as my influence extends the action of the signers of the letter to you, shall be satisfactory to you.

Reluctant as you may possibly be to make farther addresses to masses of Citizens, I would respectfully suggest that you make a Speech at Dunkirk that shall interest, and gratify, all persons, and their name is legion, having an interest or feeling in favor of internal improvements, by rail roads and canals. I think it useful now to divert public attention, as far as practicable, from the exciting theme of slavery. I am persuaded it will be refreshing to hear you upon some other leading interest of the Country.

In this connection would it not be well to advert pointedly to the great road, to be commenced with vigor this very month, from Cairo to Chicago. This road is a long link in a chain from Chicago to Mobile. At this moment this road excites an absorbing interest in Illinois. It will be certainly built, for such Gentlemen as Mr [George] Griswold and others of N. Y. & Mr Havens [Franklin Haven] & others of Boston, have engaged in the enterprize, and their measures are well and wisely taken. In less than four years, the road will be completed. You are aware that the funds to build this road are derived from the public lands—can any better disposition be made of these lands, where there is reasonable certainty, as in this case, that the object to which they are devoted, will be accomplished.

I have well considered, and definite opinions upon other matters connected with the future, which, should you desire it, I shall freely communicate, whenever a fitting private opportunity shall present. I remain Yrs Very truly   Hiram Ketchum

ALS. DLC. Ketchum (c. 1792–1870) was a New York City attorney, a close friend of DW, and a leader of the Webster Whigs in the city.

1. Possibly Nathaniel F. Williams (1780–1864), a Baltimore merchant and lifelong supporter of DW. In 1851, through DW's influence, President Fillmore appointed Williams appraiser for the Port of Baltimore.

2. In wake of the controversy over the availability of Boston's Faneuil Hall to DW and his friends, New Yorkers initiated a campaign to entreat DW to speak there. See Boston *Evening Transcript*, April 22, 1851.

3. See DW to George Griswold et al., May 9, 1851, mDW 33565, published in *Works*, 6: 595.

Completion in early May of the New York and Erie Railroad provided the occasion for an extended barnstorming tour in New York by President Fillmore and the entire cabinet. New York was crucial to the Whigs' prospects for retaining the White House in 1852, and although Webster and Fillmore had understandably avoided the subject in their personal intercourse, each man naturally wished to sample—and shape—opinion in the Empire State. Moreover, at a time when northern attacks on the Fugitive Slave Law were making southerners edgy and encouraging an otherwise faltering secessionist drive in Deep South states, it was incumbent on the administration's leading men to articulate the case for compliance with the law and adherence to the Union.

The first days of the tour were lighthearted in tone, with members of the presidential party taking turns, at more than a dozen whistlestops, in speeches praising the railroad and the communities through which it ran. Webster was particularly effusive, remarking at one juncture that if "there is a more beautiful, a richer and brighter spot in the country" than western New York, "I have not seen it" (Boston Daily Advertiser, May 22, 1851). This festive mood was dampened briefly in Dunkirk when on May 16, Fletcher Webster was suddenly stricken with a violent

*and seemingly life-threatening inflammation of the throat. As the rest
of the party traveled to engagements in Buffalo, Syracuse, and Albany,
Webster remained behind with his son. (See* Daily Advertiser, *May 17,
1851, and DW to Richard M. Blatchford, May 17, 1851, in Curtis, 2:
503.) Fletcher's quick recovery enabled Webster to continue the tour,
albeit in the wake, rather than the company, of the presidential entourage.*

*Arriving in Buffalo on May 20, Webster attended several receptions
and made two major speeches, one of which paid tribute to the city's
remarkable growth and the other, before thousands of rain-drenched
but attentive Buffalonians, emphasizing the need for obedience to the
law and support for the Union. Here and throughout the tour, he repeatedly hammered at the themes of "duty" and "contract." "Higher
law" doctrine, Webster argued, was not merely folly, but "treason," and
could not be condoned.*

*Despite the radical political complexion of upstate New York, thou-
sands of citizens came to see, hear, and applaud the "defender of the
constitution." Their cheers doubtless gratified Webster and fed hopes
not only for national harmony but also for a final presidential bid in
1852.*

TO RICHARD MILFORD BLATCHFORD

Canandaigua, May 25, 1851
Sunday Morning, Seven o'clock.

My Dear Sir:

I get along slowly, as well as poorly. I do not mean poorly in health,
for my health is much improved, but I get poorly through the meeting
of such crowds of people.

Yet I seem to have no option. The President stopped everywhere, and
said something, and it would be thought churlish if I were to do less. I
shall leave this place at nine to-morrow; stop a little while, and say a
few words at Auburn. It is Governor [William Henry] Seward's residence; and everybody there, I suppose, is a Free-soiler, or nearly everybody, and I would not wish to give him or them offence.

Thence to Syracuse, that laboratory of abolitionism, libel, and treason.
Tuesday night I shall reach Albany, and stay there through Wednesday,
and, if the weather is tolerable, take the evening boat of that day. I
must do this, in order to have one day, Thursday, in New York; and then
Friday and Saturday to get to Washington. Under these circumstances,
I do not think it worth your while to come to Albany, as we should be
asleep while together. I much prefer, if you think you can spare a day,
that you should go with me to Philadelphia. I am having a nice time

here. The finest weather in the world, and entire quiet, I begin to feel about right. You saw Fletcher, I suppose, and learned what a drenching we all had in Buffalo. Yours truly always,   Daniel Webster.

Text from Curtis, 2: 509–510. Original not found.

TO HARRIETTE STORY WHITE PAIGE

Sunday Morng Astor House
[June 1, 1851]

Dear Mrs Paige,

I can really do [no] more this morning, than to thank you for your letter,[1] which I recd on my arrival here, & to say that I will answer it immediately on my arrival at Washington, for which place I set forth tomorrow morning. I am quite well, & so was Mrs. Webster at the last date. Pray give my best love to your husband & children—& to Fletcher, on whose account I was terribly frightened, at Dunkirk. It seems strange, that it so happened that I was conversing, the afternoon before, with a Lady who had lost nearly all her children. We were sympathetically melancholy, & spoke of the hard fate of seeing our children die before us. A few hours afterwards Fletcher was seized so violently, that it seemed to me highly probable that I should be childless, before morning. God, in his mercy, averted that calamity.

Send my love to Caroline[2] & her babies, & to Master Dan.[3] Yrs. affectionately,   Danl Webster

ALS. MHi. Paige (1809–1863) was the daughter of Stephen White (1787–1841), a Boston merchant, and Harriet Story (1787–1827), sister of Justice Joseph Story. She was the wife of James William Paige, half brother of the first Mrs. Webster and sister-in-law of Fletcher Webster.

1. Not found.
2. Caroline Story White Webster (1811–1886), Harriette's sister, and the wife of Fletcher Webster.
3. Fletcher's son and DW's namesake.

FROM JOHN CATRON

Nashville, June 2d. 51

D[ea]r Sir,

I have just read your 2d Speech made at Buffalo. That *you*, who broke ground, "Solitary and alone"—as a northern man, on the 7th of March 1850, could do more good, by such a Speech as you made at Buffalo, than any other man, in the present State of affairs, is not controverted by any one in this region. And you have done all that was desired—or even *expected*, which is saying a good deal. In your remenescences of Texas, and its acquisition as Slave Territory, you state the opposition you had made to it. I knew it full well. I differed with you—as slave territory I desired Texas—and from about 1820, up to the day of annexation, used all the slight power at my command, to sever the country from Spain, from the Sabine to the Del Norte, for the sake of the Negro race, and as a home for the negro in part; but mainly as a space to pass over to Mexico and the Americas within the tropics.[1] We are the ephemerals of a day, and in connection with our accidental position with negroes in our country, must look beyond that day: To Centuries. Where will Celt and Saxon be two or three hundred years hence. Not in the tropics as a progressive man and propagator of colonies by a progeny of the European Stock. Look at India—and the tropical Islands, East & west. Nay, at Mexico. Take ten women, and men, all European but native born—and succeeding from one set of parents down through ten generations, and where would the race run out? The first set of offspring w[oul]d be puny—the 2d. set more so—the 3d. less in number, and stature—the 4th without teeth or hair at thirty—& the 5th likely to be nothing. Such has been all experience since Columbus discovered the new world—and the Portuguese re-discovered older Asia. From Hecla to the pillars of Hercules, the European man has made a failure, in his attempts to occupy the tropics & supersede the native, either negro, or mongol. Hybrids are nearly mules usually; but if they propagate, they will all be of the native race very soon.

The Mexican Spaniard gets no supplies from old Spain now—nor will the swarthy, shrivelled, headless creature remain any length of time— the native race will soon absorb him. This race is cognate to the negro— there is no antagonism between the races, and the half breeds are vigorous. On the low Coasts, and in the swamps the negro will absorb the Indian. There, the white man will wear out in a single century—or less. And under the rose be it spoken: We have much Coast Country, & swamp, between the Capes of Delaware, & the Rio Del Norte, as little suited to the Saxon (almost) as the Oronoco. Let him and the negro alone for 200 years, in such localities, excluding all white and black immigrants from abroad, and where would the white man be? A look at his puny and trembling offspring will tell you—& a look at the vigorous progency of young negroes in the rice-swamps will equally prove the assumption—for theory it is not, to any man conversant with the facts.

In view of these considerations my opinion is, that the negro should be pressed west, & west—and onward, into, and through the tropics; and there be left to <themselves> himself. Once open the Channel to the Swamp Country of Mexico, as it is now opened to Africa, and an amount of negro population will be sent there each year, beyond conjecture. The policy is to scatter the negro race—over Texas, up to the Swamps, where no clothes are needed, and the Yam, & banana grow—

where he need not work. Familiarize him to the country by a sight of it—bring him back, to talk to his fellow slaves. Let the dying man,—or living man, bargain with and carry off hundreds at a time. Send the freed negroes there. Here lies the great trouble. We can[']t allow a free negro race among us where Slaves are—Liberia is too far off—too unknown. It is in condemned Africa! The negro views it as his grave; he won't go. Ten thousand can be sent to Mexico more readily than a single hundred to Africa. Why Sir, on this plan of colonizing <not> hardly a negro w[oul]d be left in Maryland—or Kentucky, or Tennessee or Virginia (most probably) in 50, or 75 years. The plan being in motion w[oul]d sweep on with increasing strength—the States—and the U. States would afford more & more aid. It would sweep clean to the ocean through our whole extent in a century.

It may be asked, w[oul]d the Mexican agree to such a Colony? When did this Anglo-Saxon ever ask the red-man twice for such a boon—for his whole Country if required, & vacant, or nearly so. I think the Indian would hardly object, if a little money was thrown in the Scale. That is, for a *little* country to begin with. Being there, I am sure, with our help, the negro can remain, & increase, & fight his way down South, if need be.

I should like to see in my day a small spot colonized with our negroes beyond the Del Norte—but under U. States protection to some extent—as to extent in *name*, it matters little.

No other way of disposing of the negroes among us that has feasibility in it has occurred to me. That this is practicable I feel sure and having thought of it very much first and last, it is presented for what it is worth. With sincere regard, I have the honour to be, Yr obt. Servt.

J Catron.

ALS. NhD.

1. In this connection, see Catron to DW, June 12, 1836, in Curtis, 1: 523–524, and Carl B. Swisher, *The Oliver Wendell Holmes Devise His-*tory of the Supreme Court of the United States: The Taney Period, 1836–64 (New York, 1974), pp. 199–201.

TO FRANKLIN HAVEN

Washington June 4. '51
Wednesday morng
6. o'clock

My Dear Sir

I arrived once more at my own house, last Evening, & glad enough to get home. You were right in supposing that there was some danger to health, in such an undertaking; but I thought I must consider myself as committed, & that I could not turn back. I have been absent twenty three days. They have not been days of idleness. What may ensue from what has occurred, during this flight, remains to be seen. When I left you at New York, I had no idea, not the slightest, that such a tour of speech-making was before. I took with me, therefore, no book, no document, & made no preparation whatever. I am now satisfied this was fortunate; & that more impression has been made by plain statement, & some degree of warmth & earnestness, than could have been produced by more elaborate discussion. The principal Speeches, viz Buffalo, Syracuse, Albany, will be printed at N. York in pamphlet form.[1] I expect the proof today. It cost me two days hard work to correct the reports.

Contrary to all expectation, my health is greatly improved. Motion & exertion have cleared off bilious, & other habits of the system, contracted by sedentary life. I feel this morning as if I could hold a plough at Marshfield, pretty well, or hoe a row of potatoes.

Mrs. Webster I found quite well, What with driving & walking, & good weather, she has, as she says, found her time to pass off agreeably.

Of course, I have seen nobody, out of my own house, as yet. If I learn any thing important I shall write to some of you. At N. York, I saw Mr [George] Ashmun, Mr [Barnabas] Bates, Mr [Charles] Lanman, Mr [Thomas] Tileston, Mr W[illiam] T[homas] Davis, &c. & they met sundry N.Y. friends. Mr Ashmun will be in Boston this week.

I have not yet seen my letters. Please remember me to Mr Curtis,[2] Mr [Peter] Harvey, & other friends. Yrs truly & sincerely   Danl Webster

ALS. MH-H.
   1. Published as *Mr. Webster's Speeches at Buffalo, Syracuse, and Albany, May, 1851* (New York,

1851).
   2. Probably Thomas Buckminster Curtis.

TO PETER HARVEY

                       Washington June 9. '51

My Dear Sir

I am obliged to you for your letter of the 6.[1] No doubt what has been done in Boston is entirely right, & wise; and I shall always be satisfied with whatever course judicious friends adopt. The general views put forth in the Courier of Saturday,[2] are exactly such as I entertain. The danger is, as there shown, that National objects will be postponed to local objects, & that Mass. may thus lose her high character as a leading, Constitutional, member of the Union.

The policy of courting the abolitionists has been long enough practised. It has always failed: & the State committee has my opinion, if it was thought worth preserving, given two or three years ago, that by yielding, more & more, to Abolition notions, the Whigs were only strengthening an enemy, who would soon become their master.

We have nothing new here. There is, at this season, & in the recess of Congress, a sort of pause, in the pressure of affairs. And as the weather is not warm yet, we get on very well. Yrs always truly

Danl Webster

ALS. RPB. Published, incorrectly dated June 3, in *W & S*, 16: 613–614.

1. Not found.

2. In a long editorial on June 7 the *Boston Courier* had argued that political success for Massachusetts Whiggery hinged on steadfast support for the Compromise of 1850 and, in proper time, concerted backing for President of "the man who has saved the Union from dissolution and arrested a civil war by his courageous patriotism."

TO THURLOW WEED

Washington June 9. 1851.

Private

My dear Sir,

Your kind and friendly letter,[1] addressed to me at Canandaigua, was returned to Albany, and placed in my hands, while sitting at dinner. [I] gave it to my man, who mislaid it and it was not looked at until after my return to this city.

I thank you for your invitation to dine, and should have been happy, had I not been engaged otherwise, to have met at your house, with the Officers of the State Government of New York. I have met the Governor, the Secretary [of State], the Comptroller[2] &c in public life, have always acted with them, and always entertained, and still entertain for them all, high regard. Whether anybody in or out of New York, would be scandalized by my association with those Gentlemen at your table, is a matter, into the probability of which, I should not enquire.

I regret my dear Sir, that your relations with the Administration, are not more confidential and cordial. But so far as this want of cordiality arises from occurrences, personal or local, in by gone times and happening between you and others, you may be quite well assured, that *I* do not partake in it. I am happy to learn what you say of your respect to myself. You are well aware My Dear Sir, that you and your friends, especially those of them who live in the city, were Gentlemen in whom I placed unbounded trust, personal and political, down to the time of nomination of Genl. [Zachary] Taylor. It would not be frank in me, not to say, that the lead, taken in that proceeding in the city of New York—gave me dissatisfaction and uneasiness.[3] But I cherish no resentments, and shall be happy, happy indeed, if things shall take such a turn, as that we think alike, and act together hereafter. Alienation and difference, and distrust, between me and my old New York friends, have caused me more regret than almost any other political occurrences.

I pray you to present me to your friends about you. And believe me with regard, truly yours.   Daniel Webster.

Copy. NhHi. Published in Van Tyne, p. 477, and, misdated June 9, 1850, in *W & S*, 16: 547–548.

1. Thurlow Weed to DW, May 24, 1851, mDW 33664.

2. Washington Hunt, Henry S. Randall, and Philo C. Fuller, respectively.

3. Abandoning their early support for DW's presidential bid in 1848, a group of New York City's most influential bankers and merchants publicly switched allegiance to Zachary Taylor and promoted DW for Vice President on a ticket headed by the hero of Buena Vista. DW was not interested in the Vice Presidency; nor was he mollified by his erstwhile backers' insistence that their approach was the best way to thwart the ambitions of Henry Clay. See DW to Richard M. Blatchford, January 30, 1848, *Correspondence*, 6: 269, and Robert F. Dalzell, Jr., *Daniel Webster and the Trial of American Nationalism, 1843–1852* (Boston, 1973), pp. 142–143.

In June Webster's political associates, with his discreet encouragement, began to organize a presidential campaign. Because Webster wished to maintain a distance from the regular Massachusetts Whig organization, a "central committee" of his supporters, meeting in Boston on June 5, drew up nominating petitions that would circulate in every Massachusetts school district. The petitions were accompanied by a cover letter bearing the signatures of Rufus Choate, Edward Everett, Franklin Haven, Peter Harvey, and fifteen more of Webster's most reliable friends. (See George Ashmun to DW, [June 5, 1851], mDW 34039; DW to Everett, June 6, 1851, mDW 33783; Philip Greely to Millard Fillmore, July 19, 1851, Fillmore Papers, NBuHi; and Robert F. Dalzell, Daniel Webster and the Trial of American Nationalism, 1843–1852 [Boston, 1973], pp. 230–232.)

As the petition campaign progressed, Webster pronounced himself satisfied (see below, DW to Haven). Maintaining forward momentum in the months to come was his next formidable challenge.

TO FRANKLIN HAVEN

Washington June 11. '51

Private

My Dear Sir

I have fully learned from your letter,[1] & other sources, what has been done in Mass, & it seems to me to be all as well, as could be. The great point, at present, is, to let it be known, in Massachusetts, & *else where*, that the friends of the Union in Mass. are determined, & *will not take any backward step, under any circumstances. When the Country is assured of this, you will see consequences.*

You are as much, my Dear Sir, in the centre of my political friends, in & about Boston, as any other person, & rather more so. You see many of them, daily. And I have thought that I would, this mor[n]ing, give you a little statement, of my present *idea* [&] *purposes*; not because any thing is definitely fixed, in my own mind, but for your consideration, & that of other friends, as you may happen to meet them, *incidentally.*

First, then, I am inclined to do little or no more hard work, this year. There is nothing urgent, or highly important, in the Department, if I stay in it: & I mean to cease labor, in great measure, & look after my health. But then, how long can I stay? If this movement in Massachusetts should make a strong impression on the Country, & especially if it should appear to receive responses from other States, will it not be proper for me to resign, & go home? I have no doubt Mr Fillmores friends urge him constantly to be a candidate; and altho' he has often said to me, & others, that he should not, I think he has been inclined, lately, to change his purpose. I infer this, partly from some appointments, which he has made, & partly from other occurrences. I do not know, however, how far [h]is opinions on decisions may be influenced, by what he has recently seen, in N.Y.

Supposing Mr Fillmore to be a Candidate, or to intend to become one, I could not, after that should [be] *ascertained,* remain in the Cabinet, with propriety.

Then, you know my catarrh comes on, in August; & before that month, or very early in it, I must go somewhere, for health.

I think, then, on the whole, to remain here, some weeks, looking for events; & possibly, tho' not certainly, running to Marshfield, for a day or two.

The President & Cabinet are invited to old Point Comfort, Norfolk &c—& may probably return by Richmond.[2] I shall not go. It is not my purpose to make any more *joint* visits. I have no *invitation* from Richmond, altho' the papers have been so full of it. Unless I should go to Richmond, I do not propose to go any where, South or North, to address the People.[3] I have said enough, & all I have to say.

At your *entire* leisure, My Dear Sir, I should like much to hear from you, in these matters. In such cases, we must yield ourselves, very much to the Counsels of friends. Yours with constant & sincere regard,

Danl Webster

ALS. MH-H. Published in *W & S*, 16: 617–618.

1. Not found.

2. Fillmore's week-long Virginia tour, June 21–28, included stops at Norfolk, Richmond, and Fredericks-

burg, where the President continued to stress the "Union" theme.

3. Despite this vow, DW spoke twice in Capon Springs, Virginia, on June 28 while vacationing with his wife at the Shenandoah Valley resort. As was the case on the New York tour a month previous, DW intertwined the "prosperity and Union" motifs, ridiculed "higher law" doctrine, and emphasized the contractual nature of obligations under the Constitution. W & S, 13: 429–441.

FROM JOHN CANFIELD SPENCER

Albany, June 23. 1851.

My dear Sir,

I am ashamed that you was obliged to telegraph me to-day to know whether your letters of the 13th inst. were received.[1] The newspapers had announced your intended departure for Boston and Marshfield, and I waited to hear of your arrival at Boston.

Besides, I really had nothing useful to say. I sounded some gentlemen on the subject of printing an appropriate edition of the Albany speech,[2] but found such an indisposition to provide the funds, that I could make no progress. Were not my own means so limited, with two families beside my own to support, the funds should be forthcoming at once. I am yet in hopes of meeting some friends from New York, who will assist in advancing the needful. I ought to add as a mere act of justice to your Albany friends, that the cost of the reception here (some $1200) taxed them to the measure of their present feeling of ability.

The kind and feeling manner in which you speak of my remarks at the dinner table,[3] impresses me deeply, and makes me regret my incapacity to do justice to the subject, and to deserve your thanks.

Perhaps you are not aware that a very respectable edition of your speeches in this State, has been printed by Mr. [Hiram] Fuller of the N. Y. Mirror,[4] including my dinner remarks, and thousands of them have been circulated here and in the vicinity. This may in some measure supply the demand, but the compliment alluded to, would be wanting.

Allow me before I close, to mention a curious anecdote connected with the N. Y. clique, which was the subject of some observations I made to you;—a clique professing devotion to you and using your name and their pretended associations with you, to subserve the views of Mr. [William Henry] Seward and to promote his abolition objects.

During some recent visit you made to New York and while you put up at the Astor House, Mr. [William C.] Hasbrouck late Speaker of our House of Assembly,[5] called there to see you, and was told by Mr. [Charles Augustus] Stetson that you was quite unwell and had retired, and Mr. [Edward] Curtis and your Son were there with you scratching your legs! Mr. Hasbrouck loitered about the Hotel, until Mr. Curtis accidentally came up, and asked him to go with him to your room; which he did, and found you as well as ever you was in your life. I think this occurred on your late arrival at N. York with the President.

The fact is, a Surveillance has been kept over you at the Astor, so as to prevent you seeing any one whom the clique did not desire you to see. There was a double object in this—that you should suppose you had no friends but these gentlemen, and that you should not hear truths that might not be palatable to them. I think this fact will explain a great deal.

Mrs. [Elizabeth Scott Smith] Spencer is much obliged to Mrs. Webster for her kind remembrance and cordially reciprocates her regards, and she charges me also to thank you for your mention of her and your goodness in calling on her. Mrs. Parker[6] speaks of your visit every time we see her, with great gratitude. Most respectfully and truly, Your friend

J. C. Spencer.

ALS. NhHi. Published in part in Van Tyne, p. 482.

1. Letters not found.

2. DW's address to the young men of Albany was published in two different pamphlet editions in 1851.

3. Spencer's effusive remarks introducing DW's brief speech at a dinner in Albany were printed in

Works, 2: 585–588.

4. *Mr. Webster's Speeches at Buffalo, Syracuse, and Albany, May, 1851* (New York, 1851).

5. Hasbrouck, representing Orange County, served as Speaker of the assembly in 1847.

6. Not identified.

FROM EDWARD EVERETT

Cambridge 26th June 1851.

Private

Dear Sir,

Col. Joseph B. Cobb[1] of Columbus Mississippi brought me a letter of introduction a day or two ago from General [Henry Stuart] Foote. He gave me some information relative to public affairs there, which may not be news to you, but which at any rate I will venture to send you. He says the *Secessionists* no where risk an open avowal of their principles in Mississippi. If they did so, they would be universally frowned upon by the People. The measure they are advocating is that of a state tax to be imposed by the Legislature on manufactures and all other articles of northern origin, brought into Mississippi for consumption. They assume that it is competent for a state to lay such a tax, and they mean, if possible, to drive the Legislature to do so. The leaders, Jefferson Davis, [John A.] Quitman &c cannot, I should think, be so ignorant as to suppose such State Legislation warranted by the Constitution of the United States. They probably do not expect, that, if attemped, it could be successfully carried through. They must contemplate the increase of excitement & irritation at the South, by such measures of counteraction on the part of Congress, or such interposition of the supreme court of the United States as might take place.

Col. Cobb (who is a son of the former Senator from Georgia, & cousin of the present Speaker of the House of Representatives of the U. States)[2] has been a whig; but he tells me the former party distinctions are now very much merged in that of Unionists & real though not avowed disunionists. It is this circumstance which has enlisted him in the support of General Foote.[3] He thinks the general has a more arduous task upon his hands than was anticipated, but believes he will carry the State in September.

The failure to arrest the first fugitives who were reclaimed in Boston[4] excited great feeling in Mississippi as throughout the South generally & materially weakened the union cause. This evil was very much repaired by the result of Sim's case. The charge of Chief Justice [Lemuel] Shaw was widely circulated in the Union papers of Mississippi, & with very happy effect. Col. Cobb made a similar remark in reference to the sayings & doings of the dinner at New York, on the 22d of February.[5] He says that the present administration particularly yourself and the President, are regarded with great favor throughout the South. Your Buffalo Speech (he said) was very widely circulated throughout Mississippi. Having received the news of General [Winfield] Scott's nomination by the Pennsylvania Convention[6] just before Col. Cobb called upon me, I alluded to that event. He said he regretted to hear it: That he respected General Scott's military character; but should be sorry to see him brought forward for the Presidency. He did not however explain himself more fully on this subject.

The movement lately commenced here, in the way of obtaining individual subscriptions to a nomination, appears to be eminently successful. Above 7000 names have been given in Boston, & the country towns are coming in strong. The professed politicians of the Atlas school throw cold water on the project; but, I believe, without much effect. A very intelligent gentleman from Lowell,[7] a member of the whig state Central Committee, told me it would go through the State. I should not be surprized if, before the meeting of the regular autumnal whig convention, a state of feeling should exist, which would lead that body to make the nomination.

You remember that I hope to receive some hints toward the preparation of an address or manifesto. Yours ever sincerely,

P.S. You have, of course, read the admirable address to the People of Mass. written by Mr B[enjamin] R[obbins] Curtis[8] & signed by most of the whig members of the legislature. It appears to me, that if at the opening of the next session of Congress, a strong memorial were presented to the Senate of the U. S. setting forth the facts stated in that address & pursuing the same line of argument; accompanied by a list of the persons who were elected or have been appointed to office in virtue of the coalition; with the statements of Mr [Henry] Wilson, Mr [William Stevens] Robinson, & some of the editorial articles of the [Boston] Commonwealth, by which the fact of the bargain will be proved by the admission of the parties to it and by which it would appear that Mr [Charles] Sumner's election was a part & a leading part of the bargain, there would be a pretty good chance that the Senate would set aside the election, on the general ground taken by the court in the case cited by Mr Curtis from 2 Virginia Cases 460.[9] Even if the senate did not set the election aside, an important purpose might be served by calling the attention of the country to the facts.

As this matter will be taken into consideration, I wish you would give it particular attention, & let me know of your opinion confidentially.

LC. MHi.

1. Cobb (1819–1858) was best known for humorous political commentaries in the press.

2. Thomas Willis Cobb and Howell Cobb, respectively.

3. Foote was running for governor of Mississippi on a Union party ticket.

4. William and Ellen Craft. See above, pp. ooo–ooo, headnote preceding DW to Millard Fillmore, November 5, 1850.

5. Toasts and speeches at a festive Washington Day dinner at Niblo's Saloon included assurances offered by Everett, in a featured address, that Bostonians intended to uphold the Fugitive Slave Law. *Boston Daily Advertiser*, February 25, 1851.

6. A Whig convention in Lancaster on June 24 had passed resolutions commending the Fillmore ad-

ministration while endorsing Winfield Scott for the party's presidential nomination in 1852. *Daily Advertiser*, June 27, 1851.

7. Tappan Wentworth.

8. Signed by 167 Whig members of the legislature, Curtis's "Address to the People of Massachusetts" detailed and denounced the Free Soil–Democratic agreement to divide state and federal offices following the elections of 1850. See Benjamin Robbins Curtis, [Jr.], *Memoir of Benjamin Robbins Curtis . . .* (Boston, 1879), 1: 138–150.

9. In his indictment of the coalition, Curtis had cited an 1825 Virginia case, *Commonwealth* v. *Callaghan et al.*, in which two justices of the peace were indicted for colluding in the disposition of local offices. Ibid., pp. 143–145.

FROM JAMES BUTLER CAMPBELL

June 28. 1851.
[Charleston, South Carolina]

Private

My Dear Sir

I shall leave this [place] in the course [of] two weeks at farthest on my way to Massachusetts and I particularly desire to meet you personally before my return to Charleston which will be by the 1st Septr. My original intention was to pass by the way of Nashville Cincinnati Cleveland and the Lakes to Boston but I am compelled to abandon that route in consequence of the cholera and the abridgement of my time. If you can give me some idea of your probable whereabouts for the month of August I shall feel obliged to you and will then make my plans so as to fall in with you. This is the anniversary of the battle of Fort Moultrie and the commanding officer there at this time [Lt. Col. John Erving] seems to me to have done a very silly thing about it. He has refused the use of some part of the Government premises for the usual annual celebration. His folly is not in the refusal but in assigning *reasons* for the refusal. Withholding Reasons is sometimes as wise in a Soldier as in a Judge. The commanding officer refused, *because* as I understand it, heretofore treasonable speeches have been spoken and Toasts drank within the curtilage of Uncle Sam. The reasons are proper enough no doubt but it would have been much wiser to have kept them to himself. The result is that a dinner has been arranged by the Hotspurs "within the shadow of the Fort" with the intent, beyond doubt of insulting, if an opportunity can be provided the officers and all others in Federal livery. I am in hopes the affair will be got rid of by discreet councils and cool heads. But the experiment is a dangerous one and a Col[l]ision with the loss of a single life or blood spilling even, would ensure the most disastrous results. I wish the powers at Washington or those holding Federal power here could truly understand how entirely it is the feeling of the Government to avoid any collision with the citizens here. If the Revolutionists among us understood their business, if their skill were in any degree equal to their zeal and professions they would not fail to get up before another Incident another "*Boston Massacre.*" But I hope they have not been endowed with perception so respondent to their principles as this and that we shall escape what I really think a ticklish affair. I am as ever yours &c.   Jas. B. Campbell

ALS. DLC.

FROM WALTER FORWARD

London July 1. 1851.

Private

My dear Sir

I had advices that some of my Pittsb[ur]g friends have left for London, &, in the hope of meeting them, left Copenhagen without your permission.[1] There was no time for obtaining it. You will, I trust, pardon this liberty. My absence will not be prolonged beyond five or six weeks.

Before leaving the U. S. I read your speech on conciliation & said to my friends that you had taken the true ground. It is gratifying to find that the people are gradually falling into this opinion & that the agitation of the slave question is subsiding.

I have for some time felt a desire to write to you upon a matter of some interest to yourself but of much greater to the country. *Your* relation & *my* relation to our worthy president deterred me; present movements in Penna make it proper that I should now do it.[2]

I wish you to be a candidate for the presidency, & this without waiting for the *imprimatur* of a national convention. I have little confidence in those conventions & have reason also to think that, if not altogether discredited, they have lost much of their weight with the country. My desire is that your pretensions should be submitted *without any, the least, acknowledgment of the jurisdiction of a national convention,* & that your friends should not entangle themselves in the least with either *general* or *sectional* movements preliminary <to the convention.> thereto. If this be well understood your friends can bring to your support much of the feeling of honest aversion that prevails against national nominations by *present bodies.* Taking a stand against them has a manliness in it which thinking men cannot but respect. And, I am sure, if the true character—the real merits[—]of those conventions were fearlessly invoked, a nomination from that source would lose its *prestige* to a great degree, if not entirely.

I know not what your strength may be, altho I know what it ought to be. My absence from the country keeps me in the dark as to the current popularity of individuals. I take it for granted that yours has not declined. I would think it to be on the increase. Is it not time then that your friends sh[oul]d be advised as to your intentions? I speak not of your submitting to be *taken up* as a candidate. It is already done—but of your allegiance to a national convention. This, I am confident, is the true question to be solved & the sooner done the better. I should be glad to hear from you, if perfectly convenient, & to know what we are to look for.

I alluded to movements in Penna. Wm. F. Johnston was elected Gov. by the popularity of Gen. [Zachary] Taylor. He & his *friends* appear to be thinking of a like experiment upon that of Gen. [Winfield] Scott. I incline to think they will make but little out of it. Time will show. With entire regard Your friend   Walter Forward

ALS. NjMoHP.

1. Forward was then serving as United States chargé d'affaires in Denmark.

2. The previous week Pennsylvania

Whigs meeting in Lancaster had renominated Free Soil governor William F. Johnston, declined to endorse the congressional compromises of 1850, and expressed support for Winfield Scott's presidential ambitions in 1852. See Henry R. Mueller, *The* *Whig Party in Pennsylvania* (New York, 1922), p. 179.

TO JOHN TAYLOR

Washington July 2. 51

I have returned, & find your letters.[1] I cannot lay out a dollar in horse flesh. And the rule is, you know, to have no trading in horses. Your horses have worked well enough together, heretofore, & I hope will do so still. Keep your own team, do your own work, do not trouble yourself about the Sawyer Place, give your whole attention to your own farm, & your o[w]n business. Then all will go well. Never mention the word horse to me.

I expect you to hire all the labor which may be necessary to carry on the farming briskly, hoeing, haying, & all the rest. Employ good men, at fair prices, & their pay shall be ready when their work is done, or as it goes on.

I enclose $100—to pay for labor. Go ahead. I hope you & your family are all well.   D.W.

ALS. MWalB. Published in *W & S*, 16: 598.

1. Not found.

The following letter to Franklin Haven reveals something of Webster's indebtedness at this time. An incurable optimist, he had counted heavily on his Union Land Company and Trinity Land Company stock for ultimate solvency. In early June, however, the Mexican Claims Commission had declined to make a direct award to the stockholders, and, as Richard S. Coxe reported on June 6 (mDW 33792), their cause was tied up in further litigation. Webster ultimately realized nothing from the investment aside from legal fees and minor sums gained through trading in Mexican scrip.

TO FRANKLIN HAVEN

Washington July 3d '51.

Private

My dear Sir,

The miserable result, of this business of the Mexican Claims, leaves me rather poorly off. Up to a very late day, a majority of the Commissioners, gave assurances of an allowance, such as would have given me from fifty to sixty thousand dollars. I never had absolute trust in men, whether judges or other men; and I have now less than ever.

The little driblets recd on scrip and the fees recd in cases, in which I was council [counsel] have enabled me, nevertheless, to pay off some things. To your Bank I have paid, the notes of Messrs [Richard Milford] Blatchford & [Samuel] Jaudon, amounting together to $2400. Mr. Blatchfords separate note of Six hundred and Six dollars, Mr [Simeon] Drapers[1] dr[a]ft, often renewed for $500. Note endorsed by Mr [Rufus] Choate $1,000 and some reduction on the notes of Mr [James Kellogg] Mills. At the Globe Bank a note endorsed by Mr Choate for $1000; and a reduction on that, endorsed by Mr Mills. I have been able to pay Mr Samuel Frothingham[2] $3500, on his mortgage upon Marshfield, partly however by the aid of the July dividend on my annuity in the Hospital office.[3] The lien upon Marshfield at the present moment is only $4000 and some odd hundred dollars. There was an old debt on Franklin; it is paid off within a couple of hundred dollars—for reasons known to you I was induced to buy the farm on which I was born; the price was $1900. Of miscel[l]aneous debts I owe little, either in or about Boston or at Marshfield but then here are the notes, and the overdraft at your bank: What can I do with them? And how am I to pay expenses from day to day? This is a pretty serious question, about which we must talk when we meet. Whether the $960 included in my check and which goes to the account of over draft, will so reduce that account, as that I may draw for another shilling—I do not know.

But I pray you my dear Sir, not to give yourself any trouble, about these affairs of mine. It is of little moment whether I run through what remains to me of life, a little more or a little less smoothly. If I may be permitted to know from day to day, that you and yours are well, and happy, and that prosperity is attendant on other Boston friends I shall enjoy, at least, one not inconsiderable source of happiness. Yours always truly   Danl Webster

LS. MH-H.

1. Draper (1804–1866), a New York businessman, was long active in Whig politics.

2. Frothingham (1787–1869) was formerly cashier of the Boston branch of the Bank of the United States.

3. In 1846 a number of DW's supporters in Boston established a $37,000 annuity in his name with the Massachusetts Hospital Life Insurance Company, the income from which—averaging $1,000 annually—was directed to DW's account. See, on this, David Sears to DW, March 21, 1846, and DW to David Sears, March 26, 1846, in *Correspondence*, 6: 130–131; 137–138.

FROM JOHN PENDLETON KENNEDY

Ellicotts Mills July 10. 1851

My dear Sir

Mrs John S. Skinner[1] is now living in Baltimore with Mrs Chancellor

Bland her mother—and, I understand, in very narrow circumstances. Her son Frederick has been, for some years, in the employ of the Government, and is now a clerk in the Interior Department, upon a small salary.[2] It has been intimated to me that he now assumes, as far as he is able, some charge in his mother's support, and that he proposes to provide her a home in his own family. He is anxious, in view of this, to get into a position of more profit than his present post, and has asked me to aid him in his purpose.

I do not know how I can better serve him than by submitting his case to you, in the hope that some opportunity will occur to you, in which, if you think him deserving of it, you may raise him into a higher grade of employment. I am sure you sufficiently appreciate his father's public stature for many yeras past, to find, in this, a motive for a kind remembrance of the widow in her present need. From what I know of Frederick Skinner's capacity for business, I think you would find him quite worthy of the favor he asks.

Allow me, my dear Sir, to impress to you, what I hear every body doing to others, the highest admiration of your timely and effective efforts to strengthen the hands of that great Conservative party in the Country which I hope is destined to unite the best men of both of the old parties, and bring us a long and happy ascendancy. Very truly my Dear Sir Yours   J. P. Kennedy

ALS. MdBP.

1. Elizabeth Davies Skinner, wife of John Stuart Davies Skinner (1788–1851), editor and author.

2. Frederick S. Skinner was serving as an agricultural clerk with the Patent Office of the Interior Department, at an annual salary of $1,600. It is not known whether DW interceded on his behalf.

FROM JOSEPH POWELL

Greeneville C[ourt] H[ouse] S C
July 18th 1851

My dear Sir

As a citizen of South Carolina and holding an Interest in the Institution of Slavery to a small extent, I deem it a duty which I owe to the country to say one word on the great topic that at present is Agitateing the North and South. The true cause is overlooked *"or if seen"* is misrepresented that is effecting the Institution of Slavery. It is not oweing to any violation of the Federal Constitution in letter or spirit, nor to any in-equality in the Laws of Congress. But it is the result of progress, an influence, *mixed*, with morals and Interest, that is totally disconnected with the Federal Constitution and the Laws of the country, and which must at no distant day, overthrow the Institution of Slavery, the causes to effect this result, are accumalateing daily, they are too numerous and potent to be resisted by any power vested by the Constitution or by any law under it. *It is the progress, the policy and the spirit of the age*— Which State Sovereignty, nor Federal Law or Federal power cannot ar rest,—*an ultimate Necessity*—produced by the natural course of things & beyond the controle of civil expediency.

That, which, Cecession, Disunion and every other Antidote, threatened by the South, (If *practicable*), must hasten and aggravate.

This every one of sound fore-cast *must know, South Carolina is aware of it*. But She has been seeking a pretext for twenty years to cut-loose from the General Government not for any real cause, But from a desire to set-up for Herself. It originated with Mr. [John Caldwell] Calhoun— after he lost all hopes for the presidency and is still adhered to by his followers. I shall not be surprised if South Carolina should be reckless enough to make an experiment. It is not the redress of any wrong that She is after, her prayer all the time is, that congress may do some-thing, that will be so palpable, that the whole South will rise-up against it in mass—or, if they can not effect their object by some thing of that sort, that, then, they will cecede, and *perhaps*, get the sympathy of the other Southern States, let South Carolina make the experiment, and Let the Executive of the *United States*, See that the Laws are fathfully Executed, and then we shall Know, the practability of these things, and I trust, that the whole country will learn a lesson by it, that will ensure peace and tranquility for all future time.

Slavery in the United States *is doomed*. Colonization is its ultimatum, and that *must be* before the third enumeration of the Federal Senses *from date*, With the Slaves of the older States where their lands are exhausted and their transportation is prohibited by State enactments, both races can not remain long together. When Slave labor becomes valuless—one or the other, must be driven out, or become dangerous to society, to Life and property—this would now be the case, were it not for the out-let to the South-West. When that shall cease—with the pressure of the increasing White population—in the rear, What then?—colonization or anihilation—*one or the other*—unless *Cecession* should succeed, and all the result contemplated should be fully realized—(Viz) the Establishment of a Southern confederacy—the conquest of the Island of Cuba and the South American States—*hardly probable*.

I feel assured that the president will do his duty—and that then, the Union shall remain as it has stood for the last seventy-five years. I shall be pleased to hear from you in answer, Yours truly   Joseph Powell

ALS. ScU. Powell (b. 1800) was an attorney in Greenville, South Carolina.

TO ROBERT B. CROES

Boston July 22. 1851

I am most exceedingly obliged to you, for your letter of the 15th of this month.[1] Your experience, in regard to this affection of Catarrh, or Asthma, is very important. The remedy which you mention I have never tried, & never heard of before. I am sure my Physicians will advise me to make an experiment of its use, & value. I shall immediately lay your letter before them;[2] & in the mean time, if you could inform me in what form, & in what doses, the "Hydriodate of Potash" was taken by you, it would increase my obligation, as the Physicians would, no doubt, be gratified to know particulars.

I have been a sufferer under this affection for fifteen years. It makes its appearance, regularly, on the 23d day of August, seldom varying a day. I have found very little benefit from the various medicines, which I have tried; but your case is so much in point, & appears so decisive, that I entertain a good deal of hope, that I may at last find relief. I shall remain here, for some time, & shall be glad to hear from you, at your convenience. Renewing the expression of my grateful & fervent thanks, I remain, Dear Sir, Very truly, Yours   Danl Webster

ALS. CtY-M. Croes (1800–1878; Rutgers 1815) was an Episcopal minister whose career was shortened by chronic asthma.

1. mDW 34518.
2. Webster in fact showed Rev.

Croes's letter to Dr. Samuel Jackson of Philadelphia, who concurred in the suggested treatment, supplementing the hydriodate of potash with iodine of iron. See DW to Millard Fillmore, July 29, 1851, mDW 34514.

NATHANIEL SAWYER TO ALPHONSO TAFT

Concord N.H. Aug. 23. 1851

My dear Sir,

Since writing to you, I have been among my relations in Boscawen, Salisbury &c. [I] found them all well, and doing well. I have seen all my Sisters, except Mrs [Nathaniel] Webster, who is with her daughter, Mrs [Horace] Eaton, the wife [of] a Clergyman in Palmyra N. York.   My Sisters hold their ages very well, particularly Mrs [David] Pettengill my Eldest. I do not see but her mind is nearly as strong as ever. My nephews the Sons of my brother Isaac, all live in Salisbury,—all thriving respectable, & among the first men in the town.

And it is very gratifying to me, that they bid fair to keep up the rank of our family;—& in point of property, add very considerable to the stock.

It has given me very singular sensations, to look over these towns, the theatre of my childhood;—view the residences of high standing, &

powerful families, one half-century ago,—now, in general, vanished to nothing,—many of them not affording a single individual, who can, with any propriety, make pretention to any considerable degree of the antient family fame.

But I have talked long enough upon this spirit depressing subject. I have not done it so much to interest you in its contemplation, as to give you an idea of the train of thought, which has occupied my mind in passing over my juvenile haunts.

At the time designated in my other letter, I again went to see the Secretary of State, & found him much better in health than on the preceding Saturday, & I was happy to find, that my former apprehension of the seriousness of his disease was very much groundless. The facts were;—he arrived from the South on Thursday,—considerably worn down by the duties of his Office, but seeing his farm look very fine he was much exhilerated, turned in among the hay makers, & helped pitch on two loads of hay,—& in the exertion hurt one of his feet,—he supposed at the time but slightly, but in the over exertion took some cold. The next morning Sat.—immediately after breakfast set off to the next town, Hill to purchase a yoke of Oxen;—on his return to his house at 12 oclock noon—he met an express from Boston with a peck of dockuments from foreign Ministers for his answers. I saw him but a moment,—was sorry that he could have no more time with me then, as it was necessary for him to dispach five important letters by the 4 o'clock mail[s. He] wished me to call on Monday morning. On Monday [I] called, & found him confined to his chamber with his Physician under the operation of an emétick. [He] was on Sunday taken with a violent pain in his foot hurt on Friday previously,—he directed his Son to wish me to call on Wednesday following. This I did & found him, to my surprise up & about his official business, looking much better than he did on Sat.—He is thinner in flesh, but I do not see that his mind <has> is impaired. It seems as strong as ever, & he is cheerful. In the course of conversation, I mentioned that his labors must have been, for some time, very great,—to discharge the duties of his Office, & make the preparation for so many speeches that he had delivered. He said his official duties, it was true were arduous,—but his speeches cost him no previous labour,—no part previously committed to writing,—asked him if that were the case with the quotations made in his speeches, he said it was, he had no recourse to books, they were produced from memory;— I expressed surprise at it. He replied "I learned those things when young, & laid them up & have now only to fetch them out."

He has a most astonishing mind; it is an immense labratory, in which he can simplyfy the most complicated matters, & hand them out, in the most clear & forceable light.

I saw him answer foreign despatches, some of which appeared long. He would take one, set in his easy chair, look it over critically & seemed to bring the powers of his mind upon it, as a whole, & after a few minutes, call his amanuensis;—first give him the address,—then commence with the matter;—every word distinctly spoken,—go on part of a sentence, when he would say, semi-colon, a comma—period. He never revises his language, if he has to relate a part of a sentence a second time. He tells me that he never makes any alterations, or looks any instrument over.

I have no more space to tell you more now,—but an addition hereafter. In the mean time, I can say, I do not believe he was to blame in the old business of which I have not room to talk to you.[1] Your friend &c   Nathl: Sawyer

ALS. DLC. Sawyer (1784–1853; Dartmouth 1805), a Salisbury native, had read law with Judge Joseph Story. He began practicing in Newburyport and later moved to Boston. In 1813 he moved west, first stopping in Kentucky and finally settling in Cincinnati, Ohio.

1. The reference is obscure.

Having planned and organized his nascent presidential campaign independently of the state Whig party through the summer of 1851, Webster looked to the party's state convention in early September for the formal launching of his candidacy. An unexpected political development, however, dictated further delay and an alternative approach.

During the summer, Massachusetts Whigs had moved toward an endorsement of Robert C. Winthrop for governor, despite the Websterites' best efforts against it. A political moderate long identified with Webster, Winthrop had voted against the fugitive slave bill in 1850 and was therefore acceptable to his party's anticompromise wing. This same vote made any association with Winthrop unacceptable to Webster, for it was sure to injure his cause in the South. Rather than accept nomination by a convention that also acclaimed Winthrop, Webster chose to defer immediate action.

TO EDWARD EVERETT

Franklin Sep. 3. [1851]

Private

My Dear Sir

My advice is, that you *do not go to* Springfield.[1] A Convention which shall nominate me, for one high office, and Mr [Robert Charles] Winthrop for another would be an inconsistency, as I think.

The late adjustment measures constitute the great, momentous question, before the Country, at the present moment. If, in regard to them, I am right, he is clearly wrong; and so, *vice versa*.

I have no time before the mail closes to speak more at length, but my opinion is clear, strong, & decisive. Yrs truly   Danl Webster

ALS. MHi.
1. At the eleventh hour Everett had been invited by the Whig State Central Committee to preside as chairman of the Springfield convention.

FROM EDWARD EVERETT

Cambridge 3 Septr. 1851

Dear Sir,

I did not think to say yesterday, that the application to attend the meeting of the Whigs at Springfield & preside came from the State Committee. After another conference with Mr. [Nathan] Hale, I see so little prospect of the resolutions being made satisfactory to your friends here, that I have signified to the Committee that I could not comply with their request. The time was too short, to wait for an answer from you to my letter of yesterday.[1] Yours, dear Sir, Sincerely,   Edward Everett.

ALS. MHi.   1. mDW 34645.

TO EDWARD EVERETT

Franklin Sep. 4. 51

Dear Sir

It might alter the case, if there could [be] a Resolution, pledging the Whigs of the State to the hearty & honest support of the Compromise, & declaring, that whoever the Convention nominate, the nomination is made in the confidence that he will act, in all things, in conformity to this sentiment.

There is another suggestion I wish to make. The Whig Platform in N. Y. is wanting in one particular.

It declares that the compromise acts may be repealed, like other laws. That is true; but then it ought to be added "That these acts of Congress being in the nature of compromise, & mutual adjustment, between different parts of the Country, they ought not to be disturbed, without the gravest & the strongest reasons."

It ought also to be put into the Resolutions as grounds for supporting the Fugitive Slave law, that all the Judicial authorities of the Country, before whom it has been brought has [have] declared it Constitutional.[1]

In great haste, *hora matutina*.
Probably I shall be in Boston on Monday. Yrs   D W

ALS. MHi.
1. The resolutions passed at Springfield included expressions of support for the Constitution, the Union, and the Fillmore administration and avowed "undiminished confidence" in Webster's statesmanship. They were silent, however, on the Compromise of 1850 and the constitutionality of the Fugitive Slave Law. *Boston Semi-Weekly Atlas*, September 13, 1851.

TO MILLARD FILLMORE, WITH ENCLOSURE

Boston Sep. 10 '.51

My Dear Sir;

I came down from Franklin on the 8th with rather bad luck. To avoid the heat, I took the Eve' Train, which met with an accident that delayed us, & left me out till late at night. I took cold, & was not well yesterday, but am pretty well today, & am going to Marshfield, by the Hingham Boat, & a carriage. I avoid the cars as much as I can.

A very important vacancy is created by Judge [Levi] Woodburys death. The general, perhaps I may say the almost universal sentiment here, is that the place should be filled by the appointment of Mr. B[enjamin] R[obbins] Curtis. Mr [Rufus] Choate is perhaps Mr. Curtis' leader, & is more extensively known, as he has been quite distinguished, in public life. But it is supposed he would not accept the place. He must be conferred with; & I should have seen him, today, but he is out of town. I shall see him as soon as possible. Every thing being put at rest in that quarter, as I presume it will be the moment I can see Mr Choate, I recommend the immediate appointment of Mr. Curtis.[1] There will be an advantage in disposing of the matter, as soon as may be. Judge [Peleg] Sprague is now on his way home from Europe. His friends, no doubt, will urge his pretensions. Judge [John] Pitman, too, the District Judge of R.I. is a learned lawyer, an able Judge, & an excellent man. If an appointment were to be made by promotion from the Bench of a District Court, it would be very difficult to overlook Judge Pitman, who has been on the Bench more years, by a good many, than Judge Sprague, & working at a much smaller salary. But in my judgment it is decidedly better to appoint a man much younger than either of these Judges. B.R. Curtis is of a very suitable age, 41; he has good health, excellent habits, sufficient industry, & love of labor; &, I need hardly add, is in points of legal attainment, & general character, every way fit for the place.

You will see by the enclosed letter from Mr C[harles] P[elham] Curtis, that Mr B.R. Curtis will accept the place, if offered to him. I shall write you again, on this subject, the moment I have seen Mr. Choate, or heard from him.

We are all horror-struck this morning by the terrible news of the death so suddenly of Mrs. [John Jordan] Crittenden.[2] Yours always truly
Danl Webster.

ALS. NBuHi. Published in part in Curtis, 2: 530–531.

1. Associate Justice Levi Woodbury died September 4, 1851. The appointment of Benjamin Robbins Curtis to succeed him was announced on September 22.

2. Maria Innes Todd Crittenden had died in Kentucky on September 8.

ENCLOSURE: FROM CHARLES PELHAM CURTIS

September 9, 1851

My Dear Sir,

It was intimated to me that you wish to know whether if the offer of the vacant seat on the Bench of the Supreme Court, were made to Mr. B[enjamin] R[obbins] Curtis, he would accept it; I feel much pleasure in being able to answer this inquiry in the affirmative.

Upon the decease of Judge [Levi] Woodbury being known here, the Bar without exception fixed on Mr Curtis as his successor. This has been manifested to Mr Curtis in various ways, & has had its just influence on his mind in leading him to the conclusion which I have stated.

Allow *me* the privilege of ancient friendship, to suggest that if the President shall be pleased to make this appointment, it is desirable that Mr C. should be apprised of it as early as convenient, for while it is on the carpet, it disqualifies him from making any new engagements. I am truly & most resp[ectfull]y your friend   C P Curtis

ALS. NBuHi.

Neither Webster nor Fillmore allowed their rival "availability" for the Whig nomination for President in 1852 to harm an excellent working relationship. The President was unfailingly gracious in his relations with the secretary of state and accommodated all of Webster's expressed needs, including frequent sustained absences from Washington. For his part, as the letter below suggests, Webster was careful to discourage any measures that might embarrass or annoy the President.

TO PETER HARVEY

Revere House, Friday,
September 13, 1851.

My Dear Sir,

It has been suggested as possible, that some of those who will dine on the common to-day, might be inclined, afterwards, to make me a call of civility and respect, in numbers. I hope this may not happen. Such an occurrence, immediately after the President's departure,[1] might be liable to misconstruction. It might be represented that it had been planned, or designed, or, if not so, that it was disrespectful to the President. My deep and sincere regard for the President, as well as my official relations to him, would make it exceedingly painful to me, if any thing should occur, in which my name should be concerned, however remotely, manifesting disrespect to him or the slightest want of kindness, or delicacy towards his feelings. Besides, I am desirous that he should get through this occasion in a manner every way the most gratifying to him.

I shall have another opportunity, ere long, of meeting the citizens of Boston. I hope it may not be necessary to show this letter, or even to suggest its existence to any one, but, nevertheless, I wish my friends to be aware of my feelings, should the case arise. Yours, truly always,

Danl Webster.

P.S. The President is not quite well this morning, and does not come down to breakfast. I presume he has experienced a little too much fatigue.

Text from *PC*, 2: 470–471. Original not found.

   1. Fillmore had come north to celebrate the opening of new railroad lines connecting Boston with Canada and the West—and to press the theme of adherence to the Constitution and the Union.

TO EDWARD EVERETT

Marshfield Sep. 27 .51

My Dear Sir

Charles Lanman is a grandson of Mr [James] Lanman, who, you may remember was in the Senate of U.S. many years ago. He is 32. to 35 years old, well educated, of a literary taste, & fond of employing both his pen, & his pencil. He has written small vols of Essays, little Books of travels, accounts of Angling Excursions, &c. His principal connexion has been with the Nat. Intelligencer. He married a daughter of Mr. [Francis] Dodge,[1] the rich merchant at Georgetown, & is independent; but he holds a clerkship[2] under Mr. [Charles Mynn] Conrad, pretty much, I believe for the sake of occupation. He is, as a friend, one of unbounded devotion, and Enthusiasm.[3] He came to me in N.H. I went with him to the Birth place, and his sketch[4] is entirely accurate. I found elderly people, who had been in the House, indeed lived in the House, after our family had left it. We ascertained, exactly its dimensions & length, & its position, in regard to the Well, and the Elm tree; & we found one of the door stops. Deal with his suggestions, as you think best; only believe him to be a faithful, reliable, good man. His sketch is very pleasing, and graphic. Yrs   D.W.

ALS. MHi.

1. Lanman married Adeline Dodge in 1849.

2. The clerkship in the War Department paid him $1,000 annually.

3. Genuinely impressed by Lanman's enthusiasm and ability, DW asked the younger man to become his private secretary, an invitation Lanman accepted early in October 1851. DW to Lanman, September 23, 1851, mDW 34749, 34750; DW to Charles M. Conrad, November 3, 1851, mDW 35077.

4. On their excursion to Franklin, Lanman sketched the house in which Webster was born, to serve as an illustration for the six-volume edition of his *Works*, currently in prepara-

tion. This sketch, however, did not appear in the published volumes. Another artist's sketch of an adjoining farmhouse, misidentified as the birthplace, appeared in Volume 1. Lanman's original drawing was printed as the frontispiece in his *Private Life of Daniel Webster* (New York, 1852). See, on this, DW to Edward Everett, October 18, 1851, mDW 34937; Everett to DW, October 18, 1851, mDW 34944; and Charles Lanman, *Haphazard Personalities* (Boston, 1885), pp. 130–131. See also Edward Everett to George Jacob Abbot, March 17, 1852, Abbot Papers, John R. Morison, Peterborough, New Hampshire.

TO WILLIAM PITT FESSENDEN

Marshfield Sep. 28. '51

My Dear Sir

Your letter of the 15th of September[1] appears to have been entrusted to private hands, & it reached me at a late day. Before I recd it, I had already seen your friend [David] Bronson,[2] & said to him what I authorised him to say to you. I wondered that none of your Maine friends had moved, & supposed they had not, until I met with Mr Bronson. And in my interview with him, he had not the candor to let me know that he had already gone South, & seen the President, on his way hither; & after I learned this, I took it for granted that the letters of your friends had been sent direct to the President. None ever came into my hands. Of course, I do not complain of this; but I confess I felt a little awkward, when the President told me, & that was the first I knew of it, that Mr Bronson had already been to see him, as your friend.

It is perceptible enough, My Dear Sir, that some of the good Whigs of Maine have no great loving kindness toward me.[3] I do not at all include you in that number, because you never manifested any want of kind feeling, or of the continuation of your regard; and therefore it is, that I wish now to renew, in the strongest terms, every sentiment of friendship & attachment, which I ever expressed to you, in my life.

As to the recent appointment,[4] I believe that the President had settled his mind upon it, before I saw him. Yours always truly   Danl Webster

ALS. NhHi.

1. mDW 34714. In this letter Fessenden had offered himself as a possible appointment to replace the late Justice Levi Woodbury.

2. Fearing he would be unable to see Webster at his Boston hotel, on September 15 Bronson left him a letter (mDW 34705), suggesting that the Maine bar and many of Webster's "personal and political friends" there supported Fessenden for the Court vacancy.

3. Maine Whigs including Fessenden had opposed the Compromise of 1850, and many had directly criticized Webster's role in effecting a settlement. At the 1852 national Whig convention, the Maine delegation threw its support—against Fessenden's wishes—to General Winfield Scott. Charles A. Jellison, *Fessenden of Maine: Civil War Senator* (Syracuse, 1962), pp. 57–60.

4. The nomination of Benjamin Robbins Curtis to the Court. See above, DW to Millard Fillmore, September 10, 1851, and Fillmore to DW, September 10, 1851, mDW 34693.

FROM DAVID SEARS

Beacon St. Monday morning
October 13. 1851

Sir,

I know not to what to attribute your returning to me in a blank envelope, my card, which I personally left at the Revere House some ten days since in making a call on yourself and Mr [William Wilson] Corcoran.

In answer to my enquiries I was informed at the Bar that these Gentlemen had left town for Providence, but that as Mr Corcoran had not paid his bill, they probably would return in a day or two. Not having since heard from Mr Corcoran leads me to believe that this was a mistake.

But there can be no mistake in the course which it has been your pleasure to adopt. I am entirely at a loss to understand it.

We are both too old to quarrel, as in our younger days we might have done, and I feel too high a respect for your position, as well as for myself, to condescend to personal crimination. I must simply view it as a melancholoy <termination> end of a long intimacy, and of that deep feeling of regard which I have ever entertained for you.

Unobtrusively I have been your friend, and whenever, in my small ability, I have had the power to serve you, I have always been prompt to do so, and altho' in one or two points it may have been my misfortune lately to differ from you in opinion, yet in expressing my sentiments on these, I have ever said, that I would not desert a political leader because we could not think alike on all things.[1]

Since my return from Europe, I have been much occupied, and principally out of town, and I leave this afternoon for Newport. I shall carry with me more of sorrow than of anger at the insult I have received, and which terminates our social relations. respectfully your obedient servant

David Sears

ALS Copy. MHi.   Thomas B. Curtis, October 27, 1850.

1. See above, p. 169, Sears to

TO DAVID SEARS

Marshfield Tuesday Eve'
[October 14, 1851]

My Dear Sir

I am dreadfully mortified. I could not, for want of time, call at your house, to return your civility, & I directed my clerk to send you *my* card, in an envelope; &, as it would appear, he returned yours![1]

I pray you,—I beseech you—my friend, one of my oldest & best friends—to excuse this blunder. Yrs always truly   Danl Webster

ALS. MHi.   Webster had expressed the intention
1. DW's clerk George J. Abbot cor-   to call personally on Sears if at all
roborated this explanation in a letter   possible before departing Boston.
to Sears on October 15, adding that   MHi, Sears Papers.

FROM JAMES LOUIS PETIGRU

Charleston, 22 Oct 1851

My Dear Sir

A word on the subject of our local politics may not be uninteresting to you. On the 13th we had an election, which turned upon Secession or No Secession—and the Secession or Revolution party have been beaten upwards of 7000 votes.[1] But it would be far too much to set this down as a Union victory. The opposition to Disunion has been made under cover of the same principles that the Secession party profess. The manifestoes of both parties are the same in the main. Nor can it be said that either of them is entitled to the credit of Sincerity exclusively. In fact their professed principles are so bad that the compliment would be, to think them insincere. But the No Secession party were joined by all the Union men, or nearly so; the rest refusing to vote—and the practical effect of their endeavours is to put down the agitation, tho they pretend that it is their intention to agitate disunion until all the South is of their party. They are blind or pretend to be blind to the evidence that the South does not join them because they are wrong. With folly that looks like impudence they proclaim that the South will be converted by their trite & shallow reasonings; as if those worn out and exploded fallacies which they have constantly in their mouths, had not been tried without effect on Mississippi & Georgia;[2] and everywhere else rejected with scorn. These are the Cooperationists who with the Union men, have taken the State from [Robert Barnwell] Rhett and broken as I think the spell that Mr [John Caldwell] Calhoun left. The worst part of that spell was the subjection of every thing to the Dominant Idea[?] of the State. There was no dissent, because dissent was against the State. Now the masses have been provoked[?] to know which is the State, and are likely to find out that the State is not a Unit. And that will be a great discovery.

Public opinion being so decidedly pronounced against a direct attempt at disunion by the State, it is doubtful whether the Convention, the members of which are already elected to decide on Secession will ever meet—and if they do meet their authority will carry very little weight.[3] May such be the end of such machinations now & forever. Yours

J. Petigru.

ALS. DLC.

1. The tally against immediate state secession was roughly 25,000 to 17,000. Two sets of figures, each flawed, were printed. See Chauncey Samuel Boucher, *The Secession and Co-operation Movements in South Carolina, 1848 to 1852* (St. Louis, 1918), p. 129, n. 160.

2. In both Georgia and Mississippi, secessionist forces suffered defeat in the fall elections, as unionist candidates for governor were elected over southern rights opponents.

3. Although the "separate action-ists" had a majority at the state convention of April 1852, they bowed to the October election returns and declined to press for secession "from considerations of expediency only," according to the convention resolutions. Rhett, who had succeeded Calhoun in the Senate, thereupon resigned his seat. Boucher, *Secession and Co-operation Movements*, pp. 133-36; John Barnwell, *Love of Order: South Carolina's First Secession Crisis* (Chapel Hill, N.C., 1982), pp. 184–186.

FROM "AN OLD FASHIONED WEBSTER MAN"

Philadelphia, Oct. 28th '51

Mr. Webster.

The privilege of an old and sincere friendship will plead my apology for this anonymous intrusion. You will see by the extracts which I enclose,[1] that the feeble Inquirer of this City, after all its professions, has abandoned you and gone over to Mr. Fillmore. This is no loss for in a few weeks from this time, it will be for [Winfield] Scott or some one else, as it has been before. It has no power or influence except among the old ladies, who go to sleep over its soporific stupidities after tea.

Your prospects are brightening in this region and if you can properly separate yourself from the Administration, every body believes they would be improved, for reasons which are obvious. Mr. [James] Cooper and his clique, are, I fear, not faithful. They are without the strength to be useful, even if well disposed, which may be doubted from recent disclosures. They have averred their readiness to go for Scott and are actually in correspondence with him and Fillmore, protesting the same allegiance to both.

The North American interest which has control of the organization of our state politics, has become openly disaffected towards [William F.] Johnston for the course pursued by some of his papers since the Election[2] and I heard the active political editor (Mr. [James E.] Harvey)[3] last night, declare himself very strongly in presence of several leading politicians. Mr. [Morton] McMichael—Scott's fugleman—it is said, has given him up and his partners insist on a Northern Civilian, as we hear on change and at the Club. It is not too late to conciliate all such people and why not do it—why not go to the sources of power and not to the Scrubs?

We can and will respond to the Massachusetts movement,[4] but must consider as to the time and manner of proceeding. It ought to be so managed, as to do you good and not harm.

An old fashioned Webster Man.

ALS. NhHi.

1. Enclosure not found.

2. Governor Johnston had been upset in his recent bid for reelection, in part because of the defection of Webster Whigs in the Philadelphia region. Several Whig newspapers, including the Harrisburg *Daily American* (edited by Johnston's brother) bitterly assailed Webster and Fillmore for allegedly sabotaging Johnston's campaign. See *Daily American*, October 16, 1851; Brownsville, Pennsylvania, *Free Press*, October 22, 1851; James E. Harvey to Millard Fillmore, October 19, 1851, and William D. Lewis to Fillmore, October 19, 1851, Fillmore Papers, NBuHi.

3. Both Harvey, Washington correspondent for the Philadelphia *North American*, and editor Morton McMichael were active behind the scenes in Pennsylvania politics. Robert L. Bloom, "Morton McMichael's *North American*," *Pennsylvania Magazine of History and Biography* 77 (April 1953): 164–180.

4. See below, Daniel Fletcher Webster to DW, November 17, 1851.

The administration's strongly expressed commitment to enforcing the Fugitive Slave Law was again challenged in late summer 1851, this time in Pennsylvania. On September 11, in the town of Christiana, a Maryland man accompanied by federal officers was slain and his son grievously wounded in their efforts to reclaim two fugitive slaves.

Reaction to the violence at Christiana was immediate and pronounced. Southerners decried the incident, demanding prompt action against the murderers. Northern conservatives blamed "fanatics of the 'higher law' creed," as the Boston Courier put it, for the episode. Sharing this anger and frustration, the administration vowed to ensure that justice was done and the law sustained.

As in the Shadrach case, however, (see above, pp. 202–207), prosecution foundered. Personality conflicts, as the letter below suggests, were part of the problem. So was the reluctance of northern juries to convict individuals under indictment. Most crippling in this case was the decision to prosecute the Christiana rioters on treason charges rather than try them for violating the Fugitive Slave Law of 1850. Webster, who viewed the incident as simple treason (he had made a similar pronouncement about the Shadrach rescue), may have dictated the decision, which was formally entrusted to the United States attorney in Philadelphia, John W. Ashmead.

Although indictments of high treason were returned against forty-one individuals, a jury declined to convict in the lead case, and all other prosecutions were subsequently dropped. The administration had nonetheless scored political points in the South.

FROM JAMES COOPER

Pottsville October 30. 1851

Private

Dear Sir:

It is not with the slightest disposition of renewing, upon its old basis, the question of the removal of the federal officeholders at Philadelphia,[1] that I now suggest to you the propriety of removing the present U. States District Attorney [John W. Ashmead] and the appointment in his place of a competent person of good character and reputation. If after the recent events in this state, demonstrating the hostility of the federal office holders to the Administration, and manifesting at the same time their total want of influence, it should not vindicate itself and its friends by their prompt removal, it would be something worse than useless for me to recommend it. I shall therefore be silent on the subject. But there are reasons for the removal of Mr Ashmead,[2] which can hardly fail in commending themselves both to you and the President.

You are aware that the persons guilty of the late outrage at Christiana are shortly to be tried for treason. In this case the State of Maryland, as well as the entire South, feels a deep interest; and the Governor of Maryland, in obedience to the prevailing sentiment has directed Mr [Robert J.] Brent, the Attorney General of the state, to appear and aid in the prosecution. Subsequently I was retained by the Governor for the same purpose.[3]

Today, I received a letter from Mr Brent, informing me that Mr Ashmead had put it out of his power to appear, without submitting to what he regards a sort of professional degradation. It seems, that when Mr Ashmead learned from Mr Brent, that by the direction of the Governor of Maryland he intended to appear and aid in the prosecution, he immediately informed the latter, that if he did so, it must be with the express understanding that he (Ashmead) was to have the entire control of the cause and the right of concluding argument to the jury. There was not, as I understand, the slightest disposition to deprive Mr Ashmead of any legitimate control in the conduct of the cause to which his official position and the responsibility necessarily devolving upon him, entitled him to exercise. But the stipulation in advance, that he was to conduct the cause in his own way, without interference on the part of special counsel is regarded as an intimation that Mr Ashmead prefers that Maryland should not be represented in Court. In the case of acquittal, whether just or not, I need not say to you, that the administration will have to bear the blame, especially if by the conduct of its attorney, other counsel have been prevented from taking part.

For the removal of Mr Ashmead there is another reason, still more weighty. It is his want of capacity. I do not speak from my own knowledge, for it so happens that I have never met him [in] Court. But I would refer you to Thomas Dunlap, Josiah Randall, John S. Riddle, John Savage & Benjamin Brewster.[4]

In making this communication, I desire it to be understood, that I have nothing of a personal character against Mr Ashmead. I only make the foregoing suggestions, in order that [you] may be informed of the state of the case, and the mischief that is to be apprehended in case the prosecution should fail. In such event it would be said at once, that the administration did not desire a conviction, and the conduct of its officer w[oul]d be pointed to as proof of the allegation.

The communication is made in *confidence*, except insofar as it may be necessary to the information of the President. Will you favor me with an answer? Very respectfully & truly yours   James Cooper

ALS. DLC.

1. See above, Millard Fillmore to DW, April 16, 1851, n. 4.

2. Ashmead is sometimes confused with his cousin, George L. Ashmead, who assisted in the prosecution of Christiana rioter Castner Hanway.

3. Cooper was subsequently designated lead counsel for the prosecution. W. U. Hensel, *The Christiana Riot and the Treason Trials of 1851: An Historical Sketch* (Lancaster, Pa., 1911), pp. 62–63.

4. Brewster, Randall, and Dunlap were leading attorneys in Philadelphia; Riddle was a prosperous commodity merchant, and Savage, among the wealthiest men in the city, was one of their circle.

FROM J. FRANKLIN REIGART

State of Pennsylvania
Lancaster City November 1st 1851

Dear Sir

I purposed addressing a line to you two weeks ago, but being aware of your absence, and having this day heard of your return to Washington, would now fulfil my intention.

On the morning of the 11th of September, a fearful tragedy occurred about 21 miles from this city, two miles South of Christiana, a small village located on the Columbia & Philadelphia rail way, Mr. Edward Gorsuch,[1] a citizen of Maryland was cruelly slain, and his two Sons, and a nephew,[2] were shot down seriously wounded, by an armed band of negroes, some 75 or 100[3] in number, aided and abetted by whites, whilst endeavouring to recover two of his fugitive slaves. The evening Cars from Philadelphia brought the news to Lancaster. I called on our County Sheriff (residing in this city) but he declined summoning a posse and repairing to the scene of action; and by the next train of Cars, on the morning of Friday Sept. 12th John L. Thompson Esqr, of this City, the Dist. Atty of our County, and myself started to Christiana. When we reached there, we found that the Justice of the Peace Joseph D Pownall Esqr, of that neighbourhood, in and for the Township of Salisbury, had been so completely horrified, that he had feared to make any arrests the day previous (immediately as he should have done) on account of the boldness of the desperate act, and being surrounded by abolitionists, he waited until the Sheriff or some other County Officer should arrive to direct or assist him. Mr. Thompson and myself in a few minutes found ourselves surrounded by some 15 or 20 abolitionists who had the celebrated lecturer [Charles Calistus] Burleigh with them. We at once discovered that if we dared to make any arrests, these men would in a few minutes instigate a party of blacks to attack us, and rescue every prisoner. I then took the affidavit of the Deputy Marshal H[enry] H. Kline who was with Mr. Gorsuch at the time of the murder, and placed the warrant in the hands of William Proudfoot the Constable of said Township. I then suggested to Mr. Thompson that he, Kline, the Constable, and myself should go down the Rail Road about two miles, where we would be able to summon a strong and reliable posse—we did so—and two Contractors on the Rail Way Messrs Evans & Boggs[4] immediately stopt their work, and gave us their assistance and whole force of men, and in an hour's time we secured some 200 good men (in an open country) who cheerfully obeyed the call, and at the imminent risk of their lives, succeeded in arresting & securing some 17 prisoners, whom we brought up to Lancaster prison the same night. These men were principally day-laborers, who were carting, digging and blasting rocks, and although the outrage was of the most exciting character, and some of the negroes when being arrested, resisted with axes— still they acted with the greatest forbearance, and did not in the least harm or injure a prisoner by a single blow.[5] These men also left their work, and acted without the least intimation or promise of any recompense for their time or services. They travelled in parties for miles around the neighbourhood, both day & night to secure those that the officers desired to arrest. They behaved as honorable men, pleased to obey their laws with vigor, and assist their Officers in the performance of their duties. Men may speak and think as they will of this matter. No set of men ever behaved under such exciting circumstances with the same bravery and prudence. Their conduct was so cool determined and prompt, that Burleigh and his desperate coadjutors were completely terror stricken, and dared not attempt a rescue.

My reason for giving you these details is for the purpose of suggesting prompt action on the part of our Government to properly reward the truly meritorious by a suitable testimonial. The affair was an extraordinary one. Of the 200 men who hastened so promptly to avenge their laws by securing the offenders before they might all escape, about 80 composed the regular posse, the others stood guard around the Hotel, to prevent an escape or rescue. Those 80 deserve pay for their services, and they are all, day laborers, who left their work to do their duties. The Government should be as prompt to recompense them liberally for their services. Their names have been furnished to the Attorney of the U. S. Dist. Court, John W. Ashmead Esqr. He should examine and attest each account, and the U. S. Marshal Mr. [Anthony E.] Roberts should be directed to pay them without further delay.

The Hon. Cabinet at Washington may consider the affair now, as a matter of dollars & cents, and act upon those Bills as a precedent for the future but I trust in God another such affair may never occur, in our Land of compromise and brotherly love and with this impression, I at the time deemed it my duty to summon an overwhelming posse at once, from the immediate neighbourhood, to prove to the Country and the world, that every good citizen of this Union, is ever ready to act in support of the Constitution and laws, and thus immediately strike terror into the ranks of any desperate fanatics, whether East or West, North or South, who would dare, by force and arms to resist the peoples laws, and murder their own brethren.

You will pardon the liberty I have taken in thus addressing you, but justice to those men, without having consulted with any one induces me to trespass upon your well known kindness of disposition. Allow me Sir to subscribe myself with the most sincere respect Very Obdtly Yrs.

J. Franklin Reigart

ALS. DLC. Reigart, an attorney, was then serving as a Lancaster city alderman.

1. Gorsuch (1795–1851) was a prominent Baltimore County, Maryland, planter and Whig.

2. Dickinson Gorsuch was the only one of Gorsuch's sons who participated in the effort to reclaim their slaves. Edward Gorsuch's cousin, Joshua Gorsuch, was injured during the melee. The nephew, Dr. Thomas Pearce, was not shot, although he did sustain a slight injury to his head.

3. Testimony varied greatly about the number of blacks who joined the Christiana riot. Reigart's estimate appears on the high end of the scale. According to a recent study, twenty-five is a more accurate estimate. See Jonathan Katz, *Resistance at Christiana: The Fugitive Slave Rebellion, Christiana, Pennsylvania, September 11, 1851: A Documentary Account* (New York, 1974), pp. 94–95, 330, n. 7.

4. Evans and Boggs have not been further identified.

5. Newspaper accounts and the testimony of individuals sympathetic to the rioters suggested that the posses rounding up suspects were less "forbearing" than Reigart claims. See W. U. Hensel, *The Christiana Riot and the Treason Trials of 1851: An Historical Sketch* (Lancaster, Pa., 1911), pp. 41–43, and Katz, *Resistance at Christiana*, pp. 123–126.

TO JOHN OSBORNE SARGENT, WITH ENCLOSURE

Nov. 7 1851

My Dear Sir

There is a class of publicans, with whom it is a standing topic, that the U. States are not a *Nation*, nor the Govt. established by the Constitution a *National* Govt.

It might, perhaps, be difficult to define, with exactness, so general a term as *National*, when applied to Govt., yet one needs to be at no loss, as to the general character of the Govt., who looks, fairly, at its enumerated powers.

I suppose it was upon some such ideas as this, that, sometime ago, I hardly know when, or on what occasion, that I drew up this little synopsis of the powers of the Govt., which I found this morning, in looking over some old papers.

I have taken the liberty to send it to you, supposing it might possibly be useful, & save you some labor, when you may have occasion to advert to the subject.[1] Yrs truly   Danl Webster

ENCLOSURE

A Govt. which possesses the exclusive power of declaring war, & making peace; of entering into Treaties & Alliances, & of sending & receiving Embassadors & public Ministers; which possesses the exclusive power of regulating Commerce, both foreign & domestic; the exclusive power of raising & supporting armies & navies; of coining money, & of fixing the value of foreign coins; of establishing uniform rules of naturalization, & a uniform standard for weights & measures; a Government, which can alone lay duties of import & tonnage, & which holds exclusive authority over the Public Domain; a Government which has power to lay & collect taxes & excises, of all descriptions, on persons of all descriptions; a Government which demands the allegiance of the People, & which is authorized to define & punish treason committed against itself; a Government, the Constitution of which every state officer, from the highest to the lowest, is, & must be, sworn to support; finally, a Govt., the Constitution & laws of which are declared to be, & are, the supreme law of the land, any thing in any state law to the contrary notwithstanding; such a Govt., whatever name we give it, does possess the essential parts & elements of National authority.

ALS. MHi.
1. Sargent, who had supported DW's first presidential campaign as editor of the *Boston Atlas*, was cur-rently co-editor of the Washington, D.C., *Republic* and might find the enclosure of use for a future editorial.

FROM DANIEL FLETCHER WEBSTER

Boston Nov 17. 1851

My dear Father,

You know how our election has terminated, as far as it has come to a termination. The probability is that Mr. [Robert Charles] Winthrop will not be chosen.[1]

I shall never cease to rejoice that your name was not connected with his at Springfield.[2]

Mr. [Peter] Harvey says he wrote you on the subject & suggested that the causes of Mr. Winthrops defeat should be stated in the Nat[ional] Intelligencer.

If you approve the idea I wish that it might be done.[3]

The convention of the 25th will be the greatest meeting ever held in Faneuil Hall, I believe.[4]

It will do the people good to have an opportunity of expressing their long pent up feelings towards you.

I don't think they could, with health, hold in much longer.

I have seen Mr. [Edward] Everett in regard to Mr. Merrill's note[5] & he says it is all thoroughly taken care of.

Aunt Harriette [Story White Paige] told Mr. [Isaac P.] Davis of the dedication to him[6] & he was much affected. He had never heard of it before.

We are all in our new house & feel comfortable.

I have to go down to Marshfield to-night to bring up a few remnants & then we shall be fixed in Town.

I propose to come to Washington soon after the 25th but Mr. [Philip] Greely has very prejudicially interfered with one of my arrangements.

I will explain when I see you.

I was glad to hear from Mother the other day.

We are all well. Your affectionate Son   Fletcher Webster

ALS. NhHi.

1. Although Winthrop captured a decided plurality of votes cast for governor, he failed to win the necessary majority for election. The coalition of Democrats and Free Soilers in the legislature that made Democrat George Boutwell governor in 1850 thereupon reelected him. *Boston Semi-Weekly Atlas*, November 11, 1851; Frederick J. Blue, *The Free Soilers: Third Party Politics, 1848–1854* (Urbana, Ill., 1973), pp. 226–228.

2. See above, pp. 270–272, DW to Edward Everett, September 3 and September 4, 1851, and Everett to DW, September 3, 1851.

3. No such article has been found.

4. See headnote preceding Charles Wainwright March to DW, November 23, 1851.

5. Possibly Samuel Merrill (1786–1869; Harvard 1807), president of the Merrimac Fire Insurance Company.

6. DW had dedicated the second volume of his *Works* to Davis, as follows: "A warm private friendship has subsisted between us for half our lives, interrupted by no untoward occurrence, and never for a moment cooling into indifference. Of this friendship, the source of so much happiness to me, I wish to leave, if not an enduring memorial, at least an affectionate and grateful acknowledgment. I inscribe this volume of my Speeches to you."

Webster's long-gestating presidential campaign was finally launched on November 25, with a mass rally at Faneuil Hall, the scene of many notable moments in his long career. Both the number of participants and their enthusiasm were impressive. It remained to be seen, however, whether in subsequent months an expression of loyalty could translate into effective organization.

FROM CHARLES WAINWRIGHT MARCH

New York Nov. 23. 51

Private

Dear Sir

We have here quite good accounts of the meeting at Faneuil Hall on Tuesday next. Depend upon it, it will be a grand affair. A gentleman who arrived here last night tells me, that the Democrats will be present in full number. A large number of Democrats go from Lyme—some from Marblehead, Watertown, and in fact many from different parts of the State. This is a feature of future great advantage. If we can lay down a platform broad enough and strong enough for the honest of both parties, we have nothing to fear.

I beg to take the liberty of remarking that the public mind is very sensitive on the question of the right of search.[1] The letter,[2] which I wrote while in Washington, has been variously criticised—by the Democratic press, with some severe strictures, as evading the real question.

I had quite a long and interesting conversation last night with Mr. [Henry Sheffie] Geyer, the new Senator of Missouri. While he says, that there is no man in the country, he would be more glad to be President than yourself or for whom he would work with more earnestness, he is obliged to confess that Mr. Fillmore is the first choice of the Whigs of Missouri. His course since he has been President has gained their good-will. But he says that you are its second choice and that you are gaining daily upon the affections of Whigs and Hunker-Democrats, between whom he thinks there will be a union before the Presidential election. While Gen. [Winfield] Scott, he says, has not, to his knowledge a political friend in the State—Mr. Geyer also says that if you satisfy the public mind, as you doubtless will, in the Spanish-Cuban affair, and "on the right of search" the track will be clear for you.

Geo: Wilkins Kendall has just come in from New Orleans. He says, that the case of [John Sidney] Thrasher[3] is exciting the deepest interest in the whole South and even may be the "cry" of the coming campaign. Thrasher has been so kind to the American captives in Havana, has supplied them with so much money, has been so bold, and even personally reckless in his attentions to them, that his imprisonment and supposed condemnation have raised a vehemence of popular feeling, difficult to be controlled. That Mr. Thrasher may have gone farther than even an active expression of sympathy towards these deluded men, I have no doubt. But at the same time, proof of the most positive kind of his connection with the invasion of the island will be required to quiet the public feeling at the South—and I fear even that will not avail.

I hope, you will pardon me for any inferences that may be drawn from my suggestions. But I know that you have gained greatly upon the public mind from the supposition that you have refused to make any concession to the pride of Spain, even against the President, and I know also that you have it in your power to greatly promote the increasing tide in your favor.

It is probable that I shall leave here Tuesday night, & be with you Wednesday morning. Ever resp[ectfull]y & truly yrs   Chs. W. March

ALS. NhHi. Published in Van Tyne, pp. 501–503.

1. The United States government's failure to prevent filibustering expeditions provoked England and France to order their naval squadrons into the Caribbean to repel any attacks on Spanish possessions. Apprehensive

that the squadrons would attempt to search American trading vessels, DW made it known to Britain that any such act "would lead to immediate war." See DW to Millard Fillmore, December 8, 1851, *Diplomatic Papers*, 2.

2. Not found.

3. Thrasher, a coadjutor of the filibuster Narciso Lopez, had been editing an antigovernment newspaper in Havana when he was jailed by the Spanish authorities, tried by court-martial, and sentenced to serve eight years at hard labor in North Africa. The case became a cause célèbre in the United States, and through the intervention of the State Department, Thrasher was freed early in 1852, in exchange for a promise never to return to any Spanish possession. See *Diplomatic Papers*, 2.

FROM EDWARD EVERETT

Boston 26 Nov. 1851

Dear Sir,

The meeting yesterday was every thing that could be wished[,] thronged, orderly, enthusiastic. The business was well introduced & well conducted. [Rufus] Choate's speech[1] by all accounts was the very height of eloquence.

Whatever can be effected by a meeting in Faneuil Hall was done yesterday. An official communication of the doings will no doubt be made to you, when you can make such response as you think best.

When you come to express yourself in public on the subject of *Intervention*,[2] it will be well to assert as warmly the right & duty of America to exercise a *peaceful* influence in favor of liberal ideas & institutions, as you oppose the policy of *violent* interference. Yours ever sincerely,

Edward Everett.

ALS. MHi.

1. The text of Choate's speech was printed in the *Boston Daily Advertiser*, November 26, 1851. See also Daniel Fletcher Webster to DW, November 26, 1851, mDW 35279.

2. Everett is referring to the debate over American relations with Austria in the wake of the abortive Hungarian Revolution. See below, Edward Everett to DW, December 9, 1851, and *Diplomatic Papers*, 2.

TO PETER HARVEY

Washington Nov. 27 .51

My Dear Sir

I thank you for your letter.[1] The "address"[2] was printed in the [Washington] "Republic" this morning. I am too modest to say what I think of it. The Speeches, as appears from the sketches which I have seen, were excellent, most excellent, *considering the subject*.

I assure you, My Dear Sir, that no political promotion, no success in life, could give my heart such a thrill, as this outpouring of kindness &

confidence by my Massachusetts friends. Enemies, factionists, & fanatics may now [do] their worst.

I know not how to thank Mr [George] Ashmun, Mr [Joshua Thomas] Stevenson, Mr [Rufus] Choate & others for their enthusiastic efforts. I do not think I shall ever try to thank either of them. They tower above all thanks of mine. Yours, most assuredly, Danl Webster

How happy it was for Mr Choate to say, that the Doors of F[aneuil] Hall were at length opened![3]

ALS. MHi. Published in *PC*, 2: 490–491.

1. Not found.

2. The Faneuil Hall convention address.

3. Choate's remark was apropos the controversy months earlier regarding the Boston city government's refusal to permit a gathering of Websterites at Faneuil Hall. See above, pp. 234–236; DW to Millard Fillmore, April 13 and April 15, 1851, Rufus Choate to DW, [April 15, 1851], and Dalzell, *Daniel Webster and the Trial of American Nationalism, 1843–1852* (Boston, 1973), pp. 229–231.

TO FRANKLIN HAVEN

Washington Nov 28. 51

Private

My Dear Sir

I have read the Speeches, & they are masterly. The whole proceeding was capital. It now only remains to follow up what has been done, & manifest a determined ADHESION.

The matter mentioned in my secret note[1] does not stand as I could wish, and as, at one time, it was determined it should stand. Still, it does not stand very bad. The particulars cannot well be stated in a letter. I must see you, & two or three other friends, not long *first*. If you cannot come here, I must meet you in N. York. Some important questions are to be settled by the early part of January. Yrs truly Danl Webster

ALS. MH-H.

1. No such note has been found, but it was probably related to Webster's discreet efforts at this time encouraging President Fillmore's formal withdrawal from the contest for the Whig presidential nomination. See below, DW to Haven, December 14 and December 28, 1851.

FROM DANIEL FLETCHER WEBSTER, WITH ENCLOSURE

Boston Nov 29. 1851.

My dear Father,

I enclose an extract from a letter of Judge Huntingdon [Elisha Mills Huntington] of Indiana written to a gentleman of this Town.

It was shown to me I suppose for the purpose of communicating its contents.

Perhaps if any occasion offers it would be well to write Mr. Huntingdon & send Mr. [Thomas Marshall] Key[1] a Speech or something. Yr affectionate Son   Fletcher Webster.

ALS. NhHi. Published in Van Tyne, p. 503.

1. Key (1819–1869; Yale 1838), a Cincinnati lawyer, was active in Democratic politics. He was the first incumbent on the Cincinnati Commercial Court when it organized in 1848.

ENCLOSURE: EXTRACT FROM ELISHA MILLS HUNTINGTON TO [?]

"You know that if I have a wish stronger than another it is that the Country should make Mr. Webster President of the U. S.

I have never failed to improve every opportunity offered me of making a friend for him & I have hailed with most heart felt joy every sign I have seen in any quarter favourable to his prospects.

But I fear that Mr. Webster does not always second with the best effect the efforts of his friends. I never hear from him in answer to my own letters, but of this I do not complain, but on more than one occasion I have introduced gentlemen from the West to him by letter, gentlemen who are ready to unite in any movement to advance his interests who have returned chilled by his cautious and cool reception.

I will mention an instance.

Judge [Thomas Marshall] Key of the Commercial Court of Cincinnati, a man of talent, young, ardent, and idolizing Mr. Webster almost as much as I do, connected with all the Keys & Marshalls of Ky. & Ohio came down purposely to visit me on the subject—to see if by concert with the leading young men of Ohio & Indiana we could not set the ball in motion.

He gave me the names of the leading men in Ohio who were anxious for it.

But he had never seen Mr. Webster & determined to visit Washington for that purpose. I gave him a letter of introduction, a general letter telling him if an opportunity offered to have a full conversation with Mr. Webster. I have not seen him since nor has he written to me but I have understood that he presented the letter was coolly but politely received, took his leave & never went back again. Judge Key is perhaps the most popular young man in Ohio & withal, one of the most shrewd. A half dozen kind words from Mr. Webster, would have made him his Champion. Now I well know the kindness of Mr. Webster's heart & I dare say he is annoyed continually by such introductions, but Key is a modest & a sensitive man. I had told him of the warmth of Mr. Webster's heart when he once knew a man worthy of his regard & I suppose he looked for some token of recognition especially as my letter assured Mr. W. of his devotion to him.

Now the amount of all this is that I can never learn from Mr. W. or from any friend in his confidence what line of policy ought to be adopted here &c &c."

Extract in DFW's hand. NhHi. Published in Van Tyne, pp. 503–504.

FROM SIMEON DRAPER

[c. November–December, 1851]

Private and Confidential

My Dear Sir,

The time has fully arrived when your friends should know, what are your wishes in regard to the future, as matters now stand. If I can see at all what the result is to be, there is no time to be lost. The power of the Administration is to be turned some where, and the Important question is *where*. One thing seems to me to be conclusive. Viz. no one situated as you are, making one of the Administration, can be supported by parties disconnected with the patronage of the Government, without the Cooperation of the Administration, (while you are in the position you are now in). Now, I see no movement made by your immediate friends which I consider of any value. Neither do I see how they can move, unless this one point is settled. If Mr Fillmore is to be a candidate, and the patronage of the Government is to be directed for him, then I need not say to you that the earlier it is known the better, and some course marked out by your friends which shall be politic and wise. I have daily letters from Washington informing me that Mr Fillmore is really in the field—that "He is in the field earlier than expected." I hear also that he is not to be a candidate, Genl [Winfield] Scott is fairly in the pool,[1] and is daily making capital. And, I confess my utter astonishment, that those who have been loud in their denunciation of old friends, and placed themselves as the chosen champions of your rights and honour, should be so utterly faithless, as to be undecided even, any, and every where except perhaps in your presence, as to doing any thing but talk. Mr [Henry] Clay of course is to take the stump, if the probability is that he cannot get a nomination of the Convention.[2] If Mr Fillmore, and Mr Clay, would put their shoulders to the wheel, instead of putting a block before it, there would be some comfort in placing things ready for battle. I hope you will bend your way to the N England festival.[3] Yours truly

S Draper

ALS. MWalB.

1. Scott's campaign, directed by

former secretary of state John M. Clayton, was launched at a public dinner in Wilmington, Delaware, on November 16. Charles Winslow Elliott, *Winfield Scott* (New York, 1937), pp. 606–609.

2. At this time Clay's health was worsening, leading him on December 17 to resign the Senate, effective September 1, 1852. In March 1852

Clay endorsed Fillmore for reelection. Clay died June 29.

3. Webster had been invited to New York for the New England Society festival commemorating the Pilgrims, scheduled for December 22. He did not attend.

FROM CHARLES WAINWRIGHT MARCH

New York Dec. 2. '51

My dear Sir

I went to Springfield Saturday evening, for a consultation with our friend Mr. [George] Ashmun. He is in great spirits and says you could carry Mass. with 20.000 majority. The late election has turned out *precisely* right. [Robert Charles] Winthrop's defeat,[1] while it removes from your friends the opprobrium of a connection with free-soilism, will excite the Whigs to a glorious triumph next year. In Springfield, every Whig fought like coeur-de-Lion and every Whig is a Webster-man.

Ashmun insists upon an immediate organisation of your friends here, as in Massachusetts. I regret exceedingly Mr. [Edward] Curtis' doubtful health, for he is head and shoulders above all your other friends here. Still, he must lay out a chart, and we will steer by it. Each day, your strength increases, and if Mr. Fillmore be not induced by Southern promises to persevere in a canvass, your name will be irresistible.

I hope to be pardoned for saying, that the outrage upon the Prometheus[2] by the English Brig, skilfully managed, will "bring down the house" in your favor. There is deep excitement on the subject here, among all classes. If you could repeat the [Johann Georg von] Hulsemann letter,[3] we shall have but little to contend against.

Ashmun longs to be with you, and will be, at the earliest possible moment. I may wait for him here, till Friday, unless Mrs. Webster needs my escort earlier.

We have turned the Democratic flank upon the Compromise Measures, and the [New York] Herald says, it is all owing to your efforts. I will see [James Gordon] Bennett before I leave and try to have an understanding with him. Ever most rcsp[cctfull]y & truly yrs   Chs. W. March

ALS. NhHi. Published in Van Tyne, pp. 504–505.

1. See above, Daniel Fletcher Webster to DW, November 17, 1851, n. 1.

2. In late November, the American steamship *Prometheus* had refused to pay port dues demanded by au-

thorities at San Juan del Norte. As it proceeded out of the harbor, it was fired on by a British warship and forced to pay a $123 fee. The American government formally protested, the British expressed regret, and the incident blew over. See Fuess, *Web-*

ster, 2: 260–261, and *Diplomatic*
Papers, 2.
  3. See above, p. 165, DW to Millard

Fillmore, October 24, 1850, and
Diplomatic Papers, 2.

LOUIS WORCESTER TO CALEB CUSHING

Peru, 2nd December 1851

My Dear Sir:

Hon. Daniel Webster, by deed dated 16th May 1839, conveyed to Richard M[ilford] Blatchford and Samuel B[ulkley] Ruggles[1] of the City of New York the following described tract of land, lying in Bureau County in the State of Illinois:

South 1/2 of Section 36. Township 16. Range 11. 320 Acres.

North 1/2 of Section 1. Township 15. Range 11. 320 Acres = 640 Acres. Known as the Webster farm, three miles west of Peru on the Peru and Princeton road—Occupied by H. W. Terry and under tolerable cultivation.

About 200 Acres of it Oak openings 200 Acres prairie land; balance bottom land worth $10. per acre cash.

Also South 1/2 of Section 34. Township 16. Range 11. 320 Acres.

East 1/2 of N. E. quarter of Section 2 and West 1/2 of N. W. quarter of Section 2, and East 1/2 of N. E. quarter of Sec. 3.

320 Acres = 640 Acres.

All of Township 15. Range 11. East of 4th P. M.

This land is of the same value and description as the foregoing: it is conveyed by Blatchford and Ruggles to Horn, Miller and Wasson, who now occupy it.

Daniel Webster, by deed dated 28th April 1841 conveyed to Herman Cope and Thomas S. Taylor[2] of the City of Philadelphia

West 1/2 of N. E. quarter Section 29.	80 Acres
N. W. quarter Section 29.	160 Acres
N. E. quarter of Section 30.	160 Acres
West 1/2 of N. E. quarter of Section 31.	80 "
East 1/2 " N. E. quarter " Section 35.	80 "
West 1/2 " N. W. " " " 28	80 "
N. E. quarter of N. W. quarter of Section 28.	40 Acres
West 1/2 of South East quarter of Section 36.	80 "
N. E. 1/4 of S. E. quarter of Section 36	40 "
South 1/2 of Section 26	320 "
All in Township 16 Range 10 East of 4th P. M.	
North 1/2 Section 35	320 Acres
South West quarter of Section 36	160 Acres
North 1/2 of N. W. quarter of Section 25	80 "

All in Township 16. Range 7. East of 4th P. M.
North East quarter of Section 35 Township 15
Range 9. East of 4th P. M.   160 Acres
This land is worth about $5. per acre. All in Bureau Co.

As nearly as I can ascertain by inquiry and examination of Records the foregoing contains a description of all the lands ever owned by Mr. Webster in this vicinity.

I think I have conducted these inquiries in such a manner that no suspicion has risen as to the person in whose behalf they were made.

I will inform you of my arrival home. Most Respectfully Yours

Louis Worcester

Person to be employed at Peru as agent George W. Gibson, Peru, Illinois

ALS. DLC. AN postscript by Cushing. Worcester (1827–1863), an attorney, had met and become friendly with Cushing through his wife's family.

1. On this, see DW to Samuel B. Ruggles, March 2 and March 23, 1839, *Correspondence*, 4: 346, 352–353, and Moses Hicks Grinnell to DW, [February 10, 1842], *Correspondence*, 5: 189–190.

2. Cope (1789–1869), an officer of the Bank of the United States for many years, negotiated with DW for titles to much of his western land in exchange for cancellation of his large debt to the Bank. See, on this, *Correspondence*, 5: 87–89. Taylor, an accountant, was employed by the Bank during these negotiations.

FROM EDWARD EVERETT

Boston 9 Decr. '51

Dear Sir,

I noticed the other day a column of remarks in the [Washington] "Union" on the subject of my letter to the President of the Convention of 25th Novr. & the policy of "intervention."[1] Nothing could be feebler or more contrary to the facts of the case, or the history of political opinions in this Country, than Major [Andrew Jackson] Donelson's comments. I thought, at first, of replying, and I may yet do so;[2]—but I think it would be better to wait awhile, and let the ground intended to be taken by [Louis] Kossuth & others become more apparent.

In the meantime I have no doubt that the following are pretty near the facts of the case. Mr. R[obert] J[ohn] Walker early conceived the idea of making capital, as a Presidential Candidate, out of the "intervention" principle; to be applied as circumstances might dictate to Cuba, Nicaragua, or France, or Hungary, or any other quarter of the globe, not forgetting the Sandwich islands. The two first named localities were the most prominent when he left the United States; and agitation in reference to both was in train. The liberation of Kossuth[3] and his success in

England—with the failure of the Cuba plot[4]—have made Hungary at present the *Champ de bataille*. Kossuth, probably without being aware of the plot, was immediately converted in England into an electioneering agent of Mr. Walker; and has no doubt come to the U. S. with instructions from him.[5] The plan of operations probably will be to get up an irresistible enthusiasm. Kossuth will act in good faith & may or may not penetrate the political designs of his backers. It will be *their* policy to demand acts of sympathy & co-operation impossible to be granted, in order to discredit the administration by their refusal, & to secure to the Democracy the credit of proposing them.

How far this game can be played is doubtful, and depends upon the skill and recklessness of the parties, and the point to which popular madness can be carried. From present appearance the frankness of the illustrious Magyar will mar the plot. He will let it be seen that he has come, not to make an American President but a Hungarian governor: — in short that he wants money, troops, & ships of War. When this is understood, I cannot but think the politicians will find they have undertaken more than they can accomplish.

It creates a position of considerable difficulty for you, but I doubt not you will be able to keep your sympathy for liberal opinions and those who maintain them beyond doubt, on the one hand;—while you maintain the neutrality of the Country and adhere to the law of nations on the other. By the last sayings of Kossuth which have reached us, it would seem that he is beginning to be aware that he has been duped. Yours ever Sincerely,

Edward Everett.

P.S. I think Mr. [Henry Augustus] Wise could tell you something of Mr. R. J. Walker's plans.

ALS. MHi.

1. Unable for health reasons to attend the Faneuil Hall convention, Everett had addressed a brief public letter to the delegates that, in addition to praising Webster, criticized advocates of "systematic intervention," or "going to war with all the nations of Christendom, for the sake of propagating our principles and forms of government." Everett's comments, which had been originally encouraged by DW, were noted disapprovingly in the Washington *Union* on December 2. See DW to Everett, November 21, 1851, *Diplomatic Papers*, 2

2. Although Everett wrote to DW's secretary, George J. Abbot, for materials relevant to the issue, for use in a rejoinder, there is no evidence that he actually composed a rebuttal. See Everett to DW, December 5, 1851, mDW 35372.

3. The exiled Hungarian leader had recently made a popular tour of England and was currently beginning a sustained, tumultuous, but ultimately fruitless campaign to win American diplomatic and material support for renewed efforts to win Hungarian independence. See Donald S. Spencer, *Louis Kossuth and Young America: A Study of Sectionalism and Foreign Policy, 1848–1852* (Columbia, Mo., 1977), and *Diplo-*

matic Papers, 2.

4. A reference to the failed Lopez filibustering expedition earlier in 1851.

5. Everett's letterbook for December 1851 details both his embrace of and ultimate retreat from this hypothesis. MHi.

TO FRANKLIN HAVEN

Washington. Dec 13. 1851

Private
My dear Sir,

Mr [George] Ashm[u]n is here and will stay a day or two longer. He has seen many gentlemen and had much conversation with them, and will have some account to give to you, and other friends. Mr [Edward] Curtis is also here, and things are approaching a decision, one way or the other. I will ask Mr Ashm[u]n to write to you before he leaves Washington.

Gen [Lewis] Cass has this moment left my room. He urges me, by all means to stay where I am. He says the times look squally, and that men of all parties have confidence &c.&c. The same is said to me from different quarters, twenty times a day, but I am growing somewhat tired of the responsibility and the labor, and these, with some trouble about my own affairs, bring me sometimes very near a resolution of leaving public duties to be discharged by others. I shall do nothing however, without the entire approbation of friends, to whom I owe so many obligations. Yours always truly   Danl Webster

LS. MH-H. Published in *W & S*, 16: 632.

Crucial to Webster's presidential prospects in 1852 was the early withdrawal of President Fillmore from the contest for the Whig nomination. Although no evidence suggests that Webster ever directly bruited the matter with Fillmore, his agents, including Congressman George Ashmun, apparently did and were assured that the President would leave the field clear for his secretary of state.

Webster underestimated the counterpressures on Fillmore. Barraged by letters from all parts of the nation—particularly from Pennsylvania and the South—praising his stewardship, and counseled by advisers such as New York editor Thomas Foote to avoid any public disavowal of his availability, Fillmore maintained a careful silence throughout the winter. Thus, on one hand, he could fairly assert he was doing nothing to advance his own interests or to cripple Webster's chances for the nomination, while on the other hand, he was free to declare himself a candidate if political currents dictated such a course.

TO FRANKLIN HAVEN

Sunday Noon, Decr. 14 .51

Private

Mr Dear Sir,

Mr [George] Ashmun leaves for home this afternoon. He *has seen many persons, & conversed with them, from the lowest to the Highest; & he thinks the coast will be clear, & known to be clear, in due time.* His visit has evidently done good, & helped much to bring things to a point. Mr [Edward] Curtis also goes to N.Y. tomorrow. I expect to be in that City some day of Christmas week, & hope to meet you there. As soon as a day is fixed, I will give you notice; &, in the mean time, will keep you acquainted with what occurs here. The Cubans, & [John Sidney] *Thrasher*,[1] & the Prometheus,[2] & Mexico,[3] & the calls of Congress keep my hands full of work. Yrs truly   Danl Webster

—I must pray you not to give a single hint to any living person, of what is contained in the lines which I have underscored.

ALS. MH-H. Published in *W & S*, 16: 630.

1. See above, Charles Wainwright March to DW, November 23, 1851, n. 3.

2. See above, Charles Wainwright March to DW, December 2, 1851, n. 2.

3. Webster was attempting to conclude a treaty with Mexico providing for the construction of a railroad over the Isthmus of Tehuantepec. He did not succeed. Fuess, *Webster*, 2: 263.

FROM EDWARD EVERETT

Boston 22 Decr. 1851

Private & Confidential

Dear Sir,

Would it not be best, before Gen. [Henry Stuart] Foote leaves Washington, to suggest to him that the time has come when the friends of the Union belonging to the Democratic party at the South ought to decide upon a course.

The Editor of the Boston Atlas writes home to his paper that the entire democracy of the South is re-organizing as such & that it scouts all Cooperation on the ground of Union.[1]

In the meantime it is more probably true, in fact it is quite plain that the democracy of the North is coalescing with the Freesoilers.

I have it from a well-informed source that the latter will put up no Candidate for the Presidency but will support the democratic Nominee.

Have Union men at the South belonging to the democracy considered in what predicament this state of things leaves you & those who think with you?

Do they care for the Union? Do they think Anti-slavery agitation shakes it? And if so, do they propose in this way to sacrifice those to whom it is owing that there is any Union feeling at the North?

I dare say all this has occurred to you & that you have already acted upon it, as far as is proper. Yours ever sincerely. Edward Everett.

P.S. We have long ago done for Hungary all that you asked to have done for Greece in 1824.[2] We sent an agent[3] in 1849 to Hungary authorized to recognize their Independence if he found they had established it.

ALS. MHi.

1. *Atlas* editor William Schouler was in Washington at this time. His dispatches reported capital gossip about possible political alignments in 1852, including hints that Union parties would form throughout the South modeled on Henry S. Foote's Mississippi "Union" coalition. See, e.g., *Boston Semi-Weekly Atlas*, December 20, 1851.

2. In a notable speech delivered in the House of Representatives on January 19, 1824, DW had made a strong moral case for the Greek in-dependence movement but stopped short of proposing American inter-vention in the Greek-Turkish conflict. See *Speeches and Formal Writings*, 1.

3. During the high tide of Ameri-can enthusiasm for the Hungarian Revolution, in June 1849, President Zachary Taylor named A. Dudley Mann as a special emissary to the rebels, authorizing Mann to weigh the situation and grant preliminary recognition to an independent Hun-gary if circumstances warranted. See *Diplomatic Papers*, 2.

In mid-November, dispatches appearing in eastern newspapers provoked a short-lived but intense public controversy over affairs in the newly organized Utah Territory. Published accounts based on the testimony of several federal officials in Utah alleged malfeasance in office by Mor-mon leaders and charged Utah Mormons with disrespect for federal authority. The tempest had many sources but flared most prominently in the wake of injudicious remarks made by Judge Perry Brocchus in Salt Lake City on September 6, which the Mormons took as insulting to their characters and their faith. Shortly thereafter Brocchus and other recent federal appointees felt compelled to leave the territory and sought public support for a crackdown against allegedly theocratic practices in Utah.

Webster's initial reaction to the controversy, expressed in the letter below, was based on a reading of the officials' formal report to the President. Later, when Webster heard the other side of the story, in dispatches from Utah governor Brigham Young and personal confer-ences with Territorial Delegate John M. Bernhisel, he concluded that the charges against the Mormons were weakly founded, and he declined to take or recommend any action against them. The controversy died down as quickly as it had arisen. (See Congressional Globe, 32d Cong., 1st *sess., pp. 211–212, 240–241, 274, and* Appendix, *pp. 84–93; and for a judicious analysis, Norman F. Furniss.* The Mormon Conflict, 1850–1859 [*New Haven, 1960*], *pp. 21–32.)*

TO MILLARD FILLMORE

Decr. 23 .'51

My Dear Sir—

The Utah report[1] has come in, & I never before read an acct. of such abominable transactions, & such a diabolical society of men & women.

When you have read it, please return it, that we may have a copy made for the H. of R.[2] Yrs truly

ALS. NBuHi. Published in *PC*, 2: 496.

1. "Report of Messrs. [Lemuel G.] Brandebury, [Perry D.] Brocchus, and [Broughton D.] Harris to the President of the United States, Washington, December 19, 1851," *Executive Documents*, 32d Cong., 1st sess., Serial 640, Document No. 25, pp. 8–22.

2. On December 15, 1851, the House had passed a resolution requesting from the executive "all such information as may be in his possession, calculated to show the actual condition of things in the Territory of Utah." *Congressional Globe*, 32d Cong., 1st sess., p. 100. Relevant documents were forwarded to the House on January 9, 1852.

TO FRANKLIN HAVEN

Washington Decr 28. 1851

Private & Confidential
My Dear Sir

The time has now come to act vigorously & decisively, in following up the object of the Boston meeting.[1] I was told yesterday, or distinctly given to understand, by one who ought to know, that early in January Mr Fillmore would publicly announce that he should not be a Candidate, at the next election. Previous intimations had pointed the same way. Now therefore is the time for movement. As soon as that takes place, which I have mentioned above, there will be a renewed attempt to make a rally on Genl [Winfield] Scott. This will be done, on the ground, that nobody but he, can obtain the votes of Ohio, & Pennsylvania. Some men, even in the South, are so easily led away by notions of *availability*, as to be already yielding their opposition to the Genl.

I think it altogether important, that you should now come to Washington, bringing some friends with you. Mr [George] Ashmun ought certainly to come for one, & Mr [Peter] Harvey for another; and it would be of the greatest service that Mr. [Edward] Everett should be here, if his health would enable him to make the journey. Perhaps also, Mr Stephenson [Joshua Thomas Stevenson], or Mr T[homas] B[uckminster] Curtis could come on. The more of such Gentlemen the better. A *council* can then be holden, at which Northern, Western, & Southern Gentlemen might consult together, & resolve on something. There are reasons why *you,* yourself, cannot be spared from this consultation. You must be here, at all events. This week will be taken up by [Louis] Kossuth, & the new year. The early part of next week should be embraced, as the proper period for setting forth, so that you may be here by the 7th or 8th. Mr [Edward] Curtis will be here this week. I should like much that some other friends should be here from N. York; but I shall write to no one, but yourself. If Mr [Hiram] Ketchum, with other friends could be here from N. York it would be well. Genl. [Samuel P.] Lyman & Mr [Richard Milford] Blatchford, I presume, are both well disposed, & would be willing to say what they thought N. York (the State) might do, & what she would not.

You will of course answer this, at your earliest convenience.

Kossuth is expected here tomorrow. We shall not be deficient, in the duty of paying him great personal respect, but shall not, I trust, run into any distinguished follies.

The weather has been exceedingly cold, with much snow & sleet, & the mails are much disordered. Yrs truly always   Danl Webster

ALS. MH-H. Published in *Diplomatic Papers*, 2.

1. The Webster-for-president meeting at Faneuil Hall on November 25.

TO HUGH MCCULLOH BIRCKHEAD

Washington Jan. 31 1852

Private

My Dear Sir,

A handsome edition of my speeches is about to issue from the press— in Boston in six volumes at three dollars a volume to subscribers. Each subscription copy has an autograph. The <present> benefit of subscriptions now making accrues to me. Several friends in Boston have subscribed freely, some of them taking three or four or five copies; something of the same sort has been done in New York, but nothing that I know of in Philadelphia or Baltimore.

I enclose, herewith, a subscription paper,[1] which if you think fit you may show to a few friends. There were several plates likenesses &c in the volumes—and the work will be ready for delivery by the first of March.[2]

Draft in Abbot's hand. CtY. Birckhead (1788–1858) was a Baltimore merchant with the firm of Birckhead & Pearce. He supervised sales in Virginia and Maryland of the new six-volume edition of DW's *Works*.

1. Enclosure not found.
2. A new paragraph, beginning

"There was," was left uncompleted in this draft.

Although Webster's energies during the winter of 1851 1852 were largely absorbed in his conduct of foreign affairs, including delicate negotiations regarding a canal across Central America, his attention was never far from politics. Despite his age, and the practical obstacles to a nomination in 1852, Webster's presidential ambitions burned as strongly as ever—perhaps more so, since he well knew this would be his last chance for the elusive prize.

Unfortunately, a long list of prominent backers in the major cities of the Eastern Seaboard did not translate into popular enthusiasm for his cause, or add up to delegate strength for the upcoming Whig National Convention. Moreover, although Webster was loathe to admit the fact, southern support for his candidacy was almost entirely lacking. With the decline of fears for the Union, his efforts in 1850 made less of a difference to southern moderates, many of whom looked to Millard Fillmore as their best hope in 1852. For his part, the President, avowedly not a candidate, nonetheless declined to withdraw from the race, a "nondecision" that was announced on January 24 by the Republic, *Fillmore's organ in Washington.*

Under the circumstances, Webster's best chance for the nomination lay in a brokered convention, in which Winfield Scott and Fillmore supporters, failing to gain the necessary majority, would each turn to Webster as their second choice. For such an event to occur, however, Webster had to demonstrate substantial delegate support of his own. As the correspondence below suggests, this proved a frustrating quest.

TO FRANKLIN HAVEN

Washington Feb. 6. 1852

Private

My Dear Sir

I wrote a hasty note to F[letcher] W[ebster] yesterday.[1] There is a good feeling here, & I think it is encreasing, but there seems to be nobody to give it direction, or to form any organization among friends. As yet we see nothing of Mr [George] Ashmun.

The R[hode] I[sland] Whig Convention, which meets on Thursday is a matter of importance. Mr [John Hopkins] Clark[e] the Whig Senator here from that State, is a zealous friend of Genl. [Winfield] Scott [who] will be nominated at the Convention,[2] if immediate & effective steps be not taken to prevent it. Some spirited & active friend should go to Providence, without loss of time, & confer with Mr [John] Whipple, Mr [Samuel] Ames &c. &c.; and another to Newport to see Mr Cranstoun,[3] Revd. Mr [John Overton] Choules, &c. &c. Pray urge the importance of this on friends in Boston. Yrs truly

AL. MH-H.

1. Letter not found.
2. Meeting in Providence on February 12, the convention chose a slate of Whig candidates for the state elections and selected four unpledged delegates (including Webster's friend Robert Bennie Cranston) to the Whig National Convention. Providence

Daily Journal, February 13, 1852.

3. Probably Robert Bennie Cranston, a former congressman active in Rhode Island politics. His brother, Henry Young Cranston, like Robert a former Whig congressman from Rhode Island, also attended the state convention as a delegate from Newport.

TO FRANKLIN HAVEN

Friday—4 P.M.
[February 6, 1852]

Confidential
My Dear Friend;

I have seen many persons today. The great complaint is, that, although Mass. began gloriously, she does not follow up her own lead. There is nobody here from Mass—of our friends—while there are foes enough, who are making all sorts of representations, calculated to answer their own ends. We are fast losing the golden moments of opportunity.

The attempt at Providence[1] should be, to prevent any nomination, & to chuse unpledged Delegates. Yrs truly   D.W.

ALS. MH-H. DW's first letter to Haven of February 6 was probably written in the morning.

1. See above, DW to Haven, February 6, 1852.

FROM JAMES WATSON WEBB

Astor House
N. York Feby 8. '52

My Dear Sir.

I find myself very unexpectedly in town this A.M. having left home at 6 P.M. yesterday, upon a pressing invitation from Mr. Ketcham [Hiram Ketchum] & others, to attend a meeting of a few of your friends at the Mayors[1] last night.

As [Moses Hicks] Grinnell and myself were considered *lucky*, in consequence of our success in 1848,[2] they left the matter pretty much to us; & it was unanimously resolved to get up a Meeting on the 4th March.[3]

The call will be out to-morrow; and I shall place a confidential man on each of [the news] Carriers['] District[s], with instructions to call at *every House*. This was our course in 1848, & we procured 3000 signatures without there being any [Zachary] Taylor party in the City. We will get not less than 10,000 to this call; & in the meantime will be *committing* men and their friends who might otherwise vacil[l]ate in their opinions.

The 4th March was the best day we could take. It avoids the Hungarian question which is now mixed up with the 22nd Feby;[4] & it is the birth day of the Constitution of which you are the recognized champion. That day therefore, can be used with effect.

I have never permitted myself to doubt that your election is a near[?] certainty if nominated; & I know, I so told them last night, that we can secure the nomination if we abandon our timid measures & play a bold game. Any other course would merit failure. Grinnell is heartily & zealously with us; and [Simeon] *Draper* will be when necessary.

Permit me now to express the hope that you will not permit any considerations whatever, [to] induce you to *write* or *speak*, until after the nomination; & not then if it can be avoided, as it assuredly can be. You are expected here by Some to speak on the 23rd![5] That would be suicide indeed. Make [Edward] Curtis go to work at once; and let the Country see that at W[ashington] the proposed movement here, is appreciated, & the campaign fairly opened. In confidence of success. Your friend

J. Watson Webb

ALS. NHi.

1. Ambrose C. Kingsland (1804–1878), a Whig.

2. A reference to their role in Zachary Taylor's presidential campaign.

3. Webb was a leading organizer of a mass rally scheduled for March 4 in New York City that would endorse Webster for the Presidency. The meeting was actually held on March 5.

4. Hungarian insurgent leader Louis Kossuth had been portrayed

by admirers as the "Washington of Hungarian Liberty." In view of this and of Webster's disinclination to offer direct American assistance to the Hungarian rebels, his political backers preferred to avoid any awkward Washington-Kossuth connections. See Donald S. Spencer, *Louis Kossuth and Young America: A Study of Sectionalism and Foreign Policy, 1848–1852*, (Columbia, Mo., 1977), pp. 8, 50, and *Diplomatic Papers*, 2.

5. See below, DW to Webb, February 11, 1852.

TO FRANKLIN HAVEN

Washington. Feby 10. 1852

Private & Confidential
My dear Sir;

At last there are indications of movements here, from which something favorable may come. You see also, what has been begun in New York;[1] but where is Massachusetts? She should be here in force and spirits. Mr [George] Ashmun has been sick, but is better, and we look for him to night. Pray come yourself, and bring others to his aid. The most miserable and false representations are sent hither from the Boston Custom House. The Collector[2] has said lately, to a gentleman who told it to me, that Mr [Franklin] Haven & Mr [Albert] Fearing were ready to go for General [Winfield] Scott. I told the gentleman, that it was all false. Pray let me hear from you. Say, by telegraph, whether you can come or not. Yours always truly   Danl Webster

LS. MH-H.   to DW, February 8, 1852.
    1. See above, James Watson Webb   2. Philip Greely, Jr.

TO JAMES WATSON WEBB
                                        Feb. 11th 52
Private & Confidential
My Dear Sir
    I duly recd your two letters, one from Tarrytown[1] & one from Astor House.[2] I feel quite obliged to you, for both, & shall take good care to regard your prudent & timely suggestions. I am under obligation to make an address to the Historical Society of New York, & propose to perform that duty about the 23. or 24 of this month.[3] The address is written, is wholly of a literary character, & will not contain a word upon any passing political subject.
    I have read, My dear Sir,—& I need not say with great interest—the Article in your paper of yesterday.[4] With very true regard, Yours
                                        Danl Webster

ALS. CtY.   *Speeches and Formal Writings*, 2.
    1. Not found.   4. See the extended editorial, "The
    2. See above, Webb to DW, Febru-   next Presidency," in the *Courier and
ary 8, 1852.   Enquirer*, February 10, 1852. It em-
    3. Webster's speech at the Histori- phasized DW's virtue, abilities, and
cal Society on February 23, "The   long service to the nation and
Dignity and Importance of History,"   warmly endorsed him for the Whig
avoided political commentary. See   nomination.

FROM CHARLES WAINWRIGHT MARCH
                                    Washington Feby. 24th [1852]
Dear Sir
    A friend of mine, Mr. J. Sidney Smith[1] of Missouri, a member of the present Senate of that State, and a probable delegate to the National Convention, has been invited by some of your New York friends to ad-

dress the meeting of the 4th of March,[2] and will attend provided I will go in with him. Mr. Smith is a young man of ardent feelings, and much more than ordinary ability and enthusiastically devoted to your cause. A speech in your favor from such a quarter and by such a person will add much, it strikes me, to the movement.

Mr. Smith tells me that he had a full conversation with Mr. [Edward Carrington] Cabell of Florida last night, who expressed himself warmly for you, Mr. Fillmore being out of the way, and that he would go on to New York now if it were deemed expedient. It is thought however by your friends here that his presence may not at this time be necessary. Smith says that [John Gaines] Miller and [Gilchrist] Porter, two of the Whig Representatives from Missouri, are also for you.

Mr. Jno. Lee came in last night from Annapolis. He says that the Whig members of the Legislature disapprove of the proceeding of the "Whig State Committee" in proposing Mr. Fillmore's name for the Presidency. They say it was unexpected and uncalled for, and that it does not reflect the opinion of the Whigs of the State. If our engagements here or elsewhere will admit of it, Mr. [George] Ashmun & I propose to go to Annapolis next week, and try if we can't get up some movement in your favor.

We see that Mr. [Peter] Harvey is with you in New York—and hope that he will come South. He is a man of energy, and practical talent, and fertile in resources—and at this present time, would be of much use to us in devising means for the prosecution of a vigorous war. Mr. Ashmun & I have paid already over $400, and have assumed the payment of other sums, and we ought not to be alone, the more particularly as we give our time and labor to the cause. We give a dinner on Thursday to your Congressional friends and others of like sentiments—and I wish and so does Mr. Ashmun that Mr. Harvey could be present.

The telegraph tells us that you made "a masterly effort" on Monday night[3]—for which we were not wholly unprepared. With my regards to Fletcher Believe me ever most resp[ect]f[ull]y yrs   Chs W. March

ALS. MH-H.

1. Smith had previously represented St. Louis County in the Missouri House of Representatives.

2. There is no evidence Smith attended the Webster meeting on March 5.

3. DW's February 23 address to the New-York Historical Society.

FROM EDWARD EVERETT

Boston 8 March 1852

Private

Dear Sir,

You are aware that the Newyork "Whig Review," originally a consistent & pretty efficient Whig Journal, has of late been wholly under the influence of Mr. [Ephraim George] Squier, & in reference to Nicaragua matters has carried on a violent war against the Administration.[1] The property of the Review has changed hands, & it is to be restored to its former character. I have been applied to to furnish a leading article, & have partly engaged to do so for the May number.[2]

The present proprietors do not seem to be willing, in anticipation of the Nominating Convention, to commit themselves very strongly to any one Candidate, but are willing to intimate a preference for you as their first choice; and I suppose they will admit a satisfactory treatment of that subject.[3]

There are, however, one or two points on which I am at a loss.

What ought to be said on the subject of party organization? Is it expedient, in the present state of public opinion, to endeavor to give a no-party complexion to the Canvass? Do we or do we not gain by that course?

What is to be said about the Protection of American Industry? The "Whig Review" is ultra protectionist, & has expended much labor upon the refutation of R[obert] J[ohn] Walker's paradoxes. Protection seems to be almost the only old Whig issue which retains any practical consequence. How ought it to be treated?[4]

I should be glad to have your views on these points as fully and as soon as you can favor me with them.

I had hoped to be able to run on to Washington for a little while about this time, but my wife's health will not admit her going with me & is such that I do not feel it right to leave home without her.

I sincerely congratulate you on the result of your visit to Newyork,[5] which seems to have been every thing that could be wished. Yours ever, Dear Sir, Sincerely,   Edward Everett

P.S. Our friends here both those engaged in navigation & the manufacturers are quite opposed to any further grant to the Ocean Steamers as unjust in principle & prejudicial in its operation.[6]

ALS. MHi.

1. See, for example, "Central America and the Administration," *American Whig Review*, 13 (March 1851): 276–288, which assailed British pretensions in Central America and sharply criticized DW for implicitly accepting British claims to the eastern half of Nicaragua.

2. See Edward Everett to Champion Bissell, March 6, April 5, 12, and 15, 1852, Everett Papers, MHi,

microfilm reel 30.

3. Everett's article, published anonymously as "The Presidency," in the May number of the *Whig Review*, surveyed the field of possible Whig presidential nominees, praising Scott, Fillmore, and Webster in turn.

4. See below, DW to Everett, March 13, 1852.

5. In late February, Webster had spent a week in New York City, attending dinners and receptions. The

highlight of the visit, however, was his February 23 address to the New-York Historical Society, tickets to which, originally given free to all society members, sold for as much as fifty dollars.

6. See above, pp. 204–205, DW to Robert Cumming Schenck, February 17, 1851, n. 1.

FROM JOHN PENDLETON KENNEDY

Baltimore March 12. 1852

My dear Sir

During your absence from the seat of Government, when the vacancy occurred in the Judgeship of this district, I wrote a few lines to the President, presenting to him the name of our friend [Jonathan] Meredith,[1] as one who, I was sure, would be very acceptable to our Bar, and, in even higher degree, to this community. He himself was then in New York, and I wrote upon my own suggestion, offering him to the consideration of the President without further participation, on his part, than an assurance which I had received by letter that he would accept the appointment if it was tendered to him. He was not therefore to be regarded in the category of *an applicant*—a position which, I was confident, he would never be willing to assume in reference to such a post. Whilst, therefore, others, who were applicants, were engrossing all that kind of influence which is derived from personal solicitation, I was better pleased to advocate an appointment which was unassisted by such influence, and rested upon an established reputation which required no such aid.

I should have written to you at once, and before I mentioned the subject to any one else, if you had been in Washington, and as I knew you were intimately acquainted with Mr Meredith, I should have said nothing more than was necessary to apprise you of his willingness to accept the appointment in ·case it were offered to him. We have no gentleman at our bar who would command more respect on the Bench, or who would administer its duties, with more advantage to the public. As I understand the matter is still in suspense, I write this letter now to acquit myself of what should have been my first duty if you had been in Washington, and to assure you, my dear Sir, of the esteem & regard with which I am very truly yours   J. P. Kennedy

ALS. MdBP.

1. Meredith (1785–1872; University of Pennsylvania 1802), scion of a prominent Philadelphia family, had moved to Baltimore and established a lucrative law practice there. A leading candidate for the vacant federal district judgeship in Maryland, Meredith was passed over because of his age, and the appointment went to Baltimore attorney John Glenn. See Jonathan Meredith to DW, March 9, 1852, mDW 36186, DW to Millard Fillmore, March 17,

1852, mDW 36246, and *Journal of the Executive Proceedings of the*   *Senate* (Washington, 1887), 8: 374–375.

TO EDWARD EVERETT

Washington 13. March 1852

Private and confidential.

My Dear Sir,

I have received your letter of the 8th of March,[1] and, though I have not had much time to consider its contents, yet I will throw out one or two suggestions, and write you again, in a few days, if any thing farther occurs to me. I bear in mind what you said last winter about the [American Whig] "Review," and am glad that it has changed hands.

To your first question, I have to say, that, in my opinion, if we have any good in store for us, it will be through the *Whig Convention*. The movements at the North, in our favor, have been taken in the name of the *Whig party*, and if we get the requisite support from the *South* it will be probably from those who are going to the regular Whig Convention to sustain Mr. Fillmore, and who will unite with us, if Mr. Fillmore steps out of the way, or if the North give so many votes against Mr. Fillmore and for other candidates as to defeat him.

To the second inquiry, concerning the propriety of connecting my name, at this late hour of the day, in any prominent way, with the protection policy, I humbly submit that it will do no good to that policy, and be without any advantage. If any body incline, at the Presidential election to take into view protection to manufactures, he will know what *my* views are, from the past; without giving offence to the friends of free trade by any fresh proclamation in favor of a Tariff for protection.

You will see of course my letter in the [Washington, D.C., National] Intelligencer[2] of this morning, which, with my speeches on those topics, with which you are familiar, will give you perhaps a few hints. In that connection I would recall to your recollection my remarks at Buffalo on foreign emigration.[3]

I understand that the tone of the "Boston Celt,"[4] the organ of large portions of the emigrants to this country, indicates a favorable feeling. Yours always truly,   Danl Webster

LS. MHi.

1. See above.

2. Webster's letter, addressed to David A. Neal, an Illinois businessman and promoter of the Illinois Railroad, spoke of the benefits of railroad construction across America. Nothing, he observed, "is more likely to keep the Government and the Union from running off the track."

3. During his New York tour in May 1851, DW had made frequent allusions to the benefits that the influx of immigrants had brought to America. In Buffalo on May 21, for example, he noted that immi-

grants "came to remain among us, and to be of us, and to take their chances among us. Let them come." *Works*, 2: 537–541.

4. *The Boston American Celt and Adopted Citizen* was a popular weekly in the Irish-American community.

FROM JOHN TAYLOR

Franklin March 15th 1852–

Mr Webster, Dear Sir

Our winter Appears to be braking up, for the last three days, the snow has settled, so that we can see Bare ground once more on the Hils, it looks reviveing. I am in hopes in one month From this day, we can plow And draw manure.

Last wednesday I went to Vandue In Andover, at the Emery Farm Where you bought some appels Several years ago, near what is cauled the hogs Back, & the Great Cut for the R. Road,

I bought Eight Tons of first quality of English hay, Friday & Saturday I drawd it all home, I have got To pay for it, $7.00 per ton.

The great oxen, I meand our gray & red ones, 6 years Old this spring. They hav not bin yoaked for Two months, they never should be again, they are in good order Now, turn them out & let them go for Beef,—

I will tell you what I would Like if you think you can possiably do it,—

Capt James Mastin [Marston][1] of Andover a man who you know well, has a nice pare of 5 year olds that are jest right, both dark Red, girt 6 ft-10 inches, horns jest alike, &, they are right all over, I can buy them now, for jest $105. I think they are worth as much as your Frost. Stears. They will way alive, 3000 pounds. I wish I knew to day—Mr Webster's Mind, I would have the Mastin oxen in my Great Barn before the Sun goes down—I will tell you what I will do, Mr Webster I will go up to Capt Mastin's And git the refusel of them for one week. If you should Conclude to buy them you Will pleas let me know by Return of mail,—all well. I am Sir, Your most Obedient Servent,   John Taylor

ALS. NhHi.
1. Marston (1783–1869) was an Andover farmer.

TO JOHN TAYLOR

Washington. March 17th 1852

Go ahead. The heart of the winter is broke, and before the first day of April all your land may be ploughed. Buy the oxen of Capt. [James] Marston if you think the price fair. Pay for the hay. I send you a check for $160, for these two objects. Put the great oxen in a condition to be turned out to be fattened. You have a good horse team, and I think in addition to this, four oxen and a pair of four year old steers will do your work. If you think so, then dispose of the Stevens oxen, or unyoke them, and send them to the pasture, for beef. I know not when I shall see you, but I hope before planting. If you need any thing such as Guano for instance, write to Joseph Breck, Esqr., Boston, and he will send it to you. Whatever ground you sow or plant, see that it is in good condition. We want no *penny royal Crops*. "A little farm well tilled" is to a farmer the next best thing to "a little wife well-willed." Cultivate your garden. Be sure to produce sufficient quantities of useful vegetables. A man may half support his family from a good garden. Take care to keep my mother's garden in the best order, even if it cost you the wages of a man to take care of it. I have sent you many garden seeds. Distribute them among your neighbours, send them to the stores in the Village, that every body may have a part of them without cost.

I am glad that you have chosen Mr. [Austin Franklin] Pike representative. He is a true man, but there are in N. H. many persons who call themselves Whigs who are no Whigs at all and no better than disunionists. Any man who hesitates in granting and securing to every part of the Country, its just and Constitutional rights, is an enemy to the whole country. John Taylor! if one of your boys should say that he honors his father & mother and loves his Brothers and Sisters, but still insists that one of them shall be driven out of the family, what can you say of him but this, that there is no real family love in him? You and I are farmers. We never talk politics—our talk is of oxen, but remember this; That any man who attempts to excite one part of this country against another is just as wicked, as he would be, who should attempt to get up a quarrel between John Taylor and his neighbour old Mr. John Sanborn or his other neighbour Capt. [Henry] Burleigh. There are some animals that live best in the fire; and there are some men, who delight in heat, smoke, combustion and even general conflagration. They do not follow the things which make for peace. They enjoy only controversy, contention and strife. Have no communion with such persons, either as neighbours or politicians. You have no more right to say that slavery ought not to exist in Virginia, than a Virginian has to say, that slavery ought to exist in N. Hampshire. This is a question left to every State, to decide for itself and if we mean to keep the States together, we must leave to every State this power of deciding for itself.

I think I never wrote you a word before upon politics. I shall not do it again. I only say love your Country and your whole Country, and when men attempt to persuade you to get into a quarrel with the laws of other States, Tell them, "that you mean to mind your own business," and advise them to mind theirs.

John Taylor! You are a free man, you possess good principles, you have a large family to rear and provide for by your labor. Be thankful to the government which does not oppress you, which does not bear you down by excessive taxation; but which holds out to you and to yours the hope of all the blessings which liberty, industry and security may give.

John Taylor! thank God morning and evening that you were born in such a Country. John Taylor! never write me another word upon politics.

Give my kindest remembrance to your wife and children; and when you look from your Eastern windows upon the graves of my family, remember that he who is the author of this letter must soon follow them to another world.   Danl Webster

LS. NhHi. Published in *PC*, 2: 515–517.

TO JOHN TAYLOR

Trenton, N. J. March 25 1852

I am here attending a Court,[1] and shall return to Washington about next Monday.

Mr. [Roswell Lyman] Colt,[2] of this State, an old friend of mine, has made me a present of three imported Hungarian cattle, one bull, one cow, and one yearling heifer. He will start them tomorrow for Boston, where they will be by the time, that you receive this letter, and I wish you to go immediately down and take them to Franklin in the cars.

Mr. Colt does not like [Louis] Kossuth, and requests that he shall not be called by that name. You may call him "Saint Stephen." I do not propose to keep these Hungarian cattle on your farm, to mix with your Stock, we will find room for them in due time on the Sawyer place or elsewhere.

I enclose you a check for thirty dollars.

When you have seen the cattle, write me and tell me how you like them.

If southern corn is cheap in Boston, you may get as much as you will want at Mr. Otis Munroe's [grain store on] Commercial Street. If you think it better to buy country corn, you may do so, and I will send you the money.

It seems time that Dr. [Luther Martin] Knight[3] should be paid something for his kind professional services to me last fall. Please speak to him on that subject, ask him to let me know what will be agreeable. He did me great good.

Tell Mr. Horace Noyes that when I get to Washington I shall send him a check for Capt. [Nathaniel] Sawyer, and write him also, respecting the Sawyer place. I hope you are all well. Take good care of St. Stephen and his two females.   Danl Webster

ls. MBBS.
1. Webster was in Trenton to participate in the celebrated "India Rubber Case"—*Goodyear* v. *Day*, his last major legal effort. See *Legal Papers*, 3.
2. Colt (1779–1856), a commercial merchant in New York City, was president of the Society for the Establishment of Useful Manufactures in Paterson, New Jersey, from 1814 until his death. A gentleman farmer,

he took a special interest in horticulture and cattle raising.
3. Knight (1810–1887; Dartmouth Medical School 1835) had established a medical practice in Franklin in 1845. It was probably Knight who attended Webster after he hurt his foot while haying at Elms Farm the previous summer. See Nathaniel Sawyer to Alphonso Taft, August 23, 1851, pp. 268–270, above.

FROM HUGH MCCULLOH BIRCKHEAD

[c. April 5, 1852]
[Baltimore, Maryland]

My Dear Sir

I notice you have retd. to Washington, after I hope, a successful effort for y[ou]r friends at Trenton[1]—had hoped to have had you stop *one night* with us—must do so next trip—always pleased to see you with Mrs. W. Our friend [John] Barney asked me to address you in his favor, for the mission to Sweden. I enclose the Letter,[2] say to him you have it & show it if asked.

I have seen this morning, Mr. Saml. S. Gaskins,[3] the person Mr. [Z. Collins] Lee[4] imploy[e]d to get subscribers to yr new work. He has only about 70 names, hopes to get more, a person from Boston last winter, went round & got names here. Mr. Gaskins' agreement with Mr. Lee was. 25cts each subscriber. He will if you wish it, deliver the work & receive pay[men]t for which will charge 25cts more, recommends 100 Copies being sent him, one fourth handsomest edition—any Copies not accounted for, he will hand over. I dont know what your arrang[emen]t is, with publishers—any service I can render, will be done with pleasure.

Many persons declined taking the work to my surprise. How would it do to send the subscription paper to Richmond. I got but a few names at Annapolis. Some say they have not $12 to spare, others the 'work is too expensive—may take it when they, see it &c &c. You may have forgotten to send me some Copies of yr late address in New York[5]—would be pleased to have them & remain very truly   Hugh Birckhead

als. DLC.
1. DW had successfully represented Charles Goodyear in a patent

suit. See *Legal Papers*, 3.
2. Enclosure not found.
3. Gaskins was then a clerk in

the county clerk's office in Baltimore.

4. Lee (1807–1859; University of Virginia), a Baltimore lawyer, was United States district attorney for Maryland.

5. Birckhead is alluding to DW's February 23 address to the New-York Historical Society, "The Dignity and Importance of History." *Speeches and Formal Writings*, 2.

FROM JOHN PLUMMER HEALY

Boston April 7, 1852

Dear Sir,

There seems to be some division in the Board of Directors, or other persons having control, or influence in the affairs of the Old Colony Rail Road, which I do not understand. Some of them appear to be quite anxious, that the matter involved in your Suit ag[ains]t the Corporation,[1] should be disposed of in a manner agreeable to you, & others manifest a disposition to fight it out to the end. Whether this difference comes from their respective feelings towards you, or from difficulties which beset the way of some of them in their action among themselves pertaining to their official management, I do not know.

Mr. [Francis Boardman] Crowninshield,[2] the President, professes to be very friendly, & to very much regret that you should suppose any communication from you to him had been unanswered. He says if you sent any note or letter to him about the relations between yourself & the corporation, he never received it. He also seems to be very desirous to dispose of this Suit, in some way satisfactory to you, & without a trial; but also [in] a way that his Board of Directors can adopt without a violation of instructions which they are under from the Stockholders.

These things I learn through Mr. [Francis Brown] Hayes,[3] their counsel. They suggest giving you a ticket for life, <over the roads> which shall entitle you personally, but no member of your family, to pass over the road. And they make some other not important propositions, such as paying a hundred dollars in settlement of the action, &c.

Upon a trial of the case, I see no reason to doubt that you will prevail. Their grounds of defence, so far as I have learned them, do not appear to me very solid.

Is it worth the while to make a settlement upon any such terms as I have alluded to? I ought to have stated, that they propose to apologise for any want, or seeming want, of courtesy in the conduct of the officers of the corporation towards you.

I have filed interrogatories to take commissions for getting the testimony of Mr. Warren & Mr. Hobbie,[4] & the cross interrogations ought to have been filed before this time. Mr. Hayes has delayed a filing in the hope of getting a settlement.

I should be glad to know what you wish to have done. If the case is to be tried, I wish to bring it to a trial at this term.

The Passenger cases[5] will not be reached before the adjourned session of the Court in June. Very truly yours   J. P. Healy.

ALS. MHi.

1. See above, pp. 245–246, DW to Isaac Lothrop Hedge, May 5, 1851.

2. Crowninshield (1809–1877; Harvard 1829) was active in law, politics, and mercantile enterprise in addition to his responsibilities at the Old Colony Railroad.

3. Hayes (1819–1884; Harvard 1839) was for many years a director of the Old Colony Railroad and later president of the Atlantic and

Pacific Railroad Company.

4. Possibly Charles Henry Warren, former president of the Boston and Providence Railroad and brother-in-law of former Old Colony Railroad president Isaac L. Hedge. Hobbie has not been identified.

5. This is presumably a reference to lower court actions precipitated by the Supreme Court's decision in *Norris* v. *Boston* (7 Howard 283).

TO ROBERT CHARLES WINTHROP

Washington April 8. 1852

Dear Sir,

I had the honor to receive your letter of the 15th of March,[1] but had no opportunity to answer it, until since my return from New Jersey.[2] I have not seen, my dear Sir, any report of remarks, purporting to have been made by me, on any of the occasions, on which I met friends socially, during my last visit to New York; nor can I recall any particular expressions used by me, in relation to consultations, between me and my late colleagues from Massachusetts, respecting the dangers of the country, before the 7th of March 1850, but I have no hesitation in declaring that I never made, nor intended to make, any particular reference to yourself, in any such observations. I could not but know the sentiments of my colleague in the Senate, Mr [John] Davis. I spoke repeatedly with Mr. [George] Ashmun, and other friends, from the north in and out of Massachusetts. It is certainly true that you was not consulted upon the subject of my speech before it was delivered, and that I did not communicate to you, personally, in advance, my views and purposes in making it. All this is due to candor & correctness. At the same time, I must say, that I am at a loss to know, what reason you had for supposing, on the 21st of February, that I was in favor of Genl. [Zachary] Taylor's platform. Before that time, and in a long conversation, with General Taylor, the only one I ever had with him on any matter of importance, I distinctly stated to him, that I did not at all concur with him in his views; that I was for one general and final adjustment of all the questions; and that, as for the admission of California, leaving all other questions equally important, to be discussed and quarreled about thereafter—which I took to be the whole of his platform, so called—I thought such a course of proceeding very likely to lead to a civil war; and I must say, my dear Sir, that I am more strongly of that opinion now, than I was then.[3]

Believe me, my dear Sir, it gave me infinite pain, to differ with you, and the rest of my colleagues, on that exigent and critical occasion. Certainly I doubted not the patriotism or good purposes of any of you. But the path of my own duties seemed plain, and I was ready to tread it at all hazards. The consequence was, that I found myself engaged, in a controversy of great moment, to be fought on a field, in which I had neither a leader nor a follower, from among my own immediate friends.

And now let me add, my dear Sir, that there is no man in whose public career, I have heretofore taken more interest and concern than in yours. I have known and appreciated, your intelligence, your patriotism, your fitness for high public employment. I have ever spoken of you, as one, from whom the country had much to expect, and I still cherish the fervent hope, that you may yet enjoy, in full measure, the rich reward of public approbation, for distinguished public services. Yours always truly   Danl Webster

LS. MHi. Published in part in *W & S*, 16: 651.

1. Winthrop's letter has not been found, but an excerpt from it was published in Robert C. Winthrop, Jr., *A Memoir of Robert C. Winthrop* (Boston, 1897), p. 152. Essentially, Winthrop sought DW's explanation for the latter's recently reported comments that he had given Winthrop no reason in early 1850 to believe his Seventh of March speech would support the Taylor administration's approach to the sectional crisis.

2. Webster had been in Trenton from March 20 through April 2 arguing Goodyear's patent infringement suit.

3. In a rejoinder dated April 14, Winthrop reiterated *his* view that DW did not unqualifiedly oppose the Taylor plan prior to February 21 and offered at some future time to "remind you of circumstances which . . . left less impression on your mind than upon my own." Winthrop, *Memoir*, pp. 153–154. Webster evidently declined any further response.

FROM CHARLES WAINWRIGHT MARCH

New York April 8. 1852

Dear Sir

[Henry Parker] Fairbanks[1] of Charlestown came in last night. He tells me that the Scott-men in Massachusetts, aided by the Custom-House, are working energetically, and boast that they will have their delegates also in the National Convention. Mr. Fairbanks says that it was through the influence of Greeley [Philip Greely], he was left out of the State

Central Committee this year, and a Scott-man substituted and that Greeley with Geo: Morey &c promise the vote of the State ultimately for [Winfield] Scott, in Convention. At the same time, Mr. Fairbanks contends, that the removal of Greeley, at this late hour of the administration would be an impolitic proceeding. But if he is not to be removed, it strikes me he should be muzzled, and Mr. [Thomas] Corwin could do it.[2] At least, his machinations should be met and thwarted.

[Palmer V.] Kellogg, the ejected marshal of the Northern District of New York,[3] has been here, on his return home from Washington. He tells me that he has none but kind feelings towards you, and that he only supports Scott as available. If the latter be not nominated in Convention he shall go for you. The Legislative-caucus[4] you will see has expressed a choice for Scott. This was not unexpected, and may not be unfortunate. It is intended more as a demonstration against Fillmore than for Scott.

The Fillmore-newspapers, the [New York] Express, Mirror &c are throwing out intimations that your friends in Convention, finding your nomination unpracticable, will go in for Fillmore. This is intended to operate elsewhere—no one of course believes it here. The Mirror has had a series of articles lately in favor of Mr. Fillmore, not injudiciously written upon the whole. [Hiram] Fuller promises, that I shall insert an equal number for you. The paper has not much circulation but has its influence nevertheless. I requested [Henry Jarvis] Raymond to let me write a series of articles in your favor, for the "Times"—but he declines, on the ground that he wishes to take no part in the nomination. He is however for Scott, but ready to be influenced by Mr. [Simeon] Draper &c.

Your friends here meet frequently at their rooms in the Astor [Astor House], and report progress. Mr. [Moses Hicks] Grinnell is very busy, enthusiastic and sanguine. He says that with thirty firm men in Convention, you can control its vote—and I make it certain that, unless we are most egregiously deceived, you will have more than forty, giving to Mr. Fillmore the unanimous South, *which he will not have*.

I saw [Henry Mills] Fuller, M. C. from Pennsylvania last night. He says that he prefers you to any man, but that his State is for Scott. Still he says there is great dissatisfaction that the State Convention should have appointed the whole delegation to the National Convention instead of leaving the matter to the Districts, as heretofore. The consequence will be in his opinion that, as some delegates had been already appointed by Districts, there will be contested cases before the National Convention. How would it do for your friends quietly to elect delegates by Districts? and insist upon the time-sanctioned custom.

Mr. [George] Ashmun writes me that he shall go to Washington early in the week. Ever most resp[ectfull]y & truly Yrs   Chs. W. March

ALS. NhHi. Published in Van Tyne, pp. 517–518.

1. Fairbanks (1809–1854) was president of the Charlestown City Council in 1852.

2. See below, DW to Thomas Corwin, May 14, 1852.

3. Appointed marshal by President Taylor in 1849 at William H. Seward's urging (and over then Vice President Fillmore's objections), Kellogg was removed by Fillmore in March 1851 and replaced by John T. Bush.

4. Scott was overwhelmingly endorsed for President by the New York Whig legislative caucus on April 8. *New York Herald*, April 9, 1852.

TO JOHN PLUMMER HEALY

Washington, April 9. 1852

My dear Mr Healey

I have your letter of the 7th.[1] This matter of the controversy with the Old Colony Rail Road, has given me considerable mortification. I think myself to have been badly treated, although I entire[ly] acquit Mr. [Francis Boardman] Crowninshield of any intentional disrespect. He is a gentleman towards whom, I have always entertained, very friendly feelings. I should be very glad now if the matter could be adjusted, upon any reasonable and proper terms; but I must decline the acceptance of any free ticket for myself alone. This would be of very little value, considering that I am at Marshfield but only a part of the year, and then, as often go to Boston by the Hingham boat, as by the rail-road. Besides, it is awkward to pull out my purse, to pay the fare for my wife, while I go clear.

The original bargain was clear, definite, and distinct, but the Directors have broken their contract, and thats the whole of it. Mr [Francis Brown] Hayes has written me a very friendly letter,[2] for which I am much obliged to him, as I will thank you to say to him. If the Directors, will give him authority to settle, in his discretion, I hereby give you the same, repeating what I have above said, that a free ticket to me alone, cannot be received, as any part of the consideration. As for giving me one hundred dollars, if it is meant to be the whole consideration, I must reject it at once. I have not brought suit to recover one hundred dollars. Upon the whole, if they will give me and my wife, free tickets, for our respective lives, you may discharge the suit.[3] Yours truly   Danl Webster

LS. MHi.

1. See above, Healy to DW, April 7, 1852.

2. Not found.

3. Evidently the railroad's directors were unwilling immediately to yield on this point. See DW to John Plummer Healy, April 24, 1852, mDW 38562, demanding that his dispute with the railroad be "closed, somehow." The ultimate disposition of the controversy is not known.

As the following letter indicates, Webster's quest for southern support in the ongoing contest for the Whig presidential nomination led him to reaffirm, in the strongest terms, his commitment to the compromise settlement of 1850—including the controversial Fugitive Slave Law.

TO GEORGE A. TAVENNER

Washington, April 9. 1852

Dear Sir:

I have the honor to acknowledge the receipt of your letter of the 8th inst.,[1] and thank you for what you are pleased to say, of my fidelity, to great national Whig principles. I trust, there is not a man in the country, who doubts my approbation of those measures, which are usually called "Compromise Measures," or my fixed determination to uphold them steadily & firmly. Nothing but a deep sense of duty led me to take the part which I did take, in bringing about their adoption by Congress, and that same sense of duty, remains with unabated force. I am of opinion that those measures, one and all, were necessary and expedient, and ought to be adhered to, by all friends of the Constitution, and all lovers of their country. That one among them, which appears to have given the greatest dissatisfaction, I mean the Fugitive Slave Law, I hold to be a law, entirely constitutional, highly proper, and absolutely essential to the peace of the country. Such a law is demanded by the plain written words of the Constitution; and how any man, can wish to abrogate or destroy it, & at the same time say, that he is a supporter of the Constitution, and willing to <support> adhere[2] to those provisions in it, which are clear & positive injunctions and restraints, passes my power of comprehension. My belief is, that when the passions of men subside, and reason and true patriotism, are allowed to have their proper sway, the public mind, north and south, will come to a proper state, upon these questions. I do not believe that further agitation, can make any considerable progress at the north. The great mass of the people, I am sure, are sound, and have no wish to interfere with such things, as are, by the Constitution, placed under the exclusive control[3] of the separate states. I have noticed, indeed, not without regret, certain proceedings to which you have alluded,[4] and in regard to <this> these I have to say, that gentlemen may not think it necessary, or proper, that they should be called upon, to affirm, by resolution, that which is already the existing law of the land. That any positive movement to repeal or alter, any or all, the compromise measures, would meet with any general encouragement or support, I do not at all believe. But however that may be, my own sentiments remain, and are likely to remain, quite unchanged. I am in favor of upholding the Constitution, in the general, and all its particulars. I am in favor of respecting its authority and obeying its injunctions; and to the end of my life, shall do all in my power, to fulfill, honestly and faithfully, all its provisions. I look upon the compromise measures, as a just[,] proper, fair, and final adjustment of the questions to which they relate; and no re-agitation of those questions, no new opening of them, no effort to create dissatisfaction with them, will ever receive from me, the least countenance or support, concurrence or approval, at any time, or under any circumstances. I am, with regard, Your obt servt

Draft, with insertions in DW's hand. NhHi. Published in *National Intelligencer*, April 17, 1852 (as April 10), and in Van Tyne, pp. 521–522, where Tavenner is identified only as "a Virginia politician."
  1. mDW 36481.
  2. Here DW inserted the words "adhere to" in place of "support."
  3. Here DW inserted the word "exclusive."
  4. Tavenner had alluded to recent "agitation," both in northern states and in Congress, for repeal of the Fugitive Slave Law.

FROM CHARLES WAINWRIGHT MARCH

New York
April 12. '52

Dear Sir

Gov. [James Chamberlain] Jones and Mr. [Presley Underwood] Ewing of Ky. arrived here Saturday night, on an invitation to be present at the "Clay Festival" this evening.[1] The invitation was given for more than an ordinary compliment. It means mischief. The most active men of the Clay Club, [Daniel] Ul[l]man, Nat[haniel Bowditch] Blunt, Nich[olas] Carroll[2] &c., propose to bring forward Gov. Jones as the man to catch Mr. [Henry] Clay's mantle as that distinguished gentleman departs—and it is not to be supposed that the Governor is ignorant of this intention. Mr. Ewing a representative from Kentucky and a protegé of Mr. Clay told me two months since in Washington that he looked upon Jones as the most available candidate for the Presidency this coming election. I do not believe however that this movement, unless earnestly responded to at the South, will have any other result than to detach some of Mr. Fillmore's friends from his cause. I have seen a great deal of Gov. Jones since he has been here, and, to do him justice, must say, that he is invariably kind in his language towards you. He says that Mr. Fillmore's nomination, which otherwise could have been secured, will now be defeated by the inconsiderate conduct of such friends as Humphrey Marshal[l], [Edward Carrington] Cabell &c.

Mr. [Simeon] Draper told me last evening that he hoped such an arrangement would be effected between your friends in this city and those of General [Winfield] Scott as to divide the delegation between you & him—that the General's friends will not be hostile to you either in the city or out of it, but would go in with yours and secure your nomination, if the South on leaving Fillmore, take you up. This is the consummation to which we would arrive, and perhaps this is the way in which it is to be easiest accomplished. I do not find among the delegates to this time elected from the State favorable to Gen. Scott any unkind feeling towards you.

I wrote Mr. [Edward] Curtis Saturday of my fears about certain districts in Massachusetts, to which I begged him to call your attention. I trust you will hold with me that it is of paramount importance to secure the proper men from Massachusetts. One traitor there could do us more injury than fifty opponents in other States—as was proved by the conduct and insinuations of [George] Lunt in the last convention.[3] I shall write Mr. [Peter] Harvey on the subject by to-days mail. Mr. [George] Ashmun will be here to-night, and I will bring the subject before him, and get him to write.

Great exertions have been made to get up an enthusiastic meeting for the Clay demonstration to-night—which so far as numbers are concerned will doubtless be successful. Ever most resp[ectfull]y & truly yrs

Chs. W. March

ALS. NhHi. Published in Van Tyne, pp. 518–519.

1.—A citywide celebration of Henry Clay's seventy-fifth birthday, the New York "Clay Festival" culminated with a well-attended rally at the Apollo Saloon. Letters from Clay's compeers, including Webster, were read, toasts were offered to the Kentuckian's health, and Governor Jones of Tennessee recounted Clay's contributions to the Union. *New York Herald*, April 13, 1852. DW's letter to the festival is in *W & S*, 16: 652.

2. Ullman (1810–1892; Yale 1829), a New York City lawyer associated with the "Silver Gray" wing of the Whig party, ran a strong but unsuccessful race for governor in 1854 on the American Party ticket. Blunt (b. 1804) was New York district attorney at this time. Carroll was a New York merchant.

3. As a delegate to the Whig National Convention in 1848, Lunt had switched his vote from Webster to Zachary Taylor. Active in the Taylor campaign, he was rewarded with the United States attorneyship in Boston —a post that DW had sought for his son Fletcher. See *Correspondence*, 6 passim.

TO FRANKLIN HAVEN

Washington, April 28. '52

My Dear Sir

You notice that a Fillmore Demonstration is proposed, in N. York. This will be entirely *personal*, & got up principally by the *officials* of the City. Perhaps an attempt may be made to give it the appearance of a

Meeting for no purpose but to sustain the compromise, & Boston may be invited to respond. Don't be caught!

Mrs W. & I are going to Boston, & hope to be at Mr [James William] Paiges next Tuesday Evening. I think I shall proceed, if nothing should prevent, to Marshfield the next morning, & stay a day at Boston, when I return.

Depend upon it, if you are not wide awake, great danger will exist of chusing, in Massachusetts, such Delegates as will, first or last, vote for Genl. [Winfield] Scott. You must all keep a bright look out. In the Plymouth & Bristol Districts, great vigilance will be necessary. Mr [Seth] Sprague[1] of Duxbury, Mr [Isaac Lothrop] Hedge, of Plymouth, & our friends in Taunton should take that business seasonably in hand. And I suppose also that the Barnstable & New Bedford District will require looking after. Indeed, there will be danger every where, if all friends are not on the alert. Yrs truly   Danl Webster

ALS. MH-H.

1. Sprague (1821–1869; Harvard 1841), the son of federal judge Peleg Sprague, was a clerk for the District Court in Boston. He was an at-large delegate to the Baltimore convention pledged to Webster.

ALEXANDER HAMILTON LAWRENCE TO GEORGE JACOB ABBOT

Washington D.C. May 5th 1852

Dr Sir,

Knowing your interest in the affairs of Mr Webster I take the liberty of addressing to you a few lines upon what I consider a very important matter, submitting it to yourself to make such use of them as you may prefer.

It seems to me to be of the most pressing importance that there should be some organization in this City of the true & known friends of Mr Webster for the purpose of securing his nomination. There is now no place to which strangers coming here can resort for correct information as to Mr Webster's prospects. There is no organized body with whom they can consult with freedom—there is no effort to send from the centre of politics any information in regard to Mr Webster's peculiar claims to the presidency—in short there is nothing said or done here that would induce a stranger to suppose that there was the least idea entertained of Mr Websters' nomination. Now this state of things is ruinous. This is the place, of all others where there should be some concerted plan of action. It is from this place that information ought to proceed. But it is especially here, where strangers are continually coming from all parts of the Country, and where the Delegates to the Convention are even now beginning to assemble, that there should be a class of persons who would make it their business to seek out and converse with these gentlemen as they come, and shew them at least that Mr Webster has some persons to sustain his pretensions.

Now I have been led to these observations by two or three occurrences that have come within my personal knowledge within a few days. I was yesterday in conversation with a gentleman that I believed to be a friend of Mr Webster, and I put the question to him. He said that he was in mind & heart in favor of Mr W. but that from what he could see here there was no sort of chance of his nomination. And he asked me what energetic, resolute, practical & trusty friend Mr W. had in Congress who was *engaged* in promoting his interests? He asked me *where* were his friends in this City? All is *apathy*, he said, both in Congress & out. Another gentleman, a stranger & a friend of Mr W., told me that when he got here he could find no person to whom to apply and with whom to consult. Another, and a *Webster Delegate* too, plainly indicated that matters looked differently here from what he expected. And I very much fear that, unless something is done more than has been done, that very Delegate will feel himself justified in casting one vote for Mr W. and then going for some one else. Now one great reason for a concerted organization here is, that the Delegates may be talked with before the Convention—that some plan should be adopted and something be understood. That Arch Devil [William Henry] Seward has had a committee here for a year. There is a regular though as yet a secret organization for [Winfield] Scott and they are working night and day. Nothing but the cunning of Seward has kept Scott from indulging in that which he believes his very particular accomplishment—*writing*. If then we are to keep up with the rest we must organize, and that too at once. Every day that is lost is doing irretrievable injury. There ought to be money—there ought to be printed matter—and more than all *now*, there ought to be *men, true men*, who will seek out those who come here and exert themselves in Mr Webster's cause. There will be Webster men enough, confessed, *if he should be nominated*—but it is only his *real* friends that will be willing to stand out as such in order to *secure* his nomination. Let us then *do* something at once.[1] Yours truly   A. H. Lawrence

ALS. CtY. Lawrence (1812–1857; Dartmouth 1833) was a Washington lawyer.

1. For evidence that this letter provoked some action, see below, George J. Abbot to DW, May 15, 1852.

Back in Marshfield by May 6 following a month of intense labor in the State Department, Webster reserved time for personal business and recreation. On the morning of May 8, accompanied by Charles Lanman, he headed for a Plymouth pond to fish for trout. Roughly a mile from

their destination, however, the transom bolt of Webster's carriage broke,
hurling both men headlong to the ground. As Webster describes the inci-
dent in the letter below to President Fillmore, he was a lucky man; but
the accident sidelined him for several weeks, and it may well have con-
tributed to his debility as the summer of 1852 approached.

TO MILLARD FILLMORE

Marshfield Sunday morning
May 9. 1852

My dear Sir,

You will have heard of my accident yesterday morning, in falling
from a carriage. The day was very fine, and I set out to make a visit to
Plymouth, ten or twelve miles distant, with Mr. [Charles] Lanman, my
clerk. We were in a large buggy or more properly, an old fashioned
phaeton, of course open in front, and with two horses. About nine miles
from home, the king-bolt, or transom bolt, as I believe they call it,
(which, from the fore part of the carriage goes down through the perch
into the forward axletree, and so connects the fore wheels and the hind
wheels,) broke, and the body of the carriage of course fell to the ground,
and threw us both out, headlong, with some violence. Fortunately, however, we were ascending a hill, and going slow; had it been otherwise,
we could hardly have escaped with our lives. In falling, I threw my
hands forward to protect my head from the ground, and this brought
the whole weight of the body upon the hands and arms, turning back
the hands, and very much spraining the wrists. The shock of the whole
system was very great. My head hit the ground, though very lightly, and
with no injury, except a little scratching of the forehead upon the
gravel. Nor was there any internal injury. It was thought, at first, that no
bone was injured in any degree, but I think, now that one of the bones,
in the wrist, on the left hand, was slightly fractured, but not so as to be
dislocated, or be put out of place. It may probably make that wrist stiff
for some time. We got another carriage, and came home as soon as I felt
well enough, foreseeing that my bruised limbs would be more swollen
and painful to day, than they then were. In point of fact, the pain, tho'
very severe last night, has abated this morning, but the swelling has not.
I cannot use my hands at all, and am quite afraid it will be several days
before I shall be able to leave my room.

A similar accident happened to me more than twenty years ago, and
from that time I have generally been quite careful to avoid the like occurrence, by the use of a chain, or some other contrivance, to supply
the place of the bolt temporarily, in case the bolt should break. With the
exception of that used yesterday, there is not a carriage on our premises,

great or small, double or single, which has not this security, but the unlucky carriage of yesterday was not built originally for my use, and I had omitted to see to this important particular. It is quite a mercy that the consequences of the fall were not more serious. I had hardly left the village where it happened, before I heard that Mr. Webster had broken his thigh, that the fall had deprived him of his senses &c &c which induced me to cause telegraphic messages to be sent in various directions.

I shall of course, my dear Sir, keep you advised of the progress of things. Yours always truly   Danl. Webster By Chas. Lanman.

LS by proxy. NBuHi. Published in PC, 2: 528–530. Webster furnished further details of the accident in a letter to Fillmore on May 12 (mDW 36794) and thereafter provided periodic reports on his recovery. See, e.g., DW to Fillmore, May 19, 1852, below, and May 24, 1852. mDW 36890. For Lanman's account of the accident and its aftermath, see *The Private Life of Daniel Webster* (New York, 1852), pp. 173–175.

Boston collector Philip Greely, Jr., had been a thorn in Webster's side since 1850. Although not publicly identified as a Free Soiler, Greely was sympathetic to the Seward wing of the Whig party, and despite claims to the contrary in letters to Webster and Fillmore, he worked covertly against the administration.

Since joining the cabinet Webster had periodically tried, without success, to have Greely muzzled or removed, but the President declined to intervene. Secretary Corwin, to whom the letter below is addressed, also failed to act in the face of growing evidence that Greely was using his office to advance Winfield Scott's presidential prospects in Massachusetts.

TO THOMAS CORWIN

Marshfield May 14th 1852

Private & Confidential
My dear Sir,

The last movement of Greeleys [Philip Greely] is a miserable mixture of evasion and coercion. What right in the world has he to engage persons in the public service, on any other terms, than such as are prescribed by law. Some of the "aids" are very poor and he has starved them into a false admission, and now wishes to bind the rest by this admission of theirs. I must confess my mortification, in finding that so worthless an incumbent cannot be removed from office, nor is my mortification a whit less than that of the great body of the Constitutional Whigs of Massachusetts. I must be permitted to make once more a declaration, which I hoped it would not be necessary to repeat, that the Collector of Boston, is in heart a thorough Free-soiler, and exercises his official influence, in all cases in which he thinks he shall be able to avoid detection, in opposition to the Administration, and its principal leading measures. Yours truly   Daniel Webster by Charles Lanman

LS by proxy. DLC.

FROM GEORGE JACOB ABBOT

Washington, May 15
2 1/2 o'clk.

Dear Sir,

A meeting of your friends has just been held at Mr. [Alexander Hamilton] Lawrence's office. Messrs. [George] Ashmun and [Edward] Curtis, Senator [John] Bell and others were present.

Assurances have been received from Georgia, that when it could be stated that Southern representation in the Convention would be *effectual*, that a Southern delegation would be sent. This Statement must come from authentic sources. It is to be prepared and submitted at a meeting on Monday at 10 o'clk. Mr. Bell's remarks were decided and inspiring.

There were several gentlemen present—who have lately travelled through the South, & who concurred in the opinion that there was the right feeling; it only needed development. Mr. Bell regretted that a[n] organ had not been established at the Southwest a year since. In a confidential interview he stated to Dr. Smith[1]—that he was preparing himself for a speech of the right kind. *This* he does not wish known till the hour comes. As to his *sentiments* he has no concealment about them, having told Mr. Fillmore that his preference was for yourself. Very respectfully—and truly yours,   G. J. Abbot.

ALS. John R. Morison, Peterborough, New Hampshire.
   1. Possibly Dr. Peter Smith, a phy- sician active in Webster's campaign for the Whig nomination.

TO MILLARD FILLMORE

Boston. May 19. 1852

My dear Sir,

Yesterday being a fair day, for a wonder I came up from Marshfield in the cars, but am sorry to say, that I suffered more from the jarring of the cars, than I had anticipated. My shoulders and arms were full of pain, and to be sure of right treatment, I immediately sent for Dr. [Jonathan Mason] Warren & Dr. [John] Jeffries,[1] who held a consultation. They thought that in my anxiety to get well enough to travel soon, I had made too many applications, of ice-water, liniments, poultices &c

&c, and they recommend an abstinence from everything, of that kind, and to be content with the simple use of the sling, and as much rest in the limbs, as I could obtain. As I suggested in a former letter,[2] might be the case, the shock seems to have summoned into action, all the rhuematic tendencies of the system, and appearances of bruises, and much discoloration are visible in parts where there was no actual local hurt. I can walk with ease and strength, but I cannot put on, or take off my hat, nor without difficulty raise a cup of tea to my mouth. I can sign my name, though not without effort. My anxiety to get to Washington is extreme, and if there were a good vessel going to Baltimore, and a fair prospect of settled weather, I should be inclined to embark, so much do I dread the shaking of the cars. The Doctors think, however, that they can put me in condition for travelling in the ordinary way, by Monday the 24th, when I propose to leave Boston, if, in the mean time, things go on prosperously.

Mr [William] Hunter[3] sends me the despatches, and I am glad to see that things go on without much difficulty. Our great trouble is Mexico. The Government of that country seems to act, as if it intended to provoke the United States, to take another slice of its territory, and pay for it, for the benefit of persons, concerned in the Government. Yours truly

Danl Webster

LS. NBuHi. Published in *PC*, 2: 531–532.

1. Warren (d. 1867) was a Boston surgeon and member of the Harvard Medical School faculty. Jeffries (1796–1876; Harvard 1815) was a prominent Boston physician. Both attended Webster during his last months.

2. DW to Fillmore, May 12, 1852, mDW 36794.

3. Hunter (1805–1886) had been clerk in the State Department since 1829. DW named him chief clerk in 1852, a position Hunter held for the rest of his life.

FROM EDWARD EVERETT

Boston 11 June 1852.

Dear Sir,

I had a conversation with N[athan] Hale yesterday, & found what may be inferred from the columns of the [Boston] Advertiser of late, that he is quite sanguine of a favorable result at Baltimore next Wednesday. A friend lately from the South, not a politician but a man of shrewdness, expresses himself to the same effect. I am sorry that I shall not be able to go on. Knowing how likely it was that such would be the case, I expressed a wish to be excused, when first informed of my appointment as a delegate;—but friends here thought it would be as well to let my name stand, till a substitute could be appointed, which was not till the other delegates met. I cannot bear confinement in a room for any length of time;—nor safely venture into any meeting where a protracted session may be expected & no means of retreat. A very reliable person will take my place, probably Mr. [Albert] Fearing.

Enthusiastic meetings have been held in Boston the last two evenings,[1] and a most numerous delegation of your friends will proceed to Baltimore.

General [Franklin] Pierce's nomination[2] took every body by surprize, himself apparently as much as any one. This is the common version of the affair;—but there are some appearances that it was a matter arranged before hand. This I can scarce believe. It seems impossible that the purpose of nominating Genl. P.—if thus pre-arranged,—could have been concealed for 30 ballotings & then have broken out with such vigor.

With the best wishes that all may go right next Wednesday, I remain as ever sincerely yours,   Edward Everett.

P.S.—I have just received a note from Mr. [Rufus] Choate. He says that he will be at Newyork tomorrow to meet the friends who may be there, on the way to Baltimore.

ALS. MHi.

1. Webster Whigs had met at Cochituate Hall. *Boston Daily Advertiser*, June 9, 10, and 11, 1852. On June 11, a Webster meeting in Cambridge named some 100 "delegates" to attend the Whig National Convention to lobby for DW's nomination. *Advertiser*, June 14, 1852.

2. On June 5 the Democrats meeting in Baltimore had nominated New Hampshire's Franklin Pierce for President on the forty-ninth ballot.

FROM CHARLES SLAUGHTER MOREHEAD

Frankfort June 11th 1852

My dear Sir,

Amid the thousands of letters which you must be receiving from admiring and devoted friends, I have felt reluctant to obtrude upon your time, and write now only to express my deep regret of my inability to attend the approaching Whig national Convention. Our Supreme court is now in session and I am necessarily detained in attendence on it. Our delegates are virtually instructed to vote for Mr Fillmore, and I have no hesitation in saying that you are the second choice of the state. We can carry the state for either of you. While I have no objection to Mr Fillmore, my preference is known to be decidedly and unequivocally for you, and when I have expressed it as I freely do, I am met constantly with the question can we elect him? I believe we can, if we can elect any one, and I have done all that was in my power to remove an impression of this kind.

I believe most sincerely that nothing could give more moral force and power to our party than to select for its candidate for the highest office the best qualified, most experienced, the ablest and purest man in our ranks. Defeat under such a leader would be better ultimately than success with one whose chief recommendation was his availability. Our opponents have brought to a low standard, their estimate of qualification and merit. I trust that we will present a sterling contrast by elevating our standard to the height of one who is universally acknowledged to be the first man of the nation.

I tender to you my unfeigned good wishes for your nomination, and in such an event my poor services shall be exerted without stint in your behalf. I remain My Dear Sir, very truly your friend   C S Morehead

ALS. KyU.

TO DANIEL FLETCHER WEBSTER

Friday 1 o clock
[June 11, 1852]

Dear Fletcher

I have yrs of yesterday, containing an acct. of the meet[in]g &c.[1] I had intended, before its receipt, to say something on the political contents of your last.

It seems to me, with great deference, that things are not in a good way. Nobody does any thing, on our side.

Notwithstanding all the "good feeling," results appear always adverse. You say, today, that the Atlas Clique have managed to elect their own Delegates, as you fear; & that Mr [Peter] Harvey condemns the whole set.[2] But what does Mr Harvey propose to do?

Really, I am tired of hearing any thing upon this subject, unless it is a proposition *to do something.* If my friends wish to meet to consult *for action,* I will meet with them, at any time, if not confined to my home. But I have had eno[ugh] of cheering prospects, & sicken[in]g results. When is "the meeting"[3] to be called—? & where held?

I wish you, & Mr Harvey, would go & pass an hour with Mr [Edward] Everett—& come to some conclusion, ab[ou]t something. Yrs   D.W.

ALS. NhHi. Both *W & S,* 12: 643 and Van Tyne, p. 524 date the letter [May 1852].

1. The meeting of Webster Whigs at Boston's Cochituate Hall, June 9–11.

2. A week earlier the Maine Whigs had selected delegates to the national convention and disappointed the Webster forces by naming a set of delegates favorable to Winfield Scott. See *Boston Daily Atlas,* June 5 and 12, 1852, and *Boston Daily Ad-*

vertiser, June 9, 1852.
   3. Presumably a meeting of Web-

ster partisans to plot strategy for
the Baltimore convention.

FROM JOHN TAYLOR

Elms Farm—N. Hamp
Franklin June 14th, 1852

Dear Sir

As I have nearly compleated my springs work, I will now Inform you—how much we have done, and the number of acers, which I have under Cultivation. Manure drawd out, 400 loads.

First—fifteen acers of corn.

2d, seven acers of potatoes.

3d, sixteen acers of oats.

4th, five acers of winter wheat

5th, five acers of winter rye.

6th, three quarters of an acre of peas.

7th, one acre of white beans.

This week I shal sow my turnips and Bulk wheet.

All our crops have come up Extrodanary well. I have 24 acers which I shal hoe twice. I have taken, great care to have all this work done, in the best order.

Mr Webster

Rest assured, that I shal do every thing on my Part—towards secureing good Crops, I pray that we may Have our labours crownd with Good sucsess.

It is quite dry, and verry Cold, cold knights—and mornings. Feed is short in our paisters. The Great Field looks well, the Grass is one fut high, and looks Butiful, if we have rain Sone, I think we may cut a fair crop of hay.

To day we are plowing for Buck Wheat, I find the ground Verry dry, this morning we had conciderable frost but has Not hurt the corn much —I fear we shal have a cold Season.

Saint Stephen—is in fine helth—he fattens and groes large every Day—and let me say to You Sir—and say the truth, all that he has to eat, from Day to day, is a small Cock of dry hay, in the morning, & the same in the Eavning. No dinner except his manger. And that is maid of solid Whiteoak.

The lady cow—does well, and is Verry handsome—she gives seven quarts of milk per day.

The younger Heifer, groes finely &, has taken the Bool. I am, Sir, Your most Obedient Servant. John Taylor

ALS. NhHi.

FROM [?]

New York June 17/52

My dear Sir,

I once wrote you about the [William Henry] Seward clique in this city, aiming to injure you during the pending of the compromise bill. If you should be fortunate enough to get the nomination <of> at Baltimore, (which I earnestly pray you may) I would as a friend suggest the propriety of your sending a copy of your speeches,[1] to the Mayor [Ambrose Kingsland] of this city, requesting him to present it to the Mercantile Library Association &, a copy to the Apprentices Library—also send a copy to the Mercantile Library for young men, at Cincinnati Ohio. You will at once see the propriety of the suggestion, & numbering among them so many thousand of various classes, the benefit of such a donation will be felt in *time* to come. It is the prevailing opinion among leading & intelligent democrats that "Daniel Webster is the only man that [can] beat Mr. [Franklin] Pierce, for he will poll a heavy democratic vote, being in the broadest acceptation an american, & the man of the times." Yrs Truly— ★

AL. NhHi.
  1. DW's *Works*, recently issued in six volumes.

Webster's last serious hope for the Presidency died by degrees in Baltimore from June 16 to 21. At the outset of the Whig convention, his chances seemed reasonably good—perhaps on a par with both Scott and Fillmore—despite the relatively few pledged Webster delegates. It was clear, for example, that together the Webster and Fillmore forces constituted a majority. Further, Fillmore had already written a letter of withdrawal to be carried by his convention manager, George Babcock of New York, and used as the situation required.

The nomination passed Webster by nonetheless. Despite the fervent efforts of Rufus Choate and other Websterites in Baltimore, no substantial bloc of southern delegates would abandon the President. By Saturday, June 19, after six fruitless ballots had been taken the previous evening, former congressman John Barney journeyed to Washington and bluntly told Webster his chances were nil. It was time, he said, to direct a switch to the President. Meanwhile, in Baltimore, Fillmore men were offering a deal in which the bulk of the President's delegates would vote for Webster if the latter could reach the forty-delegate mark on Monday—some eight more votes than Webster had been able to muster through the Saturday voting. If the necessary votes could not be found, the proposal ran, Webster men should then shift to the President.

The Webster-Fillmore alliance was never consummated. Convinced that any movement to Fillmore would be politically disastrous back in Massachusetts, Webster's leading men declined the offer—even when confronted with Webster's own letter on Monday morning (see below, DW to Fillmore, [June 21], releasing his delegates and presumably encouraging their shift to the President.

Fillmore himself attempted to withdraw the same morning (see below, Fillmore to DW, June 21), but his own belated move to help Webster was also in vain. Ultimately, enough Webster delegates shifted to Scott on June 21 to ensure the general's nomination on the fifty-third ballot.

TO HON. [NAME TORN OFF]

Sunday Eve'.

[June 20, 1852]

Private & Confidential
My Dear Sir

I have recd. yr note, & considered its contents. I hardly know whether I can say, that this question of the nomination ought now to be terminated, in some way. I confess, I did not suppose that my old personal friends, Messrs [John Alsop] King, [William Lewis] Dayton, & [Simeon] Draper would persist in a course, which is calculated to drive my friends in the Convention, to put an end to the Controversy, by voting for a candidate whom these Northern Gentlemen are opposed to, with some warmth. But they seem inclined to hold on, & to hold out. I have nothing to say, by way of complaint, or reproach, though I confess I feel some degree of unexpected regret. They must judge for themselves; but the honor of the Whig party requires an immediate decision of the controversy. Yrs truly   D Webster

ALS. NhD.

TO MILLARD FILLMORE

[June 21, 1852]

Private
My Dear Sir

I have sent a communication to Baltimore, this morn[in]g to have an end put to the pending controversy. I think it most probable you will be nominated before 1 o clock. But this is opinion merely. Yrs   D.W.

ALS. NBuHi. *W & S*, 16: 647, dates the letter June 1852; Van Tyne, p. 531, dates it June 17, 1852.

FROM MILLARD FILLMORE

Washington June 21. [1852]

My Dear Sir,

I have your note[1] saying that you had sent a communication this morning to Baltimore to have an end put to the pending controversy.

I had intimated to my friends, who left last evening and this morning, a strong desire to have my name withdrawn, which I presume will be done unless the knowledge of your communication shall prevent it. I therefore wish to know whether your friends will make known your communication to mine before the ballotting commences this morning? If not I apprehend it <will> may be too late to affect any thing. I am truly and sincerely yours   Millard Fillmore

ALS. NBuHi.
1. See above, DW to Fillmore, [June 21, 1852]. Fillmore received

Webster's note at 9:30 A.M. and responded immediately.

TO RICHARD MILFORD BLATCHFORD

Washington June 22. 1852

My Dear Mr Blatchford,

The result of the Baltimore convention is certainly bad enough. It shows a great deal of folly, and a great deal of infidelity.

Our friends, one and all, did their best; I hear, particularly of your zealous and persevering efforts with the delegations of the Northwest. Indeed I am under infinite obligations to you all.

For myself I possess my soul in patience, and shall see you soon to thank you personally. Yours always Faithfully   Danl. Webster

P.S. In the meantime say to Mr [Moses Hicks] Grinnell, Mr [Hiram] Ketchum, and Mr [John Eliot] Thayer, and all other friends, whom you may see, that I can never be sufficiently grateful for their unparalleled efforts. I have written to Gen [James Watson] Webb.[1] Yours always truly   D.W.

Copy. MHi. Published in W & S, 16: 657.

1. See below, DW to Webb, June 22, 1852.

TO JAMES WATSON WEBB

Washington June 22. 1852

Be assured, My Dear General Webb that the regret which I feel for the result at Baltimore is infinitely less on my own account than on account of those faithful and vigorous friends who have made such efforts in my behalf. I know you are all disappointed and mortified, and that it is, which causes me great distress. Many hopes were blasted, many warm affections wounded, and not a few breasts filled with indignation, with the folly and treachery of pretended friends.

I am going to the North, My Dear Sir, and, before I return shall visit you and Mr. [Moses Hicks] Grinnell, as well as other friends, to express my heartfelt gratitude for your kindness, as well as my admiration of the ability and perseverance with which the contest was conducted. In the meantime, I am with much regard, Your obedient and humble servant, Danl Webster

LS. DLC.

FROM EDWARD EVERETT

Boston 22 June 1852

Dear Sir,

I hope you will not allow yourself to be greatly disturbed by the disappointment of our hopes at Baltimore. However desirable success may have been for the Country at large or your friends, you are the individual who has least reason to regret it. Assuming that election would have followed nomination, what could the Presidency add to your happiness or fame? Even before the office had been let down by second rate and wholly incompetent persons, the example of Mr [James] Madison shows that even repeated election to the office is of very little moment to a great constitutional statesman.

He had a powerful majority in Congress;—this will be the reverse with any whig who may be chosen for the next President; and few things I should think would be more annoying than to carry on the government in face of a powerful, and what would be not less certain, a spiteful opposition at the Capitol.

It would have given me the utmost pleasure to have taken part in the proceedings of the Convention, as your friend;—but I foresaw—what the event abundantly exhibited,—a state of things entirely beyond my present state of health.

It is a source of some satisfaction to your friends here,—amidst so much to grieve and disgust them,—that so many of the delegates who voted for you did so to the last.

Upon the whole, I hope you will bear in mind that if there is no one in the Country (as your friends think) who could have filled the office so much to the public interest and honor, there is, and for that reason, no one who is so little dependent upon office, even the highest,—for influence or reputation.

Praying my kindest remembrance to Mrs W. I remain, my dear Sir, as ever Sincerely & affectionately yours,   Edward Everett

ALS. MHi. Published in part in Samuel Frothingham, *Edward Everett: Orator and Statesman* (Boston, 1925), p. 319.

The failure of his final bid for the Whig presidential nomination profoundly dispirited Webster. It also revived his periodically expressed inclination to depart Washington. His feeble showing in the balloting at Baltimore, combined with the prospect of a hot summer's difficult labor in the capital, inspired Webster to consider and then propose a change of venue—specifically, a plan by which he would replace Abbott Lawrence in the London mission.

Webster nourished the idea for approximately a month. Ultimately, however, a variety of forces kept him on as secretary of state. Caroline Webster strongly opposed a move to London. President Fillmore emphasized the delicacy and importance of negotiations still pending with Great Britain, Nicaragua, Mexico, and Peru, while offering assurances that much of this labor could be conducted away from Washington. Finally, Webster himself began to recognize some of the drawbacks of a change of posts: the complications of moving across the Atlantic; the awkwardness of having to take, rather than give, orders; and the prospect of an early recall should the Democrats capture the White House in the November elections. By late July, the urge to change his role had passed, and Webster formally declined Fillmore's offer (DW to Fillmore, July 25, 1852, mDW 37352).

TO DANIEL FLETCHER WEBSTER

July 4. 52

Secret

My Dear Son

I confess I grow inclined to cross the seas. I meet, here, so many causes of vexation, & humiliation, growing out of the events connected with the convention, that I am pretty much decided & determined, to leave the Department early in August, & either go abroad, or go into obscurity. You may mention this to Mr [James William] Paige, but to no other soul. We leave on Tuesday.[1] Yrs affectionately   Danl Webster

ALS. NhHi. Published in *Diplomatic Papers*, 2.

1. Webster departed Washington on July 6 en route to Salisbury and Franklin, New Hampshire, via Philadelphia, New York, and Boston.

Although the national Whig party would not have Webster, Massachu-
setts expressed a very different sentiment. In the aftermath of the Balti-
more convention, Webster was treated to a tumultuous, heartfelt display
of affection and loyalty in his home state. Preferring to travel quietly
back for a July sojourn at his Elms farm in Franklin, Webster was per-
suaded by friends to attend a reception in his honor scheduled for July 9
in Boston. What Webster saw and heard on his arrival touched him
deeply. The entire city, it semed, had turned out to welcome its leading
son. Webster busts and portraits hung everywhere in the central city.
Shops, closed for business, were festooned with "the garb of a national
holiday" (Curtis, 2: 629). A military escort accompanied the Webster
entourage into town, and the secretary of state, riding in a resplendent
carriage drawn by six gray horses, was cheered at every turn. At Boston
Common, following a tribute delivered by J. Thomas Stevenson, Webster
rose to the occasion with a gracious and poignant speech recounting
Massachusetts's signal contributions to the Constitution and the Union.
The reception marked his final public appearance in Boston.

TO FRANKLIN HAVEN

Astor House, July 7, 1852

My Dear Sir,

I have just telegraphed to you, that we have arrived in safety.

My present intention is to leave for Boston, in the train of to-morrow afternoon, and after a night's rest there, to go to Roxbury[1] the next morning. It is not necessary that the manner of my getting to Roxbury should be known. A night's rest will be useful. If an address is made to me, I must make some reply. As to going to Springfield on some future occasion, that is [not] to be thought of. I have no wish to meet public assemblies, called together for the mere purpose of paying me personal respect. I acquiesce, of course, in the events which have happened, and have no wish to attract public attention, merely as one who has held public station. I am satisfied. My friends have done what they could, and no man will ever hear me complain. I shall ever honor Massachusetts, and consent to meet you and your friends on Friday, mainly for the purpose of expressing my sense of her favor and kindness to me.

If any other plan suggests itself to you, I pray you to give me a telegraphic message early to-morrow. Yours, always truly,   Dan'l Webster.

Text from *PC*, 2: 534–535. Original not found.

1. On his way from New York to Boston, Webster spent a day in Roxbury, Massachusetts, at the home of his old friend Samuel H. Walley.

FROM EDWARD CURTIS

New York 12th July 1852

My dear Sir—

I had an interview with Mr J[ohn] C[leve] Green, the other day, and learned that there was *one hundred* dollars due from each, of several persons, who were subscribers to the Webster fund, and who had failed to complete the payment of their respective subscriptions. Some of them *failed*, in business, and, some others have rather backed out. But some, it is thought, will pay upon being specially waited upon, and Mr Green agreed with me, to send Mr [George] Griswolds son [John N. Alsop Griswold] to these delinquents, and try to get the small balance due.

I presume you will have no objection to send me an order on Mr. Green to receive, for you, any balance of funds that may have been intended for you.[1]

Another topic—A gentleman of considerable wealth and influence, in this City, asked me, privately, to ascertain "what sum of money would put Mr. Webster *out of debt?*" I replied that I did not know. He said he thought you owed some debts that might be properly settled & paid off, by some confidential friend of yours for less than the face of them,— and he would like to take a part in an effort to relieve you, though he did not know what others would do. You will oblige me, by answering my request briefly in regard to Mr. Green by *return* mail.[2] I wish to leave this City, as soon as I get your reply. It is very hot; I am very feeble, & must get to some cooler place.

If you cannot answer, in respect to the amount required to discharge the *"Public Debt,"* that subject may be <thought of> considered by you, for a few days, and I will renew our correspondence on that point, and communicate the *result* to the gentleman who spoke to me on the subject. This I could do by letter, from Vermont, Saratoga, or wherever I may wander.

Your Boston Common Speech[3] has gratified all your friends in these parts, as reported by the Telegraph. Yours truly   Edward Curtis.

P.S. I send you this morning's Herald. You will see Mr. [Frederick Augustus] Tallmadges letter.[4]

The dignified position you took, in respect to the Whig nomination from your Bedroom window[5] as corrected by yourself, & published throughout the Country, is safe, & worthy of *yourself*.

If the Massachusetts Delegates make any open charge of deception or fraud against the Baltimore Convention, it would not then be unfit for *yourself* to lead us all to a proclamation of opposition to Scott. But, as I understand it, they make no such charge. If Scott is to be defeated, (and nothing but *that* will ever restore the flow of my water) it will be done without any act or word of your's. But, I ought not to obtrude my impressions upon you and so, I hold up. Yours truly   E. Curtis.

ALS. NhD. Athough dated July 12, the letter was actually completed and sealed two days later, a point noted in Curtis's diary entry of July 14, 1852, in Edward Curtis Diary, NhD.

1. By early October some $3,100 had been collected and transmitted to Webster from this fund.

2. No response from DW to this request has been found.

3. DW's July 9 address at the Boston reception in his honor.

4. For several days New York and Boston papers had been debating the veracity of reports originating with former New York congressman Frederick Augustus Tallmadge that Webster had assured him privately on July 8 that he would acquiesce in the Scott nomination. On July 14 the *New York Herald* printed a letter from Tallmadge reaffirming this account. DW made no public statement endorsing or repudiating Tallmadge's report of their conversation.

5. Responding to a squadron of well-wishers who serenaded him at home in Washington on the evening of Scott's nomination, Webster observed that the convention had "exercised its wisest and soundest discretion" and that he had no "personal feelings" about its choice to lead the Whig party. For a text of his remarks, see Curtis, 2: 622.

TO JAMES WILLIAM PAIGE

Franklin July 14th 1852
Wednesday Evg. 7 oclock

My dear Sir,

There is no stopping people's talk. Of course I cannot go to the British Provinces, until I resign my present situation. If I should do that early next month, I might go to New Brunswick or Halifax, to see how far a cool and moist atmosphere might relieve my catarrh. I cannot think of remaining in Washington through August and September, and as so long an absence from my post would no doubt be complained of, resignation seems to be the only alternative. And then you know I have talked of other things, but upon the whole, and after much reflection, although not without some hesitation, I am pretty much settled, in the idea of private life.

Whether it will be wise in me to go to Washington in the Fall, and live there as a private man for the Winter, or whether it will be better to provide some residence in Boston, remains to be considered. My lease of the house at Washington, will not be out until next Spring or Summer. I have a little, but not much business in the Court. Washington is not disagreeable to me as a place of residence, but still, other things being equal, I should prefer being nearer my Kith & Kin.

I am sorry his mother thinks Willie[1] cannot come and see me at this time. Fletcher & his son[2] have promised to come up on Friday, and if you can spare a day, it will give me pleasure to see you here. The matting has all come safe. Yours truly always,   Danl Webster

LS. Mrs. James McD. Garfield, South-   1894).
boro, Massachuetts.   2. Daniel Fletcher Webster, Jr.
    1. James William Paige, Jr. (1835–   (1840–1865).

Widespread dismay among Whigs over Winfield Scott's nomination for the Presidency virtually ensured the party's crushing defeat in the November elections. Disgusted with Scott but reluctant to vote Democratic, many conservative Whigs hoped Webster would accept a separate nomination under "Union" or "American" party auspices. But was the secretary of state agreeable to such a plan?

Webster never answered this question. Despite pleas from supporters that he denounce the Baltimore nomination, and inquiries about his willingness to head a third-party ticket, Webster maintained silence throughout the summer of 1852. Privately, he spoke in bitter tones of his failure at Baltimore, disparaged the Whig nominee, and praised the Democratic presidential candidate, Franklin Pierce of New Hampshire. But publicly he said nothing beyond dissociating himself from all draft movements.

FROM [?]

N. Y July 14/52

My dear Sir—

The Scott men are resorting to all kind of expedients to elect Genl. [Winfield] Scott, by attempting to impress upon the country that you had committed yourself to the support of their ticket. A Mr. Talmadge [Frederick Augustus Tallmadge] of this city is out in a letter to show you signified your intention to sustain the Whig party & argues that you go for *Scott*.[1] It is too contemptible to treat seriously. I hope you will accept a nomination if tendered to you. No matter what your opponents may say or do. Had Scott not recd. the nomination it was agreed to break up the convention. This is one of the reasons why I feel anxious to have you accept in common with thousands of others, to prevent if possible the election of Scott under any contingency. A moments reflection will satisfy you that the suggestion is not ill advised nor impolitic. You have every thing to gain & nothing to loose. Had you not been treacherously dealt with you could not do it, but, what stronger reasons can be assigned to warrant you in meeting the wishes of your friends & foiling the ambitious scheming of your opponents. Yrs sincerely   ★

AL. NhHi. Published in Van Tyne, pp. 534–535. Van Tyne tentatively attributed the letter to Charles W. March. The handwriting is not March's, but appears to be that of the sender of the June 17 letter printed above, p. 330.

1. See above, Edward Curtis to DW, July 12, 1852, n. 4.

FROM "NEWOB AMANUENSIS"

Louisville July 19th 1852

I observe by some remarks in the Public Journals that they are endeavouring to nominate you as a Candidate for the Presidency by the Native American Party. This Party, like [the] Free Soil & Abolition Party, have never in their political character done any thing else, than weaken the Whig Party,—instead of convincing the People of the justness of their views & policy, it has created a great deal of useless enmity among both the foreign & native population, without gaining a political influence strong enough to elect more than one or two important Candidates comparatively.

Your Ostracism by the Whig Convention was the effect of your support of the Fugitive Slave Bill, and is perhaps, the result of one of the most useful and independent acts of your life—and the People of the United States, will consider it so, as soon as they can understand its object & effect. I should dislike to hear of your acceptance as Native American Candidate for the Presidency for two reasons, one is we can never have a Whig Party in the United States, if we sustain its schisms, and if we do not sustain that part of the policy of the Democracy that never opposes the nomination of its Conventions—coute qué coute[1]—however we may dislike individuals and individual members—we can never create & perpetuate Whig policy—if we have no Whig party—if we do not make efforts to create & sustain a party, that we can sustain its policy instead of sustaining schisms that destroy its influence.

Your individuality by your support of the Fugitive Slave Bill, became as distinctive among the Abolitionists of the United States, as Mr [Henry] Clays did among the Democrats & Free Traders, and although yours may not exist injuriously politically as his did during his life,—although yours may not exist long enough to prevent you being considered in 1856 if you live, yet to yourself and Mr Clay this individuality was the most honorable to yourselves—of your independent sentiments, as Freemen, that you either ever experienced. We (Rational or Practical Abolitionists) should regret to see you accept a nomination by any other Party than the Legitimate Whig Party—Aut Caesar, Aut Nullus—is your motto. We never wish you to become a political automaton for an infinitesimal portion of the Whig & Democratic Party to use to your disappointment & political destruction. Clays & Websters are too few in the United States. Yours Very Respectfully   Newob Amanuensis

ALS. DLC.
    1. *coûte qué coûte*, i.e. "cost what it may."

FROM MILLARD FILLMORE

Washington City,
July, 24th 1852

My Dear Sir,

I wrote you hastily on the 20th and yesterday received yours of the 21st,[1] dated at Boston, from which I infer that you had not received mine at the time of writing. I promised in that communication to write you further on the subject of the proposed reciprocity of trade between us and the British Provinces,[2] and with that view I consulted the members of the Cabinet at our weekly meeting on Wednesday, all of whom seemed to be averse to making it the subject of treaty stipulation. I have reflected much on the subject since, and with a view of obtaining some necessary information have requested the Secretary of the Treasury to report to me the amount and value of the Articles proposed to be interchanged free of duty, which had been exported or imported into Canada within the last three years. I have not yet received his report; but this subject involves questions of such delicate and vital <character> importance that I think if the negotiation is to be entered upon at all, it will be indispensible that it be done here, where the whole matter can be weighed in all its bearings. The following questions well deserve consideration.

First The express power having been given by the Constitution to Congress, to regulate commerce with foreign nations, and to lay and collect duties, has this deprived the treaty-making power of authority so to regulate commerce, as to declare that no duty shall be collected on a particular article imported into this country from abroad?

Secondly Assuming that the treaty making power may stipulate to admit certain articles free of duty, is it expedient to exercise that power at this time and in this case?

Thirdly What effect would such a treaty stipulation have upon that clause in our commercial treaties which declares, that no higher duty shall be imposed upon any goods imported from the country with whom the treaty was made, than is charged upon goods of the same kind imported from any other country? For instance, would such a stipulation as this which proposed to admit hemp and wool free of duty from Canada justify Russia or England in claiming the same privileges for their hemp and wool?

Fourthly. What will be the effect upon the wool growing and hemp raising portions of the United States, if we permit the hemp and wool from Canada to come in free?

Fifthly and lastly. What is to be the effect of such a measure upon the general principle of protection, which it has been our policy to maintain, so far as necessary to encourage the industry of the country?

It seems to me that these questions require such consideration before we enter upon a negotiation of this kind as can only be had by a mutual and free interchange of sentiment at the council board, and I am rather averse to negotiating upon this subject under a state of things that looks a little like coercion on the part of Great Britain, in reference to our fisheries.[3] I had intended to have written you more fully but have been too busy. These questions however will suggest to you the difficulties that surround this case. You will recollect that our opinion has been that the question of reciprocal trade should be settled by legislation and not by treaty. I am your obt servt   Millard Fillmore

LS. NhHi. Severance, *Fillmore Papers*, 1: 376–377.

1. Millard Fillmore to DW, July 20, 1852, mDW 37311; DW to Fillmore, July 21, 1852, mDW 37319.

2. The issue of reciprocity in trade between the United States and the Canadian provinces had been pressed by the British in the late 1840s without result, partly because protectionists in Congress resisted such an agreement, and partly because the issue was overshadowed by the slavery debate. As secretary of state,

Webster was amenable to a trade agreement with the Canadians, but nothing was settled in his lifetime. Ultimately, a reciprocity treaty was fashioned and ratified by the Senate in 1854. See Lester Burrell Shippee, *Canadian-American Relations, 1849–1874* (New Haven, 1939), chaps. 2–4; *Diplomatic Papers*, 2.

3. Canada had threatened to exclude American fishermen from its territorial waters. See *Diplomatic Papers*, 2.

FROM JOHN L. STEPHENS

LaGrange Ga.

August. 3 1852

Sir, the people of Ga. are dissatisfied with the nominations made by the two National parties for President. And a large portion of them (I can say a majority of them) are anxious to present your name to the American people for that office, as their first choice. And being determined not to support either of the present Candidates we are desirous to know before our opposition Convention meets on the 18th inst. whether you would accept a nomination if tendered you by that Convention of the State.[1] We desire to know this before the meeting of that Convention because should you refuse to accept the nomination it will embarriss our movements by placing us under the necessity of calling another Convention. We are determined not to support [Winfield] Scott or [Franklin] Pierce & hope you will give us an assurance that we can make use of your name. Your Humble Servant John L. Stephens

ALS. DLC. Stephens (c. 1815–1856), half brother of Georgia congressman Alexander H. Stephens, was an attorney and planter in LaGrange, Georgia. His interest in a Webster nomination was doubtless tied to his brother's political ambitions.

1. The so-called Tertium Quid bloc, led by Congressman Stephens, met in Macon on August 17–18 and nominated a ticket of Webster and Georgia senator Charles J. Jenkins. Following DW's death on October 24, voters in Georgia were told that Webster-Jenkins ballots would be transferred to Millard Fillmore and John J. Crittenden.

FROM JAMES WATSON WEBB

Pokahoe Augt. 10. 1852

My Dear Sir,

It has occurred to me that a strong and decided leader in the [New York] Courier & Enquirer, expressive of the expectations of this commercial metropolis in regard to the Fisheries,[1] and what should be the ultimatum of our Country in the premises, would materially aid you in your pending negotiations. If you think so, and are willing to prepare such an article, or an outline of it, I need not say how happy I shall be to publish it, & of course, not suffer its paternity to be known.[2]

I hope that you will not be detained long in Washington; and that when next you visit New York, you will not fail to make me the long promised visit. [Winfield] Scott stock is below par; & I do not think any support of him by your friends now, will give him a chance of success. Yours Ever J. Watson Webb

New York Augt. 11/52

I open my letter in consequence of the rumours from W[ashington] that you are about to retire. If so, I have *faith* that it is "all right." But what a[n] Ass F[illmore] is, to give you the right to withdraw just now!

But be this as it may, now is the time to write the article I ask, & to *compel* the Administration to adopt your views in regard to the Fisheries. Of course, it would not be policy to say *now* whence the Article comes.

ALS. DLC.

1. See above, Millard Fillmore to DW, July 24, 1852, n. 3.

2. The editors have found no answer to Webb's request. Three weeks earlier, however, DW had arranged for the publication of a document, under his signature, discussing the recent seizures of American ships in Canadian waters. The article (published in the *Boston Courier*, July 19, 1852) rejected Britain's recently asserted strict construction of the Convention of 1818, under which Ameri-

can fishermen had been operating for more than thirty years without obstruction. For the text, see *Diplomatic Papers*, 2. See also *New York Times*, July 20, 1852, and DW to Millard Fillmore, July 17, 1852, mDW 37272.

TO EDWARD EVERETT

Washington Aug. 14. '52

Private

My Dear Sir

The President offered me the mission to England, before I went north. For a time, I was inclined to think favor[ably on] the idea, thinking a voyage might benefit <of> my health, & possibly enable me to avoid my annual catarrh. But on reflection, I adopted a different view. My general reasons were, that I thought it might look like a *job*, resembling Mr [George] Cannings Embassy to Portugal.[1] I have been some years in a position to give instructions on Diplomatic matters, not to receive them. I have been also a Candidate for the Presidency, & the Party has nominated another person. From this, I did not feel like taking employment, or seeking shelter in any other employment.

These reasons are personal to myself; but there are others which had their influence, &, as I thought, should have weight with any distinguished Whig. The Administration is near its close, & I have no belief in its being followed by Whig successors. Whoever goes to England will be immediately recalled. The Party will demand this, whatever may be the personal inclinations of the incoming President. Your name was spoken of by the President, but it seemed to be taken for granted that you would not accept the place. Perhaps I was wrong in so doing, but I did express that opinion to the President myself. On my return, I found the mission had been offered to Mr [Joseph Reed] Ingersol[l], that he had agreed to accept it, & was nominated to the Senate.[2] Yrs truly   Danl Webster

ALS. MHi.

1. Political opponents greeted George Canning's nomination as English minister to Lisbon in 1814 by attacking the government for creating a makework "job" in a time of fiscal stringency. The issue was pressed throughout Canning's brief and relatively uneventful tenure in the Portuguese capital. Commenting on this episode in his July 25 letter to President Fillmore (mDW 37352) declining the London mission, DW observed that Canning's "character suffered from [the criticism] with the better part of the English people."

2. Abbott Lawrence submitted his resignation on May 14, effective October 1, or at the discretion of the President. Ingersoll was nominated for the embassy post on August 10 and confirmed on August 21. *Journal of the Executive Proceedings of the Senate* (Washington, 1887), 8: 438, 442.

Washington Aug. 15, 1852

My dear Sir,

I am very much obliged to you for your friendly letter of the 3d ult,[1] which I have not had time before to acknowledge. I know your talents and character; I know the truly patriotic sentiments of your breast; I value most highly your good opinion and regard; and the good opinion and regard of other men like you. As to the rest, I have little to say. The [h]oi *polloi* of the Whig party, especially in the north and east, were, in March 1850, fast sinking into the slough of freesoilism and abolitionism. I did what I could to rescue the country from the consequences of their abominable politics. I disdain to seek the favor of such persons, and have no sympathy with their opinions. You are of the South, my dear Sir, and I of the North; but if the degrees of latitude, which divide us, were ten times as many as they are, your thoughts, and my thoughts, your hopes and my hopes for the good of the country would still rush together in a warm, glowing sentiment and a fervent prayer for the preservation of the Union. God help the right.

In regard to your friend, Mr. Charles Warley[2] let me say that I shall be most happy to be useful to him. Inform me where he now is, and I will send him letters, which shall make him known in England and France.

I pray you to remember me most kindly to all the members of your Family, and believe me, with entire regard, Your obedient and humble servant

Copy. NhHi. Published in *W & S*, 16: 662–663.

1. Petigru to DW, July 3, 1852, mDW 37178.

2. Warley has not been further identified. Petigru had indicated that Warley was planning a Euro- pean journey and would appreciate being "entrusted with a dispatch." Given DW's response, it is conceivable that he misunderstood the request, believing Warley to be seeking letters of introduction.

Kalorama August 17. 1852
Wind N.E. cold rain storm

Dear Sir

Some seventeen years ago, I think it was in the year 1835, while I was a resident of Philadelphia I called several of my friends together—Natives of New England & we agreed to urge upon all our acquaintance the nomination for the coming presidential election a candidate to be

denominated the Constitutional-Union candidate—& yourself was selected as the man most suitable for the station. Our influence was not
much & our candidate was passed over for one who was thought to be
by others more available.

It appears to me that a great many persons in the United States have
had a desire for the last 15 years to form a party to be called the Constitutional Union party & place yourself at the head of it. The present
year has seemed to me more favorable for the formation of such a
party and there seems to be a necessity for it now since the recent abolition convention at Pittsburg[1] because if those opinions prevail this
Union *must* be dissolved.

To preserve the Union I should think all the friends of the Union
ought to unite under one leader.

The Whig party & the democratic party contain Unionists—& secessionists and abolitionists—persons diametrically opposite in political
opinions—while the free soil party is united in opinion & feeling &
action. Now if the Union Whigs & Union Democrats would unite under
one head they might present a formidable front to their opponents.

The Whig party was formed some twenty years ago by the friends of
Henry Clay to carry out his views—one of which was to oppose the election of military chieftains to the office of President of the United States
but the party has been made use of to do what it was organized to
prevent.

After the success of one military chieftain sufficient number of [An-
drew] Jackson men joined the Whig party to defeat Henry Clay & elect
General [William Henry] Harrison—& the same thing was repeated in
the election of Genl. [Zachary] Taylor and now under the name of the
Whig party men are rallying to elect the General in Chief of the Army,
one who is at present exercising the highest military command, to be
president of the U. S.

History is replete with examples in all ages of the world where the
liberties of the people have been taken away by military chieftains who
have been placed at the head of civil affairs by the people themselves.

The present military commanders may do us no harm, but the
example of electing them is left as a precedent for future aspirations and
to produce future presidents, future wars must be fomented & to carry
these on successfully a strong government will be called for & then the
liberties of the people will be gradually usurped.

Therefore all good men & particularly all good whigs should vote
against any military chieftain for Chief Magistrate.

Another objection to the Whig candidate is that he is a native of a
state that has already furnished more than her share of presidents.

Our government has now existed since the adoption of the federal constitution 64 years and at the end of the next presidential term will be
68 years of which Virginia has furnished—

Washington—   8 years
Jefferson   8   ”
Madison—   8   ”
Monroe   8   ”
Harrison & Tyler   4   ”
Taylor—   4   ”   40 years

Carolina has furnished
Jackson   8—
Polk   4
& now Virginia has a candidate for 4   ”
Southern presidents—<48> 56 years
While the North has given
    the Adams   8—
    Van Buren   4   12   ”
                     ————   ———————
                                      68   ”

Death deprived us of the services of General Taylor by which event we
have a northern president for 2 years but this does not alter the election
for a Virginian was placed above a New Yorker and it required the interposition of Providence to give us the present Northern President.

A part of the Whig policy as introduced by Mr Clay was what he denominated "the American <policy> System"—this system under Mr
Clay embraced but *one idea* which was a tariff for protection of American manufactures. Now the Constitutional Union party under your lead
would embrace a more enlarged American System. The true American
System embraces the whole business of the American Union—the cotton
fields of Carolina as well as the cotton mills of Manchester N. H.

The fishing banks of the North and the Guano banks of the Southern
coast the gold mines of California & the Copper mines of lake Superior.

The rights of property & the rights of labor are all to be protected by
this enlarged American System.

The free soil system proposes to free all the blacks from their present
system of labor. This freedom would deprive them of the right to the
soil which they now have secured to them by law in the States where
slavery exists.

The planters own the land; slaves being free would have no right to
the support from the land which the law now gives them unless a further encroachment should be made upon the rights of property by
siezing the lands of the planters & dividing them among the blacks. Fol-

lowing up this idea the factories must be siezed at the North and divided among the operatives.

The Constitutional Union party should be formed to protect all rights as they exist to prevent the breaking up the very foundations of society to promote the general welfare and to guard against all foreign aggression.

But all these subjects require to be touched with the delicate hand of a Master so that while we protect our own rights we inflict no wrong upon any foreign nation—for this purpose statesmen of the first order should be selected into whose hands the destinies of the nation are to be placed.

The present time seems favorable to the formation of such a party. There are in fact but two parties in the country—those who wish to preserve the Union as it is—constitute one party and those who wish to form a new Union or at any rate wish to destroy the present Constitution form the other party. The anti-Constitutionalists under the name of free soil have already named their candidate—it now remains for the union party to name their candidate. Then there will be four candidates in the field. Those who prefer a military leader or who still cling to the name of Whig as the old party did to the name of federalist will vote the Whig ticket. Those who stick to the name of democrat will vote the democratic ticket while all those who wish to destroy the existing state of things will vote the free soil ticket. All those who love the Constitution & the Union more than they love party names will vote for the Constitutional Union Candidate & this party should be the largest party for it is to be presumed that the great body of the people have the good of their country at heart.

If there be not an-other candidate put forth a great many citizens will not have a chance of voting, for they will not vote for either of the three candidates already named.

In most of the States a plurality elects. Therefore if there be 4 candidates & 2100 voters—the one may have—526—525—525—524 respectively have one vote over one fourth of the number given will elect. This gives a fair chance to the friends of each candidate to exert themselves for their favorite.

Under all the circumstances of the case I think you should permit your friends to place the following ticket before the public
"Union Constitutional Candidate"
for President
Daniel Webster of Massachusetts
for vice President
Alexander [H.] Stevens [Stephens] of Georgia

Several sheets of paper might be written in favor of this party but this can be done after the party is formed & the candidates named. Respectfully   C. Fletcher

ALS. DLC. A native Virginian, Fletcher was then serving as a clerk in the Pension Office in Washington.

1. On August 11 Free Soilers had met at Pittsburgh's Masonic Hall to nominate New Hampshire senator John P. Hale for the Presidency and to reaffim the party's opposition to the Fugitive Slave Law of 1850 and to any further admission of slave states into the Union.

Financial troubles marred Webster's final days. A dependable government salary combined with substantial earnings as a lawyer and the continuing largesse of friends and associates failed to clear his many debts. Webster's ledger with Caleb Cushing offers a particularly telling glimpse of a man who lived exceptionally well, whose earnings by the standards of the day were high, yet who was constitutionally incapable of meeting—or even facing—long-standing financial obligations.

Cushing had loaned Webster more than $5000 in the late 1830s and early 1840s and then spent a fruitless decade seeking repayment. All he got for his requests were numerous counterrequests for patience and further promises to pay sometime in the future. (See Claude M. Fuess, The Life of Caleb Cushing [New York, 1923], 1: 231–235; 2: 83–91.) In the letter below, he came as close as he ever would to demanding a settling of accounts. Webster may have been moved by the emotion evidenced in the letter, but he responded as before—with promises. Following Webster's death in October, Cushing presented the estate's executors with an itemized statement of their accounts, but there is no evidence that he was ever repaid any substantial part of what he had loaned.

FROM CALEB CUSHING

Newburyport 11 Sept. 1852

Dear Sir:

On receiving your letter of the 30th ult.[1] I immediately wrote to you intreating [an] interview on your arrival in Boston; and I am grievously disappointed in having missed you there & in finding here today, on my return from Court at Springfield, no reply from you.

What I ask of you regarding our account is:

1. To have the debt liquidated <& funded>. I have never been able to conceive why for so many years you have refused to do this.

2. To have security for the principal. Why, out of the large estate you have, you should be unwilling to do this, I cannot conceive.

3. To receive the interest annually as upon any other regular investment.

I really need the principal. If you cannot conveniently pay that, my propositions are, it seems to me, most reasonable, such as a brother, or son, or the dearest friend, might address to you.

I must beg you, therefore to relieve me from the loathsome task of continual solicitation as to this thing, year after year, & month after month; & to dispose of it now at once; for I am half-desperate from the troubles in which I am involved by friends in whose favor I have not only stripped myself of the means of subsistence but became involved in controversies for which there is no possible end but death.

I have taken the office I now hold from sheer necessity; and I must of course attend to its duties.[2] The business of the Court has been so arranged for the Fall Circuit, that there is the minimum number of a bare quorum for each County; and I have no longer any control of my time for nine months to come, except a probable week or two in December or January.

It is not materially possible for me to go to Marshfield. I must proceed directly to Lenox on Monday to the business there next week[, it] is a capital trial. I cannot make any engagement away from there; otherwise I might propose an interview in Boston for Sunday the 19th.

I see but one way to arrange this business, and to avoid leaving it to further indefinite procrastination. It is to employ an intermediate agent to adjust the amount. Will you send a person of your own selection to Lenox? Or shall I select & send one to Marshfield?

Hoping to hear from you at Lenox, I am yours truly   CC.

ALS draft. DLC. Published in part in Fuess, *Webster*, 2: 90–91.

1. Not found.

2. Cushing had been appointed an associate justice on the Massachusetts Supreme Court in May 1852.

TO MILLARD FILLMORE

Marshfield, Sept. 12th 1852

My Dear Sir,

I suppose that by this time you must have returned from Berkeley [Springs], and hope you have had a pleasant and refreshing visit.

My march hither was rapid from Washington, using the boat where I could, and when in the cars travelling by night, to save my eyes from the glare of the sun. I was quite sick nearly all day in New York, and unable to sit up; but feeling better towards evening, took the Fall river boat, arrived at Boston the next morning, Sunday, at 7 o'clock, and came immediately home in a coach.

I have thus been here a week; and the state of my health is pretty much this; the catarrh is upon me, in its various forms, alternating, as usual, but as yet not so severe and heavy as on former occasions. My general health is not so much prostrated. If the weather be wet or damp, I must stay in the house, and have a little fire to prevent fits of sneezing and nose blowing; when the sun is very bright, I am obliged to avoid going out on account of my eyes, except, indeed, when the sea is calm, I go in the boat, and am protected by an awning. The bracing air of the ocean, I find very beneficial.

Mr. [George Jacob] Abbot from the Department joined us night before last, and Mr. [Richard Milford] Blatchford, who is fond of the sea and of boats, & content with fishing on a small scale. We talk of every thing but law and politics, and one advantage of my condition is, that it excuses me from looking into any newspaper.

I have talked much of an excursion to Maine, Penobscott, St. John's &c, but at present am inclined to stay where I am. Mr. [William] Hunter says I shall receive, in a day or two, the Nicaragua papers translated. I am anxious to see what the Nicaragua proposition is, although, I presume, it will be found quite inadmissible.[1] Yours always truly,

Danl Webster

LS. NBuHi. Published in *PC*, 2: 552.
1. DW is referring to negotiations with Nicaragua regarding the Web-

ster-Crampton agreement of April 30, 1852. See *Diplomatic Papers*, 2.

TO MILLARD FILLMORE

Marshfield, Sept. 22/52
Wed. Eve.

Private & Confidential
My Dear Sir,

Early on Monday morning I went to Boston, for further medical advice & direction, and returned early on Tuesday morning. I travelled in a carriage instead of the cars. Although the weather was fair & the roads smooth, I did not escape some fatigue.

The state of my health at this hour is this. The catarrh is still hanging about me, but very lightly, and I do not regard it. My other complaint[1] is by far the more serious, and requires the utmost care both from me and my physicians. I have never experienced so bad, or so long continued an attack. It destroys appetite, deranges all internal operations, and keeps me weak and prostrate.

In some respects the weather has been quite unfavorable, for though fair, it has been cold, with harsh and gusty northwest winds, sweeping along the coast. So that, although my house is pretty much surrounded by salt water, and the sea is immediately before me, I have not sniffed a particle of sea breeze for ten days. The Doctors say, I shall get along with patience and care, & recommend entire quiet, and strict regimen.

For my part, my Dear Sir, I must confess that unless in some weeks longer this disease can be got under some check or control, I shall feel my case to be a bad one; even while I dictate this letter, I feel a degree of uneasiness, almost amounting to positive pain, prevailing through the whole system of the stomach and bowels. If I check it by medicine, immediate constipation ensues, making matters still worse, so that I am driven to the only resource which is, extremely careful diet.

I read as little as possible, write nothing but my name, will not be talked to on general subjects, and endeavor, as far as possible for the time, to sink the character of a *thinking* being. Lord Fitzgerald,[2] one of Mr. Peal's Cabinet, who did not much love labor, was asked by the clerks, if he would peruse certain papers, he said, "no." "Will your lordship allow us to read them to you?" "No." "The subject is important. Will your lordship please think of it till Monday?" "No, I will not *think* for anybody."

So poor Mr. [Theodore Sedgwick] Fay has lost his last chance.[3] My heart grieves for him and his family. He is one of the most interesting, able and deserving of our public men abroad. Yours truly,   Danl Webster

LS. NBuHi.
1. Diarrhea, lack of appetite, and the continuing discomfort occasioned by the distention of his bowels and stomach.

2. Sir Peter George Fitzgerald (1808–1880) was vice treasurer of Ireland in Sir Robert Peel's last cabinet, 1841–1846. *DNB.*

3. Secretary of legation in Berlin since 1837, Fay had applied fruitlessly for a promotion since 1851. When no better position opened for him, Webster wrote to Fillmore on October 8, 1852, suggesting that Fay be transferred to London. Nothing came of this or other efforts on Fay's

behalf during Fillmore's administration. However, Edward Everett intervened with incoming president Franklin Pierce in early 1853, and Fay was appointed first minister resident to Switzerland in March. Everett later told George J. Abbot that DW had "much at heart the promotion of Mr. Fay." The appointment by Pierce, he observed, executed "the last wishes of Mr. Webster, relating to a public man." See DW to Fillmore, October 8, 1852, mDW 37957; Fillmore to DW, September 27, 1852, mDW 37892; and Everett to George J. Abbot, February 26, 1853, Abbot Papers, CtY.

TO MILLARD FILLMORE

Marshfield, Sepr. 28 1852

Private
My Dear Sir,
I did not leave my room yesterday, nor my bed more than five minutes at a time, on account of a violent attack of *constipation*, in my stomach

& bowels, with great pain, and much swelling of the parts. It came on early, & notwithstanding all that could be done by hot flannels, swathing, castor oil &c. it was seven at night, before we could break it up. I then went to sleep, & slept to a late hour today. What is to be the further progress of these evils, or what their end, I cannot foresee.

I sent to Boston, for my principal Physician, [Dr. John Jeffries] who will be here today. He is a personal friend, & I hope he will disguise his errand, under the pretense of a social visit, so that a *talk* may not be raised in the Newspapers. While I write this, I am free from pain, but excessively weak.

I write to nobody but you any thing important about my health. To all others, I give the general answer, that it is the season for my Catarrh, but that the disease is light. Yrs always truly   Danl Webster

ALS. NBuHi. Published in *PC*, 2 : 554.

TO CALEB CUSHING

Marshfield Sept. 30. 52

My Dear Sir

I hope you can turn the enclosed[1] to some account. It is the best I can do, till I see you. Whoever takes this may rely on its being met with punctuality, *if I live*.

I do not expect to be able to get to Boston for some days. Yrs always truly   Danl Webster

ALS. DLC. Published in part in Claude M. Fuess, *The Life of Caleb Cushing* (New York, 1923), 2: 91.

1. Enclosure not found. It was a note for $2,500, payable in six months.

TO MILLARD FILLMORE

Marshfield Sep. 30. 52

Private

My Dear Sir

Dr. [John] Jeffries has been down, & staid two nights, & has freely consulted with Dr. [John] Porter,[1] our local Physician. Their statement is more favorable than I expected, for I have been much alarmed, & that alarm has not also subsided yet. I will send you a copy of their statement, as soon as I can get one of them to make it out. Yrs always truly
                                        Danl Webster

ALS. NBuHi. Published in *PC*, 2: 555.
   1. Porter (1795–1865), a Duxbury

physician, was Charles Henry Thomas's brother-in-law.

Having arranged his finances as best he was able, and increasingly sensi-
tive to the gravity of his condition, Webster turned his attention as much
as possible to simple pleasures at Marshfield. As the following note to
his employee, Thomas Hatch, suggests, small signs of home mattered to
Webster. In this instance, he requested Hatch to move his small boat
with a mast and flag to a point on Marshfield pond where the flag would
be visible from his bedside. A ship lantern at the top of the pole would,
under this instruction, be lighted at six P.M. each day and taken down
in the morning, so long as the master of Marshfield lived. Thus, from
his rooms, Webster could observe the flag by day and at night had the
reassurance of the lantern gleaming in the dark.

TO THOMAS D. HATCH

[c. October 3, 1852]

Mr Hatch, I have *A Secret to reveal to you.*

I want you to light a lamp on the home squadron.[1] "My light shall
burn & my flag shall fly as long as my life lasts."

Do you see to this Mr. Hatch & let nobody know of it & take them by
surprise in the evening by six o'clock. There is no one here in my room
but you & I & William[2] & if he mentions it I will put a brace of balls
through him.[3]   D.W.

ANS.NhHi. Published in *W & S*, 16: 668–669, tentatively dated October 1. Van Tyne, p. 543, following a notation by Peter Harvey, dated it October 20, 1852.

1. The "home squadron" was DW's appellation for one of his boats.

Hatch called the boat "Cruiser."

2. Probably William Johnson, Webster's black servant.

3. For Hatch's account of DW's instructions, as later recounted to George Ticknor, see Curtis, 2: 684–685.

TO MILLARD FILLMORE

Marshfield Oct 4 .'52
Monday 1 oclock

Private

My Dear Sir;

I thank you for your kind & sympathizing letters, respecting my
health. The Doctors have agreed to have another conference, before they
make any statement. The reason is, that although all who know Dr
[John] Jeffries & Dr [John] Porter have entire confidence in them, yet
friends in Boston insist that they shall be permitted to send down a
medical man of high national reputation, in his Profession; & they have
proposed either Dr. [John Collins] Warren, Senior or Dr [James] Jackson.
Of course, I could not object to this, & in a day or two I shall see them

here. The great object, at present, is to check the tendency to inflam-
[m]ation, & distension, in the stomach & lower bowels. To this end,
leeches have been applied, liberally, & it is thought with good effect. I
feel, today, as if I might regard myself as rather on the mending hand;
but how long this may last, I know not. I observe that many of the con-
ductors of the Press, &, most especially, my devoted & excellent friend,
Mr Brooks of the Express,[1] is infinitely concerned about my condition.

I trust you & your Family are all well. Yrs always truly   Danl Webster

ALS. NBuHi. Published in part in
PC, 2: 556.
   1. James and Erastus Brooks co-
edited the *New York Express*, a moderate Whig paper sympathetic to DW.
DW was probably here referring to
Erastus, who served as Washington
correspondent for the paper.

TO MILLARD FILLMORE

Marshfield, Oct. 8 1852

Private & Confidential
My Dear Sir,

The Physicians assembled here on the 6th inst. and explored and
scrutinized me, from top to toe, as if I had been the subject of a *post
mortem* examination. The result of their opinion was, that the inflammation of the stomach and bowels, was gradually giving way to the
exhibition of medicines, and the effect of diet and regimen.

But they do not encourage me to hope for any rapid progress in recovery. They recommend a change in diet, and the use of plain, nu-
tritious food, so far as I have appetite for it, but there is difficulty in obtaining this appetite. It is a great while since I have been hungry. The
case is somewhat complicated. Last year, at the breaking of my catarrh,
I experienced occasional pains in my feet, which gave me a twinge, not
known to my forefathers. All these went off, however, at that time, with
the catarrh itself. They have returned, in some measure, this year, and
give occasional trouble to the feet by short paroxysms of pain, and by
producing, not infrequently, a considerable degree of swelling.

In the actual state of things, I get little exercise, except walking within
doors. Indeed, I believe I have been off the farm but once, since I came
here, and that was, when I made a forced march to Boston, for
consultation.[1]

The Doctors insist on steady quiet and repose; but say, nevertheless,
that it is not injurious to dictate three or four hours every morning to a
clerk upon subjects not very anxious, or absorbing. What they insist on,
mainly, is, that, I shall not show myself to more callers, and inquirers,
each, with a whole budget of questions; and to this I strictly conform.
Yours always truly,   Danl Webster

P.s. Mr. W[illia]m A Bradley has been here two or three days, almost the sole guest in the house. If you fall in with him, he will tell you, what he thinks of my present state of health, & its prospects.

LS. NBuHi. Published in *PC*, 2: 557.

1. Webster had traveled to Boston on September 20 to consult Dr. Jeffries and visit with his friends George Ticknor and George Ticknor Curtis. He was very weak and by all accounts looked poorly. The following day he returned to Marshfield. For Dr. Jeffries's recollection of DW's symptoms in his final month of life, see "An Account of the Last Illness of the Late Hon. Daniel Webster," *American Journal of the Medical Sciences*, New Series, 25 (January 1853): 110–120. For a first person chronicle of DW's final weeks, see the series of letters written from Marshfield by George J. Abbot to his wife Annie, beginning September 29, 1852. John R. Morison, Peterborough, New Hampshire.

Webster's public silence on the presidential question understandably encouraged rumors that he would welcome a third-party movement on his behalf. It also provoked dozens of letters seeking inside information, or trying to persuade him to follow a particular course of action. All of the letters were ignored, but in the absence of any direct rejection of a draft, Webster campaigns in several states were undertaken, with varied support and enthusiasm.

At Marshfield on August 4 Webster had discussed politics with George T. Curtis, leader of a Webster-for-president drive in Massachusetts. He told Curtis that he would not "invite or encourage" an independent candidacy, nor would he "interfere to prevent any portion of the people from casting their votes for him, if they should see fit to do so" (Curtis, 2: 651–652). Despite Webster's further comment that he wanted no activity on his behalf in Massachusetts, and a strong lobbying campaign by Webster Whigs in the state (including Edward Everett, Rufus Choate, and George Ashmun) against any third-party effort, Curtis pushed on, keynoting an August 16 rally at the Tremont House in Boston.

Such activities alarmed Whigs in many states, especially given Winfield Scott's obvious political weakness. In New York, several of Webster's old associates, led by Moses Hicks Grinnell, wrote him urging a public repudiation of all third-party efforts. That Webster was of more than one mind about an appropriate response is reflected in the two draft letters below, neither of which appears to have been sent. Having assayed a mild, noncommittal response, Webster thought better of it and drafted the letter (printed below) that reflected his continuing bitterness over the results of the Baltimore convention and his refusal to play the dutiful soldier on behalf of a political party that was dying as surely as he was.

FROM MOSES HICKS GRINNELL, WITH ENCLOSURE

October 9, 1852

My Dear Sir,

I enclose a communication from some of your friends in this City, it breathes the sentiments of your friends here. I send it to you with a heart full of interest and solicitude for your happiness. Sincerely your friend   M. H. Grinnell

ENCLOSURE: FROM MOSES HICKS GRINNELL ET AL.

September 24, 1852

Dear Sir,

After much consideration we have thought it not improper to address to you a few words on the present aspect of political affairs with the Whig party. We venture to do this in the confidence that you will receive this from us, as prompted only by our sincere interest in whatever affects your position before the Country, now as ever regarded by us as that of our most eminent Citizen.

Of the ill success which attended the efforts to promote the honor and safety of the Country, by presenting you as the Candidate of the great Whig party for the Presidency, we can only say, that it has occasioned to us, at least as much sorrow and chagrin as to any others of your friends political or personal, and the more that every day adds to the conviction which we expressed always and every where before the nomination, that the triumph of the Whig party would be assured under the auspices of your great name.

With all these feelings, however, we confess that we have observed with much solicitude the movements made by many of your friends, in various parts of the Country to connect your name with the impending Canvas for the Presidency. We can anticipate no result from them at all suitable to your dignity, or at all likely to correspond with their wishes. If the matter should come to the point of a nomination and the formation of electoral tickets, we can see no prospect of any other issue, than a most false record of the state of feeling in the Country towards you, an issue most unfortunate for the Country, and gratifying only to that faction whom your patriotism and great public services have made your enemies.

Nor do we think it unworthy of notice that all the best considered and effective efforts in your behalf before the meeting of the Convention took the shape of presenting your name to the ordeal of that body's selection from the candidates proposed by the Whig party, a shape suggested, as we then believed, no less by a wise policy than by a just sense of political fidelity. In the disaster which has fallen upon our hopes and plans, we do not find any warrant to disregard the observance of that good faith towards the successful competitor, which in a different result we should rightfully, have claimed from his friends.

The best reflections we have been able to give to this whole subject, have induced us to think that sound and sober public opinion, which should never be lightly regarded, deems a public disclaimer from you of any favor towards movements further connecting your name with the coming Presidential election, as required by your past and present eminent position whether as a Whig or a Statesman; that such is our own feeling we respectfully submit to you, and beg you to consider that whatever may be your decision, we shall never cease to acknowledge the great obligations which the Country and the Whig Party have always owed to you, and shall ever remain your sincere friends and obedient Servants,

> M[oses] H[icks] Grinnell
> W[illia]m M[axwell] Evarts
> A[mbrose] C Kingsland
> T[homas] Tileston
> James S. Thayer[1]
> J[ames] Watson Webb
> C[harles] A[ugustus] Stetson

Copy. NhHi. Published in Van Tyne, pp. 537–539, 541.

1. Thayer (1818–1881; Amherst 1838), lawyer and businessman, was then serving as public administrator of New York City.

TO MOSES HICKS GRINNELL, WITH ENCLOSURE

Marshfield Oct 12' 1852

My dear Mr. Grinnell,

I received your note of the 9th inst.,[1] only yesterday with its enclosure; to which enclosure you will herewith receive an answer Your's with constant regard.   Daniel Webster

ENCLOSURE: TO MOSES HICKS GRINNELL ET AL.

Marshfield, Oct. 12. 1852

Gentlemen,

I received only yesterday your communication of the 24th of September;[2] and among a great number of similar letters, it is the only one I answer.

There is no equal number of Gentlemen in the United States, who possess more of my deep attachment and regard than the signers of your letter, I would do almost anything to comply with your request. But if I were to do what you suggest, it would gratify not only you and your friends, but that great body of implacable enemies, who have prevented me from being elected President of the United States. You all know this; and, how can I be called upon to perform any act of humiliation for their gratification, or the promotion of their purposes?

But, Gentlemen, I do not act from personal feeling. It is with me a matter of principle and character, and I have now to State to you that no earthly consideration could enduce me to say anything or do anything from which it might be inferred directly or indirectly that I concur in the Baltimore nomination, or that, I should give it, in any way the sanction of my approbation. If I were to do such act, I should feel my cheeks already scorched with shame by the reproaches of posterity.

As to the proceedings of my friends, I encourage nothing, I discourage nothing. I leave them entirely free to judge of their own course. Probably they think they see indications that within a fortnight the Whig party in the United States will have become merely Historical. With the highest respect and the warmest attachment I remain, Gentlemen, Most truly Yours   D.W.

Copy. NhHi. Published in *W & S*, 16: 666–667. This draft letter dictated by DW was never signed or sent. Nor, apparently, was the subsequent draft by George Jacob Abbot, below—or a third draft composed by Edward Everett and submitted for Abbot's consideration. See Abbot Papers, CtY, and Abbot to Everett, October 12, 1852, Everett Papers, MHi.

1. See above.
2. See above.

TO MOSES HICKS GRINNELL ET AL.

Marshfield, Oct 13 1852

Gentlemen;

I received only yesterday your communication of the 24th of September.[1]

I beg you to believe me sincerely grateful for the assurances of attachment, political and personal contained in your letter.

In respect to the subject of it, I have now to say to you, and to others who have addressed similar letters to me, that I entertain no new opinions, and have no sentiments to express, inconsistent with those which I have, heretofore, publicly declared in the strongest manner; and to which I now, and shall always, adhere in their whole length and breadth.

I refer you Gentlemen to my published Works; and, more especially to my speeches in Fanueil Hall, and at Marshfield, on the 20th of September 1842, and the 1st of September 1848 respectively.[2] With the highest respect and the warmest attachment I remain Gentlemen Most truly Yours   Daniel Webster

Copy. NhHi. Published in *W & S*, 16: 667–668. The copy contains this comment: "Written at the especial request & in consequence of the importunity of Mr. Edward Curtis, and never sent."

1. See above, Moses Hicks Grinnell et al. to DW, September 24, 1852.

2. See *Works*, 2: 117–140, 421–446. Both are reproduced in *Speeches and Formal Writings*, 2. In the 1842 speech, defending his decision to remain in the cabinet following the

mass resignation of the Clay Whigs in September 1841, DW insisted that he was "a Massachusetts Whig, a Faneuil Hall Whig," and would remain so as long as he breathed. In the 1848 speech, Webster disparaged Zachary Taylor's qualifications for the Presidency but called the alternatives—(Lewis Cass and Martin Van Buren)—unacceptable and urged the citizens of Marshfield to cast Whig ballots in the coming elections.

FROM WILLIAM A. BRADLEY

Washington 14 Oct. 1852

My Dear Sir,

I remained three days in New York waiting the return of Major Sanford,[1] whose good offices I wished to secure in the matter of business you confided to Mr. [Richard Milford] Blatchford and myself.[2] He did not return and I was compelled to depart without seeing him.

I had an interview however with Mr. [Samuel] Jaudon & Mr. Blatchford, in which I explained to them fully, the whole transaction, and we agreed upon a plan of operations, which, I confidently expect, will lead to a most satisfactory adjustment of the matter. Of the result Mr. B[latchford] I presume will immediately advise you.

Another business matter, of some importance to you has been settled, I refer to the Kinney and Patriotic Bank affair,[3] from this you are released, as I am informed the parties have either settled or agreed upon the terms of a settlement.

I beg to express to Mrs. Webster and yourself my grateful thanks for your more than kindness during my sojourn at your paradise of Marshfield. The only drawback to my perfect enjoyment whilst there was your indisposition, which I most anxiously hope will be but temporary. I have the honor to be most sincerely yours   W A Bradley

ALS. NhHi.

1. Probably John F.A. Sanford, formerly an agent for the Clamorgan Land Association, then living in New York City.

2. "The matter of business" has not been identified.

3. No extant documentary evidence fully details this matter, but its essentials likely involved a three-

cornered arrangement of debts among DW, Henry Lawrence Kinney, and the Patriotic Bank of Washington, D.C. Kinney owed money to Webster in 1849, and the latter was in debt to the Patriotic Bank. Evidently Webster transferred to the bank the note he held from Kinney, as partial or full repayment of his own obligation to the bank. The 1852 settlement between Kinney and the Patriotic Bank thus left Webster in the clear. See Caleb Cushing to Kinney, March 9, 1849, mDW 29143, and Kinney to DW, March, 3, 1850, mDW 29868. On Kinney, see *Correspondence*, 4, passim.

FROM JAMES DWIGHT

New York Oct 14th 1852

Dear Sir,

I notice by our Papers this morning that you are now, suffering, or have lately suffered, severely, from dissentarry. Below, I hand you a Receipt for the cure of this complaint, which has proved more certain than any other Remedy I have ever known. A sincere wish that you may speedily be restored to your usual health, & a full belief that the medicine specified below will produce this effect, must be my excuse for addressing you at this time. I am, with great respect, very truly yours,

James Dwight

Take one pint Cognac brandy (best kind), & put it into a 1 1/2 pint bottle, & make it very sweet, (almost a syrrup) with pulverised loaf sugar; then take, a parcel of wheat flour, & parch it very carefully, on a flat shovel, laid on some cinders; stir it from time to time, so that it does not burn, until it becomes of a light brown colour; then put into the prepared brandy 4 heaped up table spoonsful of it, & *shake it up, thoroughly*, before using. Dose, in a severe case of dissentarry, two thirds of a wine glass once in half an hour, & in milder ones, a table spoonful once in half an hour.

The addition of the parched flour, causes the brandy to become a powerful tonic—it has produced more cures in severe bowell complaints (in Columbus, Georgia) where I live, than any other medicine I have ever known. It was used in the Revolutionary army with great effect, as a cure for dissentarry.

ALS. DLC. Dwight (1784–1863), the son of former Yale president Timothy Dwight, was a merchant based in Columbus, Georgia, at this time.

TO MILLARD FILLMORE

Marshfield Oct. 15. '52

Private & Confidential
My Dear Sir

I thank you for [from] the bottom of my heart, for your kind letter.[1] Your letters are always kind. I have been in great danger, & am in danger now. I am attended, nearly every day, by two Physicians; & yet, strange as it may seem, when I have got through the night, I can sit an hour at the Table, & write a letter, & sign others. I dont foresee the result. I am in the hands of God; & may he preserve & bless you, & yrs. ever more.   Danl Webster

ALS. NBuHi. Published in *PC*, 2: 558.

1. Millard Fillmore to DW, October 13, 1852, mDW 38027.

FROM FRANKLIN HAVEN

Boston Oct 15 1852

My Dear Sir

I recd your letters of the 12th inst.[1] whilst I was spending the day at Beverly.

Your suggestion in regard to the "aliunde" note, is quite right.[2]

You ought not to be, *and shall not be*, troubled with the matter. Had some parties (S[amuel] Appleton and one or two others) fulfilled their engagements an end would have been put to it before now.

As it is, I trust the matter will be made right before long. I pray that you will never think of it again.

The $1500 note due on the 26th inst. is guaranteed, *one half* by Mr. Mills.[3] Mr. M is the endorser of the $1950 due next Jan[uar]y. Mr. J[ohn] P[lummer] Healey's receipt for Passenger money,[4] is to cover the $3500 note, due Nov 21/—I refer to these matters now, because from the tenor of your letter, I do not know but that it is your wish that I should state them.

I hope that you will not suffer any thing to rest upon your mind that is not entirely pleasant and consistent with your comfort, whilst you are seeking repose at Marshfield. Always and Faithfully Yrs,

Franklin Haven

ALS. NhHi.

1. Only one letter dated October 12 has been found: mDW 38004.

2. DW's "aliunde" note of roughly $2,400 due at Haven's Merchants' Bank was to be paid, according to Webster, "from other funds than mine." DW to Haven, October 12,

1852, mDW 38004.

3. Possibly John Mills (1787–1862), a lawyer and former United States district attorney and Massachusetts legislator from Springfield.

4. Legal fees due DW from the passenger cases of 1849. See *Correspondence*, 6: 76n.

MEMORANDUM BY EDWARD CURTIS ON INSCRIPTION FOR WEBSTER'S GRAVE, WITH ENCLOSURE

Marshfield October 15th 1852

Friday Evg. at 9 o'clock, Mr. Webster sent his colored servant, William [Johnson], to request me to come to him, in his chamber. I entered the Chamber, immediately, & found Mr. Webster sitting in a chair, ready to go to bed. He gave me his hand; and obeying his motion I sat down by his side. He then withdrew from under his night clothes, the accompanying paper, and asked me to hand him a pen with ink in it. I did so. On the second page of the paper after the word "production" he made the letter *a*, and put the like mark before the passage, in his hand writing beginning with the words, *"This belief enters"* &c. &c. He then handed me the pen, & requested me to insert after the word "Universe" in the sixth line of the first page, those words which are therein inserted, in my hand writing—to wit: "in comparison with the apparent insignificance of this Globe." He then said I wish you to make a fair copy of this, and to understand that I intend to have this inscribed on the monument at my tomb. I wish to bear testimony to this faith. It may do some good. I shall make a request, that Mrs Webster shall be laid at my side, at the grave (here he was much affected by emotion but instantly recovered). He said, he would like to have me speak with Mrs. Webster, on these subjects. Mr. W. again took me by the hand, & saying he w[oul]d be glad to see me in the morning & bade me "good night."

ENCLOSURE:

"Lord, I believe; help Thou mine unbelief."[1]

Philosophical argument, especially that drawn from the vastness of the Universe, in comparison with the apparent insignificance of this Globe, has sometimes shaken my reason for the faith that is in me; but my heart has assured, and reassured, me, that the Gospel of Jesus Christ must be a Divine Reality.

The Sermon on the Mount cannot be a merely human production. This belief enters into the very depth of my conscience. The whole history of man proves it. Danl. Webster

AD. DLC. Enclosure is a copy, in Edward Curtis's hand.

1. Five days earlier, Webster had asked George J. Abbot to read aloud several sections of the New Testament, including the ninth chapter of the Gospel according to Mark, where a man, bringing his child to Jesus to be cured, was told: "If thou canst believe, all things are possible, to him that believeth; and straightaway the father of the child cried out, with tears, Lord, I believe, help Thou mine unbelief." Webster then dictated the inscription for his tomb, the revised version of which is printed here. See Curtis, and George J. Abbot to his wife Annie, October 10, 1852, two letters. John R. Morison, Peterborough, New Hampshire.

GEORGE JACOB ABBOT TO ANNA TAYLOR GILMAN EMERY ABBOT

Marshfield, Oct. 15th 1852
Friday Eve.

My Dearest Annie,

"The disease makes progress"—so says Dr.[John] Jeffries. The seat of the disease now enlarges. It is a "sub acute inflammation of the peritoneum." Dr. Jeffries came up at 7 o'clock last evening—& returned to Boston at 2 o'clock. He comes again tomorrow evening. Mr. W. went down about 9 o'clock—remained several hours. He went down & up the stairs twice to day.

At times he is cheerful & natural as ever. Mrs. [Harriette Story White] Paige came down with Dr. Jeffries. Mrs. [Edward] Curtis came two days ago. [Richard Milford] Blatchford came yesterday & went away this morning in the violent storm.

Both gentlemen are obliged to talk with Mr. W. on business. It is considered very desirable that he should settle his affairs. Every day he attends to business—more or less.

While Mrs. Paige was bathing his head this morning, as he was sitting in his chair, He picked up one of the hairs that fell from his head, & remarked, "See how the thread of my life is spinning out." And again he said to her, My heart is full, I have many things to say to you all, but I cannot—& then burst into tears. In a moment he drew himself up—& said I will be brave & manly, I will die firm. The "effusion" Dr. Jeffries says is greater now than it was on Tuesday. He measures one inch more around his body than he did then.

Mrs. Paige, said while she was in the room with him he quoted a sentence from Caesar,[1] after looking as it were into vacancy, for some time, about dying. I put it down here so as to remember it hereafter.

He called me into his chamber this morning, & took me by the hand & told me to give his love to you & to the children.

This morning he told Mrs. Webster that he thought he could not live very long. Now & then as he sits in the room, he gives expression to a wit[t]icism or joke—or a cheerful phrase—a rhyme or two as usual.

It is sad—very sad—thus to see a great mind passing away from the earth.

The termination will probably be sudden. He may possibly live weeks, but as I compare the progress of disease as marked by his appearance from day, to day, I cannot expect it.

And now with love to the children, & to you most affectionately ever

G. J. Abbot

ALS. John R. Morison, Peterborough, New Hampshire. Anna Abbot (1815–1861), who became George Jacob Abbot's wife in 1841, was a daughter of Nicholas Emery, of Portland, Maine.

1. Harriette Story White Paige, in a detailed account of Webster's last days (MHi, Paige Papers) wrote under date of October 15: "He related an anecdote of Octavius Caesar, and what he said about leaving this world—the last time a friend saw him;—this anecdote I hope to recover, but its true import I have lost." The Roman biographer Suetonius records that Augustus, on the day that he died, asked assembled friends

if he had played his part in the comedy of life well, adding a theatrical tag, one version of which reads, "If the spectacle of my life has pleased you, applaud." Ivar Lissner, *The Caesars: Might and Madness*, translated from the German by J. Maxwell Brownjohn (New York, 1958), p. 82.

TO MILLARD FILLMORE

Sunday, Oct. 17. 52
[Marshfield]

My Dear Sir

I have had two comfortable nights, on the whole, since I wrote you, though last night I had an excessively painful attack, which cost Dr [John] Jeffries, with his oil, morphine, & squills, two hours to subdue. I went to sleep, & slept sweetly. This [is] a beautiful, brilliant, but very cold October morning, and now, (11 oclock) I feel uncommonly well & strong. Some symptoms are decidedly better. They measure me, like an ox, & find, that there is a small, but positive diminution of the distension of the stomach & bowels. We must see, now, ere long, what turn things will be likely to take.

I keep up with Lobos;[1] & on that subject do not intend to be caught.
Yrs always truly   Danl Webster

ALS. NBuHi.

1. DW is referring to the diplomatic controversy over American rights to guano on Peru's Lobos Islands in the south Atlantic. See Kenneth E. Shewmaker, " 'Untaught Diplomacy': Daniel Webster and the Lobos Islands Controversy," *Diplomatic History*, 1 (Fall 1977): 321–340, and *Diplomatic Papers*, 2.

TO MILLARD FILLMORE

Monday Morn[in]g. 18. Oct

My Dear Sir

By the blessing of Providence, I have had another, comparatively, good night; the afternoon attack coming later, & not lasting so long; & then an excellent sleep. At this hour, (10 oclock), I feel easy, & strong, & as if I could go into the Senate, & make a speech! At one, I shall sink all away—be obliged to go to bed, at three, & go thro the Evening spasms. What all this is to come to, God only knows. My Dear Sir, I should love to pass the last months of your Administration, with you, around your Council Board. But let not this embarrass you. Consider my Resignation as always before you, to be accepted, any moment you please. I hope God, in his mercy, may preserve me; but his will be done! I have every thing right about me, & the weather is glorious.

I do not read the newspapers; but my wife sometimes reads to me the contents of some of them.

I fear things do not look very well for our side.[1] Yrs truly always,
Danl Webster

ALS. NBuHi. Published in *Diplomatic Papers*, 2 and in *PC*, 2: 560, which follows with a letter from George J. Abbot to Fillmore, October 21, 1852, stating: "You will be deeply pained to learn that within the last few hours the disease under which the Secretary of State is laboring, has taken an unfavorable turn, and that no hopes are entertained for his recovery. The last letter written by his own hand, was addressed by him to you on Monday [October 18]."

1. DW alludes to evidence that Winfield Scott would be decisively defeated in the approaching presidential election and that the Whig party as a whole would suffer from Scott's weak showing .

FROM EDWARD BURCHELL

Alex[andri]a V[irgini]a
Oct 19th 1852

Honoured Sir—

I a very humble member of the Whig party, take the liberty of forwarding the enclosed slip,[1] the contents of which it is presumable you have seen ere this time, and in Gods name and the name of the grate & glorious Whig party, beseech you to ponder it well. O Sir the sentiments it contains are big with consequences to your own world renound fame; as well as to the destiny of this grate Country; in the comeing Presidential Election. Hoping and praying that he who disposes of the hearts of all men, may so direct and dispose of yours as to cause you to give the influence of your mighty name to the Election of him who has been so fairly chosen to be the proud standard bearer of the Whig party; then will you be beloved and honoured by all living Whigs and their posterity rise to bless your name. In the language of scripture what your hands find it to do do quickly. Yours with every sentiment of respect
Edward Burchell

ALS. DLC. Burchell (1797–1866) was a tax collector in Alexandria.

1. Enclosure not found.

NOTES BY GEORGE JACOB ABBOT DESCRIBING
THE SIGNING OF WEBSTER'S WILL

Marshfield, October 21
Thurs. 8 2/3 o'clock P.M.

At this hour, Mr. [James William] Paige summoned Dr. [John] Jeffries, Mr. [Charles Henry] Thomas[1] and Mr. [George Jacob] Abbot to go up into Mr. Webster's room, to witness the signing & sealing of his will. Mr. G[eorge] T[icknor] Curtis and Mr. Ed[ward] Curtis preceded the above-named gentlemen, and entered the room alone. In a short time they were called into the chamber. Mr. Webster was lying in bed, perfectly calm & collected. He said are you all there? There were then in the room, Mr. Paige, Mr. G. T. Curtis, Mr. Thomas, Dr. Jeffries, Mr. Ed. Curtis, & Mr. G. J. Abbott. "Come here," said Mr. Webster, in loud, firm & distinct tone of voice—Mr. P. Messrs C. stood round him—"do you say on your honor as Gentlemen, that my Wife approves the Will, (or, has it been read to her, & does she approve it?) Mr. Ed. Curtis said, in a firm tone, "she does approve it, I know it." "Where is she"? said Mr. Webster. Some one answered "In the next room". "Ask her", said Mr. Webster, "to come <& kiss me> & tell me that she approves it." Mr. E. Curtis went to call Mrs. Webster from the adjoining room, the door separating the two rooms being open.

He returned, in a moment, & said, she was not able to be present. Mr. Webster then repeated "ask her to come & kiss me & tell me that she approves it." Mrs. Webster came in <attend> supported by Mr. Paige, in great distress. She knelt down by Mr. Webster's side, & he asked her, "if she had read, or heard, <Mr. Webster> his will & approved it." She answered, that she did approve it. Mr. <Fletcher> Webster than asked if Fletcher knew it, & approved it. Mr. Paige replied, "Entirely." "Where is Fletcher," said Mr. Webster. Fletcher had been sent for, from the office, which was close at hand. "Where is Fletcher? Where is Fletcher?" repeatedly asked Mr. Webster.

Fletcher came in hastily & said, "Here I am Father." "My Son" said Mr. Webster, "do you know & approve my Will." "Entirely," said his son. Then, said Mr. Webster, "this is my last Will & Testament."

Mr. G. T. Curtis asked, "shall I affix your seal, Sir"? Yes, said Mr. Webster, prepare it all ready for my signature. When this was completed, "Now raise me up." He was then supported by pillows, & Mr Thomas held him, & the Will was placed before him by Mr. G. T. Curtis. "Hold the paper a little squarer, Brother Curtis," said Mr. W. "You are not accustomed to hold papers to sick men." He then took the pen from Mr. Curtis' hand, & signed his name, in a bold hand—bolder Mr. Curtis says than he commonly writes.

As soon as he had signed the will, he said, putting his hands together, "Thank God, for strength to [do] a sensible act."!

* * * * * * * * *2

AD. John R. Morison, Peterborough, New Hampshire.

1. Thomas (1807–1894) was the son of John Thomas, from whom Webster had purchased Marshfield in 1832. From that time until his death, Webster relied on Thomas to supervise the grounds at Marshfield.

2. The remaining few short paragraphs of Abbot's notes recount Webster's ensuing expressions of religious faith, followed by mentions of his household, his nieces, and a brief farewell to his wife.

DANIEL WEBSTER'S LAST WILL AND TESTAMENT

[October 21, 1852]

In the name of Almighty God!—

I, Daniel Webster of Marshfield in the County of Plymouth and Commonwealth of Massachusetts, Esquire, being now confined at my house with a serious illness, which, considering my time of life is undoubtedly critical, but being nevertheless, in the full possession of all my mental faculties, do make and publish this my last Will and Testament.

I commit my soul into the hands of my heavenly Father, trusting in his infinite goodness and mercy.

I direct that my mortal remains be buried in the family vault at Marshfield, where monuments are already erected to my deceased children and their mother. Two places are marked for other monuments, of exactly the same size and form. One of these, in proper time, is to be for me, and perhaps I may leave an Epitaph. The other is for Mrs. Webster. Her ancestors and all her deceased kindred lie in a far distant city. My hope is, that after many years, she may come to my side, and join me and others whom God hath given me. I wish to be buried without the least show or ostentation, but in a manner respectful to my neighbours, whose kindness has contributed so much to the happiness of me and mine, and for whose prosperity I offer sincere prayers to God.

Concerning my worldly estate, my will must be anomalous and out of the common form, on account of the state of my affairs. I have two large real estates. By marriage settlement, Mrs. Webster is entitled to a life-estate in each, and after her death they belong to my heirs. On the Franklin estate, so far as I know, there is no incumbrance, except Mrs. Webster's life-estate. On Marshfield, Mr. Samuel Frothingham has an unpaid balance of a mortgage, now amounting to twenty five hundred dollars. My great and leading wish is, to preserve Marshfield, if I can, in the blood and name of my own family. To this end, it must go in the first place to my son, Fletcher Webster, who is hereafter to be the immediate prop of my house, and the general representative of my name and character. I have the fullest confidence in his affection and good sense; and that he will heartily concur in any thing that appears to be for the best. I do not see under present circumstances of him and his family, how I can now make a definite provision for the future beyond his life. I propose therefore to put the property into the hands of Trustees, to be disposed of by them as exigencies may require.

My affectionate wife, who has been to me a source of so much happiness, must be tenderly provided for. Care must be taken that she has some reasonable income. I make this will upon the faith of what has been said to me by friends, of means which will be found to carry out my reasonable wishes. It is best that Mrs. Webster's life-interest in the two estates be purchased out. It must be seen what can be done with friends at Boston and especially with the contributors to my life-annuity. My son-in-law Mr. [Samuel Appleton] Appleton[1] has most generously requested me to pay little regard to his interests or to those of his children; but I must do something, and enough to manifest my warm love and attachment to him and them. The property best to be spared for the purpose of buying out Mrs. Webster's life-interest under the marriage settlement is Franklin; which is a very valuable property, and which may be sold under prudent management, or mortgaged, for a considerable sum. I have also a quantity of valuable land in Illinois, at Peru, which ought to be immediately seen after. Mr. Edward Curtis and Mr. [Richard Milford] Blatchford and Mr. Franklin Haven know all about my large debts, and they have undertaken to see at once whether they can be provided for, so that these purposes may probably be carried into effect.

With these explanations, I now make the following provisions, namely,

Item. I appoint my wife Caroline LeRoy Webster, my son Fletcher Webster, and R. M. Blatchford Esquire of New York to be the Executors of this will. I wish my said Executors, and also the Trustees hereinafter named, in all things relating to finance and pecuniary matters, to consult with my valued friend Franklin Haven, and in all things respecting Marshfield with Charles Henry Thomas, always an intimate friend, and one whom I love for his own sake and that of his family; and in all things respecting Franklin with that true man John Taylor; and I wish them to consult, in all matters of law, with my brethren and highly esteemed friends Charles P[elham] Curtis and George T[icknor] Curtis.

Item. I give and devise to James W[illiam] Paige and Franklin Haven of Boston and Edward Curtis of New York, all my real estate in the towns of Marshfield in the State of Massachusetts and Franklin in the State of New Hampshire, being the two estates above mentioned, to have and to hold the same to them and their heirs and assigns, forever, upon the following trusts namely; *first*, to mortgage, sell or lease so much thereof as may be necessary to pay to my wife Caroline LeRoy Webster the estimated value of her life-interest, heretofore secured to her thereon by marriage settlement as is above recited, if she shall elect to receive that valuation in place of the security with which those estates now stand charged. *Secondly*, to pay to my said wife from the rents and profits and income of the said two estates the further sum of five hundred dollars per annum during her natural life. Thirdly, to hold, manage and carry on the said two estates, or so much thereof as may not be sold for the purposes aforesaid, for the use of my son Fletcher Webster during his natural life, and after his decease, to convey the same in fee to such <one> of his male descendants as a majority of the said Trustees may elect, they acting therein with my son's concurrence, if circumstances admit of his expressing his wishes, otherwise, acting upon their own discretion; it being my desire that his son Ashburton Webster take one and his son Daniel Webster Jr. the other of the said estates.

Item. I direct that my wife Caroline LeRoy Webster have and I hereby give to her the right at all times during her life, to reside in my Mansion House at Marshfield, when she wishes to do so, with my son, in case he may reside there, or in his absence; and this I do, not doubting my son's affection for her or for me, but because it is due to her that she should receive this right from her husband.

Item. I give and bequeath to the said James W. Paige, Franklin Haven and Edward Curtis, all the Books, Plate, Pictures, Statuary and Furniture, and other personal property now in my Mansion House at Marshfield, except such articles as are hereinafter otherwise disposed of, in trust to preserve the same in the Mansion House for the use of my son Fletcher Webster during his life, and after his death to make over and deliver the same to the person who will then become the owner of the estate of Marshfield, it being my desire and intention that they remain attached to the house while it is occupied by any of my name and blood.

Item. I give and bequeath to my said Wife all the furniture which she brought with her on her marriage, and the silver plate purchased of Mr. Rush,[2] for her own use.

Item. I give, devise and bequeath to my said Executors all my other real and personal estate, except such as is hereinafter described and otherwise disposed of, to be applied to the execution of the general purposes of this Will, and to be sold and disposed of, or held, and used at Marshfield, as they and the said Trustees may find to be expedient.

Item. I give and bequeath to my son Fletcher Webster all my Law Books, wherever situated, for his own use.

Item. I give and bequeath to my son-in-law Samuel A. Appleton my California gold watch and chain, for his own use.[3]

Item. I give and bequeath to my grandaughter Caroline LeRoy Appleton, the Portrait of myself by [George Peter Alexander] Healy which now hangs in the south east parlor at Marshfield, for her own use.

Item. I give and bequeath to my grandson Samuel Appleton my gold snuff-box with the head of General Washington, all my fishing-tackle and my Selden and Wilmot guns, for his own use.

Item. I give and bequeath to my grandson Daniel Webster Appleton my Washington Medals,[4] for his own use.

Item. I give and bequeath to my grandaughter Julia Webster Appleton the clock presented to her grandmother by the late Hon. George Blake.[5]

Item. I appoint Edward Everett, George Ticknor, Cornelius Conway Felton, and George Ticknor Curtis, to be my literary Executors; and I direct my son, Fletcher Webster, to seal up all my letters, manuscripts and papers, and at a proper time to select those relating to my personal history and my professional and public life, which in his judgment should be placed at their disposal, and to transfer the same to them to be used by them in such manner as they may think fit. They may receive valuable aid from my friend George J[acob] Abbot Esq. now of the State Department.

Item. My servant William Johnson is a freeman.[6] I bought his freedom not long ago for six hundred dollars. No demand is to be made upon him for any portion of this sum, but so long as is agreable I hope he will remain with the family.

Item. Monicha [Monica] McCarty, Sarah Smith and Ann Bean, colored persons now also, and for a long time in my service, are all free. They are very well deserving, and whoever comes after me must be kind to them.

Item. I request that my said Executors and Trustees be not required to give bonds for the performance of their respective duties under this Will.

In testimony whereof, I have hereunto set my hand and seal at Marshfield, and have published and declared this to be my last Will and Testament, on the twenty first day of September in the year of our Lord Eighteen hundred & fifty-two.

Danl Webster

Signed, sealed, published and declared by the said Testator as and for his Last Will & Testament, in the presence of us, who, at his request and in his presence, and in the presence of each other have set our names hereto as subscribing witnesses, the word "one" being erased in the third line from the bottom of the fifth page before signing   George J. Abbot John Jeffries   Charles H. Thomas

Plymouth ss. At a Court of Probate holden at Scituate within and for said County on the last tuesday of November 1852

The foregoing Instrument purporting to be the last Will and Testament of Daniel Webster late of Marshfield in said county Esquire deceased, having been presented to me for probate by Fletcher Webster and R. M. Blatchford two of the Executors therein named, and it appearing by the written consent of the said Fletcher Webster an heir at law of said deceased and Samuel A. Appleton the father and guardian by nature of Caroline LeRoy, Samuel, Julia Webster and Daniel Webster Appleton, the only other heirs at law of said deceased, that no person interested, intends to object to the probate thereof. Now, Charles H. Thomas, whose name is subscribed to said Instrument as a witness, being present, made oath, that he saw the said deceased sign and seal and heard him declare the said Instrument to be his last Will and Testament—that he and George J. Abbot and John Jeffries subscribed their names together as witnesses to the execution thereof in the Testator's presence, and that he was then of sound and disposing mind. I do therefore approve and allow of the said Instrument as the last Will and Testament of the said deceased, and do decree, that it have full force and effect as such, and that a Letter Testamentary be issued to the said Fletcher Webster & R. M. Blatchford as sole Executors thereof (Caroline LeRoy Webster, named Executor therein having declined the trust) they giving Bond according to law for the faithful discharge of their duties as such.   Aaron Hobart, Judge of Probate

ADS. MH-L. Although the document is dated September 21, 1852, conclusive evidence indicates that it was actually prepared beginning October 17 and signed on October 21. See note attached to DW's quill pen in Abbot Papers, CtY, G. J. Abbot to Edward Everett, October 22, 1852, Everett Papers, MHi, microfilm reel 14-A, and above, Notes Taken by George Jacob Abbot on Occasion of the Signing of Webster's Will, October 21, 1852.

1. Appleton (1811–1861), a business partner of James W. Paige and his uncle, Nathan Appleton, had married Julia Webster in London in

1839. She died in 1848.

2. Not identified.

3. See Charles Vose, et al., to DW March 28, 1850, mDW 30142, and DW's reply April 15, mDW 30259.

4. See DW to Robert Lewis, April 19, 1828, mDWs, and to [Bushrod Washington], May 24, 1828, mDW 7092.

5. Blake (1769–1841; Harvard 1789) was a Boston lawyer and politician. He and his wife were close friends of Webster and Grace Fletcher Webster.

6. See DW to David A. Hall, January 1851, mDW 32371.

GEORGE JACOB ABBOT TO MILLARD FILLMORE

Marshfield, October 23, 1852
Saturday morning—half-past
five o'clock.

Dear Sir,

Mr. Webster has been growing more feeble since yesterday morning. He has frequent attacks of vomiting, greatly reducing his strength. During the night, he had two severe attacks, at twelve and half-past two o'clock. He is, at this hour, quietly sleeping. He retains the perfect possession of his mind, and is entirely conscious of his situation. I have the honor to be, Sir, very respectfully your obedient servant, G. J. Abbot

Text from *PC*, 2: 561. Original not found.

MILLARD FILLMORE TO MEMBERS OF THE CABINET

Executive Mansion
Washington City
Monday m[orn]ing
October 25. 1852

Gentlemen,

The painful intelligence received <by me> yesterday <at the seat of Government> enforces upon me the sad duty of announcing to the Executive departments the death of the Secretary of State. Daniel Webster died at Marshfield in Massachusetts on Sunday the 24th of October between two and three o'clock in the morning.

Whilst the irreparable loss brings its natural sorrow to every American heart, <it> and will be <received> heard far beyond our <confines> borders with mournful respect wherever civilization has <found a> nurtured men who find in <great> transcendent intellect and faithfull patriotic service a theme for praise, it will <& is received> visit with more poignant emotion his colleagues in the administration, with whom his relations have been so intimate and so cordial.

The fame of our illustrious statesman belongs to his country; the admiration of it to the world.

The record of his wisdom will inform future generations, not less than its <teachings have> utterance has enlightened the present. He has bequeathed to posterity the <fruitful treasure> richest fruits of the experience and judgment of a great mind conversant with the greatest national concerns. In these his memory will endure as long as our country shall continue to be the home and guardian of freemen.

The people will share with the Executive departments in the common grief which bewails his departure from amongst us.

In the expression of individual regret at this afflicting event, the <several> Executive departments of the Government will be careful to manifest every <public> observance of honor which custom has established as appropriate to the memory of one so <exalted> eminent as a public functionary and so distinguished as a citizen.

The Acting Secretary of State[1] will communicate this sad intelligence to the Diplomatic Corps, <at W> near this government, and through our ministers abroad to foreign governments. The members of the Cabinet are requested as a further testimony of respect for the deceased to wear the usual badges of mourning for thirty days. I am, Gentlemen Your obt. servt.

AD draft. MdHi.

1. Charles Mynn Conrad, secretary of war.

VERDICT RENDERED BY THE PHYSICIANS

Oct 25 1852

"It was found on examination, that Mr. Webster died of Disease of the Liver. The immediate cause of death was Hemmorhage from the Stommach and Bowels, owing to a morbid state of the Blood consequent on the above disease. There was also dropsy of the abdomen."[1]

Extract. NBuHi. The autopsy report was furnished to President Fillmore by George J. Abbot.

1. For a full discussion of Webter's final illness and the cause of his death, see John Jeffries, "An Account of the Last Illness of the Honourable Daniel Webster," *American Journal of the Medical Sciences*, New Series, 25 (January 1853): 110–120.

MEMORANDA FOR ACCOUNT OF WEBSTER

[December 31, 1852]

Daniel Webster   To C. Cushing   D[ebto]r

Int[erest] at 6% to Dec: 31. 1852

1839		
June 19	To Balance due this day as per a/c rendered	$2412.59
	Interest 13 yrs: 6 mos: 12 days	1959.29
1841		
June 29	Cash as per receipt	2000
1842	Int[erest] 11 yrs: 6 mos: 2 d[ay]s	1380.66
Feb. 5	Amount of due Bill of date	2000
1843	Int[erest] 10 yrs: 10 mos: 26 d[ay]s	1308.55
May 20	Bal[ance] due of loan as follows	

1842 M[ar]ch 7 Amt of loan $350
1846 May—Cr[edit] by cash   200
     "   " 20 Balance due $150
     "   "   " Int[erest] to date   87.50

                                                      237.50

Int[erest] 6 yrs: 7 mo[nth]s: 11 d[ay]s   98.04

                                               11396.63

		Cr[edits]		
1851 Oct. 24	By Cash		$2500	
	Nett proceeds note for			
	$2500—6 m[onths]		$2423.75	
	Int[eres]t on 2 above items			
	1 y[ear] 2 m[onths] 7 d[ay]s		350.34	
1852 Dec	Proceeds of D. Websters acceptance			
	for $2500 sold by Rob[er]t			
	Farley for		1250	
1852 Dec: 31	Balance due C. Cushing this day			6524.09
				4872.54

AD in Cushing's hand. DLC.

SCHEDULE OF PROPERTY AT ELMS FARM, BY JOHN TAYLOR

Decem—1852—

Scedgule of Personal property on the late Hon Daniel Webster's Elms
Farm In Franklin N. Hamps[hire]

First—Hay seventy tons	70—00	
2d	Corn fodder & oat straw	12 do—
3d	Corn one hundred & fifty bushels	150—
4th	Oats two hundred fifty bushels	250—
5th	Potatoes two hundred bushels	200—
6th	Wheat—30 bushels	30—
	Cattle	
First—four oxen	4—	
2d	five cows	5—
3d	four two year old heifers	4—
4th	one pare two year old steers	2—
5th	Eleven yearlings	11—
6th	Nine calves	9—
7th	Two Bools	2
		37
8th	two horses	2—

9th	Fourteen Sheep	14—
10th	Four pigs to keep over	
	Farming tools—	
First	Two ox carts	2
	Two ox slcads	2
	One Double horse waggon	1
	One Double horse Slay	1
	One single Express waggon	1
	Three good plows	3
	Two harrows	2
	One Seed Sower	1
	One Winnering mill	1
	Two iron bars	2
	Seven draft chains	7
	five Steel shovels	5
	Ox youks rings stapels	
	Bows & co	5
	Hay forks, manure Fork, rakes, hoes	
	& other Smaul farming tools to[o]	
	Numerous to mention	

One two horse Carrage With
Shase top,   1
One New nice Buggy   1
Four Harnesses   4

Bill of Cattle Deliverd to Tilden Ames[1] on Elms Farm N.H. By order of—Hon Daniel Webster on August 3d 1852—

	First 6, Large oxen	6—
	2d, 16, four year Olds	16
	3, one Cow	1
	4th, 3 two year old heifers	3
	5, 1 yerling Bool	1
Sept	Cattle drove my self from Elms Farm, to Marshfield—	
	one large pare of oxen	2
	Two, pare of 3 year old Stears	4
	Two, 3 year old heifers	2
	One 2 year old stear	1
		36—

AD. NhHi.

1. Ames (1795–1867) was a Marshfield farmer and cattle drover.

The stock mentioned were presumably to be moved from the Elms to Marshfield.

INVENTORY OF WEBSTER'S ESTATE

[January 1, 1853]

To the Judge of Probate for the County of Plymouth. An Inventory of the Estate of Hon: Daniel Webster, late of Marshfield, in said County of Plymouth, deceased. Appraised under Oath by the subscribers, duly Appointed to that service, by the Hon: Judge of Probate for said County

		Real Estate	Dolls	Cts
Item	1	Homestead Farm, including all the Uplands and Marsh, from the branch of the River near Seth Peterson's, to the mouth of Cut River, together with the Dwelling House—Cottages, and all other buildings thereon, containing about One Thousand Acres.	30,000	00
"	2	The Island Farm, together with Dwelling House and all buildings thereon, containing about One hundred and forty two Acres.	3,500	00
"	3	One Undivided half of Factory and Mill property, purchased of Duxbury Manufacturing Company, with Dwelling House, and all other buildings thereon.	1,500	00
"	4	30 Acres of Land in Marshfield, adjoining the land of Capt. Peleg Thomas.	450	00
"	5	About 10 Acres of Upland and Swamp in Duxbury, purchased of Dr. John Porter, and C[harles] H[enry] Thomas	50	00
			35.500	00

		Personal Estate	Dolls	Cts
Item	1	All the Furniture in the Dwelling House—Silver and Plated Ware excepted.	2749	75
"	2	All the Silver and Plated Ware	2682	60
"	3	5000. Books in Library, together with Book Cases & Furniture	4474	00
"	4	Sundry—Family Portraits, consisting of Busts, Pictures and Engravings, amtg to 126 pieces in all	324	25
"	5	112 10/12 Doz: bottles and 8 Demijohns of Wine	727	00
"	6	70. Head of Neat Cattle, consisting of Oxen—Cows—Bulls—Young Cattle and Calves.	1896	00
"	7	7. Horses.	665	00
"	8	62. Sheep and 3 Lamas.	155	00

"	9	27. Hogs and Pigs.	270	oo
"	10	146. Poultry—such as Geese—Turkies—Ducks—		
"		Hens & c	51	50
"	11	6. Carriages—6 Harnesses and 4. Riding Saddles	768	oo
"	12	Farming Utensils such as Waggons Carts		
		Garden Engine—Roller &c &c.	442	oo
"	13	4. Boats—1. Skiff and 2. Old Dories.	283	oo
"	14	8. Guns—together with Gunning & fishing		
		Apparatus	146	oo
"	15	Produce of the Farm on hand, consisting of		
		Hay—Grain and Vegetables.	3300	50
"	16	2. Gold Watches and Chains.	375	oo
"	17	1. Pew and Shed at South Meeting House in		
		Marshfield	75	oo
		Total Amt of Real and Personal Estate Dolls	54884	60

Jany 1st 1853.

Seth Sprague
Geo. P. Richardson
C. H. Thomas Appraisers

Plymouth ss

At a Court of Probate holden at Plymouth on the third Monday of February 1853 Fletcher Webster one of the Executors of the last Will & Testament of Daniel Webster made oath that the foregoing Inventory contains the whole of the Estate of said deceased so far as the same has come to his hands and knowledge.   M Bates Jr Reg. Probate

Plymouth ss

At a Court of Probate held at Plymouth on the third Monday of February 1853 the foregoing Inventory having been duly sworn to, it is ordered that the same be accepted and recorded.   Aaron Hobart J[udge] Probate

Copy. Registry of Deeds, Plymouth County, Massachusetts.

Calendar, 1850–1852

Compiled by Mary Virginia Anstruther and Alan Berolzheimer.

Items in italics are included in this volume. Diplomatic correspondence from the records of the Department of State has not been calendared here. It is discussed in *Diplomatic Papers*, 2.

1850

Jan 1   To Mary Scott. ALS. PP. mDW 29698. Acknowledges a Christmas gift; explains why he changed his mind about coming to dinner

Jan 1   Account with John Plummer Healy, to July 1, 1850—$1738.50 (including balance of $1,045.83 from account July 1, 1846 to Oct 1, 1849), plus "services 14 yrs a $500 per year"—$7,000. AD. NhD (Claims on DW's Estate). mDWs.

Jan 1   Account with C. Woodward for cooking stove, etc., through Jan 7, 1851. AD. NhHi. mDW 39741.

Jan 1   Promissory note to Jared Coffin for $3460. ADS by DFW (for himself and DW). NhD (Claims on DW's Estate). mDWs.

Jan 3   From Edward Everett.   3

Jan 4   To [Daniel S.?] Dickinson. AN. NhD. mDWs. Requests his presence at dinner.

Jan 4   To Peter Harvey. Telegram. NhHi. mDW 29706. Advises him to come to Washington next week.

Jan 5   To John S. Haight. ALS. WHi. mDW 29707. Denies he owes Haight anything and indeed recollects losing money "by your father."

Jan 5   Draft on Samuel P. Lyman for $1,000 payable to self. DS (signature crossed). MHi. mDW 40369.

Jan 7   To George Washington Warren. ALS, MH–BA. mDWs. *W & S*, 16: 528. Asks Warren for an account of the Bunker Hill monument to be used in a new edition of his speeches.

Jan 7   Memorials of Albert T. Goodwin and others for protection against foreign infraction of patent rights. DS. DNA, RG 46. From Goodwin, mDW 51658; from Thomas Blanchard (mDW 51662); from Levi C. Wadleigh and others (mDW 51671); from Samuel Cox and others (mDW 51674); from Henry Y. Gilson and others (mDW 51678); from citizens of Burlington, Vt. (mDW 51682).

Jan 8   To Dwelly Baker. ALS. NhD. mDW 29708. Alludes to the burning of "the Island house" and warns him to be careful with fires.

Jan 8   To Charles Henry Thomas. ALS. MHi. mDW 29710. Inquires about the burning of "the Island house."

Jan 8   From Robert Bowne Minturn to Caroline Le Roy Webster. ALS. MH–H. mDW 29712a. Presents gifts from the Middle East to her and DW.

Jan 9   To [Peter Harvey]. ALS. NhHi. mDW 29713. *W & S*, 16: 529. Discusses various senatorial proceedings, including appointments and "a useless debate Genl. Cass has caused."

[Jan 9]   To William Henry Seward. AL. NRU. mDW 29014. Accepts an invitation to dine.

Jan 9   To [?]. ALS. NhHi. mDW 39269. Encloses a letter "lest Mr Harvey should have come south."

Jan 9   From Edward Everett.   4

Jan 9   From William Henry Furness. ALS. NhHi. mDW 29725. Van Tyne, pp. 389–390. Urges DW to speak out against slavery.

Jan 9   From Charles March. ALS. NhHi. mDW 29728. Van Tyne, pp. 390–391. Is sending DW Ceylon wine.

Jan 9   From William C. Munger. ALS. NhD. mDW 29731. Asks for public documents.

Jan 10   To Charles March. Printed. *PC*, 2: 349. Acknowledges March's gift of Ceylon wine.

Jan 10   To Charles Augustus Stetson. ALS. NhD. mDW 29733. Accepts Stetson's offer of venison and asks for peas and fish.

Jan 10   To William D. Ticknor. Printed. Charles Hamilton, Auction No. 42, June 4, 1970. Discusses plans for a new edition of "my speeches."

Jan 10   To Charles Porter Wright. ALS. NhD. mDW 29736. *PC*, 2: 349. Discusses farm matters; asks him to write more frequently.

Jan 11   To [David Dudley] Field. ALS. NhD. mDW 29737. Discusses the docket position of a case (*Williamson et ux* v. *Berry*) now pending before the Supreme Court.

Jan 13   To Franklin Haven. ALS. MH–H. mDW 29739. Asks to have the proceeds of a note endorsed by his longtime client "James G." credited to his account.

Jan 13   To Franklin Haven.   5

[Jan 14]   To Levi Woodbury. AL. DLC. mDW 29743. Invites him to dinner.

Jan 14   From Robert Dobbign. ALS. MWalB. mDW 29745. Seeks DW's professional assistance in the recovery of assets due the estate of Richard Powers.

Jan 14   From Alexander Gilchrist. ALS. NhHi. mDW 29747. Asks for government documents.

Jan 14   Petition of citizens of Boston in relation to the transmission of the mail to California. DS. DNA, RG 46. mDW 51834.

Jan 14   Petition of P.P.F. Degrand and others praying a charter for the purpose of constructing a railroad and establishing a line of telegraph from St. Louis to San Francisco. DS. DNA, RG 46. mDW 51862.

Jan 16   From William O. Bartlett.   6

[Jan 18]   To [Richard Smith]. ALS. UPB. mDWs. Will see him tomorrow or Monday about "the little note."

Jan 18   To Charles Augustus Stetson. ALS. NhD. mDW 29757. Acknowledges receipt of venison and other provisions; notes the Senate's approval of a resolution affecting expenditures for the collection of custom revenue.

[Jan 18]   To Daniel Fletcher Webster. ALS. NhHi. mDW 29758. Reports being heavily engaged in court; has heard nothing yet about appointments.

Jan 19   To [Edward Duncan Ingraham]. Copy. NhD. mDWs. Thanks Ingraham for a copy of his book (*A sketch of the events which preceded the capture of Washington by the British, on the twenty-fourth of August, 1814*).

Jan 19   To John Taylor. Printed. *PC*, 2: 349–350. Reports the Revere

House wants potatoes; authorizes Taylor to buy cattle and inquires about other farm business.

Jan 19   To Charles Porter Wright. ALS. NhD. mDW 39264. Asks whether he has potatoes to spare for the Revere House.

Jan 21   To John Plummer Healy. ALS. MHi. mDW 29760. Discusses financial matters; asks what the Massachusetts legislature will do about "the Passenger Tax business."

Jan 21   From George Wallace Jones (with DW to Daniel Fletcher Webster, [c. Jan 22, 1850]). ALS. NhHi. mDW 29764. Reports property they own jointly in Illinois is now very valuable and advises reopening the case of *Lapsley* v. *Adams*.

[c. Jan 22]   To Daniel Fletcher Webster (enclosure: George Wallace Jones to DW, Jan 21, 1850). ALS. NhHi. mDW 29763. Asks him to send papers requested by Jones concerning *Lapsley* v. *Adams.*

Jan 22   Resolution by DW to grant a quarter section of land to every male citizen of the United States on certain conditions. DS. DNA, RG 46. mDW 51171.

Jan 22   Petition of Sarah Nichols, widow of a Revolutionary soldier, praying a pension. DS. DNA, RG 46. mDW 51805.

Jan 23   To [William H.] Winder. AL. NhD. mDWs. Cannot accept a dinner invitation because of another engagement.

Jan 23   To Charles Porter Wright. Printed. *PC*, 2: 350. Authorizes the sale of two boats; asks about hay and "the fatting oxen."

Jan 24   To Franklin Haven.   8

Jan 25   To Edward Curtis. Printed. *PC*, 2: 351–352. Advises that he and Mrs. Webster will be coming to visit this evening.

Jan 25   To John Plummer Healy. ALS. MHi. mDW 29771. Encloses checks to pay off two notes; hopes the Supreme Court will recess in March.

Jan 25   To Daniel Fletcher Webster. Copy. NhHi. mDW 29774. Van Tyne, p. 391. Regrets being financially unable to support Fletcher's proposed California venture; finds all last year's earnings went to pay debts.

Jan 25   Bill from John Pettibone for $6.75 for coal, through Jan 26. AD. NhHi. mDW 40498, 40379.

Jan 26   To Thomas Jefferson Rusk. ALS. TxU. mDWs. Asks for a critical assessment of his argument relative to the claims of the Union Land Company against Mexico.

Jan 26   From Josiah Sturgis (enclosures: petition of Josiah Sturgis and others, Feb 13, 1850; list of vessels assisted by U.S. revenue cutter Hamilton, [n.d]). ALS. DNA, RG 46. mDW 51643. Argues in support of his petition asking that the Navy pension law be extended to the U.S. Revenue Service.

Jan 27   To Peter Harvey. Copy (incomplete?). NhHi. mDW 29776. *W & S*, 16: 531. Printed extract (from same letter?). *PC*, 2: 352–353. Will support [William] Haydon[Hayden]'s nomination (for Boston postmaster) despite his connection with the Boston *Altas*; expresses reluctance to see the incumbent port surveyor at Boston turned out to make room for Fletcher.

Jan 27   Receipt for $150 paid to Washington merchant Edward Simms. ADS. NhHi. mDW 40371.

Jan 28   From Charles Colburn (with enclosures). LS. DNA, RG 46.

mDW 51722. Submits anew his petition requesting payment for the full term of his enlistment in the Navy.

Jan 28   From Thomas Jefferson Rusk. AL. TxU. mDWs. Thinks DW has conclusively supported his argument regarding the claim of the Union Land Company against Mexico.

Jan 28   Petition of Collins Stevens and others, lastmakers of Boston, praying to be protected against foreign infraction of their patent. DS. DNA, RG 46. mDW 51996.

Jan 31   To [Waddy?] Thompson. ALS. NhD. mDW 29779. Feels flattered by "Miss Wright's" remarks in her note to Thompson.

Jan 31   From Nathaniel Coffin (with DW to [Thomas Ewing], Feb 18, 1850). ALS. DLC. mDW 29781. Writes about filling the vacancy in the U.S. district court in Illinois.

Jan 31   Bill from W. M. Morrison for $6.50, for books and a gold pen. AD. NhHi. mDW 40409.

[Jan?]   To [Samuel Jaudon]. ALS. NHi. mDW 29785. Advises Jaudon to return immediately to Washington; describes the president's attitude toward "the Mexican payments."

Feb 1   To Daniel Fletcher Webster. ALS (close and signature missing). NhHi. mDW 29788. ALS copy. MHi. mDWs. Van Tyne, pp. 391–392. Discusses "the passenger tax business"; warns the Massachusetts legislature not to attempt an evasion of the Supreme Court's ruling (*Norris* v. *Boston*).

Feb 1   From J. J. Sanford (with memorial of citizens of Cecil County, Maryland, Feb 13, 1850). ALS. DNA, RG 46. mDW 51850. Expresses support for the bill to give away public land to actual settlers, as proposed by DW.

Feb 2   To Daniel Fletcher Webster. ALS. NhHi. mDW 29375. Van Tyne, pp. 387–388. Expects Curtis to see the president tomorrow (regarding the Boston port surveyorship); reports the Senate is busy with the Bradbury, Cass, and Clay resolutions.

Feb 2   To Charles Porter Wright. ALS. MH–H. mDWs. Van Tyne, pp. 731–732. Discusses the sale and trading of steers.

Feb 2   From John Peirce, Jr. (with accompanying papers). ALS. DNA, RG 46. mDW 51736. Argues in support of his petition for restoration of his rank and back pay as professor of mathematics in the Navy.

Feb 4   To Waddy Thompson. ALS. NhD. mDW 29791. Plans to be in court today around noon.

[Feb 4]   To Daniel Fletcher Webster. ALS. NhHi. mDW 29388. Van Tyne, p. 388. Reports the president appears likely to reappoint [John] McNeil (surveyor for Boston).

[Feb 5?]   To Mary Elizabeth Wilson Sherwood. Printed. "A Breakfast at Mr. Webster's," *Appleton's Journal* 13 (Feb 20, 1875): 240. Invites her to breakfast.

Feb 6   To David Dudley Field. ALS. NcD. mDW 29794. Discusses court business; hears "no bad news."

Feb 6   To Sarah Hartshorne. ALS. NhD. mDW 29795. Does not have time to answer her question on a legal matter.

Feb 6   To John Plummer Healy. ALS. MHi. mDW 29798. Asks Healy to cash the enclosed check and use the money to pay a note.

Feb 9   To Hamilton Rowan Gamble. ALS. MoSHi. mDW 29801. Has little hope for "our case" (*Mills et al.* v. *County of St. Clair et al.*).

Feb 9   To [?]. ALS. NjP. mDW 29800. Answers an inquiry concerning published copies of the debate with Hayne.

Feb 12   To [Peter Harvey]. ALS. NhHi. mDW 29802. Discusses certain promissory notes; tells Harvey, "In the meantime, *don't be frightened*" about the political situation.

Feb 12   To Samuel Kirkland Lothrop.   9

Feb 13   To Peter Harvey. ALS. NhHi. mDW 29804. Van Tyne, p. 392. Predicts the current Constitutional crisis will be resolved peacefully without disunion.

Feb 13   Memorial of citizens of Cecil County, Maryland, praying that a portion of the public domain may be reserved for actual settlers. DS. DNA, RG 46. mDW 51845.

Feb 13   Memorial of Charles Colburn praying payment for the full term of his enlistment in the Navy. DS. DNA, RG 46. mDW 51767.

Feb 13   Petition of Josiah Sturgis and others, officers of the revenue cutter *Hamilton*, praying that the pension laws may be extended to the Revenue Service. DS. DNA, RG 46. mDW 51645.

Feb 13   Petition of citizens of Roxbury, Mass. in favor of cheap postage. DS. DNA, RG 46. mDW 51843.

Feb 14   To Peter Harvey.   10

Feb 14   To Franklin Haven. ALS. MH–H. mDW 29807. Declares he never doubted "[Philip] Greeley's representations were all false."

Feb 14   Account with John Purdy for $13 for coal, through Mar 9. ADS. NhHi. mDW 40373.

Feb 15   To William Henry Furness.   11

Feb 15   To James William Paige. ALS. Mrs. Irvin McD. Garfield, Southboro, Mass. mDWs. Has sent Paige's letter on to [William Morris] Meredith and expects an answer in a day or two.

Feb 15   To Charles Augustus Stetson. ALS. NhD. mDW 29814. Describes the Senate's mood regarding appointments; comments on recent speeches by Clay and Berrien.

Feb 15   From A. J. Martin. ALS. NhD. mDW 29816. Requests documents.

Feb 16   To Edward Everett. ALS. MHi. mDW 29818. *PC*, 2: 355. Is working on a new edition of his speeches; thinks the disunion "clamor" is abating and advises "our side" to keep cool.

Feb 16   To John Plummer Healy. ALS. MHi. mDW 29819. Introduces Welcome Farnham of Waterford, Mass., and asks that he be assisted in his business with the Massachusetts legislature.

Feb 16   To John Taylor. ALS. MWalB. mDW 29821. Explains the difference between turkeys and turkey buzzards; sends papers for distribution among Taylor's Franklin neighbors.

Feb 16   From William Morris Meredith.   13
Feb 17   To James William Paige.   12

Feb 17   To Charles Porter Wright. ALS. NhHi. mDW 29825. *PC* 2: 355–356. Discusses farm business and the importance of settling his Marshfield debts.

[c. Feb 18]   To Thomas Ewing (with Nathaniel Coffin to DW, Jan 31, 1850). ANS. DLC. mDW 29784. Speaks highly of both Coffin and "Judge [Samuel D.] Lockwood."

Feb 18   To James William Paige.   13
Feb 18   From Edward Everett.   13

Feb 18   From John Taylor. ALS. Robert and Richard Upton, Concord, N.H. mDW 29836. Reports on farm matters.

Feb 18   Petition of Little & Brown asking the patronage of the government to the "Life & works of John Adams, second Prest. of the U.S." which they propose to publish. DS. DNA, RG 46. mDW 51684.

[Feb 19, 1850?]   To [Elizabeth Collins] Lee. ANS. DLC. mDWs. Reports that Z. Collins Lee has been nominated U.S. attorney for Maryland.

[Feb 19]   To William Henry Seward. ALS. NRU. mDW 29838. Asks to be sent for should "our case" be called up by the Supreme Court.

Feb 21   To Roswell L. Colt. ALS. Phi. mDW 29840. Declares "we" will not permit the government to be broken up.

Feb 21   To Tilson Fuller. ALS. NhD. mDW 29843. Reports Sarah Nichols's petition has been referred to the proper committee.

Feb 21   To William Cabell Rives. ALS. DLC. mDW 29845. Introduces Isaac Ilsley Cummings of Portland, Me., now in Paris for medical studies.

Feb 22   To [Joseph] Blunt. ALS. NhD. mDWs. States he was "never more disappointed in my life, than in the result of Mr Le Roy's cases"; discusses his fees.

[Feb 24]   To William Morris Meredith. ALS. PHi. mDW 29847. Notes the recent death of General John McNeil; will come to the Interior Department tomorrow to talk about the Boston surveyorship.

Feb 24   *To Daniel Fletcher Webster.*   16

Feb 25   Deed transferring property in Mineral Point, Wis., from the U.S. government to DW. Copy. Deed Book P: 355–356. Register of Deeds, Grant County, Wisconsin.

Feb   28   From David Dudley Field. ALS. NhHi. mDW 29849. Encloses his letter, mentioned in DW's note of the day before, as well as the communication to which it was an answer (neither found).

[Feb]   To Caleb Cushing. ALS. DLC. mDW 29851. Refers to Joseph Knox as a lawyer in Rock Island, Ill. recommended to him by "Judge [Stephen] Douglas."

Feb   From William Henry Furness.   16

[Feb?]   To William Henry Seward. ALS. NRU. mDW 29853. Doubts "our case" will be reached this week, and proposes deferring their consultation "till a dryer morning."

[March 1]   To Peter Harvey.   19

[March 1]   To [Charles Henry Warren].   20

March 1   Bill from John Pettibone for $19 for ice tickets, through June 10. AD. NhHi. mDW 40388.

March 2   From Waddy Thompson.   21

March 3   From Henry L. Kinney. ALS. NhHi. mDW 29868. Wants to settle his business affairs; invites DW to come to Corpus Christi.

March 4   From R[ichard?] B. Barker.   21

March 5   From Benjamin Douglas Silliman.   22

March 6   From David Piper. ALS. NhHi. mDW 29876. Asks for documents and a copy of whatever speech DW may make on the Compromise bill.

March 7   To Willim W. Corcoran. ALS. DLC. mDW 29878. [William W. Corcoran], *A Grandfather's Legacy; containing a sketch of his life and obituary notices of some members of his family, together with letters from his friends* (Washington, 1897), pp. 84–85. Asks if his dinner invitation might be postponed until next week.

[March 7]   Heads for 7th of March Speech. Printed. Lanman, pp. 119–120.

[March 7]   Notes for 7th of March speech. AD. NhHi. mDW 29881. Van Tync, pp. 393–403.

[March 8]   To Caleb Cushing from DW and Caroline Le Roy Webster. AL in Caroline Le Roy Webster's hand. DLC. mDW 29917. Invite him to dinner.

March 8   To Robert Morrison. ALS. NhHi. mDW 29919. Will be sending garden seeds and encloses a check to pay for more.

March 8   To John Taylor. ALS. MWalB. 29922. Encloses money to pay for a steer; complains of being short of cash.

March 8   From William Anderson. ALS. DLC. mDW 29925. Expresses delight with the 7th of March speech; argues for colonization as the best solution to the slavery problem.

Mar 9   To William W. Corcoran. ALS. DLC. mDW 29929. [William W. Corcoran], *A Grandfather's Legacy* (Washington, 1897), p. 85. Thanks Corcoran for his complimentary note on the 7th of March speech and for the enclosure which accompanied it.

Mar 9   To Franklin Haven. ALS. MH–H. mDW 29931. Discusses personal finances; complains of the humiliation and poverty inflicted by his debts.

Mar 9   To James J. May. ALS. MS. mDW 8507. Asks that a $1,000 draft be credited to his account.

March 9   To Robert Charles Winthrop. ALS. MHi. mDW 29933. Encloses something due Winthrop "a long while."

March 9   From Edwin Bowman Raffensperger. ALS. NhD. mDW 29934. Requests a copy of the 7th of March speech.

March 10   To Edward Everett.   24

[c. March 10]   Corrected proof sheets of 7th of March speech. Printed, with MS revisions by DW. NhD. mDW 29938.

March 11   To Edward Everett. LS. MHi. mDW 29942. Discusses the editing of his speeches.

March 11   From Henry Alexander Scammell Dearborn.   25

March 11   From Lewis Henry Morgan. ALS. NhD. mDW 29948. Asks for a copy of the 7th of March speech.

March 11   From John Taylor.   26

March 11   From Jonathan Mayhew Wainwright. ALS. DLC. mDW 29954. Expresses admiration for the 7th of March speech and thinks DW has again rescued the Union.

March 12   To Franklin Haven.   27

March 12   From Samuel Turell Armstrong. ALS. NhHi. mDW 29957. PC, 2: 357. Thinks DW's speech is likely to do "great good."

March 12   From Isaac P. Davis. ALS. NhHi. mDW 29959. Reports DW's speech is strongly approved in "my quarter"; mentions the activities of some mutual friends.

March 12   From Edward Everett.   27

March 12   From John Strother Pendleton.   32

March 12   From William L. Sloss. ALS. NhD. mDW 29975. Requests copies of the 7th of March speech and other documents.

March 12   From John Speed Smith. ALS. NhHi. mDW 29977. Declares
that the line of the Missouri Compromise should be "the *fixed* &
perpetual boundary between the free & slave states," and that DW
will become "the *first man* in the Union" if he proposes the idea.

March 12   From L[arue P.?] Stockton, ALS. NhD. mDW 29979. Requests a copy of the 7th of March speech on behalf of the Rochester
Atheneum and Mechanics Association.

March 12   From [John Taylor]. AL incomplete. Robert and Richard
Upton, Concord, N.H. mDW 29981. Acknowledges a check to pay
for a steer.

March 12   *From William H. Winder.*   33

March 12   Account with John Howlett for gardening service and plants,
through Apr 4. AD. NhHi. mDW 40375.

March 13   From Edward Everett. LC. MHi. mDW 29986. Will attend the
Faneuil Hall meeting if health permits; expects DW's view on returning fugitive slaves will cause the most dissatisfaction among
"our people" of any part of his speech.

March 13   From Calvin Hitchcock. ALS. NhHi. mDW 29988. Van Tyne,
pp. 403–404. Comments on the treatment of slavery in the Bible and
and offers a Biblical perspective on the issue of slavery in the Northwest Territory.

March 13   From William Ingalls. ALS. NhHi. mDW 29992. Thinks
DW's speech will help allay sectional "excitement" and lead to conciliation.

March 13   From John J. Morris. ALS. NhD. mDW 29994. Requests a
copy of the 7th of March speech.

March 13   From Samuel Lewis Southard, [Jr.]. ALS. NhHi. mDW 29996.
Thanks DW for his "glorious speech."

[March 15?]   To Peter Harvey. ALS. NhHi. mDW 30057. Van Tyne, pp.
405–406. Plans wide distribution of the speech in Massachusetts.

March 15   To Redding & Company. ALS. NhD. mDW 29998. Writes
about printing a revised edition of the 7th of March speech.

March 15   From William Key Bond. ALS. NhHi. mDW 30000. Thanks
DW for his "moral courage" and believes the "salutary and healing
influences" of the speech are already being felt.

March 15   From Michael Ritts. ALS. NhD. mDW 30002. Requests a
copy of the 7th of March speech.

March 15   From D. Jerome Sands. ALS. NhD. mDW 30004. Asks for a
copy of the speech.

March 15   From Branch Archer Saunders (enclosure: poem). ALS.
NhHi. mDW 30006. Praises DW's defense of the Constitution, and
declares "the South loves the Union."

March 15   From A. Howard Scott. ALS. NhD. mDW 30010. Requests
copies of the 7th of March speech and geological reports about "the
western & southwestern Territories."

March 15   Sheriff's deeds (3) selling off lots of land in Prophetstown,
Ill. to satisfy a judgment at the Sept 1846 term of the circuit court
against James Craig and Daniel Webster. Copies. County Recorder,
Whiteside County, Illinois. mDWs.

March 16   To Charles Porter Wright. Printed. PC, 2: 357–358. Gives instructions for putting up beef and declares "We must have cheaper
labor."

March 16   From Sidney Breese.   34

March 16   From William T. Shafer. ALS. NhD. mDW 30016. Requests
a pamphlet copy of the 7th of March speech.

March 16   From Benjamin F. Stickney. ALS. NhHi. mDW 30018. Praises
DW's speech, especially for its assault on the Abolitionists.

March 17   To Alfred G. Benson, ALS. David R. Proper, Deerfield, Mass.
mDWs. Transmits his acknowledgments to Mr. Eggleston for the
latter's proffered "testimonial of respect."

March 17   To Franklin Haven. ALS. MH–H. mDW 30020. Discusses fin-
nancial matters; expects a new edition of the 7th of March speech
to be out next week.

March 17   To Calvin Hitchcock. Copy. NhHi. mDW 30022. *PC*, 2: 359–
360. Expounds on the differences in spirit between the Old and New
Testaments.

March 17   To John Taylor. ALS. NhHi. 30025. *PC*, 2: 358. Discusses
farm business.

March 17   To George Ticknor. Printed. *PC*, 2: 358–359. Expects to be detained in Washington by the California vote and court business; admits his speech has become controversial.

March 17   To Daniel Fletcher Webster. ALS. Frederick H. Johnson, Jr.,
Norwich, Vt. mDWs. Alludes to an article in the Boston *Advertiser*
signed "C"; speaks disdainfully of his "revilers."

March 17   From Richard V. Gaines. ALS. NhD. mDW 30027. Asks for
a pamphlet copy of the 7th of March speech.

March 17   From William Giles Jones.   35

March 17   From E. A. Penniman. ALS. NhD. mDW 30033. Requests a
copy of the 7th of March speech.

March 18   From John Overton Choules.   37

March 19   To Lodi Manufacturing Company. Printed extract. NhD.
mDW 30035. Reports on his use and recommendation of poudrette
fertilizer.

March 19   To Redding & Co. ALS. NhD. mDWs. Sends a copy of his 7th
of March speech to be printed.

March 19   To [Charles Porter Wright]. ALS. NhHi. mDW 30037. *PC*, 2:
360. Inquires about oxen and other farm matters.

March 19   From John R. Thomson. ALS. NhD. mDW 30040. Reports
DW's speech has been well received in New Jersey.

March 20   From J. George Heist. ALS. NhD. mDW 30043. Requests a
copy of the 7th of March speech.

March 21   To Thomas Buckminster Curtis.   38

March 21   To Franklin Haven. ALS. MH–H. mDW 30045. Discusses financial matters; hopes a new edition of his speech will be available
in Boston this week.

March 21   To William Winston Seaton. ALS. NhD. mDW 30047. Reports
great demand for the speech; thinks "the alarm" is now subsiding.

March 21   To Daniel Fletcher Webster. ALS. NhHi. mDW 30049. Van
Tyne, p. 405. Intends to send copies of his recent speech to members
of the Massachusetts legislature; reports it is in heavy demand in
the South and West.

March 21   From Edward Everett. LC. MHi. mDW 30051. Thanks the
Websters for kindness shown his daughter Charlotte.

March 21   From Nathaniel Greene Pendleton.   39

March 22   To Robert Field Stockton. Printed . *W & S*, 16: 535–536; *A Sketch of the Life of Commodore Robert F. Stockton* (New York, 1856), Appendix E, p. 69. Requests Stockton's comments on the 7th of March speech.

March 22   To [George?] Talcott. ALS. Mrs. George O. Hilliard, Jr., Westfield, N.J. mDW 30058. Introduces [Richard Milford] Blatchford, [Samuel] Jaudon, and "Mr Morgan" who have business with "your department [Bureau of Ordnance?]."

March 22   From Edward Everett.   40

March 22   From William B. Inge. ALS. DLC. mDW 30069. Thanks DW for vindicating the Constitution and the rights of the South.

March 23   To Franklin Haven.   42

March 23   From Daniel Fletcher Webster, Jr. ALS. NhHi. mDW 30075. Reports on his activities, and asks after his grandparents.

March 25   To [U.S. Patent Office]. ANS. CSmH. mDW 30078. Asks that flower seeds be sent to Samuel Jaudon.

March 25   From Calvin Hitchcock. ALS. NhHi. mDW 30079. Analyzes the Old Testament's treatment of slavery; calls for the refutation of Biblical arguments used in defense of slavery.

March 25   From Thomas Handasyd Perkins et al.   44

March 25   From Robert Field Stockton. Printed. [Samuel John Bayard], *A Sketch of the Life of Com. Robert F. Stockton* (New York, 1856), Appendix E, pp. 69–79. Contends that slavery is a moral question and that the Federal government has no authority to interfere with it.

March 25   Account with Milo Furbush & Co. (with Milo Furbush & Co. to DW, Jan 10, 1851), through Nov 15. AD. NhHi. mDW 40467.

March 26   From James W. Allen. ALS. DLC. mDW 30108. Analyzes slavery and the territorial issue from a Southern viewpoint; discusses the sectional division in the Methodist church; warns of the divisive influence of the Abolitionists.

March 26   From Thomas Allen. ALS. DLC. mDW 30116. Praises DW's "national view" of slavery and "its kindred subjects."

March 26   From "Several '*Conscientious*' Virginians." ALS. CSmH. mDW 30018. Praise the "patriotic spirit" of DW's speech; argue that slavery is expressly sanctioned by both testaments of the Bible.

March 26   From Alexander H. Stevens. ALS. NhD. mDW 30123. Praises DW's speech; criticizes a Taylor administration appointee.

March 26   Draft on Samuel Jaudon for $1,200 payable to self. DS. MHi. mDW 40377.

March 28   To Peter Harvey. Copy. MHi. mDW 30126. *PC*, 2: 363. Finds "the letter" (from Thomas H. Perkins et al., Mar 25) personally flattering; is optimistic about the situation in Washington.

March 28   To Franklin Haven. ALS. MH–H. mDW 30130. Reports on the "Unity Land Company" claims case; regards the case as "safe."

March 28   To Samuel Tenney. ALS. NhD. mDW 30131. Encloses payment due on an insurance premium.

March 28   Edward Curtis to Peter Harvey.   45

March 28   From Aaron Hobart. ALS. NhD. mDW 30132. Encloses notice of a mass meeting at Plymouth; thinks DW's speech will help preserve the Constitution and the Union.

March 28   From Edward A. Newton. ALS. NhHi. mDW 30134. Reports

DW's speech is generally approved by "enlightened and independent men."

March 28   From James Bankhead Thornton.   46

March 28   From Charles L. Vose et al. LS. NhHi. mDW 30142. *PC*, 2: 361. Present DW with a gold chain from California, and a watch.

March 31   To Daniel Fletcher Webster.   48

March 31   From William Morris Meredith. ALS. NN. mDW 30147. Acknowledges a copy of the 7th of March speech.

[April 1]   To [Franklin Haven]. ALS. MH–H. mDW30148. *PC*, 2: 364. Takes note of Calhoun's death.

April 1   To [John Plummer Healy]. ALS. MHi. mDW 30150. Instructs Healy to pay his only remaining note endorsed by Rufus Choate, before asking Choate to endorse another "about the middle of the month."

April 1   To Mr. and Mrs. Robert Charles Winthrop. ALS. MHi. mDW 39243. Reminds them of a dinner invitation on Thursday.

April 1   From Linus Child.   49

April 2   To John Plummer Healy. ALS. MHi. mDW 30155. *W & S*, 16: 537. Encloses payments due on some notes; reflects on Calhoun's death.

April 2   From Sir Henry Lytton Bulwer. ALS. DLC. mDW 30158. Thanks DW for a copy of the 7th of March speech.

[April 3]   To Daniel Fletcher Webster.   53

April 3   From Edward Everett.   51

April 3   From Henry Plympton and Nathaniel F. Cunningham. ALS by Plympton, signed also by Cunningham. NhHi. mDW 30169. Commend the 7th of March speech.

April 4   From Daniel Lord. ALS. DLC. mDW 30173. Praises DW's speech for its "statesmanly" view of the subject.

April 4   From Robert Bowne Minturn. ALS. NhHi. mDW 30175. Acknowledges a copy of DW's speech, and expresses approval of its "every sentiment."

April 5   From Charles Pelham Curtis. ALS. DLC. mDW 30179. Identifies George Ticknor Curtis as the author of the "Boston letter"; asks to be provided with letters of introduction for his forthcoming trip to England.

April 5   From Charles March. ALS. NhHi. mDW 30182. Acknowledges a copy of the 7th of March speech.

[April 6]   To [Edward Curtis?]. ALS. NN. mDW 30184. Asks him to check DW's mail and forward any letters to Baltimore.

April 6   From John McLean. AL (signature removed). NhD. mDW 30187. Thinks amending the (Fugitive Slave) act of 1793 is preferable to reporting a new bill.

April 6   Speech at anniversary celebration of the Maryland Historical Society. Printed. *Baltimore Weekly Sun*, Apr 9, 1850.

April 7   To Peter Harvey.   53

April 8   To John Plummer Healy. ALS. MHi. mDW 30192. Hopes his credit at Merchants' Bank is sufficient to pay a note given to John Taylor.

April 8   To John Pendleton Kennedy. ALS. MdBP. mDW 30193. Asks that his remarks to the Maryland Historical Society be edited before they are published.

expansion of the country to the Pacific under "the arch of the Union."

April 16   To Franklin Haven. ALS. MH–H. mDW 30267. Asks that his bank account be protected in anticipation of a deposit to be made by May 1st.

April 16   To John Taylor. Copy. NhHi. mDW 30269. Tells him to go ahead with plowing and seeding according to plan.

April 17   From Isaac Hill.   69

April 17   From Benjamin H. Magruder. ALS. NhHi. mDW 30274. Expresses satisfaction with DW's 7th of March speech and asks that copies be sent to various individuals.

April 17   From John Tyler.   71

April 18   To Samuel P. Lyman. ALS. NRU. mDW 30284. Will examine "Mr. Archer's letters" for possible publication when he comes to New York.

April 18   To Daniel Fletcher Webster. ALS. NhHi. mDW 30285. *PC*, 2: 366. Reports he may be appointed to the Committee of Thirteen, but will not serve.

April 19   To [Richard Milford Blatchford?]. ALS. DLC. mDW 30286. Plans to leave Washington next week.

April 19   Ballotings for Committee of Thirteen on [John] Bell's and [Henry] Clay's resolutions. Printed D with MS insertions. DNA, RG 46. mDW 52006.

April 19   Receipt from G[ilbert] L. Thompson for 10 shares in the scrip of the Union Land Company. ADS. NhD. mDW 40380.

April 20   To Isaac Hill.   72

April 20   From Nathaniel William Taylor (with Taylor to DW, Nov 20, 1850). ALS. NhHi. mDW 31704. Praises DW's 7th of March speech; assails DW's detractors, especially those in the religious press.

April 22   From Alfred Conkling. ALS. NhD. mDW 30303. Thinks the 7th of March speech clarified the issues for both sides and is further demonstration of DW's intellectual power.

April 22   From Charles Manly. ALS. NhHi. mDW 30307. Praises the 7th of March speech for its eloquence and "conservative temper."

April 2, 24   Minutes by James A. Pearce of two meetings of a special committee assigned to investigate the April 17 disturbances on the Senate floor. AD. MdHi. mDWs.

April 23   Petition of citizens of Fall River, Mass., for the right of trial by jury for fugitive slaves. DS. DNA, RG 46. mDW 52000.

April 23   Resolution by DW relative to the expediency of adopting measures for increasing the coinage of the U.S. AD. DNA, RG 46. mDW 51169.

April 24   To Daniel Fletcher Webster. ALS. NhHi. mDW 30309. Van Tyne, pp. 410–411. Comments on the Committee of Thirteen and his travel plans.

April 24   From Henry Alexander Scammell Dearborn. ALS. NhHi. mDW 30313. Discusses the minting of coins; attacks Abolitionist politicians and argues for the colonization of blacks.

April 24   From Ralph Emerson.   73
April 25   To Franklin Haven.   74

April 25   From John Cameron (enclosure: poem dedicated to DW). ALS. DLC. mDW 30327. Dedicates the enclosed poetic lines to DW.

April 25   From William Plumer, Jr.   75
April 25   Account with Simms & Son for $121.72 for liquor and cheese,
    through Sept 28. AD. MAnP. mDW 40413.
April 26   From Richard Rush. ALS. MHi. mDW 30340. Van Tyne, p.
    411. Thanks DW for a copy of the 7th of March speech.
April 27   Opinion on title to land in California. ADS. Larry D. Lewis,
    Springfield, Mass. mDW 30342.
April 27   Receipt from G[ilbert] L. Thompson for 5 shares of Union Land
    Company scrip. ADS. NhD. mDW 40381.
April 28   To Roswell L. Colt. ALS. PHi. mDW 30347. Gives directions for
    shipping trees and swans to Marshfield.
April 30   From John Henry Hopkins.   77
April 30   From Myron Lawrence. ALS. DLC. mDW 30354. Reports the
    Massachusetts legislature has rejected resolutions condemning DW's
    position and directing him to support the Wilmot Proviso.
April   To Peter Harvey. Copy. NhHi. mDW 30356. Van Tyne, p. 408.
    Emphasizes the need to put his speech into "the hands of the People."
April   To Daniel Fletcher Webster. Printed. PC, 2: 366–367. Asks to hear
    more frequently from Fletcher and his family.
April   From Robert Hallowell Gardiner et al. Signatures only. NhHi.
    mDW 30362. See's DW's reply, June 17.
[April]   From John [Strother] Pendleton (enclosure: John Cole to Pendle-
    ton, Apr 11, 1850). ALS. DLC. mDW 30364. Encloses a letter com-
    plimentary of DW's speech and claims it to be similar to many he
    has seen from different parts of Virginia.
[Apr-May?, 1850]   To [Peter Harvey?]. ALS. NhHi. mDW 38475. Re-
    ports that "the Advertiser, & other papers, which have sustained my
    [7th of March] Speech, are now all backing out."
[May 1]   To Moses Stuart.   79
May 1   To Willie Person Mangum.   80
May 1   From Edward Everett. LC. MHi. mDW 30372. Invites DW to
    dine.
May 2   To William Winston Seaton. Printed. Josephine Seaton, William
    Winston Seaton of the "National Intelligencer" (Boston, 1871),
    p. 306. Speaks briefly of snipe-shooting.
May 2   From Moses Stuart.   81
May 3   From Dudley C[otton] Hall et al. (with Hall to DW, May 7,
    1850). Copy. DLC. mDW30392. Express satisfaction with the 7th of
    March speech and DW's efforts to preserve the union.
May 3   Promissory note for $1,000 payable to Rufus Choate. DS. MHi.
    mDW 40383.
May 4   From Edward Bishop Dudley.   82
May 4   From Francis Lieber. ALS. NhHi. mDW 30379. Wants to send a
    copy of the 7th of March speech to a "distinguished statesman and
    friend of mine" in Germany; thinks Dante's description of Virgil as a
    fountain of speech applies even more fittingly to DW.
May 4   Promissory note for $1,000 payable to John Plummer Healy. DS.
    MHi. mDW 40384.
May 5   To Willie Person Mangum.   83
May 5   From Thomas Green Clemson. ALS. NhHi. mDW 30383. Van
    Tyne, pp. 411–412. Thanks DW for his eulogy of Calhoun.
May 6   To [Hamilton Fish] from DW and George Morey. ALS by Morey,

signed also by DW. DLC. mDW 30385. Advocate Robert Lane Colby's appointment as New York state commissioner at Boston.

May 6   To Caroline Story White Webster. ALS. NhHi. mDW 30387. *PC*, 2: 324. Regrets being unable to "come down" and take leave of her and the children.

[May 7]   To [Richard Milford Blatchford]. ALS. DLC. mDW 30309. Reports on his recent visit to Marshfield.

May 7   From Dudley C[otton] Hall (enclosure: Hall et al. to DW, May 3, 1850). ALS. DLC. mDW 30394. Forwards the copy of a letter signed by citizens of Medford, Mass.

May 8   To William Ballard Preston. ALS. DNA, RG 45. mDWs. Expresses hope that Captain [Silas Horton] Stringham may receive the command of either "the Brazilian, or Californian Station."

May 8   To Worcester Webster. ALS. NhHi. mDW 30395. Van Tyne, p. 732. Asks Webster to help him pay off a note due immediately by discounting the enclosed and placing the proceeds to "my credit" by the 15th.

May 8   From J. M. Phillis. ALS. NhHi. mDW 30398. Asks for speeches and an autograph.

May 8   From Daniel Fletcher Webster (with ANS by DW). ALS. NhExP. mDW 30400. Asks DW to introduce Edward Seager to the secretary of the Navy.

May 9   To [William Ballard Preston] (with Daniel Fletcher Webster to DW, May 8, 1850). ANS. NhExP. mDW 30401. Introduces Edward Seager.

May 9   From Edward Everett. LC. MHi. mDW 30402. Wants to help with the new edition of DW's works; fears the slavery crisis will be weathered, but "in a way to aggravate rather than allay the permanent tendencies to disunion."

May 11   To Peter Harvey.   83

May 12   Elizabeth Washington Wirt to DW and Henry Clay. ALS. DNA, RG 45. mDWs. Asks for letters from DW and Clay to the secretary of the Navy in support of her son's application.

May 13   To J. Morrison Harris. ALS. NNPM. mDW 30406. Thanks the Maryland Historical Society for an honorary membership.

May 13   To [John Plummer Healy?]. ANS. NhD. mDWs. Notes that a draft for $900 has arrived.

May 13   To George Gorham Williams. ALS. NhD. mDW 30407. Declines an invitation from the Story Association.

May 13   To Charles Porter Wright. ALS. NhD. mDW 30409. *PC*, 2: 368–369. Orders the delivery of a cow to Samuel Frothingham and the spreading of guano over grassland.

May 14   To H. J. Anderson. ALS. DLC. mDW 30412. Acknowledges Anderson's complimentary letter; pledges to stand on the principles of his speech.

May 14   To John Hill Hewitt. ALS. GEU. mDW 30414. Acknowledges a patriotic song dedicated to him by Hewitt.

May 14   To Frederick Perry Stanton. ALS. DLC. mDW 30415. Calls H. J. Anderson's "a remarkable letter."

May 16   From Charles Porter Wright (with reply [c. May 18]). ALS.
NhHi. mDW 30426. Makes suggestions regarding the application of
guano; notes that DW's town tax will be due June 1.

May 17   Agreement with W[illiam] A. Bradley and Gilbert L. Thompson
regarding promissory notes and Union Land Company scrip. DS.
NN. mDW 40514.

May 18   To Charles B. Calvert et al. ALS. MdHi. mDW 30425. Declines
an invitation to speak at the annual fair of the Maryland State Agricultural Society.

[c. May 18]   To Charles Porter Wright (with Wright to DW, May 16,
1850). ALS. NhHi. mDW 30428. Agrees to Wright's suggestions regarding guano.

[May 19]   To Edward Everett (enclosure: Nassau William Senior to
Everett, Jan 29, [1850]). ALS. MHi. mDW 30440. Returns a letter
from which he has taken an extract for use in his reply to the people
of Newburyport.

May 19   To Peter Harvey. Printed. *PC*, 2: 370. Plans to answer "the
Newburyport letter" with a full statement on the fugitive slave bill,
and hopes it will be widely published.

May 19   To Daniel Fletcher Webster. ALS. NHi. mDW 30444. Denies
"the story of my remarks in the cars" and suggests that [Philip]
Greely be so informed.

May 20   To William A. Whitehead. ALS. NjHi. mDWs. Accepts honorary
membership in the New Jersey Historical Society.

May 20   Petition of citizens of Wiscasset, Maine, in favor of the establishment of a congress of nations for amicable settlement of international difficulties. DS. DNA, RG 46. mDW 51656.

May 21   To George Wallace Jones. Invitation to dine. Ia–HA. mDW
30452.

May 21   From C. M. Anstell. ALS. DLC. mDW 30454. Congratulates DW
for his defense of the Union and for destroying the Nashville convention.

May 21   From Edward Everett. LC. MHi. m DW 30457. Sends a letter from "Mr [Henry] Hallam" of England; comments on reports
the president will support the compromise proposed by the Committee of Thirteen; chides the *Atlas* for its editorial inconsistency.

May 22   To Thomas Ewing. ALS. NhD. mDW 30459. Recommends
James Morse for a position under the Census act.

May 22   From Julia A. Moor (enclosure: poem). ALS. NhHi. mDW
30462. Encloses a poem written in memory of DW's children.

May 23   From Henry Willis Kinsman. ALS. NhHi. mDW 30466. Describes George Lunt as unfit for the office he now holds (U.S. attorney for Massachusetts).

May 23   Peition of Ziba Baker for a pension. DS. DNA, RG 46. mDW
51794.

[May 24]   To [?]. ALS. DLC. mDW 30470. Writes regarding "the treaty
with England."

May 24 To [?]. Printed. Curtis, 2: 421–422. Explains his position on the Texas resolutions of March and December, 1845.

May 25 From Edward Everett. LC. MHi. mDW 30474. Offers suggestions about the debates on "the Cuba business."

May 25 Opinion on patent of William Blake. ADS. NhD. mDW 30471.

May 26 To Richard Milford Blatchford. Printed. Curtis, 2: 445. Is delighted by the good news from "Mary"; sends him a speech to read; reports "Mary Scott is with us for a week or two."

May 26 To John Plummer Healy. ALS. MHi. mDW 30475. Sends money to pay off a note; promises a copy of his answer to the Newburyport letter.

May 26 From Thomas Worcester. ALS. DLC. mDW 30477. Praises the 7th of March speech, and thinks it provides the only true basis for preserving the Union.

May 27 To Peter Harvey. ALS. Fruitlands Museum, Harvard, Mass. mDWs (typed copy). Reports the status of nominations now before Congress.

May 27 To Franklin Haven. ALS. MH–H. mDW 30480. Accepts Haven's proposition relative to a $5,000 note.

May 29 To [Peter Harvey]. ALS. NhHi. mDW 30481. Van Tyne, p. 414. Discusses a financial matter; notes [Horace] Mann's displeasure with "my [Newburyport] letter."

May 29   To Peter Harvey.   102

[p/m May 29] From Hugh M. Nelson. ALS. NhHi. mDW 30485. Thinks the 7th of the March speech has allayed sectional passions; declares the Union to be essential to national prosperity.

May 30 To John Heard, Jr. ALS. NhHi. mDW 30488. Writes regarding "Mr. Birney's communication"; advises on the status of "yr bill."

May 30   From Moses Stuart.   103

May 31 To John Plummer Healy. ALS. MHi. mDW 30494. Discusses a money matter.

May To [George Ticknor?]. Printed. Curtis, 2: 421. Denies there are inconsistencies between his 7th of March speech and one he made in 1845 regarding Texas, and asks him to write an article making that point clear.

[May] From Thomas Handasyd Perkins. ALS. MHi. mDW 30497. Invites him to Brookline for a visit.

June 1   To [George Ticknor].   105
June 2   To Peter Harvey.   107

June 2 To [Peter Harvey]. ALS. NhHi. mDW 30502. Van Tyne, pp. 415–416. Approves the *Courier's* editorial position and also Stuart's pamphlet; underscores the need for conciliation.

June 2 To Charles Augustus Stetson. ALS. NhD. mDW 30507. Thinks of visiting Harper's Ferry.

[June 2] To Robert Charles Winthrop. ALS. MHi. mDW 30509. *PC*, 2: 372. Declines an invitation because of plans for a trip to Virginia.

June 3   To Dudley Cotton Hall et al.   108
June 3   To [Peter Harvey?].   109

June 3 To [Peter Harvey?]. ALS. NhHi. mDW 30513. Is preparing a reply to "the Medford letter."

June 3 To John Plummer Healy. ALS. MHi. mDW 30517. Asks him to pay a note for $224 due "Mr. Hovey."

June 3 To Moses Stuart. Printed. *PC*, 2: 370–371. Comments favorably on Stuart's *Conscience and the Constitution*; thinks his arguments relative to the Old Testament and slavery will correct much error.

June 3 From Sylvester Graham. Printed. *Letter to the Hon. Daniel Webster on the Compromises of the Constitution* (Northampton, 1850).

June 3 Fugitive Slave Bill.   110

June 3 Memorial of A[lfred] G. Benson praying the establishment of a steam transportation line between the U.S. and China via the adjacent islands. DS. DNA, RG 46. mDW 51839.

[June 4] To Peter Harvey. Copy. NhHi. mDW 30522a. Van Tyne, p. 417. Reports his fugitive slave bill has been laid before the Senate; expects Moses Stuart's book will make a great impression on the public.

June 4 To John S. Walker. ALS. NhExP. mDW 30523. Declines to address the New Hampshire state fair but thinks he might attend "your meeting."

[June 5] To [Peter Harvey?]. ALS. NhHi. mDW 30525. Praises yesterday's *Courier*; declares "We are all in, for this contest, & we must fight it out."

June 5 From Parker Noyes. ALS. NhHi. mDW 30526. Praises the 7th of March speech; compares Abolitionists and Free Soilers to locusts.

June 5 From Henry Whiting Warner.   112

June 6 To Caleb Cushing. ALS. DLC. mDW 30533. Strongly advises Cushing to go to Rock Island and offers to pay his expenses.

June 6 From Francis Lieber.   113

June 7 To [Edward?] Curtis. ALS. NhD. mDW 30539. Reports his efforts on behalf of Jonathan Prescott Hall's nomination (U.S. attorney for southern New York).

[June 7?] To Daniel Fletcher Webster. ALS. NhHi. mDW 30623. *PC*, 2: 533. Discusses plans for monuments to be placed in his cemetery plot.

June 7 From Abraham Watkins Venable. ALS. NhHi. mDW 30543. *PC*, 2: 371–372. Recalls conversations in which Calhoun praised DW's statesmanship.

June 7 Bill from Havenner & Bros. for $5 for bread tickets. ADS. NhHi. mDW 40396.

June 10 To Samuel Lawrence.   114

June 10 To Daniel Fletcher Webster. ALS. NiHi. mDW 30549. Van Tyne, pp. 417–418. Hopes Fletcher can get along with "Mr Coffin"; is writing a letter to "the Kennebec people."

June 10 Testimonial for James W. Simonton. Printed. Hamilton, *Graham*, 3: 479–480. Supports Simonton's proposal to establish the *California Intelligencer*.

June 10 From Elisha Mills Huntington. ALS. DLC. mDW 30551. Supports DW's view of the slavery problem; is alarmed by the Nashville convention.

June 10 Promissory note for $2,500 payable to Fletcher Webster. DS. MHi. mDW 40386.

June 10 Memorial of citizens of Massachusetts, praying that provision be made for continuing the experiments on American coal commenced by Professor Johnson in 1843. DS. DNA, RG 46. mDW 51856. Printed D. DNA, RG 46. mDW 51852.

June 11   To William Cabell Rives. ALS. DLC. mDW 30555. Introduces
Thomas Kunber, Jr. of Philadelphia.

[June 12]   To Daniel Fletcher Webster.   *117*

June 12   From Samuel Atkins Eliot.   *115*

June 12   From Jonathan Prescott Hall. ALS. Dr. George L. Hamilton,
West Hartford, Ct. mDWs. Will do his best for Henry Sargent,
a student in DW's law office.

June 13   To John Plummer Healy, ALS. MHi. mDW 30566. Encloses a
check to pay "Mr. Breck."

June 13   To George Ticknor.   *117*

June 13   To George Washington Warren and William W. Wheildon.
ALS. MHi. mDWs. *Works*, 6: 565. Calls for the defense of the Constitution and the Union; offers a toast to be read at the 75th anniversary of the battle of Bunker Hill.

June 14   To Samuel Atkins Eliot.   *119*

June 14   To Edward Everett. ALS. MHi. mDW 30570. Asks him to furnish Choate with letters of introduction to persons in England.

June 14   To James O. Harrison and H. T. Duncan. ALS. DLC. mDW
30571. Declines an invitation to a fair at Lexington, Ky.

June 14   To George Ticknor. ALS. DLC. mDW 30573. Curtis, 2: 428–
429. Thinks Mann has been "put in a mousetrap"; suggests Ticknor
write additional articles on "my speech" and on the consequences of
making too many new states.

June 14   Promissory note for $3,200 payable to James K. Mills. DS. MHi.
mDW 40389.

June 14   Account with John Pettibone for $27 for ice tickets, through
July 6. AD. NhHi. mDW 40393.

June 15   To Richard Milford Blatchford. ALS. NN. mDW 30576. *W & S*,
16: 550. Refers Blatchford to this morning's *Intelligencer* for his
view of the "let alone policy" on New Mexico; hopes to prevent recur-
curence of the Clay–Benton quarrel.

[June 15?]   To Edward Curtis. ALS. NhD. mDW 31970. Reports [Jona-
than Prescott] Hall's confirmation as U.S. attorney for southern New
York.

June 15   To Daniel Fletcher Webster. ALS. NhHi. mDW 30579. Authorizes him to use "the 'Edward' "; thinks of taking down "the old
House."

June 15   To [?]. ALS. DLC. mDW 30575. Refers to today's *Intelligencer*
for his view of the "let alone" policy regarding New Mexico.

June 16   To Mary Ann Sanborn. LS. NhD. mDW 30581. Encloses a
check for $100.

June 17   To Robert Hallowell Gardiner et al. (with DW to George Ticknor, June 18, [1850]). Printed (with autograph signature). MHi.
mDW 30585. MeHi. mDWs. *Works*, 6: 566–575. Denounces northern and southern extremists and defends his own efforts to bring
about reconciliation; emphasizes that New Mexico is unfit for
slave agriculture, and believes the issue is unnecessarily inflam-
matory.

[June 18]   To [Peter Harvey?]. AN. MWalB. mDW 30496 and mDWs.
Sends inscribed printed pamphlet of his correspondence with the
citizens of Newburyport, with the caution not to let any printer get

hold of it before the letters are published in the Newburyport newspaper.

June 18   To Samuel Lawrence.   119
June 18   To George Ticknor (enclosure: DW to Robert Hallowell Gardiner et al., June 17, 1850). ALS. MHi. mDW 30588. Asks him not to show the enclosed to any printer before it is published in Maine.
June 18   From Joseph T. Adams. ALS. DNA, RG 46. mDW 51994. Writes regarding the petition of P. P. F. Degrand and others for a charter to build a railroad and telegraph to San Francisco.
June 18   From Samuel Atkins Eliot.   120
June 18   From Edward Everett. LC. MHi. mDW 30589. Gives the names of persons to whom he is providing letters of introduction for Choate; reports giving a speech in Charlestown.
June 19   To Citizens of New York. Printed. Van Tyne, p. 418. Acknowledges their letter expressing support for the 7th of March speech.
June 19   To [Franklin Haven]. ALS. MH–H. mDW 30591. PC, 2: 374–375. Comments on prospects for the Omnibus bill; thinks of giving a speech.
June 19   To Charles Porter Wright. Printed. PC, 2: 375. Gives instructions for planting turnips, and asks for a long letter from Charles Henry Thomas on farm matters.
June 19   From Samuel Lawrence, with enclosure.   120
June 20   From William Appleton. ALS. NhHi. mDW 30600. Promises to see that the "old gentleman" is cared for; reports N[athan?] Appleton is improving.
June 20   From William A.[?] Crocker (enclosure: petition of manufacturers of copper and others engaged in the trade, praying a change of the duties on copper). ALS. DNA, RG 46. mDW 51692, 51697. Transmits the petition.
June 23   To Hubbard Winslow. Printed. Van Tyne, p. 419. Acknowledges his "encouraging letter"; pledges to stand on his convictions.
June 24   To Rufus Choate. ALS. George Alpert, Boston, Mass. mDW 30602. Makes suggestions for Choates's visit to England.
June 24   Promissory note for $666 payable to DW by Richard Milford Blatchford. DS (signature crossed). MHi. mDW 40391.
June 25   From Richard Green Parker. ALS. NhHi. mDW 30605. Praises the 7th of March speech and declares it has earned DW the title of "Pacificator."
June 25   Sheriff's deed selling off a track of land in Prophetstown, Ill. to satisfy a Sept 1846 judgment against James Craig and Daniel Webster. Copy. County Recorder, Whiteside County, Ill. mDWs.
June 26   To Alpheus Spring Packard et al. AL. MeB. mDW 30609. Declines an invitation to speak during the Bowdoin College commencement.
June 26   To Francis Sawyer et al. ALS. MHi. mDWs. Thanks them for endorsing his 7th of March speech; calls on patriots to rally around the Union.
June 27   From Jefferson Borden (enclosure: petition of citizens of Fall River, Mass. praying a modification of the tariff). ALS. DNA, RG 46. mDW 51688. Encloses a petition signed by individuals from "all parties in this vicinity."
June 28   To Daniel Fletcher Webster. ALS. NhHi. mDW 30611. Van

Tyne, p. 716. Reports speaking in the Senate yesterday in reply to [Pierre] Soulé; asks to have $500 raised for him at once.

June 29   To J. Vincent Bowne et al. ALS. MSaE. mDW 30614. Declines an invitation to the Independence Day celebration at Salem, but offers a toast to be read.

June 29   To Edwards Amasa Park. ALS. CtY. mDW 30610. Comments on Park's sermon before the convention of Congregational ministers.

June 29   To Julius Rockwell. ALS. Lenox Library, Lenox, Mass. mDW 30617. Acknowledges a list of names and asks for others to whom "my speech" might be sent.

[June?]   To Richard Milford Blatchford (with Blatchford to [Thurlow Weed], [n.d.]). ALS. NRU. mDW 30619. Alludes to "a certain business" involving Thurlow Weed; remarks that Weed has not yet printed "my Newburyport letter."

[June, 1850?]   To Edward Curtis. Printed, PC, 2: 373. Writes from the Astor House advising Curtis to let nothing "separate you from that devotion to your own health which the case requires."

July 1   From Samuel Webber. Copy. NhHi. mDW 30629. Believes DW's 7th of March speech has helped overcome sectional prejudice; reports it is generally approved in the region of Charlestown, N.H.

July 1 (?)   From Isaac P. Davis (enclosure: William Berkeley to Governor of New England, June 12, 1644) ALS. OGK. mDW 32007. Encloses a copy of a letter from early colonial times concerning runaway slaves.

July 3   To Francis Bowen. ALS. CSmH. mDW 30631. Reports "the article" ("The California and Territorial Question," *North American Review* 71 [July, 1850], 221–268) is greatly commended.

July 3   Draft on Samuel P. Lyman for $1,000 payable to self. DS. MHi. mDW 40394.

[July 8]   To Richard Milford Blatchford. ALS. DLC. mDWs. Printed. Thurlow Weed Barnes, ed., *Memoir of Thurlow Weed* (Boston, 1884), p. 183 (misdated July 2). Reports the president is very ill; notes speeches by Truman Smith and William Henry Seward.

July 8   To Harry Hibbard. AL. NhHi. mDW 30642. Invites him to dinner.

July 9   To Peter Harvey. ALS. NhHi. mDW 30644. Van Tyne, p. 419. Approves Samuel Atkins Eliot's nomination (U.S. representative from Massachusetts); is mortified by John M. Marston's recall (U.S. consul at Palermo).

July 10   To Harry Hibbard from Charles Brickett Haddock, for DW. ALS. NhHi. mDW 30645. Postpones their dinner engagement due to "the melancholy event" (Zachary Taylor's death).

July 10   From Taylor Lewis. ALS. NhD. mDW 30647. Is sending DW his *Plato against the Atheists*; makes suggestions for DW's study of Cicero.

July 12   From James Lyons. ALS. DLC. mDW 30669. Advises DW to accept the reported State Department appointment.

[July 13]   To [Edward Curtis]. AN. NN. mDW 30671. Invites him to breakfast.

July 14   To Robert Rutherford Morris. ALS. NHi. mDW 30672. Offers condolences on the death of Hannah Morris.

July 15   From William Segar Archer. ALS. DLC. mDW 30674. Urges DW to become secretary of state and thus save the Whig Party from extinction.

July 16   To Franklin Haven.   126

July 16   To Franklin Haven. ALS. MH–H. mDW 30681. Asks that a note be discounted and the proceeds credited to his account.

July 16   From Edward Everett.   126

July 16   Daniel Fletcher Webster to Peter Harvey.   128

July 17   From James Kellogg Mills.   128

[c. *July 18*]   *To [Millard Fillmore].*   129

July 18   From Friend Humphrey. ALS. DLC. mDW 30693. Hopes DW will consent to become secretary of state.

July 18   From Nathan Sargent. ALS. DLC. mDW 30695. Praises DW's speech of yesterday (on the Compromise bill). See *Speeches and Formal Writings*, 2.

July 18   A bill for the erection of a monument to the memory of Zachary Taylor, late President of the U.S. AD. DNA, RG 46. mDW 51167.

July 18   Diploma of corresponding member of the Geographical and Statistical Society of Mexico. Printed D with MS insertions. NhHi. mDW 30699.

[July 19]   To Millard Fillmore. ALS. NBuHi. mDW 30701. Van Tyne, p. 421. Agrees that Samuel Bulkley Ruggles would be right for the Post Office.

[July 19]   To Millard Fillmore. ALS. NBuHi. mDW 30705. Thinks Thomas Corwin would accept an appointment (Secretary of the Treasury).

[*July 19*]   *To [Peter Harvey?].*   129

July 19   From William H. Macfarland. ALS. NhHi. mDW 30708. Praises DW's recent speech; hopes Fillmore has offered DW the State Department.

July 19   Memorial of Elisha Putnam praying for pension. Printed. DNA, RG, 46. mDW 51815.

July 19   Petition of citizens of Fall River, Mass., praying a modification of the tariff. DS. DNA, RG 46. mDW 51687.

July 19   Petition of manufacturers of copper and others engaged in the trade praying a change of duties on copper. DS. DNA, RG 46. mDW 51692.

July 20   To Millard Fillmore. ALS. NBuHi. mDW 30711. Asks whether he should call this morning.

July 20   To Nathan Sargent. ALS. IHi. mDW 30713. Acknowledges Sargent's complimentary notice of "my recent speeches."

July 20   From Thomas L. Smith. ALS. G. Hartley Webster, Harvard, Mass. mDWs. Reports pervasive, non-partisan hope that DW will "take the helm."

July 20   From Moses Stuart. ALS. DLC. mDW 30715. Comments on DW's most recent speeches and his appointment to the State Department; inquires about Fillmore and the new cabinet.

July 20   Confirmations of DW et al. ADS. DNA, RG 59. mDW 55165.

July 21   To Richard Milford Blatchford. Printed. *PC*, 2: 378. Sometimes
feels "I have done a very foolish thing"; anticipates a "hot and anxious summer."

July 21   To Peter Harvey. ALS. NhHi. mDW 30719. *Diplomatic Papers*,
2. States he accepted the cabinet position only upon the urgings of
others and against his personal wishes.

July 21   To Franklin Haven.   130

July 22   To George Nixon Briggs (with DW to William R. King, July 22,
1850). LS copy. DNA, RG 46. mDW 51628. AL draft. PP. mDW
30727. *Cong. Globe*, 31st Cong., 1st sess., p. 1432. Resigns from the
Senate.

July 22   To Edward Everett. ALS. MHi. mDW 30728. Reports having decided to become secretary of state; suggests that Everett's son-in-law
look for a house in Washington near his.

[July 22]   To Millard Fillmore. ALS. NhD. mDWs. Wishes to be sworn in
tomorrow if it can be arranged.

July 22   To William R. King (enclosure: DW to George Nixon Briggs,
July 22, 1850). LS. DNA, RG 46. mDW 51626. *Cong. Globe*, 31st
Cong., 1st sess., p. 1432. Asks that his letter of resignation be laid
before the Senate.

July 22   DW's commission as secretary of state. Printed DS with MS insertions. DNA, RG 59. mDW 56921. DS with MS insertions. NhHi.
mDW 30729.

July 23   To George V. Brown. LS. MHi. mDW 30731. Announces he has
assumed office as secretary of state.

July 23   To William B. Kinney. LS. NjHi. mDWs. Announces he has assumed office as secretary of state.

July 23   To Daniel Fletcher Webster. ALS. NhHi. mDW 30732. *PC*, 2:
379. Describes his return to the State Department; reports on the
new cabinet.

July 23   From [Sir Henry Lytton Bulwer]. AL draft. UkLPR. mDW
30734. Contends that the Hise treaty (with Nicaragua regarding the
Isthmian canal) conflicts with the Clayton-Bulwer treaty and urges
that it be carefully reviewed.

July 23   DW's oath of office as secretary of state. DS. DNA, RG 59.
mDW 55178.

[July 24]   To Daniel Fletcher Webster. ALS. NhHi. mDW 30738. Van
Tyne, p. 422. Briefly describes his office routine; sees brightened
prospects for the Compromise.

July 25   To Henry Sargent from Daniel Fletcher Webster. ALS. Dr.
George L. Hamilton, West Hartford, Ct. mDWs. Informs Sargent
that DW would like to hire him as scribe and clerk.

July 25   Application from Caleb P. Smith, for the Meredith Bridge, New
Hampshire *Belknap Gazette*—public printer (ALS. DNA, RG 59.
mDW 53582).

July 25   Recommendation from James Bell, for the Meredith Bridge *Belknap Gazette*—public printer (ALS. DNA, RG 59. mDW 53628).

July 26   To Franklin Haven. ALS. MH–H. mDW 30739. *PC*, 2: 379–380.
Comments on the attitude of northern Congressmen, especially from
Massachusetts, on the Compromise bill.

July 26   To Franklin Haven. ALS. MH–H. mDW 30742. Alludes to
Haven's "private note" and thinks friends should do "things at their
own time, & in precisely their own manner."

July 26   To Henry Sargent from Daniel Fletcher Webster. ALS. Dr.
George L. Hamilton, West Hartford, Ct. mDWs. Has had two messages from DW wanting to know if Sargent will accept the job as
his secretary.

July 27   To Mrs. Francis Markoe, from DW and Caroline Le Roy Webster. AL. DLC. mDW 30743. Accept a dinner invitation.

July 27   From Chevalier Johann Georg Hülsemann. Copy. NhHi. mDW
30744. Van Tyne, pp. 447–448. Refers to past difficulties in Aus-
trian-American relations and suggests they meet for a frank discussion and try to reach an understanding.

July 27   Application from Charles I. Wilson, for the *Chicago Journal*—
public printer, endorsed by S. Lisle Smith, July 28 (ALS. DNA, RG
59. mDW 53564).

July 28   To George Ticknor. Printed. Curtis, 2: 463–464. Reports uncertain prospects for the Compromise bill; notes "the great point of difficulty is the Texan boundary."

July 29   Promissory note for $1,000 payable by J. B. Gray (with DW to
Charles Levin, Feb 7, 1852). DS. Erwin Lodge, Philadelphia, Pa.
mDWs.

July 29   Account with T. Bastianelli & Co. for $14.32 for clothing, etc.,
through Sept 28. AD. NhHi. mDW 40428.

July 29   Bill from M. Vail for $2.50 for coat. ADS. NhHi. mDW 40483.

July 30   To Millard Fillmore.   132

July 30   To Millard Fillmore. LS. NBuHi. mDW 30751. Reports receiving a paper indicating what [Alexander de] Bodisco plans to say on
behalf of the diplomatic corps.

July 30   To Millard Fillmore. LS. NBuHi. mDW 30753. Encloses an extract from a letter from "Mr. Green" explaining a charge for $250.

July 30   To [James Smith?] Thayer. ALS. DLC. mDW 30754. Invites
him for dinner.

July 30   From Herrick Aiken. ALS. DNA, RG 48. mDWs. Denounces the
incumbent commissioner of patents as incompetent and urges his
replacement by Jonathan Dennis of Washington.

July 30   From Thomas Abbot Merrill (with endorsement identifying
missing enclosure). ALS. NhHi. mDW 30758. Sends DW a review to
read, as an offering from an old friend who does not seek office.

[c. July 31]   To Charles Henry Thomas. Printed, Gershom Bradford, "The
Unknown Webster," *Old Time New England*, 49 (Fall 1953): 62.
Duxbury Clipper, Dec. 30, 1965. Comments on his official work, his
relations with Fillmore, and the character of the cabinet.

July 31   From Willaim A. Weeks. ALS. DNA, RG 59. mDW 56858. Is
forwarding despatches returned for want of proper addresses; acknowledges receipt of State Department seals.

July 31   Notice of Henry Sargent's appointment as State Department
clerk. LS. Dr. George L. Hamilton, West Hartford, Ct. mDWs.

[July] [1850]   To James William Paige. ANS. Mrs. Irvin McD. Garfield,
Southboro, Mass. mDWs. Sends him a copy of "my *last* speech in
Congress," on the Compromise bill.

[Aug 1]   To Millard Fillmore. ALS. NBuHi. mDW 30760. Recommends
calling a cabinet meeting.

Aug 1   To Peter Harvey. Telegram. NhHi. mDW 30763. Urges Albert
Fearing's election (to Congress).

Aug 1   To Edward Hooker. LS. CtY. mDW 30763a. States that it is contrary to government policy to appoint negroes or mulattos to office;
advises that the consular agent at Mayaguez, Puerto Rico, is to be
removed.

[Aug 1]   To Francis Markoe (enclosure: Caroline Le Roy Webster to
DW, [Aug. 1, 1850]). ALS. DLC. mDW 30764. Encloses a note from
Mrs. Webster excusing herself from a dinner engagement because of
illness.

Aug 1   To [William H.?] Winder. ALS. NhExP. mDW 30767. Thanks
him for a basket of "Sparkling Moselle."

Aug 1   From William L. Yancey. ALS. NcD. mDW 30769. Apologizes for
past criticism and admits his attitude toward DW has changed
greatly.

[Aug 1]   From Caroline Le Roy Webster (with DW to Francis Markoe,
[Aug 1, 1850]). ALS. DLC. mDW 30765. Reports she feels ill and
will be unable to dine with Mr. and Mrs. Markoe.

Aug 1   Account with C. Miller for $185.14 for meat, through Sept 28.
DS. NhHi. mDW 40419.

Aug 1   Recommendation from John W. Howe et al., for the *Philadelphia
Daily News*—public printer (LS. DNA, RG 59. mDW 53631).

Aug 2   To Peter Harvey. Copy. NhHi. mDW 30772. Van Tyne, pp. 422–
423. Declares that Albert Fearing "must come" to Congress.

Aug 2   From A. Calderon de la Barca. Translation. DNA, RG 59. mDW
56504. Accuses the U.S. government of failing to act decisively
against filibustering expeditions organized and launched against
Cuba from the United States.

Aug 3   To Millard Fillmore. LS. NBuHi. mDW 30774. Advises withdrawal of the Buckingham Smith nomination (secretary to the U.S.
legation in Mexico).

Aug 3   To Millard Fillmore. ALS. NBuHi. mDW 30776. Van Tyne, p.
423. Reports the North is greatly disturbed at the loss of the "omnibus" Compromise bill; advises the preparation of a message.

Aug 3   To William Alexander Graham. ALS. NcU. mDW 30780. Hamilton, *Graham*, 3: 340. Introduces Francis Lieber.

Aug 3   From John B. Ashe. ALS. NhD. mDW 30781. Expresses satisfaction with the views of the president and the cabinet on the Texas
boundary problem and will communicate them to an influential
member of the Texas legislature.

[Aug 4]   To [Franklin Haven]. ALS. MH–H. mDW 31009. *W & S*, 16:
556–557. Expects the territorial questions to be mostly settled and
the remaining cabinet seats filled before Congress adjourns.

Aug 5   To Peter Hansbrough Bell. Printed. *Cong. Globe*, 31st Cong., 1st
sess., pp. 1526–1527. Explains the U.S. government's position regarding the situation in New Mexico.

Aug 5   From Sir Henry Lytton Bulwer. Copy. UkLPR. mDWs. Requests
information regarding the seizure of the Brig *Joseph Albino* at San
Francisco.

Aug 5   From Truman Smith. ALS. NhD. mDW 30787. Makes suggestions regarding appointments; expects Congress will resolve current issue according to DW's views and pledges his support.

Aug 5   Recommendations from Roger Sherman Baldwin, for Frederick
W. Northrop—consul at Belfast or Glasgow (ALS. CtY. mDW
30783); from Solon Borland, for the Little Rock *Arkansas State Gazette and Democrat*—public printer (ALS. DNA, RG 59. mDW
53652); from Henry Clay, for the *Knoxville* (Tenn.) *Whig*—public
printer (ALS. DNA, RG 59. 53595); from Mrs. H. Balch Macomb, for
J. A. Williamson—any position (ALS. NhHi. mDW 30784).

Aug 6   To Millard Fillmore. ALS. NBuHi. mDW 30791. Van Tyne,
p. 423. Makes suggestions regarding the letter to Governor [Peter
Hansbrough] Bell of Texas; is just completing the message to
Congress.

Aug 6   To Franklin Haven. LS. MH–H. mDW 30794. Accuses "our New
England friends" of unnecessarily provoking southerners, "on whom
we have relied for the protection of our industry."

Aug 6   To Elisha Whittlesey. LS. OClWHi. mDW 30795. Thanks him
for a letter from James Young commenting on the Washington portrait which hangs in the State Department.

Aug 6   From Charles Henry Thomas. ALS. NhHi. mDW 30797. *PC*, 2:
380–382. Reports on DW's cattle and the general state of the Marshfield farm.

Aug 6   Presidential message on Texas and New Mexico—drafted by
DW. Printed. *Cong. Globe*, 31st Cong., 1st sess., pp. 1525–1526.

Aug 7   To Millard Fillmore. ALS. NBuHi. mDW 30802. Transmits
[Daniel Dewey] Barnard's nomination (U.S. minister to Prussia).

[Aug 7]   To Millard Fillmore. ALS. NBuHi. mDW 30804. Van Tyne,
p. 421. Reports the president's message has been well received.

Aug 7   To Peter Harvey.   132

Aug 7   To Charles Augustus Stetson. ALS. NhD. mDW 30811. Thanks
Stetson for fish and the offer of wine; discusses travel plans.

Aug 7   To Worcester Webster. Typed copy. NhD. mDW 30814. Hopes to
be in New Hampshire in another month.

Aug 7   From Edmund M. Evans. ALS. DNA, RG 59. mDW 54989. Accepts appointment as secretary to the president, with authority to
sign land patents in his name.

Aug 7   From William A. Weeks. ALS. DNA, RG 59. mDW 56860. Reports forwarding despatches to London; is expecting others to arrive
with the *Cambria*.

Aug 8   To George P. Fisher. LC. DNA, RG 76. mDWs. Encloses despatches and papers relative to the seizure and detention of the Bark
Yeoman by Brazilian authorities.

Aug 8   To John Alexander McClernand. Printed. *W & S*, 16: 557. Replies
to an inquiry concerning Robert M. Walsh's claim for compensation
while serving as chargé d'affaires in Mexico.

Aug 8   From Pierre Fleurimont (enclosures: petition, affidavits, etc.).
LC. CaOOA. mDW 30816. Copy. UkLPR. Petitions for redress for
damages and injury caused when British soldiers forcefully removed
deserters from his house in Sault Ste. Marie, Michigan.

Aug 8   From Robert Walsh. ALS. MHi. mDW 30830. Reports his activity
as U.S. consul at Paris.

Aug 8   From William A. Weeks. ALS. DNA, RG 59. mDW 56861. Reports having forwarded despatches just received from the U.S. legation at London.

Aug 8   Recommendation from Hamilton Fish, for Daniel Dewey Barnard—U.S. minister to Prussia (Presscopy. DLC. mDW 30815).

[Aug 9]   To Franklin Haven. ALS. MH H. mDW 30832. W & S, 16: 557–558. Reports on the appropriation and Texas boundary bills and on prospective cabinet nominees Charles Mynn Conrad and Thomas McKean Thompson McKennan.

Aug 9   To John E. Thayer & Brother [Nathaniel Thayer]. ALS. MHi. mDW 30835. Expresses mortification at the recall of John M. Marston but supposes nothing can be done now.

Aug 9   From [Sir Henry Lytton Bulwer]. AL draft. UkLPR. mDW 30836. Advises caution in the appointment of U.S. consuls in Canada.

Aug 9   From Sir Henry Lytton Bulwer. LS. DLC. mDW 30839. AL draft UkLPR. mDW 30842. Suggests they get together for a conversation on topics of mutual concern.

Aug 9   From Charles Augustus Davis.   *133*

Aug 9   From Peter Hamilton. Copy. DNA, RG 59. mDW 56529. Reports securing witnesses from among the "Contoy prisoners" for the upcoming trial of Narciso Lopez.

Aug 10   To Franklin Haven.   *135*

Aug 10   To John P. Gaines. LS. Or–Ar. mDWs. Is having a packet of books forwarded to Gaines in compliance with a joint resolution of Congress.

Aug 10   To Samuel Lawrence. Copy. NiHi. mDW 30853. Van Tyne, p. 424. Calls Eliot's nomination "excellent"; reports "The Machine of the Government seems beginning to move again."

Aug 10   To Moses Stuart. Printed. PC, 2: 383–384. Comments on the president and the cabinet and on the progress of the Compromise bills; reports Stuart's book is being well received in southern circles.

Aug 10   "The Question Settled." Unsigned editorial. *Daily National Intelligencer*, Aug 10, 1850.

Aug 10   Application from Walter Newman Haldeman, for the *Louisville* (Ky.) *Morning Courier*—public printer (ALS. DNA, RG 59. mDW 53589).

[Aug 11]   To [Peter Harvey]. ALS. NhD. mDW 30855. Van Tyne, pp. 431–432 (in error as to date and recipient). Reports on developments relative to the Texas boundary and California bills; would prefer "a respectable Democrat" to the election of a Whig with Abolitionist or Free Soil tendencies.

Aug 12   To Charles E. Sherman. Draft. CtY. mDW 30861. Withdraws as legal consultant in certain cases because of his official status in the government.

Aug 12   To Charles Henry Thomas. ALS. NhD. mDW 30864. Gershom Bradford, "The Unknown Webster," *Old-Time New England*, 49 (Fall, 1953): 62–63. Discusses farm business; assesses the position of the Massachusetts congressional delegation on the Texas bill and specifically derides "our own worthy representative" (Orin Fowler) for his vacillating stand.

Aug 12   From Robert Greenhow. ALS. DNA, RG 59. mDW 56174. Asks the U.S. govenment to assist Mexico in establishing the ratio of the Mexican *vara* to the yard by providing it with a "graduated standard."

Aug 12   From Robert Greenhow (enclosures: [Robert P. Letcher] to [Jose Maria de Lacunza], Aug 5, 1850; Lacunza to Letcher, Aug 6 1850). ALS. DNA, RG 59. mDW 56718. Reports on his mission to Mexico in search of documents pertaining to claims pending before the U.S. board of commissioners in Washington.

[Aug 13]   To Millard Fillmore. LS. NBuHi. mDW 30868. Reports Thomas McKean Thompson McKennan is starting for Washington today.

Aug 13   To Joel Furrill. LS. NhD. mDWs. Discusses a financial matter relating to the estate of Enoch L. Hatch, deceased U.S. consul to the Sandwich Islands.

Aug 13   To Peter Harvey. Printed. *W & S*, 16: 561. Reports on the Texas boundary and California bills; expects both will pass.

Aug 13   To Truman Smith. ALS. CtHi. mDW30871. Agrees with Connecticut chief justice Thomas Scott William's high opinion of "your speech" (in the Senate, July 8, on the Compromise bill).

Aug 14   To John Jordan Crittenden. ALS. MHi. mDW 30872. Invites him to dine today at five.

Aug 14   To Millard Fillmore. ALS. NBuHi. mDW 30874. Returns a letter from Daniel Dewey Barnard.

Aug 14   To [Peter Harvey?]. ALS. NhHi. mDW 30876. Van Tyne, p. 424. Urges Harvey and Fearing to vote for Samuel Atkins Eliot and then come south; reports Ashmun is giving a "masterly speech" on Texas.

Aug 14   Bill for $2.50 from M. Titcomb for brandy. AD. NhHi. mDW 40398.

Aug 15   To George Folsom. ALS. RPB–JCB. mDWs. Introduces John Carter Brown of Rhode Island who will be travelling in Europe.

Aug 15   To William Cabell Rives. ALS. RPB–JCB. mDWs. Introduces John Carter Brown.

Aug 15   To George Ticknor. Printed. Curtis, 2: 471–472. Fears a close vote on the Texas bill; reports on the cabinet; describes the president's character and temperament.

Aug 15   From George P. Fisher. LS. DNA, RG 76. Inquires about documents needed by the commission established to adjust claims against Brazil.

Aug 16   To Millard Fillmore. ALS. NBuHi. mDW 30877. Reports "the new Secretaries" have been sworn into office; is inquiring about "Mr. Dickinson's suggestions."

Aug 16   To Peter Harvey. Copy. NhHi. mDW 30879. Van Tyne, pp. 424–425. Wishes Clay would visit Boston; declares Eliot is needed in Washington; reports the cabinet is now complete.

Aug 16   From Joseph W. Beck. ALS. DNA, RG 59. mDW 54927. Accepts appointment as justice of the peace for the District of Columbia.

Aug 16   From [Sir Henry Lytton Bulwer]. AL draft. UkLPR. mDW 30881. Encloses a copy of a despatch on the status of Greytown in a dispute between Nicaragua and Costa Rica.

Aug 16   From John McLean.   137

Aug 17   To Millard Fillmore. ALS. NBuHi. mDW 30885. Writes concerning nominations of judges for Minnesota and Oregon.

Aug 17   From [Sir Henry Lytton Bulwer]. AL draft. UkLPR. mDW
30888. Encloses an extract from a memorandum on the negotiations
for the Clayton-Bulwer treaty; suggests other papers be laid before
the Senate

Aug 17   From Sir Henry Lytton Bulwer. Copy. UkLPR. mDWs. Writes
concerning an agreement negotiated by John Middleton Clayton for
British, French and American intervention to prevent hostilities between the Dominican Republic and Haiti.

Aug 17   From Deming Jarves. ALS. NhHi. mDW 30891. PC, 2: 384.
Presents DW with a large flint glass bowl.

Aug 17   Bill from Walter & Peck for provisions, through Sept 27. DS.
DLC. mDW 40417.

[Aug 19?]   To Millard Fillmore. LS. DLC. mDW 30893. Praises James
Brown Clay's service as U.S. chargé d'affaires to Portugal; suggests
that Clay be asked to complete negotiations for a convention with
that country.

Aug 19   To George P. Fisher. LS. DNA, RG 76. Reports that an application will be made to the Brazilian Minister of Foreign Affairs for papers required by the commission appointed to adjust claims against
Brazil, established under the treaty of Jan 27, 1849.

Aug 19   To Francis Hall. LS. MBU. mDW 30895. Thinks Hall's recommendation ought to be enough to enable "Mr Melvin" to retain his
position.

Aug 19   To Deming Jarves. LS. draft. NhHi. mDW 30896. Van Tyne,
pp. 426–427. Thanks Jarves for the flint glass bowl.

Aug 19   From Thomas Donoho. ALS. DNA, RG 59. mDW 54981. Accepts appointment as justice of the peace for the District of
Columbia.

Aug 20   To [Sir Henry Lytton Bulwer]. Copy. UkLPR. mDWs. Replies to
Bulwer's inquiry about U.S. cooperation with Britain and France to
prevent hostilities between the Dominican Republic and Haiti.

Aug 20   From Anthony Hyde. ALS. DNA, RG 59. mDW 55029. Accepts
appointment as justice of the peace for Washington, D.C.

Aug 20   Application from Lampkin & Adams, for the Athens, Georgia
Southern Whig—public printers (LS. DNA, RG 59. mDW 53719).

[Aug 21]   To [Millard Fillmore]. ALS. NBuHi. mDW 30900. Reports "Mr.
Ketchum" will leave for the East tomorrow in a "very important
matter"; suggests that employment be found for "Mr. Collier" in
New York.

[Aug 21]   To Millard Fillmore. ALS. NBuHi. mDW 30903. Reports he is
"doing the needful, respecting outfits, etc."

[Aug 21]   To Millard Fillmore. ALS. NBuHi. mDW 30905. Suggests "this
Gentleman" may be "a little touched, in his mind & faculties."

[Aug 21? 1850]   To Daniel Fletcher Webster. ALS. NN. mDW 39177.
Asks Fletcher to "be more sparing of your Telegraphs," since they
cost DW "a mint of money."

Aug 21   From Benjamin Robbins Curtis. ALS. DLC. mDW 30907. Acknowledges with thanks a copy of DW's speech of July 17th.

Aug 21   From Edward Everett. ALS. MHi. mDW 30914. Strongly protests [John] Miller's removal as despatch agent in London; advises
against R[obert] H[owe] Gould's appointment to any position.

Aug 21   From William A. Weeks. ALS. DNA, RG 59. mDW 56862. Reports forwarding despatches bound to and from the U.S. legation at London.

Aug 21   Recommendation from Hamilton Fish, for Francis S. Lippitt—U.S. district court judge in California (Presscopy. DLC. mDW 30918).

Aug 22   To Millard Fillmore. ALS. NBuHi. mDW 30919. Reports the department heads are planning to confer; thinks something should be done for Indiana, "in the person of Mr [Courtland] Cushing."

[Aug 22]   To [Millard Fillmore]. ALS. NBuHi. mDW 30944. Defends Ashmun; reports consulting with him this morning on ways to rally friends."

Aug 22   To William Alexander Graham. LS. NcU. mDW 30922. Hamilton. *Graham*, 3: 365. Advises him of a meeting of department heads at the State Department this afternoon.

Aug 22   To Peter Hamilton. Copy. DNA, RG 59. mDW 56528. Approves Hamilton's actions relative to the Contoy prisoners.

Aug 22   To Robert Cumming Schenck. LS fragment. MeWC. mDW 31980. LC. DNA, RG 59. Advises him of James Lugenbeel's terms of service as U.S. agent in Liberia.

Aug 22   To [Edward D.] Sohier and [Charles A.] Welch. ALS. MBSpnea. mDW 30923. Is amazed to learn that "Mr Greenough" is suing him.

Aug 22   From Henry Clay. LS. ViU. mDW 30926. Responds to the president's proposal that his son James Brown Clay return to Lisbon to negotiate a convention with Portugal.

Aug 22   From Thomas Corwin (with DW to Sir Henry Lytton Bulwer, Aug 24, 1850). Copy. DNA, RG 79. Writes regarding the British Brig *Joseph Albino*, seized by customs authorities at San Francisco in December, 1849.

Aug 22   From Joseph Mayo. ALS. NhHi. mDW 30928. Acknowledges a copy of DW's July 17th speech; praises his defense of the Union and Southern rights.

Aug 22   From Richard Rush. ALS. DLC. mDW 30932. Reflects on his service as U.S. minister to France; expresses concern for the Union.

Aug 22   From Charles Augustus Stetson. ALS. NcU. mDW 31018. Hamilton, *Graham*, 3: 383–384. Speaks critically of the circumstances of Capt. Robert Field Stockton's resignation from the Navy and demands that something be done.

Aug 22   Application from John Watkins—superintendent of the branch mint at New Orleans (ALS. DLC. mDW 30936).

Aug 23   To James Brown Clay. LS. DLC. mDW 30938. Asks him to return to Lisbon and negotiate an agreement with Portugal respecting claims.

Aug 23   To Millard Fillmore. ALS. NBuHi. mDW 30942. Transmits papers and letters.

Aug 23   To Herman Day Gould. LS. LU–Ar. mDW 30946. Reports that a certified copy of an act for the relief of Benjamin T. Smith has been transmitted to the commissioner of pensions.

Aug 23   From Abbott Lawrence. LC. MH–H. mDWs. Will continue his practice of writing private letters to the secretary of state; discusses the importance of the upcoming London Exhibition for U.S. commerce; thinks the U.S. will have to use gold to pay off its trade debt with Europe.

Aug 23   *From Alphonso Taft.*   137
Aug 23   Application from B. R. McKennie & Co., for the *Nashville*
         (Tenn.) *True Whig*—public printers (ALS. DNA, RG 59. mDW
         53591).
Aug 24   To Sir Henry Lytton Bulwer (enclosure: Thomas Corwin to DW,
         Aug 22, 1850). Copy. UkLPR. mDWs. Encloses the treasury secre-
         tary's reply in the case of the *Joseph Albino.*
Aug. 24   To Edward Everett. ALS. MHi. mDW 30951. Announces the
         reappointment of John Miller (despatch agent at London); promises
         to look out for Gould.
Aug 24   From Charles March. ALS. NhHi. mDW 30952. Presents some
         Madeira wine.
[Aug 25]   To [?]. ALS. NhHi. mDW 31264. Reports action in Congress
         on "the [Texas] bill."
Aug 25   From Cornelius Conway Felton. ALS. NhHi. mDW 30954. Sends
         a copy of the Daily Advertiser "containing a short communication
         (written by myself) upon the *Captatio verborum* question which Mr.
         Mann has so absurdly and ignorantly raised."
Aug 25   Recommendation from William C. Dawson, for the Athens,
         Georgia, *Southern Whig*—public printer (ALS. DNA, RG 59. mDW
         53721).
Aug 26   To Millard Fillmore. ALS. NBuHi. mDW 30957. Van Tyne, pp.
         427–428. Discusses the appointment of a secretary of the interior;
         encourages Fillmore to consider the credentials of Charles J. Jenkins
         of Georgia.
Aug 26   To Millard Fillmore. ALS. NhExP. mDW 30961. Comments on
         policy of providing outfits for missions overseas; advises "you are
         not bound to fill vacancies, unless you think the public service re-
         quires you to do so."
Aug 26   To [Peter Harvey?]. ALS. NhHi. mDW 30963. Complains of
         rheumatism; sees good prospects for "the [Compromise] Bills."
[*Aug 26*]   *"The Important Week" (Editorial).*   140
Aug 28   To William Alexander Graham. LS. NcU. mDW 30976. Hamil-
         ton, *Graham*, 3: 375. Cannot see Graham today but will call at his
         department tomorrow.
Aug 28   To [Henry D.] Moore. ALS. PHC. mDW 30977. Van Tyne, p.
         633. Thanks him for two bottles of liniment, stating that "once a
         year, at least, & sometimes oftener, I have a turn of lumbago."
Aug 28   From John Macpherson Berrien. ALS. DNA, RG 59. mDW
         53722. Asks DW to peruse a letter and see if there is any way he can
         accommodate the writers.
Aug 28   From William Alexander Graham. ALS. NcU. mDWs. Hamil-
         ton, *Graham*, 3: 375. Wishes to see him today on a subject of "some
         public importance."
Aug 28   From William Cabell Rives. ALS. CLU. mDW 30979. Writes re-
         garding asylum for Hungarian exile Bertalan Szmere.
Aug 29   To Millard Fillmore. LS. NBuHi. mDW 30982. Transmits
         Charles Howard Edward's nomination to be "Clerk to the Commis-
         sioner under the Convention with Brazil."
Aug 29   From William H. Morell. ALS. DNA, RG 59. mDW 56863.
         States that J. E. Kennedy of Boston has been given a passport, as
         courier for Liverpool.

Aug 29   From Amos Tuck and John L. Hayes. LS. DNA, RG 76. State the claim of the owners of the schooner *John* against Britain.

Aug 30   To William Alexander Graham. LS. NcU. mDWs. Hamilton, *Graham*, 3: 377. Invites him to call at the State Department before 2 p.m.

Aug 30   To Anne Charlotte Lynch. AL. NN. mDW 30984. *Memoirs of Anne C. L. Botta*, written by her friends (New York, 1894), p. 366. Thanks her for a bouquet.

Aug 30   To Mary Scott. AL. UPB. mDWs. Sends her a bouquet of flowers given to him by Anne Charlotte Lynch.

Aug 30   From Alfred Ray. ALS. DNA, RG 59. mDW 55080. Accepts appointment as justice of the peace for Washington, D.C.

Aug 30   Application from John Johnston—despatch bearer (Typed copy. MiD. mDW 30986).

Aug 31   To Edward Claudius Herrick. LS. CtY. mDW 30995. Agrees to transmit with the diplomatic mail a packet for Abbott Lawrence from the American Association for the Advancement of Science.

Aug 31   From Edward Everett. ALS. MHi. mDW 30991. Sends the two volumes of his *Orations and Speeches* "to be published today" as an example of "typography and getting up"; comments on the "vast & complicated" nature of the American governmental system.

Aug 31   Application from John Crumby—appraiser in New York custom house (ALS. DLC. mDW 30997).

Aug 31   Recommendations from Benjamin Robbins Curtis, for George Ticknor Curtis—U.S. attorney in Massachuetts (ALS. DLC. mDW 31000); from Samuel R. Thurston, for the Oregon City *Oregon Spectator*—public printer (ALS. DNA, RG 59. mDW 54453).

[Aug]   To Millard Fillmore (with reply). ALS. NhD. mDW 31008. Submits the draft of his letter notifying Robert Walsh of his recall (U.S. consul at Paris).

[Aug/Sept]   To Charles Augustus Stetson. ALS. Mrs. N. R. Buchsbaum, Baltimore, Md. mDW 31011. Cannot go north before the House votes on the Texas boundary bill.

[Aug]   From Millard Fillmore (with DW to Fillmore, [Aug, 1850]). ALS. NhD. mDW 31008. Concurs with DW's proposal to recall Robert Walsh.

Aug   From Ebenezer Price et al. LS. NhHi. mDW 31012. *Correspondence between Daniel Webster and his New Hampshire Neighbors* (Washington, 1850), pp. 3–6. Express support and gratitude for DW's defense of the Union.

[Aug]   Bill from Dennis [illegible] for $424.25 for carriage hire and supplies. AD. NhHi. mDW 40403.

Sept 1   To Charles Augustus Stetson. ALS. DLC. mDW 31016. Expresses disapproval of the way in which Commodore Robert Field Stockton was driven out of the Navy.

Sept 2   To William Alexander Graham (enclosure: Charles Augustus Stetson to DW, Aug. 22, 1850). ALS. NcU. mDW 31017. Hamilton, *Graham*, 3: 383–384. Transmits a letter from Stetson about the resignation of Stockton from the Navy.

Sept 2   To William Alexander Graham. LS. NcU. mDW 31021. Introduces William J[oseph] Hubbard of Boston.

Sept 2   To Franklin Haven. ALS. MH–H. mDW 31022. Discusses a financial matter; plans to go north once the House has decided "the
important questions before it."

Sept 2   From John McCutchen. ALS. DNA, RG 59. mDW 55072. Accepts
appointment as justice of the peace in Washington, D.C.

Sept 3   To Don Mariano Arista. Draft. NhIli. mDW 31023. Van Tyne,
pp. 429–430. Accepts membership in the Geographical and Statistical Society of Mexico.

Sept 3   To John Macpherson Berrien. Draft. DNA, RG 59. mDW 53724.
Explains why he cannot appoint Lampkin & Adams printers of the
law.

Sept 3   To Thomas Corwin. LS. DLC. mDW 31026. Introduces Samuel
Kettell of the *Boston Courier* and Chandler R. Ransom of the *Boston
Bee* as loyal supporters of the Administration; commends the *Boston
Advertiser*.

Sept 3   To Millard Fillmore. LS. NBuHi. mDW 31028. Van Tyne, pp.
428–429. Introduces William J[oseph] Hubbard, here on a matter
concerning France and the Sandwich Islands.

Sept 3   To William Alexander Graham. LS. Nc–Ar. mDWs. Hamilton,
Graham, 3: 384. Introduces the editors of the *Boston Courier* and
the *Boston Bee*, both Administration supporters, and also commends
the *Boston Advertiser*.

Sept 3   To Hannibal Hamlin. LS. DNA, RG 46. mDW 52024. Encloses
papers pertaining to the appointment and confirmation of William
N. Adams as U.S. consul at Santiago de Cuba.

Sept 3   From John Macpherson Berrien (with ANS by DW). ALS. DNA,
RG 59. mDW 53723. Inquires whether DW has the authority to appoint Lampkin & Adams printers of the laws.

Sept 3   From Theodore S. Fay. ALS. DLC. mDW 31032. Introduces Dr.
H. Adami, son of a senator from Bremen, Germany.

Sept 3   Department of State circular on Cuban invasion. Printed D.
DNA, RG 59. mDW 55152.

Sept 3   Bill from Thomas Pursell for $6.12 1/2 for six "waiters" (trays).
ADS. NhHi. mDW 40411.

Sept 4   From John Miller to William S. Derrick. ALS. DNA, RG 59. mDW
56866. Transmits despatches and returns a bag which by mistake
had been mailed direct to the U.S. legation in London instead of
being addressed to the despatch agent at Boston, thereby incurring
heavy postage.

Sept 4   From William A. Weeks. ALS. DNA, RG 59. mDW 56864. Reports placing the London despatches in the charge of S. R. Spaulding.

Sept 4   Receipt for advance of $114 to G[ilbert] L. Thompson. DS. NhD.
mDW 40381.

Sept 4   Account with John Pettibone for coal and for ice tickets, through
Dec 23, 1851. AD. NhHi. mDW 40405.

[Sept 5]   To Franklin Haven. ALS. MH–H. mDW 31034. *W & S*, 16: 561.
Comments on the status of the Texas bill in the House; sees "a fearful crisis."

[p/m Sept 5]   To Samuel Jaudon. ALS. NHi. mDW 31036. Sees no need
for Jaudon and Blatchford to come to Washington merely because of
"the matter, to which you refer."

Sept 6   To William Duer. ALS. NhD. mDW 31038. Invites him to dine.
Sept 6   To Millard Fillmore. LS. NBuHi. mDW 31039. Writes regarding
the commercial agency at Curaçao.
Sept 6   From Charles Allen. ALS. DLC. mDW 31041. Reports his impressions of Thomas D. Sargent and advises that other references
be obtained.
Sept 6   From Charles Pelham Curtis. ALS. DLC. mDW 31044. Discusses
the appointment of a new U.S. attorney for Massachusetts; is cha-
grined that five Massachusetts Congressmen contributed to the defeat of the Texas bill.
Sept 6   From William A. Weeks. ALS. DNA, RG 59. mDW 56865. Reports receiving and forwarding despatches to and from Britain.
Sept 7   To Millard Fillmore (enclosure: John W. Davis to Zachary Taylor, Feb 18, 1849). LS. DNA, RG 46. mDW 51204. Transmits the report of the commissioner to China for communication to the Senate
in accordance with a resolution of Sept 5, 1850.
Sept 7   To Alexander H[ugh] H[olmes] Stuart. LS. ViHi. mDW 31049.
Alexander F. Robertson, *Alexander Hugh Holmes Stuart 1807–1891*
(Richmond, Va., 1925), p. 52. Asks whether Stuart will accept nomination to be secretary of the interior.
Sept 7   From William Alexander Graham. ALS. Nc–Ar. mDWs. Sends
copy of a private letter by Commander L. M. Powell of the U.S. ship
John Adams describing operations of British cruisers "in the suppres-
sion, or pretending to suppress it," of the slave trade on the coast of
Africa.
Sept 7   From David Spangler Kaufman. ALS. NhD. mDW 31047. Asks
assurances that Fillmore's message and DW's letter to the governor of Texas were not intended to be menacing.
[Sept 8]   To Samuel Jaudon. ALS. NN. mDW 31054. Asks when he may
expect to hear regarding "a confidential matter."
Sept 8   From Ladislaus Ujhazimff (with English translation). ALS.
DLC. mDW 31056. Expresses gratitude for Szmere's appointment as
bearer of despatches from Paris to the U.S.; asks DW to use his in-
fluence on behalf of other Hungarian exiles.
Sept 8   Promissory note for $1,000 payable to Rufus Choate. DS. MHi.
mDW 40407.
Sept 9   To Stephen Arnold Douglas (with Anthony Ten Eyck to James
M. Mason, June 28, 1852; enclosure: memorandum in support of
Ten Eyck's memorial to Congress). Copy. DNA, RG 59. mDW 55643.
Submits information relative to Anthony Ten Eyck's tenure as U.S.
commissioner to the Sandwich Islands.
[Sept 9]   To Samuel Jaudon. ALS. NN. mDW 31063. Asks for something-
definite concerning "the subject we have written about."
[Sept 9]   To [?]. ALS. NhD. mDW 25820. Advises him to join [William]
Duer in taking charge of "this Texan bill" in the House.
Sept 9   From Amos B. Corwine. (with DW to Fillmore, Feb 15, 1851).
Extract. DNA, RG 46. mDW 51247. Discusses difficulties arising
from the "Contribution Tax" imposed on Americans doing business
in Panama.
Sept 10   To Thomas H. Bayly (enclosure: draft of bill to reorganize the
State Department). Copy. DNA, RG 46. mDW 51185. Submits recom-

mendations for the reorganization and enlargement of the State Department staff.

Sept 10   To John McClernand (enclosure: DW to Thomas H. Bayly, Sept 10, 1850). LS. DNA. RG 46. mDW 51183. Encloses a copy of a letter to the chairman of the House Ways and Means Committee.

Sept 10   To Peter Harvey.   *143*

Sept 10   From Alexander H[ugh] H[olmes] Stuart. ALS. NhHi. mDW 31065. Agrees to become secretary of the interior.

Sept 11   To Millard Fillmore. ALS. NBuHi. mDW 31068. Van Tyne, pp. 430–431. Discusses the appointments of Philip H. Greely, Jr. as customs collector and William Hayden as postmaster in Boston.

Sept 11   To Mrs. H[arriet?] Webster. LS. NhD. mDWs. Says he cannot "effect anything" unless "Dr. Dalton" comes to Washington, but he will give his aid.

Sept 11   From G[eorge] B[artle] (with AN by DW). Telegram. NBuHi. mDW 31072. "He [Alexander H. H. Stuart] accepts."

Sept 12   To Franklin Haven.   *144*

Sept 12   To Stephen Pleasonton. LS. NhD. mDW 31085. Writes concerning the estate of George C. Betton, a mariner who died on St. Helena in April, 1849.

Sept   12   From [Sir Henry Lytton Bulwer]. AL draft. UkLPR. mDW 31087. Offers congratulations (on the passage of the Compromise bills?); makes observations regarding the Canadian reciprocity bill.

Sept 12   From Gilbert C. Russell (with DW to Fillmore, Jan 17, 1851). Copy. NBuHi. mDW 32196. Defends his requests to look at papers at the State Department which pertain to the [Joseph?] De la Francia claim.

Sept 13   To Hugh Birckhead. LS. MdHi. mDW 31089. Asks whether Birckhead has received the letter he wrote to him a few days ago.

Sept 13   To Peter Harvey.   *146*

Sept 13   To Gilbert C. Russell (with DW to Fillmore, Jan 17, 1851). Copy. NBuHi. mDW 32197. Denies permission to look through State Department files for papers relevant to the De la Francia claim.

Sept 13   From Edward Everett, with extract from Abbott Lawrence to Everett, Aug 16, 1850.   *146*

Sept 13   From Albert Fearing. ALS. NhHi. mDW 31101. Introduces Marshal [Francis] Tukey; reports general satisfaction in Boston with the territorial settlement.

Sept 14   To William B. Lewis. ALS. NhHi. mDW 31103. Notes the recently approved Compromise measures; gives assurances of the Administration's future conduct.

Sept 14   To the U.S. Senate. LS. DNA, RG 46. mDW 51607. Transmits the Rev. R[alph] R[andolph] Gurley's report on Liberia.

Sept 14   To Robert Wheaton. LS. NNPM. mDW 31107. Writes regarding Erick Glad's claim against France.

Sept 14   From Angel Calderon de la Barca. ALS. DLC. mDW 31110. Promises to do what he can for "Mrs Graffam's son."

Sept 14   From Caleb Cushing.   *149*

Sept 14   Application from Henry Alexander Scammell Dearborn—collector or postmaster at Boston, or some other position (ALS. NhHi. mDW 31116).

[Sept 15, 1850]   To Daniel Fletcher Webster. AL. Dr. George L. Hamilton, West Hartford, Ct. mDWs. "Will look after the interests of "Mr. Ropes," "Mr. [Francis] Tukey," and "Mr. Lincoln"; will not retain resentment against "Mr. Greenough" who attempted to "disgrace & distance me"; reports "a very good spirit" on the tariff; commends Henry Sargent.

Sept 15   To [?].   *150*

Sept 16   To Peter Harvey. ALS. NhHi. mDW 31123. *PC*, 2: 389. Comments on any plans there may be for his reception in Boston, and asks that [Samuel Atkins] Eliot be invited.

Sept 16   From John Page. ALS. DNA, RG 59. mDW 55051. Accepts appointment as justice of the peace in Washington D.C.

Sept 16   From Fitz Henry Warren. ALS. DNA, RG 59. mDW 53997. Encloses a letter from J[ohn] Wright on behalf of the Madison *Wisconsin Statesman*.

Sept 16   Account with Isaac Hill for firewood, through June 4, 1851. ADS. NhHi. mDW 40537.

Sept 17   To Millard Fillmore. ALS. NBuHi. mDW 31126. Advises sending [Courtland] Cushing's nomination (U.S. chargé d'affaires to Ecuador) to the Senate.

Sept 17   To James A. Pearce. LS. MdHi. mDW 31128. Replies to a request that copies of documents be made for the editor of the Alexander Hamilton papers.

Sept 17   From William Erigena Robinson. ALS. NhD. mDW 31130. Asks for a delay in any proceeding to extradite Joseph Brennan, a fugitive wanted in Ireland.

Sept 17   From William A. Weeks. ALS. DNA, RG 59. mDW 56868. Reports forwarding despatches received from the U.S. legation at London.

[rec'd Sept 17]   Application from William W. Wyman, for the Madison *Wisconsin Statesman*—public printer (AL with signature page missing. DNA, RG 59. mDW 54014).

Sept 17   Agreement with G[ilbert] L. Thompson respecting 5 shares of Union Land Company stock. DS. NhD. mDW 40381.

Sept 18   To Millard Fillmore. LS. NBuHi. mDW 31132. Recommends the reappointment of Joseph R. Croskey as U.S. consul at Cowes and Southampton.

Sept 18   To Peter Harvey. ALS. NhHi. mDW 31136. Introduces William A. Bradley, who is coming to Boston on "important business."

Sept 18   To Alexander Ramsey. LS. MnHi. mDW 31138. Is glad to hear good news about the Whig Party in Minnesota.

Sept 18   To Robert Charles Winthrop. Printed. *PC*, 2: 389–390. Asks him to inform Frothingham as to what might be done for a destitute woman named "Mrs. [Caroline L.] Eustis."

Sept 18   From Jeremiah van Rensselaer. DS. DLC. mDW 31141. Resolutions of Detroit Common Council thanking Clay, Cass and DW for their efforts to resolve sectional controversy.

Sept 18   From William A. Weeks. ALS. DNA, RG 59. mDW 56869. Reports on despatches forwarded to and from the State Department.

[Sept 19]   To Millard Fillmore. ALS. NBuHi. mDW 31144. *PC*, 2: 390. *Diplomatic Papers*, 2. Prepares Fillmore for his meeting with Amin Bey of Turkey.

Sept 19   To Millard Fillmore. ALS. NBuHi. mDW 31148. Recommends
the immediate withdrawal of George A. Porter's nomination (U.S.
consul at Tripoli).

Sept 19   To Robert M. Patterson. LS. DNA, RG 104. mDW 57149. Asks
for the information requested by Thomson Hankey, Jr., deputy governor of the Bank of England.

Sept 19   From Sir Henry Lytton Bulwer. ALS draft. UkLPR. mDW
31150. LS. UkLPR. mDW 31156. Discusses difficulties created by
[Ephraim George] Squier's treaty with Nicaragua.

Sept 19   From Robert Walsh. ALS. NhHi. mDW 31161. Protests his removal as U.S. consul at Paris.

Sept 20   To Caleb Cushing. LS with postscript in DW's hand. DLC. mDW
31165. Fuess, *Cushing*, 2: 88. Speaks despondently of his debts;
wishes to settle matters between them.

[Sept 20]   To Millard Fillmore. ALS. NBuHi. mDW 31168. Advises the
immediate withdrawal of the Porter nomination.

Sept 20   To [Millard Fillmore]. LS. NBuHi. mDW 31170. Identifies
George A. Porter as a former consul at Constantinople.

Sept 20   To Millard Fillmore. LS. NBuHi. mDW 31172. Asks if his clerk
might copy a list of consuls.

Sept 20   From James H. Causten. ALS copy. DLC. mDW 31174. Discusses his claim against Mexico.

Sept 20   From Charles March. ALS. NhHi. mDW 31180. Inquires about
DW's plans to return north.

Sept 20   Account with William H. Harrover for $6.70 for tinware,
through Jan 14, 1851. AD. NhHi. mDW 40477.

Sept 21   To Ebenezer Price et al. Draft revised by DW. NhHi. mDW
31182. *Correspondence Between Daniel Webster and His New Hampshire Neighbors* (Washington, 1850), pp. 7–10. Emphasizes the
blessings of the Union; reminisces about his family and friends
around Salisbury.

Sept 21   From James Brown Clay. ALS draft. DLC. mDW 34740. Explains his views of the negotiations with Portugal; will return to
Lisbon only to conclude the convention and with no desire to remain
longer.

Sept 21   From Horatio J. Harris. ALS. DNA, RG 59. mDW 56531. Reports hearing declarations, but having little hard evidence of another
military expedition against Cuba.

Sept 22   From Amos B. Corwine (with DW to Fillmore, Feb 15, 1851).
Extract. DNA, RG 46. mDW 51254. Reports evidence that authorities
of New Grenada are seeking to "oppress" Americans in Panama.

Sept 22   From Caleb Cushing. ALS. MWalB. mDW 31189. Writes regarding Rock Island; reports he is having "Mr. [William] Brackett's
claims" investigated.

Sept 23   To Millard Fillmore. ALS. NBuHi. mDW 31191. Reports his
clerks are still working on a synopsis of the applications for foreign
and territorial appointments.

Sept 23   To Chevalier Johann Georg Hülsemann. LS. Austrian State Archives, Vienna. mDW 31193. Agrees to see him at the State Department.

Sept 23   To William Henry Seward. LS. NRU. mDW 31194. Invites him
to dinner.

Sept 23 *From Henry Alexander Scammell Dearborn.*   *151*

Sept 23 From John Henry Hopkins. ALS. NhHi. mDW 31203. Expresses concern about the "enormous and increasing evil" of unrestricted immigration, and submits for DW's consideration the manuscript of an article he has written on the subject.

Sept 23 From A. G. Rice. ALS. DNA, RG 59. mDW 56872. Will sail on Oct 5, and asks that despatches for Paris or London be sent to his New York hotel.

Sept 24 To Sir Henry Lytton Bulwer. Copy. UkLPR. mDWs. Expresses mortification upon seeing a letter from Ephraim George Squier in the *New York Herald* relative to the treaty with Nicaragua.

[Sept 24] To William W. Corcoran. ALS. DLC. mDW 31206. Asks him to see whether Senator [Daniel Stevens] Dickinson might report and pass "the [Mexican indemnity] Bill" this morning.

Sept 24 To James A. Pearce. LS. MdHi. mDW 31208. Replies to an inquiry relative to public documents to which the state of Alabama is entitled.

Sept 24 From [Anonymous]. AL. NhHi. mDW 31211. Accuses Marcus J. Gaines of slandering Whig candidates and Millard Fillmore, and urges his removal as U.S. consul at Tripoli.

Sept 24 From Daniel Fletcher Webster. ALS. NhHi. mDW 31214. Recommends "[Albert?] Fitz" as one capable of providing the State Department with intelligence on "a new Cuban expedition."

Sept 25 To the U.S. Senate (enclosure: J. Randolph Clay to John Middleton Clayton, Aug 13, 1850). LS. DNA, RG 46. mDW 51611. Transmits a letter containing additional information on the guano trade between Peru and the United States.

Sept 25 From [Sir Henry Lytton Bulwer]. AL draft. UkLPR. mDW 31217. Encloses the draft of a letter respecting "Mr. Squier's publication."

Sept 25 From Robert M. Patterson (enclosures: list of questions directed at Thomson Hankey, Jr., and statement of the value of California gold deposited at the U.S. Mint). Draft. DNA, RG 104. mDW 57151. ALS. DLC. mDW 31219. Submits information requested by Thomson Hankey, Jr of the Bank of England regarding the amount of California gold deposited in the Mint; submits questions of his own regarding silver imported into Britain and Europe from the U.S. and South America.

Sept 26 To Daniel Stevens Dickinson. Printed. John R. Dickinson, ed., *Speeches, Correspondence, etc. of the Late Daniel S. Dickinson* (2 vols., New York, 1867), 2: 448–449. Advises him to discount "idle objections" to the nominee for collector at New Bedford (William T. Russell).

Sept 26 *To [Edward Everett].*   *154*

[Sept 26] To [Peter Harvey]. ALS. NhHi. mDW 31268. Will be conferring with [Thomas Jefferson] Rusk regarding [William] Hayden's nomination (postmaster at Boston).

[Sept 26] To [Peter Harvey]. ALS. NhHi. mDW 21367. Advises that "the [Post-Office and Post-Roads] Committee" will recommend Hayden's confirmation.

Sept 26 From Sir Henry Lytton Bulwer. Copy. UkLPR. mDWs. Tells DW he has informed the British government of the U.S. intention to ap-

point an agent to the Dominican Republic to offer mediation with
Britain and France.

Sept 26   From Ambrose Dudley Mann. LS. DNA, RG 59. mDW 55889.
Reports on the negotiations for a convention with Switzerland.

Sept 26   From Prentice & Weissinger. LS. DNA, RG 59. mDW 53725. Ask
whether they are expected to print the laws.

Sept 26   From Daniel Fletcher Webster. ALS. NhHi. mDW 31225. Conveys the recommendation of "Dr. [John Overton] Choules" that
"[Timothy] Coggenshall" be appointed postmaster at New Bedford.

Sept 27   To Daniel Stevens Dickinson. ALS. ICN. mDWs. ALS facsimile.
NhD. mDW 31227. PC, 2: 392. Expresses high esteem for Dickinson, and praises his "noble, able, manly, and patriotic, conduct, in
support of the great measures of this session."

Sept 27   To Peter Harvey. ALS. MBBS. mDW 31230. Comments on the
upcoming Massachusetts State Whig Convention at Worcester; reports "many things remain yet undone."

Sept 27   To Franklin Haven. ALS. MH–H. mDW 31231. PC, 2: 390–391.
Sees little prospect for tariff reform; regrets Ashmun is leaving Congress; reports the president enjoys the goodwill and confidence of
those around him.

[Sept 27]   To [Robert Charles Winthrop]. ALS.MHi. mDW 31236. Wishes
to see him for a few minutes.

Sept 27   From [Anonymous]. AL. NhHi. mDW 31237. Warns that
[George] Harrington, chief clerk at the Treasury, has been spying for
"the Seward clique" and suggests S[ilas?] H. Hill as a suitable replacement.

Sept 27   From Aquilla K. Arnold. ALS. DNA, RG 59. mDW 54917. Accepts appointment as justice of the peace for Washington, D.C.

Sept 27   From Richard H[enry] Bayard. ALS copy. DLC. mDW 31240.
Accepts appointment as U.S. chargé d'affaires in Belgium.

Sept 27   From Sir Henry Lytton Bulwer. AL draft. UkLPR. mDW 31242.
Copy. UkLPR. mDWs. Advances a proposal by Costa Rica that the
U.S. and Great Britain arbitrate its boundary dispute with Nicaragua.

Sept 27   From Sir Henry Lytton Bulwer. Copy. UkLPR. mDWs. Transmits a memorandum on "Portions of Mr. [Ephraim George] Squier's
treaty with Nicaragua which seem to require amendment."

Sept 27   From Charles W. Cutter. ALS. DLC. mDW 31247. Reports an
allegation that DW opposed Abbott Lawrence's confirmation; asks
why the Administration is retaining Democrats in office.

Dec[Sept] 28   To Daniel Stevens Dickinson. ALS. ICN. mDWs. John R.
Dickinson, ed., Speeches, Correspondence, etc. of the Late Daniel S.
Dickinson (2 vols., New York, 1867), 2: 456–457. Requests Dickinson to consider favorably a bill, already passed by the House, to fill
in the gap in the pubished debates and proceedings of Congress.

[Sept 28]   To Millard Fillmore. ALS. NBuHi. mDW 31251. Advises the
immediate withdrawal of the Zerubbabel Snow nomination (associate justice, Utah).

Sept 28   To John Plummer Healy (enclosure: Healy's commission as
U.S. district judge, Sept 28, 1850). Printed LS with MS insertions.
MHi. mDW 31253. Informs Healy of his appointment as U.S. dis-
trict judge for southern California.

Sept 28   To Humphrey Howe Leavitt. LS. NhD. mDW 31256. Requests facts in the case of Guido J. W. F. Fuhrmann, a convicted robber now petitioning for presidential pardon.

Sept 28   To Mary Webster Sanborn. .LS. NhD. mDW 31259. Will be glad to see "you and Alice [Bridge Webster Gregg]" when he goes to New York.

Sept 28   From Sir Henry Lytton Bulwer. ALS draft. UkLPR. mDW 31260. Reminds DW of his promise for a letter regarding "the conduct & letter of Mr. [Ephraim George] Squier."

Sept 28   Application from [George E.] Senseney and [C. A. B.] Coffroth, for the *Winchester* (Va.) *Republican*—public printers (LS. DNA, RG 59. mDW 53622).

Sept 28 [1850?]   Form for acceptance of invitation from the president. AN. NhD. mDWs.

[Sept 29]   From Moses Kelly. ALS. MeHi. mDWs. Asks that estimates of the appropriation needed to implement the bounty land bill be sent in today.

Sept 30   From [Sir Henry Lytton Bulwer]. AL draft. UkLPR. mDW 31262. Recommends that [Joseph W.] Livingston, U.S. consul to Nicaragua, be ordered to remain silent on "these troublesome questions."

Sept 30   From Paul Stevens. ALS. DNA, RG 59. mDW 55099. Accepts appointment as justice of peace for Washington, D.C.

Sept 30   From Thomas U. Walter (with Walter to Hamilton Fish, Jan 31, 1870; enclosure: John Boulton to Walter, Sept 26, 1850). ALS. DNA, RG 59. Discusses his claim against Venezuela respecting nonpayment for construction of a breakwater at La Guayra.

Sept 30   Account with William B. Todd for $8 for two hats, through Oct. 1. DS. NhHi. mDW 40415.

[Sept]   To [?]. ALS. NhD. mDW 31265. Asks him to write down "a general form for the amendment of the law, on the point spoken of today."

[Sept, 1850?]   To [?]. ALS. NhD. mDW 25819 (as Apr–Jun 1844). Suggests that he and some other "leading *Northern* Gentlemen . . . take a lead on this Texan Bill."

Sept   From Robert Brookhouse and William Hunt. LS. DNA, RG 76. Discuss the *Seamew* and *Tigris* claims against Britain.

Sept   Account with Henry Barron for carpentry, building supplies, etc., through Apr 24, 1851. AD. NhHi. mDW 40512.

[Sept?]   Memorandum of tax claims on Rock Island lands owned or formerly owned by DW. ADS by William Brackett. DLC. mDW 40344.

[Sept?]   Recommendation from Julius T. Clark et al., for the *Wisconsin Statesman*—public printer (LS. DNA, RG 59. mDW 53995).

Oct 1   To [Franklin Haven]. ALS. MH–H. mDW 31269. Plans leaving soon for Boston; is drawing on "your [Merchants'] Bank" at "H[arvey?]'s" suggestion.

Oct 1   From Perry E. Brocchus. ALS. DNA, RG 59. mDW 54947. Accepts appointment as associate U.S. justice for Utah Territory.

Oct 1   Recommendation from Thomas J. Rusk, for the Victoria *Texian Advocate*—public printer (ALS. DNA, RG 59. mDW 53689).

Oct 1   Memorandum re appropriation in the Civil and Diplomatic Bill of Sept 30, 1850, "for the expenses of the Agent of the Sublime Porte." DS and AD. DNA, RG 59. mDW 56687–56690; 56691–56698.

Oct 2 To Jonathan Prescott Hall. Copy. DNA, RG 59. mDW 56533. Reports that the steamers *Creole* and *Fanny*, now in New York, may be destined for an invasion of Cuba.

Oct 2 *To Peter Harvey.* 155

Oct 2 To [Peter Harvey?]. ALS. NhHi. mDW 31270. Asks when he should agree to meet "the People of Boston."

Oct 2 To [Peter Harvey]. ALS. NhHi. mDW 38453. States "Your advice seems good, therefore I shall draw on the Bank for what I want."

Oct 2 To Daniel Fletcher Webster. ALS. NhHi. mDW 31279. *PC*, 2: 394. Wishes to have a coach with horses and driver available during his stay at Marshfield.

Oct 2 From Peter Hamilton. Copy. DNA, RG 59. mDW 56534. Reports evidence that an expedition against Cuba is being organized in the Mobile, Ala. region.

Oct 2 From Logan Hunton. Copy. DNA, RG 48. Reports on prosecutions pending in U.S. Circuit Court in New Orleans as a result of the recent expedition against Cuba.

Oct 2 From William A. Weeks. ALS. DNA, RG 59. mDW 56871. Reports on despatch mail forwarded to and from the State Department.

Oct 2 Circular re official visit of Amin Bey. Draft. DNA, RG 59. mDW 56699.

Oct 3 To Millard Fillmore. ALS. NBuHi. mDW 31281. *PC*, 2: 394. *Diplomatic Papers*, 2. Will send him a copy of Hülsemann's note; predicts there will be a quarrel with Austria.

Oct 3 Receipt for $150 paid Henry Barron for building a dining room. ADS. NhHi. mDW 40426.

Oct 4 from William Hunter (enclosure: President Zachary Taylor's message regarding Hungary, Apr 3, 1850). ALS. NhHi. mDW 31284. Van Tyne, p. 452. *Diplomatic Papers*, 2. Recommends a response to Hülsemann's note in a way that will appeal to "the public mind."

Oct 4 From John M. Moore. ALS. DNA, RG 59. mDW 55066. Accepts appointment as principal clerk of surveys in the General Land Office.

Oct 4 From Theodore Sedgwick (enclosure: documents regarding case of Cristobal Madan). Presscopy. DLC. mDW 31302. Copy. DLC. mDW 31307. Contends that Madan was wrongly convicted by a Cuban military commission, and asks the U.S. government to intercede on his behalf.

Oct 4 From Alexander H[ugh] H[olmes] Stuart. LS. DNA, RG 59. mDW 54994. Requests that a commission be issued for Simeon Francis, recently appointed Indian agent in Oregon.

Oct 5 From Daniel Stevens Dickinson. Printed. *PC*, 2: 393. Acknowledges DW's complimentary letter (of Sept 27) and, in turn, praises DW's statesmanship.

Oct 5 *From Edward Everett.* 156

Oct 5 From William A. Weeks. ALS. DNA, RG 59. mDW 56873. Reports forwarding despatches just received from London.

Oct 6 To Richard H[enry] Bayard. ALS. DLC. mDW 31323. Promises Bayard the Brussels mission will be his once Thomas G. Clemson can be recalled.

Oct 6 Application from Francis G. Baldwin, for the Columbus, Mississippi *Primitive Republican*—public printer (ALS. DNA, RG 59. mDW 53552).

Oct 7   From Ambrose Dudley Mann. ALS. DNA, RG 59. mDW 55891. Relates the recent history of Switzerland.

Oct 7   From Henry Sargent. ALS. DLC. mDW 31326. Reports the Grand Vizier of Turkey is anxious that Amin Bey should bring home maps, charts, and other mementos of his travels.

Oct 7   From John Wilson. ALS. DNA, RG 59. mDW 55135. Accepts appointment as principal clerk of public lands in the General Land Office.

Oct 7   Application from Coker Fifield Clarkson, for the Brookville *Indiana American*—public printer (ALS. DNA, RG 59. mDW 53877).

Oct 8   *To Edward Everett.*   159

Oct 8   From Millard Fillmore. LS. DNA, RG 59. mDW 54458. Recommends that the *California Courier* and *The Oregonian* be appointed to print the laws, etc.

Oct 8   From Phillips Pharick. ALS. NhHi. mDW 31333. Reminds DW of letters promised John D. Wolfe, who is about to visit Europe.

Oct 9   From Edward Everett. LC. MHi. mDW 31335. Introduces W[illiam] G[iles] Dix.

Oct 9   From Jonathan Prescottt Hall (enclosure: Hugh Maxwell to Hall, Oct 4, 1850). Copy. DNA, RG 59. mDW 56537. Encloses the report of the New York port collector relative to the rumored Cuban expedition.

Oct 10   From Robert G. Campbell. LS. DNA, RG 59. mDW 54965. Accepts appointment as secretary to sign in the president's name all patents for land sold or granted by the U.S. government.

Oct 11   From Richard H[enry] Bayard. ALS copy. DLC. mDW 31337. Would prefer to leave early in December for his post in Brussels.

Oct 11   From Sir John H. Pelly. Printed. DNA, RG 76. Proposes that an umpire be appointed to arbitrate negotiations for U.S. purchase of the possessory rights of the Hudson's Bay Company and Puget Sound Agricultural Company south of the 49th parallel.

Oct 12   Application from W. J. F. Morgan, for the Paris, Texas *Western Star*—public printer (ALS. DNA, RG 59. mDW 53557).

Oct 14   *To Millard Fillmore.*   159

Oct 14   From Edward Everett. ALS. MHi. mDW 31348. Thinks [Ezra] Lincoln's assurances were given in good faith but admits he himself has little influence over "those [Whigs] who control matters here"; is peeved at not being offered DW's Senate seat.

Oct 14   From Enoch Train & Company. LS. DLC. mDW 31352. Invite DW to the launching of the packet ship *Daniel Webster*.

Oct 14   From Thomas Cogswell Upham. ALS. NhHi. mDW 31355. Presents a copy of his latest book (*American Cottage Life* [Brunswick, Maine, 1850]).

Oct 14   Recommendations from William A. Pratt et al., for the Sault Ste. Marie, Michigan *Lake Superior Journal*—public printer (LS. DNA, RG 59. mDW 53846).

Oct 15   From Charles Pelham Curtis. ALS. DLC. mDW 31357. Inquires about the authority of commissioners appointed to enforce the Fugitive Slave Law.

Oct 15   From William Hunter (enclosure: draft by Hunter of a reply to Chevalier J. G. Hülsemann's note of Sept 30). ALS. NhHi. mDW

31359. Van Tyne, p. 452. Recommends that a reply to Hülsemann's note be delivered promptly.

Oct 15 Application from Worcester Webster—mail inspector for New England (ALS. NhHi. mDW 31393).

Oct 16 From Caleb Cushing. ALS. DLC. mDW 31395. Apologizes for forwarding a letter to "Mr Cheever," care of DW.

Oct 16 From Joseph S. Fay. ALS. DNA, RG 60. mDWs. Writes regarding the failure of U.S. authorities in Boston to arrest the fugitive slave [William] Craft.

Oct 17 To [?]. AL (signature removed). NhHi. mDW 31397. Invites him to visit Marshfield together with Fearing, Haven, and Harvey.

Oct 17 *From Millard Fillmore.*   162

Oct 17 From John Plummer Healy. ALS. MHi. mDW 31403. Reports Henry Randall v. DW in the circuit court is scheduled for trial in a few days; comments on a note due S. K. Bayley.

Oct 18 From Thomson Hankey, Jr. ALS. DLC. mDW 31405. Estimates the value of California gold exported to Europe at $16,500,000.

Oct 18 Promissory note for $3,000 payable to Merchants' Bank. DS. MHi. mDW 40430.

Oct 19 To Richard Milford Blatchford. Printed. Curtis, 2: 480. Complains of asthma; plans a visit to New Hampshire.

Oct 19 To Millard Fillmore. ALS. NBuHi. mDW 31408. Plans a visit to New Hampshire to seek relief for his cold.

Oct 19 From Broughton D. Harris. ALS. DNA, RG 59. mDW 55043. Accepts appointment as secretary for Utah Territory.

Oct 19/20 To Millard Fillmore (enclosures: Robert Walsh to DW, Sept. 19, 1850; James B[rown] Clay to DW, Sept 21, 1850). LS. NBuHi. mDW 31417. Van Tyne, pp. 434–436. Discusses the Fugitive Slave Law; U.S. representatives at Brussels and Paris; James Brown Clay's negotiations with Portugal; and the selection of judges to serve in California.

Oct 20 To Thomas Corwin. ALS. DLC. mDW 31431. Asks when [Thomas] Butler King (appointed port collector for San Francisco) is to embark for California.

Oct 20 To Edward Everett. LS. ViU. mDW 31435. *Diplomatic Papers*, 2. Asks Everett to draft a reply to Hülsemann, and suggests a general theme.

Oct 20 From Bradley B. Meeker. ALS. DNA, RG 59. mDW 55068. Accepts appointment as associate judge for Minnesota Territory.

Oct 21 To Richard Milford Blatchford. Printed. Curtis, 2: 480. Reports his arrival at Franklin.

Oct 21 From James Cooper. ALS. DLC. mDW 31439. Announces plans for a public dinner to be held at Philadelphia in DW's honor.

Oct 21 From Edward Everett. ALS. MHi. mDW 31443. Agrees to draft a reply to Hülsemann.

Oct 21 Application from John Miller McKee, for the *Knoxville* (Tenn.) *Register*—public printer (ALS. DNA, RG 59. mDW 53587).

Oct 22 To Richard Milford Blatchford. Printed. Curtis, 2: 481. Describes the fall scenery around Elms Farm.

Oct 22 *From Charles Wainwright March.*   166

Oct 23 To Richard Milford Blatchford. Printed. PC, 2: 396. Describes a morning fog; reports receiving a visit yesterday from Governor Isaac Hill.

Oct 23   To Frankin Haven. ALS. MH–H. mDW 31445. Discusses a note signed by Blatchford and Jaudon.

Oct 23   *From Millard Fillmore.*   163

Oct 23   From Robert Greenhow. LS. DNA, RG 59. mDW 56187. Reports no progress in his efforts to secure documents from the Mexican government; plans to leave Mexico soon for California.

Oct 23   From John Plummer Healy (with DW to Fillmore, Oct 24, 1850). ALS. NBuHi. mDW 31451. Explains why he cannot accept a federal judgeship in California.

Oct 24   To Edward Curtis. Printed. PC, 2: 397. Is resting and avoiding callers, but expecting to see "General [Franklin] Pierce and other friends from Concord tomorrow."

Oct 24   *To Millard Fillmore with enclosure: Charles Wainwright March to DW, Oct 22.*   165

Oct 24   To Millard Fillmore (enclosure: Healy to DW, Oct 23, 1850). LS. NBuHi. mDW 31453. Recommends Charles B. Goodrich for U.S. district judge in southern California.

Oct 24   To Daniel Fletcher Webster. ALS. NhHi. mDW 31463. PC, 2: 396. Reports his health has improved.

Oct 24   From Edward Everett (enclosure: draft for reply by secretary of state to Chevalier Johann Georg Hülsemann, revised by DW, Oct 24, 1850). ALS. MHi. mDW 31486. Encloses, with explanation, his draft for DW's reply to Hülsemann.

Oct 24   From Joshua Fansant. ALS. DLC. mDW 31512. Invites DW to the annual fair of the Maryland Institute for the Promotion of the Mechanic Arts.

Oct 24   From Francis S. Lathrop et al. LS. DLC. mDW 31514. Invite DW to a Union meeting in New York on Oct 31.

Oct 24   From [Abbott Lawrence]. Draft. DLC. mDW 31515. Discusses postal relations between the U.S., Britain, and France and asks for instructions.

Oct 24   From Thomas Cogswell Upham. ALS. NhHi. mDW 31529. Proposes that the principle of binding arbitration be incorporated into all future treaties negotiated by the U.S.

Oct 24   Recommendation from Day O. Kellogg, for the *Troy* (N.Y.) *Whig*—public printer (ALS. DNA, RG 59. mDW 53625).

Oct 25   *To Millard Fillmore.*

Oct 25   To Daniel Fletcher Webster. ALS. MH–H. mDW 31535. Expects no difficulty in "the [Craft] slave case" but warns the marshal must be prepared to use force if necessary.

Oct 26   From Daniel Fletcher Webster. ALS. NhHi. mDW 31541. Accuses Almon W. Griswold and Philip H. Greely of improper behavior and recommends punitive action; encloses relevant correspondence.

Oct 26   *Thomas Buckminster Curtis to David Sears.*   167

Oct 26   Promissory note for $1,200 payable to Richard Milford Blatchford. DS (signature crossed). MHi. mDW 40431.

Oct 26   Promissory note for $1,200 payable by Samuel Jaudon. DS (signature crossed). MHi. mDW 40432.

[Oct 27]   To Peter Harvey. ALS. NhHi. mDW 31544. Is expecting Harvey, Haven, and others at Franklin on Tuesday; reports 120 people from Concord attended "our frolic yesterday."

[Oct 27]   To Daniel Fletcher Webster. Copy. NhHi. mDW 31539. Van Tyne, p. 605. Invites Fletcher to a dinner he is planning at Franklin; is pleased to hear of [William] Appleton's nomination for Congress.

Oct 27   *From Moses Stuart.*   170

Oct 27   *David Sears to Thomas Buckminster Curtis.*   169

Oct 28   To [Edward Everett]. ALS. MHi. mDW 31550. Asks that Everett's draft of the reply to Hülsemann be sent to him at Franklin.

Oct 28   To Francis A. Fisher and T[homas] J. Lovegrove. LS. DLC. mDW 31551. Regrets their letter was delayed in reaching him.

Oct 28   To Francis S. Lathrop et al. Printed. *Works*, 6: 577–579. Praises the objectives of their Union party meeting in New York; defends the Compromise measures; warns against lawlessness and the renewal of "past agitation and useless controversy."

Oct 28   To Little & Brown. ALS. NhHi. mDW 31553. Asks them to send him a set of the United States Statutes and bill the State Department.

Oct 28   To William Cabell Rives. LS. DLC. mDW 31557. Introduces Lt. William S. Drayton, U.S. Navy, of South Carolina.

Oct 28   From Henry Boyce. ALS. DNA, RG 59. mDW 54943. Accepts appointment as U.S. district judge for western Louisiana.

Oct 28   *From Millard Fillmore*   172

Oct 29   *To Millard Fillmore.*   173

Oct 29   To Nathan Kelsey Hall. ALS. NBuHi. mDW 31566. Recommends that "a respectable public office" be conferred on former governor Anthony Colby of New Hampshire.

Oct 29   To Little & Brown. LS. Mrs. Mary L. Hamelberg, Columbus, Ohio. mDW 31569. Plans to meet "Mr. [James] Brown" at the Revere House.

Oct 29   From Alexander Hugh Holmes Stuart. LS. DNA, RG 59. mDW 54957. Asks that a commission be issued for George Butler, recently appointed agent for the Cherokee Indians.

Oct 29   Memorandum on William Hoyt. Printed. *PC*, 2: 398. Reminisces about Hoyt, "for many years teacher of our country school in Salisbury."

Oct 31   Application from Columbus Drew, for the Jacksonville *Florida Republican*—public printer (ALS. DNA, RG 59. mDW 53696).

Oct 31   Contract with Little & Brown for printing the laws. AD copy. DLC. mDW 31570.

[Oct?]   From Charles Stark Newell et al. LS. CtY. mDWs. Welcome DW back to Massachusetts; would like him to meet them and the public at Lawrence.

Oct   Recommendation from Elizabeth Washington Wirt, for Dabney Carr Wirt—purser, Navy Department (ALS. DNA, RG 45. mDWs).

Oct   Memorandum and circular concerning visit by Amin Bey. DS. DNA, RG 59. mDW 56687. Draft. AD in DW's hand. DNA, RG 59. mDW 56691.

[Oct]   Proposed circular on defense of the Constitution, with explanatory notes by Daniel Fletcher Webster and Caroline Story Webster. Draft. NhD. mDW 31580. *New England Magazine* 4 (June, 1886), 511–515.

Nov 1   From Fitz Henry Warren. LS. DNA, RG 59. mDW 55113. Reports
that George R. Trotter, recently appointed deputy postmaster for Lexington, Ky., has posted bond.

Nov 1   Recommendations from Benjamin H. Epperson, for the Victoria
Texian Advocate, and the Paris, Texas *Western Star*—public print-
ers (ALS. DNA, RG 59. mDW 53686); from Thomas J. Rusk, for the
Texian Advocate—public printer (ALS. DNA, RG 59. mDW 53689).

Nov 2   Agreement with Stephen Sawyer for the purchase of a farm in
Franklin, N.H. AD by Webster (signature removed), signed also by
Sawyer. NhHi. mDW 40435.

Nov 2   Receipt for $200 paid Stephen Sawyer in partial fulfillment of
their agreement of Nov 2, 1850. DS. NhHi. mDW 40438.

Nov 2   Account with James Colburn for $55.89 for building supplies,
through Nov 25. AD. NhHi. mDW 40445.

Nov 3   To Richard Milford Blatchford. Printed. *PC*, 2: 399–400. Reflects
on his stay at Elms Farm; calls the Union meeting "A stirring occasion, but fears a decisive split in the Whig party.

Nov 3   Memoranda for John Taylor.   175

Nov 5   To James Brown Clay. LS. DLC. mDW 31604. Conveys the president's views on the negotiations with Portugal and Clay's own position.

Nov 5   To Millard Fillmore.   177

Nov 5   From Edward Everett. LC. MHi. mDW 31612. Provides an item of
information and offers to do whatever else he can to spare DW "an
evening's labor."

Nov 5   From Bladen Forrest. ALS. DNA, RG 59. mDW 54992. Accepts
appointment as justice of the peace for Washington, D.C.

Nov 5   From William Hickey. ALS. DLC. mDW 31614. Requests "a
few earnest words" for the forthcoming edition of "my little book"
(*The Constitution of the United States, with an alphabetical analysis*
[4th edition, Philadelphia, 1851]).

Nov 5   Promissory note for $779.96 payable to John Taylor. DS. DLC.
mDW 40439.

Nov 6   To Richard Milford Blatchford. ALS. NhD. mDW 31617. Describes the Sawyer farm and the terms for its purchase; has arranged
affairs at the Elms for the coming year.

Nov 7   To William Prescott. ALS. NhHi. mDW 31621. Van Tyne, p. 440.
Excuses himself from answering a question; asserts his life-long ob-
jective has been the preservation of the "Institutions of our Fathers."

Nov 7   From William Kinney et al. LS. CtY. mDWs. Invitation to DW to
be present at a "Union Mass Meeting" in Staunton, Va., on Nov 25.

Nov 7   Application from Thomas Swelling—public printer and U.S.mar-
shal for eastern Texas (ALS. DNA, RG 59. mDW 53555).

Nov 8   To Morris Ketchum. ALS. NhD. mDW 31623. Agrees to provide
Ketchum's son with letters for his tour of Europe.

Nov 8   From Daniel Moreau Barringer. ALS. NhD. mDW 31629. Reports
the release of the last of the Contoy prisoners; emphasizes the efficiency of the British intelligence-gathering system.

Nov 8   From Francis S. Lathrop et al. LS. DLC. mDW 31634. Report
DW's letter (Oct 28, 1850) was read and enthusiastically received at
the Union meeting in New York.

Nov 8   Memorandum on cattle at Marshfield. AD. NhHi. mDW 31625.
Van Tyne, pp. 652–653.

Nov 9   From Alexander Hugh Holmes Stuart. LS. DNA, RG 59. mDW
54998. Asks that a commission be issued for Abram M. Fridley, recently appointed agent for the Winnebago Indians.

Nov 10   From Alfred G. Benson, ALS. DLC. mDW 31636. Asks when DW
will be in New York so that the committee of the Union meeting at
Castle Garden might wait on him.

Nov 11   *To Anthony Colby.*   *179*

Nov 11   To Millard Fillmore. LS. DNA, RG 94. mDWs. Recommends Hasket Derby for appointment to West Point.

Nov 11   To [Leonard Eugene] Wales et al. ALS. NhExP. mDWs. Printed
copy. DLC. mDW 31638. Praises John Middleton Clayton, while excusing himself from a reception in Clayton's honor.

Nov 11   From Josiah Randall et al. LS. DLC. mDW 31640. Invite him to
a meeting of "Friends of the Constitution and the Union" in Philadelphia.

Nov 12   From James Watson Gerard. ALS. NhHi. mDW 31642. Suggests
that George Matthew be recommended to the British government as
a successor to Sir Henry Lytton Bulwer, and requests DW to help secure Matthew's preliminary appointment as secretary to the British
legation.

Nov 12   Account with Alfred Lee for $13.85 for grains and meal,
through July 1, 1851. AD. NhHi. mDW 40529.

Nov 13   *To Thomas Corwin.*   *180*

Nov 13   To Millard Fillmore. ALS. NBuHi. mDW 31651. *PC*, 2: 402–
403. Is preparing a family burial vault in the cemetery located near
the Marshfield farm.

Nov 13   To Millard Fillmore. ALS. NBuHi. mDW 31654. *W & S*, 16:
575–576. *Diplomatic Papers*, 2. Comments on Whig losses in Massachusetts; is sending him a draft of the reply to Hülsemann; thinks
the time is right to demonstrate "the temper and spirit" of U.S. foreign policy under Fillmore.

Nov 13   To William Alexander Graham. LS. NcU. mDW 31657. Hamilton, *Graham*, 3: 481–482. Demands the withdrawal of official patronage from the *Boston Atlas*.

Nov 13   From Edward Everett. ALS. MHi. mDW 31659. Cites a remark
attributed to Joseph II of Austria and discusses his draft of the reply
to Hülsemann.

Nov 13   From Edward Everett. LC. MHi. mDW 31664. Thinks he has
found the source of the remark made by Joseph II in 1820.

[c. Nov 13]   To George Ashmun. ALS. NhD. mDW 38206. Would like to
see him to discuss "the business in the H. of R."; learns that
[Charles Wentworth] Upham is not chosen for Congress.

Nov 14   To Francis S. Lathrop et al. Printed. *PC*, 2: 404. Calls for united
patriotic resistance to the "open schemes of disunion."

Nov 14   To Josiah Randall et al. Copy. NhHi. mDW 31666. *PC*, 2: 403–
404. Regrets that official duties will prevent his attendance at the
Union meeting in Philadelphia.

Nov 14   Recommendation from William Welch, for the *Wisconsin
Statesman*—public printer (ALS. DNA. RG 59. mDW 53982).

Nov 15   To Millard Fillmore. ALS. NBuHi. mDW 31670. Introduces Gilman Marston, whom he thinks might accept a California judgeship.

Nov 15   To Millard Fillmore (enclosure: press clipping).   180

Nov 15   To Charles Henry Thomas. ALS. MB. mDW 31677. Asks him to take "young Mr. Alden" to the Boston postmaster regarding a job.

Nov 15   From Joseph S. Fay (with DW to John Jordan Crittenden, Nov 22, 1850; enclosure: affidavit of Willis H. Hughes, Nov 15, 1850). ALS. DNA, RG 60. mDWs. Calls for the prosecution of those who obstructed Willis Hughes's efforts to recover the fugitive slaves William and Ellen Craft in Boston.

Nov 15   From Robert Moore. ALS. DNA, RG 59. mDW 54455. Accepts appointment to publish the laws in Oregon Territory, while complaining that the compensation is inadequate.

Nov 15   From Hugh O'Neal. ALS. DNA, RG 59. mDW 55053. Accepts appointment as U.S. attorney for Indiana.

Nov 15   From Fitz Henry Warren. LS. DNA, RG 59. mDW 55045. Reports that George W. Hamersly, newly appointed postmaster at Lancaster, Pa., has posted bond.

Nov 15   From Robert Charles Winthrop. ALS. MHi. mDW 31679. Thanks DW for a gift.

Nov 16   To Benjamin F. Ayer.   182

Nov 16   To Edward Curtis. ALS. NN. mDW 31683. Reports "the Plate, Copy right, &c—are all bought, for $2,000 . . . Dr. Choules did the business."

Nov 16   To Millard Fillmore. ALS. NBuHi. mDW 31684. Van Tyne, p. 443. Praises the New Hampshire Whigs; thinks Freesoilism can be killed in New England; rejoices at James Louis Petigru's acceptance (U.S. attorney for South Carolina).

Nov 16   From John Macpherson Berrien. ALS. DLC. mDW 31686. Urges that immediate action be taken on behalf of claimants under the Florida treaty.

Nov 16   From Charles Devens, Jr. (with DW to John Jordan Crittenden, Nov. 22, 1850). ALS. DNA, RG 60. mDWs. Returns some papers; promises to submit a report in a few days.

Nov 17   From J. B. Conyngham et al. LS. CtY. mDWs. Enclose copy of the proceedings of the Young Men's Union Meeting held in Wilkes Barre, Pa. on Nov 11.

Nov 17   From Edmond J. Forstall. ALS. DLC. mDW 31689. Reports a proposal by President-elect Arista that Mexico become a U.S. protectorate, in order to "reorganize and regenerate" that country and reassert the preponderance of the white race.

[Nov 18]   From Charles Pelham Curtis. ALS. DNA, RG 60. mDWs. Comments on the behavior of U.S. marshal Charles Devens, Jr. in the Craft fugitive slave case.

Nov 18   From Charles Devens, Jr. (enclosure: affidavit of Charles Devens, Jr., Nov 18, 1850). ALS. DNA, RG 60. mDWs. Submits an affidavit defending his actions in the Craft case.

Nov 18   From Joseph S. Fay (with DW to John Jordan Crittenden, Nov 22, 1850). ALS. DNA, RG 60. mDWs. Discusses the Craft incident; suggests that the government's action in this case could affect the elections to the Georgia State Convention later in the month.

[c. Nov 18]   From Joseph S. Fay (with Seth J. Thomas to Fay, Nov 18,

1850). ANS. DNA, RG 60. mDWs. Believes Thomas would agree that
Willis Hughes was dissatisfied with Devens's efforts to recover the
Crafts.

Nov 18 Application from Henry Alexander Scammell Dearborn—U.S.
consul at Havana (ALS. NhHi. mDW 31696).

Nov 18 Recommendation from Franklin Pierce, for Albert G. Allen—
clerkship (ALS. NN. mDW 31699).

Nov 19 From Samuel F. Train. ALS. DNA, RG 45. mDWs. Asks if it
would be wise to petition the secretary of the Navy regarding his
appointment as purser.

Nov 19 Remarks at Astor House to a delegation of New York merchants
and the Committee of Safety. Printed. *Boston Semi-Weekly Atlas*,
Nov 23, 1850.

Nov 20 From C. H. S. de la Figanière. LS. NhHi. mDW 31700. Solicits
DW's orders for wine.

Nov 20 From Nathaniel William Taylor (enclosure: Taylor to DW, Apr
20, 1850). ALS. NhHi. mDW 31702. Explains why he is just now
mailing the enclosed to DW.

Nov 20 From Robert Wheaton. ALS. NNPM. mDW 31707. Encloses a
letter from "Mr Fleury of Paris" regarding Erick Glad's claim on the
French government.

Nov 20 Application from Quincy K. Underwood, for the Helena, Arkansas *Southern Shield*—public printer(ALS. DNA, RG 59. mDW
53645).

Nov 21 From John C. Clark. LC. DNA, RG 206. Writes regarding petitions from defendants indicted for trespassing on government lands.

Nov 21 From Charles Wainwright March (enclosure: press clippings).
ALS. NhHi. mDW 31709. Reports DW's visit and reception at New
York have drawn universal praise.

Nov 22 To John Jordan Crittenden (enclosures: Joseph S. Fay to DW,
Nov 15; Fay to DW, Nov 18; Charles Devens, Jr. to DW, Nov 18;
Charles Pelham Curtis to [DW], [Nov 18]). LS. DNA, RG 60. mDWs.
Encloses papers pertaiing to Charles Devens, Jr. and the attempted
recovery of the fugitive slaves, William and Ellen Craft.

Nov 22 To Jacob Snider, Jr. LS. PPAmP. mDW 31711. Thanks Snider
for his "acceptable 'representative.' "

Nov 22 From Alexander Hugh Holmes Stuart. LS. DNA, RG 59. mDW
55078. Asks that a commission be issued John B. Preston, newly appointed surveyor general of public lands in Oregon.

Nov 23 To William Kinney et al.   184

Nov 23 From Richard M. Corwine. ALS. DLC. mDW 31712. Encloses a
letter of introduction from John I. Bryan.

Nov 23 From James Lee (with abstract of reply). ALS. OGK. mDW
31716. Calls attention to [Alexander J.] Cotheal's appointment (commercial agent, River Djeb).

Nov 23 From Charles Wainwright March (enclosure: press clipping).
ALS. NhHi. mDW 31718. Reports a "glorious Union meeting" in
Manchester, and also plans for a New York delegation to attend the
Faneuil Hall meeting.

Nov 23 Account with Duval & Brother for $158.13 for clothing, through
June 12, 1851. ADS. NhHi. mDW 40546.

Nov 24 To Richard Milford Blatchford. LS. DLC. mDWs. Expects Fillmore's message will be well received, and exhorts those who like it "to defend and commend it."

Nov 24   To Millard Filmore. LS. NBuHi. mDW 31721. *W & S*, 16: 579. Approves "the general character" of Fillmore's message; is sending recommendations for a few changes and additions.

Nov 25   From Ambrose Dudley Mann. LS. DNA, RG 59. mDW 55917. Reports having just concluded a convention with the Swiss Confederation.

Nov 25   From James Watson Webb. ALS. NhD. mDWs. Praises the draft of DW's reply to Hülsemann; expresses entire agreement with DW's view of the slavery issue.

Nov 25   Application from Richard J. Smith, for the Bowling Green, Kentucky *Warren Intelligencer*—public printer (ALS. DNA, RG 59. mDW 53752).

Nov 26   From John Johnston. Typed copy. MiD. mDW 31725. Applies for a passport.

Nov 26   From Charles March. ALS. NhHi. mDW 31726. Introduces Robert Bayman of I. Howard March & Company.

Nov 26   From William Strong. Copy. DNA, RG 46. mDWs. Argues that salaries paid the judiciary in Oregon are inadequate and urges that the problem be brought to the attention of Congress.

Nov 26   Application from T. A. Butterfield, for the Racine, Wisconsin *Commercial Advertiser*—public printer (ALS. DNA, RG 59. mDW 53584).

Nov 26   Recommendation from Aaron F. Perry, for the Columbus *Ohio State Journal*—public printer (ALS. DNA, RG 59. mDW 53692).

Nov 26   Account with P. M. Pearson & Co. for $10.50 for coal, through Dec 14. DS. NhHi. mDW 40450.

Nov 27   To Joseph Blunt. LS. NhD. mDW 31728. Offers to assist in the Van Rensselaer case.

Nov 27   From Alexander Hugh Holmes Stuart. LS. DNA, RG 59. mDW 55039. Asks that a commission be issued for James E. Heath, recently appointed commissioner of pensions.

Nov 27   From Alexander Hugh Holmes Stuart. LS. DNA, RG 59. mDW 55105. Asks that a commission be issued for Elias S. Terry, recently appointed recorder of the General Land Office.

Nov 27   From William A. Weeks. ALS. DNA, RG 59. mDW 56874. Reports forwarding the London despatches aboard the *Cambria*; mentions a minor difficulty involving a despatch bearer.

Nov 27   Recommendation from A. G. Hobson et al., for the Bowling Green, Kentucky, *Warren Intelligencer*—public printer (ALS by Hobson, signed also by others. DNA, RG 59. mDW 53733).

Nov 27   Receipt for $3.50 paid Abel Tandy for work on barn and fences. ADS. NhHi. mDW 40440.

Nov 28   To Millard Fillmore. ALS. NBuHi. mDW 31729. Returns the proofs of the annual message; predicts it will be well received by "all true Whigs."

Nov 28   To John Taylor. Printed. *PC*, 2: 405. Discusses farm business.

Nov 28   To Caroline Le Roy Webster. ALS. NhD. mDW 31731. Asks whether she wants to employ "Hannah"; is arranging and decorating the house and meeting occasionally with Congressmen.

Nov 28   To Charles Porter Wright. ALS. NhHi. mDW 31734. Van Tyne,
pp. 683–684. Discusses the butchering of hogs and cattle.

Nov 28   Application from Evans & Vernon, for the Wilmington *Delaware
Republican*—public printer (LS. DNA, RG 59. mDW 53566).

Nov 29   To Peter Harvey.   186

Nov 29   To Logan Hunton. Copy. DNA, RG 59. mDW 56541. Forwards
information received from the Spanish Minister concerning an alleged new attempt to invade Cuba.

Nov 29   From William A. Weeks. ALS. DNA, RG 59. mDW 56876. Reports forwarding despatches received from London.

Nov 29   Account with Edward Simms for liquor and cheese, through
Dec 31. AD. NhHi. mDW 40459.

Nov 29   Account with Edward Simms for liquor, etc., through June 5,
1851. AD. NhExP. mDW 40524.

Nov 30   From Calhoun Benham. ALS. DNA, RG 59. mDW 54933. Accepts appointment as U.S. attorney for northern California.

Nov 30   From Ambrose Dudley Mann. Typed copy. DNA, RG 59. mDW
55919. Discusses the convention he has just negotiated with Switzerland.

Nov 30   From R. C. Pailey et al. LS. CtY. mDWs. Invite DW to attend a
public meeting in Bath, Me. on Dec 16 in support of the Union and
enforcing the laws.

Nov 30   Account with Edwin Green for $93.50 for bedstead, etc.,
through Dec 11. ADS. NhHi. mDW 40464.

[Nov]   To [Millard Fillmore]. ALS. NBuHi. mDW 31745. Encloses "slips"
from the *Boston Atlas* commenting on Whig losses in Massachusetts.

[Nov]   From George Shattuck. ALS. NhHi. mDW 31747. Presents gift of
a "mess" of potatoes.

Dec 1   To William D. Merrick. ALS. NhD. mDW 31749. Acknowledges
Merrick's approving letter; promises to do what he can for "Mr. [Na-
thaniel F.] Williams."

Dec 1   To James William Paige. ALS. MHi. mDW 31751. Reports his
speeches are nearly all ready for the press but he wants to consult
further with Curtis.

Dec 1   From Crane & Rice. ALS. DNA, RG 59. mDW 53734. Accept appointment to publish the laws in the San Francisco *California
Courier*.

Dec 2   To Millard Fillmore. ALS. NBuHi. mDW 31752. Van Tyne, p.
444. Recommends that the message be sent to Congress today; reports "enough of nullification reading" in the morning papers.

[Dec 2]   To Millard Fillmore. ALS. NBuHi. mDW 31574. Van Tyne, p.
444. Reports the message has been well received by Congress; thinks
it bodes well for the Administration.

Dec 2   From Isaac P. Davis. ALS. NhHi. mDW 31942. Submits information about Plymouth Colony and sends Joseph Hunter's *Collections
concerning the early history of the founders of New Plymouth, the
first colonists of New England* (London, 1849).

Dec 2   Recommendation from Elisha Whittlesey, for the Pittsburgh
Daily Commercial Journal—public printer (ALS. DNA, RG 59. mDW
53713).

Dec 2 [1850–1851]   From Randall Hunt. Telegram. NhHi. mDW 38654.

Reports that DW's services may be required on behalf of New Orleans in a suit involving John McDonough's will.

Dec 3   To Henry Lytton Bulwer. Copy. DNA, RG 76. mDWs. Transmits
information regarding the seizure of the brig *Joseph Albino* by customs authorities at San Francisco.

Dec 3   To Caleb Cushing. Dictated letter. DLC. mDW 31757. Agrees to
see him at the State Department.

Dec 3   From Samuel K. George. Typed copy. DNA, RG 59. mDW 57028.
Reports on a guano contract let by the Peruvian government.

Dec 3   Application from Anderson & Stith, for the *Holly Springs* (Miss.)
Gazette—public printer (LS. DNA, RG 59. mDW 53598).

Dec 4   To Millard Fillmore. ALS. NBuHi. mDW 31760. Reports the president's message is generally commended by the diplomatic corps.

Dec 4   From Francis Ives, Henry Kollock Harral, and Elisha Smith Aber-
nethy. LS. CtY. mDWs. Invite DW to a Union Mass Meeting in
Bridgeport, Conn. on Dec. 20.

Dec 4   From Daniel Le Roy. ALS. NhHi. mDW 31762. Introduces Frederick Schuchard, who is supporting an applicant for U.S. consul at
Leghorn.

Dec 4   Applications from Adolphus Heilmann, for the German-Language
Buffalo (N.Y.) *Telegraph*—public printer (ALS. DNA, RG 59. mDW
53676); from John D. Logan, for the Victoria *Texian Advocate*—
public printer (ALS. DNA, RG 59. mDW 53690; from William W.
Wyman, for the Madison *Wisconsin Statesman*—public printer
(ALS. DNA, RG 59. mDW 53985).

Dec 4   Recommendation from Christopher Harris Williams, for the Jackson *West Tennessee Whig*—public printer (ALS. DNA, RG 59. mDW
53716).

Dec 4   Promissory note for $500 payable to Richard Milford Blatchford.
DS (signature crossed). MHi. mDW 40441.

Dec 4   Account with David A. Baird for $39.63 for fixing windows, etc.,
through Dec 20. ADS. NhHi. mDW 40455.

Dec 5   To Franklin Haven.   *186*

Dec 5   From John S[teele] Tyler. ALS. DLC. mDW 31769. Discusses the
choice of counsel in the "Brutus case" (*Barnard* v. *Adams*, 10
Howard 270, 1850).

Dec 5   Application from [Jerome] Fuller & Seward, for the *Albany*
(N.Y.)*State Register*—public printer (LS. DNA, RG 59. mDW
53674).

Dec 5   Recommendation from Joseph R. Underwood, for the Bowling
Green, Kentucky, *Warren Intelligencer*—public printer (ALS. DNA,
RG 59. mDW 53730).

Dec 6   To Mary A. Boardman. ALS. NHi. mDWs. Has no unfilled offices
to offer her friend.

Dec 6   To Millard Fillmore. ALS. NBuHi. mDW 31773. Will see him tomorrow regarding the South Carolina resolutions.

Dec 6   From Joseph Balestier. ALS. DNA, RG 59. mDW 56082. Discusses
his plans for negotiating a convention with the "Radjah of Sarawak."

Dec 6   From Joseph Ripley Chandler. Presscopy. DLC. mDW 31775.
Draws attention to an earlier application by John G. Pierie to be commercial agent in Mayaguez, Porto Rico.

Dec 6   From James Louis Petigru. ALS. DLC. mDW 31776. Reports little outward public opposition to his appointment as U.S. attorney for South Carolina; finds that "disunion" is the pervading sentiment and that Calhoun's opinions have greatly influenced popular attitudes in the state.

Dec 6   From John S. Williams. ALS. DNA, RG 59. mDW 55012. Reports Rufus R. Haines has been appointed postmaster at Bath, Maine.

Dec 6   Receipt for $51.95 paid Moses Copp. ADS. NhHi. mDW 40443.

Dec 7   *To Thomas Corwin, with reply Dec 7.*   *187*

Dec 7   To George Evans et al. LS. DNA, RG 76. mDW 57092. Adopts their suggestion that a special messenger be sent to Mexico to cause the government to comply with requisitions for documents addressed to it pursuant to the 15th Article of the treaty of Guadaloupe Hidalgo.

[Dec 7]   To Millard Fillmore. ALS. NBuHi. mDW 31782. Transmits a letter from "Major Downing"; expresses his feeling that "torrents of praise" in response to Fillmore's message "will not be likely to turn your head."

Dec 7   To Franklin Haven. ALS. MH–H. mDW 31784. Encloses a note from [Thomas] Corwin regarding Mexican scrip; sends new promissory notes to replace others falling due.

Dec 7   *To Whitemarsh Benjamin Seabrook.*   *188*

[Dec 7]   To Ichabod Smith Spencer. Copy. NhHi. mDW 31789. Van Tyne, p. 747. Praises Spencer's recent sermon on the Fugitive Slave law; argues that obedience to established government is a Christian duty.

Dec 7   To John S[teele] Tyler. LS (with postscript in DW's hand). NhD. mDW 31793. Discusses the problem of scheduling arguments in the *Brutus* case.

Dec 7   To John Collins Warren. Printed. *PC*, 2: 406. Edward Warren, *The Life of John Collins Warren* (2 vols., Boston, 1860), 2: 55. Praises Warren's part at the Faneuil Hall meeting; reports the proceedings are to be published and extensively circulated.

Dec 7   To Charles Porter Wright. ALS. NhHi. mDW 31797. *PC*, 2: 405. Asks him to send Dr. John Collins Warren some ears of corn; briefly discusses other farm business.

Dec 7   From Samuel K. George. Typed copy. DNA, RG 59. mDW 57030. Doubts the U.S. government can do much to lower guano prices short of buying or seizing the Chincha Islands.

Dec 8   To [Thomas B. Curtis]. ALS. MB. mDW 31798. *W & S*, 16: 581 (as to George Ticknor Curtis). Expresses delight with the outcome of the Union meeting in Faneuil Hall.

Dec 8   Application from F[ranci]s G. Baldwin, for the Columbus, Mississippi *Primitive Republican*—public printer (ALS. DNA, RG 59. mDW 53575).

Dec 9   From Lewis Cass. ALS. NhD. mDW 31802. Returns DW's reply to Hülsemann, calling it "pungent" and "unanswerable."

Dec 9   From James Brown Clay. ALS copy. DLC. mDW 31806. Explains his decision to return to the United States.

Dec 9   From Edward Everett. ALS. MHi. mDW 31811. Sends notes from Dr. Holland and Lord Aberdeen; discusses "the question of peace or war in Europe"; thinks it "a pity" that the South places so much importance on the Fugitive Slave bill.

Dec 9   Application from John Bailhache, for the *Alton* (Ill.) *Telegraph and Democratic Review*—public printer (ALS. DNA, RG 59. mDW 53560).

Dec 9   Account with Samuel Kirby for $80.50 for furniture and repairs, through May 13, 1851. ADS. NhHi. mDW 40544.

Dec 10   To Richard Milford Blatchford. ALS. DLC. mDW 31815. *PC*, 2: 406–407. Regrets the continuance of acrimonious sectional controversy, but predicts peace will be restored "to a considerable extent."

Dec 10   To Millard Fillmore. ALS. NBuHi. mDW 31819. Will see Fillmore tomorrow regarding judgeships for California, Oregon, and New Mexico.

Dec 10. From Charles March. ALS. NhHi. mDW 31821. Sends a quarter cask of Madeira wine, the gift of his brother, the consul [John Howard March].

Dec 10   Recommendation from Henry Dodge, for William W. Wyman and the Madison *Wisconsin Statesman*—public printer (ALS. DNA, RG 59. mDW 53993).

Dec 10   Promissory note for $2,500 payable to self at Merchants' Bank in Boston. DS. MHi. mDW 40446.

Dec 11   To Richard H[enry] Bayard (enclosures: letter of credence; diplomatic passport). LS. DLC. mDW 31823. Encloses documents and instructions for Bayard's assignment as U.S. chargé d'affaires in Belgium.

Dec 11   To Solomon W. Downs. LS. DNA, RG 46. mDW 51176. Urges Congress to act soon on the bill providing for the reorganization of the State Department.

Dec 11   To Edward Everett. LS. MHi. mDW 31829. Inquires about a letter addressed by Joseph II of Austria to his minister to the Netherlands; and about "Mr. Lee's correspondence" and relevant comments by Alexander Everett.

Dec 11   To Millard Fillmore. LS. DNA, RG 46. mDW 51229. Submits copies of official correspondence relating to Brazil, as requested by the Senate resolution of Aug 28, 1850.

Dec 11   From William A. Weeks. ALS. DNA, RG 59. mDW 56877. Reports having forwarded the London despatches care of Edward A. Crowninshield.

Dec 12   To Millard Fillmore. ALS. NBuHi. mDW 31831. Advises him to send "a *congratulatory* message."

Dec 12   From Theodore Parker.   *189*

[c. Dec 13]   To Millard Fillmore. ALS. NBuHi. mDW 31837. Introduces John Hogan of St. Louis.

Dec 13   To Charles Augustus Stetson. ALS. NhD. mDW 31839. Comments on the expense of supplying his dinner table with fish.

Dec 13   From Edward Everett. ALS. MHi. mDW 31844. Discusses a quotation attributed to Joseph II of Austria.

Dec 13   From Asahel Huntington. ALS. NhHi. mDW 31848. Admits that his initially negative reaction to the 7th of March speech has gradually changed to full agreement with DW's view of the sectional crisis; praises Fillmore's annual message to Congress.

Dec 13   From Ichabod Smith Spencer. Copy. NhHi. mDW 31851. Requests permission to publish DW's letter to him of Dec 7; presents a copy of his book (*A Pastor's Sketches; or Conversations with Anxious Inquirers Respecting the Way of Salvation* [New York, 1850]).

Dec 13   From William A. Weeks. ALS. DNA, RG 59. mDW 56878. Reports receipt and forwarding of despatches from London.

Dec 13   Recommendations from Joseph P. Caldwell, for the Salisbury, North Carolina *Carolina Watchman*—public printer (ALS. DNA, RG 59. mDW 53612); from John Hogan, for the *St. Louis Intelligencer*—public printer (ALS. DNA. RG 59. mDW 53727).

Dec 14   To Baring Brothers & Company. LS duplicate. DLC. mDW 31852. Authorizes Richard H[enry] Bayard to draw on them for salary and contingent expenses as U.S. chargé d'affaires in Belgium.

Dec 14   From Hugh Maxwell. Copy. DNA, RG 59. mDW 56542. Writes regarding the steamers *Creole* and *Fanny*, vessels suspected of being fitted for an illegal invasion of Cuba.

Dec 14   Promissory note for $3,200 payable to self at Merchants' Bank in Boston. DS. MHi. mDW 40448.

Dec 15   To Millard Fillmore. ALS. NBuHi. mDW 31853. Advises that a proclamation relative to the Texas boundary settlement will be ready for him tomorrow.

Dec 15   From Richard H[enry] Bayard. ALS copy. DLC. mDW 31767. Acknowledges his commission and other official papers; will leave for his post at Brussels on Dec 22.

Dec 15   From [Sir Henry Lytton Bulwer]. AL draft. UkLPR. mDW 31855. Asks him to read over the draft of a letter to be sent to the British chargé d'affaires in Central America.

Dec 16   To George Perkins Marsh. ALS. VtU. mDW 31856. Introduces Alfred Douglas of Albany.

Dec 17   To Edwin David Sanborn. LS. NhD. mDW 31859. Acknowledges a copy of "your agricultural address" (before the New Hampshire State Agricultural Society) calling it a "model for the New Hampshire farmers."

Dec 17   To Hugh McLeod. LC. DNA, RG 59. mDWs. Printed. Cora Montgomery, *Eagle Pass or Life on the Border* (New York, 1852), pp. 86–87. Replies to the memorial from inhabitants of Eagle Pass, Texas, demanding that the U.S. government intervene with Mexico regarding the abduction of Manuel Rios.

Dec 17   Recommendations from John A. Rockwell, for the *Norwich* (Conn.) *Courier* and the *New Haven Palladium*—public printers ALS. DNA, RG 59. mDW 53568).

Dec 18   To Jenny Lind. Dictated note. NhHi. mDW 31862. Encloses two letters of introduction, and hopes they may meet again after her return from the South.

Dec 18   To Daniel Fletcher Webster. ALS. NhHi. mDW 31864. Asks if [Albert?] "Fitz" might like to carry a treaty to Lima, Peru.

Dec 18   From Henry Dimock. ALS. DNA, RG 59. mDW 54018. Inquires about his compensation for printing the laws in the Washington, North Carolina *North State Whig*.

Dec 18   From Roland Dubs (with DW to Thomas Corwin, Feb 27, 1851). ALS. DNA, RG 206. Discusses the illegal discharge of an American seaman at Maracaibo by the brig *Maria* in November, 1850.

Dec 18   Application from Isaac Munroe, for the Baltimore *Patriot*—public printer (ALS. DNA, RG 59. mDW 53899).

Dec 18   Recommendation from J. Bowman Sweitzer, for the *Pittsburgh Gazette*—public printer (ALS. DNA. RG 59. mDW 53667).

Dec 18   Account with John Mills for $14.75 for boots and repairs, through Jan 20, 1851. AD. NhHi. mDW 40471.

Dec 18   Account with John Pettibone for $25 for ice tickets, through Mar 4, 1851. ADS. NhHi. mDW 40494.

Dec 19   To Charles M[ynn] Conrad. LS. Ronald von Klaussen, Florida. mDWs. Asks him to obtain verification of the alleged violation of U.S. territory at Sault Ste. Marie, Mich., by British soldiers in search of a deserter.

[Dec 19]   To Millard Fillmore. ALS. NBuHi. mDW 31865. Discusses the appointment of a judge in California.

[Dec 19]   To Millard Fillmore. ALS. NBuHi. mDW 31868. Wishes to discuss "the vacant Pursership."

[Dec 19]   From James Cooper. ALS. DNA, RG 59. mDW 53578. Advises that the Pennsylvania newspapers he is recommending to publish the laws have supported DW and the administration.

Dec 19   From Daniel Fletcher Webster. ALS. NhD. mDWs. Reports that Peter Harvey is on his way to Washington; inquires about the patent case *Sizer et al.* v. *Many*; says the Brandon *Vermont Union Whig* is "*the* paper in Vermont."

Dec 19   Recommendations from James Cooper, for the *Philadelphia Daily News, Pittsburgh Gazette, Lancaster Examiner and Herald,* and Harrisburg *Whig State Journal*—public printers (ALS. DNA, RG 59. mDW 53603).

Dec 20   To William Thomas Carroll. ALS. DNA, RG 267. mDWs. Asks when No. 70 will be reached in the Supreme Court; also for the number of *Sizer* v. *Many*, and when it will be reached.

[Dec 20]   To Millard Fillmore. LS. NBuHi. mDW 31870. Discusses the appointment of Hugh N. Smith as secretary of New Mexico Territory.

Dec 20   From Joseph Ripley Chandler. Press copy. DLC. mDW 31872. Presents a memorial from Philadelphia on behalf of the incumbent U.S. consul at Paris (Robert Walsh).

Dec 20   From Millard Fillmore. LS. ViU. mDW 31873. *Diplomatic Papers*, 2. Signifies his approval of DW's reply to Hülsemann.

Dec 20   From Henry S. Foote. ALS. DNA, RG 59. mDW 53551. Encloses letters (not found) from "excellent Whig *Union* editors" in Mississippi.

Dec 21   To Edward Everett. ALS. MHi. mDW 31875. Agrees with "Mr. Beaumont's" view of the future of France; reports the Hülsemann letter, revised and enlarged, has been copied and despatched.

Dec 21   To Franklin Haven. ALS. MH–H. mDW 31879. Discusses a matter of personal finance.

Dec 21   To Chevalier Johann Georg Hülsemann. LS. Austrian State Archives. mDW 31881. *Diplomatic Papers*, 2. Defends U.S. policy and especially the actions of the U.S. minister to Austria during the Hungarian uprising; affirms the philosophical basis of the American constitutional system and U.S. foreign policy.

Dec 21   To Asahel Huntington (with Huntington to Daniel Fletcher

Webster, Jan 2, 1857). Copy. NhHi. mDW 31924. Van Tyne, p. 445. Thinks Huntington's reaction to the 7th of March speech was typical of that of many Whigs.

Dec 21   To John Alexander McClernand. LS. NhD. mDW 31927. Suggests the State Department reorganization bill be allowed to stand on its own merits, without the addition of "incongruous matter of any kind."

Dec 21   To Ichabod Smith Spencer (with Spencer to Daniel Fletcher Webster, Nov 11, 1851). Copy. NhHi. mDW 31929. Van Tyne, pp. 444–445. Authorizes the publication of his letter to Spencer of Dec 7 and thanks him for a book.

Dec [21?]   To Charles Augustus Stetson. Telegram. Private owner, Massachusetts. mDWs. Has written a note to Sir Henry Bulwer; can only stay in New York "from Monday one o'clock till Tuesday morning"; Stetson to advise others.

Dec 21   From [Ernest André Olivier] Sain de Bois Le Comte (with Sir Henry Lytton Bulwer to DW, Dec 21, 1850). Copy. UkLPR. Calls on the United States to join Britain and France in mediating the war between Santo Domingo and Haiti.

Dec 21   From [Sir Henry Lytton Bulwer] (enclosures: Bulwer to [?] Upsher (Britsh consul at Port-au-Prince), Dec 21, 1850; Bois Le Comte to DW, Dec 21, 1850). AL draft. UkLPR. mDW 31933. Copy. UkLPR. mDWs. Makes suggestions for drafting instructions to the U.S. representative in Santo Domingo relative to the war with Haiti.

Dec 21   From John P. Gaines. ALS. DNA, RG 59. mDW 55004. Accepts appointment as territorial governor of Oregon.

Dec 21   From John P. Gaines. ALS. Or–Ar. mDWs. Acknowledges DW's letter of Aug. 10, 1850, regarding volumes shipped to the government of Oregon.

Dec 23   From Daniel Dewey Barnard. ALS. NhD. mDW 31938. Discusses matters concerning various U.S. diplomatic representatives in Europe.

Dec 23   From Ichabod Goodwin. ALS. DNA, RG 107. Asks DW to use his influence on behalf of Captain H. B. Judd, who is seeking transfer to one of the Army's new cavalry regiments.

Dec 23   From James Alphonsus McMaster. ALS. DLC. mDW 31943. Accuses Abbott Lawrence of making anti-Catholic statements, and asks if his remarks reflect the official sentiments of the Fillmore cabinet.

Dec 24   From Daniel Fletcher Webster, with enclosure. ALS. NhD. mDWs. Discusses the weather; sends a letter to be forwarded to Henry Sargent.

Dec 25   From William A. Weeks. ALS. DNA, RG 59. mDW 56879. Reports having forwarded despatches to London aboard the *America*.

Dec 26   From Asahel Huntington. ALS. NhHi. mDW 31947. Views the constitutional crisis of 1850 from the perspective of the Plymouth colonists; endorses DW's efforts to return national thinking to "first principles."

Dec 26   From Ambrose Dudley Mann. ALS. DNA, RG 59. mDW 55928. Reports the Swiss Congress has ratified the convention with the U.S.; comments briefly on related matters.

Dec 27   From Joseph Balestier (enclosure: Balestier to [William S.

Walker], Dec 15, 1850). ALS. DNA, RG 59. mDW 56084. Reports he
was unable to go to Sarawak and encloses a copy of his letter to the
captain of the U.S.S. *Saratoga*.

Dec 27   From Ambrose Dudley Mann (enclosures: Henri Druey to
Mann, Dec 13, 1850; reports of the committee of both houses of the
Swiss Congress relative to the treaty with the United States. ALS.
DNA, RG 59. mDW 55934. Transmits various papers and documents
pertaining to the convention he has just negotiated with Switzerland.

Dec 27   From Richard Rush. ALS. DLC. mDW 31950. Comments on
speeches by DW and Bulwer at the recent commemoration in New
York of the landing of the pilgrims at Plymouth.

Dec 27   Application from Rufus Hosmer, for the *Detroit Daily Advertiser*—public printer (ALS. DNA, RG 59. mDW 53864).

Dec 28   To Jesse D. Bright. LS. OrHi. mDW 31954. Finds no evidence
of charges against former governor of Oregon Joseph Lane in
State Department files.

Dec 28   From Robert G. Corwin (enclosure: William Greene to Corwin,
Dec 19, 1850). ALS. DLC. mDW 31956. Encloses a letter regarding
appointment to public office.

Dec 29   To Harriette Story White Paige. ALS. Mrs. Irvin McD. Garfield,
Southboro, Mass. *PC*, 2: 408–409. Discusses tripe.

Dec 29   To Charles Porter Wright. Printed. *PC*, 2: 407–408. Refers to
"the letter about guano" sent to Wright recently; discusses its
application.

Dec 30   To Millard Fillmore. LS. DNA, RG 46. mDW 51228. Transmits
official correspondence between the State Department and the Austrian chargé d'affaires, as requested by a Senate resolution of Sept
26, 1850.

Dec 31   To Charles Augustus Stetson. LS. Private owner, Massachusetts.
mDWs. Will be able to send Stetson a printed copy of his "New
England Dinner Speech" in a few days.

Dec 31   To William McKendree Gwin from Henry Sargent, for DW. ALS.
CU–BANC. mDWs. Reports the U.S. has no consul at Rialejo (Nicaragua) nor any plans at present to send one.

Dec 31   From Crane & Rice. ALS by proxy. DNA, RG 59. mDW 53897.
Accept appointment to publish the laws in the *California Courier*,
but report that the pamphlet containing the laws has not yet reached
them.

Dec 31   From Ambrose Dudley Mann. ALS. DNA, RG 59. mDW 55951.
Forwards documents from the Federal Council of the Swiss Confederation.

[Dec]   To John Taylor (enclosure: Thomas S. Pleasants to Thomas
Branch, Dec 11, 1850). ALS. NhHi. mDW 31959. Calls Taylor's attention to the enclosed commentary on guano and its application.

[1850]   To Richard Milford Blatchford. ALS. CtY. mDW 31965. Reports
spending the day working on his speeches with Everett; extols James
Watson Webb's article in the *Morning Courier & New York Enquirer*.

[1850]   To Clement Moore Butler. ANS inscription. PHi. mDW 31968.
Inscription on pamphlet copy of 7th of March speech.

[1850]   To Millard Fillmore. ALS. NBuHi. mDW 31971. Introduces
[Charles Brickett?] Hadduck.

[1850?]   To Harriette Story White Paige. ALS. Mrs. Irvin McD. Garfield,

Southboro, Mass. mDWs. Sends his family's epitaphs for her consideration.

[1850?]   From Charles Fox. ALS incomplete. DLC. mDW 38379. Mentions publishing a new book, and the death of his son; learns there is no vacancy at present for a chaplain.

[1850]   Account with D. McClelland for $39.50 for printing and engraving, Dec 3, 1849–Dec 31, 1850. DS. NhHi. mDW 40457.

[1850?]   Inscriptions for cemetery monuments at Marshfield. Printed. Curtis, 2: 331–332.

[1850]   Memorandum of events, September, 1849–April, 1850. AD. NhHi. mDW 31973. Lists his Supreme Court cases, Jan–April; notes precisely how long it took to deliver his 7th of March speech, and that it was ignored in the South Carolina press.

[1850–1851]   To Henry Sargent. ANS. Dr. George L. Hamilton, West Hartford, Ct. mDWs. Asks him to call after church.

[1850–1851?]   To John [?]. ANS. Dr. George L. Hamilton, West Hartford, Ct. mDWs. Asks for his fishing rod from "Mr. Bradford."

[1850–1851]   To B. Wilcox, from Henry Sargent, for DW. ALS. NBuHi. mDW 39230. Answers an inquiry regarding DW's 1826 eulogy of Adams and Jefferson.

[1850–1852]   To George Jacob Abbot. ALS. CtY. mDW 31977. Asks for Abbot's letter to Mr. Griswold, and also for [Hiram] Ketchum's letter.

[1850–1852]   To George Jacob Abbot. ALS. John R. Morison, Peterborough, N.H. mDW 31979. Instructs him to send "Mr. Adam's letter to "Mr [Edward?] Curtis (enclosed) at the Committee Room."

[1850–1852]   To [Millard Fillmore]. ALS. NBuHi. mDW 31981. Encloses a letter addressed to Everett by a friend.

[1850–1852]   To Nathan Kelsey Hall. ANS. NBuHi. mDW 31983. Recommends Joseph K. Hartwell for a clerkship.

[1850–1852]   To Henry Hallam. Draft in George Jacob Abbot's hand. CtY. mDW 31985. Introduces the Rev. W[illiam] C[hauncey] Fowler (former professor of Rhetoric and Oratory at Amherst College).

[1850–1852]   To Franklin Haven. ALS. MH-H. mDW 38527. Discusses a financial matter involving Rufus Choate.

[1850–1852]   To [Daniel?] Le Roy. NNPM. mDW 31987. Expresses disappointment that Le Roy and his daughters were not there for dinner, but he will be glad to see them at tea.

[1850–1852]   To Francis Markoe, Jr. ANS. NN. mDW 31989. Encloses an anonymous note accusing Markoe of electioneering in the Senate and advises him to be cautious.

[1850–1852]   From [Anonymous] (with DW to Markoe, [1850–1852]). ALS. NN. mDW 31990. Accuses Markoe of electioneering in the Senate and demands his removal from office.

[1850–1852]   From William Appleton. ALS. CtY. mDW 38197. Informs him of a "Mr. Sanders from Tennessee," editor of a Webster Whig newspaper, and a "Mr. Patten of Charleston, S.C.," who desire to see DW.

[1850–1852]   From George Bancroft. ALS. mDW 38214. Has received DW's parcel; can't remember "whether I was to send a Photograph or not."

[1850–1852]   From Millard Fillmore. ALS. DLC. mDW 32008. Is prepared to see DW this morning at eleven.

[1850–1852?] Speech at public school festival. Draft in George Jacob
    Abbot's hand. CtY. mDW 31991.

1851

Jan 1   From John Taylor (with DW to Edward H. Hadduck, Jan 3,
    1851). ALS. NhHi. mDW 32009. Asks DW to write Hadduck on be-
    half of his son, Henry Taylor.
Jan 1   From Samuel Wood. ALS. NhHi. mDW 32011. Inquires about pur-
    chasing an Ayrshire cow and also about sweet turnips as cattle
    feed.
Jan 1   Application from Thomas H. Bringhurst for the *Logansport*
    (Ind.) *Journal*—public printer (ALS. DNA, RG 59. mDW 53870).
Jan 2   To Sarah Goodridge. ALS. MHi. mDW 32013. Sends a check in
    partial payment of a debt.
Jan 2   To J[oseph?] Howard & Son. LS. NBLiHi. mDW 32014. Writes re-
    garding their claim against New Granada for a shipment of gold
    dust seized in Panama.
Jan 2   To Charles Porter Wright. Printed. *PC*, 2: 409. Gives instructions
    for butchering and curing meat.
Jan 2   From E[rastus] C. Benedict. ALS. ViU. mDWs. Commends DW's
    Hülsemann correspondence.
Jan 2   From Sir Henry Lytton Bulwer. LS. DLC. mDW 32017. Will cor-
    rect the report of "my speech" and send it to DW tomorrow.
Jan 2   From Edward Everett. LC. MHi. mDW 32019. Comments on DW's
    reply to Hülsemann and offers to do research for him; praises his re-
    cent speech in New York.
Jan 2   From John Plummer Healy.   190
Jan 2   Recommendations from Richard Wigginton Thompson, for the
    Madison (Ind.) *Daily Banner*; Brookville, *Indiana American*; Terre
    Haute, Ind. *Wabash Express*; *New Albany* (Ind.) *Gazette*; and *Vin-
    cennes* (Ind.) *Gazette*—public printers (ALS. DNA, RG 59. mDW
    53882).
Jan 3   To E[dward] H. Hadduck (with John Taylor to DW, Jan 1, 1851).
    AL copy. NhHi. mDW 32010. Describes Henry Taylor as honest and
    capable, and an experienced drover.
Jan 3   To [Abbott Lawrence]. AL. NhD. mDWs. Apologizes for not writ-
    ing sooner; reports a calm Congress; is concerned that if imports
    continue at the present rate "we shall have a catastrophy"; wants to
    know what England is likely to do about gold and silver; notes that
    Fillmore's administration is "harmonious."
Jan 3   To George Washington Nesmith. Printed. *PC*, 2: 409–410. De-
    clares "Your friend Fowler, being a good Union man, is safe"; in-
    quires about the use of lime and plaster on potato fields.
Jan 3   from James H. Causten (with DW to Andrew Jackson Donelson,
    Jan 8, 1851). Copy. DLC. mDW 32065. Asks the State Department to
    assist him in obtaining documents needed in a Texas claim case.
Jan 4   To Stephen Pleasonton. Copy. DLC. mDW 32025. Discusses salary
    and expenses due James Brown Clay, former U.S. chargé d'affaires
    in Portugal, and charges for newspapers.

Jan 4   Recommendation from David Alexander Bokee, for the *Albany*
(N.Y.) *State Register*—public printer (ALS. DNA, RG 59. mDW
53670).

Jan 5   To Richard Milford Blatchford. Printed. *PC*, 2: 410. Wishes to
repay advances made by Blatchford and others in anticipation of
fccs in the passenger case.

Jan 5   To Apollinairie Antoine Maurice, Comte d'Argout. Facsimile.
Godsey's Magazine, 128 (March, 1894): 353–355. mDW 32028.
Introduces Thurlow Weed; speaks philosophically of the past,
present, and future.

Jan 6   To George William Frederick Howard (7th Earl of Carlisle). ALS.
NRU. mDW 32031. Thurlow Weed Barnes, ed., *Memoir of Thurlow
Weed* (Boston, 1884), p. 199. Introduces Thurlow Weed.

Jan 6   To Charles William Wentworth (3rd Earl of Fitzwilliam). ALS.
NRU. mDW 32033. Introduces Thurlow Weed.

Jan 6   To John Winthrop. AL copy. NhHi. mDW 32035. Agrees to be retained as counsel in *J. B. Piagio* v. *The Tow Boat Shark*.

Jan 6   From William Adams. ALS. NhHi. mDW 32038. Encloses his discourse on civil government; reflects on DW's role in the recent crisis
with a quotation from Pliny.

Jan 6   From Edward Everett. LC. MHi. mDW 32043. Encloses a letter
from "Mr. [Joshua?] Bates" on French and German politics.

Jan 6   From Elizabeth A. McNeil. ALS copy. NhHi. mDW 32045. Asks
DW to asslst in the adjustment of a debt due the government from
the estate of her late husband, a former surveyor of the port of
Boston.

Jan 6   From Walter Underhill. ALS. DNA, RG 76. mDWs. Requests information about the claims allowed U.S. citizens under the recent
treaty with Brazil.

Jan 6   Recommendation from William C. Dawson, for the Macon
Georgia Journal and Messenger—public printer (ALS. DNA, RG 59.
mDW 53964).

Jan 7   To John Davis (1787–1854) and Joseph Grinnell. ALS draft.
NhHi. mDW 32047. Introduces Tilden Ames, the bearer of a petition
for an appropriation for dredging a new outlet for the North River at
Marshfield.

Jan 7   To Millard Fillmore. LS. NBuHi. mDW 32050. Sends a volume of
New York statutes containing the law on habeus corpus.

Jan 7   To Millard Fillmore. LS. NBuHi. mDW 32052. Thinks the removal
of Chief Justice Aaron Goodrich of Minnesota ought to be the subject of a special message to the Senate.

Jan 7   To Millard Fillmore. Dictated letter. NBuHi. mDW 32057. Notes
that all the nominations for justices in the District of Columbia mentioned in the report submitted to "the ex-mayor" are old appointments.

Jan 7   From Millard Fillmore. ANS. NBuHi. mDW 32056. Encloses a list
of nominees for justices of the peace in Washington, D.C.

Jan 7   Application from William W. Wyman, for the Madison *Wisconsin
Statesman*—public printer (ALS. DNA, RG 59. mDW 53998).

Jan 7   Recommendation from William King Sebastian, for the Helena,
Arkansas, *Southern Shield*—public printer (ALS. DNA, RG 59.
mDW 53665).

Jan 7   Account with I. Hill for $156.38 1/2 for firewood, through Feb 12, 1852. DS. NhHi. mDW 40599.

Jan 8   To Sir Henry Lytton Bulwer. LS. UkLPR. mDW 32059. *Diplomatic Papers*, 2. Acknowledges Bulwer's note announcing that certain duties now levied at San Juan de Nicaragua are to be revoked as of Jan 31, 1851.

Jan 8   To Sir Henry Lytton Bulwer. LS. UkLPR. mDW 32060. Responds to a request for the extradition of George Matthews, explaining some details of the extradition law of Aug 12, 1848.

Jan 8   To Andrew Jackson Donelson (enclosure: James H. Causten to DW, Jan 3, 1851). LS. DLC. mDW 32063. Draws Donelson's attention to a demand for documents relative to a claim against "the late Government of Texas for the schooner Mary Elizabeth and cargo."

Jan 8   To Edward Everett.   192

Jan 8   To James Watson Webb. ALS. CtY. mDW 32069. *Diplomatic Papers*, 2. Acknowledges "your remarkable article" on the Hülsemann correspondence; recollects their discussion in New Hampshire of Austrian affairs.

Jan 8   From Angel Calderon de la Barca (with DW to Fillmore, Feb 8, 1851). Translation. DNA, RG 46. mDW 51233. Urges that Congress be called upon to make immediate settlement of the *Amistad* claim.

Jan 8   From George Washington Nesmith.   192

Jan 8   From John H. Sherburne. ALS. NhD. mDW 32074. Asks DW's assistance in obtaining the approval of the French government for the disinterment of John Paul Jones's remains for eventual burial in the United States.

Jan 7   Account with I. Hill for $156.38 1/2 for firewood, through

Jan 8   Recommendations from Solon Borland, for the Little Rock *Arkansas State Gazette and Democrat*—public printer (ALS. DNA, RG 59. mDW 53902); from John H. Clarke et al., for the *Providence* (R.I.) *Daily Journal* and the *Newport* (R.I.) *Daily News*—public printers (ALS by Clarke, signed also by others. DNA, RG 59. mDW 54020); from William A. Gorman, for the *Vincennes* (Ind.) *Gazette*—public printer (ALS. DNA, RG 59. mDW 53880).

Jan 8   Receipt for $2.55 paid the Washington Branch Railroad for cartage. DS. NhHi. mDW 40461.

Jan 9   To Edward Curtis. ALS. NhExP. mDWs. Asks him to "come at 6 & take Mr. Corwin's place."

[Jan 9] To Millard Fillmore. AL. NBuHi. mDW 32078. Offers to see him at the State Department or the White House.

Jan 9   To George Ticknor. ALS. NjMoHP. mDW 32080. *W & S*, 16: 584. Discusses arrangements for the new edition of his works.

Jan 9   To James Wilson (with Albert Fitz to [Wilson], [n.d]). LS. NhHi. mDW 32082. Introduces Albert Fitz and recommends him for public employment.

Jan 9   From Nathan Kelsey Hall. LS. DNA, RG 59. mDW 53955. Discusses newspapers appointed to print the laws in Georgia.

Jan 9   Account with Clagett, Newton, May & Co. for $13.23 for dry goods, through May 15. DS. NhHi. mDW 40548.

Jan 10   To Sir Henry Lytton Bulwer. LS. UkLPR. mDW 32085. Gives assurances that U.S. colors were never displayed over Tigre Island by

authority of the U.S. government and that steps will be taken to see
that they are removed.

Jan 10   To Millard Fillmore. Dictated letter. NBuHi. mDW 32087. Will
introduce him to the new chargé d'affaires for Sweden and Norway,
[M.G.] de Sibbern, tomorrow.

[Jan 10]   To Millard Fillmore. ALS. NBuHi. mDW 32360. Is having Gen.
[Emilio de] Alvea summoned with regard to "the Buenos Ayres
business."

Jan 10   To Nathan Kesley Hall. LS (with postscript in DW's hand).
NhD. mDW 32089. Reports that no Georgia newspapers have as yet
been appointed to print the laws.

Jan 10   To Robert M. McLane. LS. DNA, RG 233 mDWs. Calls attention
to the present scarcity of silver and suggests that Congress find a
remedy.

Jan 10   To Thomas Abbot Merrill. ALS. NhD. mDW 32091. *PC*, 2: 411–
412. Acknowledges a letter; recalls their college days at Dartmouth.

Jan 10   From Rufus Choate (enclosure: statement by George S. Hillard
et al., U.S. Circuit Court, Mass. District). ALS. DLC. mDW 32095.
Comments on the administration of justice in the Massachusetts district of the U.S. Circuit Court; recommends George Ticknor Curtis
for a position if there is to be "a change in the office."

Jan 10   From Millard Fillmore. ALS. DLC. mDW 32108. Severance, *Fillmore Papers*, 1: 337. Discusses the applicability of habeus corpus
in fugitive slave cases, and also the matter of a jailer's authority to
hold a fugitive slave in a county jail.

Jan 10   From Millard Fillmore. ALS. DLC. mDW 32110. Returns a despatch and suggests that a protest be filed with the Argentine
minister.

Jan 10   From Milo Furbush & Co. (enclosure: DW's account for gro-
ceries, Mar 25–Nov 15, 1850). LS. NhHi. mDW 40465. Acknowledge DW's check for $150 and ask him to remit the full amount of
the remaining balance due.

Jan 10   From William Alexander Graham. LS. DNA, RG 76 mDWs.
Transmits papers and returns others relative to the capture of the
brig *Volusia*.

Jan 10   Recommendation from Samuel Atkins Eliot, for "Dr. Bugbee"—
a position in California. (ALS with ANS by DW. DLC. mDW 32106).

Jan 10   Receipt for $13.13 paid the Washington Branch Railroad for cart-
age. DS. NhHi. mDW 40463.

Jan 11   To Sir Henry Lytton Bulwer. LS. UkLPR. mDW 32112. Informs
him that the official thanks of the British government have been re-
layed to an American captain for assisting a British vessel in distress.

Jan 11   To Sir Henry Lytton Bulwer. LS. UkLPR. mDW 32113. Applies
for the extradition of Ira C. Jones, wanted in Lowell, Mass. for
counterfeiting.

Jan 11   To Millard Fillmore. ALS. NBuHi. mDW 32115. Van Tyne, p.
445. Reports on the balloting for U.S. Senator in Massachusetts.

Jan 11   From Thomas Corwin (with DW to Sir Henry Lytton Bulwer,
Jan 14, 1851 enclosure: Corwin to [John Adair], Jan 11, 1851).
Copy. UkLPR. mDW 32153. Transmits a copy of his instructions to

the U.S. customs collector at Astoria, Ore., relative to the seizure of the British ship *Albion* in April, 1850.

Jan 12   To William Adams. Printed. *PC*, 2: 412–413. Praises the style and thought in Adams's "Christianity and Civil Government."

Jan 12   From John Middleton Clayton (enclosure: F. Schwarzenburg to Chevalier Johann Georg Hülsemann, Nov 5, 1849, French text with English translation). ALS. NhHi. mDW 32121. *Diplomatic Papers*, 2. Commends DW's reply to Hülsemann and comments on "mistakes" which appear in Hülsemann's note to DW.

Jan 13   To Sir Henry Lytton Bulwer. LS. UkLPR. mDW 32140. Reports the State Department has no information about the fate of George Shapcott.

Jan 13   Application from Charles Hopkins—clerkship (ALS with ANS by DW. DLC. mDW 32143).

Jan 13   Recommendations from Joseph Ripley Chandler, for Samuel J. Oakford—U.S. consul at Tumbez, Peru (Presscopy. DLC. mDW 32142).

Jan 14   To Sir Henry Lytton Bulwer. LS. UkLPR. mDW 32147. Reports the U.S. government has no authority to intervene in a Maine decision invalidating the claim of a New Brunswick man to land on the Aroostook River.

Jan 14   To Sir Henry Lytton Bulwer. LS. UkLPR. mDW 32149. Reports an American agent will be sent to cooperate with agents of Britain and France in mediating the war between Haiti and the Dominican Republic.

Jan 14   To Sir Henry Lytton Bulwer (enclosure: Thomas Corwin to DW, Jan 11, 1851). LS. UkLPR. mDW 32151. Transmits correspondence pertaining to the seizure of the British ship *Albion* by customs authorities at Astoria, Ore.

Jan 14   To James Linen. LS. CSt. mDW 32156. Declines an invitation to the annual festival of the New York "Burns Club."

Jan 14   Recommendation from Jeremiah Clemens, for the Huntsville, Ala., *Southern Advocate*—public printer (ALS. DNA, RG 59. mDW 53860).

Jan 15   To Joseph Blunt. LS. NNMus. mDW 38275. Advises Blunt to see [William T.] Carroll before his case (*Van Rensselaer* v. *Kearney*) comes up for argument before the Supreme Court.

Jan 15   To Rufus Choate. AL copy. DLC. mDW 32158. Inquires about the distribution of complaints among the commissioners of the U.S. Circuit Court in Boston; asks if the incumbent U.S. attorney for Massachusetts is competent.

Jan 15   To John Middleton Clayton. AL draft. NhHi. mDW 32162. LS. DLC. mDW 32165. *Diplomatic Papers*, 2. Sees firm evidence that the Austrian government knew of the private instructions to Ambrose Dudley Mann.

Jan 15   To [Edward Curtis]. ALS. NN. mDW 32168. Is expecting him for dinner, and asks whom else he should invite.

Jan 15   To Miner, Lawrence & Co. LS. DNA, RG 76. Encloses copies of papers they requested relating to the brig *Louisa Beaton*.

Jan 15   From Sir Henry Lytton Bulwer. Copy. UkLPR. mDWs. Requests an estimate of the number of British subjects in the U.S. on Mar 31, 1851.

Jan 15   From Sir Henry Lytton Bulwer. Copy. UkLPR. mDWs. Transmits a request by the British government that the Hudson's Bay Company's establishment at Nisqually be authorized as a port of delivery.

Jan 15   From Edward Everett. ALS. MHi. mDW 32171. Makes suggestions for the new edition of DW's works and agrees to prepare a "biographical notice"; comments on the recent seizure of the *Niagara* at Boston for attempted smuggling.

Jan 15   From Christopher Richardson. Copy. UkLPR. mDW 32175. Urges settlement of claims against the U.S. filed by owners of the British ship *Francis & Eliza*.

Jan 16   To Millard Fillmore. LS. NBuHi. mDW 32177. Sends a copy of the instructions given H.M. consul at Haiti and the draft of instructions to be given Robert Walsh, recently appointed U.S. agent to Haiti and the Dominican Republic.

Jan 16   To Millard Fillmore. ALS. NBuHi. mDW 32179. *W & S*, 16: 585–586. Cites evidence that the Austrian government somehow knew of the secret instructions given to Ambrose Dudley Mann.

Jan 16   To George Ticknor. Printed. Curtis, 2: 537. *Diplomatic Papers*, 2. Responds to Ticknor's assertion that his Hülsemann letter is "boastful and rough."

Jan 16   From William W. De Forest & Co. LS. NhD. mDW 32183. Protest the removal of Joseph Graham, U.S. consul at Buenos Ayres, and his replacement by E. A. Saunders, whose family are "Abolitionists of the most rabid kind."

Jan 16   From Millard Fillmore. ALS. NhHi. mDW 32185. Van Tyne, pp. 456–457. Comments on the evidence that the Austrian government somehow knew of the private instructions to Ambrose Dudley Mann.

Jan 16   From James A. Hamilton et al. LS. NjMoHP. Invite DW to address a Union meeting in Tarrytown, N.Y.

Jan 16   From N. Biddle Van Zandt. ALS. DNA, RG 59. mDW 55115. Accepts appointment as justice of the peace for Washington, D.C.

Jan 16   Account with G. E. Kirk for $5 for paint, painting, etc., through Apr 12. ADS. NhHi. mDW 40595.

Jan 17   To Millard Fillmore. LS. NBuHi. mDW 32188. Van Tyne, p. 447, errs both as to date and recipient of the instructions. Agrees to incorporate Fillmore's words into the instructions to Walsh at Haiti.

[Jan 17]   To Millard Fillmore. ALS. NBuHi. mDW 32190. Claims he made "the change" (removal of Graham as U.S. consul at Buenos Ayres) unwillingly, but that "Ketchum, & some of the Union Comee. seemed resolved to take no denial."

Jan 17   To Millard Fillmore (enclosure: Gilbert C. Russell to DW, Sept 12, 1850), and reply, Sept 13, 1850). ALS. NhD. mDWs. LS. NBuHi. mDW 32193. Van Tyne, pp. 446–447. Explains his decision to deny Gilbert Russell permission to look through State Department files for papers relative to the [Joseph] De la Francia claim.

Jan 17   From Benjamin B. French. ALS. DNA, RG 59. mDW 54996. Accepts appointment as justice of the peace for Washington, D.C.

Jan 17   From George Griswold.   *194*

Jan 17   Recommendations from James Cooper, for various Pennsylvania newspapers—public printers (ALS, DNA, RG 59. mDW 53837).

Jan 18   To Sir Henry Lytton Bulwer. LS. UkLPR. mDW 32202. Cannot

supply him with estimates of the number of British subjects now
living in the United States.

Jan 18   To Jose Maria Medrano. Printed. Sumner Welles, *Naboth's
Vineyard: The Dominican Republic 1844–1924* (2 vols., New York,
1928), 1: 122. Introduces Robert M. Walsh, special agent of the
United States to the Dominican Republic and Haiti.

Jan 18   To Benjamin Franklin Perry. LS. A-Ar. mDWs. Typed copy. A-Ar.
mDW 32203. Acknowledges a copy of Perry's Union speech; asks
which South Carolina papers might be appointed to print the laws.

Jan 18   To Charles Augustus Stetson (enclosure?: memo on nominations before the Senate). ALS.ViU. mDW 32204. Promises to keep
him informed on the status of nominations; doubts that [Hiland?]
Hall's nomination is in any danger.

Jan 18   To Robert M. Walsh. Copy. UkLPR. mDWs. Gives Walsh instructions for his mission to the Dominican Republic and Haiti.

Jan 18   To Robert M. Walsh. Printed. Sumner Welles, *Naboth's Vineyard: The Dominican Republic 1844–1924* (2 vols., New York,
1928), 1: 113–115. Gives Walsh additional instructions.

Jan 18   From Millard Fillmore. AL. DLC. mDW 32207. Severance, *Fillmore Papers*, 1: 338. Returns "Mr. Dennison's letter."

Jan 18   From D[avid] Saunders. ALS. DNA, RG 59. mDW 55089. Accepts appointment as justice of the peace for Washington, D.C.

[Jan 19]   To Millard Fillmore. ALS. NBuHi. mDW 32208. Forwards despatches just received from abroad.

Jan 19   To James Watson Webb. ALS. CtY. mDW 32211. Reminds Webb
of their dinner engagement.

Jan 20 [1851?]   To Robert P. Anderson. ANS. NhHi. mDW 38191. Asks
Anderson to deliver "whatever Documents there may be belonging to
me, in the Senate" to John A. Rockwell and John W. Allen.

Jan 20   To Thomas Buckminster Curtis.   *196*

Jan 20   To John Osborne Sargent. Invitation. MHi. mDW 32216.

Jan 20   From Daniel Dewey Barnard. LC. N. mDWs. Suggests [Henry
S.] Sanford or Peter A. Porter as choices for secretary of legation at
Berlin.

Jan 20   From Henry Augustus Boardman. ALS. NhHi. mDW 32217.
Praises the Hülsemann letter and recommends its general dissemination in Europe; requests DW to prevail upon the *National Intelligencer* to assist in circulating his own pamphlet on the Union.

Jan 20   From R[obert] H. Clements. ALS. DNA, RG 59. mDW 54975.
Accepts appointment as justice of the peace for Washington, D.C.

Jan 20   From Samuel Finley Breese Morse. ALS. ICHi. mDW 32220.
Diplomatic Papers, 2. Introduces Henry D. J. Pratt; lauds DW's
"noble and American position" on the slavery controversy, and his
"admirable rebuke" of Hülsemann.

Jan 20   From Robert White. ALS. DNA, RG 59. mDW 55129. Accepts
appointment as justice of the peace for Washington, D.C.

Jan 20   Application from Robert Lefavour—Army paymaster (Copy.
DNA, RG 92. mDW 57097).

Jan 20   Recommendations from O[rsamus] Cole, for the *Milwaukee
Sentinel & Gazette*, and the Madison *Wisconsin Express*—public
printers (ALS. DNA, RG 59. mDW 53941).

Jan 21 To Edward Everett (enclosure: Edward Curtis to DW, Jan 21, 1851). ALS. MHi. mDW 32221. *PC*, 2: 413–414. Asks Everett to take charge of the new edition of his works.

Jan 21 To Charles Augustus Stetson. ALS. NhD. mDW 32225. Discusses the meaning and design of his family's coat of arms.

Jan 21 From Edward Curtis (with DW to Edward Everett, Jan 21, 1851). Printed. *PC*, 2: 414. Hopes Everett will take charge of the publication of DW's works.

Jan 21 Recommendations from Rufus Choate, for George W. Cooley— U.S. district judge in California (ALS. PP. mDW 32228); from D. Cooper, for the St. Paul *Minnesota Chronicle and Register*—public printer (ALS. DNA, RG 59. mDW 53858).

Jan 21 U.S. Senate resolution ordering an inquiry into the expediency of reorganizing the Department of State. DS. DNA, RG 46. mDW 51179.

Jan 22 From Thomas Corwin (with DW to Sir Henry Lytton Bulwer, Jan 24, 1851). Copy. UkLPR. mDW 32243. States that Astoria must remain Oregon's sole port of entry until Nisqually shall be so designated by an act of Congress.

Jan 22 From Henry Dilworth Gilpin. ALS. NhHi. mDW 32230. Praises DW's Hülsemann correspondence and his speech to the New England Society at New York.

Jan 22 From J[ohn] K[earsley] Mitchell. ALS. NhHi. mDW 32233. Commends "the style & sentiment" of DW's letter to Hülsemann.

Jan 22 Recommendations from G. Blainache and Justin Butterfield, for the Rock Island, Ill. *Advertiser*—public printer (ALS by Blainache, signed also by Butterfield. DNA, RG 59. mDW 53889); from Joseph R. Underwood, for the Bowling Green, Kentucky, *Warren Intelligencer*—public printer (ALS. DNA, RG 59. mDW 53950).

Jan 22 U.S. Senate Bill #421 "to Reorganize the Department of State." Printed D. DNA, RG 46. mDW 51178.

[Jan 23?] To Millard Fillmore. ALS. NBuHi. mDW 32365. Advises withholding John Strother Pendleton's nomination (chargé d'affaires in Argentina) on the chance he might be better qualified for a different post.

Jan 23 To Franklin Haven. LS. MH–H. mDW 32236. Asks if "Mr. May" has sent "all the scrip which was in your bank."

Jan 23 To Hiram Ketchum. ALS. NhD. mDW 32237. Reports the President is inclined to reverse the decision affecting the Buenos Ayres consulate.

Jan 23 To William Strong. LS. PPAmP. mDW 32240. Feels he cannot order the U.S. minister to France to make further inquiry in the case of Alex Schubart.

Jan 24 To Sir Henry Lytton Bulwer (enclosure: Thomas Corwin to DW, Jan 22, 1851). LS. UkLPR. mDW 32241. Relays the Treasury secretary's decision regarding ports of entry for Oregon.

Jan 24 To Charles M[ynn] Conrad (enclosures: Robert Lefavour to DW, Jan 20, 1851; testimonials for Lefavour). LS. DNA, RG 92. mDW 57095. Testifies to the good character of the individuals who signed the enclosed testimonials on behalf of Robert Lefavour.

Jan 24 To Thomas Buckminster Curtis.   *196*

Jan 24   To [Samuel Dinsmoor]. LS. NhD. mDW 32248. Reports 140 additional copies of the laws passed at the 1st session of the 31st Congress are being sent to New Hampshire.

Jan 24   To Millard Fillmore. LS. NBuHi. mDW 32240. Has written De Forest & Co. and others regarding "a subject" (dismissal of Joseph Graham as U.S. consul at Buenos Ayres), with the promise to correct any mistake.

Jan 24   To Millard Fillmore (with reply, c. Jan 24). ALS. NBuHi. mDW 32251. Expresses concern about the jealousy among the New York Whigs.

Jan 24   To Edward Kent. ALS. NhHi. mDW 32252. Introduces Lt. George H. Page, U.S. Army.

Jan 24   From Mariano Arista (with English translation). LS in Spanish, NhHi. mDW 32254. Observes that the Mexican Congress will not accept any changes in the Tehuantepec treaty; urges that Robert Perkins Letcher be retained as U.S. minister to Mexico; is sending him an atlas prepared by the Mexican Geographical and Statistical Society.

Jan 24   From Thomas Cadwalader. ALS. DLC. mDW 32260. Thinks DW's recent speech to the New England Society of New York was particularly relevant to "the present political crisis."

Jan 24   From Edward Everett. ALS. MHi. mDW 32264. Agrees to oversee the publication of DW's works, but advises he is thinking of spending a few months abroad later in the year.

[c. Jan 24]   From Millard Fillmore (with DW to Fillmore, Jan 24, [1851]). ANS. NBuHi. mDW 32251. Declares that the Administration must stand on the principles of his message to Congress and recognize as friends those "who go with us."

Jan 24   From John Bannister Gibson. ALS. NhHi. mDW 32267. Acknowledges copies of DW's speech to the New England Society of New York and his Hülsemann correspondence.

Jan 24   Recommendations from James G. King and William A. Newell, for the *Trenton State Gazette* and the *Newark Daily Advertiser*—public printers (ALS by King, signed also by Newell. DNA, RG 59, mDW 54022).

Jan 25   To Millard Fillmore (with reply, Jan 25 [1851]). Dictated letter. DLC. mDW 32269. Severance, *Fillmore Papers*, 1: 339. Encloses notes from the Spanish minister concerning the *Amistad*.

Jan 25   To Millard Fillmore. LS. NBuHi. mDW 32272. Discusses various diplomatic appointments.

Jan 25   To J. B. Gardiner (with handwritten extract from DW's speech on the President's Protest, delivered in the Senate on May 7, 1834). ALS. NcU. mDW 32275. Answers a question by referring Gardiner to his Senate speech of May 7, 1834.

Jan 25   From Mariano Arista (with English translation). LS in Spanish. NhHi. mDW 32277. Warns that the Mexican Congress may refuse to ratify the Tehuantepec treaty.

Jan 25   From Joseph Balestier. ALS. DNA, RG 59. mDW 56088. Reports having received "no advices from the Government," nor notice of the arrival of a government ship.

Jan 25   From Millard Fillmore (with DW to Fillmore, Jan 25, 1851). ALS. DLC. mDW 32270. Severance, *Fillmore Papers*, 1: 338. Fears it may be politically unwise to press the *Amistad* claims on Congress now, but will adhere to the treaty whatever the risk.

Jan 25   From Nathan Kelsey Hall. ALS. DNA, RG 59. mDW 54024. Advises that the *Newark Daily Advertiser* and the *Trenton State Gazette* are recommended to publish the laws in New Jersey.

Jan 25   From Sergio Texcira de Macedo. Printed. Curtis, 2: 562–564. Complains of a breach of diplomatic etiquette at the dinner recently given by DW.

Jan 26   From Joseph Balestier (enclosure: statement of Javanese exports to the U.S. 1845–1850). ALS. DNA, RG 59. mDW 56090. Describes the commerce and commercial system of Java and its dependencies.

Jan 26   From Sir Henry Lytton Bulwer (enclosure: draft of a proposed reply from DW to Sergio Texeira de Macedo, in Bulwer's hand). ALS. DLC. mDW 32283. Curtis, 2: 565. Comments on the misunderstanding with Macedo which transpired at DW's private dinner.

[Jan 26]   From Sir Henry Lytton Bulwer. ALS. DLC. mDW 32290. Curtis, 2: 565. Reports remonstrating with Macedo over his complaint of a slight at DW's dinner.

Jan 26 [1851?]   From William S. Derrick. ALS. Dr. George L. Hamilton, West Hartford, Ct. mDWs. Informs DW where to find lists of "the French claims referred to by your correspondent."

Jan 27   To Roger Sherman Baldwin. LS. Ct. mDW 32295. Asks him to see what might be done about reimbursing Governor [Charles] Elliott (of Bermuda) for assistance rendered a shipwrecked American.

Jan 27   To Sir Henry Lytton Bulwer. LS. UkLPR. mDW 32298. Calls attention to a "singular correspondence" between H.M. consul at Charleston and the governor of South Carolina.

Jan 27   To James A. Hamilton et al. ALS draft. NjMoHP. mDW 32299 and mDWs. LS. NN. *Boston Atlas*, Feb 1, 1851, and *Works*, 6: 582–586. Warns of the dangers of secession and disunion, and emphasizes that forceful resistance to the laws constitutes treason.

Jan 27   To Edward William Johnston. LS. DNA, RG 76. mDW 57093. Transmits correspondence concerning the deportation of Americans from California in 1840 and their subsequent release by the Mexican government.

Jan 27   To Sergio Texeira de Macedo. ALS draft. DLC. mDW 32302. Curtis, 2: 564. Notes his ignorance of the Treaty of Vienna, and explains that the recent dinner at which Macedo was a guest was a private affair, not governed by diplomatic protocol.

Jan 27   From Sir Henry Lytton Bulwer. ALS. DLC. mDW 32304. Curtis, 2: 565. Approves DW's reply to Macedo, but suggests that the tone be softened somewhat.

Jan 27   From Abbott Lawrence. ALS. DLC. mDW 32308. *Diplomatic Papers*, 2. Is seeking to give DW's Hülsemann letter wide circulation in England and Europe.

Jan 27   From Timothy R. Young and Andrew Johnson. ALS by Johnson, signed also by Young NhD. mDW 32311. Ask DW to state publicly his views on the disposition of the public domain, and send him a copy of a bill now before the House, asking if it embraces his ideas on the subject.

Jan 27   Recommendations from Benjamin Franklin Perry, for the

Greenville, S.C. *Southern Patriot*, the Columbia *South Carolinian*, and the *Charleston* (S.C.) *Courier*—public printers (ALS. DNA, RG 59. mDW 54029).

Jan 28 To Angel Calderon de la Barca. DS. Archivo General de Indias, Seville, Spain. mDW 32315. Receipt for interest on the Spanish debt.

Jan 28 To Logan Hunton. Copy. DNA, RG 59. mDW 56544. Orders him to look out for a steamer suspected of carrying rifles for the Cuban filibusters.

Jan 28 From Sergio Texeira de Macedo. Printed. Curtis, 2: 564–565, Accepts DW's explanation of diplomatic protocol.

[Jan 28] From Daniel Fletcher Webster. ALS. NhHi. mDW 32317. Advises that a large sum may be due DW on the East Boston shares now held for him by Thayer & Brother.

Jan 29 To A[ndrew] P[ickens] Butler. LS. DNA, RG 46. mDWs. Calls attention to William Strong's complaints about the inadequacy of salaries paid judges in Oregon.

Jan 29 To William Alexander Graham. ALS draft. NhD. mDWs. Introduces A[lfred] G. Benson of New York, who has part of a claim still pending.

Jan 29 To Morris Ketchum. AL draft. DLC. mDW 32321. *W & S*, 16: 595. Reports the President is inclined to reinstate Joseph Graham as U.S. consul at Buenos Ayres.

Jan 29 To R[obert] Toombs. ALS. NhD. mDW 32324. Asks him to give the writer of the enclosed note five minutes' conversation.

Jan 29 To [Charles K. Williams]. LS. Vermont State House. mDWs. Reports additional copies of laws from the 1st session of the 31st Congress are being sent to Vermont.

Jan 29 From J[oseph] R. Flanigen. ALS. DNA, RG 59. mDW 53824. Accepts appointment to publish the laws in the *Philadelphia Daily News*.

Jan 29 From William Freret. ALS. DNA, RG 59. mDW 56547. Having been warned of another expedition against Cuba, promises full vigilance to see that the neutrality laws are not broken.

Jan 29 From Logan Hunton. ALS. DNA, RG 59. mDW 56545. Promises every precaution to prevent movements in support of the suspected Cuban filibusters.

Jan 29 From Abbot Lawrence. ALS. DLC. mDW 32326. Reports on the dissemination of DW's Hülsemann correspondence; comments on the bullion question, also on allegations in the British press that free traders in England raised money to spend in support of the U.S. tariff law of 1846, and are continuing to do so to prevent its alteration.

Jan 29 From Daniel Phillips. ALS. NhHi. 32330. Reports remarks alleged to have been made about DW to E. P. Little at a meeting.

Jan 29 From Edward Stubbs. ALS. NhHi. mDW 32332. Reports evidence relative to a financial transaction occurring during DW's earlier term as secretary of state.

Jan 30 To Franklin Haven. LS. MH–H. mDW 32335. Asks Haven to inquire for him about a balance which may be due on his East Boston shares.

Jan 30 To Franklin Haven (enclosure: DW to [John Eliot Thayer], Jan

30, 1851). LS. MH–H. mDW 32339. Asks him to see Thayer regarding the East Boston shares.

Jan 30   To [John Eliot Thayer] (with DW to Franklin Haven, Jan 30, 1851). LS copy MH–H. mDW 32342. Asks him to consult with Haven about the East Boston shares.

Jan 30   From Cranston & Norman. LS. DNA, RG 59. mDW 53740. Accept appointment to print the laws in the *Newport* (R.I.) *Daily News.*

Jan 30   From Ebenezer Brewer Foster & Co. LS. DNA, RG 59. mDW 53738. Accept appointment to publish the laws in the *Boston Courier.*

Jan 30   From Fuller & Seward. LS. DNA, RG 59. mDW 53826. Accept appointment to publish the laws in the *Albany* (N.Y.) *State Register.*

Jan 30   From White & Co. LS. DNA, RG 59. mDW 53736. Accept appointment to publish the laws in the *Pittsburgh Gazette.*

Jan 30   Application from Joseph G. Brown, for the Sault Ste. Marie *Lake Superior Journal*—public printer (ALS. DNA, RG 59. mDW 53843).

Jan 30   Recommendations from Jackson Morton and E[dward] C[arrington] Cabell, for the Tallahassee *Florida Sentinel* and the *Florida Republican*—public printers (ALS by Morton, signed also by Cabell. DNA, RG 59. mDW 54027).

Jan 30   Account with John M. Donn & Brother for $68.75 for chandelier, divan, etc., through Mar 21. DS. NhHi. mDW 40492.

Jan 31   To William McKendree Gwin. LS. CU–BANC. mDW 32344. Asks if the California congressional delegation would object to Ogden Hoffman's appointment as U.S. district judge.

Jan 31   To Elizabeth A. McNeil. Dictated letter. NhHi. mDW 32346. States that her request has been referred to the secretary of the treasury.

Jan 31   From Sir Henry Lytton Bulwer. Copy. UkLPR. mDWs. Sends him correspondence respecting the claim of a British ship run down by a U.S. ship of war.

Jan 31   From Sir Henry Lytton Bulwer. Copy. UkLPR. mDWs. Explains his instructions to the British consuls in the South regarding the use of their influence to secure justice for Blacks.

Jan 31   From Roswell L. Colt. ALS. DLC. mDW 32347. Acknowledges copies of DW's speech to the New England Society of New York and his Hülsemann correspondence.

Jan 31   From Edward Everett. ALS. MHi. mDW 32351. Discusses the editing of the forthcoming edition of DW's works.

Jan 31   From Thomas Hale. ALS. DNA, RG 59. mDW 53828. Accepts appointment to print the laws in the Windsor *Vermont Journal.*

Jan 31   From Lee, Mann & Co. LS. DNA, RG 59. mDW 53817. Accept appointment to print the laws in the *Rochester* (N.Y.) *Daily American.*

Jan 31   From Scott & Bascom. LS. DNA, RG 59. mDW 53832. Accept appointment to print the laws in the Columbus *Ohio State Journal.*

Jan 31   From Wright & Cook. LS. DNA, RG 59. mDW 53830. Accept appointment to print the laws in the Meredith Bridge, New Hampshire, *Belknap Gazette.*

Jan 31   Application from Charles W. Denison for the Benicia *California Gazette*—public printer (ALS. DNA, RG 59. mDW 53914).

Jan 31   Recommendations from W. G. Coffin, for the Sault Ste. Marie
          Lake Superior Journal—public printer (ALS. DNA, RG 59. mDW
          53856); from Volney E. Howard, for the Victoria *Texian Advocate*—
          public printer (ALS. DNA, RG 59. mDW 53895).
Jan 31   Receipt for $10 paid Martin & Colclazer for "Services at house
          regulating Hacks at $5.00 each." DS. NhHi. mDW 40473.
[Jan]   To William Bingham Baring, 2nd Baron Ashburton. ALS. NRU.
          mDW 32355. Introduces Thurlow Weed.
Jan   To Richard H. Bayard. LS. DLC. mDW 32357. Introduces Charles
          H. Russell and family.
[*Jan*]   *To Millard Fillmore.*   194
Jan   To David A. Hall. LS. NN. mDW 32371. *W & S*, 16: 583. Encloses
          a deed of manumission for former slave William Alexander Johnson,
          and asks to have it properly recorded.
Jan   To Charles Johnson McCurdy. LS. PP. mDW 32379. Introduces
          Charles H. Russell and family.
Jan   To William Cabell Rives. LS. NRU. mDW 32374. Introduces Thur-
          low Weed.
[Jan?]   From George S. Gideon. ALS. DLC. mDW 32377. Asks for a copy
          of DW's letter to Hülsemann.
[Jan]   Form for letters introducing Thurlow Weed. AL. NhD. mDWs.
Feb 1   To Hannibal Hamlin. Copy. NBuHi. mDW 32381. Asks that the
          Senate give early consideration to John Howard Payne's nomination
          for U.S. consul at Tunis.
Feb 1   To Hiram Ketchum. ALS. NhD. mDW 32382. Feels he has no
          right to interfere in the New York senatorial election by complying
          with Ketchum's request that it be postponed.
Feb 1   From [Sir Henry Lytton Bulwer]. AL draft. UkLPR. mDW 32385.
          Suggests that they find a way to smooth over the difficulties created
          by recent correspondence between H.M. consul at Charleston and the
          governor of South Carolina.
Feb 1   From Henry Dimock. ALS. DNA, RG 59. mDW 53806. Accepts ap-
          pointment to print the laws in the Washington, N.C. *North State
          Whig.*
Feb 1   From William Freret. Copy. DNA, RG 59. mDW 56548. Reports
          on the surveillance of the steamer *Fanny* at New Orleans.
Feb 1   From Willam Alexander Graham. Typed copy. DNA, RG 59. mDW
          56422. Asks for copies of Joseph Balestier's despatches relative to
          the conduct of Commodore Vorhees.
Feb 1   From Edward Kent. Copy. UkLPR. mDWs. Expresses his belief
          that the participation of Americans in the slave trade has been com-
          pletely eliminated, although vigilance is needed to maintain its
          suppression.
Feb 1   From J. Howard March. ALS. NhHi. mDW 32387. Acknowledges
          DW's "friendly letter."
Feb 1   From Sherwin & Sherwood. LS. DNA, RG 59. mDW 53821. Accept
          appointment to print the laws in the *Greensborough* (N.C.) *Patriot.*
Feb 2   From Henry Reaver. ALS. DNA, RG 59. mDW 55084. Accepts ap-
          pointment as justice of the peace for Washington, D.C.
Feb 2   From Edward M. Samuel (with ANS by DW). ALS. WaU. mDW
          32390. Hails Benton's defeat for re-election and predicts other Whig

victories in the Missouri elections; expresses interest in a government position.

Feb 3   *To Edward Everett.*   197

Feb 3   To Edward Everett. LS. MHi. mDW 32398. *PC*, 2: 415. Discusses plans for the new edition of his works.

Feb 3   To Millard Fillmore. ALS. NBuHi. mDW 32400. *Diplomatic Papers*, 2. Comments on the Nicaraguan crisis and recommends sending William Hunter there as a political agent.

Feb 3   To Millard Fillmore (enclosure: J. H. Pelly to DW, Oct 11, 1850). LS. DNA, RG 46. mDW 51242. Encloses papers relative to the possessory rights of the Hudson's Bay Company and the United States in Oregon, as requested by a Senate resolution of Jan 30, 1851.

Feb 3   To Edward Stubbs. ALS. PP. mDW 32404. *W & S*, 16: 595–596. Denies harboring any feeling of hostility, but insists that Stubb's turning over of confidential information to a political foe (Ingersoll) was indefensible.

Feb 3   From H. Collier, for Wright, Ferris & Co. ALS. DNA, RG 59. mDW 53813. Accepts appointment to publish the laws in the *Cincinnati Gazette*.

Feb 3   From D[orson] E. Sykes. ALS. DNA, RG 59. mDW 53819. Accepts appointment to publish the laws in the *Norwich* (Conn.) *Courier*.

Feb 3   From Moses Taylor and Isaac Townsend. LS. CtY. mDWs. Ask DW to attend a public dinner in New York in honor of Washington's birthday and the Union.

Feb 4   To Edward Everett. ALS. MHi. mDW 32406. *PC*, 2: 416. Thanks Everett for agreeing to oversee the publication of the new edition of his works; discusses the selection of a title.

[Feb 4?]   To Millard Fillmore. ALS. NBuHi. mDW 32362. Feels compelled to abandon the idea of sending [William] Hunter [Jr.] to Nicaragua, and asks that someone else be found.

Feb 4   To William Alexander Graham (enclosures: Joseph Balestier to John Middleton Clayton, Apr 30, 1850; Balestier to Clayton, June 24, 1850; convention with the Sultan of Borneo, June 23, 1850; Balestier to Clayton, July 13, 1850; Balestier to P. F. Voorhees, June 24, 1850; Balestier to Vorhees, June 25, 1850; Balestier to Clayton, July 20, 1850; Balestier to Vorhees, July 18, 1850; Balestier to Clayton, July 22, 1850). Typed copy. DNA, RG 59. mDW 56423. Transmits copies of despatches requested by Graham.

Feb 4   To Nathan Kelsey Hall. LS. NBuHi. mDW 32408. Introduces "Mr Marsh," the editor of the *Boston Daily Bee*.

Feb 4   From Hamilton Fish. ALS. DLC. mDW 32409. Introduces Major General John Taylor Cooper of Albany.

Feb 4   From [Abbott Lawrence]. Draft DLC. mDW 32411. Comments on George W. Atwood's claims against the British government.

Feb 4   From [Abbott Lawrence]. Draft. DLC. mDW 32415. Encloses a copy of his note to Palmerston reporting Atwood's charges against British officials at Rio de Janeiro.

Feb 4   Recommendation from Albert G. Watkins, for Samuel Eckle— U.S. consul at Talcahuan, Chile. (ALS. NhD. mDW 32418).

Feb 5   To Isaac N. Coffin. LS. NjMD. mDWs. Relays information on the Revolutionary War service of Capt. Edwin Hull of the Virginia line.

Feb 5 To Jacob Merritt Howard. ALS. MiD. mDW 32422. Asks him to recommend a successor to the incumbent U.S. marshal for Michigan (Charles H. Knox).

Feb 5 To James William Paige. ALS. Mrs. Irwin McD. Garfield, Southboro, Mass. mDWs. Discusses the publication of his works, noting the participation of Everett and George Jacob Abbot.

Feb 5 From Joseph Reed Ingersoll. ALS. DLC. mDW 32426. Cannot think of anyone suitable to be named U.S. commissioner to China.

[Feb 5?] From Jacob McGaw. Printed. *PC*, 2: 417–418. Thinks DW delivered a crushing response to Hülsemann; asks if he'll visit Bangor this summer.

Feb 5 Application from Wheeler & Simpson, for the Augusta, Maine *Kennebec Journal*—public printer (LS. DNA, RG 59. mDW 53862).

Feb 5 Recommendation from William Schouler, for "Mr. Clegg"—a minor diplomatic post (ALS. NhHi. mDW 32429).

[Feb 6] From Sir Henry Lytton Bulwer. LS. DLC. mDW 32472. Postpones their meeting for a day because of a headache.

Feb 6 From John Middleton Clayton. ALS. NhD. mDW 32475. Asks DW to find employment for a clerk at the State Department; draws attention to the extradition treaty with Mexico now pending in the Senate.

Feb 6 From Edward Everett. LC. MHi. mDW 32478. Discusses editorial matters pertaining to the publication of DW's works.

Feb 6 From [Abbott Lawrence]. Draft. DLC. mDW 32482. Comments on the projected trans-isthmian canal and the need to preserve peace among the Central American republics.

Feb 6 Notes on *Van Rennselaer* v. *Kearney*. AD. NhHi. mDW 32432.

Feb 7 To Daniel Stevens Dickinson. Printed. John R. Dickinson, ed., *Speeches, correspondence, etc., of the late Daniel S. Dickinson* (2 vols., New York, 1867), 2: 464. Responds to Dickinson's request that his wife and daughter be furnished with letters for their trip to Cuba.

Feb 7 To William Schouler. LS. NhD. mDW 43286. States that the diplomatic posts sought by Clegg have been filled.

Feb 7 From William C. Conant. ALS. DNA, RG 59. mDW 53815. Accepts appointment of the Rutland *Vermont Union Whig* to print the laws.

Feb 7 From Henry Holland. ALS. NhD. mDWs. Thinks DW's Hülsemann letter may initiate a new style of diplomacy; comments on British and European affairs.

Feb 8 To Edward Everett. ALS. MHi. mDW 32487. *PC*, 2: 418. Decides on a title for his works; agrees to provide letters of eminent individuals for inclusion with the speeches.

Feb 8 To Millard Fillmore (enclosures: Angel Calderon de la Barca to DW, Jan 8, 1851; Calderon to DW Aug 14, 1850). LS. DNA, RG 46. mDW 51232. Encloses correspondence pertinent to the *Amistad* case as requested by a Senate resolution of Feb 1, 1851.

Feb 8 From Edward Everett. ALS. MHi. mDW 32496. Discusses annotations and alterations to the text of DW's Plymouth address and other editorial questions.

Feb 8 From William Freret (enclosure: Report on observations by John F. Grichen of the *Fanny*, Feb 7, 1851). Copy. DNA, RG 59. mDW

56551. Reports there is no evidence yet that the *Fanny* is connected with the rumored Cuban expedition.

Feb 8   From Logan Hunton. Copy. DNA, RG 59. mDW 56549. Reports no evidence that the *Fanny* is connected with the rumored Cuban expedition.

Feb 8   From Hannibal Hamlin. ALS. DNA, RG 59. mDW 54033. Seeks information relative to the appointment of the *Hartford* (Conn.) *Daily Courant* to publish the laws.

Feb 8   From Johnston & Cavis. LS. DNA, RG 59. mDW 53811. Accept appointment of the Columbia *South Carolinian* to publish the laws.

[Feb 8]   From M. P. Simons. ALS. DLC. mDW 32504. Has come from Philadelphia to collect portraits to take to the world's fair in England. and hopes DW will consent to sit (for a photograph).

Feb 8   From Truman Smith. ALS. DNA, RG 59. mDW 54035. Asks that a commission of appointment to publish the laws be sent to the *Hartford Daily Courant*.

Feb 8   From J. G. Moore to [Henry Sargent]. ALS. NhD. mDWs. Asks for the names of people nominated for judges in New Mexico; thinks DW "does not appear to trouble himself whether I receive knowledge of what is going on in the Department or not," and says "I may not entrench where I am not welcome."

Feb 8   Recommendations from William S. Derrick, for James H. Birch—justice of the peace for Washington, D.C. (ALS. NBuHi. mDW 32488); from M[armaduke] Shannon, for the *Vicksburg* (Miss.) *Whig*—public printer (ALS. DNA, RG 59. mDW 53935).

Feb 9   From C[olumbus] Drew. ALS. DNA, RG 59. mDW 53799. Accepts appointment of the Jacksonville *Florida Republican* to print the laws.

Feb 9   From William Plumer, [Jr.] ALS. NhHi. mDW 32508. Commends DW's Hülsemann letter and his speech to the New England Society of New York; asks for his recollections of William Plumer, Sr.

Feb 10   To [Ernest André Olivier] Sain de Bois le Comte. Draft. CtY. mDW 32511. Communicates the Supreme Court's decision in the case of *La Jeune Nelly. United States* v. *Baptiste Guillem*, 11 Howard (1850) 47.

Feb 10   From Knowles & Anthony. LS. DNA, RG 59. mDW 53808. Accept appointment of the *Providence* (R.I.) *Daily Journal* to print the laws.

[Feb 11]   To Millard Fillmore. ALS. NBuHi. mDW 32514. Van Tyne, p. 447. Encloses the draft for an "answer to the Senate" and also various newspapers and cards.

Feb 11   To Daniel Appleton White. LS. MSaE. mDWs. Has requested that White be appointed visitor to West Point for the annual examination of the cadets.

Feb 11   From Joseph Clisby. ALS. DNA, RG 59. mDW 53797. Accepts appointment of the Tallahassee *Florida Sentinel* to publish the laws.

Feb 11   Report of the secretary of state showing the disbursements for the services of that department, including foreign missions, during the year ending June 30, 1850. AD, DNA, RG 46. mDW 51619.

Feb 11   Report of the secretary of state with lists of the clerks and other persons employed in that department during the year 1850. AD. DNA, RG 46. mDW 51622.

Feb 12   To George Cadwalader. LS. PHi. mDW 32516. Reports Cadwalader is being recommended for appointment as visitor to West Point.

Feb 12   To Millard Fillmore. LS. DNA, RG 46. mDW 51243. Submits information concerning drafts by the Mexican government on the U.S. Treasury as requested by a Senate resolution of Feb 10, 1851.

Feb 12   From Edward Everett. ALS. MHi. mDW 32521. Discusses editorial matters.

Feb 12   From Perry & Elford. LS. DNA, RG 59. mDW 53803. Accepts appointment of the Greenville, South Carolina *Southern Patriot* to publish the laws.

Feb 12   From Q[uincy] K. Underwood. ALS. DNA, RG 59. mDW 53793. Accepts appointment of the Helena Arkansas *Southern Shield* to publish the laws.

Feb 13   From George Cadwalader. ALS. PHi. mDW 32525. Will accept appointment as visitor to West Point should it be offered to him.

Feb 13   From Francis Lieber.   199

Feb 13   From Joseph Gilbert Totten. ALS. PHi. mDW 32531. Promises to show DW's letter recommending George Cadwalader's appointment as visitor to West Point to the secretary of war.

Feb 13   From Henry Wood. ALS. DNA, RG 59. mDW 53801. Accepts ap-Accepts appointment of the Helena, Arkansas *Southern Shield* to publish the laws.

[Feb 14]   To Millard Fillmore. ALS. NBuHi. mDW 32532. Proposes introducing him to ex-president Paez of New Granada and party at noon.

Feb 14   To [Millard Fillmore]. LS. NBuHi. mDW 32535. Will accompany General Paez to the White House this noon, and acknowledges Paez as former president of Venezuela, not New Granada.

Feb 14   To Millard Fillmore. Dictated letter. NBuHi. mDW 32537. Transmits documents pertaining to the Swiss convention.

Feb 14   To [William Plumer, Jr.]. LS. NhD. mDW 32539. *PC*, 2: 419–420. Briefly recalls his memories of William Plumer, Sr.

Feb 14   From F. S. Lathrop et al. LS. CtY. mDWs. Invite DW to the Union Festival to be held in New York on Feb 22.

Feb 14   From William M. Richards et al. (enclosure: list of donors). LS. NhHi. mDW 32542. *PC*, 2: 419. Present DW with a carriage equipped with horses and harness.

Feb 14   From Cadwalader Ringgold. ALS. DNA, RG 59. mDW 46722. Asks to be reimbursed for expenses incurred on a special mission to California.

Feb 14   From John Trumbull Van Alen. ALS. NhD. mDW 32546. Reports the Hülsemann correspondence is being printed for circulation throughout Europe; comments on "anarchy and confusion" in Ecuador and recommends that the U.S. acquire the Galapagos Islands.

Feb 14   From Robert M. Walsh. ALS. DNA, RG 59. mDW 56286. Reports on his mission to Haiti and the Dominican Republic.

Feb 14   From [William] G. Woodruff. ALS. DNA, RG 59. mDW 53789. Accepts appointment of the *Arkansas State Gazette & Democrat* to print the laws.

Feb 14   Report of the Secretary of State relative to the resolution of the

Senate calling for information about the expediency of adopting a graduated scale of diplomatic salaries. AD. DNA, RG 46. mDW 51617.

Feb 15 To Edwin Bartlett. ALS. NhD. mDW 32552. Inquires where he might buy quality guano and the probable price.

Feb 15 To Millard Fillmore (enclosures: Amos B. Corwine to DW, Sept 9, 1850; Corwine to Thomas M. Foote, Aug 26, 1850; Corwine to DW, Sept 22, 1850). LS. DNA, RG 46. mDW 51245. Transmits correspondence relative to U.S. transit privileges across Panama as requested by a Senate resolution of Feb 10, 1851.

Feb 15 To Gales & Seaton (enclosure: William E. Channing to DW, May 14, 1828), Printed. W & S, 10: 98. Encloses letter extracts for publication in the *National Intelligencer.*

Feb 15 To John Taylor. ALS. Mrs. Farwell A. Brown, Lebanon, N.H. mDWs. Gives directions for preparing land and planting potatoes and turnips.

Feb 15 To O. C. Tiffany. ALS. MdHi. mDWs. Thanks him for some excellent hams and orders two dozen more.

Feb 15 To [?]. ALS. IaDaM. mDW 32551. Asks that his account be left as is until his return from Boston.

Feb 15 From Thomas Hale. ALS. DNA, RG 59. mDW 54037. Requests that copies of the *Republic* containing the laws of Congress be sent to him.

Feb 16 To Charles Porter Wright. ALS. NhHi. mDW 32553. *PC*, 2: 420. Inquires about ashes; outlines plans for using guano at Marshfield.

Feb 16 *From Levi C. Turner.*   200

Feb 17 To Sir Henry Lytton Bulwer. LS. UkLPR. mDW 32559. Encloses copies of the proceedings in the cases of the ships *Spitfire* and *Martha.*

Feb 17 *To Peter Harvey.*   204

Feb 17 *To Robert Cumming Schenck.*   204

Feb 17 *From Charles Pelham Curtis.*   203

Feb 17 From Millard Fillmore. ALS. DLC. mDW 32562. Will see him if no response is received regarding "the rescue of a slave in Boston."

Feb 17 *From N[athaniel] G[ookin] Upham.*   205

Feb 17 Recommendation from James Duane Doty, for the Madison *Wisconsin Statesman*—public printer (ALS. DNA, RG 59. mDW 53984).

Feb 18 *To Charles Devens, Jr.*   206

Feb 18 To T[homas] M. Rodney. ALS. NhExP. mDWs. Acknowledges two despatches received from Rodney at Matanzas.

Feb 18 From De Bruyn Kops. ALS. NhHi. mDW 32566. Argues against a proposition, now before the Senate, to devalue silver currency.

Feb 18 *Presidential proclamation on enforcement of the Fugitive Slave Act in Boston.*   206

Feb 19 To Thomas H. Bayly (with DW to Duff Green, Mar 11, 1851). Copy. NcD. mDW 32902. Explains the U.S. government's financial obligation to Mexico under the treaty of Guadalupe Hidalgo and the method by which installments are paid.

Feb 19 To Charles Ward. LS. MSaE. mDW 32570. Acknowledges Ward's despatches describing recent occurrences in Zanzibar, and states that an officer will visit him to obtain additional information.

Feb 19   From [Abbott Lawrence]. Draft. DLC. mDW 32572. Makes suggestions regarding the coinage of the United States.

Feb 19   From Sherman & Harris. LS. DNA, RG 59. mDW 53795. Accept
appointment of the *Trenton State Gazette* to publish the laws.

Feb 19   Applications from G. W. Gillett, for the *Sheboygan* (Wisc.) *Mercury*—public printer (ALS. DNA, RG 59. mDW 53943); from John
B. Porter, for the Wilmington *Delaware State Journal*—public
printer (ALS. DNA, RG 59. mDW 53744).

Feb 19   Account with Daniel Campbell for $16.75 for livery supplies,
through May 10. ADS. NhHi. mDW 40542.

[Feb 20]   To [Millard Fillmore]. ALS. NBuHi. mDW 32589. Will come
over once the Boston mail arrives.

Feb 20   To Millard Fillmore (enclosures: documents relating to the
Contoy prisoners, and to any projected expedition against Cuba).
LS. DNA, RG 46. mDW 51585. Transmits documents as requested by
a Senate resolution of Jan 17, 1851.

Feb 20   To Moses Taylor et al. LS draft. NhHi. mDW 32591. Curtis,
2: 490–491. *Works*, 6: 586– 590. Comments on the career and character of George Washington: condemns "the dark, unwholesome,
troubled current of secession," and also the Boston slave riot.

Feb 20   From Charles Devens, Jr. Telegram. DLC. mDW 32602. Reports
E. Wright, accused as a participant in the Boston slave riot, has been
bound over for trial.

Feb 20   From Edward Everett. LC. MHi. mDW 32604. Is planning a
short visit to Washington.

Feb 20   From Joseph Hume. ALS. NhHi. mDW 32605. Commends DW's
Hülsemann letter; appeals on behalf of the Florida bondholders.

Feb 20   From [Robert Walsh]. Copy. NBuHi. mDW 32607. Defends his
conduct and bitterly protests his removal as U.S. consul at Paris.

Feb 21   To Millard Fillmore. Dictated letter. NBuHi. mDW 32611. Reports no further papers on John Rutherford are on file at the State
Department.

Feb 21   To Millard Fillmore. Dictated letter. NBuHi. mDW 32613. Sends
him nominations for consuls at Belfast and Sonneberg.

Feb 21   From Thomas T. Kinney. ALS. DNA, RG 59. mDW 53791. Accepts appointment of the *Newark Daily Advertiser* to publish the
laws.

Feb 21   From G. J. Robbins (enclosure: resolution of the Board of Directors, Institution for the Instruction of the Deaf and Dumb). ALS.
NhHi. mDW 32615. Encloses a resolution thanking DW for providing Harvey P. Peet with letters of introduction for his trip to Europe.

Feb 21   From J[ohn] Sainsbury. ALS. DLC. mDW 32617. Offers to sell
his historical collection to some public institution in the U.S.

Feb 22   From John Connell. Printed. *A Letter to the Hon. Daniel Webster, upon the propriety of establishing an Annual National Jubilee,
to commemorate the adoption of the Constitution of the United
States* (Wilmington, Del., 1851).

Feb 22   From Joseph Henry. ALS. DNA, RG 59. mDWs. Inquires about
an Englishman named Snape, to whom he has given temporary employment at the Smithsonian Institution on the strength of a letter
of introduction from Lord Brougham to DW.

Feb 22   To Joseph Henry. Dictated note. DSI. mDW 32620. Reports

"that he knows no more of the gentleman referred to, than he has
learned from Lord Brougham's letter."

Feb 22 From Swain & Sherwood. LS. DNA, RG 59. mDW 53906. Report having not yet received the issues of the *Republic* containing the
laws of Congress.

Feb. 22 Recommendation from James H. Duncan, for the *Lowell*
(Mass.) *Daily Journal and Courier*—public printer (ALS. DNA, RG
59. mDW 53910).

Feb 22 Account with Hook & Co. for $17.25 for coach repairs, through
June 28. ADS. NhHi. mDW 40526.

[Feb 23] To Millard Fillmore. ALS. NBuHi. mDW 32621. Expects
Everett here soon; asks for the return of some despatches.

Feb 23 From Benjamin Robbins Curtis. ALS. DLC. mDW 32750. Recommends George B. N. Tower for appointment to West Point; comments
on the Boston slave riot.

Feb 23 From Henry Alexander Scammell Dearborn.   207

Feb 24 To George P. Fisher. LS. DNA, RG 76. Transmits documents pertaining to claims of U.S. citizens against Brazil.

Feb 24 To John A. McClernand. LS. IHi. mDWs. Asks that a provision
for an increase in the State Department's work force be included in
the General Civil and Diplomatic bill now before Congress.

Feb 24 From James H. Birch. ALS. DNA, RG 59. mDW 54935. Accepts
appointment as justice of the peace for Washington, D.C.

Feb 24 From Millard Fillmore. Copy. DNA, RG 59. mDW 55840. Letter
of credence authorizing DW to negotiate with the Portuguese minister to the U.S. regarding claims against Portugal.

Feb 24 From Logan & Sterne. LS. DNA, RG 59. mDW 53779. Accept appointment of the Victoria *Texian Advocate* to publish the laws.

Feb 24 From Nathaniel Sawyer. ALS. NhHi. mDW 32761. Van Tyne,
pp. 3–5. Discusses their common ancestry.

Feb 24 Applications from Charles W. Brewster, for the *Portsmouth*
(N.H.) *Journal of Literature and Politics*—public printer (ALS.
DNA, RG 59. mDW 53952); from J. C. Gibbes—public office (ALS.
NhHi. mDW 32758).

Feb 24 Recommendation from John M. Jewell, for the *Vicksburg*
(Miss.) *Whig*—public printer (ALS. DNA, RG 59. mDW 53937).

Feb 24 Receipt for $5 paid S. Carusi for subscription to "Birth night
assembly." AD. NhHi. mDW 40481.

Feb 25 To Benedict & Boardman. LS. NhD. mDW 32766. Discusses the
retainer they might expect from clients in a case recently decided
against them.

[c. Feb 25] To [Charles M. Conrad] (with Hasket Derby to DW, Feb 25,
1851). ANS. DNA, RG 94. mDWs. Would be glad if Derby could be
appointed to West Point.

Feb 25 To George Lunt. LS. MNS. mDW 32768. Authorizes Lunt to hire
Rufus Choate or Charles G. Loring to aid in the slave riot
prosecutions.

Feb 25 From Joseph Abraham et al. DNA, RG 59. mDWs. *Cincinnati
Commercial*, May 19, 1851. *Diplomatic Papers*, 2. Protest that the
convention recently concluded with Switzerland discriminates
against Jewish Americans.

Feb 25 From Luther Severance. ALS. DNA, RG 59. mDW 55652. Emphasizes the high cost of living in the Sandwich Islands, and supports former U.S. Commissioner Anthony Ten Eyck's claim for additional compensation.

Feb 25   Application from Hasket Derby—appointment to West Point (ALS. DNA, RG 94. mDWs).

Feb 26   To Millard Fillmore. LS. NBuHi. mDW 32769. Submits the nomination of Andrew Rothwell for justice of the peace for Washington, D.C.

Feb 26   To James Tappan. Printed. *National Intelligencer*, March 10, 1851. *Works*, 1: xxi–xxii. Recalls people he once knew in Salisbury, and his days as Tappan's pupil.

Feb 26   From David F. Douglas, ALS. DNA, RG 59. mDW 54983. Accepts appointment as U.S. marshal for northern California.

Feb 26   From Robert Cumming Schenck.   210

Feb 26   Account with John Pettibone for $35.25 for ice tickets, through May 16. AD. NhHi. mDW 40522.

Feb 27   To Thomas Corwin (enclosure: Roland Dubs to DW, Dec 18, 1850). LS. DNA, RG 206. Transmits the register of the brig *Maria* in case proceedings should be initiated against her master, John Perry.

Feb 27   From Grafton Baker. ALS. DNA, RG 59. mDW 54921. Accepts appointment as chief justice of New Mexico.

Feb 27   From J[ames] H. Duncan. ALS. DNA, RG 59. mDW 53912. Is sending letters advocating the appointment of the *Lowell* (Mass.) *Daily Journal & Courier* to publish the laws.

Feb 28   To J[oseph?] Howard & Son. LS. NBLiHi. mDW 32755. Transmits letters exonerating U.S. consul to Panama Amos B. Corwine of culpability in the seizure of their shipment of gold.

Feb 28   To William B. Kinney. ALS. NjHi. mDWs. Recommends Capt. J. Nash to Kinney's attention.

Feb 28   To George Perkins Marsh (with DW to Fillmore, Mar. 10 1851). AD. DNA, RG. 46. mDW 51599. Works, 6: 591–594. Instructs him to call upon the Sublime Porte at Constantinople to permit the emigration of Kossuth and other Hungarian exiles to the U.S.

Feb 28   From James S. Calhoun. ALS. DNA, RG 59. mDW 54961. Accepts appointment as governor of New Mexico.

Feb 28   From Franklin Haven.   210

Feb 28   From Henry D. Moore. ALS. NhD. mDW 32777. Calls DW's attention to documents left by "several Friends" from Philadelphia.

Feb 28   From William A. Weeks. ALS. DNA, RG 59. mDW 56880. Reports forwarding of despatches just received from the U.S. legation at London.

[Feb]   To Millard Fillmore (with ANS by Fillmore; and Daniel Fletcher Webster to Caroline Story White Webster). ALS. NhHi. mDW 32779. Van Tyne, p. 457. Asks him to read over Fletcher's draft of the letter to George P. Marsh at Constantinople.

[Feb]   Caroline Story White Webster from Daniel Fletcher Webster (with DW to Fillmore, [Feb, 1851]). ALS. NhHi. mDW 32780. Van Tyne, p. 457. Expects "this letter," his draft of DW's letter to Marsh, will please her.

[Feb]   From Sir Henry Lytton Bulwer. LS. DLC. mDW 32782. Asks that his draft of a note on the Mathew correspondence be returned.

[Feb]   From Millard Fillmore (with DW to Fillmore, [Feb, 1851]). ANS.
NhHi. mDW 32799. Van Tyne, p. 457. Calls Fletcher's draft of the
letter to Marsh "capital."

Feb   Receipt for $10 paid Colclazer & Martin for "regulating Hacks."
DS. NhHi. mDW 40479.

March 1   To Millard Fillmore. LS. NBuHi. mDW 32784. Discusses vari
ous diplomatic appointments; reports Benton is very ill.

March 1   To [Millard Fillmore]. ALS. NBuHi. mDW 32790. Introduces
"Mr. Willie" [Tolman Wiley?], a member of the Boston bar.

March 1   To William P. Lunt. ALS. MHi. mDWs. Will keep Lunt in mind
should a vacancy occur.

March 1   To [William Cabell Rives]. LS. DLC. mDW 32793. Introduces
Lt. D. M. Frost, U.S. Army.

[March 1]   To [Luther Severance]. Draft. NhHi. mDW 32794. Van Tyne,
pp. 458–460. Discusses the war-making powers of the president in
the context of an incident between France and the Sandwich Islands; gives Severance instructions regarding U.S. policy on Hawaiian independence.

March 1   To John Taylor. LS. NjMoHP. mDW 32804. Discusses farm
matters.

March 1   From George Ashmun. Printed. Curtis, 2: 493. Reports the
House of Representatives is quite incensed by Rep. Charles Allen's
attack on DW.

March 1   From S. Siegfried. ALS. DNA, RG 59. mDW 53783. Accepts appointment of the Morgantown, Va. *Monongalia Mirror* to publish the
laws.

March 1   Memorandum of George Ashmun describing John Otis's story
of being asked by Charles Hudson and Philip Greely to remonstrate
with President Fillmore against DW's appointment as secretary of
state. Printed. Curtis, 2: 493.

March 1   Recommendation from J[ames] M. H. Beale, for the *Weston*
(Va.) *Sentinel*—public printer (ALS. DNA, RG 59. mDW 53960).

March 2   To Franklin Haven.   211

March 2   To [?]. ALS. MH–H. mDW 32807. Asks him to make a financial arrangement with Haven in anticipation of a retainer he is expecting from New Orleans.

March 3   To Millard Fillmore. ALS. NBuHi. mDW 32812. Fears various
treaties and nominations may be delayed by the present "state of
business in Congress."

March 3   To Millard Fillmore. LS. DNA, RG 46. mDW 51586. Responds
to a Senate resolution inquiring about the abduction of an American
citizen into Mexico from New Mexico.

March 3   To William Alexander Graham. LS. NcU. mDW 32814. Hamilton, *Graham*, 4: 49–50. Describes C. W. Cutter as a foe of abolitionists and free soilers, and advises that he be allowed to deal with
"evil influence" at the Portsmouth Navy Yard.

March 3   From George Jacob Abbot. ALS. MHi. mDW 33126. Discusses
the preparation of DW's works for the press; releases samples of the
proofreader's work.

March 3   From John McLean. ALS. MHi. mDW. 32819. Asks that Joshua
H. Hayward, now at the Boston custom house, be found a more
suitable position.

March 3   From James B. Reynolds. ALS. NhD. mDW 32822. Predicts
DW's reputation will remain untarnished by present political assaults; draws attention to his application to be U.S. consul at Havana.

March 3   From Robert M. Walsh (enclosures sent with despatch of Mar.
16 refiled with despatches of Mar 3, 1851). ALS. DNA, RG 59. mDW
56190. Reports on his mission to Haiti and makes observations regarding the emperor and Haitian domestic affairs.

March 3   Bill for $20 for subscription to four Washington Assemblies.
Printed with MS insertions. NhHi. mDW 40486.

March 4   To Charles Porter Wright. ALS. NhHi. mDW 32825. Asks when
ploughing will begin; requests that he be sent the plan for farming
they drew up.

March 4   Application from J[oseph] L. Locke & Co., for the *Savannah*
(Ga.) *Republican*—public printers (LS. DNA, RG 59. mDW 53962).

March 4   Recommendation from J[ohn] Wales, for the Wilmington
Delaware State Journal—public printer (ALS. DNA, RG 59, mDW
53866).

March 5   To Joseph Abraham et al. LC. DNA, RG 59. mDWs. *Cincinnati
Commercial*, May 19, 1851. *Diplomatic Papers*, 2. Acknowledges
their letter of Feb 25 objecting to the Swiss convention; assures he
will not approve any measure which may infringe on the rights of
"any class of our fellow citizens."

March 5   To Edward Everett. LS. MHi. mDW 32827. Agrees to see
Everett tomorrow.

March 5   To Millard Fillmore. LS. NBuHi. mDW 32829. Will call tomorrow with Don Luis de la Rosa, the newly-arrived Mexican minister
to the U.S.

March 5   To Duff Green. AL. NcU. mDW 32831. Agrees to see Green on
Friday.

March 5   From George Jacob Abbot. ALS. MHi. mDW 32832. Discusses
editorial questions affecting the publication of DW's works.

[c. March 5]   From Heath, Elliott, Scott & Co. LS. DNA, RG 59. mDW
53786. Accept appointment of the *Richmond* (Va.) *Whig and Public Advertiser* to publish the laws.

March 5   Recommendation from Hugh Birckhead, for the *Baltimore
Patriot*—public printer (ALS. DNA, RG 59. mDW 53908).

March 6   From Thomas Jefferson Rusk. Invitation. TxU. mDWs.

March 6   From Sir Henry Lytton Bulwer. Copy. UkLPR. mDWs. Inquires
about the claim of Thomas Rider against the U.S. for unjust imprisonment at Tampico in 1847.

March 6   From W[illiam] M[orris] Meredith et al. LS. MHi. mDW 32834.
Ask DW to accept an invitation to address a church benefit near
Philadelphia.

March 7   To Millard Fillmore. ALS. NBuHi. mDW 32836. Suggests criticism of [William] Easby (nominated for commissioner of public
buildings) be brought to the attention of the secretary of the interior.

March 7   To Millard Fillmore. LS. NBuHi. mDW 32840. Advises regarding nominations for office in New Mexico.

[March 7/8]   To Millard Fillmore. LS. NBuHi. mDW 32842. Encloses
"Mr. Lyman's 'memorandum.'"

March 7   To Franklin Haven. LS. MH–H. mDW 32844. Discusses a financial matter.

March 7   To Henry Hibbard. LS. MHi. mDWs. Tells Hibbard that Robert P. Letcher was instructed to ascertain the "temperature of the Rio del Monte mine at its bottom and at the surface of the earth," but that no word has since been received from the Mexican legation.

March 7   To John Taylor. LS. MBBS. mDW 32847. Expresses concern on hearing of illness in Taylor's family, and sends him money as assistance.

March 7   To Charles Porter Wright. LS. NhD. mDW 32848. Van Tyne, p. 747. Suggests that "Mrs. Baker" go stay with John Taylor and family for a few days.

March 7   From Abbott Lawrence (enclosure: Lawrence to Palmerston, Mar 7, 1851). Copy. UkLPR. mDWs. Sends him a note he wrote to Palmerston regarding the capture and loss of the schooner John.

March 7   From Griffith Owen. ALS. DLC. mDW 32849. Invites DW to deliver an address at the Musical Fund Hall in Philadelphia.

March 8   To Millard Fillmore. Dictated letter. NBuHi. mDW 32851. Will call this morning at eleven.

March 8   From H[enry] A[ugustus] Boardman (with AN by DW). ALS. DLC. mDW 32853. Urges DW to address the church benefit in Philadelphia.

March 8   From Millard Fillmore. AL. DLC. mDW 32857. Severance, Fillmore Papers, 1: 339–340. Advises a joint consultation with the secretary of the navy before replying to Lady Jane Franklin's letter relating to the missing ships of the Arctic search expedition commanded by her husband Sir John Franklin.

March 8   Notice of $1000 promissory note due at Merchants' Bank. DS. MHi. mDW 40488.

March 9   To Richard Milford Blatchford. Printed. PC, 2: 421. Reports "a very amiable" reply from Vienna; expects the despatch to Marsh will be published in a few days.

[March 9]   To Edward Curtis. ALS. NN. mDW 32859. Asks him to come up and meet James William Paige.

March 9   To [Edward Everett]. ALS. MHi. mDW 32861. Declares: "This is beautifully written" and has evoked fond remembrances.

March 9   To Franklin Haven. LS. MH–H. mDW 32862. Asks that his letter to Haven of July 12, 1850 be published.

March 9   To John Plummer Healy (enclosure: promissory note for $1000). LS. MHi. mDW 32864. Requests him to ask Choate to endorse the enclosed note.

March 9   To John Taylor. LS. MBBS. mDW 32868. W & S, 16: 597–598. Gives directions for preparing a potato field, which are to be followed "exactly and to the letter."

March 9   From Charles Porter Wright. ALS. NhHi. mDW 32872. Reports on his farm activity.

March 10   To John P[rescott] Bigelow.   212

March 10   To James Hervey Bingham. AN. CSmH. mDW 32875. Invites Bingham to dinner.

March 10   From Solon Borland. ALS. NhHi. mDW 32886. Complains that DW solicited but then ignored his advice respecting the appointments of a U.S. attorney and U.S. marshal for Arkansas.

March 10   To Solon Borland. Copy. NhHi. mDW 32877. Assures Borland that no slight was intended in the selection of U.S. attorney and U.S. marshal for Arkansas.

March 10   To Sir Henry Lytton Bulwer. LS. UkLPR. mDW 32881. States that Congress will again be asked for funds to pay the claim of Thomas Rider, unjustly imprisoned by U.S. military officials in Mexico.

March 10   To [Edward Everett]. AL. NhD. mDWs. Sends papers from Abbott Lawrence and discusses the preparation of his volume of speeches.

March 10   To Millard Fillmore. ALS. NBuHi. mDW 32883. Asks when Amin Bey might call to bid his official farewell.

March 10   To Millard Fillmore (enclosure: DW to George P. Marsh, Feb 28, 1851). LS. DNA, RG 46. mDW 51587. Encloses papers respecting "the liberation of Kossuth and his companions," as requested by a Senate resolution of Mar 8,1851.

March 10   To Elisha Whittlesey. AL. OClWHi. mDW 32885. Invites him to dinner.

March 10   From Sir Henry Lytton Bulwer. Copy. DNA, RG 59. mDW 56558. Reports [Narciso] Lopez may be organizing another invasion of Cuba.

March 10   From [Duff Green]. ALS draft. NcU. mDW 32890. Discusses the payment of installments due Mexico under the treaty of Guadalupe Hidalgo.

March 10   From Samuel P. Lyman.   214

March 11   To [George Jacob Abbot]. ALS. CtY. mDW 32898. Asks him to purchase a watch for Caroline.

March 11   To Millard Fillmore. LS. NBuHi. mDW 32899. Asks when Don Felipe Molina, the new Costa Rican envoy, might present his credentials.

March 11   To Duff Green (enclosure: DW to Thomas H. Bayly, Feb 19, 1851). LS. NcU. mDW 32901. Encloses a letter addressed to the chairman of the House Ways and Means Committee respecting the payments due Mexico under the treaty of Guadalupe Hidalgo.

March 11   From Asa Cummings. ALS. DNA, RG 59. mDW 53746. Accepts appointment to print the laws in the Portland, Maine *Christian Mirror*, providing it does not impinge on his editorial independence.

March 11   From Pennsylvania Legislature. Copy. DLC. mDW 32909. *Diplomatic Papers*, 2. Resolution of thanks for DW's letter to Hülsemann of Dec 21, 1850.

March 11   Recommendation from Joseph R. Chandler, for Cornelius Mc-Caullay—U.S. consul at Belfast (ALS. DLC. mDWs).

March 11   Promissory note for $1000 payable to Rufus Choate. DS. MHi. mDW 32867. Inscribed: "This note not used but #3 given in its place."

March 11   Promissory note for $1000 payable to Rufus Choate. DS. MHi. mDW 40490. Inscribed #3.

March 12   To Richard Milford Blatchford. Printed. PC, 2: 421–422. Describes the Morgan horse; wants to know "who is successor to Brigham."

March 12   To Millard Fillmore, with reply. LS. NhD. mDWs. DW asks if Amin Bey, the agent of the Sublime Porte, may be presented with a specimen of California gold. Fillmore thinks it not authorized, but suggests that a request could be submitted to Congress.

March 12   To Chevalier Johann Georg Hülseman. Draft. NhHi. mDW 32910. Reasserts the position taken in his note to Hülsemann of Dec 21, 1850.

March 12   To [Enrique Antonio Mexia]. LS. CU–BANC. mDW 32607. Invites him to dinner.

March 12   To Daniel Fletcher Webster. ALS. NhHi. mDW 32914. *PC*, 2: 421. Asks him to look up and send a kitchen roaster.

March 12   From George Jacob Abbot. ALS draft. CtY. mDW 32916. Reports his interview with former U.S. consul Charles Ward on the state of affairs with Muscat and Zanzibar.

March 12   From George C. Bates. ALS. DLC. mDW 32931. Severance, *Fillmore Papers*, 1: 342–44. (where the subject of the letter is wrongly identified). Asks for instructions to proceed with a fugitive slave case.

March 12   From John D. Defrees. ALS. DNA, RG 59. 53918. Asks whether he should continue printing the laws under appointment given the Indianapolis *Indiana State Journal* in January, 1850.

March 12   From U.B. Spencer. ALS. DNA, RG 59. mDW 53777. Accepts appointment of the *Centreville* (Md.) *Times* to pubish the laws.

March 12   From Daniel Fletcher Webster. ALS. NhHi. mDW 32933. Insists that remarks attributed to "Mr. Benson" are untrue; reports DW's letter to Haven has been published.

March 12   From William A. Weeks. ALS. DNA, RG 59. mDW 56881. Reports on despatches now under the charge of Theodore Neal of Salem.

March 12   Recommendation from Joseph R. Chandler, for [Samuel J.] Oakford—U.S. consul at Tumbez, Peru (ALS. DNA. mDWs).

March 12   Warranty deed transferring property in Franklin, N.H. from Daniel Osgood to DW. Registry of Deeds, Merrimack County, New Hampshire. Book 105, p. 28.

March 13   To Millard Fillmore. ALS. NBuHi. mDW 32935. Submits his draft of "the *finale* of the Austrian correspondence.

March 13   To Peleg Sprague. LS. MDuHi. mDWs. Inquires for information which might determine if Joab Bartlett is eligible for a presidential pardon.

March 13   To John Taylor. LS. NhHi. mDW 32937. Gives instructions for spreading guano; inquires about the health of Taylor's family.

March 13   From W. F. Bang & Co. LS. DNA, RG 59. mDW 53916. Inquire whether they are to publish the laws for the second session of the 31st Congress as well as the first, in the *Daily Republican Banner and Nashville Whig*.

March 13   From Millard Fillmore (enclosure: [DW to Hülsemann, Mar 12, 1851, in part], draft in Fillmore's hand, revised by DW). ALS. DLC. mDW 32938. Returns DW's draft of a note to Hülsemann with some additions.

March 13   From Smith & Sayward. LS. DNA, RG 59. mDW 53781. Accept appointment of the Bangor, Maine *Daily Whig and Courier* to publish the laws.

[March 13]   Recommendation from Friend Humphrey, for H. M. Humphrey—a position (ALS. DLC. mDW 32941).

[March 14]   To Millard Fillmore. ALS. NBuHi. mDW 32943. Submits a revised draft of his note to Hülsemann, which has caused him much "vexation & bother."

March 14   To Franklin Haven. LS. MH–H. mDW 32945. Thanks Haven for his replies to the attacks against DW in the House of Representatives.

March 14   To William Cabell Rives. LS. InU–Li. mDW 32956. Introduces Josiah P. Cooke of Boston.

March 14   To Upjohn & Co. LS. NhD. mDW 32957. States that plans for enlarging the Capitol are not yet decided, and invites their suggestions.

March 14   From Lemuel G. Brandenburg. ALS. DNA, RG 59. mDW 54945. Accepts appointment as chief justice of Utah.

March 14   From Millard Fillmore. AL. DLC. mDW 32949. Severance, *Fillmore Papers*, 1: 340. Returns DW's draft of the note to Hülsemann.

March 14   From A[ndrew] Rothwell. ALS. DNA, RG 59. mDW 55086. accepts appointment as justice of the peace for Washington, D.C.

March 15   To [Ernest André Olivier] Sain de Bois Le Comte. Typed copy. DLC. mDW 32950. Expresses regret and good wishes on Bois Le Comte's retirement as French minister to the U.S.

March 15   Millard Fillmore from Edward A. Saunders et al. (endorsed by DW "Private files"). LS. DLC. mDWs. Protest Joseph Graham's removal as U.S. consul at Buenos Ayres.

March 15   To Chevalier Johann Georg Hülsemann. LS. Austrian State Archives, Vienna. mDW 32951. Expresses gratification for Austria's desire for friendly relations, while reaffirming the position taken in his note of Dec 21, 1850.

March 15   From Duff Green. ALS draft. NcU. mDW 32954. ALS copy NcU. mDW 32958. Urges that the last installment due Mexico under the treaty of Guadalupe Hidalgo be paid through the agency of "Mr. Marks."

March 15   From J[ames] A. Kennedy. ALS. DNA, RG 59. mDW 55022. Accepts appointment as justice of the peace for Washington, D.C.

March 15   From John Taylor. Printed. *PC*, 2: 422–423. Reports on his farming; asks if he should buy a certain pair of oxen.

March 15   From Daniel Fletcher Webster. ALS. NhHi. mDW 32965. Can Report nothing on "Mr. Hale" but finds that [George P.] Sanger is a law partner of Charles G. Davis, a defendant in the Shadrach rescue case.

March 15   From Daniel Fletcher Webster. ALS. NhHi. mDW 32968. Responds to allegations he offered to obtain Timothy Darling a consulship for $200.

March 15   From Daniel Fletcher Webster. ALS. NhHi. mDW 32972. Comments on "Mr. McIntyre's" charges against "Gowen & Wells'"; reports all is well at Marshfield.

March 15   Application from Henry Major—diplomatic position (ALS. NhHi. mDW 32962).

March 16   To H[enry] A[ugustus] Boardman. Draft. DLC. mDW 32976. Declines an invitation to speak at the church benefit in Philadelphia.

March 16   From Amin Bey. Translation. DNA, RG 59. mDW 56703. Expresses gratitude for the hospitality shown him during his visit to the United States.

[c. March 16] To Amin Bey. Copy. DLC. mDW 31738. *Diplomatic Papers*, 2. Bids Amin Bey farewell on his return to Turkey.

March 16 From [Sir Henry Lytton Bulwer]. AL draft. UkLPR. mDW 32982. Refuses to divulge the source of his information about a possible invasion of Cuba, and asks that his letter not be made public.

March 16 From Edward Everett. ALS. MHi. mDW 32979. Will heed DW and Abbot's editorial suggestions; reports Bancroft's advice that the U.S. take a firm stand on Nicaragua.

March 16 From Robert M. Walsh (enclosures: copies of notes exchanged with the Haitian foreign minister). ALS. DNA, RG 59. mDW 56220. Reports on his negotiations with Haiti.

March 17 To Millard Fillmore. ALS. NBuHi. mDW 32986. Van Tyne, p. 461. Introduces John S. Riddle of Philadelphia as a staunch friend of the Administration.

March 17 To Millard Fillmore. Dictated letter. NBuHi. mDW 32990. Reports that papers relative to the barque *Pedimonte* were sent to Fillmore on Mar 14th.

March 17 To William Alexander Graham. ALS. Nc–Ar. mDW 32992. Invites Graham to dine with himself and Captain [Robert Field] Stockton.

March 17 To [Nathan] Hale. ALS. MHi. mDW 32994. Explains the government's actions regarding Kossuth and the Hungarian exiles.

M[arch] 17 To L[uther] R. Marsh. LS. NhD. mDWs. Is happy to learn that "things are not so bad as I feared" regarding a law suit; states "it is quite proper that Bro. Niles should go into the public service at Sing Sing."

March 17 To William Cabell Rives. LS. DLC. mDW 32995. Informs Rives that [Thomas] Ritchie has sold his interest in the Washington, D.C. *Union*, and encloses a letter for Ritchie's Paris correspondent; describes Ritchie as a staunch Union supporter.

March 17 To Daniel Fletcher Webster. ALS. NhHi. mDW 32997. Is recommending Daniel Webster Fessenden for a clerkship; agrees also to recommend "Mr. March" and to see about a postmaster for Fitchburg; asks him to send "Mr. Benson's letter, if it be right."

March 17 John Overton Choules to Daniel Fletcher Webster. ALS. DNA, RG 59. mDW 56882. Asks where he should pick up his despatches; asks also for a letter of introduction to anyone in England, especially " in the great farming interest."

March 17 Application from Stephen A. Hurlbut—a job (ALS. DLC. mDW 32999).

March 18 To Ogden Hoffman, Jr. Printed DS with MS insertions. . CSmH mDWs. Encloses a commission appointing David P. Douglas U.S. marshal for northern California.

March 18 To John Taylor. ALS. MBBS. mDW 33002. *PC*, 2: 423. Inquires about Taylor's family; asks for measurements of each of his oxen.

March 18 From Lewis Cass. ALS. NhHi. mDW 33005. Van Tyne, pp. 461–462. Calls the letter to Marsh regarding the Hungarian exiles a "model" state paper.

March 18   From Edward Everett. LC. MHi. mDW 33007. Discusses the
editing of the two Bunker Hill speeches for DW's works.

March 18   Account with John B. Kibbey & Co. for $15.67 for provisions,
through Dec 29. AD. NhHi. mDW 40586.

March 19   To William Cabell Rives (enclosure: newsclipping from the
National Intelligencer on the recall of Bois Le Comte). ALS. DLC.
mDW 33012. Van Tyne, p. 462. Expresses regret at Bois Le Comte's
recall but is looking forward to the arrival of his successor.

[March 19]   From [Sir Henry Lytton Bulwer]. ALS. DLC. mDW 33017.
Thanks DW for showing him some correspondence.

March 19   From Sir Henry Lytton Bulwer. Copy. UkLPR. mDWs. Encloses correspondence relative to the possessory rights of the Hudson's Bay Company in Oregon, and requests that the issue be
resolved.

March 19   From William R. Lount. ALS. DNA, RG 48. mDWs. On behalf
of squatters on government lands in Alabama, asks if the bounty
land warrants issued to war veterans are "receivable at the Land
Office in payment for their lands."

March 19   From John S. Watts. ALS. DNA, RG 59. mDW 55121. Accepts
appointment as associate justice of the New Mexico supreme court.

[March 20]   To Millard Fillmore. LS. NBuHi. mDW 33019. Will introduce Don Felipe Molina, the new Costa Rican minister, to Fillmore
at noon.

March 20   To Millard Fillmore. Dictated letter. NBuHi. mDW 33021.
Transmits a copy of the address Molina plans to deliver when he
meets the president.

March 20   To Isaac Hill. ALS. NhHi. mDW 33023. Asks if there is anything he or Caroline can do for Hill.

March 20   To George Perkins Marsh. LS. VtU. mDW 33024. Introduces
Lucius C. Duncan of New Orleans.

March 20   To John Taylor. LS. MBBS. mDW 33026. Asks about oxen.

March 20   From M[erwin] R. Brewer et al. (with AN by DW). LS. DLC.
mDW 33027. Van Tyne, p. 462. Invite him to a birthday festival in
honor of Henry Clay.

March 20   From James Butler Campbell.   215

March 20   From Duff Green (with memorandum by Green; and Green to
Fillmore, Mar 20, 1851). ALS copy. NcU. mDW 33034. Submits
Marks' proposition for payment of the last installment of the Mexi-
can indemnity.

March 20   From H[orace] Mower. ALS. DNA, RG 59. mDW 55063. Inquires about his appointment as associate justice of the New Mexico
supreme court.

March 20   Department of State circular on Austrian correspondence.
Printed D. DNA, RG 59. mDW 55154.

March 21   To Sir Henry Lytton Bulwer. LS. UkLPR. mDW 33037. Accepts Bulwer's comments on the possessory rights of the Hudson's
Bay Company in Oregon and would like to discuss the matter with
him.

March 21   To Edward Everett. LS. MHi. mDW 33038. *PC*, 2: 425–426.
Discusses the editing of his Bunker Hill speeches.

March 21   To Millard Fillmore. ALS. NBuHi. mDW 33040. Refers to this morning's *Republic* for the text of Judge [Peleg] Sprague's charge to the Boston grand jury.

March 21   To Albert R. Hatch. LC. DNA, RG 59. Authorizes him to forward "the works" remaining in the office of the clerk for the U.S. district court in Portsmouth, N.H.

March 21   To Joseph Henry. LC. DNA, 59. Conveys information relative to the Magnetic Observatory at Toronto.

March 21   To Charles King. LS. NNC. mDW 33042. Reports that the State Department is forwarding a set of documents to Columbia College.

March 21   To William M. Richards et al.   217

March 21   To Peleg Sprague. ALS. MDuHi. mDW 33051. Pronounces Sprague's charge to the Boston grand jury "sound, lawyer-like, & able."

March 21   From H[orace] Mower. ALS. DNA, RG 59. mDW 55062. Accepts appointment as associate justice of the New Mexico supreme court.

March 21   From Josiah Randall. ALS. DLC. mDW 33052. Demands the removal of the incumbent collector and surveyor in the Philadelphia custom house.

March 22   To Sir Henry Lytton Bulwer. LS. UkLPR. mDW 33055. Thanks him for a statement on import duties prepared by the Board of Trade.

March 22   To Sir Henry Lytton Bulwer (enclosure: John Jordan Crittenden to DW, Mar 22, 1851). LS. UkLPR. mDW 33056. Transmits a note from the attorney general relative to the prospective sale of a "girl of color" said to be a British subject.

March 22   From Sir Henry Lytton Bulwer. Copy. UkLPR. mDWs. Wishes to know if DW will negotiate about proposed commercial regulations to be established between the U.S. and Canada.

March 22   From John Jordan Crittenden (with DW to Bulwer, Mar 22, 1851). Copy. UkLPR. mDW 33057. Advises that the case of a girl of color, alleged to be a British subject, is essentially a judicial question the decision of which belongs to the courts.

March 22   From [Edward Everett]. LC. MHi. mDW 33059. Discusses the make-up of volume one of DW's works; sends letters from friends in England.

March 22   From James B. Howell. ALS. DNA, RG 59. mDW 53774. Accepts appointment of the *Valley Whig and Keokuk* (Ia.) *Register* to publish the laws.

March 22   From Daniel Fletcher Webster. ALS. NhHi. mDW 33061. Advises hiring Horace Green Hutchins to assist Lunt in the prosecution of the slave rescue cases.

March 23   To Millard Fillmore. ALS. NBuHi. mDW 33063. Van Tyne, p. 464. Sends over Campbell's letter reporting on secessionist sentiment in South Carolina.

March 23   To William P. Hill.   219
March 23   From Washington Hunt.   219

March 24   To William Freame Johnston. Draft. CtY. mDW 33074. Asks that the Pennsylvania legislature be given his thanks for their resolutions in support of his Hülsemann letter.

March 25   From Duff Green. ALS drafts and copy. NcU. mDW 33076,
33080, 33084. Advises the appointment of Marks to arrange payment of the last installment on the Mexican indemnity.

March 25   From William L. Hodge (with DW to Bulwer, Mar 26, 1851).
Copy. UkLPR. mDW 33090. Reports the Treasury Department has
decided to make restitution for the condemnation and sale of the
Albion.

March 26   To Sir Henry Lytton Bulwer (enclosure: Hodge to DW, Mar
25, 1851). LS. UkLPR. mDW 33088. Transmits a letter from the acting secretary of the treasury announcing the Department's decision
in the *Albion* case.

March 26   From George Jacob Abbot. ALS. CtY. mDW 33092. Submits a
list of DW's speeches of which he does not have copies.

March 27   To Millard Fillmore. ALS. NBuHi. mDW 33093. Encloses a
letter from Fletcher Webster.

March 27   To John Henry Manners (5th Duke of Rutland). Copy. NhHi.
mDW 33095. Van Tyne, p. 634. Introduces John Overton Choules, a
clergyman from Rhode Island.

March 27   To Charles Porter Wright. LS. NhHi. mDW 33098. *PC*, 2:
426.   Discusses farm matters.

March 27   From [Sir Henry Lytton Bulwer]. AL draft. UkLPR. mDW
33100. Warns that the Canadian government may retaliate if some
reciprocal trade agreement cannot be reached.

[March 28]   To Richard Milford Blatchford. Printed. *PC*, 2: 426–427. Is
suffering from overwork; looks forward to going north.

March 28   To Millard Fillmore. LS. NBuHi. mDW 33105. Asks him to
meet with the Peruvian chargé d'affaires, [Juan Ygnacio de] Osma.

March 28   To W[illiam?] C. Miller. LS. InU–Li. mDW 33108. Sends the
address for the U.S. consul at Bordeaux.

March 28   To Daniel Fletcher Webster. ALS. InU–Li. mDW 33109. Has
sent Choules a courier's passport and a letter of introduction to the
Duke of Rutland; will be coming north in April.

March 28   From [Anonymous] (with ANS by DW). AL. DLC. mDW
33110. Encloses a clipping from the *Tribune*, and accuses DW's New
York friends of supporting a newspaper which is hostile to him.

March 28   From Sir Henry Lytton Bulwer. Copy. CaOOA. mDW 33112.
Identical to the letter from Bulwer of Mar 22, 1851, mDWs.

March 28   From Edward Everett. LC. MHi. mDW 33118. Discusses
strategy for marketing DW's works.

March 28   From Freeman Hunt. ALS. ViU. mDWs. Agrees to provide
back issues of the *Merchant's Magazine*, and explains the intent of
his journal.

March 28   From Felipe Molina. Copy. UkLPR. mDWs. Asks the U.S. to
arbitrate a territorial dispute between Costa Rica and Nicaragua
under the Clayton-Bulwer Treaty of 1850.

March 28   Application from Alfred Dietah, for the Chicago *Commercial
Advertiser*—public printer (ALS. DNA, RG 59, mDW 53920).

March 29   To Sir Henry Lytton Bulwer. LS. UkLPR. mDW 33121. Transmits a presidential exequatur recognizing George Aiken, H.M. consul
in California.

March 29   From L[ewis] C[harles] Levin. ALS. NhD. mDW 33122. Introduces Jules Coutin of France, here to study American railroads.

March 31   To [Edward Everett]. ALS. MHi. mDW 33124. Agrees to
Everett's suggestion about a speech; will leave for the north this
afternoon.

March 31   From David H. Campbell. ALS. DLC. mDW 33128. Offers a
"Southern" plan for the abolition of slavery.

March 31   From Crane & Rice. LS. DNA, RG 59. mDW 53756. Accept appointment of the San Francisco *Daily California Courier* to publish
the laws.

March 31   From Charles Pelham Curtis.   220

March 31   From Edward Everett. ALS. MHi. mDW 33138. Sends part
two of his biographical sketch of DW; asks what speeches from the
13th and 14th Congresses DW wants omitted from his works.

*March 31   From George Lunt, with enclosure: Rufus Choate to Lunt,
March 29, 1851.*   221

March 31   From James Hervey Otey. Copy. NhHi. mDW 33142. Thanks
DW for testimonial letter; praises DW's efforts on behalf of the
Union.

March 31   From owners of the British ship *Francis & Eliza*. Copy. DLC.
MDW 32816. Petition for the payment of a long-standing claim
against the U.S. government.

March 31   From N[athaniel] S. Richardson. ALS. DLC. mDW 33145.
Asks DW to endorse the newly published *Church Review*.

March 31   From Peleg Sprague. LS. DLC. mDW 33148. Acknowledges
DW's letter complimenting his charge to the Boston grand jury.

March 31   From Robert M. Walsh (enclosures: news clippings and
copies of notes exchanged with the Haitian foreign minister). ALS.
DNA, RG 59. mDW 56227. Reports the conclusion of the three western diplomats, that force must be used against Haiti, and that
Britain and France are planning a blockade of the island.

March 31   Recommendation from R[obert] W[ard] Johnson, for the
Little Rock *Arkansas Democratic Banner*—public printer (ALS.
DNA, RG 59. mDW 53886).

[March]   To [District Attorney of Mississippi]. Draft revised. NhHi.
mDW 33150. Comments on the mistrials of former senator John
Henderson, accused of complicity in the Lopez expeditions.

March   To H[enry] S[tuart] Foote. Copy. NhHi. mDW 33154. Van Tyne,
p. 460. Submits estimates of the appropriation necessary for a minister plenipotentiary to San Salvador, Honduras, and Costa Rica.

[March]   From Samuel K. Thurston. ALS. DNA, RG 76. mDWs. Comments on the right of the Hudson's Bay Company to trade in Indian
country south of the 49th parallel.

[pre-April 1]   To [?]. ALS. NN. mDW 39318. Fears "you have forgotten
Mr. Mathias' letter"; reminds him that "I go to Harrisburg, on
Tuesday."

April 1   From Alpheus Felch. ALS. MiD. mDW 33156. Wishes to apply
for a passport.

April 1   From John P. Gaines. ALS. Or–Ar. mDWs. Answers a request for
copies of the laws of Oregon.

April 1   Receipt for $80 paid Peter Slevin for wages. DS. DLC. mDW
40496.

April 2   From Millard Fillmore. AL. DLC. mDW 33157. Severance, *Fillmore Papers*, 1: 340–341. Wishes to see DW regarding the letter

from the Mexican chargé d'affaires on the Tehuantepec route.

April 3   From Fitz Henry Warren. LS. DLC. mDW 33159. States that Morris E. Fuller, newly-appointed postmaster at Rockton, N.Y., has posted bond.

April 3   Application from Thomas Palmer and Edward Pickett, for the Jackson, Mississippi *Flag of the Union*—public printer (LS. DNA, RG 59. mDW 53932).

April 4   To Millard Fillmore. LS. NBuHi. mDW 33160. Van Tyne, pp. 464–465. Reports his meeting with the Pennsylvania legislature; finds Gov. Johnston is opposing the enactment of a law which would allow federal prisoners to be held in state and local jails.

April 4   To Millard Fillmore (enclosure: George Lunt to DW, March 31, 1851, enclosing Choate to Lunt, Mar 29, 1851). LS. NBuHi. mDW 33164. Is trying to learn why Choate withdrew from the slave rescue case; considers others who might assist Lunt.

April 4   To Millard Fillmore. LS. NBuHi. mDW 33176. Admits overlooking the resignation of the U.S. marshal for Georgia, and suggests a successor.

April 4   To George Lunt (with Henry Sargent to Fillmore, Apr 5, 1851; enclosure: W. Laflin to James B. Robb, Apr 4, 1851).   226

April 4   From Sir Henry Lytton Bulwer. Copy. UkLPR. mDWs. Asks DW to provide any information about "evil-disposed" Americans who might try to disrupt the world's fair in London.

April 4   From W[illiam] C[hanning] Gibbs (with AN by DW).   225
April 4   From Daniel Fletcher Webster (with ANS by DW).   228
April 4   From Daniel Fletcher Webster.   228

April 5   To [Millard Fillmore] (with DW to Fillmore, Apr 6, 1851). LS. NBuHi. mDW 33198. Reports that Robert Rantoul was denied an adjournment of the Senate, requested so he could prepare his argument on the constitutionality of the Fugitive Slave law.

April 5   From H[enry] D[ilworth] Gilpin. ALS. NhHi. mDW 33190. Promises to do what is necessary regarding the Mexican awards.

April 5   From Swain & Sherwood. LS. DNA, RG 59. mDW 53929. Report not yet receiving certain issues of the *Republic*.

April 6   To Millard Fillmore with enclosure: DW to Fillmore, April 5, 1851.   229

April 6   To William Alexander Graham. ALS. NcU. mDW 33199. Hamilton, *Graham*, 4: 67. Asks what North Carolina has done to show its support for the Compromise.

April 7   To Peter Harvey. Telegram. NhHi. mDW 33200. Van Tyne, p. 468. "No reception. I will come up from Marshfield."

April 7   To Peter Harvey. Printed. PC, 2: 427. Would prefer that any reception for him at Boston should come on his return from Marshfield.

April 7   To H[enry] W[ashington] Hilliard. Copy. NhHi. mDW 33201. Van Tyne, pp. 468–469. Explains why it might be better for Hilliard not to take a diplomatic assignment before the coming presidential canvas.

[April 7, 1851]   To Francis Schroeder. ALS. NHi. mDWs. Introduces S[amuel] Starkweather of New York.

April 7   To Charles Porter Wright. ALS. NhHi. mDW 33204. Will arrive at Marshfield in a few days, and asks that the house be made ready.

April 7   From [George Jacob Abbot]. AL draft. CtY. mDW 33206. Applies for reimbursement for expenses incurred in his interview with the former consul in Zanzibar.

April 7   From John R. Riddle. ALS. DLC. mDW 33208. Writes regarding patronage and the Philadelphia custom house.

April 7   From William Sweatt (with AN by DW). ALS. NhHi. mDW 33211. Van Tyne, p. 545. Reminisces about Salisbury, N.H. and his memories of DW's parents.

April 7   From Jesse Turner. ALS. DNA, RG 59. mDW 55103. Accepts appointment as U.S. attorney for western Arkansas.

April 7   Application from Simeon Francis, for the Springfield *Illinois Journal*—public printer (ALS. DNA, RG 59. mDW 53891).

April 7   Promissory note for $500 payable to Richard Milford Blatchford. DS. MHi. mDW 40500.

April 7   Treasury Department circular asking consuls and commercial agents for information about trade. Printed D. DNA, RG 59. mDW 55155.

April 8   From Robert M. Walsh. ALS. DNA, RG 59. mDW 56240. Comments on the opening of the Haitian Chambers and Emperor Soulouque's accession to the throne.

April 8   Application from James and William Witherspoon, for the Marshall, Texas *Star State Patriot*—public printer (LS. DNA, RG 59. mDW 53958).

April 9   To Millard Fillmore.   230

April 9   From Sir Henry Lytton Bulwer. Copy. UkLPR. mDWs. Asks DW to address the claim of an American seaman whose life insurance indemnity has been fraudulently acquired by someone else.

April 9   From Edward Everett. LC. MHi. mDW 33219. Refers to speeches he is thinking of omitting from DW's works.

April 9   From Jermain & Brother. ALS. DNA, RG 59. mDW 53772. Accept appointment to publish the laws in the Adrian *Michigan Expositor*.

April 10   From William Cabell Rives. ALS. DLC. mDW 33221. Encloses a note for Thomas Ritchie; comments on Bois Le Comte's recall and the unsettled state of French politics.

April 10/13   From Robert M. Walsh (enclosure: proclamation by the Emperor of Haiti, Apr 1, 1851). ALS. DNA, RG 59. mDW 56248. Comments critically on Haitian society and government, calling it "so absurd a caricature of civilization"; reports his efforts to prevent Haiti from sending agents to London, Paris and Washington to negotiate a peace settlement.

April 11   To John Taylor. ALS. MBBS. mDW 33225. States that Asa Hewitt, Jr. will be coming to Franklin to work on trees, gardens, etc.

April 11   From John T. Bush. ALS. DNA, RG 59. mDW 54953. Accepts appointments as U.S. marshal for northern New York.

April 11   From Caleb Eddy et al. LS. MWalB. mDW 33234. Invite DW to a reception at Faneuil Hall.

April 11   From Millard Fillmore   231

April 11   Opinion. AD and ANS. NhHi. mDW 33226. Regarding the Constitutional power of the New York legislature to pass a bill entitled "An act to provide for the completion of the Erie Canal enlargement, & the Genessee Valley and Back River canals"; with covering note to Fletcher Webster asking him to copy it in a fair hand.

April 11   Receipt for $12.86 paid the Washington Branch Railroad for transportation and charges on a carriage, with fixtures and whip. DS. NhHi. mDW 40502.

April 12   To William Sweatt. Copy. NhHi. mDW 33238. Van Tyne, pp. 634–635. Acknowledges Sweatt's letter of reminiscences.

April 12   From William Plumer, Jr. ALS draft. Nh. mDW 33240. Refers to New Hampshire's participation in an expedition against the Spanish West Indies in 1740; mentions a tract in Epping, N.H. known as "the Cuba lands."

April 12   Recommendations, from Caleb B. Smith to William S. Derrick, for the Indianapolis *Indiana State Journal*, and the Terre Haute *Wabash Express*—public printers (ALS. DNA, RG 59. mDW 53884).

April 12   Mortgage deed assigning property in Duxbury, Mass. to the Duxbury Manufacturing Company. DS. NhD. mDW 40504. Copy. Book 242: 144–145. Recorder of Deeds, Plymouth County, Massachusetts. mDWs.

April 12   Warranty deed transferring a cotton factory, grist mill, etc., in Duxbury, Mass. to DW from the Duxbury Manufacturing Company. DS. NhD. mDW 40508. Copy. Book 242: 143–144. Recorder of Deeds, Plymouth County, Massachusetts. mDWs.

April 13   To Richard Milford Blatchford. Printed. *PC*, 2: 428. Expects "the meeting" will come on Thursday but has not heard so officially.

April 13   To Millard Fillmore.   232

April 14   From Thomas L. Roan. ALS. DNA, RG 393. mDWs. Asks DW to support his petition for discharge from the Army.

April 14   From James Shields. ALS. PHi. mDW 33245. Introduces Herman Engelbach, who wishes to obtain a passport.

April 15   To Richard Milford Blatchford. Printed. *PC*, 2: 431. Reports being in the midst of a "furious northeaster."

April 15   To Edward Everett. ALS. MHi. mDW 33246. Will look over the biographical sketch; decides to omit various speeches from the works.

April 15   To Millard Fillmore.   234
April 15   To Millard Fillmore.   235

April 15   To George G. Smith et al. AL draft. NhHi. mDW 33255. Curtis, 2: 499–500. Comments on the Boston alderman's denial of the use of Faneuil Hall for his reception; defends his public conduct, and predicts "fanaticism and folly" will be short-lived.

April 15   From W. C. Ballard. ALS. DLC. mDW 33259. Stresses the need to emphasize the ethical aspects of the Compromise and the folly of those who appear bent on destroying the Union.

[April 15]   From Rufus Choate.   236

April 15   From Jonathan Prescott Hall. Copy. UkLPR. mDWs. Finds no evidence of a conspiracy by criminals to disrupt the exhibition at London.

April 15   From Y. M. Lampkin. ALS. DNA, RG 59. mDW 53768. Accepts appointment of the Athens, Georgia *Southern Herald* to publish the laws.

April 16   From Millard Fillmore.   237

April 17   From Edward Everett. ALS. MHi. mDW 33268. Reports on the preparation of DW's works for the press.

April 17   From William B. Figures to William S. Derrick. ALS. DNA, RG
59. mDW 53770. Accepts appointment to print the laws in the
Huntsville, Alabama *Southern Advocate*.

April 17   From Charles Wainwright March.   238

April 18   To Millard Fillmore.   239

[April 18]   To [?]. Printed. W & S, 16: 609. Reports being detained at
Marshfield by a violent storm.

April 18   From Francis Brinley (enclosure: Preamble and resolutions
of Boston Common Council, Apr 17, 1851). ALS. NhHi. mDW 33279.
Van Tyne, p. 472. Encloses a resolution of regret over the refusal of
the mayor and aldermen to permit the use of Faneuil Hall for DW's
reception.

April 18   From Thomas J. Rusk. Typed copy of photostat. TxSjM.
mDWs. States that J. George Woldert, who desires a passport, has
been a U.S. citizen since the annexation of Texas.

April 18   From Moses Stuart. ALS. NhD. mDW 33285. Comments on
anti-slavery politics in Massachusetts; asks if his son might be appointed an Army surgeon.

April 18   Recommendation from A.W. Fletcher to William S. Derrick,
for the *Logansport* (Ind.) *Journal*—public printer (ALS. DNA, RG
59. mDW 53876).

April 19   To Francis Brinley. AL draft. MSaE. mDW 33291. Curtis, 2:
500–501. Acknowledges the resolutions of the Boston Common Council; declares he will not again enter Faneuil Hall until it is open to all
who believe in union and liberty.

April 19   From Henry Alexander Scammell Dearborn. ALS. NhHi. mDW
33298. Van Tyne, pp. 472–473. Condemns the conduct of the Boston
aldermen in their treatment of DW and earlier of Fillmore.

April 21   To Richard Milford Blatchford. ALS. ICHi. mDW 33302. Will
ensure that "the deed" is properly executed and forwarded once it
reaches him.

April 21   To [Samuel P. Lyman]. ALS. MiU. mDWs. Inquires about the
price of Mexican scrip, saying he must dispose of some of his
holdings.

April 21   To Charles Porter Wright. Printed. *PC*, 2: 431–432. Discusses
oxen and other farm matters.

April 21   From Edward Everett. ALS. MHi. mDW 33306. Inquires about
DW's speech in New York on Sept 28, 1840.

April 21   From David Henshaw. ALS. NhHi. mDW 33310. *PC*, 2: 432–
434. Dismisses the Boston aldermen's action as "a pitiful attempt . . .
to annoy you"; regards the state's outlook on national affairs as nar-
rowly sectional.

April 21   From Henry Washington Hilliard. ALS. NhHi. mDW 33314.
Suggests it might be in the Administration's best political interest
to give him the overseas post he wants.

April 21   From Josephine [Hosmer?]. ALS. NhHi. mDW 33322. Offers
some political advice.

April 21   From Henry B. Rogers et al. (enclosure: Order of the Boston
City Council, Apr 21, 1851). LS. NhHi. mDW 33326. Van Tyne,
p. 473. Invite DW to deliver an address at Faneuil Hall.

April 21   From [James Wilson]. AL draft. NhHi. mDWs. Complains that
the Administration has overlooked his claim to office.

April 21   From Prentice & Weissinger. LS. DNA, RG 59. mDW 53764. Accept appointment of the *Louisville* (Ky.) *Journal* to publish the laws.

April 22   From N[athaniel] S. Richardson. ALS. DLC. mDW 33329. Seeks DW's approval of an article in the *Church Review* on "Loyalty to the American Constitution."

April 23   To Edward Everett. ALS. MHi. mDW 33332. Admits to being quite disturbed by the Faneuil Hall episode; thanks Everett for writing to Hale; discusses editorial problems.

April 23   To Franklin Haven. ALS. MH–H. mDW 33335. Asks Haven to honor some drafts, and be sure everything is all right.

April 23   To Henry B. Rogers et al. ALS. MB. mDW 33339. Harvey, *Reminiscences of DW*, p. 192. Coldly refuses their invitation to speak at Faneuil Hall.

April 23   To George Stimpson, Jr. ALS. Convent of the Holy Cross, West Franklin, N.H. mDW 33342. Thanks him for a gold pen.

April 23   To [John Taylor]. ALS. MWalB. mDW 33343. *PC*, 2: 434–435. Gives instructions for farm work to be done at the Elms.

April 23   From David S. Donaldson to William S. Derrick. ALS. DNA, RG 59. mDW 53766. Accepts appointment of the Terre Haute *Wabash Express* to publish the laws.

April 23   From Millard Fillmore. ALS. NhD. mDWs. Discusses the Indian problem with Mexico, and thinks, with Letcher, that DW's response to the Mexican minister, de la Rosa, should be modified; thinks a chargé should be despatched to Nicaragua immediately; reports on a letter that "Sir Henry [Bulwer?]" thinks was a forgery "intended to give Genl. Cass the Irish vote and magnify his services on the compromise measures."

April 23   From Robert M. Walsh (enclosures: L. Dufrene to [Walsh et al.], Apr 19, 1851; Walsh et al. to [Dufrene], Apr 19, 1851). ALS. DNA, RG 59. mDW 56265. Reports that the tripartite proposal has been "positively rejected" by Haiti; counsels the use of force against Haiti.

April 23   Recommendation from Washington Hunt, for Peter Rowe— despatch bearer (ALS. PHi. mDW 33345).

April 24   From Edward Everett. ALS. MHi. mDW 33349. Comments on the "Faneuil Hall affair"; reports volume one of DW's works is nearing completion.

April 25   To William S. Derrick. ALS. NhD. mDW 33353. Gives instructions in anticipation of an attempted invasion of Cuba.

[April 25]   To Millard Fillmore. ALS. NBuHi. mDW 33354. *Diplomatic Papers*, 2. Reports on preparations for the arrest of "several offenders" in the conspiracy to invade Cuba, but fears little can be done here to restrain "these lawless people."

April 25   To Millard Fillmore. AL, draft. NhD. mDWs. Thinks "Mr. Wilson" and [John] O'Sullivan (Cuban filibusters) should be arrested.

April 25   From L[ewis] C[harles] Levin. ALS. DLC. mDW 33356. Offers to arrange a reception by Philadelphia's working men when DW reaches the city on Monday.

April 26   From Isaac G. Seymour to William S. Derrick. ALS. DNA, RG 59. mDW 53762. Accepts appointment of the *New Orleans Commercial Bulletin* to publish the laws.

April 26   From Richard G. Smith. ALS. DNA, RG 59. mDW 53760. Accepts appointment of the Bowling Green, Kentucky *Warren Intelligencer* to publish the laws.

April 26   From Henry L. Tilden. ALS. DNA, RG 59. mDW 55111. Accepts appointment as U.S. marshal for Minnesota Territory.

April 26   Applications from Thomas C. Hambly—"a commissionership to California" (ALS. DLC. mDW 33358); from Daniel Palmer—military storekeeper (ALS. DNA, RG 156. mDWs).

April 27   To Richard Milford Blatchford. Printed. *PC*, 2: 435. Announces his return to Washington.

[April 27]   To Thomas Corwin (with Thomas C. Hambly to DW, Apr 26, 1851). ANS. DLC. mDW 33358. Asks if anything can be done for Hambly.

April 27   To Charles Porter Wright. ALS. NhHi. mDW 33361. *PC*, 2: 435. Gives instructions for packing and shipping pork; wishes to be kept fully informed on the progress of the farm.

April 27   From Richard Rush. ALS. DLC. mDW 33363. Is disappointed he missed seeing DW in Philadelphia; sends a token of appreciation.

April 28   To Millard Fillmore. ALS. NBuHi. mDW 33366. Promises to "look after Mr. Squiers, forthwith."

April 28   To William Alexander Graham. Typed copy. DNA, RG 59. mDW 56461. States that a draft payable to claimants in the *Josephine* and *Ranger* cases has been turned over to the Treasury.

April 28   To Franklin Haven. ALS. MH–H. mDW 33368. *Diplomatic Papers*, 2. Discusses the matter of a draft; thinks evils resulting from recent territorial acquisitions are now beginning to be felt.

April 28   From Charles Gibbons. ALS. NhHi. mDW 33372. Complains about Administration patronage policies in Pennsylvania.

April 28   From Giles M. Hillyer. ALS. DNA, RG 59. mDW 53754. Accepts appointment of the *Natchez* (Miss.) *Courier* to publish the laws.

April 28   From John Miller McKee. ALS. DNA, RG 59. mDW 53758. Accepts appointment of the *Knoxville* (Tenn.) *Register* to publish the laws.

April 28   From John Taylor. ALS. NhHi. mDW 33374. *PC*, 2: 436. Reports on farm activity at The Elms.

April 28   Recommendation from David Bronson, for the Bath, Maine *Northern Tribune*—printing for the Treasury and Navy Departments (ALS. DLC. mDW 33370).

April 28   To [Edward Everett]. LS. MHi. mDW 33383. Discusses editorial matters.

April 29   To Richard Milford Blatchford. ALS. DLC. mDW 33377. *PC*, 2: 436–437. Hears that Savannah is to be the rendezvous for the Cuban invasion force; describes a stroll through the Washington market.

April 29   To [Millard Fillmore]. LS. NBuHi. mDW 33386. *PC*, 2: 437. Reports the draft for a reply to Don Luis de la Rosa has been given to the copyist and will be brought to him tomorrow.

April 29   From Phillip Clayton. ALS. DNA, RG 59. mDW 53718. Encloses articles critical of the Compromise clipped from the Athens, Ga. *Southern Herald*, a newspaper that has been appointed to publish the laws.

April 29   From James Cooper (with DW to Fillmore, May 1, 1851).
NhD. mDW 33435. Criticizes the Fillmore administration's patronage policy in Pennsylvania.

April 29   From Edward Everett (with ANS by DW). ALS. MHi. mDW
33390. Inquires about DW's Andover speech of November, 1843.

April 29   From George P. A. Healy.   240

April 29   From O[gden] Hoffman. ALS. NhHi. mDW 33396. Asks for official approval of his appointment to assist in the prosecution of the
Cuban conspirators.

April 29   From Robert Field Stockton (with AN by DW). ALS. DLC.
mDW 33398. Asks if something can be done for Bernard Maguire,
a cripple with political friends, who faces dismissal from the Philadelphia custom house.

April 29   Memorandum on recall of Joseph W. Livingston, U.S. consul at
San Juan de Nicaragua. AD. NBuHi. mDWs.

April 29   Warranty deed transferring property in Marshfield, Mass. from
Gershom B. Weston to DW. Copy. Book 242: 250–251. Recorder of
Deeds, Plymouth County, Massachusetts.

[April 30]   To Richard Milford Blatchford. Printed. *PC,* 2: 437. *Diplomatic Papers,* 2. Predicts the Cuban expedition "will all blow out"
and describes the conspirators as "a set of geese."

April 30   To George Ticknor Curtis (with ANS by Curtis to William
Wetmore Story). LS. TxU. mDW 33401. Answers a request for the
letters addressed to him by Justice Joseph Story.

April 30   To William Alexander Graham. Typed copy. DNA, RG 59.
mDW 56462. Refers to reported difficulties with the Sultan of Zanzibar, and recommends sending warships to investigate.

April 30   To Peter Harvey. Telegram. NhHi. mDW 33402. Expects the
ship *Nantucket* to be righted soon and asks who should captain "the
other vessel."

April 30   To Franklin Haven. LS. MH–H. mDW 33403. Dicusses the
sale of some scrip, indicating he will comply with "Mr. May's suggestions."

April 30   To Ogden Hoffman. Draft revised by DW. NhHi. mDW 33404.
Notifies Hoffman that his appointment as associate counsel in the
prosecutions against the Cuban conspirators has been approved; encloses an advance of $500, with a receipt to be signed and returned.

April 30   To William Winston Seaton. Printed. Josephine Seaton, *William Winston Seaton of the "National Intelligencer"* (Boston, 1871),
p. 307. Recommends Marshfield salt beef for a good lunch.

April 30   To [John Taylor]. LS. MBBS. mDW 33406. *PC,* 2: 438. Discusses farm business.

April 30   From George P. Fisher. Copy. DNA, RG 76. Announces his decision denying Bradford Barnes's claim against Brazil, and returns
some papers.

April 30   From Josiah Randall. LS. DLC. mDW 33408. Discusses patronage matters in Pennsylvania.

April 30   From William A. Weeks. ALS. DNA, RG 59. mDW 56884. Reports the arrival of despatches from London.

[April?]   From Sir Henry Lytton Bulwer. Copy. UkLPR. mDWs. Asks DW
to ensure that a man in Missouri accused of inducing a slave to escape receives a fair trial.

May 1 To Don Mariano Arista. Draft. NhHi. mDW 33410. Copy. NhHi. mDW 33424. *Diplomatic Papers*, 2. Comments on Robert P. Letcher's possible return to Mexico as U.S. minister; ratification of the Tehuantepec treaty; and payment of the Mexican indemnity.

May 1 To Millard Fillmore (enclosure: James Cooper to DW, Apr 29, 1851). ALS. NhD. mDW 33432. Encloses a letter critical of Administration patronage practices in Pennsylvania.

May 1 To John P. Gaines. LS. Or–Ar. mDWs. Transmits the attorney general's opinion on points raised in Gaines' letter of Feb 6, 1851.

May 1 From Edward Everett.   241

May 1 From Millard Fillmore. ALS. NhD. mDW 33452. Wishes to discuss Pennsylvania politics.

May 1 From Joseph C. G. Kennedy. ALS. DNA, RG 48. mDWs. Wishes to conduct a study abroad of British census methodology in connection with the preparation of an abstract of the last U.S. census.

May 1 From M[armaduke] Shannon. ALS. DNA, RG 59. mDW 53752. Accepts appointment of the *Vicksburg* (Miss.) *Whig* to publish the laws.

May 1 Account with N. A. Telegraph Co. for $18.44, through May 27. ADS. NhHi. mDW 40516.

May 2 To Richard Milford Blatchford. Printed. *PC*, 2: 439–440. Mentions his present preoccupation with Latin American affairs; is particularly delighted with "my wagon."

May 2 To Millard Fillmore. ALS. NBuHi. mDW 33453. Encloses an article from the *Journal of Commerce*, and suggests it ought to be published in the *Republic*.

May 2 From Edward Everett. ALS. MHi. mDW 33456. Discusses the organization of the volumes of DW's works.

May 2 From Pablo Noriega de la Guerra. ALS. DNA, RG 59. mDW 55057. Accepts appointment as U.S. marshal for southern California.

May 2 From William F. Switzler. ALS. DNA, RG 59. mDW 53750. Accepts appointment of the Columbia *Missouri Statesman* to publish the laws.

May 2 From John Taylor. Printed. *PC*, 2: 440. Reports buying an ox and turning some cattle out to pasture.

May 2 From Daniel Fletcher Webster. AL incomplete. NhHi. mDW 33459. Comments on "the [Massachusetts Whig] Committee at Large" and thinks DW's friends should have nothing to do with it.

May 2 From Daniel Fletcher Webster.   244

May 2 Recommendations from P[hilip] Clayton to William S. Derrick, for the *Augusta* (Ga.) *Chronicle and Sentinel*, Milledgeville, Georgia *Southern Recorder*, Macon *Georgia Journal and Messenger*, Savannah *Republican*, Columbus (Ga.) *Enquirer*, and the Griffin, Georgia *American Union*—public printers (ALS. DNA, RG 59, mDW 53946).

May 3 To [Edward Everett]. AL. MHi. mDW 33467. Acknowledges Everett's report on "the movements in South Carolina"; discusses revising manuscripts.

[May 3] To Millard Fillmore. LS. NBuHi. mDW 33694. Encloses a letter from Buckingham Smith, secretary to the U.S. legation at Mexico City, which if credible, "is very important."

May 3 To George P. Fisher. LS. DNA, RG 76. mDWs. Acknowledges

Fisher's letter and the return of papers in the case of the barque *Yeoman*.

May 4   To Millard Fillmore. ALS. NBuHi. mDW 33469. Reports having appointed A. Newbold Le Roy to be bearer of despatches to Mexico, and indicates his plans to send documents there; will take up the topic of Nicaragua on Tuesday.

May 4   To [Peter Harvey?] LS. NhHi. mDW 33473. Van Tyne, p. 474. Wishes to tell him something that cannot be put in writing.

May 4   To Peter Harvey.   244

May 4   To Daniel Fletcher Webster. ALS. NhHi. mDW 33479. Scoffs at [William] Schouler's notions about their correspondence and promises to send Fletcher copies.

May 4   From John Arnold Rockwall. ALS. NhHi. mDW 33481. Quotes Complimentary remarks by Baron Roenne on DW's reply to Hülsemann.

May 4   From Charles Porter Wright. ALS. NhHi. mDW 33485. Reports on activity at Marshfield.

May 5   To Don Mariano Arista. Draft. NhHi. mDW 33489. Copy. NhHi. mDW 33494. Discusses the problem of sending a minister to Mexico.

May 5   To Richard Milford Blatchford. ALS. Private owner, Massachusetts. Reports giving up professional engagements and plans to remain at work until his annual catarrh strikes; finds U.S. foreign relations are unusually quiet.

May 5   To Richard Milford Blatchford. Printed. *PC*, 2: 442, Wishes to see Blatchford for a private talk.

May 5   To Millard Fillmore. ALS. NBuHi. mDW 33498. Will try to see him once it stops snowing.

May 5   To Millard and [Abigail Powers] Fillmore. AL. NN. mDW 33500. Accepts a dinner invitation.

[May 5?]   To Peter Harvey. ALS. NhHi. mDW 33523. Expects the verdict in "Mr. Brigg's case" will be late but favorable.

May 5   To Isaac L. Hedge.   245
May 5   To Myron Lawrence.   246

May 5   To George Little. LS. Nc–Ar. mDWs. Transmits the president's pardon of Thomas Burge, convicted of robbing the mail in 1850.

May 5   To [Charles Augustus Stetson?] .ALS. NhD. mDW 33509. Alludes to his political difficulties in New York; thinks it may be time to give a public statement of his political views.

May 5   To Daniel Fletcher Webster. ALS. NhHi. mDW 33511. Van Tyne, p. 475. Speaks critically of the Massachusetts Whig Central Committee.

May 5   From Hiram Ketchum. ALS. MHi. mDW 33513. Van Tyne, p. 474. Introduces Henry R. Dunham, bearer of a letter and invitation asking DW to visit New York.

May 5   From George L. Prentiss. ALS. DLC. mDW 33517. Reminds DW of a promise to write a testimonial on the late S. S. Prentiss.

May 6   To [Edward Everett]. ALS. MHi. mDW 33521. *PC*, 2: 442. Proposes to dedicate each volume of his works to some friend.

May 6   From Millard Fillmore. ALS. NhD. mDWs. Can see him later.

May 6   From George W. Knox. ALS. DNA, RG 59. mDW 55018. Accepts appointment as U.S. marshal for western Arkansas.

May 6   From Robert M. Walsh. ALS. DNA, RG 59. mDW 56274. Reports

conferring with Dominican leaders regarding the pacification of the
island.

May 7   To Stephen Merrill Allen. ALS. Charles G. Douglas III, Concord,
N.H. mDWs. Hopes to see Massachusetts restored to "her true character and position"; has written Fletcher regarding "Mr. Jenks."

May 7   To [Richard Milford Blatchford]. Printed. Curtis, 2: 502. Feels
he ought to join "the jaunt on the Erie Railroad."

May 7   To Edward Everett. ALS. MHi. mDW 33524. Asks if his dedication to Isaac P. Davis is "proper & graceful."

May 7   To Peter Harvey. Telegram. NhHi. mDW 33527. Van Tyne, pp.
460–461. Asks him to come to New York.

May 7   To Franklin Haven. LS. MH–H. mDW 33529. Wishes to see
Haven and other Boston friends in New York; is planning an excursion over the Erie railroad.

May 7   To Franklin Haven. LS. MH–H. mDW 33533. Asks if he might
add $2000 to "this account."

May 7   To Charles Augustus Stetson. ALS. NhD. mDW 33535. Indicates
his plans for an excursion over the Erie railroad; asks Stetson to save
a room for him.

May 7   Alexander Hugh Holmes Stuart from DW et al. LS. DNA, RG 48.
mDWs. Recommend approval of Joseph C. G. Kennedy's proposal
for a study of British census methodology.

May 7   To Elisha Whittlesey. LS. DNA, RG 217. mDW 57239. Reports
the papers of the commission to adjust Mexican claims have not yet
been deposited at the State Department.

May 7   From Edward Curtis. ALS. DLC. mDW 33543. Urges DW to
speak when he comes to New York.

May 7   From John Pendleton Kennedy. ALS. MdBP. mDWs. Asks when
DW might be able to attend a dinner of the Maryland Historical
Society.

May 7   From José Maria Medrano (with Robert M. Walsh to DW, June
10, 1851). LS. DNA, RG 59. mDW 56224. Discusses the Walsh mission and the Dominican Republic's desire for good relations with
the U.S.

May 7   From John Taylor. Copy. NhHi. mDW 33546. Reports having
purchased a pair of oxen for $125.

May 7 & [n.d.]   *Works of Daniel Webster* dedication. Drafts in DW's and
other hands. MH–H. mDW 33536.

[May 8]   To Richard Milford Blatchford. ALS. NhExP. mDW 33548. Asks
for a list of topics in case he should be called upon to speak during
his tour of New York.

May 8   To Sir Henry Lytton Bulwer. LS. UkLPR. mDW 33551. Expresses
confidence that a British subject charged in Missouri with inducing
a slave to run away will receive a fair trial in the state's courts.

May 8   To Lewis Cass. LS. NcD. mDW 33553. Introduces Charles Ellis
of Richmond, Va.

May 8   To John Jordan Crittenden. Copy. DLC. mDW 33554. Thanks
him for a pair of Kentucky hams.

May 8   To Edward Everett. ALS. MHi. mDW 33555. Reports he will accompany Fillmore on an excursion over the Erie railroad to western
New York.

May 8   To John Pendleton Kennedy. LS. MdBP. mDW 33557. Declines

Kennedy's invitation because of a commitment to visit New York with the president.

May 8   From Millard Fillmore (with William Alexander Graham to Fillmore, May 8, 1851). ANS. DNA, RG 59. mDW 56724. Comments on the propriety of paying the expense account presented by Commander [Cadwalader] Ringgold.

May 8   From James Piper (enclosure: press clipping). ALS. NhHi. mDW 33558. Comments on the secessionist threats in South Carolina.

May 9   To William Alexander Graham. Copy. MdHi. mDW 33563. *Diplomatic Papers*, 2. Proposes a move toward opening commercial relations with Japan.

May 9   To George Griswald et al. Draft revised by DW. NhHi. mDW 33565. Copy. NhHi. mDW 33569. *Works*, 6: 595. Thinks he may accept their invitation to visit New York.

May 9   To Peter Harvey. Copy. NhHi. mDW 33573. *PC*, 2: 443. Plans conferring with some Boston friends in New York on Tuesday, May 13.

May 9   To Franklin Haven.   247

May 9   To Daniel Fletcher Webster. LS. NhHi. mDW 33579. Van Tyne, p. 475. Agrees that the *Atlas'* plan for refounding the Massachusetts Whig party ought to be fully exposed, and ridicules "its absurdity."

May 9   From Edward Everett. ALS. MHi. mDW 33584. Comments on the practice of dedicating published works; discusses more scripts to omit from DW's manuscript.

May 10   Emperor of Japan from Millard Fillmore. LS (countersigned by DW). PHi. mDWs. Severance, *Fillmore Papers*, 1: 344–345. Proposes that Japan and the U.S. conclude agreements on trade, the treatment of shipwrecked persons, and coaling privileges for American vessels in Japan.

May 10   From Hiram Ketchum.   248

May 10   Application from Charles Sexton, for the Willow River (Hudson), Wisconsin *St. Croix Inquirer*—public printer (ALS. DNA, RG 59. mDW 53939).

[May 11]   To Richard Milford Blatchford. Printed. *PC*, 2: 443. Looks forward with dread to his upcoming trip, especially the necessity of speech-making.

May 12   To Franklin Haven. Telegram. MH–H. mDW 33595. Will be happy to see Haven and Harvey.

May 12   From Edward Everett (with DW to Everett, May 14, [1851]). ALS. MHi. mDW 33598. Expresses approval of DW's dedication to Isaac P. Davis; recommends the ommission of three speeches from the published works.

May 12   From M[yron] Lawrence. ALS. NhHi. mDW 33601. Praises DW's self-sacrifice for the Union; thinks the Massachusetts Whigs are beginning to realize their errors.

May 13   From Alexander Kelsey et al. Printed LS. DLC. mDW 33603. Invite DW to visit Rochester, N.Y. and present his views on public issues.

May 13   From Isaac H. Wright. LS. DLC. mDW 33624. Invites DW to the anniversary celebration of the Ancient and Honorable Artillery Company.

May 14   To [Edward Everett] (with Everett to DW, May 12, 1851). AN.

MHi. mDW 33600. Thinks the three speeches referred to by Everett in his letter of May 12 should not be published.

May 14 From C[ornelius] C[onway] Felton. ALS. MHi. mDW 33626. Introduces A. Hammond Whitney.

May 14 From Augustus N. Le Roy. ALS. DNA, RG 59. mDW 56499. Reports he is preparing to embark for Mexico; reports also that 60 Americans have been jailed at Tehuantepec.

May 15 To Franklin Haven. Telegram. MH–H. mDW 33629. Declares: "Quite well never better."

May 15 From Ogden Hoffman, Jr. ALS. DNA, RG 59. mDW 55033. Accepts appointment as U.S. district Judge for northern California.

May 16 From S[ilas] H[orton] Stringham (enclosure: Navy Department regulations, Apr 10, 1845). LS. NhD. mDW 33630. Objects to the navy secretary's order forbidding him to fly "a broad pennant" as commander of the Gosport Navy Yard.

May 17 To Richard Milford Blatchford. Printed. Curtis, 2: 503. Expresses alarm at Fletcher's attack of illness; reports giving a speech at Dunkirk last night.

May 17 To Harriette Story White Paige. ALS. Mrs. Irvin McD. Garfield, Southboro, Mass. mDWS. Writes of Fletcher's sudden illness; will go to Buffalo tomorrow.

May 20 To Caroline Story White Webster. ALS. NhHi. mDW 33637. PC, 2: 444. Explains why he has kept Fletcher with him longer than expected.

May 20 From William H. Russell. ALS. DLC. mDW 33640. Reports on his interview with President Arista and the general state of U.S. relations with Mexico.

May 21 To G[eorge] W[ashington] Lay. ALS. Daniel Webster Birthplace, West Franklin, N.H. mDW 33644. Invites Lay to visit him in Washington; plans a speech in Buffalo tomorrow.

May 21 To Hanson A. Risley et al. ALS. NcD. mDW 33646. Thanks them for their part in "the late celebration."

May 21 To H[arriet C.] Risley. ALS. NcD. mDW 33648. Thanks her for the hospitality shown him during his stay at Buffalo.

May 21 From Nathaniel Horton et al. LS. DLC. mDW 33651. Invite DW to give the Fourth of July address at Newburyport.

May 21 From Benjamin Loder et al. DS. DLC. mDW 33655. Resolution of the Board of Directors of the New York and Erie Railroad Company.

May 21 From A[lvah] Worden et al. LS. DLC. mDW 33657. Invite DW to a public meeting at Canandaigua, N.Y.

May 22 From [Sir Henry Lytton Bulwer]. AL draft. UkLPR. mDW 33660. Encloses a letter on the policy of Central America.

May 22 From Augustus N. Le Roy. ALS. DNA, RG 59. mDW 56501. Reports his arrival off Vera Cruz.

May 22 Application from C[harles] P. Bertrand, for the Little Rock *Arkansas Whig*—public printer (ALS. DNA, RG 59. mDW 53967).

May 23 Recommendation from B[enjamin] F. Copeland, for the *Boston Daily Journal*—public printer (ALS. DNA, RG 59. mDW 53976).

May 24 From John Canfield Spencer et al. LS. DLC. mDW 33661. *W & S*, 4: 265. Invite DW to a public dinner at Albany and to give an address if he feels up to it.

May 24   From Thurlow Weed. ALS. DLC. mDW 33664. Invites DW to
dine with "the state officers" in Albany; gives assurances of high personal regard despite their differences on political questions.

May 24   Application from S[amuel] Ryan, Jr. & Co., for the *Green Bay*
(Wisc.) *Spectator*—public printer (ALS. DNA, RG 59. mDW
54168).

May 25   To Richard Milford Blatchford.   250

May 26   From Richard Milford Blatchford (with DW to Haven, [May
27, 1851]). ALS. MH-H. mDW 33668. Asks him to endorse some
notes to cover others due May 29th; praises DW's Buffalo speech.

May 26   From Alexander Hugh Holmes Stuart: LS. DNA, RG 59. mDW
55109. Requests that a commission be issued appointing Henry J.
Thornton commissioner on private land claims in California.

May 26   From Alexander Hugh Holmes Stuart. LS. DNA, RG 59. mDW
55097. Asks that a commission be issued appointing John Canfield
Spencer commissioner on private land claims in California.

[May 27]   To Richard Milford Blatchford. Printed. *PC*, 2: 438. Announces his arrival at Albany; has dispatched the notes to Boston.

[May 27]   To Franklin Haven (enclosure: Blatchford to DW, May 26,
1851). ANS. MH–H. mDW 33670. Forwards some notes.

May 27   From Edward Everett. ALS. MHi. mDW 33674. Encloses a report of the Buffalo speech for revising; comments on Massachusetts
congressional elections.

May 27   Application from Bates & Crawford, for the Montgomery *Alabama Journal*—public printer (LS. DNA, RG 59. mDW 53971).

May 29   To Edward Everett. LC. MHi. mDW 33678. Asks that "Mr.
Tidd" be omitted from the Charleston speech.

May 29   To Edward Everett. LS. MHi. mDWs. States "The Buffalo
speech will be revised by me immediately and printed in pamphlet
form."

May 29   To Millard Fillmore. ALS. NBuHi. mDW 33679. *PC*, 2: 444.
Reports that Fillmore's visit to New York has left a favorable impression.

May 29   To David A. Hall. LS. NjP. mDW 33681. Acknowledges Hall's
letter with its "most agreeable news."

May 29   To Franklin Haven. LS. MH–H. mDW 33682. Mentions an exciting day in Albany; expresses his dissatisfaction with "Mr. Dana."

May 29   To John B. Townsend. LS. NHi. mDW 33683. Regrets he
missed seeing Townsend and his mother while in Albany.

May 29   From Thomas Corwin. Copy. UkLPR. mDWs. Discusses trading
privileges of Canadian ships under the Act of Sept 26, 1850, and
needs to know whether reciprocal privileges will be offered American ships in Canada.

May 29   Recommendations from H[enry] W[ashington] Hilliard, for the
Montgomery *Alabama Journal*—public printer (ALS. DNA, RG 59.
mDW 53973); from William A. Weeks, for Elijah Williams—despatch bearer (ALS. DNA, RG 59. mDW 56885).

May 30   From Frederic De Peyster et al. ALS by De Peyster, signed also
by others. DLC. mDW 33684. Invite DW to speak at the anniversary
of the New York Historical Society.

May 30   From Benjamin Carr Sargeant et al. ALS by Sargeant, signed
also by others. NhHi. mDW 33687. Invite him to visit Lowell.

[May] To [Edward Curtis?]. ALS. NN. mDW 33690. Expects Fillmore "will try his chances" (for the presidency?); asks what his own demeanor should be on the tour (of New York).

[May?] To Franklin Haven. Printed. *PC*, 2: 438–439. Requests the loan of Wilson's *Rural Cyclopedia*.

[May?] From Daniel Fletcher Webster. ALS. NhHi. mDW 33698. Advises regarding the sale of DW's farm in Peru, Ill.

June 1 To [Edward Everett]. ALS. MHi. mDW 33701. Suggests that the Buffalo and Albany speeches be revised before publication with DW's other works; reports the Buffalo speech is having a good effect.

June 2 From Myron Lawrence. ALS. DLC. mDW 33715. Reports on a meeting in Charlestown where he defended DW's views; thinks the Massachusetts Whigs are "awakening to a right sense of their duty."

June 2 Applications from B[enjamin] Fahnestock & Co., for the Pittsburgh *West Pennsylvania Stateszeitung*—public printer (LS. DNA, RG 59. mDW 53980); from Charles S. Willett, for the New York *Evening Mirror*—public printer (ALS. DNA, RG 59. mDW 53974).

June 3 To John Minor Botts. Printed. Curtis, 2: 508–509. Notes an error in the report of his Buffalo speech; again stresses that slavery is strictly the responsibility of the states.

June 3 To Franklin Haven. LS. MH–H. mDW 33722. Refers to some difficulty with "Mr. Schaumberg's acceptance."

June 3 From Sir Henry Lytton Bulwer. UkLPR. mDWs. Transmits observations by Sir John Pelly denying the Hudson's Bay Company is engaged in illicit trade with Indians in Minnesota.

June 3 From Sir Henry Lytton Bulwer. Copy. UkLPR. mDWs. Requests DW to investigate a case in which Maine citizens allegedly interfered with British attempts to extradite a criminal.

June 3 From Edward Everett. ALS. MHi. mDW 33725. Discusses editorial matters.

June 3 From Augustus N. Le Roy. ALS. NhHi. mDW 33729. Comments on prospects for Mexican ratification of the Tehuantepec treaty; strongly advises that Letcher's influence is needed in Mexico.

June 4 To Millard Fillmore. ALS. NBuHi. mDW 33733. Reports his return to Washington.

June 4 From H[iram] Fuller. ALS. CtY. mDW 33739. Discusses plans for pamphlet editions of DW's recent New York speeches; reports the Buffalo speech is having a "glorious effect in New England."

June 4 From William H. Morell (enclosure: Morell to George Bancroft, May 30, 1851). ALS. DNA, RG 59. mDW 56887. Writes regarding the delivery of items contained in a despatch bag received from abroad.

June 5 To William Cabell Rives. LS. DLC. mDW 33742. Introduces William H. Le Roy.

[June 5] From George Ashmun. ALS. DLC. mDW 34039. Reports on a political meeting chaired by Everett, and declares Massachusetts' course is *"irrevocably fixed."*

June 5 From Samuel A. Cartwright (with synopsis). LS. MhHi. mDW 33743. Defends slavery on racial grounds.

June 5   From Robert Wilson Gibbes. ALS copy. ScU. mDW 33774. Asks whether a Colombian bond acquired by his father in 1830 might yet be redeemed.

June 5   From Harriet C. Risley. ALS. NcD. mDW 33776. Speaks fondly of DW's recent visit to Dunkirk, N.Y.

June 5   From W[illiam] A. Walker. ALS. DLC. mDW 33778. Requests a copy of "your great speech on the Compromise."

June 6   To Caleb Cushing. LS. DLC. mDW 33780. Fuess, *Cushing*, 2: 88. Hopes to see Cushing regarding his debts; states the results of the Mexican Claims Commission have "utterly astonished me."

June 6   To Edward Everett. LS. MHi. mDW 33782. Discusses the dedication of his works.

June 6   To Edward Everett. LS. MHi. mDW 33783. Agrees to Everett's editorial suggestions.

June 6   To Millard Fillmore. ALS. NBuHi. mDW 33786. Introduces former Congressman [Andrew Jackson] Ogle of Pennsylvania.

June 6   To Franklin Haven. LS. MH–H. mDW 33789. Encloses a check to cover D[avid] A. Hall's acceptance.

June 6   To Franklin Haven. LS. MH–H. mDW 33790. Writes regarding notes secured by Mexican scrip.

June 6   To Franklin Haven. Telegram. MH–H. mDW 33791. Asks him to inform Ashmun and Harvey that the president will not be going north again this summer.

June 6   From Thomas Corwin (with DW to Bulwer, June 9, 1851). Copy. UkLPR. mDW 33800. Discusses reciprocal privileges for U.S. and Canadian ships in the ports of either nation.

June 6   From Richard S. Coxe. ALS. DLC. mDW 33792. Answers DW's inquiries regarding the Union Land and Trinity Land Companies.

June 6   Account with Richard Cruit for $4 for horseshoes, through July 21. ADS. NhHi. mDW 40574.

June 7   To Sir Henry Lytton Bulwer. LS. UkLPR. mDW 33795. Applies for the extradition of three forgers who have escaped to Canada.

June 7   To [Citizens of Easton, Pa.]. AL, composed by Henry Sargent. NhD. mDWs. Commends them for their Union sentiment, but regrets he cannot deliver an address; quotes from Washington's farewell address, "The Unity of government which constitutes you one people . . . is the main pillar in the edifice of your *real independence.*"

June 7   Recommendation from Joseph R. Chandler, for J. M. Fuchs—despatch bearer (ALS. DLC. mDWs).

June 8   To Millard Fillmore. ALS. NBuHi. mDW 33797. Encloses a letter concerning Ketchum, and hopes Ketchum can be gratified.

June 9   To Sir Henry Lytton Bulwer (enclosure: Corwin to DW, June 6, 1851). LS. UkLPR. mDW 33799. *Diplomatic Papers*, 2. Transmits a letter from the secretary of the treasury on U.S.-Canadian commercial relations.

June 9   From [Edward Everett]. LC. MHi. mDW33811. Discusses editorial matters.

June 9   From John Plummer Healy. ALS. MHi. mDW 33813. Discusses court business.

June 9   From Charles Lanman (enclosure: notes for a trip to the
          sources of the Potomac). ALS. NhHi. mDW 33816. Offers sugges-
          tions for DW's proposed trip to the Allegheny mountains.
June 9   From William A. Weeks. ALS. DNA, RG 59. mDW 56894. Re-
          ports the arrival of despatches from London.
June 10   To John H. Aulick. True copy. MdIIi. mDW 33820. Official in-
          structions for Aulick's expedition to Japan, including the negotiation
          of a treaty of amity and commerce and a coaling agreement.
June 10   To Samuel Atkins Eliot. LS. MH–Ar. mDW 33826. Gives John
          Jordan Crittenden's full name and promises to answer Eliot's other
          questions later.
June 10   From Jonathan Prescott Hall. Copy. UkLPR. mDWs. Reports
          no evidence of Charles Tyng's participation in a slave transaction of
          the brig *Martha*.
June 10   From William Wetmore Story. ALS. NhHi. mDW 33827. In-
          quires for letters to DW from Justice Story.
June 10   From Robert M. Walsh (enclosures: Jose Maria Medrano to
          [DW], May 7, 1851; Medrano to Walsh, May 7, 1851). ALS. DNA, RG
          59. mDW 56276. Reports on his mission to Haiti and the Dominican
          Republic.
June 11   To Stephen Merrill Allen. ALS. NhD. mDW 33831. Expresses
          concern about the political situation in Massachusetts and stresses
          the importance of making "fit and proper nominations" for the fall
          elections.
June 11   To Sir John Fiennes Crampton. LS. UkLPR. mDW 33833. Re-
          ports reaching an understanding with the Nicaraguan minister, and
          hopes Bulwer can be in Washington next week.
June 11   To Millard Fillmore. LS. NBuHi. mDW 33834. Wishes to talk
          over Nicaraguan and Mexican matters.
June 11   To Franklin Haven.   256
June 11   To David Henshaw. Copy. NhHi. mDW 33841. Van Tyne, pp.
          477–478. Thanks him for his letter; believes that "there are many
          men at the North, who do not speak out what they wish, but who
          really desire to break up the Union"; but that things "begin to look
          better."
June 11   To John Taylor. ALS. MBBS. mDW 33844. Harvey, *Reminis-
          cences of DW*, p. 301. Fears the cold weather may affect his crops.
June 11   From John Minor Botts. ALS. MeHi. mDW 33846. Asks for an
          interpretation of the Constitutional right of trial by jury.
June 11   From William A. Weeks. ALS. DNA, RG 59. mDW 56890. Re-
          ports the arrival of despatches from London.
June 12   To Thomas Corwin. Draft (with ANS by DW). DLC. mDW
          33848. Encloses the translation of a note received from the French
          minister in Washington regarding money allowed as due to the own-
          ers of the French ship *Edward*. (DW corrected the word "legiti-
          mately" to "lawfully" in this letter sent up by a bureau head for his
          signature: " 'Legitimately,' as used here is not English. It is an am-
          bitious Americanism. 'Legitimate' means of *lawful origin*. We are
          most sure of writing good English when we use the plainest words.")
June 12   To Benjamin Carr Sargeant et al. AL draft. NhHi. mDW 33850.
          Van Tyne, pp. 701–702. Accepts an invitation to visit Lowell.
[June 12?] To [?] (with DW to Corwin, June 12, 1851). ANS. DLC.

mDW 33848. Van Tyne, pp. 701–2. Encloses draft of his June 12 letter to Thomas Corwin, "that you may see an instance of my daily corrections of drfts of papers, Sent up from the heads of Bureaus. Everybody is afraid of homely words."

June 13 To George S. Gideon. LS. NhD. mDW 33852. Fears the rain will have spoiled fishing in the mountains for tomorrow morning.

June 13 From King & Fuller. LS. DNA, RG 59. mDW 53969. Request a book of the laws to determine if they omitted any from those already published in the *Milwaukee Sentinel and Gazette.*

June 13 Promissory note for $2500 payable to self at Merchants' Bank in Boston. DS (signature crossed). MHi. mDW 40518.

June 14 To [Francis] Granger. ALS. DLC. mDW 33854. Reports his safe return to Washington; thinks of visiting Annapolis.

June 14 To John Osborne Sargent. Invitation in DW's hand. MHi. mDW 33858.

June 14 From Sir Henry Lytton Bulwer. ALS. DLC. mDW 33864. Will be glad to talk with him about Nicaragua; discusses Greytown and the trans-isthmian canal.

June 14 From Joseph R. Chandler. ALS. DLC. mDWs. States that J. M. Fuchs will leave on June 25 for Europe.

June 14 From James M. Crane. ALS. DNA, RG 59. mDW 53948. Asks to be sent the volume of laws promised when the San Francisco *Daily California Courier* was appointed to be public printer.

June 14 From J[ohn] Delafield (with reply, [June], 1851). ALS. NhD. mDW 33872. Invites DW to the New York State Agricultural Society fair at Rochester.

June 14 From Hiram Fuller. ALS. CtY. mDW 33876. Discusses the printing of DW's Buffalo and Albany speeches; thinks Massachusetts is finally coming to her senses.

June 14 From Cadwalader Ringgold. ALS. DNA, RG 59. mDW 56725. Submits vouchers and other evidence of expense incurred on a government mission to California.

June 14 From Alexander Hugh Holmes Stuart. LS. DNA, RG 59. mDW 55133. Requests that a commission be issued appointing James Wilson U.S. commissioner for private land claims in California.

June 14 Recommendation from William A. Weeks, for William Bartlett, Jr.—despatch bearer (ALS. DNA, RG 59. mDW 56891).

June 15 To Franklin Haven. LS. MH–H. mDW 33879. Asks how money might be found to provide for the circulation of his Albany speech, particularly in the south.

June 15 To Franklin Haven. LS. MH–H. mDW 33883. Will send proceeds from the sale of his Mexican scrip once the injunction against its sale is removed.

June 15 To John Taylor. ALS. Mrs. Farwell A. Brown, Lebanon, N.H. mDWs. Commends Taylor for hard work; will spend a day at Franklin "at commencement of the warm weather."

June 15 To [Samuel Finley] Vinton. LS. NNC. mDW 33884. Explains the difficulty in appointing Converse Goddard to the post now held by Walter Forward (chargé d'affaires in Denmark); expresses his high opinion of Vinton.

June 16 To Edward Curtis. Printed. *PC*, 2: 373–374. Reports not much is happening in Washington; contemplates a visit to Virginia Springs.

June 16 [Edward] Curtis from DW and Caroline Le Roy Webster. ALS by DW, signed also by Caroline. NHi. mDW 33890. Send congratulations to a wedding party.

June 16 To Edward Everett. ALS. MHi. mDW 33892. Asks Everett to think of a motto which might be used with the dedication of his Albany speech.

June 16 To Millard Fillmore. ALS. NBuHi. mDW 33896. States that Curtis is recommending "[Maxwell?] Woodhull" for naval officer at New York.

June 16 To Millard Fillmore. LS. NBuHi. mDW 33899. Suggests that Washington Ingrams might be eligible for executive clemency.

June 16 To [Sarah Preston Everett] Hale. ALS. MNS–S. mDWs. Offers his and Caroline's condolences on the death of her daughter Sarah.

June 16 To George Ticknor. ALS. NhD. mDW 33902. Is glad that Ticknor and his friends are making things uncomfortable for the *Atlas* and Horace Mann.

June 16 To Daniel Fletcher Webster. ALS. NhHi. mDW 33904. Van Tyne, pp. 479–480. Mentions his plans for returning north and the publication of his Albany speech in pamphlet form.

June 16 From Thomas Fitzgerald. ALS. NhD. mDW 33907. Expresses admiration for DW's efforts to save the Union; reports DW's popularity is rising in the west.

June 16 From Hiram Fuller. ALS. CtY. mDW 33911. Sends copies of the New York speeches, and recommends that a large supply be sent to Pennsylvania.

June 16 From Hiram Fuller. Telegram. CtY. mDW 33913. "Tomorrow morning with a proof copy of the pamphlet."

June 16 From Charles Sexton. ALS. DNA, RG 59. mDW 53742. Accepts appointment of the Willow River (Hudson) *St. Croix Inquirer* to publish the laws.

June 16 Recommendations from William Appleton, for William Bartlett, Jr.—despatch bearer (ALS. DNA, RG 59. mDW 56891).

June 17 Application from William Bartlett, Jr.—despatch bearer (ALS. DNA, RG 59. mDW 56892).

June 18 To Homer Bostwick. Draft. CtY. mDW 33914. Accepts with thanks Bostwick's *The Causes of Natural Death and How to Keep Young.*

Jun 18 To Millard Fillmore. ALS. NBuHi. mDW 33915. Asks him to meet with the Peruvian chargé d'affaires.

June 18 To Millard Fillmore. ALS. NBuHi. mDW 33918. Suggests sending the ratified Swiss Convention to Europe with Ashmun.

June 18 To James P. Walker et al. LS. NjP. mDW 33921. Promises to visit Lowell later in the summer.

June 18 From Edward Everett. LC. MHi. mDW 33924. Discusses the choice of a motto for the Albany speech; comments on an article about Britain's recognition of the independence of the Sandwich Islands.

June 18 From Millard Fillmore. AL. DLC. mDW 33927. Severance, *Fillmore Papers*, 1: 346. Agrees to see DW and the Peruvian chargé d'affaires.

June 19   To Millard Fillmore. ALS. NBuHi. mDW 33928. Introduces
"Mr. Lookinland, from Vermont."

June 19   To Franklin Haven. LS. MH–H. mDW 33930. Wants to see
him in Boston next week; will see that the money from the Mexican
scrip is sent once a favorable decision is rendered.

June 19   To Ely Samuel Parker. PPAmP. mDW 33932. Thanks him for
Parker's book *League of the Iroquois*.

June 19   To Col. Warren. Private owner. Massachusetts, mDWs. Asks
him "to dine with us today, rather extemporaneously."

June 19   From George Jacob Abbot. ALS. CtY. mDW 33934. Asks that
his application to prepare the *Annual Register* for 1851 be with--
drawn.

June 19   From Robert Balmanno. ALS. NhHi. mDW 33935. Invites DW
to subscribe to a testimonial for Mary Clarke, author of *The Complete Concordance of Shakespeare*.

June 19   From John McLean. ALS. NhHi. mDW 33937. Protests move to
oust William Sprague as Indian agent.

June 20   To Millard Fillmore. ALS. NBuHi. mDW 33941. Decides to remain in Washington until after July 4th.

June 20   To Franklin Haven. Telegram. MH–H. mDW 33944. Will be
detained in Washington until after the 4th of July by ceremonies at
the Capitol.

June 20   From Hiram Fuller. ALS. CtY. mDW 33945. Discusses revising
DW's Albany speech for publication in a pamphlet edition.

June 20   Account with Joseph Morrill for $7.75 for masonry, through
June 30 (paid by Samuel George). DS. NhD. mDW 40576, 40557.

June 21   To Abbott Lawrence. LC. MH–H. mDWs. Transmits his answer
to "Baron Goldsmid," chairman of the Committee of Mexican Bondholders in London.

June 21   To Luther Severance. Copy. H–Ar. mDW 33949. Orders that
Russian citizens be rendered "lawful aid and assistance" by U.S.
consuls at Honolulu and Lahaina.

June 21   From Charles Wainwright March. ALS. NhHi. mDW 33954.
Van Tyne, pp. 480–481. Reports Whig sentiment in Pennsylvania;
emphasizes the political importance of DW's visit to New Hampshire; wishes that DW's rebuke of Abbott Lawrence's anti-Catholic
remarks might be published.

Jun 21   Recommendations from John Bell, for John S. Brien—commissioner for the settlement of California land claims (ALS. DLC. mDW
33951).

June 21   Bill from S. Alvin Farley for $5.45 for bricks ordered by Samuel
George. AD. NhD. mDW 40520.

[June 22]   To Richard Milford Blatchford. Printed. *PC*, 2: 445. Reports
his trip north will be delayed but is contemplating taking Caroline
to Virginia in the meantime.

[June 22]   To Millard Fillmore. LS. NBuHi. mDW 34038. *Diplomatic Papers*, 2. Reports Great Britain and France have decided to blockade
Haiti.

June 22   To Peter Harvey. ALS. NhExP. mDW 33958. Thanks him for a
salmon.

June 22   To Franklin Haven. LS. MH–H. mDW 33959. *PC*, 2: 445–446.

Will remain here for ceremonies at the Capitol; contemplates an excursion to the Shenandoah.

[June 22]   To Daniel Fletcher Webster. ALS. NhHi. mDW 33965. *PC*, 2 : 375. Plans going first to Marshfield, then to New Hampshire; is drafting his address for the 4th of July ceremony at the Capitol

June 22   From Sir Henry Lytton Bulwer. Copy. UkLPR. mDWs. Suggests that Haiti be invited to enter into a peace agreement with the U.S., Britain, and France, while it continues to negotiate with the Dominican Republic.

June 22   From Sir Henry Lytton Bulwer. Copy. UkLPR. mDWs. Reports that Britain and France have agreed to blockade Haiti if it resumes aggression against the Dominicans.

June 22   Account with Joseph Clark for $14.14 for nails, etc., through July 16. AD. NhD. mDW 40559.

June 23   To Alexander Hugh Holmes Stuart Copy. DNA, RG 217. mDW 57241. States that David F. Douglas and Pablo Noriega, newly appointed marshals for California, have received their commissions.

June 23   Recommenation for Paul Jennings. ADS. NcU. mDW 33968. Praises Jennings's service in the Webster household and states that formerly he was body servant to James Madison.

June 23   From John Canfield Spencer.   258

June 24   From Sir Henry Lytton Bulwer. Copy. UkLPR. mDWs. Warns that Canada is prepared to take "certain measures" if the U.S. doesn't agree to reciprocal commercial privileges.

June 24   Recommendation from James S. Wallace, for A. DeKalb Tarr—a consulship (ALS. NhD. mDWs).

June 25   From Sir Henry Lytton Bulwer. ALS. DLC. mDW 33975. Looks forward to seeing DW at Capon Springs.

June 25   From William A. Weeks. ALS. DNA, RG 59. mDW 56893. Reports hiring a boat to pick up despatches from a steamer anchored in Boston Harbor.

June 26   From Edward Everett.   259

June 27   To George Jacob Abbot. ALS. CtY. mDW 33983. Discusses some page proof corrections.

June 27   To Hiram Ketchum. ALS. NhD. mDW 33985. Expresses his high opinion of James Watson Webb.

June 27   To the President of the Board of Trustees of Watson Town. Printed copy. Mr. Boyd B. Stutler, Charlestown, W. Va. mDW 33989. Acknowledges resolutions of welcome; reflects on his stay at Capon Springs.

June 27   To Daniel Fletcher Webster. ALS. MHi. mDW 33990. *PC*, 2 : 446–448. Describes Capon Springs and the surrounding countryside.

June 27   From Sir Henry Lytton Bulwer. LS. DLC. mDW 33998. *Diplomatic Papers*, 2. Proposes they negotiate a general convention about Greytown and other Central American issues.

June 27   From John McGregor. ALS. NhHi. mDW 34011. Introduces William Eppes Cormarth.

June 27   From Daniel Fletcher Webster. ALS. NhHi. mDW 34014. Van Tyne, p. 483. Asks him to meet with Edward Riddle for a conversation on the Exhibition at London.

June 27   From Daniel Fletcher Webster. ALS. NhHi. mDW 34018. Asks what might be done to prevent or delay "Dr. Barker's" removal from his position at the Boston Custom House.

June 28   From C[olumbus] Alexander. ALS. DNA, RG 59. mDW 53537. Is unable to give bond for the printing of the *Biennial Register*.

June 28   From James Butler Campbell.   261

June 28   From William S. Clark et al. ALS by Clark, signed also by others. DLC. mDW 34028. Invite DW to a public dinner.

June 28   From Patrick Henry et al. Printed letter. DLC. mDW 34031. Invite him to address a Union meeting and barbecue at Canton, Miss.

June 28   From E[lias] P. West. ALS. DNA, RG 59. mDW 55123. Accepts appointment as U.S. attorney for New Mexico.

[June 29]   To John Taylor. ALS. Dr. Francis H. Herrick, Oakland, Calif. mDW 34023. Van Tyne, p. 716. Plans several visits to Franklin; asks that his boat and fishing tackle be prepared for use.

June 30   From N[athan] Hale. ALS. CtY. mDW 34035. Comments on the extent and impact of railroads on travel in America, focusing on George Washington's journeys.

June 30   From John Jones. ALS. DNA, RG 59. mDW 55024. Accepts appointment as U.S. marshal for New Mexico.

[June]   To John Delafield (with Delafield to DW, June, 14, 1851). NhD. mDW 33873. Doubts he can attend the New York State Agricultural Society fair at Rochester.

[June]   To Hiram Fuller. ALS. NhD. mDW 35635. Writes regarding the proofs for the pamphlet edition of his New York speeches.

June   From James P. Walker et al. Copy. NjP. mDW 34042. Invite DW to visit Lowell.

June   Receipt for $60 paid Samuel George for labor and supplies purchased by him. AD. NhD. mDW 40528, 40560.

July 1   To Francis Markoe. DS. DLC. mDW 34043. Markoe's appointment as principal clerk in the State Department.

July 1   From Walter Forward.   262

July 1   Receipt for $2.50 paid Ira Greely for lime. ADS. NhD. mDW 40533.

July 1   Receipt for $18 paid for rental of pew in New Trinity Church, Washington. DS. DLC. mDW 40531.

July 1   Receipt for $28.63 paid Walker & Shadd (eating house). DS. NhHi. mDW 40535.

July 2   To [Clement H.] Butler. ALS. PHi. mDW 34048. Inquires about Bishop George Berkeley's stanzas on America ("America or the Muse's Refuge").

July 2   To J. W. Preston et al. AL draft in Sargent's hand, signed by DW. NhD. mDWs. LS. NhD. mDW 34050. Cannot attend their Independence Day celebration in Springfield, Mass.; knows that the spirit of Union will "overcome the bitterness of distrust and alienation."

July 2   To John Taylor.   264

July 3   To Franklin Haven. LS. MH–H. mDW 30633. W & S, 16: 620–621. Announces his return to Washington from Capon Springs; states that his draft for the 4th of July oration is now in the hands of the copyists.

July 3   To Franklin Haven.

July 3   To Franklin Haven. LS. MH–H. mDW 34063. Discusses his personal finances.

July 3   From John Howard Payne. ALS. NhD. mDWs. Is sending DW
tabulated information on the French political parties.

July 4   To Gideon & Co. LS. CtY. mDW 34064. Asks that the copy of
"my address" left with them last night be sent to George Jacob Abbot.

July 4   From Henry Alexander Scammell Dearborn. ALS. NhHi. mDW
34284. Announces DW's election as an honorary member in the
Massachusetts Society of the Cincinnati.

July 4   Henry A. Holmes to Charles Johnson McCurdy (with McCurdy
to DW, Mar 1, 1852). Extract. NhD. mDW 36125. Asks if he would
agree to forward money and jewels for Kossuth to Abbott Lawrence
in London.

[July 4]   From Francis Aurelius Pulszky. LC (in Hungarian). HuOSzK.
mDWs. Discusses Kossuth and the Hungarian liberation struggle,
and requests DW to transmit a letter to the President.

July 4   From William B. Gooch et al. LS. DLC. mDW 34286. Invite DW
to visit West Dennis, Mass.

July 4   From William J. Young (enclosure: press clippings). ALS.
NhHi. mDW 34289. Comments on the public land policy, the danger
of landlordism and the valor of the working man, and seeks DW's
views on behalf of the New York City Industrial Congress.

[July 4]   Speech at laying of cornerstone of addition to the Capitol:
opening remarks. AD draft. NhD. mDW 34065.

[July 4]   Passage from speech at laying of cornerstone of addition to
Capitol. AD draft (with ANS and AN, by Charles Lanman, the latter
with DW's signature). NN. mDWs. Facsimile of small section of this
draft at NjP, mDW 34067.

[July 4]   Passage from speech at laying of cornerstone of addition to
Capitol. AD draft. MdHi. mDW 32623.

[July 4]   Speech at laying of cornerstone of addition to Capitol. Drafts.
CtY. mDW 34608, 34180.

[July 4]   Speech at laying of cornerstone of addition to Capitol. Corrected proofs. CtY. mDW 34258.

[July 4]   Account in DW's handwriting of the proceedings on the occasion of the laying of the cornerstone of the addition to the Capitol,
deposited beneath the cornerstone. Printed. Curtis, 2: 521.

July 5   To Sir Henry Lytton Bulwer. LS. UkLPR. mDW 34295. Agrees to
the proposed allied blockade of Haiti, but warns that American participation is contingent upon prior Congressional approval.

July 5   To Sir Henry Lytton Bulwer. LS. UkLPR. mDW 34298. Reports
Fillmore's approval of Bulwer's proposal for ending the conflict between Haiti and the Dominican Republic.

July 5   To Robert Wilson Gibbes. LS. ScU. mDW 34300. Replies to
Gibbes's inquiry about a bond issue by the former Republic of Co-
lombia.

July 5   From William B. Gooch. ALS. DLC. mDW 34302. Reports plans
for DW's reception at West Dennis, and suggests his presence is
needed to counter the spread of free-soilism on Cape Cod.

July 5   From Robert Perkins Letcher. ALS. DLC. mDW 34304. Reports
DW's recent speeches are having great effect, and that Clay is in
poor health; finds general apathy in Kentucky toward the coming
elections.

July 5   Application from W. F. Lyons, for the Cincinnati *Citizen*—public printer (ALS. DNA, RG 59. mDW 53978).

July 6   From Robert Perkins Letcher. ALS. CtY. mDWs. Praises DW's Capon speech; thinks all the Virginia speeches together with the New York speeches should be published in pamphlet form.

July 7   To Millard Fillmore. LS. NBuHi. mDW 34308. Asks whether the commission appointing Cornelius McCaullay U.S. consul at Belfast should now be forwarded.

July 7   To Franklin Haven. ALS. MH–H. mDW 34311. Asks him to look after some financial business.

July 7   To R[ichard] Smith. LS. NN. mDW 34312. Discusses a note.

July 7   From Hudson E. Bridge. ALS. NhD. mDWs. Invites DW to lecture before the St. Louis Mercantile Library Association.

July 7   From Sir Henry Lytton Bulwer. AL draft. UkLPR. mDW 34314. LS. DLC. mDW 34322. Discusses negotiating an agreement with the U.S. on Central American affairs.

July 7   From John H. B. Latrobe. Printed. Curtis, 2: 523–524. Recalls an incident twenty years ago when they were together in Annapolis.

July 7   Receipt for $3.50 paid Samuel Lewis for a gold watch key. AD. NhHi. mDW 40540.

July 8   To Millard Fillmore. LS. NBuHi. mDW 34328. *Diplomatic Papers*, 2. Reports the arrival of Augustus N. Le Roy with despatches from Mexico; stresses the importance of settling the Nicaraguan problem soon.

July 8   To John K. Porter. ALS. NN. mDW 34330. Asks that copies of his Albany speech be distributed among the young men who arranged his reception there.

July 8   From Henry Lunt. Printed. *W & S*, 4: 319–320. Recalls the original stone-laying ceremony at the Capitol on Sept 18, 1793.

July 8   From Joseph B. Varnum, Jr. ALS. CtY. mDW 34333. States that money to pay for completing the Capitol was loaned to the government by Maryland on George Washington's personal credit.

July 9   To Edward Curtis. LS. NN. mDW 34335. Van Tyne, pp. 478–479. Asks Curtis to recommend someone for appointment as Naval Officer (at the New York custom house).

July 9   To William B. Gooch et al. CtY. mDW 34336. Accepts their invitation to West Dennis on the understanding he will not be expected to give a speech.

July 9   From Sir Henry Lytton Bulwer. AL draft. UkLPR. mDW 34339. LS. DLC. mDW 34347. *Diplomatic Papers*, 2. Replies to DW's suggestion that they meet with Marcoleta, the Nicaraguan representative.

July 9   From William Alexander Graham. Copy. UkLPR. mDWs. Sends him gold and silver medals to be given to British, French, and Spanish seamen who rescued American seamen from the *Somers*.

July 9   From J[ose] de Marcoleta. ALS. NhHi. mDW 34353. Proposes they meet informally with Bulwer to discuss the problem of Greytown.

July 9   From L[ewis] H[enry] Morgan. ALS. CtY. mDW 34356. Requests a copy of DW's speech at the Capitol.

July 9   From George Ticknor. Printed. G. S. Hillard, ed., *Life, Letters, and Journals of George Ticknor* (2 vols., Boston, 1876), 2: 272–273. Thanks DW for a copy of his Albany speeches; relays a fishing invitation from Sir Edmund Head, Lieutenant-Governor of New Brunswick; contrasts his current position with being a student at Dartmouth College fifty years ago.

July 9   From Tench Tilghman. ALS. DLC. mDW 34357. Sends a letter written by Washington, and asks DW to return it once he has read it.

July 10   To Sir Henry Lytton Bulwer. ALS. DLC. mDW 34360. *Diplomatic Papers*, 2. Is not feeling well due to the heat; will have Hunter meet with Marcoleta regarding Nicaragua.

July 10   To Millard Fillmore. ALS. NBuHi. mDW 34362. Wishes to see him about some consulships; suggests sending E. Ritchie Dow to China.

July 10   To Russell Hinckley. ALS. WaU. mDWs. Acknowledges his friendly letter; is sending copies of the Albany speech and offers to send more of it or other speeches.

July 10   To John H. B. Latrobe. ALS. MdHi. mDW 34366. Curtis, 2: 524. Recalls their sojourn together at Annapolis twenty years ago.

July 10   To Cameron F. McRies. ALS. NhD. mDW 34370. Acknowledges his warm letter; promises a copy of his Capon Springs speech.

July 10   To Jose de Marcoleta. Copy. NhHi. mDW 34372. *Diplomatic Papers*, 2. Responds to Marcoleta's proposal for a meeting between themselves and Bulwer.

July 10   From Millard Fillmore. ALS. NhD. mDWs. Is reading despatches; concurs with DW on the consul at Acapulco; will make a recommendation on the extradition treaty with Prussia; wonders who to send on a mission to China.

July 10   From Theodore Frelinghuysen. ALS. NjR. mDWs. Introduces "Mr. Kimball," who comes to Washington in search of employment.

July 10   From John Pendleton Kennedy.   265

July 10   From Alexander Hugh Holmes Stuart. LS. DNA, RG 59. mDW 55095. Asks that commissions be issued appointing A. A. Skinner and E. A. Starling Indian agents in Oregon.

July 11   To [Robert Balmanno]. Copy. Uk. mDW 34373. Agrees to subscribe to a testimonial honoring the Shakespearian scholar Mary Clarke.

July 11   To Millard Fillmore. LS. NBuHi. mDW 34374. Sends letters of application and recommendation for district attorney in California.

July 11   From Jose de Marcoleta. LS. NhD. mDW 34376. Accepts an invitation to accompany DW and Caroline by steamship to New York.

July 12   To Charles Porter Wright. ALS. NhHi. mDW 34378. Indicates his plans for coming north; asks about the farm.

July 12   From John W. Ashmead. ALS. NhD. mDW 34380. Reports the plans of the Native American Party in Pennsylvania; declares that Scott could not carry this state.

July 12   From Sir Henry Bulwer. Copy. UkLPR. mDWs. Requests a letter relative to the case of James Dempsey.

July 12   From Robert Monroe Harrison. LS. NhD. mDWs. Introduces Walter George Stewart, colonial secretary of Jamaica.

July 12   From Charles King. ALS. DLC. mDW 34382. Invites DW to the Columbia College commencement exercises.

July 12   From C. H. Powell. ALS. CtY. mDWs. Asks for a pamphlet form of DW's recent 4th of July oration; tells how he went from Plymouth Rock to Marshfield some years ago, but DW was not at home.

July 12   Account with Havenner & Bros. (bakers) for $20 for tickets, through Dec 16. AD. NhHi. mDW 40588.

July 12   Bill from John Mills for $4.75 for glazing shoes and repairing boots. ADS. NhHi. mDW 40550.

July 14   To Millard Fillmore. ALS. NBuHi. mDW 34384. Decides not to go abroad "while clouds lower at the North."

July 14   To Abbott Lawrence. Copy. UkLPR. mDWs. Transmits medals to be given to British seamen who rescued the crew of the *Somers*.

July 14   To Luther Severance. Copy H–Ar. mDW 34400. Draft. NhHi. mDW 34388. Van Tyne, pp. 484–486. Expresses the U.S. government's opposition to recent French actions in the Sandwich Islands.

July 14   To William B. Gooch et al. *Works*, 6: 596–599. *Cape Cod Magazine*, May 1921, pp. 15–17. Reflects on his acquaintance with Cape Cod; declares that Massachusetts's welfare and prosperity depend upon the preservation of the Union.

July 14   From William L. Hodge (with DW to Bulwer, July 15, 1851). Copy. UkLPR. mDW 34411. Advises him of the conditions under which vessels from Prince Edward Island will be admitted to U.S. ports on an equal footing with American ships.

July 14   From Henry Lunt. ALS. MHi. mDW 34406. Expresses delight at his mention in DW's July 4th address at the Capitol; relates an anecdote of George Washington.

July 14   From Charles E. Sherman. ALS. DLC. mDW 34408. Requests permission to make copies of public records pertinent to "my case."

July 15   To Sir Henry Lytton Bulwer (enclosure: William L. Hodge to DW, July 14, 1851). LS. UkLPR. mDW 34410. Encloses a letter from the acting secretary of the treasury concerning port privileges for ships from Prince Edward Island.

July 15   From Robert B. Croes (with DW to Fillmore, July 29, 1851). Copy. NBuHi. mDW 34518. *PC*, 2: 450. Prescribes a cure for catarrh.

[July 16]   To Sir Henry Lytton Bulwer. LS. Major M. F. Hobbs, Swindon, England, deposited in Corpus Christi College Library, Cambridge. mDW 34413. Reports he cannot leave home today.

July 16   Account with Alfred Lee for $6.78 for corn and oats, through Nov 4. AD. NhHi. mDW 40571.

July 16   Account with John Pettibone for $30.75 for ice tickets, through Nov 1. AD. NhHi. 40499.

July 17   To Henry Alexander Scammell Dearborn. LS. NN. mDW 34415. Expresses gratification for his election to honorary membership in the Massachusetts Society of the Cincinnati.

July 17   From Franklin Pierce. ALS. NhHi. mDW 34418. Writes regarding a debt claimed by "Mrs. Taggard" against DW.

July 18   To George Jacob Abbot. ALS. CtY. mDW 34421. Asks him to correct a phrase in his July 4th speech at the Capitol.

July 18   To Edward Everett. LS. MHi. mDW 34422. *Diplomatic Papers*, 2. Refers to the difficulty with France in the Sandwich Islands, and asks Everett to search his correspondence for relevant information.

July 18   To Millard Fillmore. ALS. NBuHi. mDW 34426. Is on his way

to Boston; reports Walter Forward will return to Copenhagen after
spending a few days in London.

July 18   To Charles Porter Wright. Copy. MHi. mDW 34428. Expects to
be in Boston tomorrow and will inform Wright when he is coming
to Marshfield.

July 18   From Joseph Powell.   2GG

July 18   From John Thomas (enclosures: letters of recommendation).
ALS. OGK. mDW 34433. Describes Charles Loring Elliott as an artist
of great talent and suggests that he be allowed to paint DW's portrait.

July 19   From Millard Fillmore. ALS. DLC. mDW 34437. *Diplomatic Papers*, 2. Comments on problems connected with the Tehuantepec
treaty, especially the danger that the railroad contractors may use
force in defense of their grant.

July 19   From Millard Fillmore. ALS. DLC. mDW 34441. Severance,
Fillmore Papers, 1: 348. Reports only two attended the last cabinet
meeting; encloses a letter from Kossuth regarding DW's Hülsemann
correspondence.

July 20   To Edward Everett. LS. MHi. mDW 34443. Would like to see
him on Monday.

July 20   From M[ary] A[nn] Binney. ALS. DLC. mDW 34444. Presents a
set of volumes authored by "Dr. [Horace] Binney."

July 21   To George Jacob Abbot. LS by proxy. CtY. mDW 34446. Asks for
copies of his July 4th address to meet the large demand in Boston.

[July 21]   To George Jacob Abbot (with DW to Gales & Seaton, July 21,
1851). ANS, CtY. mDW 34456. Asks him to deliver the enclosure to
Gales & Seaton and to put the second Capon Springs speech "in a
shape to be safe."

July 21   To Edward Everett. LS. MHi. mDW 34447. Asks him to review
the draft of a letter to Luther Severance.

July 21   To Millard Fillmore. LS. NBuHi. mDW 34448. *PC*, 2: 451–452.
Discusses the issues of Tehuantepec and the Sandwich Islands, and
his own plans to remain in seclusion at Marshfield.

July 21   To Gales & Seaton (with DW to George Jacob Abbot, [July 21],
1851). ALS. CtY. mDW 34455. Asks them to "write over" the second
Capon Springs speech and make it right.

July 21   From Edward Everett. ALS. MHi. mDW 34465. Gives a summary of his official correspondence on the recognition of Hawaiian
independence.

July 21   From W[ilson] M. Kidd. ALS. NhD. mDWs. Asks for clarification of DW's position on the constitutionality of the acquisition of
slave territory.

July 21   From Mary Webster Sanborn. ALS. NhD. mDWs. Asks DW to
attend the Dartmouth College commencement.

July 21   Promissory note for $3500 payable to self. DS (signature
crossed). MHi. mDW 40552.

July 21   Promissory note for $3400 payable to self. DS. MHi. mDW
40554.

[July 22]   To [George Jacob Abbot]. ALS. CtY. mDW 34472. Encloses
some lines for insertion in the printed edition of the second Capon
Springs speech.

July 22   To George Jacob Abbot. Telegram. Mr. John R. Morison, Peterborough, N.H. mDW 34474. Reports having written Abbot twice regarding the Capon Springs speech.

July 22   To Robert B. Croes.   268

July 22   To Edward Curtis. ALS. NN. mDW 34479. Has written Gales & Seaton; is leaving for Marshfield this morning.

July 22   From Charles Atkinson. ALS. DLC. mDW 34480. Asks that the Rock Island Railroad be granted a right-of-way across DW's Peru, Ill. property.

July 22   From Millard Fillmore. Copy. DNA, RG 206. mDWs. Agrees that [Absalom] Fowler, U.S. attorney for Arkansas ought to resign because of his role as attorney to a claimant to lands at the Hot Springs.

July 22   From T. B. Miner. ALS. NhD. mDWs. Discusses the practice of bee-keeping; praises DW's "moral courage" in his defense of the Union.

July 22   From Edwin David Sanborn. ALS. NhD. mDWs. Invites DW to the Dartmouth commencement, the 50th since his graduation in 1801.

July 22   From Alexander Hugh Holmes Stuart. Copy. DNA, RG 206. mDWs. Encloses correspondence relative to Absalom Fowler's defense of a claimant to land at the Hot Springs of Arkansas.

July 23   To George Jacob Abbot. LS by proxy. CtY. mDW 34482. Discusses the revision of the Capon Springs speech.

July 23   To Millard Fillmore. LS. NBuHi. mDW 34484. PC, 2: 452–454. Describes his Marshfield estate and its environs.

July 23   From Charles Atkinson. ALS. DLC. mDW 34492. Encloses a deed he forgot to send with his letter of yesterday.

July 23   From Sir Henry Lytton Bulwer. Copy. UkLPR. mDWs. Officially protests the illegal execution of a British citizen in San Francisco last month.

July 23   From Edward Everett. ALS. MHi. mDW 34496. Returns DW's Sandwich Island papers; speaks critically of Severance and Rives.

July 24   To George Jacob Abbot (with ANS by Abbot). Telegram. CtY. mDW 34500. Orders the printing of the Capon Springs speech suspended until further notice.

[July 24?]   To Daniel Fletcher Webster. ALS. NhHi. mDW 39154. PC, 2: 454. Invites him to join in a morning ride; asks him to have some birds shot for dinner.

July 25   From James Butler Campbell (with DW to Fillmore, July 29, 1851). ALS. NBuHi. mDW 34520. Reports on anti-secessionist activity in Charleston.

July 25   From Jonathan Prescott Hall. ALS. NhD. mDWs. Reports one or two hundred Creoles wish to return to Havana from New York in the aftermath of the Principe uprising.

July 25   From Benjamin Carr Sargeant. ALS. NhHi. mDW 34502. Asks when it might be convenient for DW to visit Lowell.

July 26   From George Jacob Abbot. ALS. NhHi. mDW 34504. Encloses reports of the Capon Springs speech; has ordered its printing stopped.

July 26   From Millard Fillmore. ALS. DLC. mDW 34506. Severance, Fillmore Papers, 1: 349. Expects to see Letcher soon; is planning a few days' stay at Virginia Springs.

July 26   From Alexander Hugh Holmes Stuart. LS. DNA, RG 59. mDW
55016. Asks that a commission be issued Francis W. Lea, recently
appointed Indian agent for the Pottawatomie Indians.

July 27   From George Jacob Abbot. ALS. NhHi. mDW 34509. Reports a
large number of speeches are ready for distribution.

July 28   To George Jacob Abbot. Telegram. CtY. mDW 34511. "Mr.
Seargent says the West denies, letter is with you he has not it."

July 28   From William S. Crocker. ALS. NhD. mDWs. Asks that his son
and a friend be given a letter to the U.S. minister at Berlin.

July 28   From Charles Lanman (enclosure: extract from *Der Boston
Mercur*, July 12, 1851). ALS. NhD. mDWs. Reports growing support
for DW's nomination for president in the German press and among
"the more enlightened . . . Germans of the Union."

July 28   From "C.S." ALS. NhHi. mDW 34512. Van Tyne, pp. 486–487.
Calls for the formation of a Union party under DW's leadership.

July 28   From Moses Stuart. ALS. NhD. mDWs. Comments on DW's
recent speeches and on presidential politics.

July 28   From William Wigglesworth. ALS. NhD. mDWs. Quotes a
prophecy in verse taken from an almanac printed at Salem in 1783.

July 29   To [Edward K. Collins?]. Draft. NhD. mDWs. Acknowledges
Collins' offer of free passage aboard one of his ships; endorses the
principle of government subsidization of American trans-Atlantic
steamship service.

July 29   To Millard Fillmore (enclosures: Robert B. Croes to DW, July
15, 1851; James Butler Campbell to DW, July 25, 1851; Samuel Jackson to DW, [July, 1851?]). ALS. NBuHi. mDW 34514. Reports his
health is improving; comments on a cure for catarrh, and on the
news from Cuba about the uprising.

July 29   To John Taylor. LS. MHi. mDWs. *PC*, 2: 455–456. Reports on
farming at Marshfield, his fishing, etc.

July 29   From John Wingate Thornton. ALS. DLC. mDW 34523. Quotes
poetry by Herbert.

July 30   To Millard Fillmore. Telegram. NOsU. mDW 34526. "Take care
of your health—I am improving."

July 30   From Judah P. Benjamin. ALS. NBuHi. mDWs. Typed summary. OCAJ. mDWs. Encloses a card in advance of its publication
which he declares contains only facts already known to the public
(about the Tehuantepec Grant).

July 30   From Sir Henry Lytton Bulwer. Copy. UkLPR. mDWs. Expresses
confidence that the U.S. government will prevent another invasion
of Cuba.

July 30   From Joseph L. Heywood. ALS. DNA, RG 59. mDW 55035. Accepts appointment as U.S. marshal for Utah.

July 30   From Charles Wainwright March. ALS. NhD. mDWs. Urges
DW to make a tour of northern New England.

July 30   From John A. Rockwell. ALS. NhD. mDWs. Invites DW to address the Phi Beta Kappa Society.

July 30   Recommendation from Samuel Lord, for William M. Thack-
ford—Navy Agent at Portsmouth, N.H. (ALS. NhD. mDWs).

July 31   From Thomas Otis Le Roy & Co. LS. NhD. mDWs. Accuse
"messrs. Tathams" of seeking the removal of commissioner of Patents Thomas Ewbank.

July 31   From Boyd Reilly. ALS. NhD. mDWs. Encloses a letter from
Hiram Powers; comments on the eagle as an American emblem.

July 31   Application from H. G. Luther—despatch bearer to Mexico City
(ALS. DNA, RG 59. mDW 56896).

[July]   To Richard Rush. ALS. NjP. mDW 34527. Invites him to dine and
meet General Scott.

[July]   From Samuel Jackson (with DW to Fillmore, July 29, 1851). Extract. NBuHi. mDW 34522. Prescribes a cure for catarrh.

[July]   From Robert Montgomery Martin. Copy. DNA, RG 48. Asks for
assistance in preparing a work on the United States for publication
in England.

[Aug 1]   To [Millard Fillmore]. Copy. MHi. mDW 34530. Discusses the
appointment of a U.S. consul at Palermo.

Aug 1   To Millard Fillmore. LS. NBuHi. mDW 34523. *Diplomatic Papers*,
2. Comments on sending a U.S. minister to Mexico.

Aug 1   To Millard Fillmore. LS. NBuHi. mDW 34536. *PC*, 2: 456–457.
Is prepared to meet Corwin in New York or come to Washington
if necessary, but hopes to remain in New England "for some considerable time."

Aug 1   To a Gentleman of North Carolina. Printed. Curtis, 2: 520–521.
Clarifies comments he made at Capon Springs on the question of
secession.

Aug 1   To Nathan Kelsey Hall. ALS. NhD. mDW 34539. Calls attention
to a newspaper item.

Aug 1   From Seth M. Blair. ALS. DNA, RG 59. mDW 54937. Accepts appointment as U.S. attorney for Utah.

Aug 1   From W[illiam] Hunter. ALS. NhD. mDWs. Reports on administrative matters in the State Department and a meeting with Letcher;
comments on the report of a Mexican decree of Nov 6, 1846.

Aug 1   From William Henry Le Roy. Telegram. NhD. mDWs. Will be
unable to meet Caroline due to the death of his brother-in-law.

Aug 1   Recommendation from William A. Weeks and John Plummer
Healy, for H. G. Luther—despatch bearer (ANS by Weeks, signed
also by Healy. DNA, RG 59. mDW 56896).

Aug 2   To Samuel T. Tisdale (with Tisdale to Daniel Fletcher Webster,
Jan 21, 1853). Copy. NhHi. mDW 34542. *PC*, 2: 457–458. Is sending him an Alderney heifer; expresses gratitude for Tisdale's hospitality.

Aug 2   From Millard Fillmore. ALS. NhD. mDWs. Discusses Mexican
affairs and reports Letcher is ready to return; asks who should be
sent to China, and states he is thinking of appointing a U.S. district attorney for southern California.

Aug 2   From William W. Greenough. ALS. NhD. mDWs. Reports on a
meeting held to determine Boston's interest in steam navigation; asks
DW's views regarding government subsidization of steamship
service.

Aug 2   From Ambrose Dudley Mann. ALS. DNA, RG 59. mDW 55955.
Encloses the report of the political department of the Swiss Confederation for 1850.

Aug 2   From Alexander Hugh Holmes Stuart. LS. DNA, RG 59. mDW
55055. Asks that a commission be issued for James H. Norwood, recently appointed Indian agent.

Aug 2   From Fitz Henry Warren. LS. DNA, RG 59. mDW 54931. Reports the appointment of Crawford Bell as postmaster at Evansville, Ind.

Aug 3   From George Jacob Abbot. ALS. NhD. mDWs. Reports DW's speeches have been circulated throughout the country.

Aug 3   From George Ticknor. ALS. NhD. mDWs. Reports Sir Edward Head's desire to see DW, and asks to be informed whenever he decides about going to New Brunswick.

Aug 4   To Richard Milford Blatchford. Printed. *PC*, 2: 458–459. Invites Blatchford to accompany him to New Hampshire.

[Aug 4?]   To [John Taylor]. ALS. MBBS. mDW 34544. Expects to be in Franklin soon.

Aug 4   From Edward Codman & Co. (enclosure: DW's account with Codman & Co., Apr 11, 1848–July 28, 1851). LS. NhD. mDWs. Informs DW of a balance due on his account.

Aug 5   To Millard Fillmore. ALS. NBuHi. mDW 34545. *Diplomatic Papers*, 2. Is plagued by visitors and diarrhea; discounts the Cuban rumors as "substantially groundless."

Aug 5   To William R. Lawrence. ANS. CtHi. mDW 34551. Expresses his regards.

Aug 5   To Edwin David Sanborn. ALS. NhD. mDW 34552. *PC*, 2: 460. Gives extreme fatigue as his excuse for not attending the Dartmouth commencement.

[Aug 5]   To John Taylor. ALS. NhD. mDW 38930. Doubts whether "we shall go up tomorrow"; asks him to "take good care of all that goes up."

[Aug 5]   To John Wingate Thornton. AN. NhD. mDWs. Inscription on title page of pamphlet "Mr. Webster's Address at the Laying of the Corner Stone of the Addition to the Capitol, July 4, 1851."

Aug 5   From L[uther] Bradish. ALS. NhD. mDW 34553. Asks whether DW will accept the invitation to address the New-York Historical Society.

[Aug 5]   From Rufus Choate. ALS. NhD. mDWs. Explains he cannot visit DW at the Revere House because of ill health.

Aug 5   From Edward Curtis. ALS. NhD. mDWs. Has arranged to meet Corwin at New York and bring him to Franklin.

Aug 5   From Edward Everett. LC. MHi. mDW 34556. Reports on progress in the publishing of DW's works.

Aug 5   Bill from Joseph Clark for nails etc. ordered in part by Samuel George, June 22 to July 16. AD. NhD. mDW 40559, 40561.

Aug 6   To R[obert?] P. Anderson. LS. MSaE. mDW 34558. Asks for the volumes of the *Congressional Globe* containing the debates of the 28th and 29th Congresses.

Aug 6   To Edward Everett. LS. MHi. mDW 34559. Has sent to Washington for the volumes of the *Congressional Globe* Everett requested.

Aug 6   To Millard Fillmore (enclosure: R[obert] B[ennet] Forbes to DW, Aug 6, 1851). LS. NBuHi. mDW 34560. *PC*, 2: 461. Comments on the revision of the Mexican treaty of 1848, and the choices for a representative to China and a district attorney for southern California; thinks of going to New Hampshire; notes the Kentucky elections "look bad."

Aug 6   To [John Taylor]. ALS. MBBS. mDW 34567. Says to look for him on the early train tomorrow.

Aug 6   From R[obert] B[ennet] Forbes (with DW to Fillmore, Aug 6,
         1851). ALS. NBuHi. mDW 34564. Makes suggestions regarding a
         representative to China; comments on consular matters.
Aug 6   From William B. Gooch et al. LS. DLC. mDW 34568. Invite DW
         to a public dinner at Dennis, Mass.
Aug 6   From William Alexander Graham. Copy. UkLPR. mDWs. Reports
         the Treasury's acceptance of a claim by the heirs of James Dempsey.
Aug 6   From Willaim A. Weeks. ALS. DNA, RG 59. mDW 56895. Re-
         ports receiving packages and letters for London but no bearer's pass-
         port, and asks for one in the name of Henry P. Oxnard.
Aug 7   From Edward Everett. LC. MHi. mDW 34571. Corrects a refer-
         ence DW made to John Fries in his Albany speech.
Aug 9   Charles Johnson McCurdy to Henry A. Holmes (with McCurdy
         to DW, Mar 1, 1851). Extract. NhD. mDW 36125. Cannot comply
         with the request of "your friend" (Kossuth).
Aug 10   To Millard Fillmore. ALS. NBuHi. mDW 34573. *Diplomatic Pa-
         pers*, 2. Discusses the problem of buying off U.S. treaty obligations
         to protect Mexico from Indian attacks; regrets that Corwin may re-
         sign from the Cabinet.
Aug 11   To Franklin Haven. LS. MH–H. mDW 34577. Reports his ac-
         tivity at Franklin; discusses financial matters.
Aug 11   To S[olomon] W[right] Jewett. LS. Mr. and Mrs. Tilden Wells,
         Delaware, Ohio. mDWs. Declines an invitation to the state fair at
         Middlebury, Vt.
Aug 11   To Charles Porter Wright. ALS. NhHi. mDW 34583. Orders beef
         and fish hooks sent to him at Franklin.
Aug 11   From Thomas Corwin. ALS. NhD. mDW 34585. Decides not to
         come to New Hampshire; expresses loathing for public life and a de-
         sire to retire.
Aug 12   From Edward Kent. Copy. UkLPR. mDWs. Explains irregulari-
         ties that occurred in the sale of the brig *Dolusia* and the issuance
         of the relevant documents at Rio de Janeiro.
Aug 13   To [George] Hutchins. ALS. ICHi. mDW 34587. Asks that vari-
         ous items of houseware be sent to him at Franklin.
Aug 14   To John Taylor. ALS. MHi. mDWs. Asks Taylor to bring the
         mail to him at Center Harbor the day after tomorrow.
Aug 14   From Millard Fillmore. ALS. NjMoHP. mDW 34588. Reports an
         enthusiastic reception for him at White Sulphur Springs; thinks of
         replacing Buckingham Smith as secretary of the U.S. legation at
         Mexico City; wants to consider the appointment to China further
         before offering it to "Mr. [Daniel Converse] Goddard."
Aug 14   From John Wilson et al. LS. NhHi. mDW 34590. Expresses the
         views of the California Whig State Central Committee on general
         political matters.
Aug 15   From Edward Everett. LC. MHi. mDW 34593. Advises about
         the publication of DW's Capon Springs speech.
Aug 16   To Robert Perkins Letcher. Draft. NhHi. mDW 34595. *Diplo-
         matic Papers*, 2. Discusses U.S. relations with Mexico and Letcher's
         current mission.
Aug 17   To Robert Bradley. ALS. Fryeburg Academy, Fryeburg, Me.
         mDW 34599. Introduces Daniel Fletcher Webster and Richard Mil-
         ford Blatchford.

Aug 17   From Millard Fillmore. ALS. DLC. mDW 34600. *Diplomatic Pa-pers*, 2. Emphasizes the need to buy out of the U.S. treaty obligation to defend Mexico against Indian attacks; hopes Corwin will not resign.

Aug 19   To George Jacob Abbot. ALS. CtY. mDW 34603. Writes about the publication of his Capon Springs speech.

Aug 19   To Millard Fillmore. ALS. NBuHi. mDW 34605. *Diplomatic Papers*, 2. Reports on his tour of the White Mountains; his health; Forward's wish to be recalled from Denmark; and considers the problem of replacing Corwin.

Aug 20   From R[obert] M[ontgomery] Martin (enclosure: Printed list of Martin's writings). ALS. DLC. mDW 34610. Requests information to be used in a comprehensive work on the United States to be published in England.

Aug 21   To E[dward] C[odman] & Co. Printed copy. NhD. mDW 37639. Orders brandy shipped to John Taylor at Franklin; promises to ad-just his account when he returns to Boston.

[Aug 22]   To John Plummer Healy. ALS. MHi. mDW 38649. Gives in-structions about mail; reports "We have [had] a grand time, & seen grand sights" (on a trip to the White Mountains).

Aug 22   From Edward Everett. LC. MHi. mDW 34616. Asks whether DW wants the tariff speech of July 25, 1846, included among his pub-lished works.

Aug 23   To Richard Milford Blatchford. Printed. *PC*, 2: 464–465. Com-ments on their friendship, his health, and his present effort to ward off his catarrh.

Aug 23   To Edward Everett. ALS. MHi. mDW 34618. Comments on the speeches Everett inquired about; awaits the onslaught of his catarrh.

Aug 23   To Millard Fillmore. ALS. NBuHi. mDW 34622. Fears the ar-rival of his catarrh; comments bitterly on the secessionist character of South Carolina; reluctantly admits that Robert M. Walsh may be the best choice as secretary to the Mexican mission.

Aug 23   *Nathaniel Sawyer to Alphonso Taft.*   268

Aug 25   To Richard Milford Blatchford. Printed. *PC*, 2: 466. Reports the catarrh has spared him so far.

Aug 25   From Edward Everett. ALS. MHi. mDW 34628. Charles Lan-man, *Haphazard Personalities* (Boston, 1885), p. 137. Asks him to indicate which speeches ought to be included in volume five of his works.

Aug 25   From Joseph Hume. ALS. CtY. mDW 34632. Urges that Con-gress settle the claims of Florida bond holders residing in England.

Aug 26   To Richard Milford Blatchford. Printed. *PC*, 2: 466. Reports his catarrh has not yet appeared.

Aug 26   To Joseph Burnett. ALS. DLC. mDW 38290. Reports "the bottles of medicine all came safe," and requests two or three boxes of soda powders.

Aug 26   To Edward Everett. ALS. MHi. mDW 34633. Wishes that his at-tacks on Ingersoll and Dickinson in his defense of the Treaty of Washington be softened.

Aug 26   To Charles Porter Wright. ALS. NhHi. mDW 34635. *PC*, 2: 466–67. Lists cattle he is planning to have sent from Franklin to Marshfield.

Aug 26 To William C. Zantzinger. ANS. NhD. mDWs. Asks to have "my salary for this month" paid to William S. Derrick, the acting secretary of state.

Aug 26 From William L. Hodge. Copy. UkLPR. mDWs. Transmits Treasury Department instructions to admit vessels from Prince Edward Island into U.S. ports on equal footing with U.S. vessels.

Aug 27 To Franklin Haven. ALS. MH–H. mDW 38506. Discusses financial matters.

Aug 27 To Franklin Haven. Printed. *PC*, 2: 467–468. Reports the catarrh so far "holds off."

Aug 29 To Edward Everett. ALS. MHi. mDW 34639. Offers to send Abbot to help with the editorial work; enjoins Everett not to overlook the Girard's Will speech.

Aug 29 To Edwin David Sanborn. ALS. NhD. mDW 34640. Invites Sanborn to bring his wife to Franklin for a visit.

Aug 31/Sept 1 To Richard Milford Blatchford. Printed. *PC*, 2: 468–469. Complains of gout; begins to detect symptoms of the catarrh.

Aug 31 To Edwin David Sanborn. ALS. NhD. mDW 34642. Looks forward to seeing the Sanborns at Franklin.

[Aug] To Richard Milford Blatchford. Printed. *PC*, 2: 463. Begins to hope the catarrh may pass him by this year.

Sept 1 To James Adams. ALS. CtY. mDWs. Transmits a paper (not found) to Adams at the Bank of Washington, and asks him "to do the needful with it."

Sept 2 To [George?] Bartle. ALS. NhD. mDW 38215. Asks for "a good penknife"; hopes to escape the worst of the catarrh.

[p/m Sept 2] To John Plummer Healy or Daniel Fletcher Webster. ALS. MHi. mDW 34813. Asks that $1000 in bills be sent to him at Franklin through John Taylor.

Sept 2 From Edward Everett. ALS. MHi. mDW 34645. Asks whether he should agree to preside over the Whig State Convention at Springfield.

Sept 2 From Millard Fillmore. ALS. DLC. mDW 34649. *Dipomatic Papers*, 2. Comments on the recent Lopez expedition and reports what action he has taken to prevent further attacks on Cuba from American ports; comments on the matters involving Forward, Corwin, and Walsh.

Sept 3 To [Edward Curtis?]. ALS. NN. mDW 34653. Reports on his health.

[Sept 4?] To Daniel Fletcher Webster. ALS. NhHi. mDW 34669. Van Tyne, p. 464. Expects to be visited by the committee on the railroad celebration at Boston; asks that some poultry be sent to him at Franklin.

Sept 4 Account with William B. Todd for $13 for three servants' and one coachman's hats, through Dec 13. AD. NhHi. mDW 40590.

Sept 5 From C.H.S. de la Figanière. ALS. NhHi. mDW 34671. Has received wine ordered by DW and asks where it should be shipped.

Sept 6 To Henry Sargent. LS. Dr. George L. Hamilton, West Hartford, Ct. mDWs. May need Sargent's services in Boston.

Sept 6   From Bangs Brothers & Co. ALS. NhHi. mDW 34673. Seek DW's
legal opinion in a matter concerning a land grant to Iowa for improvements on the Des Moines River.

Sept 6   From J[ames] H. R. Washington. ALS. DLC. mDW 34677. Invites DW to a fair at Macon sponsored by the Southern Central Agricultural Association.

Sept 6   Agreement respecting DW's deed to the Sawyer Farm in Franklin, N.H. Draft in DW's hand, signed by George Washington Nesmith. MHi. mDWs. DS. MHi. mDWs.

Sept 8   To Millard Fillmore. ALS. NBuHi. mDW 34679. *Diplomatic Papers*, 2. Thinks Fillmore's course on Cuba is "extremely right"; is
suffering from gout and his anti-catarrh regimen; hopes Corwin will
not resign; reports ordering Forward recalled from Denmark; declares he will not accept an invitation to "the Boston celebration."

Sept 9   To Hervey Ely. LS. NRU. mDW 34683. Will not be attending
the agricultural fair in Rochester.

Sept 9   From Charles Pelham Curtis (with DW to Fillmore, Sept 10,
1851). ALS. NBuHi. mDW 34688. Reports Benjamin Robbins Curtis
will accept appointment to the Supreme Court and that his nomination is unanimously supported by the Boston Bar.

Sept 10   To Millard Fillmore.   272

Sept 10   To Francis Markoe. ALS. DLC. mDW 34689. Doubts Fillmore
will appoint a U.S. minister to Denmark before Congress meets.

Sept 10   From Edward Everett. LC. MHi. mDW 34691. Writes regarding
the inclusion of various speeches in DW's works.

Sept 10   From Millard Fillmore. ALS. DLC. mDW 34693. Curtis, 2: 531–
532. Has declined the Boston invitation because of the Cuban situation; asks if Benjamin Robbins Curtis might be right to succeed the
late Justice Woodbury on the Supreme Court.

Sept 11   To Edward Everett. LS. MHi. mDW 34697. Wishes to talk over
the results of the Whig State Convention; suggests that his Baltimore
speech of 1843 ought not to be published with his other works.

Sept 12   From Millard Fillmore. ALS. DLC. mDW 34699. Curtis, 2: 532–
533. Reports the Cuban situation now appears under control and decides to come to Boston after all.

Sept 12   From Robert Bennet Forbes (with Forbes to Daniel Fletcher
Webster, Sept 12, 1851). Presscopy. Forbes Papers, Capt. Robert
Bennet Forbes House, Milton, Mass. mDWs. Asks that the U.S. con-
sul at Hong Kong be granted a leave of absence.

Sept 12   Robert Bennet Forbes to Daniel Fletcher Webster (enclosure:
Forbes to DW, Sept 12, 1851). Presscopy. Forbes Papers, Capt.
Robert Bennet Forbes House, Milton, Mass. mDWs. Asks Fletcher to
deliver the enclosed to DW.

Sept 13   To Peter Harvey.   273

Sept 14   To John Taylor. ALS. MBBS. mDW 34702. Harvey, *Reminiscences of DW*, p. 303. Discusses farm business.

Sept 15   To Richard Milford Blatchford. Printed. PC, 2: 471–472. Mentions his health, his activities at Marshfield, and his refusal of the
invitation to the Boston railroad celebration.

[Sept 15]   To Justina van Renssalaer (postscript to Caroline Le Roy Webster to Justina van Renssalaer, [Sept 15, 1851]). ANS. NHi. mDW
34711. Acknowledges "your kind inquiries."

[Sept 15]   Justina van Renssalaer from Caroline Le Roy Webster (with ANS by DW). ALS. NhHi. mDW 34707. Reports on DW's health.

Sept 15   From James Wilson. ALS. DLC. mDW 34718. Thanks DW for helping him win appointment as U.S. commissioner in California on private land claims.

Sept 15   Application from William Pitt Fessenden—Associate Justice of the U.S. Supreme Court (ALS draft. MeB. mDW 34712. ALS. NhHi. mDW 34714).

Sept 15   Recommendation from D[avid] Bronson, for William Pitt Fessenden—Associate Justice of the U.S. Supreme Court (ALS. MeB. mDW 34705).

Sept 16   From W[orthington] G. Snethen. ALS. DLC. mDW 34725. Requests permission to search State Department files for documents needed in support of his clients' claim against Brazil.

Sept 16   Recommendation from Edward J. Phelps, for Samuel Shethar Phelps—Associate Justice of the U.S. Supreme Court (ALS. NhHi. mDW 34721).

Sept 18   From Edward Everett. ALS. MHi. mDW 34733. Discusses editorial matters.

Sept 18   Promissory note for $1750 payable to Daniel Fletcher Webster. DS. MHi. mDW 40565.

Sept 19   To John Taylor. ALS. NhD. mDW 34737. Discusses farm business, emphasizing the need to "stick close to the Potatos."

Sept 22   To George S. Boutwell. Printed. PC, 2 : 472–473. Presents copies of his New York speeches.

Sept 22   To Edward Everett. ALS. MHi. mDW 34744. Comments on editorial matters, asking that General Cass be spared and not ridiculed.

Sept 22   To Nathan Kelsey Hall. ALS. NBuHi. mDW 34745. Discusses personnel changes at the State Department; advises Joel Eastman's appointment as mail agent.

Sept 2   To [Franklin Haven]. ALS. MBBS. mDW 34748. Is preparing to visit him at Beverly.

Sept 22   From John G. Smith. ALS. DNA, RG 76. mDWs. Writes regarding a claim against Britain for the seizure of the *Portsmouth* off Sierra Leone in 1805.

Sept 22   Recommendation from [?] Hughes, for William W. Wyman—public printer (ALS. DNA, RG 59. mDW 53991). [Madison *Wisconsin Statesman*].

Sept 23   To Charles Lanman. ALS. NcD. mDW 34750. Asks that a clerk be sent to Boston to help him; is weak from catarrh; reports the president's visit has made a favorable impression in Boston.

Sept 23   From Edward Everett. LC. MHi. mDW 34752. Discusses speeches to be included among DW's published works; hopes Curtis will be appointed to the Supreme Court.

Sept 24   To A[llen] Ferdinand Owen. Draft. CtY. mDW 34753. Orders him to make a detailed report on the recent Lopez expedition, and to ensure that the American prisoners are given a fair trial.

Sept 24   To Henry Sargent. LS. NhD. mDWs. Informs Sargent he has been selected as bearer of despatches to A. Dudley Mann, whom he will find either in London or in Paris; gives instructions.

Sept 25   To [Edward Everett]. ALS. MHi. mDW 34757. Asks that the

Oregon speech of August, 1848 be included in his works; recalls the circumstances of the "Oregon arrangement."

Sept 25   To Charles Lanman. ALS. MH–H. mDW 34749. Declares he must have a clerk.

Sept 25   From D[aniel] M[oreau] Barringer. ALS. DLC. mDW 34758. Comments on Spanish reaction to the recent Lopez expedition and his own efforts to preserve harmony between the U.S. and Spain.

Sept 25   From Charles Wainwright March. Telegram. MH–H. mDW 34762. States that Curtis is going to Boston tonight.

Sept 26/[27]   To Richard Milford Blatchford. ALS. MH–H. mDW 34763. PC, 2: 473. Reports spending a few days in Beverly with Haven; is looking for Edward Curtis.

Sept 26   From Edward Everett. LC. MHi. mDW 34766. Asks about giving titles to the 7th of March and 17th of July, 1850 speeches, and also for information on Oregon for inclusion in DW's memoir.

Sept 26   From B[radford] Sumner. ALS. DLC. mDW 34768. Reports the sum due today is $905.73.

Sept 27   To [Edward Everett]. ALS. MHi. mDW 34769. PC, 2: 473–474. Discusses the choice of a title for the 7th of March speech.

Sept 27   To [Edward Everett].   274

Sept 27   From William C. Zantzinger (enclosures: William M. Morell to Zantzinger, Sept 9, 1851, and reply, Sept 10, 1851). ALS. NhHi. mDW 34776. Calls for changes in the New York despatch agency.

Sept 28   To James Brown. ALS. MH–H. mDW 34784. Asks for books.

Sept 28   To William Pitt Fessenden.   275

Sept 28   To Millard Fillmore. ALS. NBuHi. mDW 34790. PC, 2: 474–475. Reports Fillmore's visit to Boston has made a favorable impression; feels weak from catarrh and "the Harrisburg Diarrhea."

Sept 28   To Fanklin Haven. ALS. MH–H. mDW 34794. Reports Curtis is in Boston and will remain there "so long as business shall require."

Sept 29   From Edward Everett. ALS. MHi. mDW 34799. Discusses editorial changes in the 7th of March speech; ridicules the abolitionists; asks whether various diplomatic papers not yet presented to Congress should also be included in DW's works.

Sept 29   From William Alexander Graham. ALS. OGK. mDW 34803. Announces Charles H. Ladd's appointment as Navy Agent at Portsmouth.

Sept 30   To Richard H. Ayer. Printed. W & S, 16: 626–627. Accepts an invitation to stay with Ayer during his visit to the New Hampshire state fair; speaks of their long friendship.

Sept 30   Memorandum of the Austrian Government regarding the release of Kossuth from Turkey, endorsed by DW. AD. NhHi. mDW 34806. *Diplomatic Papers*, 2.

[Sept]   From James Bailey (with DW to Bailey, Oct 4, 1851). Copy. UkLiU. mDW 34839. Transmits an autograph request.

Oct 1   To Franklin Haven. ALS. MH–H. mDW 34816. Declares the time has come for decisive action (on his presidential candidacy).

Oct 1   From William A. Weeks. ALS. DNA, RG 59. mDW 56897. Writes about the forwarding of despatches.

Oct 2   From Millard Fillmore. ALS. DLC. mDW 34819. Curtis, 2: 551 (in part). Severance, *Fillmore Papers*, 1: 354–356. Expresses satisfaction with his Boston visit; comments on consular appointments; reports Britain and France may use warships to prevent filibusters from reaching Cuba.

Oct 2   From William Wetmore Story. ALS copy. TxU. mDW 34823. Copy (dated Oct 3, 1851). NhHi. mDW 34835. Van Tyne, pp. 635–636. Requests permission to publish some of DW's correspondence with Justice Story.

Oct 3   To Franklin Haven. LS. MH–H. mDW 34825. Asks if a loan might be arranged to save the Boston Daily Bee from bankruptcy.

Oct 3   To [Franklin Haven] (enclosure: press clippings). ALS. MH–H. mDW 34828. Feels unable to comply with Curtis's suggestion that he give an opinion of a certain matter.

Oct 3   To William Wetmore Story. LS. TxU. mDW 34833. Van Tyne, p. 636. Refuses permission to publish his private letters to Justice Story.

Oct 4   To James Bailey (enclosure: Bailey to DW, [Sept, 1851]). ALS. UkLiU. mDW 34838. Responds to a request for an autograph.

Oct 4   To Caleb Cushing. LS. DLC. mDW 34840. Promises to honor an engagement before leaving for the south.

Oct 4   To [Edward Everett]. ALS. MHi. mDW 34842. Will meet him in Cambridge or Boston, whichever is convenient.

Oct 4   To Edward Everett. LS. MHi. mDW 34844. Returns "the manuscript biography" with comments and suggested alterations, saying it "far exceeds my expectation."

Oct 4   To Millard Fillmore. LS. NBuHi. 34848. Diplomatic Papers, 2. Discusses the possibility British warships may stop American vessels under pretense of their containing Cuban invaders, and recounts the recent history of U.S.-European contention over the island.

Oct 4   To [George S.] Gideon & Co. LS. NhD. mDW 34854. Discusses the payment of a draft.

Oct 4   To J[ames] H. R. Washington. Draft. CtY. mDW 34908. Encloses his response to an invitation to attend an agricultural fair at Macon.

Oct 6/8   To [F. D. Anderson et al.]. Draft incomplete. CtY. mDW 34855. Van Tyne, pp. 748–749. Expounds on the significance of the temperance movement, but declines an invitation to a temperance celebration in Maryland.

Oct 6   To Mark A. Cooper. Printed. Works, 6: 599–600. Contrasts the farming systems of north and south; advocates the preservation of the individuality of states under a union based on the Constitution; reports he cannot attend the agricultural fair in Macon.

[c. Oct 7]   From Benjamin Robbins Curtis. ALS. DLC. mDW 34858. Accepts appointment to the U.S. Supreme Court.

Oct 7   From J[ames] T[rask] Woodbury. ALS. NhHi. mDW 34861. Invites him to the dedication of a monument on the Acton, Mass. town common.

Oct 8   From John H. Genin. Printed circular. NhHi. mDW 34863. Solicits a contribution to the "Kossuth Fund" to honor the Hungarian with a testimonial.

Oct 9   From Patrick Hall. ALS. MHi. mDW 34867. Seeks clarification of the naturalization laws.

Oct 9   Sheriff's deed selling off property seized from DW and James

Craig in Whiteside County, Ill. Copy. County Recorder, Whiteside
County, Illinois.

Oct 10   From Millard Fillmore. ALS. DLC. mDW 34870. Curtis, 2: 552
(in part). Severance, *Fillmore Papers*, 1: 356–358. Has ordered
strict enforcement of the neutrality laws to prevent Americans from
intervening in a revolt in Mexico; reports France has decided to join
Britain in using warships to protect Cuba from invasion; suggests
sending Joseph Blunt to China.

Oct 10   From Henry Lunt. ALS. OGK. mDW 34874. Reports DW's 4th of
July address has been enthusiastically received in Illinois; comments
on the threat of secession.

Oct 11   To Millard Fillmore. LS. NBuHi. mDW 34878. Encloses a letter
from Nathaniel Thayer, Jr. regarding John M. Marston, former U.S.
consul at Palermo.

Oct 11   To Millard Fillmore. ALS. NBuHi. mDW 34881. *PC*, 2: 476. Reports attending the New Hampshire state fair at Manchester and his
plans to come south; is suprised to hear he is expected to speak at
Baltimore.

Oct 11   To Millard Fillmore. LS. NBuHi. mDW 34884. *Diplomatic Papers*, 2. Introduces "Mr. Cook" from Alabama, who wishes the government to do something for his son, now imprisoned by Spanish
authorities for participation in the Lopez expedition.

Oct 11   From William S. King. ALS. DLC. mDW 34887. Discusses new
methods of ripening and preserving pears.

Oct 12   To Millard Fillmore. LS. NBuHi. mDW 34890. *Diplomatic Papers*, 2. Comments on the possibility that American merchantmen
may be stopped by British and French warships looking for individuals "bound to Cuba, and with hostile purposes"; recommends Blunt
for the China mission.

Oct 12   To Franklin Haven. ALS. MH–H. mDW 34894. Asks that "the
President's letter to me" be sent to Marshfield.

[Oct 12]   To George Washington Nesmith (with ANS by Nesmith). ALS.
NhD. mDW 34896. Invites him to visit Marshfield.

Oct 13   To W[illiam] P[rescott] Smith. LS. NhD. mDWs. Defers giving a
definite reply to an invitation to address the Maryland Institute.

Oct 13   From Edward Everett. ALS. MHi. mDW 34898. Makes some inquiries apropos of DW's memoirs; is sending a young Hungarian
artist to sketch DW's Marshfield house.

Oct 13   From Edward Everett. LS. MHi. mDW 34902. Introduces Hungarian artist A. Strausz, whom Little & Brown is sending to sketch
the Marshfield house.

Oct 13   *From David Sears.*   276

Oct 13   From C. S. Wayne. ALS. NhHi. mDW 34904. Asks for an autograph on behalf of Psi Delta Society at Waterville College.

Oct 14   To Edward Everett. ALS. MHi. mDW 34906. Encloses something
and asks what objection there might be "to stating the whole of it."

Oct 14   *To David Sears.*   277

Oct 14   From Hesekiah D. Batchelder (with DW to John Taylor, [Oct
20, 1851]). ALS. MBBS. mDW 34910. Submits a bill for a horse and
carriage and other services.

Oct 14   From Edward Everett. ALS. MHi. mDW 34912. Inquires about a document, cited in a Webster speech, in which Madison defends the constitutionality of the tariff.

Oct 14   From William Holmes (with reply, [c. Oct 15, 1851]). NhHi. mDW 34915. *PC*, 2: 478–479. Quotes poetry written by his father describing the qualities of a fine cow.

Oct 14   From Alfred Wheeler. ALS. DNA, RG 59. mDW 55127. Accepts appointment as U.S. attorney for southern California.

Oct 15   To [Edward Everett]. LS. MHi. mDW 34918. Replies to editorial queries.

[c. Oct 15]   To [William Holmes] (with Holmes to DW, Oct 14, 1851). AL draft. NhHi. mDW 34917. *PC*, 2: 479. Thanks him for a poem.

Oct 15   To J[ames] T[rask] Woodbury. Printed. *Works*, 6: 601. Declines an invitation to the dedication of a monument to Isaac Davis, a minuteman slain at the Battle of Concord in 1775.

Oct 15   From Joshua Bates. LS. DLC. mDW 34922. Introduces Henry Bingham Mildmay.

Oct 15   From Edward Twisleton. ALS. NhD. mDWs. Thanks DW for answers regarding the common schools of New England.

Oct 16   To Richard Milford Blatchford. ALS. NSchU. mDW 34924. Is working on the speech volumes; inquires about "Mr. Spencer's arbitration."

Oct 16   To George S. Boutwell. Printed. *PC*, 2: 479–480. Concurs with Boutwell's view of the Union as "a political necessity" and cites pertinent resolutions passed by the town of Acton in 1776.

Oct 16   To [Caleb Pratt]. ALS copy. NhHi. mDW 34926. *PC*, 2: 480. Sends him the inscriptions which are to appear on the monuments for Julia and Edward in the cemetery at Marshfield; asks him to put the words on paper in the proposed form, "before they are cut on the stone."

Oct 16   From George Ticknor. ALS. NN. mDWs. Gives citations for the British Parliamentary debates in 1835 over the foreign enlistment bill.

Oct 16   From Henry Varner. ALS. NhHi. mDW 34929. Presents a bust of DW carved in ivory.

Oct 17   To Caleb Cushing. ALS. NN. mDW 34931. Offers to meet him at the Revere House.

Oct 17   To Downing & Sons. ALS. NhHi. mDW 34933. Encloses a check.

Oct 17   Certification of Samuel Appleton's half interest in the Marshfield Manufacturing Company. ADS. CtY. mDW 40567.

Oct 17   Bill from W[ashington] O Berry & Beach for metal repairs, through Dec 17. ADS. NhHi. mDW 40580.

Oct 18   From Edward Everett. ALS. MHi. mDW 34944. Asks if Lanman's sketch accurately portrays the house in which DW was born; calls for the dedications of the first five volumes of DW's works.

Oct 18   To Edward Everett. LS. MHi. mDW 43937. *PC*, 2: 480–481. See Charles Lanman, *Haphazard Personalities* (Boston, 1885), pp. 130–131. Describes the house in which he was born, and states that Lanman's sketch is an accurate representation.

Oct 18   To Edward Everett. LS. MHi. mDW 34934. Encloses dedications for all six volumes of his works and explains his adaptation of three lines of verse by George Canning.

Oct 18   To Israel W. Putnam. LS. Gardiner Public Library, Gardiner, Me.
mDW 34941. Expresses delight with "your discourse on Gen. Dearborn's Life and Character."

Oct 18   To Henry A. Scudder. Printed. *Constitution of the Cape Cod
Association, with an account of the celebration of its first anniversary* (Boston, 1852), p. 77. Declines an invitation to attend the
anniversary celebration of the Cape Cod Association.

Oct 18   From James Mathers. ALS. NhHi. mDW 34947. *PC*, 2: 481.
poses questions on the nature and theory of government.

Oct 18   From Fritz Henry Warren. LS. DNA, RG 59. mDW 54939. Asks
that Dexter C. Bloomer, newly appointed postmaster at Seneca Falls,
N.Y., be issued his commission.

Oct 18   From J[ames] T[rask] Woodbury. ALS. NhHi. mDW 34949.
Urges DW to reconsider his decision not to attend the dedication of
the Isaac Davis monument at Acton.

Oct 20   To [Richard Milford Blatchford]. ALS. NhD. mDWs. Invites
him to breakfast.

Oct 20   To William Cabell Rives. LS. DLC. mDW 34951. Introduces
"Dr. Olmstead," a recent graduate of the medical school of New
York.

[Oct 20]   To John Taylor (with Hesekiah Batchelder to DW, Oct 14,
1851). ALS. MBBS. mDW 34910. Directs the partial payment of
Batchelder's bill and promises to pay the rest when he comes to New
Hampshire.

Oct 20   From William Channing Gibbs. ALS. OGK. mDW 34956. Presents copies of a sermon on the "Errors of Ultraism," recently
preached at the Episcopal Church in Newport, R.I.

[Oct 20]   From [National Union Party organizers]. AD. DLC. mDW
34958. Manifesto calling for DW's nomination for president.

Oct 20   Application from William A. Crafts—State Department position
(ALS. DLC. mDW 34952).

Oct 21   From Charles D. Smith et al. LS. DLC. mDW 34962. Desire to
take DW's measurements so they may present him with a new suit
of clothes.

Oct 21   Account with L. A. Huntington for $41 for tailoring, through
May 20, 1852. AD. CtY. mDW 40615.

Oct 22   To Millard Fillmore. ALS. NBuHi. mDW 34964. *PC*, 2: 482. Reports being detained by a case pending in U.S. circuit court in Boston; is disappointed by Judge [Alfred] Conkling's opinion on the
forceful rescue of fugitive slaves.

Oct 22   To Charles K. Williams. LS. Vermont State House—Governors'
Papers. mDW 34967. Recommends he consider pardoning Christian
Meadows, a convicted thief now incarcerated in the Vermont State
Prison in Windsor.

Oct 22   From James Louis Petigru.   277

Oct 23   From Edward Everett. LC. MHi. mDW 34975. Suggests references on Britain's foreign enlistments bill.

Oct 23   From Hiram Hill. ALS. DLC. mDW 34977. Requests the return
of the testimonials in support of his application for a position in the
Boston custom house.

Oct 23   From Samuel F. Train. ALS. DLC. mDW 34979. Acknowledges
DW's support for his application to be a purser in the Navy.

Oct 24   From Abbot Lawrence. Printed. Hamilton Andrews Hill, *Memoir of Abbott Lawrence* (Boston, 1883), pp. 216–217. Recommends that Postal Convention with Britain of December, 1848, be annulled.

Oct 27   From Edward Everett (with reply, [c. Oct. 29, 1851]). ALS. MHi. mDW 34984. Asks whether Cass's letters ought to be published along with DW's in the diplomatic papers.

Oct 27   From Edward Everett (with reply, [c. Oct 29, 1851]). ALS. MHi. mDW 34990. Inquires whether DW wrote out the argument for Wheaton in *Gibbons* v. *Ogden,* or whether Wheaton wrote it out from his own notes; also whether DW was the author of Tyler's message transmitting the Treaty of Washington to the Senate.

Oct 27   From Samuel Jaudon. ALS. DLC. mDW 34994. Alludes to his financial difficulties; promises to support DW's presidential campaign.

Oct 27   From H[oratio] G. Parker. ALS. DLC. mDW 34997. Requests copies of DW's speeches "touching our affairs with Mexico."

Oct 27   Application from Holloway & Davis, for the *Richmond* (Ind.) *Palladium*—public printers (LS. DNA, RG 59. mDW 54358).

Oct 28   From "An old fashioned Webster Man."   278

Oct 28   From Fitz Henry Warren. LS. DNA, RG 59. mDW 55014. Notifies him of various postal appointments.

Oct 28   Application from Witherspoon & Co., for the Marshal, Texas *Star State Patriot*—public printer (LS. DNA, RG 59. mDW 54091).

Oct 29   To John Barney. ALS. NbO. mDW 35002. Agrees to taste some wine.

[Oct 29]   To [Edward Everett]. ALS. MHi. mDW 35003. Asks Everett to look over his letters to "the Southern Agricultural meeting" before "these pages go to the press."

[c. Oct 29]   To [Edward Everett] (with Everett to DW, Oct 27, 1851). LS. MHi. mDW 34993. *PC,* 2: 482–483. Replies to various editorial inquiries.

[c. Oct 29]   To [Edward Everett] (with Everett to DW, Oct 27, 1851). AN. MHi. mDW 34987. Thinks Cass's letters should be omitted from the diplomatic volume.

[Oct 29]   To Edward Everett. ALS. MHi. mDW 35006. Makes a correction in his letter to the Southern Central Agricultural Association.

Oct 29   From Edward Everett. LC. MHi. mDW 35007. Introduces George M. Hobbs, a recent Harvard graduate, who wishes to apply for a clerkship in the State Department.

Oct 29   From William S. King. ALS. DLC. mDW 35009. Reports plans to provide educational facilities for farmers in Massachusetts, New Hampshire, and Vermont, and asks DW to submit a paper on agricultural improvement for publication in the *Journal of Agriculture.*

Oct 29   From C[handler] E. Potter. ALS. NhHi. mDW 35013. Seeks historical and genealogical information pertaining to the Salisbury area and DW's ancestors.

Oct 30   From James Cooper.   280

Oct 30   From William A. Weeks. ALS. DNA, RG 59. mDW 56898. Writes regarding the forwarding of despatches.

[c. Oct 30?]   Poem "To the Hon. Daniel Webster" by Anne Charlotte Lynch. AD. ViU. mDWs.

Oct 30   Account with Daniel Campbell for $21.63 for livery supplies, through Jan 9, 1952. ADS. NhHi. mDW 40597.

Oct 31   To Sir John Fiennes Crampton. LS. UkLPR. mDW 35021.
Promises to communicate resolutions of thanks for the Legislative
Council of Canada to Congress and the New York and Vermont legis-
latures for contributions to a library for the Canadian parliament.

Oct 31   To Edward Curtis. ALS. NN. mDW 35002. Reports "a little
poaching, not much"; asks Curtis to come to Washington as soon
as possible, to talk about things "I cannot write about."

Oct 31   To John F. Darby. LS. MoHi. mDW 35023. Agrees to provide
"Mr. Dawson" with a courier's passport.

Oct 31   To Anne Charlotte Lynch. Printed. *Memoirs of Anne C. L. Botta*
(New York, 1894), p. 336. Thanks her for her poem "To the Hon.
Daniel Webster."

Oct 31   To [John Osborne] Sargent. Invitation. MHi. mDW 35025.

Oct 31   From Edward Everett. LC. MHi. mDW 36026. Submits a draft;
infers that England may have suspended the foreign enlistments
bill to allow British subjects to enlist with Spain to protect Cuba.

Oct 31   From William J. Young. ALS. CSmH. mDWs. On behalf of the
"Industrial Congress" of New York, asks for a copy of the "Latest
Bounty Land Law" and amendments, and for DW's views on the bill.

Oct 31   From Daniel Fletcher Webster. ALS. NhHi. mDW 35028. Reports
a large printing of "your speech" is ready; detects the beginning of
"a ground swell" (of support for DW's nomination for president).

Nov 1   To Louisa Cheney. ALS. NhD. mDW 35059. Franklin Benjamin
Sanborn, *Henry D. Thoreau* (New York, 1882), pp. 94–95. Fears
former Concord friends feel alienated from him by their attachment
to such "vagaries" as abolitionism, free-soilism, and transcenden-
talism.

[Nov 1]   To Millard Fillmore. LS. NBuHi. mDW 35046. Will be late to
this morning's Cabinet meeting, because of an appointment with
Hülsemann.

Nov 1   To Samuel P. Lyman (with ANS by DW). LS. NhD. mDW 35066.
Describes the official arrangements for Thurlow Weed's trip abroad.

Nov 1   From Charles Augustus Davis. ALS. NhHi. mDW 35069. Advances proposals for a "passover" to the Pacific across Mexico, and
for a railroad from Maine to the Gulf of Mexico.

Nov 1   From Jonathan Prescott Hall. ALS. DNA, RG 17. mDW 57211.
Requests funds to pay expenses arising from the prosecution of three
individuals indicted in the Cuban conspiracy.

Nov 1   From J. Franklin Reigart.   282

Nov 1   From Fitz Henry Warren. LS. DNA, RG 59. mDW 54949. Requests that a commission be issued to Norborne C. Brooks, recently
appointed postmaster at Staunton, Va.

Nov 3   To C[harles] M[ynn] Conrad. CoDU. mDW 35077. Asks that "Mr.
Newcomb" be appointed to the position vacated by Lanman.

Nov 3   To Millard Fillmore. Invitation. NBuHi. mDW 35079.

Nov 3   To William Aexander Graham. Invitation. NcU. mDW 35081.

Nov 3   To William Alexander Graham. LS. CtHi. mDW 35082. Recommends "Mr. [Samuel F.] Train."

Nov 3   To Peter Harvey. LS. NhD. mDW 35083. Regrets to say that the
courier's passport requested for George O. Hovey has been given to
someone else.

Nov 3   To Annie F. Wilson. LS. NN. mDW 35085. Encloses payment on a note; offers congratulations on the prospective marriage of her sister Mary.

Nov 3   From Joseph W. Furbur. ALS. DNA, RG 59. mDW 55002. Accepts appointment as U.S. marshal for Minnesota.

Nov 3   From Nathan Kelsey Hall. LC. DNA, RG 28. mDW 57066. Requests three sets of the acts of the 29th, 30th, and 31st Congresses.

Nov 3   From Alexander Hugh Holmes Stuart. LS. DNA, RG 59. mDW 54987. Asks that a commission be issued for William H. Emory, recently appointed surveyor to the Mexican boundary commission.

Nov 3   Application from W. H. P. Denny, for the Lebanon, Ohio *Western Star*—public printer (ALS. DNA, RG 59. mDW 54044).

Nov 3   Account with William T. Dove for $42.50 for coal, through Dec 15. ADS. NhHi. mDW 40569.

Nov 4   To Edward Everett. Telegram. MHi. mDW 35087. "Your dispatch received & agricultural letter with others mailed yesterday."

Nov 4   To John Strother Pendleton. LS. MHi. mDW 35088. Asks for a statement of Pendleton's expenses as chargé d'affaires in Argentina.

Nov 4   From Angel Calderon de la Barca. ALS. NhD. mDW 35091. Demands that the U.S. give a formal apology for the assaults on the Spanish consul at New Orleans.

Nov 4   From Sir John Fiennes Crampton. Copy. UkLPR. mDWs. Inquires about the legality of a duty levied on British ships at Portsmouth.

Nox 4   From Chevalier Johann George Hülsemann (enclosure: press clipping). AL. NhHi. mDW 35102. Van Tyne, p. 490. Encloses a clipping entitled "The Liberation of Kossuth," taken from an English newspaper.

Nov 4   Account with Alfred Lee for Grain. AD. NhHi. mDW 40571.

Nov 5   From Nathan Kelsey Hall. LC. DNA, RG 59. mDW 57066. Encloses a paper for filing at the State Department.

Nov 5   From Seth Salisbury. ALS. DLC. mDW 35106. Thanks DW for his note replying to an invitation to visit Bradford County, Pa.

Nov 5   Recommendation from John Dowling, for the Columbus, Mississippi *Primitive Republican*—public printer (ALS. DNA, RG 59. mDW 54106).

Nov 5   Receipt for $1.44 paid A. Kleiber for milk. ADS. NhHi. mDW 40573.

Nov 6   To Edward Everett. Telegram. MHi. mDW 35108. Has mailed "Marston's note in Goodrichs case."

Nov 6   To John Plummer Healy. ALS. MHi. mDW 35109. Discusses business.

Nov 6   To Charles Scott Todd. Copy. NhHi. mDW 35111. PC, 2: 483. Acknowledges Todd's friendly letter and would be glad to see him.

Nov 6   From John Tyler. Printed. *William & Mary Quarterly* 8 (January 1910): 173–176. Praises DW's efforts on behalf of the Union, but takes exception to John Canfield Spencer's criticism of the President's role in the Ashburton negotiations.

Nov 7   To Richard Milford Blatchford. Printed. PC, 2: 483–484. Is attending to the publication of his works and preparation of the president's annual message.

Nov 7   To John Osborne Sargent.   284

[Nov 7]   To Nathaniel F. Williams. LS. NhD. mDW 35122. Agrees to meet Williams and his friends, but warns he cannot promise to comply with their wishes.

Nov 7   From Charles March. ALS. NhHi. mDW 35124. Is sending him some vintage wine.

Nov 8   To Annie F. Wilson. LS. NhD. mDW 35127. Thanks her for forwarding a note and for her good wishes.

Nov 8   Application from W. P. F. Morgan, for the Paris, Texas *Western Star*—public printer (ALS. DNA, RG 59. mDW 54448).

Nov 9   To Charles Porter Wright. Printed. *PC*, 2: 484. Discusses farm business.

Nov 9   From Charles Augustus Stetson. Telegram. NOsU. mDWs. Election news.

Nov 10   To D. D. Addison. LS. ICHi. mDW 35129. Reports evidence of Henry Daggett's Revolutionary War service.

Nov 10   To Millard Fillmore. LS. DNA, RG 217. mDW 57214. Submits Jonathan Prescott Hall's request for funds to pay for the prosecution of individuals accused in the Cuban conspiracy.

Nov 11   To Peter Harvey. Telegram. NhHi. mDW 35130. Asks: "How have the elections gone?"

Nov 11   From William W. Campbell. ALS. DLC. mDW 35131. States that George B. Mathew, British consul at Charleston, wishes to call on DW.

Nov 11   From Samuel Lawrence. ALS. DLC. mDW 35135. Advocates the negotiation of a reciprocity treaty with Canada.

Nov 11   Ichabod Smith Spencer to Daniel Fletcher Webster (with DW to Spencer, Dec 21, 1850). ANS. NhHi. mDW 31930. Encloses the copy of a letter from DW to himself.

Nov 12   To Richard Milford Blatchford. Printed. *PC*, 2: 485. Thanks Blatchford for following "the passenger-money business" and for calling on Mrs. Curtis and Caroline; is enjoying a quiet life in Washington with Curtis.

Nov 12   To John Southgate. LS. NcD. mDW 35138. Reports on payments due claimants in the *Ranger* case against Ecuador.

Nov 12   To Charles Porter Wright. LS. NhHi. mDW 35139. *PC*, 2: 485–486. Makes suggestions for the storage of turnips, and discusses other farm business.

Nov 12   From Sir John Fiennes Crampton. Copy. UkLPR. mDWs. Sends a copy of Palmerston's instructions to British warships regarding expeditions against Cuba.

Nov 12   From Robert Perkins Letcher. LS. DNA, RG 60. mDWs. Authorizes the payment of $1000 to William R. Glover, charged to George W. Slacum's expense account.

Nov 13   To Angel Calderon de la Barca. UkLPR. mDWs. Responds to Calderon's complaints about the outrages committed by a riotous mob against the Spanish consulate in New Orleans.

Nov 13   To Charles March. Printed. *PC*, 2: 487. Acknowledges March's gift of wine.

Nov 13   To Charles Porter Wright. Printed. *PC*, 2: 486–487. Gives instructions for spreading various fertilizers and asks if he has enough oxen.

[c. Nov 13]   From Angel Calderon de la Barca. Translation. UkLPR.

mDWs. Is confident DW's reply regarding the sack of the Spanish consulate in New Orleans will be sufficient to reestablish friendly relations between the U.S. and Spain.

Nov 13   From Edward Everett. LC. MHi. mDW 35142. Has moved back to Boston; comments on the recent elections.

Nov 13   From Sir John Fiennes Crampton (with DW to Graham, Nov 14, 1851). Copy. DNA, RG 78. mDWs. *On the establishment of An Universal System of Meteorological Observations, by Sea and Land* (Washington, 1851), p. 1. Invites the U.S. to cooperate with Britain in establishing a system of meteorological observation, and sends a pamphlet on the subject.

Nov 14   To Leslie Combs. LS. NhD. mDWs. Reports that appeals have been made to the Spanish government on behalf of Robert H. Breckenridge and other prisoners from the Lopez expedition.

Nov 14   To Sir John Fiennes Crampton. LS. UkLPR. mDW 35144. Has transmitted Crampton's note together with the enclosed pamphlet to the secretary of the navy.

Nov 14   To William Alexander Graham (enclosure: Crampton to DW, Nov 13, 1851). LS. DNA, RG 78. mDWs. *On the Establishment of an Universal System of Meteorological Observations, by Sea and Land* Washington, 1851), p. 2. Transmits a communication from Crampton proposing Anglo-American cooperation to establish a uniform system of meteorological observation.

Nov 14   From Charles Wainwright March. ALS. NhHi. mDW 35146. Van Tyne, p. 501. Comments on the recent Massachusetts elections and and their implications for DW's presidential campaign.

Nov 14   From William A. Weeks. ALS. DNA, RG 59. mDW 56899. Reports on the forwarding of despatches from Boston.

Nov 15   To Millard Fillmore. LS. NBuHi. mDW 35148. States that the records of the Havana trials have been translated and that an abstract will be sent to him.

Nov 15   To Chevalier Johann Georg Hülsemann. Draft. NhHi. mDW 35151. *Diplomatic Papers*, 2. Promises to look into the matter referred to by Hülsemann earlier in the day.

Nov 15   From Millard Fillmore. ALS. DNA, RG 217. mDW 57217. Suggests that the money requested by Jonathan Prescott Hall might be taken from the Judiciary Fund.

Nov 15   From John Plummer Healy. ALS. MHi. mDW 35152. Discusses miscellaneous business matters; reports on a political meeting and suggests that Boutwell and Winthrop have about even chances.

Nov 15   From Chevalier Johann Georg Hülseman. AL. NhHi. mDW . 35155. *Diplomatic Papers*, 2. Complains that his private conversations at the State Department have been appearing in print.

Nov 15   Application from McCreary & Sterrett, for the *Parkersburg Gazette & West Virginian Courier*—public printer (LS. DNA, RG 59. mDW 54078).

[Nov 16]   To Millard Fillmore. ALS. NBuHi. mDW 35158. Returns a letter; thinks Clayton and Harvey have been in a quandary since the Pennsylvania elections.

Nov 16   From Benjamin Robbins Curtis. ALS. DLC. mDW 35160. Benjamin R. Curtis, ed., *Memoir of Benjamin Robbins Curtis, LL.D.* (2 vols., Boston, 1879), 1: 157–158. Comments on the exercise of judicial power and the role of the Supreme Court.

Nov 16   From George M. Everly. ALS. DNA, RG 156. mDWs. Asks whether the U.S. government might be interested in buying rights to an invention in gunnery.

Nov 16   From John Taylor. ALS. NhHi. mDW 35164. PC, 2: 488. Reports on the first appearance of winter and DW's cattle at Elms Farm.

Nov 17   To Robert F. Aberdeed. ALS. NhD. mDW 35167. Has seen Aberdeed's letter to "my friend & relative" Nathaniel Sawyer of Cincinnati on family ancestry.

Nov 17   To Sir John Fiennes Crampton. ALS. UkLPR. mDWs. Thanks him for his "good offices" regarding DW's correspondence with Calderon, which has been satisfactorily closed.

Nov 17   To Elisha Whittlesey. LS. DNA, RG 217. mDW 57236. Asks if money from the Judiciary Fund might be used to furnish U.S. attorney Jonathan Prescott Hall with the funds he wants.

Nov 17   From Thomas N. Carr. ALS. DLC. mDW 35169. Advises the U.S. government to subsidize a steamship service to northwestern Africa or risk losing the African trade to England.

Nov 17   From M. C. Ege (with an AN by DW). ALS. NhHi. mDW 35172. Requests the loan of $100.

Nov 17   From Edward Everett. LC. MHi. mDW 35174. Asks whether the quotation from Plato in the Girard's Will speech ought to be put in the original Greek; is thinking about inserting " 'Mr. McGregor's letter' in our little address."

Nov 17   From Daniel Fletcher Webster.   285

Nov 18   From Robert M. Harrison. Copy. UkLPR. mDWs. Thanks the British naval commander and a ship captain in Jamaica who rescued American seamen from an "unfortunate vessel."

Nov 18   From Caroline Le Roy Webster. ALS. NhHi. mDW 35181. Discusses miscellaneous family matters, including the whereabouts of a mustard fork and sugar tongs.

Nov 18   From Thomas Corwin (with DW to Crampton, Nov 19, 1851). Copy. UkLPR. mDW 35186. Replies to an inquiry about admeasurement fees levied on foreign vessels by customs officials at Portsmouth.

Nov 19   To Sir John Fiennes Crampton (enclosure: Corwin to DW, Nov 18, 1851). LS. UkLPR. mDW 35185. Encloses the response of the secretary of the treasury to Crampton's inquiry about fees levied on British vessels at Portsmouth.

Nov 19   To Dickins & Coombs. LS. DLC. mDWs. Reports finding no evidence of Joseph Parrott's Revolutionary War service.

Nov 20   From B[enjamin] W. Bonney. LS. DLC. mDW 35188. Invites him to a commemoration of the Pilgrims' landing, sponsored by the New England Society of New York.

Nov 20   From John L. Hayes. ALS. DLC. mDW 35191. Presents the views of the iron manufacturers of New York and New England on the tariff and a reciprocity agreement with Canada.

Nov 20   From George Washington Warren (enclosure: printed proceedings of a Webster meeting, Charlestown, Mass.). ALS. NhHi.

mDW 35199. Forwards an account of a large Webster meeting held Nov 17th in Charlestown.

Nov 21   To Edward Curtis. ALS. NN. mDW 35201. Asks him to confer with J. Ring on a matter of apparent interest to "many of our N. York friends."

Nov 21   To Edward Everett. LS. MHi. mDW 35204. *Diplomatic Papers*, 2. Detects a growing clamor for a more aggressive foreign policy and suggests that Everett consider whether some response might be made.

Nov 21   To Franklin Haven. ALS. MH–H. mDW 35206. *W & S*, 16: 629. Gives his approval of the address to be presented at the Faneuil Hall meeting; has made some suggestions to Everett.

Nov 21   To Charles King. LS. MH–H. mDW 35210. Will try to attend a memorial meeting for James Fenimore Cooper, providing prominent literary figures—Ticknor, etc.—also come.

Nov 21   From C[harles] Edwards Lester. LS. NhD. mDW 35213. Promises DW the support of *The Herald of the Union* and in turn asks for a testimonial which might be circulated privately among potential advertisers.

Nov 22   To [Edward Everett]. ALS. MHi. mDW 35216. Suggests that Sheriden's Encomium on Washington's policy of neutrality ought to be read at the Faneuil Hall meeting.

Nov 22   From Sir John Fiennes Crampton. Copy. UkLPR. mDWs. Thanks the U.S. government and the people of Boston for the cordiality shown Lord Elgin during his visit to the city in celebration of the completion of a Canada-to-New England railroad.

Nov 22   From Hugh Maxwell. LS. DNA, RG 59. mDW 56710. Asks that Samuel La Farge be paid for gathering intelligence on the Cuban invaders.

Nov 22   Application from George A. Fitch, for the Kalamazoo *Michigan Telegraph*—public printer (ALS. DNA, RG 59. mDW 54051).

Nov 22   Recommendation from John H. B. Latrobe, for "Col. Capron"— public office (ALS. DLC. mDW 35218).

Nov 22   Receipt for $5 paid Edward Ambush & Co. for whitewashing. ADS. NhHi. mDW 40575.

Nov 23   To Franklin Haven. ALS. MH–H. mDW 35219. Is busy with the annual message; wants the Hülsemann letter and his Buffalo speech widely disseminated, especially in the west and south, and among the foreign population.

Nov 23   From Ambrose Dudley Mann. LS. DNA, RG 59. mDW 55956. Will make every effort to hasten exchange of ratifications of the Swiss Convention.

Nov 23   From Charles Wainwright March.   286

Nov 24   To Thomas Aspinwall. LS. NhD. mDW 35226. Gives instructions for his use of official funds as U.S. consul at London.

Nov 24   To Philip Ricard Fendall. LS. NhD. mDW 35229. Cannot conveniently provide him with copies of the rules for estimating and assessing damages established under the convention with Mexico of 1839.

Nov 24   To Millard Fillmore. LS. NBuHi. mDW 35232. Forwards a despatch just received from Rives.

Nov 24   To Millard Fillmore. LS. NBuHi. mDW 35234. Requests the return of the Rives despatch.

[Nov 24]   To Millard Fillmore. LS. NBuHi. mDW 36236. *PC*, 2: 488–489.
Comments on the president's message.

Nov 24   To Millard Fillmore. ALS. NBuHi. mDW 35239. *Diplomatic Papers*, 2. Comments on Hülsemann's allegation that a private note has been leaked to "Mr. Grund."

[Nov 24]   To Millard Fillmore. ALS. NBuHi. mDW 35243. *PC*, 2: 489.
Encloses a letter from Francis Lieber.

Nov 24   From Daniel Fletcher Webster. ALS. NhD. mDW 35246. Various political comments.

Nov 24   From Charles Porter Wright. ALS. NhHi. mDW 35250. *PC*, 2: 489. Reports on harvesting turnips and collecting kelp.

Nov 25   To Millard Fillmore. Printed. *PC*, 2: 490. Advises omitting a passage on consular law from the annual message.

[Nov 25]   To [Millard Fillmore] (enclosure: Harvey to DW, Nov 25, 1851). ALS. NBuHi. mDW 35252. Asks if he can be of any service while they await the printed proof of the annual message; briefly mentions the Massachusetts elections.

Nov 25   From Joseph Balestier. ALS. DNA, RG 59. mDW 56101. Reports on his diplomatic and commercial mission to Southeast Asia.

Nov 25   From Edward Everett. ALS. OGK. mDW 35256. Advises "a conciliatory course" toward Fillmore.

Nov 25   From Peter Harvey (with DW to Fillmore, [Nov 25, 1851]). Telegram. NBuHi. mDW 35255. "Against the Whigs. Boutwell will be Governor."

Nov 25   From Charles Wainwright March. ALS. NhHi. mDW 35260. Expects the Faneuil Hall meeting to be a great success.

Nov 25   Recommendation from James Butler Campbell, for the son of "the Revd. Mr. Yates."—a position (ALS. DNA, RG 45. mDWs).

Nov 25   Bill for $8.50 owed William Wall for a coat. NhHi. mDW 40593.

Nov 26   To Sir John Fiennes Crampton. LS. UkLPR. mDW 35263. Acnowledges H.M. government's thanks for the reception accorded Lord Elgin at the Boston festival in September.

Nov 26   To T[homas] H[artley] Crawford. LS. DLC. mDW 36265. Asks for a statement of facts to determine if two convicted criminals are eligible for clemency.

Nov 26   To Philip Ricard Fendall. LS. NhD. mDW 35267. States that his request for copies of the laws of Brazil has been forwarded to the Brazilian legation.

Nov 26   From J[ohn] C. Clark. LC. DNA, RG 206. Asks for instructions relative to the appointment of additional counsel to aid in the prosecutions growing out of the Syracuse slave riots.

Nov 26   From John L. Dimmock. ALS. DLC. mDW 35269. Forwards a recommendation for John C. Hoyt of Newburyport.

Nov 26   From Edward Everett.   288

Nov 26   From Daniel Fletcher Webster. ALS. NhHi. mDW 35279. Comments on the Massachusetts Whig Convention, and says in relation to William Schouler, editor of the Boston *Atlas*, "The cur is unwillingly whipped in, but whipped in he is"; asks about the omission of a word in a letter to Haven.

Nov 26   From William A. Weeks. ALS. DNA, RG 59. mDW 56900. Reports on despatches forwarded through Boston.

Nov 26   Recommendation from Reverdy Johnson, for C. H. Capron—
government employment (ALS. DLC. mDW 35275).

Nov 27   To Sir John Fiennes Crampton. LS. UkLPR. mDW 35283. Acknowledges his note transmitting a communication from the Haitian
government.

[Nov 27]   To Millard Fillmore. ALS. NBuHi. mDW 35284. *Diplomatic
Papers*, 2. Has directed the publication of "the substance of Mr. Wad-
dell's letter"; is drafting a letter to Barringer on behalf of the prisoners of the Lopez expedition.

Nov 27   To Peter Harvey.   288

Nov 27   To Franklin Haven. ALS. MH–H. mDW 35288. *PC*, 2: 490. Expresses great personal satisfaction with "the Address" (at the Faneuil
Hall meeting).

Nov 28   To John C. Clark. LS. DNA, RG 206. mDWs. States that a letter
has been sent to the U.S. attorney for northern New York concerning
the appointment of additional counsel to aid in the Syracuse slave
riot prosecutions.

Nov 28   To Franklin Haven.   289

Nov 28   To Charles A. Smith & Co. ALS. NhD. mDW 35294. Thanks
them for the gift of a suit of clothes.

Nov 28   From G. B. Newcomb. ALS. DLC. mDW 35295. Asks DW for
useful hints for inclusion in a study guide for students at academies
and common schools.

Nov 29   From George Ashmun. ALS. DLC. mDW 35296. Believes the
Faneuil Hall meeting was a success; looks forward to the President's
message; thinks Fillmore should be content "with the glory which is
secure."

Nov 29   From Daniel Fletcher Webster (enclosure: abstract from Elisha
Huntington to [?], [1851]).   289

Nov 30   To George Washington Burnap. LS. MHi. mDW 35304. *W & S*,
16: 630–631. Acknowledges two volumes of Burnap's discourses;
speaks highly of his other literary work.

Nov 30   To [Franklin Haven]. ALS. MH–H. mDW 35306. *W & S*, 16:
629–630. Is certain a straight Whig presidential ticket cannot be
elected; reports great discord at the Democratic caucus of last
evening.

[Nov 30]   From [Abbott Lawrence]. Draft. DLC. mDW 35312. Recommends that Congress appropriate funds for "the American Department" at the London Exhibition.

Nov 30   From Charles Porter Wright. ALS. MBBS. mDW 35310. Reports
on the kelp harvest.

[Nov?]   To [John Plummer Healy]. AN. MHi. mDW 35311. Asks Healy
to see that a note is paid.

[Nov-Dec, 1851]   From Simeon Draper.   291

Dec 1   To Philip Ricard Fendall. LS. DNA, RG 76. Encloses the translation of a note relative to Fendall's request for copies of Braziian laws.

Dec 1   To John B. Floyd. LS. ViW. mDWs. Informs him that the packet
accompanying his letter of November 28 will be forwarded to
Mexico.

Dec 1   From Edward Everett. ALS. MHi. mDW 35320. Inquires about the
inclusion of certain names with the second Bunker Hill speech.

Dec 1   From Daniel Fletcher Webster. ALS. NhHi. mDW 35324. Is suffering from a cold; reports briefly on his family.

Dec 1   Application from Coker Fifield Clarkson, for the Brookville
Indiana American—public printer (ALS. DNA, RG 59. mDW
54103).

Dec 2   To [John Smith] Phelps. ALS. NhExP. mDW 38799. Invites him
to dinner.

Dec 2   *Louis Worcester to Caleb Cushing.*   293

Dec 2   From Justin Butterfield. ALS. DNA, RG 59. mDW 55020. Asks
for the reissuance of a commission lost by S. D. King, newly-
appointed surveyor general of California.

[Dec 2]   From [Abbott Lawrence]. Draft. DLC. mDW 35031. Hamilton
Andrews Hill, *Memoir of Abbott Lawrence* (Boston, 1883), pp. 206–
226. Reports his impressions of Ireland.

Dec 2   *From Charles Wainwright March.*   292

Dec 2   From J[oseph] L. White. (enclosure: Resolution of the Board of
Directors of the Pacific Ship Canal Co., Dec 1, 1851). Copy. UkLPR.
mDWs. Discusses the outrage committed by a British vessel against
the *Prometheus* at San Juan de Nicaragua, and urges DW to take
action.

Dec 2   Applications from W[illaim] H. Cranston, for the *Newport* (R.I.)
Daily News—public printer (ALS. DNA, RG 59. mDW 54109);
from Charles Sexton, for the Willow River (Hudson) *St. Croix*
(Wisc.) *Inquirer*—public printer (ALS. DLC. mDW 35331).

Dec 3   To Edward Everett. LS. MHi. mDW 35340. Stands by his decision regarding the names of individuals to be included with the
second Bunker Hill speech.

Dec 3   To Millard Fillmore. LS. NcU. mDW 35348. *Diplomatic Papers*, 2.
Regards the *Prometheus* incident as serious and advises sending warships to the Central American coast.

Dec 3   To Millard Fillmore. LS. NBuHi. mDW 35350. *PC*, 2: 492. Reports there is a letter from [John] Thrasher at the State Department;
recommends publishing the report of the Utah delegation.

Dec 3   To Millard Fillmore. LS. NBuHi. mDW 35353. *PC*, 2: 493. Is
sending the despatches to Barringer at Madrid by special courier.

[Dec 3]   To Millard Fillmore. ALS. NBuHi. mDW 35355. Introduces
"Mr. Warner, an ardent Whig from Natchez."

Dec 3   To Rev. [?]. White. ALS. PHi. mDWs. Complies with a request
for his autographs; briefly discusses the Faneuil Hall meeting.

Dec 3   To [?]   ANS. NN. mDW 35339. Extends good wishes.

Dec 4   To Francis Dodge. ALS. NN. mDW 35357. Invites him to dine.

Dec 4   To Edward Hamilton. LS. Or–Ar. mDWs. Acknowledges a copy of
the *Executive Journal of Oregon* for Jan 1 to Oct 6, 1851.

Dec 4   To Peter Harvey. ALS. CSmH. mDW 35358. Is expecting Harvey
for dinner tomorrow.

Dec 4   To Franklin Haven. LS. MH–H. mDW 35359. Declares "the Carter Grant" is worthless and that the title has been repudiated.

Dec 4   To Franklin Haven. ALS. MH–H. mDW 35360. *W & S*, 16: 631.
Declares that the time has come to do what must be done and that
all will be well if Massachusetts stands firm.

Dec 4   Draft for $2000 payable to self. DS. NhD. mDW 40577.

Dec 5   To Angel Calderon de la Barca. Draft. CtY. mDW 35364. Encloses an accordance signed by insurance company officials recommending John C. Hoyt's appointment as Spanish vice-consul at Key West.

Dec 5   To Millard Fillmore. ALS. NBuHi. mDW 35414. *PC*, 2: 493. Reports a letter from the governor-general of Cuba on the Thrasher case is now being translated.

Dec 5   To Abbott Lawrence. LC. MH–H. mDWs. Directs Lawrence to suggest the immediate return of Bulwer to the U.S., or the appointment of another minister with full powers, to prevent the *Prometheus* affair from "extending to a dangerous extent."

Dec 5   To Elisha Whittlesey. LS. OClWHi. mDW 35366. Writes about $20.08 donated to the fund for the construction of a monument to George Washington at Nantes.

Dec 5   From Roswell L. Colt (with reply, [Dec 8, 1851]). ALS. DLC. mDW 35368. Suggests that charcoal be used in marking the boundary between California and Mexico; advises DW to remain in office until the *Prometheus* difficulty is resolved.

Dec 5   From Edward Everett. LC. MHi. mDW 35372. Writes regarding his reply to the *Union* on interventionism and American foreign policy.

Dec 5   Application from S. Siegfried, for the Morgantown, Virginia *Monongalia Mirror*—public printer (ALS. DNA, RG 59. mDW 54392).

Dec 5   Promissory note for $2400 payable to John Plummer Healy. DS. MHi. mDW 40579.

Dec 6   From William Alexander Graham (with DW to Crampton, Dec 13, 1851). Copy. UkLPR. mDW 35418. *On the Establishment of an Universal System of Meteorological Observations by Sea and Land* (Washington, 1851), pp. 11–13. Agrees that the U.S. should join Britain in establishing a uniform system for gathering weather data.

Dec 6   Recommendation from S[amuel] W[ilson] Parker, for the *Indiana American*—public printer (ALS. DNA, RG 59. mDW 54097).

Dec 7   From Millard Fillmore. ALS. DLC. mDW 35374. Severance, *Fillmore Papers*, 1: 359. Asks if the State Department knows anything about a reported violation of the Nicaraguan treaty by H.M. consulgeneral.

Dec 7   Recommendations from E[dward] C[arrington] Cabell to William S. Derrick, for the Tallahassee *Florida Sentinel*, and the Jacksonville *Florida Republican*—public printers (ALS. DNA, RG 59. mDW 54074).

Dec 8   To Roswell L. Colt (with Colt to DW, Dec 5, 1851). AL draft. DLC. mDW 35371. LS. PHi. mDW 35376. Is forwarding Colt's proposal for marking international boundaries with charcoal to the secretary of the interior.

Dec 8   To Millard Fillmore. LS. NBuHi. mDW 35377. *Diplomatic Papers*, 2. Is doubtful the U.S. may legally intervene with Spain on Thrasher's behalf.

Dec 8   To Millard Fillmore. ALS. NBuHi. mDW 35380. *Diplomatic Papers*, 2. Denies ever intimating that the U.S. might acquiese to the visitation of American vessels by British warships sent to protect Cuba from invasion; states that Britain has been warned that such acts would lead immediately to war.

Dec 8   Thomas Jefferson Tabb to Francis Mallory (with Mallory to DW, Dec 9, 1851). ALS. NhHi. mDW 35403. Asks him to inform DW that he will accept appointment as U.S. consul at Laguna.

Dec 8   Application from O[badiah] H. Platt, for the Brattleboro *Vermont Phoenix*—public printer (ALS. DNA, RG 59. mDW 54087).

Dec 8   Recommendation from Jeremiah Clemens, for the Huntsville, Alabama *Southern Advocate*—public printer (ALS. DNA, RG 59. mDW 54067).

Dec 9   To Millard Fillmore. LS. NBuHi. mDW 35384. Recommends Leonard W. Jerome for U.S. consul at Trieste.

Dec 9   To Millard Fillmore. LS. NBuHi. mDW 35386. Refers to Story's *Conflict of Laws* for the rule of law applicable in the Thrasher case.

Dec 9   From Charles F. Briggs et al. ALS by Briggs, signed also by others. DLC. mDW 35388. Invites DW to a banquet for Kossuth in New York.

Dec 9   From Sir John Fiennes Crampton. Copy. UkLPR. mDWs. Makes suggestions that the U.S. could implement for a more effectual prevention of the slave trade.

Dec 9   *From Edward Everett.*   294

Dec 9   From Francis Mallory (enclosure: Thomas Jefferson Tabb to Mallory, Dec 8, 1851). ALS. NhHi. mDW 35401. Encloses a letter in which Tabb agrees to be nominated consul at Laguna.

Dec 9   From John S. Rockwell. ALS. DNA, RG 76. mDWs. Writes regarding the *Louisa Beaton* claims against Great Britain.

Dec 10   To Millard Fillmore. LS. NBuHi. mDW 35404. Transmits despatches recently received from Mexico; will call tomorrow.

Dec 10   From Ambrose Dudley Mann. ALS. DNA, RG 59. mDW 55960. Bitterly assails Louis Napoleon's assumption of dictatorial powers in France; reports the Swiss Federal Council has been reelected, but has not yet considered the amendments to the convention; notes that the ministerial journals of Europe are circulating an article purporting to be a reply to DW's Hülsemann letter.

Dec 10   From William H. Winder. ALS. DLC. mDW 35406. Explains seating arrangements for DW and party at the opening of the National Theatre in Washington.

Dec 11   To Sir John Fiennes Crampton. LS. UkLPR. mDW 35409. Acknowledges Crampton's proposals for more effective prevention of the slave trade.

Dec 11   From Millard Fillmore. ALS. DLC. mDW 35410. Severance, *Fillmore Papers*, 1: 359–360. Cites various legal authorities on the subject of crime and the renunciation of citizenship.

[Dec 12] To Millard Fillmore. LS, NBuHi. mDW 35411. Inquires about a reference by Fillmore to Vattel's *Law of Nations*.

Dec 12   Application from Quincy K. Underwood, for the Helena, Arkansas *Southern Shield*—public printer (ALS. DNA, RG 59. mDW 54283).

[Dec 13] To [Daniel Moreau Barringer]. Draft incomplete. CtY. mDW 35619. Instructs him regarding the Thrasher case.

Dec 13   To Sir John Fiennes Crampton (enclosure: Graham to DW, Dec 6, 1851). LS. UkLPR. mDW 35416. Submits the secretary of navy's response to Crampton's proposal for Anglo-American cooperation in systematizing the collection of weather data.

Dec 13   To Millard Fillmore. LS. DLC. mDW 35421. Advises sending the
despatches to Barringer and Letcher by special couriers.

[Dec 13]   To Millard Fillmore. ALS. NBuHi. mDW 35425. Refers to the
translation of a despatch.

Dec 13   To J. Morrison Harris. LS. MdHi. mDW 35427. States that the
letter from Maryland Historical Society will be forwarded to Sir
Richard Pakenham as requested.

Dec 13   To Franklin Haven. LS. MH–H. mDW 35428. Asks that "the
proceeds of these" be credited to his account.

Dec 13   *To Franklin Haven.*   296

Dec 13   From Chevalier Johann Georg Hülsemann (with English translation). ALS. NhHi. mDW 35434. *Diplomatic Papers*, 2. Protests the
official reception and honors accorded Kossuth in the United States.

Dec 13   From Washington Irving. ALS. CtY. mDW 35458. States that
the James Fenimore Cooper memorial meeting will be held at Trip-
ler Hall, Dec 24, 1851.

Dec 13   From Richard B. Kimball. ALS. NhD. mDW 35459. Assures DW
that his invitation to the Cooper memorial meeting comes in recognition of his standing as a literary figure.

Dec 13   From Abraham B. Kinsey. ALS. NhHi. mDW 35462. Asks for advice "as to what principles my future course should be regulated by."

Dec 14   *To [Franklin Haven].*   297

Dec 14   To Washington Irving. ALS. MH–H. mDW 35467. Is unsure he
will be able to attend the Cooper memorial meeting.

Dec 15   To Millard Fillmore. LS. NBuHi. mDW 35469. Hopes to have
the replies to two Senate resolutions ready by tomorrow; sends the
draft for a message on the *Prometheus* incident.

Dec 15   To Millard Fillmore. ALS. NBuHi. mDW 35472. *PC*, 2: 494.
Transmits the translation of a letter from the governor-general of
Cuba to Calderon; has been obliged to redraft his letter to Barringer.

Dec 15   From Ambrose Dudley Mann. LS. DNA, RG 59. mDW 55968.
Makes recommendations for the reorganization of the U.S. diplomatic establishment in Europe.

Dec 16   Recommendation from Charles E. Sherman, for the *Evansville*
(Ind.) *Daily Journal*—public printer (ALS. DNA, RG 59. mDW
54058).

Dec 16   To Millard Fillmore. LS. NBuHi. mDW 35475. Encloses despatches from Paris and Spain.

[c. Dec 16]   To [Millard Fillmore]. ALS. NBuHi. mDW 35623. *PC*, 2:
491–492. Agrees with Fillmore's changes in the Thrasher report;
expects it will be ready later in the afternoon.

Dec 16   To Chevalier Johann Georg Hülsemann. Draft. NhHi. mDW
35477. LS. Austrian State Archives, Vienna. mDW 35479. *Diplomatic
Papers*, 2. Refuses to accept Hülsemann's recent note until all allusions to confidential conversations are expunged.

Dec 16   To William R. King. DS. DNA, RG 46. mDW 52031. Reports to
Congress the amount expended under the appropriation for the expenses for the agent of the Sublime Porte.

Dec 16   To Louis Kossuth. Copy. MHi. mDW 35481. Will present Kossuth to the president when he reaches Washington.

Dec 16   From Millard Fillmore. AL. DLC. mDW 35483. Severance,
Fillmore Papers, 1: 360. Recommends sending Kossuth the joint

resolution of welcome by messenger with nothing more than a letter of concurrence.

Dec 16   From Charles Henry Thomas. ALS. NhHi. mDW 35485. Will send the pamphlet copies he found of a DW speech; reports "the *New Mill*" is in operation and he's found a man to run it.

Dec 16   Application from Charles Sexton, for the Willow River (Hudson) *St. Croix* (Wisc.) *Inquirer*—public printer (ALS. DNA, RG 59. mDW 54039).

Dec 17   From Caleb Cushing (enclosure: Cushing to DW, Dec 17, 1851). ALS. DLC. mDW 35489. *Diplomatic Papers*, 2. Presents evidence of John S. Thrasher's U.S. nationality.

Dec 17   From Chevalier Johann Georg Hülsemann. ALS. NhHi. mDW 35495. *Diplomatic Papers*, 2. Disputes DW's contention that their recent official exchanges should be treated as confidential.

Dec 17   From William T. G. Morton. ALS. MBCo. mDWs. Asks whom DW now considers to be the first to use ether in surgical operations.

Dec 18   To Richard Milford Blatchford. Printed. PC, 2: 495. Is busy with foreign affairs and the Thrasher case; reports his plans for visiting New York are unsettled.

Dec 18   To Millard Fillmore. LS. NBuHi. mDW 35498. *PC*, 2: 494. Reports assurances from Palmerston that Britain, Spain, and France have not made a treaty regarding Cuba.

Dec 18   To Chevalier Johann Georg Hülsemann. AL draft. NhHi. mDW 35501. LS. Austrian State Archives, Vienna. mDW 35504. *Diplomatic Papers*, 2. Insists that all of his conversations with Hülsemann are to be considered confidential.

Dec 18   To George Little. LS. Nc–Ar. mDWs. Transmits the president's pardon of Thomas H. Harvey, convicted of robbing the post office at Newburn [New Bern], N.C., in 1847.

Dec 18   From Millard Fillmore. ALS. Gates W. McGarrah Collection of Presidential Autographs, owned by Richard Helms, Washington, D.C. mDW 35506. Advises publication of the section of Barringer's despatch concerning the release of the "widow's son."

Dec 19   To Millard Fillmore. LS. NBuHi. mDW 35508. Advises that "Messrs. Green's" (Duff and his son) be informed regarding the payment of the Mexican indemnity.

Dec 19   To Millard Fillmore. LS. NBuHi. mDW 35511. Gives a citation from the U.S. laws.

Dec 19   To Millard Fillmore. LS. NBuHi. mDW 35514. Van Tyne, p. 506. Is Puzzled by [Duff] Green's charges he suppressed some of Rosa's correspondence; has received a letter from Rosa regarding the payment of the Mexican indemnity.

Dec 19   To George Latimer. LS copy. CtY. mDW 35517. Acknowledges his despatches; approves the appointment of Thomas Turull as consular agent at Mayaguez.

Dec 19 To S[amuel] N. Sweet. Copy. NhHi. mDW 35519. Acknowldges Sweet's friendly comments; requests a copy of his book on elocution.

Dec 19   From Abbott Lawrence. ALS. DLC. mDW 35520. Agrees that a British envoy should be sent to Washington to negotiate on Central America; thinks strong measures are needed to produce a change in British behavior there.

Dec 19   From Martin Farquhar Tupper. ALS. ICN. mDWs. Recommends that something be done to prevent the sale and dispersal of Catlin's American Museum of "aboriginal curiosities."

Dec 19   Recommendation from J[oseph] P[earson] Caldwell, for the Salisbury, North Carolina *Carolina Watchman*—public printer (ALS. DNA, RG 59. mDW 54267).

Dec 20   To Charles Benjamin. Draft. CtY. mDW 35523. Introduces J. M. Gougas of Quincy.

[Dec 20]   To Richard Milford Blatchford. Printed. *PC*, 2: 496. Reports his activity; looks forward to meeting Kossuth, but cannot go to New York before Kossuth comes to Washington.

Dec 20   To Caleb Cushing. LS. DLC. mDW 35528. *Diplomatic Papers*, 2. Discusses the Thrasher case, assuring that "we are doing everything for him which we can do."

Dec 20   To Millard Fillmore. ALS. NBuHi. mDW 35524. *Diplomatic Papers*, 2. Recommends that Gen. Henry Stuart Foote's desire that [Horace H.] Miller be appointed chargé d'affaires in Bolivia be gratified.

Dec 20   To William T. G. Morton. L.S. KU–M. mDWs. Credits Morton himself for discovering the use of ether as an anaesthetic.

Dec 20   To Augustus Schell et al. LS. NHi. mDW 35537. Will be unable to attend the New-York Historical Society's meeting until after Kossuth's visit to Washington.

Dec 20   To Charles Porter Wright. Printed. *PC*, 2: 495. Sends money; inquires about the Marshfield farm; gives instructions for curing hams.

Dec 20   Recommendations from Charles Chapman, for the Hartford *Connecticut Courant*—public printer (ALS. DNA, RG 59. mDW 54089); from Edward Everett, for Stanislas Hernisz—translating clerk at the State Department (ALS. MHi. mDW 35533).

Dec 20   Receipt for $8 paid John Mills for shoes. DS, NhHi. mDW 40582.

[Dec 21]   To [Edward Curtis]. ALS. NN. mDW 35538. Remarks on the difficulty of controlling what is written about himself; notes "the French news" (Louis Napoleon's coup and election as president for ten years).

Dec 21   To John Osborne Sargent. Dictated letter, unsigned. MHi. mDW 35540. Wishes to see him regarding the news from France about Louis Napoleon's coup.

Dec 22   To Sir John Fiennes Crampton. LS. UkLPR. mDW 35542. States that a package consigned to Crampton will be admitted duty-free by the New York custom house.

Dec 22   To Millard Fillmore. ALS. NBuHi. mDW 35543. Encloses Hunter's report on his visit with Kossuth.

Dec 22   To Millard Fillmore. LS. NBuHi. mDW 35545. Sends recommendations for [Samuel J.] Oakford's appointment as U.S. consul at Tumbez, Peru.

Dec 22   To Samuel Jaudon. ALS. NHi. mDW 35547. Remembers a financial obligation to Jaudon and asks him to send "Annie" to the State Department "to allow it."

Dec 22   *From Edward Everett.*   297

Dec 22   From William B. Rose. ALS. NhHi. mDW 35551. Praises DW's efforts on behalf of the son of "Mrs. Talbot of Louisiana."

Dec 22   Recommendation from Jacob Welsh Miller, for the *Trenton State Gazette*—public printer (ALS. DNA, RG 59. mDW 54070).

Dec 22   Mr. Webster's lines on [Henry S.] Foote. AD. NhHi. mDW 35548. Van Tyne, pp. 636–637.

Dec 22   Receipt for $5 paid James F. Jackson for a wheelbarrow. ADS. NhHi. mDW 40584.

[Dec 23]   To Edward Curtis. Printed. *PC*, 2: 439. Comments on Kossuth's visit; expresses shock at the report of "human depravity, and enormities" in Mormon Utah.

Dec 23   To Millard Fillmore.   299

Dec 23   To Millard Filmore. LS. NBuHi. mDW 35555. Submits an answer to the call from the House of Representatives for information in the Thrasher case.

Dec 23   To [Franklin Haven]. ALS. MH–H. mDW 35557. Discusses a financial matter; blames careless saving habits for many of the difficulties in his life.

Dec 23   To Franklin Haven. ALS. MH–H. mDW 35561. *PC*, 2: 497. Reports the government's reception for Kossuth will be somewhat constrained; is concerned about the news from France and thinks "Louis Napoleon will carry his purpose."

Dec 23   To Robert Perkins Letcher. ALS draft. NhHi. mDW 35564. *Diplomatic Papers*, 2. Instructs him regarding the Tehuantepec Treaty.

Dec 23   From A[lexander] H[amilton] Bullock. ALS. NhD. mDW 35570. Thanks DW for a basket of canvasback ducks.

Dec 24   To Benjamin Robbins Curtis. Printed LS with MS insertions. DLC. mDW 35572. Encloses Curtis' commission as associate justice of the U.S. Supreme Court.

Dec 24   To Charles Porter Wright. Printed. *PC*, 2: 498–499. Inquires about oxen, beef, and pork.

Dec 24   From John Taylor. ALS. NhHi. mDW 35573. *PC*, 2: 497–498. Reports on life at the farm in Franklin.

Dec 25   To [Richard Milford Blatchford]. ALS. NSchU. mDW 35576. Is embarrassed about Kossuth; marvels at the swift success of Louis Napoleon's take-over in France.

Dec 25   To James William Paige. Printed. *PC*, 2: 499. Is sending a Christmas basket and thanks him for wine; fears Kossuth's presence in Washington may cause some embarrassment.

Dec 26   To Edward Everett. Telegram. MHi. mDW 35579. "Omit the Worcester letter. Thrasher corrected, is mailed today."

Dec 26   To Abbott Lawrence. LS. MH–H. mDW 35580. Directs him to inform Palmerston that Crampton would be quite acceptable as Britain's representative in the negotiations over Central America.

Dec 26   To Abbott Lwrance. LS. MH–H. mDW 35582. Notes the growing strength of the Irish electorate in the U.S.; suggests that H.M. government be approached discreetly regarding the release of the Irish state prisoners now held on Van Dieman's Land.

Dec 26   To Edward Riddle. LS. MHi. mDW 35584. Congratulates Riddle for the successful discharge of his duties with the American exhibit at the London Exhibition.

Dec 26   From Abbott Lawrence. ALS draft. MH–H. mDWs. LC. MH. mDWs. Reports the version he's heard of Palmerston's resignation;

hopes that with Granville as a successor the U.S. can now make progress on claims and U.S.-British relations in Nicaragua.

Dec 26 Recommendation from Samuel Brenton, for the Terre Haute, Indiana *Wabash Express*—public printer (ALS. DNA, RG 59. mDW 54056).

Dec 27 From Henry Sargent. ALS. DNA, RG 59. mDW 56497. Reports on his mission as despatch bearer to Ambrose Dudley Mann.

Dec 27 From [Lemuel Shaw]. Copy. MHi. mDWs. Writes regarding Henry Savage's claim for services rendered as a public agent in Central America.

[Dec 28] To Millard Fillmore. ALS. NBuHi. mDW 35585. Van Tyne, p. 506. Reports Kossuth will not leave here before Tuesday and will require extensive lodgings for himself and his suite.

Dec 28 To Franklin Haven.   299

[Dec 28] To William Henry Seward. ALS. NRU. mDW 35881. Asks how long Kossuth will stay in Washington and how many from his suite the president should invite to dinner.

Dec 28 From William A. Weeks. ALS. DNA, RG 59. mDW 56901. Reports on despatches forwarded through Boston.

Dec 29 To Millard Fillmore. ALS. NBuHi. mDW 35591. Advises him not to entertain Kossuth at dinner on Wednesday.

Dec 29 To Franklin Haven. ALS. MH–H. mDW 35594. Alludes to a financial matter raised in "your private letter."

Dec 29 To Abbott Lawrence. LS. MH–H. mDW 35597. *Diplomatic Papers*, 2. Comments on U.S. problems with Mexico, the Central American difficulties with Britain, and the likelihood a "more war-like Administration" may succeed Fillmore's.

Dec 29 To William Cabell Rives. Draft. DLC. mDW 35602. Asks Rives to do what he can for an American naval officer recently injured in Paris.

Dec 29 To Charles Porter Wright. Printed. *PC*, 2: 499–500. Discusses ashes, oxen, and other farm business.

Dec 29 From John S. Riddle. ALS. DLC. mDW 35604. Believes most Americans sympathize with Kossuth, but are opposed to intervention; urges DW to stand firm against Kossuth's demands.

[Dec 30] To Richard Milford Blatchford. Printed. *PC*, 2: 501–502. *Diplomatic Papers*, 2. Reports calling on Kossuth; promises to turn a deaf ear to any talk of intervention.

[Dec 30] To Millard Fillmore. ALS. NBuHi. mDW 35607. *PC*, 2: 501. Has an appointment in court and may be unable to attend the reception for Kossuth.

[Dec 30] To Millard Fillmore. ALS. NBuHi. mDW 35610. *PC*, 2: 501. reports his court case has been postponed; will bring Kossuth to see the President tomorrow.

Dec 30 Recommendation from [?], for the Springfield *Illinois Journal*—public printer (ALS signatures missing. DNA, RG 59. mDW 54041).

Dec 31 To Richard Milford Blatchford. Printed. *PC*, 2: 502. Reports on Kossuth's reception by the president.

Dec 31 To Franklin Haven. LS. MH–H. mDW 35612. Asks him to renew a note.

Dec 31 From Frederic De Peyster et al. ALS by De Peyster, signed also

by others. DLC. mDW 35615. Asks for a week's notice in advance of
the day DW plans to address the New York Historical Society.

Dec 31   From John Taylor. ALS. NhHi. mDW 35617. PC, 2: 502–503.
Thanks DW and Lanman for "great presents" they sent him.

[Dec]   To Millard Fillmore. ALS. NBuHi. mDW 35621. Reports receiving
no newspapers from abroad containing mention of Fillmore's presidential message.

[1851]   To Joseph Burnett. ALS. NN. mDW 38292. Requests Burnett to
furnish Chief Justice of Massachusetts Lemuel Shaw with a preparation of "Hydriodate of Potash" according to "Mr [Robert] Croes's
prescription.

[1851]   To Millard Fillmore (enclosure: Caroline Le Roy Webster to
DW, [1851]). Printed. W & S, 16: 602. Encloses a note from Caroline
regarding a salmon she is sending for the president.

[1851]   To Peter Harvey. ALS. NjMoHP. mDW 35637. Wishes to see him
this morning.

[1851]   To Mrs. Samuel P. Lyman. ANS. MiU. mDWs. Inscription on the
cover of pamphlet Speech of Mr. Webster at the Celebration of the
New York New England Society.

[1851]   To Elisha Riggs. ALS. DLC. mDW 35638. Asks where "good
clean coal" might be found in Washington or Georgetown.

[1851]   To John Taylor. ALS. MBBS. mDW 35641. Asks "Do you not
wish that kelp was found in Merrimack River."

[1851]   To Robert Charles Winthrop. ALS. MHi. mDW 35642. Thanks
him for a remembrance.

[1851]   Elisha Huntington to [?] (with Daniel Fletcher Webster to DW,
Nov 29, 1851). Extract. NhHi. mDW 35301. Reports DW has given
would-be supporters a rather cold reception.

[1851]   From Caroline Le Roy Webster (with DW to Fillmore, [1851]).
Printed, W & S, 16: 602. Writes regarding a salmon she is sending
to the President.

[1851]   Application from Charles Cocke—a diplomatic position (ALS.
NhHi. mDW 35665).

[1851]   Dedication to James William Paige (with George Jacob Abbot to
Harriette Story White Paige, May 14, 1854). Printed page proof with
corrections by DW. Mrs. Irvin McD. Garfield, Southboro, Mass.
mDWs.

[1851]   List of largesses to DW. Ad in unknown hand. MHi. mDWs.

[1851]   Notes on Gaines v. Relf. AD. MHi. mDW 35643.

1851   Receipt for $6 paid Henry Neal for waiter's services. ADS. NhHi.
mDW 40587.

[1851?]   To Daniel Stevens Dickinson. ALS. ICN. mDWs. Reminds him
of their dinner engagement.

[1851?]   Statement of estimated cost and expenses for transportation
of three head of cattle from Murzthal, Hungary, to Bremen. AD.
DLC. mDW 40674.

[1851–1852]   To Simeon Draper. ALS. NN. mDW 35669. Wishes to
speak with "Mr. Raymond, of The [New York] Times."

[1851–1852]   To Millard Fillmore. ALS. NBuHi. mDW 35626. Will try
to see him today.

[1851–1852]   To Millard Fillmore. ALS. NBuHi. mDW 35628. Introduces [Robert A.] West of the New York *Commercial Advertiser*.

[1851–1852]   To Millard Fillmore. ALS. NBuHi. mDW 35630. Is fatigued and cannot see him until tomorrow.

[1851–1852?]   To John Plummer Healy. ALS. MHi. mDW 38645. Wishes to see him regarding "this Randall suit," of which he has no recollection.

[1851–1852]   To Charles Augustus Stetson. ALS. CtY. mDW 38872. States, "If I arrive in N.Y. tomorrow Evening, I must take the Providence Boat Wednesday Eve., on account of things in Boston."

1852

[Jan 1]   To [William Henry Seward]. ALS. NRU. mDW 35879. Asks that Kossuth be informed that he, with his suite, will be received from one to two o'clock.

Jan 1   From Sir Henry Lytton Bulwer. ALS. DLC. mDW 35672. Curtis, 2: 594. Assures him of H.M. government's wish to settle its differences with the U.S. in Central America; suggests their two countries might be able to reach an understanding on Greytown with or without the participation of the Nicaraguan representative.

Jan 1   From William Sprague. ALS. DNA, RG 59. mDW 54053. Asks that the State Department reconsider paying the Kalamazoo *Michigan Telegraph* for publishing the laws of the second session of the last Congress.

Jan 2   From Abbott Lawrence. ALS. DLC. mDW 35676. Curtis, 2: 593–594. Comments on the *Prometheus* affair; reports Bulwer is being pressed to undertake a mission to Washington to settle Anglo-American differences over Central America; thinks Britain wants to give up the Nicaraguan protectorate if it can retain its "national honor."

Jan 2   From Eben Newton. ALS. NhD. mDW 35680. Requests copies of the Webster-Hülsemann correspondence to send to his constituents.

Jan 3   From Sir John Fiennes Crampton. Copy. UkLPR. mDWs. Transmits information about blacks being kidnapped in Jamaica and imported for slavery at Norfolk and other ports.

Jan 3   From Louis Kossuth. ALS. MHi. mDW 35681. Reports the persecution of his family by Austrian authorities; asks the U.S. government to help send them relief.

Jan 3   From Ambrose Dudley Mann. LS. DNA, RG 59. mDW 55979. Reports the Swiss government needs more time to consider the convention; bitterly criticizes Louis Napoleon's usurpation of power and urges the U.S. to cut off diplomatic ties and support his republican opponents.

Jan 3   From J[ames] M. Mason. ALS. UkLPR. mDWs. States that "Mr. [Albert?] Fitz" withdrew his petition from Senate files to avoid "the *publicity* incident to the usages of legislation."

Jan 3   From John Taylor (with DW to Taylor, [c. Jan 6, 1852]). ALS. MBBS. mDW 35685. Makes suggestions for spring farm work at The Elms.

Jan 3   Recommendation from Truman Smith, for the *Hartford Daily Courant*, and the *New Haven Palladium*—public printers (ALS. DNA, RG 59. mDW 54398).

Jan 4   From Ambrose Dudley Mann. ALS. DNA, RG 59. mDW 55997. Corrects an error in his preceding despatch; comments on events in Austria and France.

Jan 5   To Abbott Lawrence, LS. MH–H. mDW 35689. Analyzes the Nicaraguan problem; mentions Kossuth's visit.

Jan 5   From James W. Bradbury et al. LS. DLC. mDW 35693. Invite DW to a dinner for Kossuth sponsored by members of Congress.

Jan 5   From Quincy K. Underwood. ALS. DNA, RG 59. mDW 54227. Accepts appointment of the Helena, Arkansas *Southern Shield* to publish the laws.

Jan 5   From Daniel Fletcher Webster. ALS. NhHi. mDW 35695. Comments briefly on the Spanish negotiations and the Kossuth visit; reports the death of Professor Moses Stuart.

Jan 5   Recommendation from Truman Smith, for the Helena, Arkansas *Southern Shield*—public printer (AL. DNA, RG 59, mDW 54294).

Jan 6   To John Appleton. LS. G. Hartley Webster, Harvard, Mass. mDWs. States that Appleton's letter calling for U.S. intercession on behalf of the exiled Irish patriots has been filed in the State Department archives.

Jan 6   To Sir John Fiennes Crampton. LS. UkLPR. mDW 35699. Applies for the extradition of Emma Andrus, recently indicted for infanticide in New York.

[c. Jan 6]   To John Taylor (with Taylor to DW, Jan 3, 1852). ALS. MBBS. mDW 35688. Harvey, *Reminiscences of DW*, pp. 305–306. Comments on Taylor's proposals for spring farm work at The Elms.

Jan 7   To Millard Fillmore. ALS. NBuHi. mDW 35701. Has an appointment at court and hopes he will not be needed at the cabinet meeting.

Jan 7   To Millard Fillmore. LS. NBuHi. mDW 35703. Thinks a remission of fine ought to be allowed the ship *St. George* if the facts stated in the enclosed papers are correct.

Jan 7   To Millard Fillmore. ALS. NBuHi. mDW 35706. *Diplomatic Papers*, 2. Suggests it would be politically advisable for the Administration to be represented at the Kossuth dinner this evening.

Jan 7   To Franklin Haven. Telegram. MH–H. mDW 35710. Asks Haven to come as soon as possible and to bring Ashmun.

Jan 7   To Franklin Haven. Telegram. MH–H. mDW 35711. Wants Haven and Ashmun in Washington by Monday.

[Jan 7]   Notes for speech at Kossuth dinner. AD. MdBP. mDW 35712.

Jan 8   To [Charles] Chapman. ALS. MWalB. mDWs. Wishes to say "a word about what you mentioned last Eve'."

Jan 9   To D. D. Addison. LS. NhD. mDW 35716. Reports evidence of the Revolutionary War service of "Lieutenant Banks."

Jan 9   To Lemuel Shaw. LS. MHi. mDWs. Advises Henry Savage to petition Congress for compensation for his services as a political agent in Central America.

Jan 9   From Millard Fillmore. AL. DLC. mDW 35717. Severance, *Fillmore Papers*, 1: 360. Wishes to see him regarding "a *confidential* matter."

Jan 9   From Isaac D. Jones. ALS. NhD. mDW 35719. Commends DW
for his defense of the Union and his public service.

Jan 9   Recommendation from John A. Wilcox, for the *Aberdeen*
(Miss.) *Independent*—public printer (ALS. DNA, RG 59. mDW
54369).

Jan 10   To Robert Morrison. ALS. NN. mDW 35722. Sends him $100;
expresses concern about reports of sickness around Marshfield.

[Jan 10]   From William Henry Seward. ALS. DLC. mDW 35724. Reports
Kossuth would be pleased to see DW, and has offered to correct statistical errors in DW's speech at the banquet.

[c. Jan 10]   Application from W. W. and S. A. Pratt, for the Jersey City
Daily Sentinel and Advertiser—public printer (LS. DNA, RG 59.
mDW 54348).

[Jan 11]   To Richard Milford Blatchford. Printed. *Diplomatic Papers*, 2.
Explains his speech at the Kossuth dinner, comments on Palmerston's retirement.

Jan 11   To Charles Porter Wright. ALS. NhHi. mDW 35727. Van Tyne,
p. 749. Expresses concern about widespread sickness in Marshfield, and authorizes the use of whatever might be needed from his
house.

Jan 11   From John W. Houston. ALS. NhD. mDW 35728. Expresses
keen admiration for Kossuth; urges the U.S. to become "the advocate and patron" of his principles.

Jan 12   To Millard Fillmore. ALS. NhD. mDW 35732. Asks him to look
over a despatch.

Jan 12   To Millard Fillmore. LS. NBuHi. mDW 35733. Has made the
changes recommended by Fillmore in the despatch to Rives.

Jan 12   To Millard Fillmore. LS. NBuHi. mDW 35735. States that Fillmore's inquiry will be addressed at once to the judges and secretary
of Utah territory.

Jan 12   To Millard Fillmore. Dictated letter. NBuHi. mDW 35727. Submits the draft of an extradition convention with Prussia and certain
other German States.

Jan 12   To Millard Fillmore. AL. NBuHi. mDW 35739. Will see him tomorrow around ten o'clock.

Jan 12   To Millard Fillmore. ALS. NBuHi. mDW 35741. Asks Fillmore
to review the accounts of Thomas Butler King; urges that the account be settled before King leaves office.

Jan 12   To Millard Fillmore. LS. DNA, RG 59. mDW 56719. Recommends that the claim of Thomas Butler King, former special and
confidential agent to California, be paid.

[Jan 12]   To [William Cabell Rives]. AL draft. NhHi. mDW 35743. *Diplomatic Papers*, 2. Comments on Louis Napoleon's overthrow of the
French Republic; explains U.S. policy toward the new regime.

Jan 12   From Millard Fillmore. AL. NhHi. mDW 35754. *Diplomatic
Papers*, 2. Wishes to discuss the appointment of Commodore Perry
to command the East India squadron with orders to negotiate a
treaty with Japan.

Jan 12   From Millard Fillmore. AL. DLC. mDW 35756. Severance,
Fillmore Papers, 1: 360–361. Orders various alterations in the despatch to Rives about U.S. recognition of Napoleon's government.

Jan 12   From Edward A. Le Roy, ALS. NhHi. mDW 35760. Is preparing to leave for Havana with his family, and asks that passports be sent at once.

Jan 12   Recommendation from John McLean, for the Brookville *Indiana American*—public printer (ALS. DNA, RG 59. mDW 54096).

Jan 13   To Robert Cumming Schenck. LS. MdBJ. mDW 35763. Introduces sons of Edward M. Greenway who are about to visit Rio de Janeiro.

Jan 13   From [Hiram Ketchum]. Extract in another hand. CtY. mDWs. Is happy DW has attended to "Dunham's business"; reports that Dunham has ordered the operatives in his foundry to attend a political meeting on Feb 4, which Ketchum hopes will be spirited and influential; admonishes DW to attend the Ascension Church on the 22nd and remain to congratulate "our mutual and most excellent friend Rev. Doct. Adams" for his exertions; sends a copy of the Syracuse *Daily Star* containing an article that "clearly gives Mr. Fillmore up."

Jan 13   Recommendation from J[acob] W[elsh] Miller, for the *Newark* (N.J.) *Daily Advertiser*—public printer (ALS. DNA, RG 59. mDW 54350).

Jan 14   To Sir John Fiennes Crampton. LS. UkLPR. mDW 35764. Replies to charges that Americans have been kidnapping and enslaving blacks from the British West Indies.

Jan 14   To Franklin Haven. Invitation. MH–H. mDW 35767.

Jan 14   To John Fanning Watson. LS. NhD. mDW 35768. Acknowledges Watson's letter and manuscript on the early settlers of New Hampshire.

Jan 14   From Baring Brothers & Co. et al. Copy. CaOOA. mDW 35769. Reply to Congressional criticism by explaining their position regarding the payment of the installments on the Mexican indemnity.

Jan 14   From C.H.S. de la Figanière to William Hunter. LS. NhHi. mDWs. Is recovering from a painful affliction but hopes to be able to see DW in Washington next week.

Jan 14   From Abbott Lawrence. LC. MH–H. mDWs. Curtis, 2: 594–595. Has informed Lord Granville that Crampton would be acceptable as the British representative in the negotiations over Central America.

Jan 14   From Millard Fillmore. ALS. DNA, RG 59. mDW 56716. Asks him to write John M. Clayton regarding Thomas Butler King's account.

Jan 14   Recommendation from Aaron M. Palmer, for the Houston *Beacon*—public printer (ALS. DNA, RG 59. mDW 54450).

Jan 15   To John Middleton Clayton. Copy. DNA, RG 59. mDW 56714. Inquires about Thomas Butler King's claims for reimbursement as a special agent to California.

Jan 15   To Charles Johnson McCurdy. LS. NhHi. mDW 35773. *Diplomatic Papers*, 2. Comments on Kossuth's visit to the U.S.; orders him to assure Austria that the U.S. will not intervene in purely European wars.

Jan 15   From S[olomon] D. Jacobs. Printed LS with MS insertions. DNA, RG 59. mDW 54951. Announces William W. Brown's appointment as postmaster at Boscawen, N.H.

Jan 15   From Abbott Lawrence. ALS. NhD. mDWs. Discusses the problem of the Irish state prisoners now confined to Van Diemen's Land.

Jan 15   From Abbott Lawrence. LC. MH–H. mDWs. Hamilton Andrews
Hill, *Memoir of Abbott Lawrence* (Boston, 1883), pp. 88–90. Comments critically on the rising interventionist spirit in America;
discusses Mexico's troubles and the "Central American Question."

Jan 15   Recommendation from Robert Goodenow, for the Augusta,
Maine *Kennebec Journal*—public printer (ALS. DNA, RG 59. mDW
54407).

Jan 16   To Charles Porter Wright. ALS. MH–H. mDW 35781. *PC*, 2:
504–505. Discusses Marshfield business.

Jan 16   From Sir Henry Lytton Bulwer. ALS. DLC. mDW 35784. Refers
to the resolution of the *Prometheus* affair; reports H.M. government
no longer sees an urgent need to send him to the U.S. to negotiate a
settlement of the Nicaraguan problem.

Jan 16   From Abbott Lawrence. LC. MH–H. mDWs. Reports that many
in Britain fear war with Louis Napoleon; they wonder what assistance the U.S. would provide in case of war.

Jan 17   To Millard Fillmore. AL. NBuHi. mDW 35788. Would be glad
to see him any time before 3 p.m.

Jan 17   To Millard Fillmore. LS. NBuHi. mDW 35790. Advises him to
disregard J[ames] H. Bennett's letter; describes John Payne Todd as
a wastrel and rather disreputable.

Jan 17   To Richard Howes. Copy. NhHi. mDW 35794. *PC*, 2: 505–506.
Recalls their past acquaintanceship; offers to recommend Howes'
appointment as U.S. district judge in southern California.

Jan 17   From William Henry Seward. ALS. DLC. mDW 35798. Reports
that John F. Winder, whom DW has agreed to appoint bearer of
despatches, is planning to leave soon for England.

Jan 17   From Elisha Whittlesey. Presscopy. DLC. mDW 35800. Invites
DW to the annual meeting of the American Colonization Society.

Jan 17   Receipt for $44 paid John M. Donn & Bro. for brackets and
chairs. DS. NhHi. mDW 40592.

Jan 18   To Millard Fillmore. ALS. NBuHi. mDW 35801. *Diplomatic
Papers*, 2. Reports favorable news just received from London concerning the *Prometheus* affair.

Jan 18   To Abbott Lawrence. ALS. MH–H. mDW 35803. Van Tyne, pp.
513–514. Approves Lawrence's handling of the *Prometheus* affair;
discusses the Nicaraguan problem.

Jan 18   From W[illiam] B. Stevens. ALS. DLC. mDW 35810. Sends
birthday congratulations.

[Jan 19]   To Millard Fillmore. LS. NBuHi. mDW 35812. Advises him
not to withhold the message on the Mexican indemnity.

Jan 19   To Lodi Manufacturing Company. Printed extract. NhD. mDW
35814. Declares that his gardener prefers poudrette to guano; orders
ten barrels of the fertilizer.

Jan 19   To [Robert Cumming Schenck]. ALS draft. MHi. mDW 35816.
Asks him to intimate to the Brazilian government that the U.S. government would not be displeased if de Sodre were retained as Brazilian chargé d'affaires at Washington.

Jan 19   To James Wilson. LS. NhHi. mDW 35821. Introduces Edward
Doane.

Jan 19   From Elisha Whittlesey. Presscopy. DLC. mDW 35820. Asks
DW to speak briefly at the meeting of the American Colonization
Society.
Jan 19   Application from D[orson] E. Sykes, for the *Norwich* (Conn.)
Courier—public printer (ALS. DNA, RG 59. mDW 54396).
Jan 20   To Daniel Fletcher Webster. ALS. NN. mDW 35825. Advises
him not to go out until the weather improves.
Jan 21   From John Middleton Clayton. ALS. DNA, RG 59. mDW 56712.
Makes recommendations regarding the payment of the balance
claimed by Thomas Butler King.
Jan 21   From William A. Weeks. ALS. DNA, RG 59 mDW 56902. Re-
ports forwarding despatches to London by the *Cambria*.
Jan 21   Recommendations from S[olomon] D. Jacobs, for the Paris,
Texas *Western Star*—public printer (ALS. DNA, RG 59. mDW
54445); from Christopher H. Williams, for the Jackson *West Ten-
nessee Whig*—public printer (ALS. DNA, RG 59. mDW 54272).
Jan 22   To Thomas Carberry. Printed LS with MS insertions. MH–H.
mDW 35827. Announces Carberry's appointment as justice of the
peace for Washington, D.C.
Jan 22   To Franklin Haven. ALS. MH–H. mDW 35828. Declares it im-
perative that Haven and Ashmun come at once because "things
are not going right here."
Jan 22   From Sir John Fiennes Crampton. ALS. DLC. mDW 35831.
Returns Bulwer's letter.
Jan 22   From Millard Fillmore. ALS. DLC. mDW 35833. Severance,
Fillmore Papers, 1: 361–362. Directs DW to draft a reply to "the
Baltimore committee."
Jan 22   From William A. Weeks. ALS. DNA, RG 59. mDW 56903. Is
planning to forward despatches to London via New York to take
advantage of the steamer schedule.
Jan 23   To Millard Fillmore. LS draft. DLC. mDW 35835. Proposes to
appoint Hardy M. Burton commercial agent at St. Thomas.
Jan 23   From Sir Henry Lytton Bulwer. ALS. DLC. mDW 35837. Curtis,
2: 595–596. Reports Crampton has been named to succeed him as
British minister at Washington, and thinks it a sensible arrangement.
Jan 23   From Sir John Fiennes Crampton. Copy. UkLPR. mDWs. Transmits the Canadian response to Treasury Department instructions
on the assessment of duties, and asks for repeal of the instructions.
Jan 24   To [Benjamin] Seaver. ALS. MHi. mDW 35841. Is mortified at
not seeing Mr. and Mrs. Blanchard; reports a very severe winter in
Washington.
Jan 24   From N[icholas] Callan. ALS. DNA, RG 59. mDW 54963. Accepts appointment as justice of the peace for Washington, D.C.
Jan 24   From Millard Fillmore. AL. DLC. mDW 35844. Severance, *Fillmore Papers*, 1: 362. Asks DW for comments on the attorney general's opinion relative to the removal of territorial judges in
Minnesota.
Jan 24   From Samuel Grubb. ALS. DNA, RG 59. mDW 55010. Accepts
appointment as justice of the peace for Washington, D.C.
Jan 25   To Samuel Jaudon. ALS. NhD. mDW 35846. *Diplomatic Papers*,
2. Thinks "the Commodore" [Perry] ought to have been more as-

sertive of his desire to command the eastern squadron; advises
Perry to see the secretary of the navy.

Jan 26 To Sir John Fiennes Crampton. LS. UkLPR. mDW 35847. States
that a package consigned to H.M. consul at New York will be admitted duty-free.

Jan 26 From Angel Calderon de la Barca. ALS. DLC. mDW 35848.
Reminds DW of a promise for a reply to his note announcing the
liberation of the prisoners (from the Lopez expedition).

Jan 26 From S[imeon] & A[llen] Francis. LS. DNA, RG 59. mDW
54225. Accept appointment of the Springfield *Illinois Journal* to
publish the laws.

Jan 26 From James Shields. ALS. MHi. mDW 35850. Asks DW to grant
an interview to the mother of an Irish patriot.

Jan 27 To Millard Fillmore. LS. NBuHi. mDW 35852. *PC*, 2: 506. Comments on laws regulating the tenure and removal of territorial judges.

Jan 27 From Seth Salisbury. ALS. NhHi. mDW 35855. Encloses the
"address to the Democracy of Bradford County" Pennsylvania; conveys the committee's high regard.

Jan 28 From James Duane Doty. ALS. WHi. mDW 35857. Discusses
law and precedent for the removal of territorial judges.

Jan 28 From William J. McCormick. ALS. DNA, RG 59. mDW 55074.
Accepts appointment as justice of the peace for Washington, D.C.

Jan 28 From William Waters. ALS. DNA, RG 59. mDW 55119. Accepts
appointment as justice of the peace for Washington, D.C.

Jan 29 From William H. Bissell et al. Printed copy. *Congressional Banquet in Honor of George Washington and the Principles of Washington* (Washington, 1852), p. 23. Invite DW to a banquet in honor of
George Washington's birthday.

Jan 29 From Thomas Carberry. ALS. DNA, RG 59. mDW 54969. Acknowledges receipt of his commission as justice of the peace for
Washington, D.C.

Jan 29 From John D. Clark. ALS. DNA, RG 59. mDW 54973. Acknowledges receipt of his commission as justice of the peace for Washington, D.C.

Jan 29 Recommendations from J[oseph] R[ogers] Underwood, for the
Louisville Daily Journal, and the Bowling Green *Kentucky Standard*—public printers (ALS. DNA, RG 59. mDW 54432).

Jan 30 To James Cunningham. LS. DLC. mDWs. States that Calderon
has been asked to intercede for John Cunningham, now imprisoned
in Cuba.

Jan 30 To H. C. Currier. ALS. MSaE. mDW 35862. Refuses an offer of
$8000 for some land, while stating he would have accepted $10,000.

[Jan 30] To William Maxwell Evarts. ALS. NhD. mDW 35863. Invites
him to dinner.

Jan 30 To Chares Porter Wright. ALS. NhHi. mDW 35865. *PC*, 2: 506–
507. Encloses money to pay various Marshfield debts; emphasizes
the need to find cheap labor and asks him to watch cattle prices.

Jan 30 From Edward Everett. ALS. MHi. mDW 35870. Describes the
Count de Gurowski as a perplexing character; advises DW to remain
on friendly terms with Fillmore; comments on rumors from Europe
on Louis Napoleon's territorial ambitions.

Jan 30   From Edward Everett. LC. MHi. mDW 35874. Introduces the
Count A. de Gurowski, a Polish nobleman.

[Jan 30]   From J[oseph] R[ogers] Underwood (enclosure: the Bowling
Green *Kentucky Standard*, Jan 17, 1852). ALS. DNA, RG 59. mDW
54434. Encloses a copy of one of the newspapers the Kentucky
Congressional delegation is recommending to publish the laws.

Jan 31   To Hugh Birckhead.   300

Jan 31   To William Maxwell Evarts. ALS. NhD. mDW 35877. Informs
him that dinner is to be at five o'clock.

[Jan]   From Sir Henry Lytton Bulwer. ALS. DLC. mDW 35889. Is planning to return briefly to Washington to negotiate a settlement of the
Central American problem; warns that Britain is anxious for a
peaceful settlement, providing it is not offensive to her honor and
dignity.

[Jan]   Notes on *Gaines* v. *Relf.* AD. NhD. mDW 35882.

Feb 1   To James Watson Webb. LS. CtY. mDW 35903. Promises to keep
the Shelbyville paper in mind; acknowedges the friendly articles in
'"your paper" (*Courier & Enquirer*); wishes to see Webb and "other
New York friends."

Feb 1   From John Jordan Crittenden. ALS. DNA, RG 59. mDW 54099.
Transmits a letter relative to the appointment of the *Indiana American* to print the laws.

Feb 1   From Charles Porter Wright. ALS. NhHi. mDW 35907. Reports
his wife is recovering slowly; discusses farm business.

Feb 2   From George P. Fisher. Copy. DNA, RG 76. mDWs. Reports on
the proceedings of the commission appointed under the convention
with Brazil.

Feb 2   Recommendation from George Washington Nesmith, for the
Concord *New Hampshire Statesman*—public printer (ALS. DNA,
RG 59. mDW 54403).

Feb 2   Account with Thomas Young for $460 for carriage and harness,
through Mar 13. ADS. NhHi. mDW 40621.

Feb 3   To [Aaron] Woodman and [Charles N.] Black. LS. MiU. mDW
35909. States instructions in the *Hercules* claim case have been sent
to the U.S. chargé d'affaires at Lima.

Feb 3   From John Dickey. ALS. DNA, RG 59. mDW 54979. Acknowledges receipt of his commission as U.S. marshal for western
Pennsylvania.

Feb 3   From Joseph Bradley Varnum, Jr. et al. LS. MHi. mDW 35911.
Invite DW to give an address in New York on Feb 21, on the life
and services of Washington.

Feb 3   Recommendations from Ephraim Hutchins, for the Concord *New
Hampshire Statesman*—public printer (ALS. DNA, RG 59. mDW
54405); from Israel Webster Kelly, for the *New Hampshire Statesman*—public printer (ALS. DNA, RG 59. mDW 54406; from
S[amuel] W. Parker, for the Brookville *Indiana American*—public
printer (ALS. DNA, RG 59. mDW 54093).

Feb 4   From Millard Fillmore. AL. DLC. mDW 35913. Severance, *Fillmore Papers*, 1: 339. Would be glad to see him before the cabinet
meeting.

Feb 4   From Giles M. Hillyer. ALS. DNA, RG 59. mDW 54378. Asks whether the *Natchez* (Miss.) *Courier* should continue publishing the laws.

Feb 4   From William A. Weeks. ALS. DNA, RG 59. mDW 56904. Reports forwarding despatches to London care of J. W. Wilson.

Feb 5   To Thomas Wren Ward et al. Copy. DLC. mDW 35915. Urges them to reconsider their decision to terminate their contract to arrange payment of the last installment on the Mexican indemnity.

Feb 5   From Ambrose Dudley Mann. LS. DNA, RG 59. mDW 56000. Comments on Swiss and French affairs; warns Louis Napoleon may be contemplating conquests in the Western hemisphere.

Feb 6   To Franklin Haven.   301
[Feb 6?]   To Franklin Haven.   302

Feb 6   To [John Lord]. ALS (in Caroline Le Roy Webster's hand). NhD. mDWs. Invites him to dine.

Feb 6   To Edward D. Mansfield. LS. OHi. mDW 35919. Informs him of H.M. government's decision not to establish a consulate in Cincinnati.

Feb 6   From Thomas Corwin (with DW to Crampton, Feb 11, 1852; enclosure: Corwin to Collectors of Customs on the Lake Frontier, Jan 29, 1852). Copy. UkLPR, mDW 35956. Encloses a copy of his order modifying instructions given collectors on the Lake Frontier in November.

Feb 6   From Thomas L. Crittenden. Copy. UkLPR. mDWs. Discusses the murder of John Adams Paine, an American seaman, aboard a British ship.

Feb 6   From Abbott Lawrence. ALS. NhD. mDWs. Reports Granville was much gratified by DW's remembrance; comments on the Nicaraguan problem.

[Feb 6]   From Comte de Sartiges. AL. NhHi. mDW 35923. Presents a portrait of the French president and a bottle of brandy.

[Feb 6]   To Comte de Sartiges. Copy. NhHi. mDW 35920. *Diplomatic Papers*, 2. Accepts a portrait of the French president; suggests "recent transactions in France" reflect "the almost unanimous choice" of the French people.

Feb 7   To John Middleton Clayton. LS. DeHi. mDW 35926. States that a copy of Clayton's letter of Jan 31 accompanies the answer which may be sent to the House of Representatives.

Feb 7   To L[ewis] C[harles] Levin (enclosure: J. B. Gray's promissory note of July 29, 1850). Erwin Lodge, Philadelphia, Pa. mDWs. Asks that J. B. Gray's notes be handed over to an attorney for collection.

Feb 7   To Joseph Bradley Varnum, Jr. Copy. NhHi. mDW 35927. Van Tyne, pp. 512–513. Explains why he declined the invitation of the committee to make a Washington's birthday address in New York.

Feb 7   From Lewis Carbery. ALS. DNA, RG 59. mDW 54967. Acknowledges receipt of his commission as justice of the peace for Washington, D.C.

Feb 7   From Alexander Hugh Holmes Stuart. LS. MH–H. mDW 35929. Asks if John Dickey is in fact U.S. marshal for western Pennsylvania; demands that the department of the interior be kept informed on changes in the judiciary

Feb 7   Recommendations from John S. Newman and S. Meredith, for the *Richmond* (Ind.) *Palladium* and the South Bend, Indiana *St.*

Joseph Valley Register—public printers (ALS by Newman, signed
also by Meredith. DNA, RG 59. mDW 54356).

Feb 8   *From James Watson Webb.*   302

Feb 9   To Millard Fillmore. ALS. NBuHi. mDW 35935. Suggests he invite Sidney Bartlett, a "most eminent lawyer at the Boston Bar,"
and his wife to dinner.

Feb 9   To Millard Fillmore. LS. NBuHi. mDW 35937. Reports that Sidney Bartlett called at the White House but there was no vacant dinner seat for Mrs. Bartlett.

Feb 9   To Ross Wilkins. LS. MiD. mDW 35939. Inquires to determine
if John H. Van Houten might be eligible for a presidential pardon.

Feb 9   From William A. Weeks. ALS. DNA, RG 59. mDW 56905. Reports forwarding despatches just received from London by the New
Haven mail.

Feb 10   To Sir Henry Lytton Bulwer. Copy. DLC. mDW 35941. Curtis,
2 : 596. Expresses high regards for Bulwer, and is glad of Crampton's appointment to succeed him as H.M. minister at Washington;
declares they will begin at once on the Nicaraguan problem.

[Feb 10]   To Millard Fillmore. ALS. NBuHi. mDW 36101. States:
"Thrasher is released."

Feb 10   *To Franklin Haven.*   303

Feb 10   To Abbott Lawrence. LS. MH–H. mDW 35948. Expresses satisfaction with Crampton's appointment as H.M. minister at Washington; thinks he and Lawrence are in substantial agreement on "the
important events of the times."

Feb 10   From Alexander Hamilton Stevens. ALS. DLC. mDW 35950.
Is sending a saddle of venison.

Feb 10   Application from John D. Defrees, for the Indianapolis *Indiana
State Journal*—public printer (ALS. DNA, RG 59. mDW 54301).

Feb 10   Recommendations from W[illis] A. Gorman, for the *Vincennes*
(Ind.) *Gazette*—public printer (ALS. DNA, RG 59. mDW 54303);
from James F. Strother and Addison White, for the *Abingdon
Virginian*—public printer (ALS by Strother, signed also by White.
DNA, RG 59. mDW 54252).

Feb 10   Report of secretary of state communicating the report of the
board of commissioners on claims against Mexico, in answer to a
Senate resolution of Feb 7, 1852. AD. DNA, RG 46. mDW 52033.

Feb 11   To Sir John Fiennes Crampton. LS. UkLPR. mDW 35952. States
that the president will receive Crampton's official letters tomorrow.

Feb 11   To Sir John Fiennes Crampton (enclosure: Corwin to DW, Feb.
6, 1852). LS. UkLPR. mDW 35954. Returns the reply of the secretary of the treasury to Canadian requests for the repeal of customs
regulations recently established for the Lake Frontier.

Feb 11   *To James Watson Webb.*   304

Feb 11   To Charles Porter Wright. Copy. MHi. mDW 35964. Considers
selling some oxen to pay outstanding bills.

Feb 11   From Samuel Bowles & Co. LS by proxy. DNA, RG 59. mDW
54223. Accept appointment to publish the laws in the *Springfield*
(Mass.) *Republican*.

Feb 11   From E[benezer] B[rewer] Foster & Co. LS. DNA, RG 59. mDW
54221. Accept appointment of the *Boston Courier* to publish the laws.

Feb 12   To Sidney Bartlett. ALS. NhD. mDW 35966. Invites Bartlett and his wife to breakfast.

Feb 12   To Richard Milford Blatchford. ALS. NhD. mDWs. *PC*, 2: 507. Will act according to Blatchford's suggestions; plans to be at the Astor on Feb 21.

Feb. 12   To [Franklin Haven]. ALS. MH–H. mDW 35968. Reports Ashmun has reached Washington at last; plans to be in New York on Feb. 21.

Feb 12   To Charles Porter Wright. ALS. NhHi. mDW 35969. *PC*, 2: 507. Asks Wright to come to New York if he can.

Feb 12   Recommendation from Aaron M. Palmer, for the *Chicago Commercial Advertiser*—public printer (ALS. DNA, RG 59. mDW 54297).

Feb 12   Account with C. Miller for $147.68 for provisions, through Apr 27. AD. NhHi. mDW 40610.

Feb 13   To Sir John Fiennes Crampton. AL. UkLPR. mDW 35971. States that Fillmore will receive him tomorrow; asks to see an advance copy of any address Crampton plans to make on the occasion.

Feb 13   To F. C. Stainback. ALS (for telegraphic transmittal). NjP. mDW 35972. Comments briefly on the effects of railroads.

Feb 13   From Abbott Lawrence. IC. MH–H. mDWs. Reports "Despotism is now in the ascendant"; discusses the U.S. trade imbalance with Europe.

Feb 14   To Thomas Birch Florence. LS. NhD. mDWs. Transmits papers concerning the death in Costa Rica of James Chase, an American citizen.

Feb 14   From John T. Bush. LS. DNA, RG 59. mDW 54955. Acknowledges receipt of his commission as U.S. marshal for northern New York.

Feb 14   From Sir John Fiennes Crampton. ALS. DLC. mDW 35973. Submits a copy of the address he plans to present to the president, and asks for critical comment.

Feb 14   From Holloway & Davis. LS. DNA, RG 59. mDW 54217. Accept appointment of the *Richmond* (Ind.) *Palladium* to publish the laws.

Feb 15   To Millard Fillmore. ALS. NBuHi. mDW 35976. Warns there may be opposition to [John] Curry's nomination for judge in California.

Feb 15   From Alexander Wilkin. ALS. DNA, RG 59. mDW 55131. Accepts appointment as secretary of Minnesota Territory.

Feb 15   From Charles Porter Wright. ALS. NhHi. mDW 35979. Discusses the marketing of cattle; cannot come to New York because of his wife's poor health.

Feb 16   To Edward Everett. LS. MHi. mDW 35983. Asks if Everett objects to an allusion to his projected social history of Rome in DW's address before the New-York Historical Society.

Feb 16   To Millard Fillmore. LS. NBuHi. mDW 35987. *PC*, 2: 508. Plans delivering a non-political address before the New-York Historical Society.

Feb 16   To Rufus W. Griswold. LS. MB. mDW 35990. Will be able to attend the commemoration of "Mr. [James Fenimore] Cooper's life and genius."

Feb 16   To C[olin] M[acrae] Ingersoll. LS. MBU. mDW 35991. Reports

that the State Department will begin distributing the first installment of the Portuguese indemnity once the money reaches the
bankers of the U.S. government in London.

Feb 16   From Schuyler Colfax. ALS. DNA, RG 59. mDW 54219. Accepts
appointment of the South Bend, Indiana *St. Joseph Valley Register*
to publish the laws.

Feb 17   To Sir John Fiennes Crampton. LS. UkLPR. mDW 35992. Promises the case of the schooner *Prince of Wales* will be given immediate attention.

Feb 17   To Sarah Weston Gales Seaton. Printed. Josephine Seaton, *William Winston Seaton of the "National Intelligencer"* (Boston,
1871), pp. 306–307. Thanks her for salt beef.

Feb 17   From Daniel Dewey Barnard. LC. N. mDWs. Reports more
cordiality from Baron Prokesch, Austrian minister at Berlin, perhaps indicating a change of feeling at Vienna toward the U.S.; says
his health is bad and he may be forced to go to Italy.

Feb 17   From Abbott Lawrence. LC. MH–H. mDWs. Has made informal
application to Granville for the release of the prisoners in Van
Dieman's Land.

Feb 17   Recommendation from Edward Stanly and J[oseph] P. Caldwell,
for the Salisbury, North Carolina *Carolina Watchman*—public
printer (ALS by Stanly, signed also by Caldwell. DNA, RG 59. mDW
54264).

Feb 17   Opinion on presidential power to remove territorial judges.
Draft. NhHi. mDW 35993.

[Feb 18]   To Millard Fillmore. LS. NBuHi. mDW 36099. Encloses despatches just received from Letcher; will send the proposal for a
new treaty once it has been translated.

Feb 18   From Edward Everett. ALS. MHi. mDW 36003. Is writing a
study of international law, not a social history of Rome as DW
thought; has finished the last proofs of the index to DW's *Works*.

Feb 18   From [Abbott Lawrence]. Draft. DLC. mDW 36007. Writes regarding the settlement of American claims against the British
government and British claims against the U.S.

Feb 18   From Thomas Ritchie. ALS. DLC. mDW 36012. Requests the
loan of Governor Pownall's "Three Memorials addressed to the
Sovereigns of Europe and America."

Feb 18   From William A. Weeks. ALS. DNA, RG 59. mDW 56906. Reports entrusting despatches to the U.S. legation at London to W.
Newhall's care.

Feb 18   Application from Perry & Elford, for the Greenville, South Carolina *Southern Patriot*—public printer (LS. DNA, RG 59. mDW
54342).

Feb 19   To William H. Bissell et al. Printed copy. *Congressional Banquet in Honor of George Washington and the Principles of Washington* (Washington, 1852), p. 23. Underscores Washington's
principles of non-interference in the internal affairs of other
countries.

Feb 19   To Millard Fillmore. LS. NBuHi. mDW 36015. Comments on a
judicial appointment in California and the appointment of a mail
agent at New York; states that Hunter will handle any communications from Mexico.

Feb 19   To Millard Fillmore. ALS. NBuHi. mDW 36018. Thinks Z. Collins Lee is highly qualified to be U.S. district judge for Maryland.

Feb 19   To Millard Fillmore. ALS. NBuHi. mDW 36021. Advises Fillmore not to act hastily in appointing a successor to Judge [Upton S.] Heath of Maryland.

Feb 19   To William L. Hodge. ALS. Universität Bremen Bibliothek. mDWs. Reminds him "to return no answer to Mr. Hunter till my return" to Washington.

Feb 19   To Charles Henry Thomas (with ANS by William S. Russell regarding the deed of trust for Caroline Le Roy Webster). ALS. MHi. mDW 36023. Asks him to determine if the deed of trust for Caroline was properly recorded.

Feb 19   From Ambrose Dudley Mann. LS. DNA, RG 59. mDW 56016. Reports Louis Napoleon is threatening Switzerland and may even attempt an invasion of the United States; discusses the dangers of absolutism in Europe; warns that America and its people are not held in high esteem by the French.

Feb 20   From John H. Aulick. LS. DNA, RG 59. mDW 56356. Acknowledges the receipt of various documents from the state department.

Feb 20   From Edward Everett. ALS. MHi. mDW 36027. Submits a copy of his letter to DW of Feb 18 in case the original should have missed him in Washington.

Feb 21   From Robert R. Coleman et al. (enclosures: printed invitation; printed copy of the Maine liquor law). LS. DLC. mDW 36031. Asks DW for remarks to be delivered or read at a meeting opposing the enactment by New York of legislation similar to the "Maine Liquor Law."

Feb 21   From Henry Grinnell. ALS. NhHi. mDW 36044. Encloses letters from Lady [Jane] Franklin, and asks whether they ought to be delivered.

[Feb 21]   From Augustus N. Le Roy. ALS. NhHi. mDW 36046. States that "Dr. Haight" will be preaching tomorrow, and offers the use of his pews; sends two bottles of Madeira wine.

Feb 21   From E[llen] S[pence]. ALS. DLC. mDW 36048. Describes herself as a widow in desperate straits; asks DW for a loan or at least advice.

[Feb 22?]   To Jonathan Prescott Hall. Printed. *PC*, 2: 508–509. Discusses the American turkey.

Feb 22   From Felix Sanierski. ALS. NhHi. mDW 36051. Discusses Poland.

Feb 23   From [?]. AL. NhHi. mDW 36055. Reports a political conversation with the editor of the *Baltimore American*; considers the choice of a successor to Judge Upton Heath.

[Feb pre-23]   From George Ticknor. Dictated notes with autograph insertions. NhD. mDW 36104. Replies to DW's questions about historians and the nature of history (for DW's use in his Feb 23 speech before the New-York Historical Society); includes, in Ticknor's hand, a note of Herodotus by Cornelius Conway Felton (mDWs).

[Feb] 23   Speech to the New-York Historical Society. Incomplete draft. CtY. mDW 32635.

[Feb 23]   Speech to the New-York Historical Society. Corrected proofs. CtY. mDW 32740. *Speeches and Formal Writings*, 2.

Feb 24   To George Ticknor. ALS. NhD. mDW 36059. Comments on his
address to the New-York Historical Society, especially acknowledges
his indebtedness to Ticknor and Cornelius Conway Felton for help
in its preparation.

Feb 24   From Edward Everett. LC. MHi. mDW 36060. Comments on
DW's speech to the New York Historical Society; Hale's statement
in the *Advertiser* on the Story correspondence; and Palmerston's
view of British relations with the U.S.

Feb 24   From Charles Wainwright March.   304

Feb 24   From M[atthew] Newkirk et al. LS. DLC. mDW 36065. Invite
DW to repeat his lecture to the New-York Historical Society in
Philadelphia.

Feb 24   Recommendations from Amory Holbrook, for the Oregon City
Oregon Spectator and the Portland *Weekly Oregonian*—public
printers (LS. DNA, RG 59. mDW 54425).

Feb 25   To Edward Everett. Telegram. MHi. mDW 32767. "Your letter
& the Advertiser received this morning."

Feb 25   To Millard Fillmore (enclosure: Everett to DW, [Feb, 1852],
extract). LS. NBuHi. mDW 36067. *PC*, 2: 510. States that Everett's
comments on Palmerston are "strictly true."

Feb 26   From Sir John Fiennes Crampton. Copy. UkLPR. mDWs. Draws
DW's attention to a claim arising from the seizure of the British
vessel *Lady Shaw Stewart* on Apr 9, 1851, at San Francisco.

Feb 26   From Edward Everett. ALS. MHi. mDW 36076. Fears Kossuth
may create more trouble; suggests using extracts from Mann's despatches to show how far the U.S. went in supporting Kossuth's
government.

Feb 26   From Hiram Ketchum. ALS. MHi. mDW 36080. Introduces
James T. Henry, editor of the (Ellicottville?) *Whig & Union*, published in Cattaraugus County, New York.

Feb 26   From "Stat Nominis Umbra." ALS. NhHi. mDW 36082. Van
Tyne, pp. 514–515. States confidentially that a decision in the
Gaines case can be expected Monday (Mar. 1).

Feb 26   Application from Dobbin, Murphy, & Bose, for the *Baltimore
American*—public printer (LS. DNA, RG 59. mDW 54394).

Feb 26   Recommendation from F. Madera, for the Morgantown, Virginia
Monongalia Mirror—public printer (ALS. DNA, RG 59. mDW
54387).

Feb 27   To Beebe & Co. Copy. DLC. mDW 36085. Acknowledges their
gift of a hat.

Feb 27   To Millard Fillmore. LS. NBuHi. mDW 36088. *Diplomatic Papers*, 2. Discusses the Tehuantepec Treaty; suggests alternative
propositions for pushing the negotiations ahead.

Feb 27   To [Justina?] Van Rensselaer. Draft. CtY. mDW 36094. Fur-
nishes her with a letter to the U.S. consul at Havana.

Feb 27   From Sir John Fiennes Crampton. Copy. UkLPR. mDWs. Calls
DW's attention to the case of the *Confidence*, run down by the U.S.
frigate *Constitution*.

Feb 28   To B[enjamin] F. Butler. LS. N. mDW 36097. Reminds Butler
of his promise to send a book containing an essay on Gray's Elegy.

Feb 28   From Jacob Chamberlin (with DW to Corwin, [c. Mar. 1,

1852]). ALS. DLC. mDW 36116. Recommends that specific rates replace the ad valorem duties established under the present tariff.

Feb 28   From Daniel Dewey Barnard. LC. N. mDWs. Writes at length
on the prospects for the expansion of democracy in Europe, strongly
criticizing the revolutionary movements as an obstacle to the progress of reform.

Feb 28   Account with Alfred Lee for $4.40 for oats and corn, through
May 30. AD. NhHi. mDW 40603.

[c. Feb]   To John Lord from DW et al. LS. NhD. mDWs. Invite Lord to
give a course of lectures on "the Saints & Heroes of the Middle
Ages."

[Feb–March]   To [William L. Sharkey]. Draft. DLC. mDW 38114. Discusses the Thrasher case, with particular emphasis on the proper
national allegiance of Americans who have established residence in
Cuba.

March 1   To B[enjamin] F. Butler. LS. N. mDW 36114. Returns a book
containing an essay on Gray's Elegy.

[c. March 1]   To Thomas Corwin (with Jacob Chamberlin to DW Feb
28, 1852). LS. DLC. mDW 36115. Encloses a letter discussing tariff
duties.

[March 1]   To [Edward Curtis?] ALS. NN. mDW 36113. Agrees that
"People here [New York] would not listen to any body a second who
should propose a No. 2."

March 1   To Franklin Haven. ALS. MH–H. mDW 36118. PC, 2: 510.
Reports things are looking well in New York; insists that Choate
must come.

March 1   From Robert Balmanno. ALS. MH–H. mDW 36120. Transmits
a list of the subscribers to the testimonial for Mary Clarke; reports
the recent discovery of a Shakespeare folio.

March 1   From Charles Johnson McCurdy (enclosure: extracts from
Henry A. Holmes to McCurdy, July 4, 1851, and reply, Aug 9, 1851).
ALS. NhD. mDW 36121. Reports an interview with Prince Schwarzenburg; comments on Kossuth's request that the U.S. assist his
family.

[March 2]   To Franklin Haven. ALS. MH–H. mDW 36128. Wants
Choate to be in New York by Friday (Mar 5); asks Haven to write
every day.

March 3   From a Compromise Whig. ALS. NhHi. mDW 36130. Accuses
U.S. marshal William Irwin of leading a pro-Scott intrigue in Pennsylvania; urges Irwin's removal from office.

March 3   From Grafton Baker. ALS. DNA, RF 59. mDW 54364. Encloses
letters relative to the appointment of public printers for the federal
government in Mississippi.

March 3   From William A. Weeks. ALS. DNA, RG 59. mDW 56907.
Reports forwarding despatches to London by the *Cambria*.

[c. March 4]   To Thomas Corwin (with Jacob Chamberlin to DW, Feb
28, 1852). LS. DLC. mDW 36115. Elcloses a letter discussing tariff
duties.

March 4   To [James Diament] Westcott. ALS. NNPM. mDW 36134. Invites him to dinner.

March 4   From Charles James Lanman. ALS. NhD. mDW 36135. Reports on an informal meeting of delegates to the Connecticut state

Whig convention, and on sentiment for DW's nomination for president.

March 4 From Ambrose Dudley Mann. ALS. DNA, RG 59. mDW 56029. Reports that Switzerland is refusing to submit to French extradition demands, and may be threatened by an attack from France; thinks Louis Napoleon suffered a set-back in the recent French elections.

March 4 From Luke P. Poland. DS. DNA, RG 59. mDW 56924. Warrant for the extradition of John Cole.

March 4 Application from Babcock & Wildman, for the *New Haven Palladium*—public printer (LS. DNA, RG 59. mDW 54400).

March 4 Report of the secretary of state, accompanied by lists of clerks and other persons employed in the department during 1851 and the amount paid to each. DS. DNA, RG 46. mDW 52041.

March 4 Report of the secretary of state showing disbursements for the year ending June 30, 1851. DS. DNA, RG 46. mDW 52045.

March 5 To William W. Corcoran. ALS. DLC. mDW 36142. *A Grandfather's Legacy; containing a sketch of this life and obituary notices of some members of his family, together with letters from his friends* (Washington, 1879), p. 105. Sends him "a bit of the loin of a moose deer."

March 5 To Millard Fillmore. ALS. NBuHi. mDW 36144. Reports Crampton has not yet called and may have been disturbed by the news from England.

March 5 To Peter Harvey. Copy. NhHi. mDW 36146. Van Tyne, p. 516. Thinks Scott is pulling away from "his native Americanism"; regards tonight's meeting in New York as crucial.

March 5 To William Henry Seward. LS. NRU. mDW 36148. Reports no progress has been made in adjusting the claims of Waldron and Smyley against the Buenos Ayres government.

March 5 To Elisha Whittlesey. LS. DNA, RG 217. mDW 57215. States that an authenticated copy of Brigham Young's oath as governor of Utah was filed at the state department in September, 1851.

March 5 To Charles Porter Wright. ALS. NhD. mDW 36149. *PC*, 2: 510. Discusses the marketing of oxen and the importance of sturdy sheep-tight fences.

March 5 Recommendation from Edward Everett, for Francis Lieber— U.S. chargé d'affaires in Switzerland (ALS. MHi. mDW 36155).

March 6 To Dr. [?] Baldwin. AN. MWA. mDW 36159. Agrees to see Baldwin at the state department today.

[March 6] To Millard Fillmore. ALS. NBuHi. mDW 36160. Asks for "Mr. [Hugh] Birckhead's letter."

March 6 From Dobbin, Murphy, & Bose. LS. DNA, RG 59. mDW 54213. Accept appointment of the *Baltimore American* to publish the laws.

March 7 To Millard Fillmore. ALS. NBuHi. mDW 36166. Reports no despatches or newspapers have been received from London dated after Feb 20, the night of the debate that caused the defeat and resignation of the ministry.

[March 7] To George Kent. Printed extract. MH–H. mDWs. Recalls Kent's late father.

March 8 To Millard Fillmore. ALS. NBuHi. mDW 36169. Sends over a letter received from Lady [Jane] Franklin.

March 8 To [William Cabell Rives]. Copy. DLC. mDW 36171. Reports

complaints that passages in Rives's despatches amount to meddling
in French domestic affairs; directs him to assure the French government that nothing disrespectful was intended or implied.

March 8   From Edward Everett.   305

March 8   From Joseph W. Furbur. ALS. DNA, RG 59. mDW 55000.
Accepts appointment as U.S. marshal for Minnesota.

March 8   From James K. Harper. ALS. DNA, RG 59. mDW 54215. Accepts appointment of the *Centreville* (Md.) *Times* to publish the
laws.

March 8   From Royal Phelps. ALS. NhHi. mDW 36179. Presents a bag
of coffee and makes suggestions for the brewing.

March 8   From Webster Woodman. ALS. NBuHi. mDWs. With the support of Boston merchants, seeks appointment as consul in
Constantinople.

March 8   From Charles Porter Wright (with marginal notes in reply).
ALS. NhHi. mDW 36182. *PC*, 2: 511–513. Discusses farm business.

March 9   To Charles M[ynn] Conrad. LS. NhD. mDWs. Copy. DNA, RG
107. mDWs. Writes in support of N[athan] A. M. Dudley's applica-
cation for an Army commission.

March 9   Recommendation from J[onathan] Meredith, for J[ohn] Glen—
U.S. district judge for Maryland (ALS copy. NcD. mDW 36186).

March 10   To Phoebe Coleman. ALS. ViU. mDW 36190. Lanman, p.
134. Sends his autograph.

March 10   To Millard Fillmore. ALS. NBuHi. mDW 36191. Knows of
no necessity for a consul or commercial agent at Quebec.

March 10   From Samuel Appleton Appleton (enclosure: press clipping).
ALS. MHi. mDW 36193. Discusses miscellaneous business; says the
children are writing to Caroline.

March 10   From John Arnold Rockwell. ALS. CSmH. mDW 36195.
Submits evidence in support of the *Louisa Beaton* claim against
England.

March 10   From [?] de Saint Anthoine. Printed LS. NhHi. mDW 36202.
Offers DW honorary membership in the Institut d'Afrique.

March 10   From Lund Washington. ALS. DNA, RG 59. mDW 55117.
Accepts appointment as justice of the peace for Washington, D.C.

March 11   To William Scott Haynes. Copy. DNA, RG 217. mDW 57244.
Explains what funding is available to finance the return home of
members of the Lopez expedition recently freed from imprisonment
in Spain.

March 11   From Nathan Kelsey Hall. LC. DNA, RG 28. mDW 57067.
Requests a copy of the recently enacted law for the relief of Rufus
Divinel.

March 11   From [?]. AL incomplete. CtY. mDW 36203. Complains that
a state department agent has refused to pay an account DW had
previously approved.

March 11   Senate confirmation of nominations for Indian agents. Copy.
DNA, RG 59. mDW 55167.

March 12   To Millard Fillmore. LS. NBuHi. mDW 36205. Promises that
Fillmore's suggestions on Oregon will be given immediate attention.

March 12   To David A. Neal. Printed. *National Intelligencer*, March 13,
1852. *W & S*, 16: 647–648. Comments on the Illinois Central Railroad and its land grant.

March 12   To Elisha Whittlesey. LS. DNA, RG 217. mDW 57216. Approves the rules proposed by Whittlesey applying to the settlement of claims on behalf of individuals captured on the Lopez expedition and imprisoned in Spain.

March 12   To Elisha Whittlesey. LS. DNA, RG 217. mDW 57242. Encloses a list of prisoners from the Lopez expedition who were sent to Spain.   307

March 12   From John Pendleton Kennedy.

March 12   From Alexander Hugh Holmes Stuart. LS. DNA, RG 59. mDW 55166. Requests the issuance of commissions for individuals whose nominations were recently confirmed by the Senate.

March 13   To Edward Belknap. Copy. CaOOA. mDW 36208. *Diplomatic Papers*, 2. Thinks U.S. treaties with Britain and New Grenada will afford ample protection for Belknap's projected trans-isthmian canal.

March 13   To Sir John Fiennes Crampton (enclosure: DW to Foxhall A. Parker, Mar 13, 1852). LS. UkLPR. mDW 36211. Encloses a copy of the orders to be sent Commodore Parker regarding the pacification of Greytown.

March 13   To Edward Everett.   308

March 13   To Foxhall A. Parker (with DW to Crampton, March 13, 1852). Copy. UkLPR. mDW 36212. Orders him to cooperate with the British naval commander in maintaining law and order at Greytown.

March 13   To John Taylor. ALS. NhHi. mDW 36218. Lyman, *Life and Memorials of DW* (New York, 1853), 2: 256–258. Quotes verses from Virgil which are suggestive of Elms Farm and Taylor's work.

March 13   From Sir John Fiennes Crampton. Copy. UkLPR. mDWs. Requests the extradition of William Henry Barrett, charged with forgery.

March 13   From John Jordan Crittenden. ALS. DNA, RG 59. mDW 54380. Reminds DW of his promise to appoint Henri F. Middleton of the Shelbyville, Kentucky *Shelby News* to publish the laws.

March 13   Recommendations from James Abercrombie, for the Huntsville, Alabama *Southern Advocate*—public printer (ALS. DNA, RG 59. mDW 54069); from Jeremiah Clemens, for the *Southern Advocate*—public printer (ALS. DNA, RG 59. mDW 54069).

March 13   Bill from William Wall for $5 for a frock coat. AD. NhHi. mDW 40606.

March 14   From W. A. Black et al. ALS by Black, signed also by others. DLC. mDW 36222. Announce DW's election to honorary membership in the Euphemian Society of Erskine College, South Carolina.

March 14   Application from S[amuel] Stokely—U.S. district judge for southern California, or governor of Utah Territory (ALS. DLC. mDW36138).

March 15   To G[eorge] W. McCleary. LS. Ia–Ar. mDW 36224. Asks him to authenticate the signature of Henry M. Salmon, notary public of Lee County, Iowa.

March 15   From Franklin S. Myers. ALS. DNA, RG 59. mDW 55060. Accepts appointment as justice of the peace for Washington, D.C.

March 15   From John Taylor.   309

March 15   From Robert Charles Winthrop. Printed extract. Robert

Winthrop, Jr., *A Memoir of Robert C. Winthrop* (Boston, 1897), p. 152. States he has uniformly denied published insinuations that DW consulted him before delivering the 7th of March speech; declares that in his own speech on Feb 21 in support of General Taylor he believed he was expressing himself in conformity with DW's views; takes exception to DW's reported remarks, finding that he is "under some misapprehension as to what occurred *before*, and what *after*, the 7th of March, 1850."

March 15   Recommendation from E[benezer] J[enckes] Penniman, for the *Detroit Daily Advertiser*—public printer (ALS. DNA, RG 59. mDW 54299).

March 16   To Sir John Fiennes Crampton. LS. UkLPR. mDW 36229. Reports a warrant has been issued preliminary to the extradition of William Henry Barrett to England for trial on a forgery charge.

March 16   To John Jordan Crittenden. LS. DNA, RG 60. mDWs. Requests the attorney general's opinion of an act of New Mexico on the holding of district courts.

[March 16]   To Millard Fillmore. ALS. NBuHi. mDW 36231. Advises writing to [Charles] Pearce at Elkton, Maryland (relative to the appointment of a U.S. district judge for Maryland).

[March 16]   To Millard Fillmore. Copy. NhHi. mDW 36688. ALS. UkLPR. mDW 36242. Van Tyne, pp. 483–484. Describes Crampton's reaction to the news from Greytown.

March 16   To H. B. Johnston. Draft. CtY. mDW 36233. Sends his autograph; emphasizes his life-long commitment to the Union.

March 16   From Amos Bacon. ALS. NhHi. mDW 36235. Offers advice to presidential candidates.

March 16   From James Points. ALS. DNA, RG 59. mDW 55076. Accepts appointment as U.S. marshal for western Virginia.

March 16   Recommendations from William R. W. Cobb, for the Huntsville, Alabama *Southern Advocate*—public printer (ALS. DNA, RG 59. mDW 54064); from Calvin Colton, for Charles S. J. Goodrich— U.S. consul at Genoa (ALS. OGK. mDW 36237).

March 17   To Sir John Fiennes Crampton. LS. UkLPR. mDW 36238. States that wine consigned to H.M. consul at New York will be admitted duty-free.

March 17   To Millard Fillmore. LS. NBuHi. mDW 36239. Is busy with Mexico and Nicaragua; hopes he will not be needed at "the meeting of the Gentlemen."

March 17   To Millard Fillmore. ALS. NN. mDW 36246. Recommends that [John] Glenn's nomination (U.S. district judge for Maryland) be sent to the Senate today.

March 17   To John Taylor.   309

March 17   From Sir John Fiennes Crampton. Copy. UkLPR. Requests that the U.S. equalize duties on coffee and tea imported indirectly from Great Britain and directly from the West Indies.

March 17   From Millard Fillmore. ALS. NNPM. mDW 36254. Returns Letcher's letter and Slacum's reports; asks that the accompanying depositions be authenticated by the district attorney.

March 17   From Samuel F. Train. Telegram. DNA, RG 45. mDWs. "Purser Ashmun from Massachusetts is dead. Cannot my application be now secured."

March 17   From R[ichard] Van Dien. ALS. DLC. mDW 36256. Describes the design of a steel plate and invites DW to subscribe for copies.

March 17   From William A. Weeks. ALS. DNA, RG 59. mDW 56908. Reports forwarding despatches to London by the *America* in care of Henry Tomes.

March 18   To Millard Fillmore. LS. NBuHi. mDW 36259. *Diplomatic Papers*, 2. Submits a revised draft of the Vega letter; thinks the U.S. must convince Mexico's "very unreasonable and unreliable" government of America's earnestness.

March 18   To William Alexander Graham. Copy. UkLPR. mDWs. Issues orders to the American naval commander at Greytown to warn a group of American settlers of the serious consequences of their application to the Nicaraguan government for guarantees of protection.

March 18   From George Griswold. LS. NhHi. mDW 36262. *W & S*, 16: 655. Offers to pay DW an additional $1000 should the U.S. district court decide in favor of Goodyear's patent.

March 18   From W[illiam] B[erkeley] Lewis. ALS. NhD. mDW 36268. Requests a copy of DW's address to the New-York Historical Society; relates an anecdote of the Webster-Hayne debate of 1830.

March 18   From Ambrose Dudley Mann (enclosures: press clippings; Report of the Swiss government to the Swiss chargé d'affaires at Paris, Mar 18, 1852). LS. DNA, RG 59. mDW 56032. Reports on French and Swiss affairs.

March 18   Application from Henry Washington Hilliard—U.S. chargé d'affaires in Switzerland (ALS. NhD. mDW 36264).

March 18   Recommendation from Lyman D. Stickney, for the *Weekly Evansville* (Ind.) *Journal*—public printer (ALS. DNA, RG 59. mDW 54062).

[c. March 19]   To John Jordan Crittenden. ALS. NcD. mDW 38119. States that Crittenden's "man at Shelbyville" has been appointed public printer; asks if he has considered the "abstraction of papers."

March 19   To G[reer] B. Duncan. Press Copy. MsBB. mDWs. Praises Duncan's handling of the *Gaines* case.

March 19   To Philip Ricard Fendall. LS. NcD. mDW 36271. Reports Fillmore is worried about the Gardiner indictments; asks for a list of witnesses whose testimony is needed.

March 19   To Millard Fillmore. LS. NBuHi. mDW 36273. *PC*, 2: 517. Sees little in Fillmore's letter to Arista which requires alteration, and thinks it will be effective.

March 19   From Thomas Aspden. ALS. DLC. mDW 36275. Solicits DW's professional services in the litigation of the Matthius Aspden estate.

March 19   From Philip Ricard Fendall. LS. DNA, RG 60. mDWs. Lists the witnesses for the United States whose testimony will be required in the Gardiner cases.

March 19   From George Kent. ALS. DLC. mDW 36277. Is still searching for an article DW requested; acknowledges DW's remembrances of himself and his parents; hopes DW will be elected president.

March 19   From Abbott Lawrence. LC. MH–H. mDWs. Will pursue the release of the Van Dieman's Land prisoners until a final decision is reached.

March 19   From A[aron] N[ichols] Skinner. ALS. CtY. mDW 36280.

Asks Ebenezer Seeley be given a letter of introduction to some prominent individual in London.

March 19   From Daniel Fletcher Webster. ALS. NhHi. mDW 36281. Reports the "same old [Massachusetts State Whig] committee is chosen"; mentions his own "controversial correspondence" with Philip Greely, Jr.

March 19   From William A. Weeks. ALS. DNA, RG 59. mDW 56910. Reports forwarding by land mail despatches just received from London.

March 20   A[lbert] H. Almy to Nathan Kelsey Hall (with Hall to DW, Mar 24, 1852). ALS. DLC. mDW 36318. Thinks J. W. White is entitled to something from the Fillmore Administration for past political services.

March 20   From Boswell & Faxon. LS. DNA, RG 59. mDW 54209. Accept appointment of the *Hartford Daily Courant* to publish the laws.

March 20   From a Californian (enclosure: press clipping). ALS. NhHi. mDW 36285. Demands that something be done to stop the influx of criminals into San Francisco.

March 20   From William C. Conant. ALS. DNA, RG 59. mDW 54211. Accepts appointment to publish the laws in the Rutland *Vermont Union Whig*.

March 21   From William Hunter. ALS. NhD. mDW 36287. Reports Fillmore has approved DW's alteration of the letter to Arista; calls Slacum entirely unfit for the mission to Mexico.

March 21   From Alexander Hugh Holmes Stuart. ALS. DNA, RG 59. mDW 54384. Agrees that the *Winchester* (Va.) *Republican* would be suitable for appointment to publish the laws.

March 22   To Richard Milford Blatchford. Printed. *PC*, 2: 518–519. Sends condolences on the death of Blatchford's daughter.

March 22   To Millard Fillmore. LS. NhD. mDWs. Encloses a letter written in support of George D. Parker's application for a midshipman's warrant.

March 22   To Charles Porter Wright. LS. NhHi. mDW 36291. *PC*, 2: 518. Proposes the construction of a small house to rent; makes suggestions for manuring and planting.

March 22   From Dick H. Austin et al. LS. DLC. mDW 36295. Announce DW's election to honorary membership in the Madison Literary Society of Madison College.

March 22   From N[athan] S[ydney] Beman (enclosure: press clippings). ALS. John R. Morison, Petersborough, N.H. mDW 36297. Inquires about the truth of reports that Protestant missionaries have been barred by treaty from Indian territory in Oregon.

March 22   From Harris, Fairbanks & Co. LS. DNA, RG 59. mDW 54203. Accept appointment of the *Cleveland Herald* to publish the laws.

March 22   From Charles Edwards Lester. ALS. DLC. mDW 36303. Asks if Charles S. J. Goodrich can expect appointment to a consulate in France or the Mediterranean area.

March 22   From Ambrose Dudley Mann. ALS. DNA, RG 59. mDW 56045. Reports France is increasing its defense expenditures, and suggests the U.S. strengthen its steam navy; warns the United States to beware of Louis Napoleon.

March 22   From Joseph F. Randolph et al., members of the legislature
and bar of New Jersey. LS. CtY. mDWs. Trenton Historical Society,
A History of Trenton: 1679–1929 (Princeton, 1929), p. 634. Invite
DW to a public dinner in his honor.
March 22   From John S. Warden. ALS. DLC. mDW 36306. Calls for
contributions from honorary members of the Euphemian Literary
Society of Mount Pleasant College.
March 22   From A[ndrew] C. Wright. ALS. DNA, RG 59. mDW 54196.
Accepts appointment to publish the laws in the Meredith Bridge,
New Hampshire *Belknap Gazette.*
March 22   Bill from W. J. Page for $24.03 for potatoes and freight on
the Connecticut & Passumpsic Railroad. AD. NhHi. mDW 40601.
March 23   To Franklin Haven. LS. MH–H. mDW 36308. Asks Haven to
look after some financial business.
March 23   From Sir John Fiennes Crampton. Copy. UkLPR. mDWs. Sub-
mits the claim of the owners of the brig *Confidence.*
March 23   From Jermain & Brother. LS. DNA, RG 59. mDW 54194.
Accept appointment of the Adrian *Michigan Expositor* to publish the
laws.
March 23   From Richard B. Kimball. ALS. CtY. mDW 36311. Requests
letters of introduction and, if possible, a courier's passport.
March 23   Application from Alexander H. Thacher—a position (ALS.
DLC. mDW 36313).
March 24   To Joseph F. Randall et al. Printed. *W & S*, 16: 642. De-
clines their invitation to a public dinner in Trenton.
March 24   From Dunckler, Wales & Co. LS. DNA, RG 59. mDW 54205.
Accept appointment of the *Detroit Daily Advertiser* to publish the
laws.
March 24   From P[eter] C. Ellmaker et al. LS. DLC. mDW 36315. Invite
DW to the anniversary dinner of the "Washington Grays" of
Philadelphia.
March 24   From [Nathan Kelsey Hall] (with A[lbert] H. Almy to Hall,
Mar 20, 1852). AN. DLC. mDW 36317. Submits a letter calling at-
tention to the political claims of J. W. White.
March 24   From Henri F. Middleton. ALS. DNA, RG 59. mDW 54200.
Accepts appointment of the Shelbyville, Kentucky *Shelby News* to
publish the laws.
March 25   To Roswell L. Colt. Draft. John R. Morison, Peterborough,
N.H. mDW 36321. Accepts the gift of Hungarian cattle and asks
that they be shipped to Boston.
March 25   To John Taylor.   *311*
March 25   To Abraham O. Zabriskie et al. AL draft incomplete. mDW
36323. Draft. CtY. mDW 36325. Accepts an invitation to meet with
the New Jersey state legislature.
March 25   From John Barney. ALS. DLC. mDW 36343. Commends
DW's address to the New-York Historical Society; speaks of wine;
expresses a desire to accompany Commodore Perry.
March 25   From McFarland & Jenks. LS. DNA, RG 59. mDW 54198.
Accept appointment of the Concord *New Hampshire Statesman* to
publish the laws.
March 25   From Abraham O. Zabriskie et al. (enclosure: list of members of a joint committee of the New Jersey state legislature). LS.

DLC. mDW 36349. Transmit a joint resolution inviting DW to meet with the house and senate of the New Jersey legislature.

March 26[25]   Notes for argument in *Goodyear* v. *Day*. AD incomplete. DLC. mDW 36330.

March 26   To W[illiam] Thomas Carroll. Telegram. DNA, RG 267. Asks that "the opinion of court in Wheeling Bridge case" be sent to him at once.

March 26   From Joseph Cable. ALS. CtY. mDW 36353. Requests a copy of DW's speech before the "New York Horticulture Society" to send to someone in Ohio.

March 26   From Daniel Fletcher Webster. ALS. NhHi. mDW 36354. Reports his correspondence with Greely is growing hot; mentions the Hungarian cattle.

March 27   To Richard Milford Blatchford (with postscript by George Jacob Abbot). LS. ViU. mDW 36358. Describes court proceedings in *Goodyear* v. *Day*; reports visiting last night at "Mr. Halsted's."

March 27   To Frances Halstead. ALS. NhD. mDWs. Thanks her for a bouquet and sends a "volume of poems of my favorite English Poet," John Milton.

March 27   To James William Paige. ALS. MH–H. mDW 36362. *PC*, 2: 519–520. Invites him to bring his family to Washington and to select from the barnyard stock at Marshfield; comments on the Hungarian cattle.

March 27   From Babcock & Wildman. LS. DNA, RG 59. mDW 54207. Accept appointment to publish the laws in the *New Haven Palladium*.

March 27   From E[benezer] B[rewer] Foster & Co. LS. DNA, RG 59. mDW 54192. Ask for copies of the *Republic* if they are to continue printing the laws in the *Boston Courier*.

March 27   From William Hunter. ALS. CtY. mDW 36366. Reports briefly on official State Department business.

March 27   From Charles Porter Wright. ALS. NhHi. mDW 36368. Discusses plans for "the Island house"; reports finding a prospective tenant for the Taylor house.

March 27[28]   To Daniel Fletcher Webster. ALS. MWalB. mDW 36371. Discusses plans for the Hungarian cattle; doubts any good can come from Fletcher's correspondence with Greely.

March 29   To George Peabody. Draft. CtY. mDW 36375. Introduces New York attorney Ebenezer Seeley.

March 29   From William Hunter. LS. CtY. mDW 36377. Refers to passport matters.

March 29   From Hiram Ketchum. Telegram. CtY. mDWs. Asks if DW will remain at Trenton until Thursday morning.

March 29   From Israel Wells et al. LS. CtY. mDWs. Praise DW's "long and unceasing labors for the elevation of the American mechanic and American labor," and request him to address the Workingmen's Association of the City of Trenton.

March 30   From Daniel Le Roy. ALS. NhHi. mDW 36378. Thinks DW's plans to purchase Caroline's marriage settlement makes sense.

March 30   From Little, Brown & Co. LS. CtY. mDW 36380. Plan immediate publication of DW's *Works*; ask if complimentary sets should be sent to "leading editors."

March 30   From Daniel Fletcher Webster. ALS. NhHi. mDW 36381.
Promises to take care of the cattle; reports paying a couple of DW's
debts; has ended his correspondence with Greely.
March 30   Recommendations from James L. Orr, for the York, South
Carolina *Yorkville Miscellany* and the Anderson, South Carolina
Southern Christian Advocate[?]—public printers (ALS. DNA, RG 59.
mDW 54344).
March 31   From Thomas Hale. ALS. DNA, RG 59. mDW 54190. Accepts
appointment of the Windsor *Vermont Journal* to publish the laws.
March 31   To George Peabody. LS. MSaE. mDWs. Introduces Ebenezer
Seeley.
March 31   From William Cabell Rives. Copy. DLC. mDW 36385. ALS.
DLC. mDWs. Insists he has written nothing which could be con-
strued as meddling in French domestic affairs; reports his relations
with French government officials, including the president, have
been cordial.
[March]   To Franklin Haven. ALS. MH–H. mDW 36393. Expresses delight with the results of "your meeting"; reports "Friends think this
an important moment."
[March?]   Inscriptions on pamphlet copies of speech before the New-
York Historical Society, to; Clement M. Butler. ANS. PHi. mDW
38118; Abbott Lawrence, Jr. ANS. Reginald Foster III, Manchester,
Mass. mDWs; Mary Scott. ANS. Lenox Library, Lenox, Mass. mDW
38127.
April 1   To Franklin Haven. ALS. MH–H. mDW 36407. Plans meeting
with Massachusetts friends in Washington; thinks things are beginning to look favorable.
April 1   From George W. Slacum. ALS. DNA, RG 60. mDWs. Reports on
his mission to Mexico to obtain depositions in the Gardiner and
Means cases.
April 1   From William A. Weeks. ALS. DNA, RG 59. mDW 56911. Reports on his handing of various despatches for overseas destinations.
April 1   Receipt for $190 paid Runyon Toms (of Trenton, N.J.) for a
horse. DS. John R. Morison, Peterborough, N.H. AD by DW, signed
by Toms. mDW 40605.
April 1   Account with Z. D. Gilman (druggist) for $16.64 for toiletries,
etc., through June 28. AD. NhHi. mDW 40636.
April 2   From Alfred Wheeler, LS. DNA, RG 59. mDW 55125. Accepts
appointment as U.S. attorney for southern California.
April 2   Recommendation from John Moore, for the Alexandria, Louisi-
ana *Red River Republican*—public printer (ALS. DNA, RG 59.
mDW 54338.
April 3   To Mrs. [?] Glover. ALS. Ronald von Klaussen, Dade County,
Fla. mDWs. Sends her a present.
April 3   To Charles Porter Wright. LS. NhHi. mDW 36409. PC, 2: 520.
Discusses farm work and the rental of houses in Marshfield.
April 3   Recommendation from Charles J. Faulkner, for the *Winchester*
(Va.) *Republican*—public printer (ALS. DNA, RG 59. mDW 54382).
April 3   Expense account of Francis Arenz as bearer of despatches to
Berlin and Vienna. Endorsed by DW. DNA, RG 59. mDW 56726.
April 3   Account with John Pettibone for $45 for ice tickets, through
June 14. AD. NhHi. mDW 40626.

April 4   To Little & Brown. Draft by George Jacob Abbot. CtY. mDWs. Encloses names of people and newspapers who should receive copies of his *Works*.

April 4   From George Catlin. ALS. NHi. mDW 38414. Marjorie Cutler Roehm, *The Letters of George Catlin and his Family* (Berkeley and Los Angeles, 1966), pp. 441–443. Discusses his proposal to sell his American collection to the U.S. government.

April 4   From George Catlin. Printed circular. NjMoHP. mDWs. Draws attention to his petition now before the two houses, and begs Congress to act on the report of the Library Committee in favor of the purchase of his Indian collection.

April 5   To Rufus Choate. ALS. MHi. mDW 36418. Asks that Choate and Healy look out for the "Passenger money case."

April 5   To Millard Fillmore. ALS. ICHi. mDW 36419. Excuses himself from a dinner engagement.

April 5   To Millard Fillmore. LS. NBuHi. mDW 36420. Reports being unable to locate "the accompaniments" to Brigham Young's letter of Sept 29, 1851.

April 5   To Millard and Abigail Powers Fillmore. AL. NN. mDW 36422. Declines an invitation to dinner.

April 5   To W. W. Gates[?]. Draft. CtY. mDW 36423. Acknowledges Gates's letter and his long support of "Whig principles."

April 5   To Charles Porter Wright. ALS. NhHi. mDW 36424. Discusses the construction of a wagon shed.

April 5   From William M. Burwell. ALS. DNA, RG 59. mDW 56360. Reports his arrival at Pensacola (en route to Mexico); explains that he is a bit behind schedule.

April 5   Recommendation from C[hristopher] H. Williams, for the Jackson *West Tennessee Whig*—public printers (ALS. DNA, RG 59. mDW 54274).

[c. April 5]   *From Hugh McCulloh Birckhead.*

April 6   To Sir John Fiennes Crampton. LS. UkLPR. mDW 36429. Applies for the extradition of Edward Welch, indicted for murder and now a fugitive in Canada.

April 6   To James L. Orr. LS. NcU. mDW 36432. Writes about the selection of newspapers to publish the laws in South Carolina.

April 6   From Millard Fillmore. Copy. UkLPR. mDWs. Has decided not to pardon convicted murderers Thomas Reid and Edward Clements.

April 6   From J[ohn] Z[acheus] Goodrich. ALS. CtY. mDW 36431. Requests a copy of DW's defense of the Treaty of Washington for a constituent.

April 6   From John H. Hill et al. Copy. VtU. mDW 36433. Submit a statement regarding the conviction of the Rev. Jonas King by a Greek court.

April 7   To the Clay Festival Association. Printed. *W & S*, 16: 652. Praises Henry Clay's patriotism and public character, but cannot attend a birthday celebration in Clay's honor.

April 7   To Millard Fillmore. LS. NBuHi. mDW 36441. Recommends the appointment of a consul at Manchester, England, and suggests Francis B. Ogden.

April 7   To Jared Sparks. LS. MH–H. mDW 36445. *W & S*, 16: 650–651. Thanks Sparks for returning a bound set of Dumas manuscripts to the State Department archives.

April 7   From George Gordon Gallup. ALS. DLC. mDW 36448. Claims
he was the first to discover sulphuric ether as an anaesthetic, and
that [William T. G.] Morton stole the secret from him.

April 7   From John Plummer Healy.   313

April 7   From William Cabell Rives (enclosure: Rives to Marquis de
Turgot, Apr 3, 1852). Extract. DNA, RC 60. mDWs. Reports papers
in the *General Armstrong* case have been laid before the French
President.

April 7   From John Arnold Rockwell. ALS. CSmH. mDW 36454. States
that claimants in the *Jones* case are anxious for an early settlement
by H.M. government.

April 7   From W[illiam] Thompson. ALS. DNA, RG 59. mDW 55107.
Accepts appointment as justice of the peace for Washington, D.C.

April 8   To Amos Bacon. Copy. NhHi. mDW 36458. *PC*, 2: 521. Declares that a president should represent "the whole people."

April 8   To Sir John Fiennes Crampton. LS. UkLPR. mDW 36460.
Responds to charges that American custom officials at Astoria
have interfered in "the trading pursuits of the Hudson's Bay
Company."

April 8   To Caleb Cushing. ALS. DLC. mDW 36463. Fuess, *Cushing*, 2:
89. Fears he may be obliged to request an extension on the due date
of a promissory note held by Cushing.

April 8   To Joseph Henry. LS. DSI. mDW 36465. Introduces Gardner
Chilson, the inventor of a heating and ventilating device.

April 8   To Morris Ketchum. ALS. NhD. mDW 36467. Presents a set of
his *Works*.

April 8   To James Watson Webb. LS. CtY. mDW 36470. Discusses the
appointment of Edward A. Hopkins as U.S. consul at Paraguay.

April 8   To Robert Charles Winthrop.   314

[c. April 8]   To [?]. Printed. *New York Times Saturday Review of Books*,
Jan 26, 1907. mDW 36457. *New England Historical and Genealogical Register*, 65 (Oct. 1911): 309. Responds to a letter of April 8
asking him to take a case: "I never engage on contingencies,
merely, for that would make me a mere party to a lawsuit."

April 8   From Charles Wainwright March.   315

April 8   From G[eorge] A. Tavenner. LS. NhHi. mDW 36481. Van Tyne,
pp. 520–521. Declares the South has taken a National stance on the
sectional conflict; warns that agitation for the repeal of the Fugitive
Slave Law will rekindle sectional conflict, and insists that Southern
rights must be respected; wonders what will unite northern and
southern Whigs in the coming presidential election.

April 9   To Franklin Haven. ALS. MH–H. mDW 36485. Warns that important time is being lost; asks that Haven and Ashmun come to
Washington at once.

April 9   To John Plummer Healy.   317

April 9   To John Strother Pendleton. LS. MHi. mDW 36494. Asks him to
advise the Buenos Ayres government that it will be expected to pay
interest if payment is delayed on the Halsey claim due to the overthrow of Governor [Juan M. de] Rosas.

April 9   To George A. Tavenner.   318

April 9   Recommedations from W[alter] Brooke and John D. Freeman,
for the *Natchez* (Miss.) *Courier* and the Jackson *Flag of the*

Union—public printers (ALS by Brooke, signed also by Freeman. DNA, RG 59. mDW 54376).

April 10   To Sir John Fiennes Crampton. LS. UkLPR. mDW 36502. Encloses copies of various documents for transmission to H.M. minister in Mexico.

April 10   To Robert Bowne Minturn, Jr. ALS. NhD. mDWs. Copy. CtY. mDW 36425. *PC*, 2: 521. Presents a set of his *Works*.

April 10   To William Cabell Rives. LS. NjMoHP. mDW 36503. Introduces A. B. Estes, now of New York.

April 10   To John Taylor. ALS dictated in part. MBBS. mDW 36504. Harvey, *Reminiscences of DW*, p. 310. Discusses the Hungarian cattle.

April 10   To Charles Porter Wright. ALS. NhHi. mDW 36507. *PC*, 2: 522. Discusses the use of oxen at Marshfield.

April 10   From William M. Burwell. ALS. DNA, RG 59. mDW 56361. Announces his arrival at Vera Cruz; says "Those I meet profess an anxiety to settle the Tehuantepec Question."

April 12   To Thomas Corwin. Copy. DLC. mDW 36508. Asks that something be done about an annoying subject [Philip Greely, Jr.?] raised in a recent letter from Fletcher Webster.

April 12   To Sir John Fiennes Crampton. LS. UkLPR. mDW 36509. Reports what steps have been taken toward the extradition of fugitive John Cole to Canada.

April 12   From George Bartle. ALS. DLC. mDW 36511. Applies for a promotion.

April 12   From Hiram Ketchum. ALS. DLC. mDW 36514. Discusses strategy for DW's presidential campaign.

April 12   From William B. Figures. ALS. DNA, RG 59. mDW 54184. Accepts appointment of the Huntsville, Alabama *Southern Advocate* to publish the laws.

April 12   From Charles Wainwright March.   *319*

April 12   From Smith & Sayward. LS. DNA, RG 59. mDW 54188. Accept appointment of the *Bangor* (Me.) *Daily Whig and Courier* to publish the laws.

April 13   To [William H.] Groesbeeck. ALS. CtY. mDW 36529. Presents a set of his *Works*.

April 13 [1852?]   To [Charles Porter Wright]. ALS. NhD. mDWs. DW likes Mr. Whiting very well, but can't "pay him such wages as he asks. We must reduce the cost of labor."

April 13   To [?]. Draft in Abbot's hand. CtY. mDW 36521. Van Tyne, pp. 516–517. Comments on support for DW's presidential campaign in the South and in New York, and discusses strategy for the rest of New England.

April 13   From Sir John Fiennes Crampton. Copy. UkLPR. mDWs. Submits correspondence and discusses the *Louisa Beaton* case.

April 14   To Samuel Jaudon. Printed, *PC*, 2: 522. Feels overwhelmed by petty annoyances.

April 14   To [John Taylor.] ALS. MBBS. mDW 36532. Harvey, *Reminiscences of DW*, p. 306. Regrets hearing of the loss of an ox; orders that oxen from Vermont be sent directly to Marshfield without stopping at Franklin.

April 14   From Robert Charles Winthrop. Printed. Robert Winthrop, Jr.,

A Memoir of Robert C. Winthrop (Boston, 1897), pp. 153–154. Disputes DW's recollection of events in February, 1850 relative to the territorial crisis.

April 14   Application from J[oseph] L. Locke & Co., for the *Savannah* (Ga.) *Republican*—public printer (LS. DNA, RG 59. mDW 54346).

April 14   Recommendation from R[obert] H. Gallahar, for the *Richmond* (Va.) *Daily Republican*—public printer (ALS. DNA, RG 59. mDW 54385).

[April 15]   To Roswell L. Colt. Draft. CtY. mDW 36536. Presents a set of his *Works*.

April 15   To Franklin Haven. Invitation. MH–H. mDW 36538.

April 15   To Caroline Story White Webster. ALS. NhHi. mDW 36539. *PC*, 2: 523. Sends a gift of money; reports his health has improved somewhat.

April 15   To [?]. ALS. NhHi. mDW 36533. Reports his health is better; is busy with foreign affairs.

April 15   From S[tephen] Adams. ALS. DNA, RG 59. mDW 54371. Discusses the appointment of newspapers to publish the laws in Mississippi.

April 15   From George Catlin. ALS. NjMoHP. mDW 36542. Appeals for help to prevent the sale of his Indian collection by his creditors.

April 15   From Charles Wainwright March. ALS. NhHi. mDW 36546. Recommends appointment of Joseph R. Curtis as visitor to West Point; anticipates a good demonstration in New York on Monday (Apr 19); reports DW's reply to Tavenner has been well received in New York.

April 15   Account with Alfred Lee for corn and cornmeal through May 22. AD. NhHi. mDW 40616.

April 16   To Millard and Abigail Powers Fillmore. AL. NN. mDW 36549. Accepts a dinner invitation.

April 16   To Nathaniel F. Williams. ALS. NhD. mDW 36550. Orders a few barrels of Bermuda seed potatoes.

April 16   To Charles Porter Wright. ALS. NhHi. mDW 39248. Van Tyne, p. 710. Expresses his dismay at Nathaniel Delano's hunting habits, and asks Wright to tell Delano "that I prefer letting it [John Taylor's house] to those who work altogether on the Farm."

April 16   From Asa Cummings. ALS. DNA, RG 59. mDW 54186. Accepts appointment of the Portland, Maine *Christian Mirror* to publish the laws.

April 16   From William A. Weeks. ALS. DNA, RG 59. mDW 56913. Reports forwarding despatches to and from England.

Apri 17   To Millard Fillmore. LS. NBuHi. mDW 36553. *PC*, 2: 523. Suggests that Fillmore invite Haven to dinner on Thursday.

[c. April 17]   To Elisha Whittlesey (enclosure: "Act of June 28, 1848"). ANS. DNA, RG 217. mDW 57247. Asks if Joseph Nourse was allowed any interest under the act.

April 17   From William Lewis Dayton. ALS. NhD. mDW 36556. Endorses DW's choice of Francis B. Ogden for U.S. consul at Manchester, England.

April 17   From G. S. Garrett. ALS. DLC. mDW 36559. Is contemplating a career in law and asks DW's advice.

April 18   To Charles Lanman. ANS. NhD. mDW 36563. Inscribes a
book on fish to "Junior Brother Angler."

[April 19]   To Franklin Haven. ALS. MH–H. mDW 36690. *PC*, 2: 513.
Invites him to dinner.

April 19   To A[ugustus] G]eorge[Hazard. ALS. NCooHi. mDW 36566.
Acknowledges Hazard's report on the Connecticut Whig convention;
approves the course of Hazard and his friends.

April 19   To [Charles] Morris. LS. MHi. mDW 36568. Asks Morris to see
what he can do about granting the wishes expressed by Kossuth in
the enclosed letter.

April 19   To Thomas Handasyd Perkins. Printed. *New England Histori-
cal and Genealogical Register*, 10 (July, 1856): 211. Thomas G.
Cary, *Memoir of Thomas Handasyd Perkins* (Boston, 1856), p. 263.
Presents a set of his *Works*.

April 19   To [?]. ALS photostat. OClWHi. mDW 36565. Acknowledges
his report on the [Ohio?] state convention; approves his actions.

April 19   From Caroline Story White Webster. ALS. NhHi. mDW 36570.
Acknowledges a gift; reports efforts to aid three seamen from a vessel which grounded off Carswell.

April 19   Quitclaim deed transferring property in Franklin, N.H. from
George Washington Nesmith to DW. DS. MHi. mDW 40608. Copy.
Deed Book 128: 494. Register of Deeds, Merrimack County, New
Hampshire.

[April 20]   To Millard Fillmore. ALS. NBuHi. mDW 36574. Reports
Haven will be unable to attend the dinner, but would nevertheless
like to pay his respects to the president.

April 20   To Millard Fillmore. ALS. NBuHi. mDW 36576. Will try to see
him today.

April 20   To Franklin Haven. ALS. MH–H. mDW 36578. Presents a set
of his *Works*.

April 20   To William R. King. LS. DNA, RG 46. mDW 52060. Report of
the secretary of state communicating statements showing the number of passengers who arrived in the U.S. from Sept. 30, 1850 to
Jan 1, 1852.

April 20   From Thomas Bailie. ALS. DNA, RG 59. mDW 54174. Accepts
appointment on behalf of the owners of the *Richmond* (Va.) *Times*
to publish the laws.

April 20   From Henry W. Gilbert to Thomas Corwin (with Corwin to
DW, [Apr, 1852]). ALS. NhD. mDW 36721. Is forwarding papers
received from Argentina; reports an extensive American interest
and presence in Buenos Ayres.

April 20   From Ambrose Dudley Mann. ALS. DNA, RG 59. mDW 56049.
Reports Austria and France are proposing a military cordon around
Switzerland; advises the U.S. to conclude a treaty with Sardinia so
as to preserve trade communications with Switzerland; reports on
politics in Berne.

April 21   To Millard Fillmore. Dictated letter. NBuHi. mDW 36579. Reports that Jacob Shuster's prison term appears to have expired.

April 21   To [Millard Fillmore]. LS. NBuHi. mDW 36580. Has received
no answer yet from the "Utah officers"; reports the resignation of the
territorial secretary of New Mexico (William S. Allen).

April 21 To Millard Fillmore. LS. NN. mDW 36582. Regrets to say that
Caroline will be unable to attend the Fillmore's dinner tomorrow.

April 21 To Dr. Peter Smith, from George Jacob Abbot for DW. Draft.
CtY. mDWs. Has sent a box of speeches and a set of DW's *Works*;
would like to know "to what points I shall direct letters to you say a
week or fortnight hence.

April 21 To John Taylor. Printed. *PC*, 2: 524. Instructs him in the care
of the Hungarian bull.

April 21 From S[amuel] Hooper. ALS. NhD. mDW 36583. Announces
DW's election to honorary membership in the Somerset Club of
Boston.

April 22 To William W. Corcoran. ALS. Riggs National Bank, Washington, D.C. mDWs. Presents a set of his *Works*.

April 22 To Millard Fillmore. ALS. NBuHi. mDW 36585. *Diplomatic
Papers*, 2. Reports a conversation with Crampton regarding Nicaragua; suggests a warship be sent to Central America to demonstrate
"an imposing appearance"; advises that now is the time to adjust
the problems with Britain.

April 22 From Hugh Birckhead. ALS. DLC. mDW 36589. Discusses the
marketing of DW's *Works*.

April 22 From F[rederick] W. Bogen. ALS. DLC. mDW 36592. Presents
a copy of his new edition of Washington's "Farewell Address."

April 22 From James M. Crane. ALS. DLC. mDW 36594. Plans visiting
Guatemala regarding "a new route" and requests a letter to the Gua-
temalan government.

April 22 From W[illiam] Lacy & Co. LS. DNA, RG 59. mDW 54182.
Accept appointment to publish the laws in the *Albany Daily State
Register*.

April 22 From George W. Slacum. Telegram. DNA, RG 60. mDWs.
Wishes to report to DW and Fillmore on his mission to Mexico.

April 22 Recommendations from William Appleton, for William Lee—
naval storekeepr (LS. DNA, RG 156. mDWs); from John G. Miller,
for the Columbia *Missouri Statesman*—public printer (ALS. DNA,
RG 59. mDW 54352).

April 23 From Sir John Fiennes Crampton. Copy. UkLPR. mDWs. Requests DW to summarize in writing the comments he made this
morning in a conversation with Crampton and de Sartiges on "a
convention" (regarding the right of search?).

April 23 From Abbott Lawrence. LS. DLC. mDW 36597. *Diplomatic
Papers*, 2. Reports an interview with the Earl of Derby concerning
the release of Irish prisoners confined to Van Dieman's Land.

April 24 To Sir John Finnes Crampton. LS. UkLPR. mDW 36605.
Informs him that a shipment of linen will be admitted duty-free by
the New York custom house.

April 24 To John Plummer Healy. ALS. NN. mDW 38562. Demands
that his business with the Old Colony Railroad be "closed, somehow."

April 24 To Daniel Fletcher Webster. LS. NhHi. mDW 36606. *PC*, 2:
525–526. Complains of the monotony of Fletcher's letters; recommends a book on medicine by "Dr. Holland," of England."

April 24 From Franklin Haven. ALS. NhHi. mDW 36612. Acknowledges the gift of a set of DW's *Works*.

April 24   From Louis Kossuth. ALS. MHi. mDW 36615. Asks the U.S.
government to arrange assistance for his family in Austria.

April 24   From Henry Wood. ALS. NhD. mDW 36618. Asks that his
newspaper, the Concord, New Hampshire *Congregational Journal,*
be appointed to publish the laws to help recoup losses suffered in
the Concord, N.H. fire of 1851.

April 25   To Nathaniel Sawyer. Draft. CtY. mDW 36622. Provides the
death dates of his mother and other family members.

April 26   To Charles Burdett. Draft. CtY. mDW 36624. Thanks Burdett
for reporting a possible abuse of the State Department's franking
privilege.

April 26   To Richard Burgess. LS. NsyU. mDW 36625. Reports uncover-
ing no evidence of Lt. Simon Summer's Revolutionary War service.

April 26   To William H. Groesbeeck. LS. NhHi. mDW 36627. Suggests
he consult "Mr. Webster's Works" for biographical information;
promises to send speeches.

April 26   To Nathan Kelsey Hall. LS. CtY. mDW 36630. Encloses a
letter "addressed to me by Mr. S. L. Magurn."

April 26   To James William Paige. MH–H. mDW 36631. Is gratified by
his election to honorary membership in the Somerset Club; plans
to head north later in the week.

April 26   To William Cabell Rives. LS. DLC. mDW 36633. Introduces
New York attorney George Wood.

April 26   To John Taylor. Printed. *PC,* 2: 526–527. Will be in Boston
early next week; discusses farm business.

April 26   To Postmaster of Windsor, Canada West. Draft. CtY. mDW
36635. Gives notice of unauthorized use of the State Department's
franking privilege.

April 26   From Jasper Harding. ALS. DNA, RG 59. mDW 54180. Accepts
appointment of the Philadelphia *Pennsylvania Inquirer and Gazette*
to publish the laws.

April 26   Recommendation from Edward Everett, from "Mr. Barney of
Baltimore"—a position (ALS. MHi. mDW 36637).

April 27   To Thomas Corwin. LS. DLC. mDW 36639. Cannot agree with
a Cabinet proposal to Congress for a board of examiners on clerks,
and declares he will submit his own report.

April 27   To William Alexander Graham. LS. NcU. mDW 36640. Hamilton, *Graham,* 4: 296. Cannot agree with a Cabinet proposal to Congress for a board of examiners on clerks, and declares he will
submit his own report.

April 27   To Charles March. Printed. *PC,* 2: 527. Presents a set of his
Works.

April 27   From Coale & Bass. LS. DNA, RG 59. mDW 54178. Accept
appointment of the *Abingdon Virginian* to publish the laws.

April 27   Application from S. Siegfried, for the Morgantown, Virginia
Monongalia Mirror—public printer (ALS. DNA, RG 59. mDW 54390).

April 27   Recommendation from James F. Morehead, for the *Greensboro*
(N.C.) *Patriot*—public printer (ALS. DNA, RG 59. mDW 54270).

April 28   To [Franklin Haven].   320

April 28   To Franklin Haven. Dictated letter unsigned. MH–H. mDW
36645. Acknowledges "a very gratifying letter"; reports nothing unfavorable has happened since "you left us."

April 28   To Robert Cumming Schenck. Draft. MHi. mDW 36646. Sees improved opportunities for trade with Argentina since the fall of [Juan M.de] Rosas; authorizes him to broach the subject of a commercial treaty to the Argentine government.

April 28   From Richard H. Bayard. ALS draft. DLC. mDW 36652. Discusses Belgian affairs; reports general acceptance of Louis Napoleon's regime and the monarchical principle in Europe; advises the U.S. to avoid entanglement in European affairs.

April 29   To George C. Bates. LS. NhExP. mDW 36656. Wishes to discuss the choice of a successor to Bates (recently resigned U.S. attorney for Michigan).

April 29   To Sir John Fiennes Crampton. LS. UkLPR. mDW 36659. *Diplomatic Papers*, 2. Explains U.S. policy regarding Cuba.

April 29   To Millard Fillmore. Dictated letter. NBuHi. mDW 36662. Inform him that Judge [O. C.] Pratt's term will expire in December.

April 29   To Millard Fillmore. LS. NBuHi. mDW 36664. Requests a memorandum of the topics Fillmore wants to discuss tomorrow.

April 29   To William Alexander Graham. Draft. CtY. mDW 36667. Asks that the U.S.S. *Saranac* be ordered to transport Robert M. Walsh and a British diplomat from Pensacola to San Juan de Nicaragua.

April 29   To Franklin Haven. LS by proxy. MH–H. mDW 36668. *Diplomatic Papers*, 2. Promises the *Evening Journal* will not be forgotten providing it holds to a "bold constitutional course."

April 29   To R[obert] M. T. Hunter. LS. DLC. mDWs. Transmits a copy of his letter to the secretary of the treasury on the subject of clerks.

April 29   To George Perkins Marsh. LS. VtU. mDWs. Orders him to investigate the case of Dr. Jonas King, acting U.S. consul in Athens, now imprisoned.

April 29   To Robert Cumming Schenck. LS. NN. mDW 36669. States that the U.S. would be gratified if Brazil were to upgrade the rank of M. de Sodre, the Brazilian chargé d'affaires at Washington.

April 29   From Champion Bissell. ALS. DLC. mDW 36672. Writes about plans to include DW's letter to Commodore Aulick on the Japan expedition in the June issue of the *American Whig Review*.

April 29   From Sir John Fiennes Crampton. Copy. UkLPR. mDWs. Is satisfied that the U.S. will consider British propositions regarding Cuba.

April 29   From Chevalier Johann Georg Hülsemann. Copy. UkLPR. mDWS. Curtis, 2: 608–609. Protests the hostility toward him exhibited by DW and the U.S. press; states that he is resigning as Austrian chargé d'affaires.

April 29   From William A. Weeks. ALS. DNA, RG 59. mDW 56914. Reports on the forwarding of despatches to and from England.

April 29   Recommendation from R[ufus] Hosmer, for the Niles, Michigan *Western Union*—public printer (ALS. DNA, RG 59. mDW 54332).

April 29   Statement of balance due on $100 owed Henry Pleasants for services rendered. AD. CtY. mDW 40612.

April 30   To William B. Gooch. LS. CtY. mDW 36674. Offers condolences on the death of Gooch's mother and sister; has written the U.S. consul at Havana regarding the appointment of Gooch's father as agent at Cardenas.

April 30   To Edward Everett Hale. LS. MdHi. mDW 36676. *W & S*, 16: 654. States that Hale's recommendations for the tabulation of data have been incorporated into the report to Congress on emigration.

[April 30]   To Charles Johnson McCurdy. AL draft. NhHi. mDW 36678. Van Tyne, pp. 523–524. Writes regarding the U.S. government's wish that Hülsemann be recalled.

April 30   From R[ichard] Smith (enclosure: receipt, Apr 30, 1852). ALS. MHi. mDW 36682. Writes regarding two promissory notes and DW's account with the Bank of the Metropolis.

April 30   Proposed basis of an arrangement for settling Central American affairs, signed by DW and Sir John Fiennes Crampton. Copy. UkLPR mDWs.

[April]   From Thomas Corwin (with Henry W. Gilbert to Corwin, Apr 20, 1852). ANS. NhD. mDW 36721. Will send over the Buenos Ayres papers mentioned in Gilbert's letter once they arrive.

April   From Daniel Eaton et al. ALS by Eaton, signed by others. DLC. mDW 36723. Make proposals for free distribution of public lands, the issuance of paper currency, and the direct election of the president and vice-president.

April   Application from Isaac Hulse, Jr.—a lieutenancy in the Marine Corps (ALS. DNA, RG 45. mDWs).

[April]   Notes on U.S. Constitution and the Washington Administration. Copy. NhHi. mDW 36693. Van Tyne, pp. 705–708.

[April?]   To William Judson. Copy. CtY. mDW 36727. Presents a set of his *Works*.

[April?]   To [?]. Draft (in another hand). DLC. mDW 35633. Presents a set of his *Works*, stating "no sentiment expressed in any of them is cherished by me more warmly than my estimate of your friendship."

[*April* ?]   *From Hugh Birckhead.*

May 1   To [William Thomas] Carroll. ALS. DNA, RG 267. mDWs. Requests the "mandate" be sent to [Greer B.] Duncan; asks when "Docket No. 125" is likely to be taken up by the Supreme Court.

May 1   To Edward Curtis. ALS. NN. mDW 36728. Sends greetings from the Gerard House, where with Mrs. Curtis, Mrs. Webster, and Charles Lanman, he is "drinking soda water, a waiting for the ineffable pleasure of a *serenade*" expected a little before midnight.

May 1   To Newbold Edgar. ALS. NN. mDW 36730. Sends an autograph for Edgar's friend.

May 1   To Franklin Haven. ALS. MH–H. mDW 36731. Expects to be in Boston soon; asks to have the enclosed note credited to his account.

May 1   To William L. Hodge. ALS. NhHi. mDW 36733. Writes regarding a draft on G[reer] B. Duncan.

May 1   To Samuel Jaudon. ALS. NHi. mDW 36734. Informs Jaudon that he expects to be in New York on Monday afternoon (May 3) and to leave on Tuesday morning, and would be glad to have "a short interview with Mr. Belmonte (August Belmont). Can you suggest this to him, very quietly & privately?"

May 1   To Charles Porter Wright. Printed. *PC*, 2: 527–528. Is leaving today for Marshfield; advises Wright to take care of himself.

May 1   From George Jacob Abbot. ALS. CtY. mDW 36735. Encloses a letter from the chief clerk; will send part of Grund's letter tomorrow.

May 1   Fom Giles M. Hillyer. ALS. DNA, RG 59. mDW 54176. Accepts
appointment of the *Natchez* (Miss.) *Courier* to publish the laws.
May 1   From L. G. Marshall. ALS. DLC. mDW 36738. Requests a copy of
the 7th of March speech.
[May 2]   To [William Thomas Carroll]. ALS. DNA, RG 267. mDWs. In-
quires about the date when the argument in a case is likely to come up.
May 2   From John Taylor. ALS. NhHi. mDW 36740. Van Tyne, p. 684.
Reports on farm matters at The Elms.
May 3   From William Maxwell Evarts. ALS. NhD. mDW 36743. Ac-
knowledges the gift of DW's *Works*; feels a hereditary responsibility
to defend the Declaration of Independence and the Constitution.
May 3   From De Witt C. Greenwood. ALS. DNA, RG 59. mDW 54172.
Accepts appointment of the *Aberdeen* (Miss.) *Independent* to pub-
lish the laws.
May 3   From Joseph Parsons. ALS. DNA, RG 59. mDW 55049. Accepts
appointment as U.S. marshal for eastern Tennessee.
May 3   From Robrt Wesselhoeft. LS. NjR. mDWs. Requests passports
for his sons.
May 3   Recommendations from Andrew Hull Foote, for John W.
Carrol—U.S. consul at St. Helena (LC. DLC. mDW 36746).
May 4   To William Cabell Rives. LS. DLC. mDW 36747. Introduces
Aaron S. Pennington and Thomas Oliver Colt.
May 4   From George W. Slacum. ALS. DNA, RG 60. mDWs. Reports
having deposited various documents pertinent to the Mears and
Gardiner cases at the State Department.
May 4   Application from G. W. Gillett, for the *Sheboygan* (Wisc.)
Mercury—public printer (ALS. DNA, RG 59. mDW 54428).
May 5   Alexander Hamilton Lawrence to George Jacob Abbot.   321
May 6   From Benjamin H. Irwin. ALS. DLC. mDW 36753. Complains of
seeing no Whig literature since moving to Illinois; asks for speeches
and public documents.
May 6   From David Tomlinson (with reply, May 11, 1852). ALS copy.
NhHi. mDW 36755. *W & S*, 16: 655. Presents a gift of sprouted
chestnuts to plant at Marshfield.
May 6   From [?] (enclosure: press clippings). AL. NhHi. mDW 36749.
Thinks DW's wealthy Boston friends should "shell out $100 to a
poor man [in Newburyport] who has worked like a Tiger for two
years *for him* & *his cause*," to finance a pamphlet for distribution
before the Whig National Convention.
May 6–8   Order of Boston City Council. Copy. NhHi. mDW 36756. Invitation to speak at Faneuil Hall.
May 7   To Benjamin Seaver. LS. NhD. mDWs. Introduces Christopher
Whiting "who has been for some years in my employment," and now
desires an appointment from the Boston city authorities "to some
subordinate office."
May 7   From Abbott Lawrence. Printed. Hamilton Andrews Hill, *Memoir
of Abbott Lawrence* (Boston, 1883), pp. 217–219. Argues for a cheap-
ening of transoceanic mail rates between the U.S. and Great Britain.
May 7   From M[ahlan] D. Phillips. ALS. NhHi. mDW 36758. Asks if DW
considers *Webster's Dictionary* "a standard of orthography."
May 7   From John Taylor. ALS. NhHi. mDW 36760. Reports he bought
a pair of oxen for $125.

May 8   From George Catlin. ALS. NjMoHP. mDW 36761. Again appeals for help to have his American Indian collection from sale and dispersal.

May 8   From Edward Everett. ALS. MHi. mDW 36766. Suggests that DW visit the frigate *Cumberland*, now lying in Boston Harbor.

May 8   From Edward McK. Hudson. ALS. DLC. mDW 36768. Announces DW's election to honorary membership in the Literary and Scientific Institute of Smithville, S.C.

May 9   To Millard Fillmore.   323

May 9   From William Hunter. ALS. DLC. mDW 36779. Reports the despatches to Brazil will be delayed because the owners of the S.S. *Brother Jonathan* have decided suddenly that the ship shouldn't stop at Rio de Janeiro.

May 9   Recommendation from Edward Everett, for George E. Rice— secretary of the legation at Madrid (LC. MHi. mDW 36778).

May 10   To John Russell et al. Printed. *W & S*, 16: 643–645. Comments on the significance of Kossuth's pending visit to Plymouth in terms of American political principles and U.S. foreign policy.

May 10   To John Taylor. Telegram. Robert and Richard Upton, Concord, N.H. mDW 36782. Advises that his visit to Franklin must be put off because of the carriage accident.

May 10   From L. M. Curtiss. ALS. DLC. mDW 36783. Inquires about reports that a wealthy Englishman has died intestate, whose lawful heirs are now in the United States.

May 10   From Jonathan Mayhew Wainwright. ALS. NhD. mDW 36785. Is preparing to leave for England on a religious mission, and requests letters of introduction.

May 11   To William Curtis Noyes. ALS by proxy. DNA, RG 267. mDWs. Is suffering from injuries and cannot be sure when he might leave home.

May 11   To David Tomlinson (with Tomlinson to DW, May 6, 1852). Copy. NhHi. mDW 36755. Van Tyne, pp. 684–685. Thanks Tomlinson for his gift of sprouted chestnuts. ·

May 11   From Millard Fillmore. DS. MHi. mDW 36790. Copy. DNA, RG 94, mDW 55841. Letter of credence empowering DW to negotiate a treaty with the Netherlands.

May 11   From William Plumer, Jr. ALS draft. Nh. mDW 36789. Wishes to draw on DW's recollections of William Plumer, Sr.

May 12   To Millard Fillmore. LS by proxy. NBuHi. mDW 36794. *PC*, 2: 529–530. Gives further details of his carriage accident and the resulting injuries; has written McCurdy regarding Hülsemann's expected departure.

May 12   To Benjamin Seaver et al. Printed. *W & S*, 16: 646–647. Expresses his feelings about speaking at Faneuil Hall.

May 12   From William M. Burwell. LS. DNA, RG 59. mDW 56362. Gives detailed report on his mission to Mexico, with observations about the rejection of the Tehuantepec treaty.

May 12   From Cornelius Conway Felton. ALS. CtY. mDW 36809. Comments on the classical allusions which appear in DW's address to the New-York Historical Society.

May 13   From John W. Allen. ALS. DLC. mDW 36812. Conveys an invitation to address the Ohio State Agricultural Society.

May 13   From Charles Augustus Stetson. ALS. MH–H. mDW 36815.
Reports the defeat of a Scott candidate in Ulster County; declares
John Botts "is out for Scott."

May 14   To Thomas Corwin.   324

May 14   To Abbott Lawrence. LS. MH–H. mDW 36820. *Diplomatic
Papers, 2.* Acknowledges Lawrence's various despatches; explains
the difficulty the U.S. faces in offering its good offices on behalf of
the Irish prisoners.

May 14   To Abbott Lawrence. Copy. UkLPR. mDWs. Reports that he and
Crampton have signed a proposition regarding Costa Rica and Nicaragua; discusses building a canal across Nicaragua.

May 14   Application from George A. Fitch, to Millard Fillmore, for the
Michigan Telegraph—public printer (ALS. DNA, RG 59. mDW
54059).

[May 15]   To Franklin Haven. LS by proxy. MH–H. mDW 36824. Is
mildly irritated that Ashmun could not wait in Washington for his
return.

May 15   To William Curtis Noyes. ALS. by proxy. DNA, RG 267. mDWs.
Will be unable to argue "our patent cause" this term, and asks that
his fee be transferred to another attorney.

May 15   From George Jacob Abbot.   325

May 15   From George Jacob Abbot. ALS. John R. Morison, Peterborough, N.H. mDW 36830. Applies for transfer to the State Department claims desk should Hunter be appointed to the vacancy caused
by the death of chief clerk William S. Derrick.

May 15   From Charles Boyle et al. ALS by Boyle, signed also by others.
DLC. mDW 36832. Announces DW's election to honorary membership in the Mechanics' Literary and Library Association of Uniontown, Pa.

May 15   From Giuseppe Fagnani. ALS. DLC. mDW 36834. Asks DW to
sit for the portrait requested by Sir Henry Lytton Bulwer.

May 15   From A Whig of the Olden Time. ALS. NhHi. mDW 36836.
Complains of corruption and bad federal appointments in California.

May 16   To Franklin Haven. LS by proxy. MH–H. mDW 36844. Hopes
to be in Boston Tuesday evening May 18.

May 16   From George Jacob Abbot. ALS. John R. Morison, Peterborough,
N.H. mDW 36845. Discusses pre-convention politics and also the
appointment of a chargé d'affaires in Greece.

May 17   To William Hunter. LS by proxy. WaHi. mDW 36849. Reflects
on the death of William S. Derrick; authorizes Hunter to inform
applicants that the vacancy has been filled.

May 17   From Edward Everett. ALS. MHi. mDW 36854. Asks him to
provide the Rev. Dr. Albro with letters of introduction; reports news
of Kossuth and his family.

May 17   Application from E. S. Smith, for the Niles, Michigan *Western
Union*—public printer (ALS. DNA, RG 59. mDW 54328).

May 18   Application from Ryan & Co., for the *Green Bay* (Wisc.)
Spectator—public printer (LS. DNA, RG 59. mDW 54430).

May 19   To Millard Fillmore.   325

May 19   To Franklin Haven. LS. MH–H. mDW 36865. Asks him to discount a draft on Gideon & Company.

May 19   To John Taylor. Telegram. MBBS. mDW 33636. Asks him to come down today or tomorrow.

May 19   From Issac A. Pennypacker. ALS. DLC. mDW 36867. Reports he was injured in an accident similar to DW's eight years ago; describes agriculture and industry in the region around Phoenixville, Pa., and invites DW to come for a visit.

May 19   Promissory note for $2000 payable to George S. Gideon & Co. DS. NhD. mDW 40613.

May 20   From Millard Fillmore. LS.NhHi. mDW 36870. Severance, *Fillmore Papers*, 1: 364–366. Van Tyne, pp. 527–528. Discusses a response to Hülsemann's letters, and also the problem of the Tehuantepec Company and Mexico.

May 22   To George P. Fox. LS. ViU. mDW 36877. Writes about his summer "Paletôt" (cloak), to be delivered to him at the Astor House.

May 22   To Benjamin H. Green and Amos Baker. Draft. CtY. mDW 36879. Declines an invitation to the Unitarian Festival.

May 22   To Jared Sparks, from Samuel R. Betts et al., with ANS by DW, May 26. LS. MH–Ar. mDWs. Request that Harvard bestow an honorary degree upon Freeman Hunt, editor of the *Merchant's Magazine*; DW concurs entirely.

May 22   From John W. Allen. ALS. NhD. mDW 36881. Reports on delegate strength in three New York wards; makes some political recommendations.

May 22   From Charles S. Daveis. LS. DLC. mDW 36885. Suggests that DW visit Portland if he is planning a trip to Franklin.

May 24   To William Thomas Carroll. Telegram. DNA, RG 267. mDWs. "Has the mandate gone? Mr. Duncan complains loudly."

May 24   To Millard Fillmore. LS. NBuHi. mDW 36890. *Diplomatic Papers*, 2. Reports his injuries are still painful; alludes to Hülsemann and to Mexico.

May 24   To [Robert Bennet Forbes]. Draft. CtY. mDW 36895. Revised draft. CtY. mDW 36898. Accepts a gift of tea, and asks that it be sent to Washington.

May 24   From Edward John Stanley, 2nd Baron Stanley. ALS. NhD. mDW 36902. Apologizes for not being able to pay attention to Ketchum when he was in England.

May 24   Application from Johnson & Chandler, for the Wilmington *Delaware Gazette*—public printer (LS. DNA, RG 59. mDW 54334).

[c. May 25]   From George W. Ashmun. ALS. DNA, RG 59. mDW 54258. Asks if J. P. Caldwell's wish that the Salisbury, North Carolina *Carolina Watchman* be appointed to publish the laws cannot be granted; requests that March be furnished with letters to Rives and to Joshua Bates.

May 25   Recommendations from James L. Orr, for the Columbia, South Carolina *Palmetto-State Banner*—public printer (ALS. DNA, RG 59. mDW 54340); from Aaron H. Palmer, for the Houston *Beacon*—public printer (ALS. DNA, RG 59. mDW 54452).

May 26   From William A. Weeks. ALS. DNA, RG 59. mDW 56915. Reports forwarding despatches to London by the *Canada*.

May 27   To John W. Allen. LS. MdHi. mDW 36904. Comments on estimates of delegate strength in New York wards.

May 28   From Robert M. Walsh. ALS. DNA, RG 59. mDW 56298. Describes preparations for his journey overland to San Jose, Costa Rica; reports Greytown is controlled by foreigners, mostly Americans.

May 30   Recommendation from Jonathan Clarke for Frederick W. Clarke—U.S. consul at Sydney, New South Wales (ALS. DLC. mDW 36907).

May 31   To Robert S. Daniels et al. Copy. MWA. mDW 36910. Declines an invitation to the Danvers centennial celebration.

May 31   To George Washington Nesmith (with AN by Nesmith). LS. DLC. mDW 36912. Offers to confer with Nesmith to see what might be done for a Salisbury man recently dismissed from a government position.

May 31   From Millard Fillmore. Dictated note. DLC. mDW 36916. Severance, *Fillmore Papers*, 1: 364. Asks DW to attend today's Cabinet meeting.

May 31   Recommendations from Edward Carrington Cabell, for the Tallahassee *Florida Sentinel* and the Jacksonville *Florida Republican*—public printers (ALS. DNA, RG 59. mDW 54417).

[May]   To [Nathan Appleton]. ALS. MHi. mDW 36918. Gives poor health as the reason he and Caroline haven't called.

[May]   To Daniel Fletcher Webster.

May   From William Anderson. ALS. DLC. mDW 36925. Submits an extract from a commentary in "my journal" on DW's recent Faneuil Hall speech.

May   Receipt for $3 paid the Boston Library for yearly assessment from May 1852 to May 1853. DS. MBAt. mDW 40618.

[May?]   From Henry Grinnell et al. LS. DLC. mDW 36929. Recommend that a special envoy be sent to the newly liberated countries of the La Plata region.

June 1   To John Taylor. Copy. MBBS. mDW 36932. Harvey, *Reminiscences of DW*, p. 306. Expects Taylor will have planted his crops; quotes some verse.

June 1–2   To Charles Porter Wright. LS by proxy. NhHi. mDW 36934. Van Tyne, p. 685. Discusses farm business; advises Wright not to work too hard.

June 1   From J[ohn] C. Clark. LC. DNA, RG 206. mDWs. Writes regarding the prosecution of individuals implicated in the filibustering movements of the steamer *Pampero*.

June 1   From D. M. Corwine. ALS. DNA, RG 76. mDWs. Writes regarding the detention of the American steamship *Quickstep* by authorities in Panama.

June 1   From Sir John Fiennes Crampton. Copy. UkLPR. mDWs. Calls attention to "the proceedings of certain adventurers from the United States at Queen Charlotte's Island."

June 1   From Abbott Lawrence. LC. MH–H. mDWs. States his desire to return home; mentions commerce with the nations of the Rio de la Plata, the Van Dieman's Land prisoners, and elections in Great Britain.

June 1   Application from Giles van de Wall, to Millard Fillmore, for the Kalamazoo, Michigan *Netherlander*—public printer (ALS. DNA, RG 59. mDW 54414).

June 2   To Millard Fillmore (with reply). Typed copy. John R. Morison,
        Peterborough, N.H. mDW 36938. Asks to be excused from the Cabi-
        net meeting because of extreme pain in his arm.
[June 2]   From Millard Fillmore (with DW to Fillmore, June 2, 1852).
        John R. Morison, Peterborough, N.H. mDW 36938. Excuses DW
        from this morning's Cabinet meeting.
June 2   From James C. Jewett (with DW to William Alexander Graham,
        June 5, 1852). Copy. DLC. mDWs. Copy. DNA. RG 59. mDW 56937,
        57021. Asks whether U.S. citizens have the right to take guano from
        the Lobos Islands.
June 2   From [Francis] Richard and [Antonio] Mouton. ALS. DLC. mDW
        36939. Seek DW's endorsement of their new *French Literary Review*.
June 2   Recommendations from Samuel Brenton, for the *Fort Wayne*
        (Ind.) *Times and People's Press*—public printer (ALS. DNA, RG
        59. mDW 54362).
June 3   To Sir John Fiennes Crampton. LS. UkLPR. mDW 36942. Prom-
        ises immediate action to restrain the lawlessness of American "ad-
        venturers" on Queen Charlotte's Island.
June 3   From Alfred Dutch. ALS. DNA, RG 59. mDW 54153. Accepts
        appointment of the *Chicago Commercial Advertiser* to publish the
        laws.
June 4   To [?] Newman. AL. CtY. mDW 36944. Invites him to dinner.
June 4   From Philip R. Ammidon. ALS. DLC. mDW 36946. Requests
        an autographed copy of DW's "Union Speech before the Senate in
        1848."
June 4   From J[ohn] Romeyn Brodhead. ALS. DLC. mDW 36948. Re-
        quests a copy of DW's remarks at festival held recently for the
        officers of the *Prince of Orange*.
June 4   From Edwin Lord (enclosure: theological dissertation). ALS.
        DLC. mDW 36950. Comments on the views expressed in his dis-
        sertation, and asks DW to look it over.
June 4   From Daniel Fletcher Webster. ALS. NhHi. mDW 36957. Thinks
        "things are about to occur" and notes "the news from Portland."
June 5   To George S. Bryan. Draft. CtY. mDW 36961. Refers Bryan to
        his Tavenner correspondence in April; calls the Fugitive Slave Act
        an "indispensable part" of the Compromise.
June 5   To Millard Fillmore. LS. NBuHi. mDW 36963. *Diplomatic Pa-
        pers*, 2. Will confer with him regarding the Tunis consulate; sends
        the draft of his letter on the Lobos Islands.
June 5   To William Alexander Graham (enclosure: James C. Jewett to
        DW, June 2, 1852). Copy: MdBP. mDW 36966. *Diplomatic Papers*,
        2. Recommends sending an armed vessel to protect American citi-
        zens who are taking guano from the Lobos Islands.
June 5   To James C. Jewett. Copy. CaOOA. mDW 36968. Copy. DNA, RG
        59. mDW 56940, 57016, 57022. *Journal of Commerce*, Aug 11,
        1852. mDW 56985. *The Farmer's Monthly Visitor*, 12 (Sept 1852),
        p. 270. Asserts that the Lobos Islands are not subject to Peru, and
        that a warship will be sent to protect American citizens desiring to
        take guano there.
June 5   To James Louis Petigru. Draft. CtY. mDW 36971. Expresses
        gratification at his high standing among the South Carolina Whigs;
        hopes to see members of their delegation to the national convention.

June 5   From F. M. Bassett. ALS. NhHi. mDW 36974. Sends seeds from
an elm tree at the site of Burgoyne's surrender.

June 5   From Sir John Fiennes Crampton. Copy. UkLPR. mDWs. Copy.
MeHi. mDWs. Sends three gold medals to be awarded to American
captains who helped rescue passengers from the British emigrant
ship *Unicorn.*

June 5   From Ambrose Dudley Mann. LS. DNA, RG 59. mDW 56055.
Reports complications regarding the exchange of treaty ratifications
with Switzerland caused by the threatening attitude of the auto-
cratic powers; notes that Louis Napoleon has interpreted the U.S.
mission to Japan as a deliberate show of strength.

June 5   Application from W[illiam] F. Switzler, for the Columbia *Missouri Statesman*—public printer (ALS. DNA, RG 59. mDW 54423).

June 7   To John Miller. LS. Lincoln College Library, Lincoln, Ill. mDW
36976. Introduces Charles Wainwright March.

June 7   To Pupils of Phillips Exeter Academy. ALS. NhExP. mDW
36979. Draft. CtY. mDW 36978. Lawrence Crosbie, *The Phillips
Exeter Academy, A History* (Exeter, The Academy, 1923), p. 87.
Presents a copy of his recent New York address; calls upon them to
honor the memory of Benjamin Abbott, founder of Phillips Exeter
Academy.

June 7   Application from J[oseph] R. Flanigen, for the *Philadelphia
Daily News*—public printer (ALS. DNA, RG 59. mDW 54421).

June 7   Promissory note for $400 payable by Daniel Fletcher Webster
(with Daniel Fletcher Webster to DW, June 8, 1852). ADS. NhHi.
mDW 37000.

June 8   To Sir John Fiennes Crampton. LS. UkLPR. mDW 36980. Acknowledges various testimonials received from H.M. government for
presentation to the captain and crew of an American vessel for
assisting a wrecked British brig.

June 8   To Sir John Fiennes Crampton. LS. UkLPR. mDW 36982. Acknowledges medals received from HM government for presentation
to three American captains for assisting in the rescue of the crew
and passengers from an emigrant ship.

June 8   To C[harles] Edwards Lester. LS. MWA. mDW 36984. Will
speak to the President regarding the Lyon consulate; encloses letters
to the U.S. minister and to the U.S. consul at Paris.

June 8   To [Ebenezer Price]. Draft. CtY. mDW 36987. Requests a copy
of Price's history of Boscawen, N.H.; asks specifically for information about the killing of Indians by Peter Bowen of Salisbury during
the French and Indian War.

June 8   From John Plummer Healy. ALS. MHi. mDW 36993. Asks him
to transmit the enclosed proposal for introduction of "House's System of Telegraphing" into Russia to the Russian minister at
Washington.

June 8   From Daniel Fletcher Webster (enclosure: promissory note payable by Daniel Fletcher Webster, June 8, 1852). ALS. NhHi. mDW
36996. Encloses a promissory note; comments briefly on politics.

June 8   Recommendation from John G. Miller, for the Columbia *Missouri Statesman*—public printer (ALS. DNA, RG 59. mDW 54355).

[June 8]   Memorandum on John Bowen of Salisbury. Draft. CtY. mDW
36990.

June 9   To William Alexander Graham. Draft. CtY. mDW 37001. Joins others in calling for Lt. Meade's restoration to the Navy.

June 9   To Nathaniel F. Williams. LS. NhD. mDW 37002. Thanks him for sending Bermuda potatoes to Marshfield.

June 9   To Charles Porter Wright. LS. NhHi. mDW 37005. Van Tyne, pp. 685–686. Discusses boats and turnips.

June 10   To William Cabel Rives. LS. DLC. mDW 37009. Introduces Charles Edwards Lester, former U.S. consul at Genoa.

June 10   From John Jordan Crittenden. ALS. NcD. mDW 37011. ALS draft. NhD. mDW 37014. Ann Mary Crittenden Coleman, *The Life of John J. Crittenden* (Philadelphia, 1871), 2: 37. Apologizes for remarks he made yesterday.

June 11   To John Jordan Crittenden. ALS. NcD. mDW 37016. Ann Mary Crittenden Coleman, *The Life of John J. Crittenden* (Philadelphia, 1871), 2: 37. Accepts Crittenden's apologies for "your remarks at the President's."

[*June 11*]   *To Daniel Fletcher Webster.*   328

June 11   To Isaac T. Wright. AL. CtY. mDW 37018. Invites him to breakfast.

June 11   From Edward Everett.   326

June 11   From J. Howard March. ALS. NhHi. mDW 37026. Acknowledges "your very kind letter"; offers to be of service while he is in England.

June 11   From Charles S. Morehead.   327

June 11   From Johnson & Chandler. LS. DNA, RG 59. mDW 54160. Accept appointment to publish the laws in the *Wilmington* (Del.) *Gazette*.

June 11   From Robert M. Walsh. LS. UkLPR. mDW 56303. Describes his difficult journey to Costa Rica; thinks the proposed arrangement will be quickly accepted by Costa Rica and Nicaragua.

June 11   Recommendation from Joseph Lane, for the Salem *Oregon Statesman*, currently published in Oregon City—public printer (ALS. DNA, RG 59. mDW 54427).

June 11   Protest for non-acceptance of a draft on G[reer] B. Duncan for $546.64 drawn in favor of William Thomas Carroll. Printed D with MS insertions. DLC. mDW 40624.

June 12   To G[reer] B. Duncan. Draft. CtY. mDW 37031. Will be glad to see Duncan when he can get to Washington; asks him to deliver a couple of letters in person.

June 12   From Ambrose Dudley Mann (enclosure: European protocol on Neufchatel, copies in English and French, May 24, 1852). ALS. DNA, RG 59. mDW 56059. Comments on the recent European protocol on Neufchatel and reports the Swiss are prepared to resist.

June 12   Recommendations for Charles M[ynn] Conrad, for the *New Orleans Commercial Bulletin* and the Alexandria, Louisiana *Red River Republican*—public printers (LS. DNA, RG 59. mDW 54412).

June 13   To John Taylor. LS. NhD. mDW 37033. Is planning a visit to New Hampshire; asks Taylor to make sure the boat on Lake Como is ready.

June 13   To Charles Porter Wright. LS by proxy. NhHi. mDW 37034. *PC*, 2: 534. Directs him to send an Alderney cow to James William Paige.

June 13   From Charles Porter Wright. ALS. NhHi. mDW 37035. Reports
on work at Marshfield.
June 13   Application from P. P. Hull & Co., for the *San Francisco Daily
Whig*—public printer (LS. DNA, RG 59. mDW 54279).
June 14   To Franklin Haven. LS. MH–H. mDW 37038. Introduces Alex-
ander Lawrence.
June 15[14]   To [Humphrey] Marshall. ALS. CtY. mDW 37039. Asks
that the "Kentucky gentlemen" he has not yet seen be brought to his
house for breakfast tomorrow.
June 14   To Elisha Whittlesey. LS. DNA, RG 217. mDW 57249. An-
nounces appointment of Benjamin G. Ferris as territorial secretary
of Utah.
June 14   From Alexander Bodisco. ALS. NhHi. mDW 37041. Replies to
DW's recent correspondence concerning Henry Evans and E. B.
Elliot.
June 14   From John T. Clark. ALS. DLC. mDW 37052. Asks where he
might obtain the latest reports on the common schools of Massachu-
setts; is seeking to awaken interest in Virginia in public education.
June 14   From Sir John Fiennes Crampton. Copy. UkLPR. mDWs.
Transmits a gold medal to be presented to an American captain for
meritorious conduct in rescuing the crew of a British ship.
June 14   From Knowles & Anthony. LS. DNA, RG 59. mDW 54115. Ac-
cept appointment of the *Providence Journal* to publish the laws.
June 14   From John Taylor.   329
June 14   Application from Shelton & Paul, for the Wadesborough *North
Carolina Argus*—public printer (LS. DNA, RG 59. mDW 54275).
[June 14]   Memorandum by Alexander Bodisco on relations between
Austria and the U.S. AD in Bodisco's hand. NhHi. mDW 37042. Van
Tyne, pp. 530–531.
June [pre-15]   From Champion Bissell. Printed. *American Whig Review*,
16, (Dec 1852): 504. Asks DW to suggest someone to write a review
of his *Works*.
June 15   To Champion Bissell. Printed. *American Whig Review*, 16
(Dec 1852): 504. Suggests that Cornelius Conway Felton write a re-
view of his *Works* for publication in the *American Whig Review*.
June 15   To Charles Loring Brace. Draft. CtY. mDW 37058. Thanks
Brace for his work on Hungary.
June 15   To [Prof.?] Pease. Printed forgery. *W & S*, 16: 655–657. *Ameri-
can Farmer's Magazine*, 9(1857): 694. Comments on the signifi-
cance of Sabbath schools; recalls a conversation he had with
Thomas Jefferson on religion.
June 15   From Millard Fillmore. Copy. DNA, RG 59. mDW 55842. Cre-
dence empowering DW to negotiate an extradition treaty with
Prussia.
June 15   From "Sylvander." LS. NhHi. mDW 37061. Declares that DW
has the unanimous support of the foreign element, and predicts he
will be elected president.
June 15   From Achsah Pollard Webster. ALS. NhHi. mDW 37064.
Thanks him for an autographed speech and for the dedication in
Volume 1 of his *Works*.
June 15   Recommendations from James S. Conger, for the *Pontiac*

(Mich.) *Gazette*—public printer (ANS. DNA, RG 59. mDW 54410); from William M. Thompson for the *Pontiac* (Mich.) *Gazette*—public printer (ALS. DNA, RG 59. mDW 54410).

June 15   Report of the Secretary of State in answer to a resolution of the Senate calling for information in relation to the Gardiner claim. AD. DNA, RG 46. mDW 52048.

June 16   To Alexander H. Lawrence. Draft. CtY. mDWs. Presents a set of his *Works*.

June 16   To Israel W. Putnam. Draft. CtY. mDW 37067. ALS. MHi. mDW 37065. *PC*, 2: 534. Acknowledges Putnam's kind expressions; will accept whatever result comes from the Baltimore convention with "a composed mind."

June 16   From Benjamin G. Ferris. ALS. DNA, RG 59. mDW 54991. Accepts appointment as territorial secretary of Utah.

June 16   From Johnson & Chandler. LS. DNA, RG 59. mDW 54163. Report they are without copies of the laws approved prior to May 26.

June 16   From Perry & Elford. LS. DNA, RG 59. mDW 54158. Accept appointment of the Greenville, South Carolina *Southern Patriot* to publish the laws.

June 16   Application from R. M. Duncan—employment (ALS. DLC. mDW 37069).

June 17   To G. B. Elkins. Draft by George Jacob Abbott. CtY. mDWs. Thanks him for his favorable letter; will accept the results of the convention with "the satisfaction resulting from the discharge of duty, regardless of popular applause, or public honors."

June 17   From [Anonymous].   330

June 17   From Joseph Clisby. ALS. DNA, RG 59. mDW 54151. Accepts appointment of the Tallahassee *Florida Sentinel* to publish the laws.

June 17   From James H. Gasner. ALS. DLC. mDW 37073. Demands a warrant to some land.

June 17   From Daniel Fletcher Webster. ALS. NhHi. mDW 37075. Is leaving today for New York; predicts much trouble if "things do not go right."

June 18   From William Bingham Baring, 2nd baron Ashburton. ALS. MHi. mDW 37079. George F. Hoar, "Daniel Webster," *Scribner's Magazine*, 26(Aug, 1899): 216. Acknowledges DW's letter on behalf of a friend; briefly comments on British politics and the state of the British economy.

June 18   From John Barney. Telegram. CtY. mDWs. Reports ballot count at Baltimore at 8:33 P.M.: "Unless Mr. Webster instructs his friends forthwith Scott will be nominated."

June 18   From George Washington Warren. Telegram. CtY. mDWs. Report on platform and Second Ballot at 8:54 P.M.

June 18   From John Barney per J. Wills. Telegram. CtY. mDWs. Report on Third Ballot at 9:03 P.M.

June 18   From John Barney per J. Wills. Telegram. CtY. mDWs. Report on Fourth Ballot at 9:08 P.M.

June 18   From John Barney per J. Wills. Telegram. CtY. mDWs. Report on Sixth Ballot. "Adjourned until nine morning."

June 18   Application from Evans & Vernon, for the Wilmington *Delaware Republican*—public printer (LS. DNA. RG 59. mDW 54419).

[June 19]   To Daniel Jenifer. ALS. John R. Morison, Peterborough, N.H.

mDW 37083. Exclaims: "My friends will stand firm. Let the South answer for the consequences. Remember the 7th of March."

[June 19]   From John Barney. ALS. CtY. mDWs. Reports that Fillmore has authorized him to tell people that "nothing will gratify him more than your selection" as Whig presidential candidate.

June 19   From Sir John Fiennes Crampton. Copy. UkLPR. mDWs. Requests the extradition of Thomas Cain, wanted for murder in Ireland.

June 19   From J. C. Morgan. ALS. DNA, RG 59. mDW 54164. Accepts appointment of the Columbia, South Carolina *Palmetto-State Banner* to publish the laws.

June 19   From [?]. AL. CtY. mDWs. Designating himself "An old Man, an old Federalist," etc., calls on DW to save the Whig Party.

[*June 20*]   *To [?]*.   331

June 20   Application from Porter & Eckel, for the Wilmington *Delaware State Journal*—public printer (LS. DNA, RG 59. mDW 54316).

June 21   To Mrs. Richard Milford Blatchford. ALS. MWiW. mDWs. Draft. CtY. mDW 36686. Presents a set of his *Works*.

June 21   To Edward Curtis and George Ashmun. Telegram. CtY. mDW 37087. Reports Fletcher, Bell, and Paige are about to go down (to Baltimore, and most likely will arrive before much has happened.

[*June 21*]   *To Millard Fillmore*.   331

[June 21]   To Franklin Haven. ALS. MH–H. mDW 38529. Asks him to come here by eight o'clock and bring "what Mass[achusetts] men you can."

June 21   From S[amuel] Austin Allibone. ALS. DLC. mDW 37091. Recommends Dr. Henry's history of Great Britain; reports hearing from Mary Clarke relative to "the *modus operandi* of her magnum opus."

June 21   *From Millard Fillmore*.   332

June 21   From D[e Witt] C. Greenwood. ALS. DNA, RG 59. mDW 54132. Reports he has not yet received a copy of the *Daily Republic*.

June 21   From Ambrose Dudley Mann. ALS. DNA, RG 59. mDW 56070. Has informed the Swiss government he must leave by July 10; thinks a sustained Prussian occupation of Neufachatel might provoke French military retaliation.

June 21   From James T. Morehead. ALS. KyU. mDW 37097. Asks that Dr. [William T. G.] Morton of Boston, a pioneer in the use of ether as an anaesthetic, be provided with recommendations for his forthcoming trip to Europe.

June 22   *To Richard Milford Blatchford*.   332

June 22   *To [James Watson Webb]*.   332

June 22   From Samuel Appleton Appleton. ALS. MHi. mDW 37102. Writes concerning salmon he has had shipped to DW from Boston.

June 22   *From Edward Everett*.   333

June 22   From George Stillman Hillard. ALS. DLC. mDW 37111. Comments on DWs' defeat for the Whig presidential nomination.

June 22   From Charles Sexton (enclosure: *St. Croix Inquirer*, Dec 2, 1851). ALS. DNA, RG 59. mDW 54000. Refuses his appointment to publish the laws in the Willow River (Hudson), Wisconsin *St Croix Inquirer* in protest of the failure of the Whig Convention to nominate DW for president.

June 22   From Samuel H. Walley. ALS. DLC. mDW 37114. Comments on DW's defeat for the Whig presidential nomination.

June 23   From James W. Lugenbeel. Press copy. DLC. mDW 37118. Resigns as U.S. commercial agent at Monrovia, and recommends that his successor be a Liberian national.

June 24   To [?]. Draft. CtY. mDW 37120. Calls upon his friends to accept the convention results as "an evil now without remedy."

June 24   From Henry Washington Hilliard. ALS. DLC. mDW 37122. Comments on the outcome of the Whig National Convention; asks for appointment to an overseas post.

June 24   From William A. Weeks. ALS. DNA, RG 59. mDW 56916. Reports forwarding despatches by the *America* in the charge of J. Livingston.

June 24   Speech before Agricultural Convention at Washington. Printed. Lanman, pp. 131–132.

June 25   To Henry F. Tallmadge. LS. NhExP. mDWs. Transmits Fillmore's remission of a penalty incurred by the Bremen Brig *Don Quixote* for violation of the Passenger Act of February 22, 1847.

June 25   To Ignacio Tolen. Copy. DLC. mDW 37125. Replies to Tolen's request for a passport and special protection as a naturalized American citizen during his trip to Cuba.

June 25   From Barstow & Judd. LS. DNA, RG 59. mDW 54166. Accept appointment of the *Syracuse Daily Star* to publish the laws.

June 25   From Robert M. Walsh (enclosures: correspondence with Bernardo Calvo, Foreign Minister of Costa Rica; decree of the Legislative Body of Costa Rica). ALS. DNA, RG 59. mDW 56306. Reports the government of Costa Rica has agreed to the proposed treaty; will now proceed to Nicaragua.

June 25   Recommendations from John Bell, for the *Nashville True Whig*—and *Brownlow's Knoxville Whig and Independent Journal*—public printers (ALS. DNA, RG 59. mDW 54261); from James Cooper, for the Harrisburg, Pennsylvania *Whig State Journal*—public printer (ALS. DNA, RG 59. mDW 54323).

June 26   To Samuel Austin Allibone. LS. CSmH. mDW 37127. Asks to see [James Pettit] Andrews's continuation of [Robert] Henry's history of England.

June 26   From J. G. Seymour. ALS. DNA, RG 59. mDW 54144. Accepts appointment of the *New Orleans Commercial Bulletin* to publish the laws.

June 26   Note for $192 due to Dennis Samallwood. ALS. NhD (Claims on DW's estate). mDWs.

June 26   Report of the Secretary of State as to the expediency of adopting a graduated scale of diplomatic salaries. AD. DNA, RG 46. mDW 52056.

June 28   To John Bell et al. AL draft. CtY. mDW 37129. Printed copy. MdHi. mDWs. Accepts invitation to a public dinner in his honor; alludes to "a great calamity (the death of Henry Clay) . . . pending over Congress."

June 28   To Sir John Fiennes Crampton (enclosure: Philip R. Fendall to DW, June 28, 1852). LS. UkLPR. mDW 37130. Encloses a letter from the U.S. attorney in Washington: recommends that Crampton agree to give testimony in the trial of an individual charged with stealing from him.

June 28   To John Jordan Crittenden. LS. DNA, RG 60. mDWs. Calls for a report in reply to a Senate resolution of June 22 "relative to affairs on the Rio Grande."

June 28   To James A. Pearce. LS. DLC. mDWs. Recommends that Congress support the publication of Charles L. Fleischmann's work on viniculture.

June 28   From Joseph H. Barrett. ALS. DNA, RG 59. mDW 54130. Accepts appointment of the *Middlebury* (Vt.) *Register* to publish the laws.

June 28   From Samuel Barstow. ALS. DNA, RG 59. mDW 54925. Accepts appointment as U.S. attorney for Michigan.

June 28   From John Bell et al. Printed Copy. MdHi. mDWs. Invite DW to a dinner in his honor to be given by various members of Congress.

June 28   From Philip Ricard Fendall (with DW to Crampton, June 28, 1852). Copy. UkLPR. mDW 37131. Asks that Crampton be requested to appear as a witness at the trial of a person charged with stealing from him.

June 28   From Thomas T. Kinney. ALS. DNA, RG 59. mDW 54140. Accepts appointment of the *Newark Daily Advertiser* to publish the laws.

June 28   From T[homas] Loring. ALS. DNA, RG 59. mDW 54134. Accepts appointment of the Wilmington, North Carolina *Weekly Commercial* to publish the laws.

June 28   From William Pennington. ALS. NhD. mDW 37133. Is dismayed by failure of the Whig National Convention to norminate DW; describes his own efforts in New Jersey on behalf of DW's candidacy.

June 28   Recommendations from Sam Houston, for the *San Antonio Ledger* and the *Nacogdoches* (Tx.) *Chronicle*—public printers (ALS. DNA, RG 59. mDW 54325).

June 29   To Charles L. Fleischmann. LS. NhD. mDW 37136. Commends Fleischmann's work on "the grape vine and its culture."

June 29   From J. J. Bruner. ALS. DNA, RG 59. mDW 54136. Accepts appointment of the Salisbury, North Carolina *Carolina Watchman* to publish the laws.

June 29   From Franklin Haven. Copy. NhHi. mDW 37138. Conveys an invitation from the Webster State Committee of Correspondence to a reception in DW's honor.

June 29   From George Henry Moore. ALS. NHi. mDWs. Sends 200 copies of an address and an engraving from the portrait by [Richard M.] Staigg.

June 29   From Charles Augustus Stetson. Copy. NhHi. mDW 37141. Van Tyne, p. 532. Will write a letter for "Col. Howard of Michigan"; offers some lines of verse "to Whig friends."

June 29   From L[ewis] Zinn. ALS. DNA, RG 59. mDW 54128. Accepts appointment of the Alexandria, Louisiana *Red River Republican* to publish the laws.

June 30   To [Thomas Aspinwall]. Draft. CtY. mDW 37124. Introduces John O'Connell, formerly of Ireland.

[June 30]   To [Jane Erwin Yeatman] Bell. ALS. T. mDWs. "The vacant place [secretary of the navy] has been offered to Mr. [John] Bell. Please telegraph him."

June 30   To Sir John Fiennes Crampton. ALS. UkLPR. mDW 37146. Invites him to funeral services for Henry Clay at the Capitol.

June 30   From Sir John Fiennes Crampton. Copy. UkLPR. mDWs. Transmits a letter and requests the assistance of the U.S. government in investigating the capture of Benjamin Boyd by Solomon Islanders.

June 30   From John J. Clyde. ALS. DNA, RG 59. mDW 54142. Accepts appointment of the Harrisburg, Pennsylvania *Whig State Journal* to publish the laws.

June 30   From Fred Krepp. ALS. DLC. mDW 37147. Seeks admission to a public academy in hopes of someday becoming a political writer.

June 30   Report of the Secretary of State in relation to the examination, promotion, classification, and compensation of the clerks in several departments. AD. DNA, RG 46. mDW 52050.

[June-pre 18]   To [?]. ALS. NN. mDW 37151. Demands that "Mr. Haven of Buffalo" be asked pointedly if New York would vote for Fillmore and against Pierce.

[June]   From [Anonymous]. AL. NhHi. mDW 37153. Asks if the Federal Government cannot force Mississippi to pay the Hawkers' Bank bonds.

July 1   To George Jacob Abbot. Telegram. John R. Morison, Peterborough, N.H. mDW 37157. "Send me to Boston Hickey's Constitution."

July 1   To Sir John Fiennes Crampton. LS. UkLPR. mDW 37158. Wants to know how a private understanding between himself and Crampton regarding Central America should happen to have appeared in print.

July 1   To Alpheus Felch. LS. MiD. mDW 30627. Advises Felch where to look to determine if the copyright to "The American Harp" has expired.

[July 1]   To [Millard Fillmore] (with ANS by Fillmore). ANS. DNA, RG 59. mDW 56730. Recommends approval of compensation requested by Henry Burtnete for services leading to the arrest and trial of individuals charged with conspiracy to invade Cuba.

July 1   To Franklin Haven. LS. MH–H. mDW 37161. Will be prepared to meet "the [Webster] committee, and their friends," on Tuesday (July 6) at the Revere House.

July 1   From Henry Burtnete (with DW to Fillmore, [July 1, 1852]). ALS. DNA, RG 59. mDW 56729. Requests $2000 for services rendered leading to the detention of the steamer *Cleopatra* and the prosecution of individuals charged with conspiring to invade Cuba.

[July 1]   From [Angel Calderon de la Barca]. AL incomplete. DLC. mDW 35661. Strongly advises the United States to make every every effort to prevent the outfitting of expeditions against Cuba; warns that future invaders will be treated with the utmost severity.

July 1   From Sir John Fiennes Crampton. Copy. UkLPR. mDWs. Assures DW he knows nothing about the publication of a document signed by themselves concerning Central America.

July 1   From Knight & Lunt. LS. NhD. mDWs. Inquire about American fishing privileges in the Gulf of St. Lawrence under the Treaty of 1818.

July 1   Account with Walker & Shadd (National eating house), from Jan. 15 to April 22, 1852. AD. NhHi. mDW 40627.

July 2   To Cornelius Conway Felton. Draft incomplete. CtY. mDW 37164. Acknowledges Felton's friendly letter; is glad Felton will be reviewing Everett's edition of DW's *Works*.

July 2   To Millard Filmore. LS. NBuHi. mDW 37165. Has decided to remain in Washington until various matters are cleared up.

July 2   To Franklin Haven. LS. MH–H. mDW 37167. Has postponed his Boston trip until after the 4th of July.

July 2   To John Taylor. LS. MBBS. mDW 37169. Orders him to send Porter Wright 200 bushels of oats.

July 2   To Charles Porter Wright. LS. NhHi. mDW 37171. Expects a light hay crop, and orders a reduction in his herd of cattle.

July 2   Receipt for $25.75 paid Moses Copp's Pavilion. DS. NhHi. mDW 40629.

July 3   To Sir John Fiennes Crampton. LS. UkLPR. mDW 37173. Agrees to assist H.M. government in trying to determine the fate of Benjamin Boyd, an Englishman believed missing in the Solomon Islands.

July 3   To Millard Fillmore. Copy. NhHi. mDW 37175. Recommends that [Samuel F.] Train be appointed to a Navy pursership.

July 3   From James Louis Petigru. ALS. NhHi. mDW 37178. Is pained by the outcome of the Baltimore convention: asks that Charles Warley be entrusted with despatches for Vienna.

July 3   Receipt for $9 paid David A. Baird. ADS. NhHi. mDW 40631.

July 4   To Edward Curtis (with memorandum by Curtis). Copy. NhD (Curtis diary). mDW 37181. NhHi. mDWs. Van Tyne, p. 533. Presents a set of his *Works* to "my Best of Friends."

July 4   To Daniel Fletcher Webster.   334

July 5   To Millard Fillmore. LS. NBuHi. mDW 37185. Discusses the problem of Nicaragua and Costa Rica.

[July 5]   To Franklin Haven. Telegram. MH–H. mDW 37188. Plans to be in New York tomorrow; asks to hear from Haven there.

July 5   To George Henry Moore. LS. NHi. mDWs. Thanks him for the copies of the address.

July 5   To Charles Augustus Stetson. LS. NhHi. mDW 37189. Van Tyne, p. 533. Reports the Detroit bar is asking that the appointment of a U.S. Marshal for Michigan be delayed; will leave for New York tomorrow.

July 5   From Sir John Fiennes Crampton. Copy. UkLPR. mDWs. Warns that H.M. government has decided to station a naval force off the British North American Provinces to prevent French and American vessels from fishing there in violation of the Treaty of 1818.

July 5   From Sir John Fiennes Crampton. Copy. UkLPR. mDWs. Transmits a silver medal for an American captain who rescued the crew of a sinking British vessel.

July 5   From Sir John Fiennes Crampton. Copy. UkLPR. mDWs. Informs DW of a decision regarding lights on British ships.

July 5   From Edward Curtis. ALS. DNA, RG 76. mDWs. Transmits documents on behalf of John Graham concerning the case of the brig *Volusia*.

July 5 Application from M[armaduke] Shannon, for the *Vicksburg* (Miss.) *Whig*—public printer (ALS. DNA, RG 59. mDW 54277).

July 5 Receipt for $100 paid R[euben] Burdine for rent. DS. NhHi. mDW 40633.

July 6 To Franklin Haven. Telegram. MH–H. mDW 37191. "I go this morning . . . let the reception be on Friday."

July 6 To Franklin Haven. Telegram. MH–H. mDW 37193. "Nothing happening, it shall be on Thursday."

[July 6] To Franklin Haven. Telegram. MH–H. mDW 37192. Has been obliged to stop at Philadelphia by an equipment breakdown.

July 6 From B. R. McKennie & Co. LS. DNA, RG 59. mDW 54146. Accept appointment to publish the laws in the *Nashville True Whig*.

July 6 From Ryan & Co. LS. DNA, RG 59. mDW 54170. Accept appointment of the *Green Bay* (Wisc.) *Spectator* to publish the laws.

[July 7] To Franklin Haven. Telegram. MH–H. mDW 37195. Reports his arrival at New York and his plans to continue on to Boston.

July 7 To Franklin Haven. 335

July 7 From Ryan & Co. LS. DNA, RG 59. mDW 54281. Request information relative to their appointment to publish the laws.

July 7 Application from Francis Vincent, for the Wilmington, Delaware *Blue Hen's Chicken*—public printer (ALS. DNA, RG 59. mDW 54320).

July 8 To George Jacob Abbott. LS. CSmH. mDWs. Asks him to send a box of spirits to Boston, care of J. W. Paige & Co.

July 8 To Millard Fillmore. LS. NBuHi. mDW 37197. Van Tyne, pp. 533–534. Discusses Letcher's despatch from Mexico.

July 8 To Franklin Haven. Telegram. MH–H. mDW 37200. Is preparing to take the train to Boston, and asks him to notify the Revere House.

July 8 To Franklin Haven. Telegram. MH–H. mDW 37201. Decides, after all, to take the boat to Boston.

July 8 To John Taylor. LS. MBBS. mDW 37202. Harvey, *Reminiscences of DW*, p. 307. Reacts to the news of Taylor's goring by the Hungarian bull.

July 8 To John Taylor. Telegram. Robert and Richard Upton, Concord, N.H. mDW 37204. Asks why Taylor has not killed the Hungarian bull for goring him; will come directly to Franklin from Boston.

July 8 From William Bigler. ALS. NhD. mDW 37206. Asks that the Pennsylvania commissioner of loans be furnished with a letter to Baring Brothers.

July 8 From W. G. Brownlow. ALS. DNA, RG 59. mDW 54149. Accepts appointment to publish the laws in *Brownlow's Knoxville Whig and Independent Journal*.

July 8 From Sir John Fiennes Crampton. Copy. UkLPR. mDWs. Discusses the strategic importance of Cuba and asks the U.S. to join Britain and France in renouncing designs of possession of Cuba and guaranteeing the island's neutrality.

July 8 From Columbus Drew. ALS. DNA, RG 59. mDW 54138. Accepts appointment of the Jacksonville *Florida Republican* to publish the laws.

July 8 From Millard Fillmore. LS. NhHi. mDW 37208. Severance, *Fill-*

more Papers, 1: 369–371. Thinks that the issues of Cuba and the Sandwich Islands might be linked in the negotiations with Britain; discusses the Peruvian claim to the Lobos Islands.

July 8   From John Graham. LS. DNA. RG 76. mDWs. Discusses his claim against H.M. government for the seizure and confiscation of the brig *Volusia*.

July 8   From William Alexander Graham. Copy. UkLPR. mDWs. Notes measures taken to assist in the search for Benjamin Boyd, disappeared in the Solomon Islands.

July 8   From William Woodruff. ALS. DNA, RG 59. mDW 54126. Accepts appointment to publish the laws in the Little Rock *Arkansas State Gazette and Democrat*.

July 9   From [Charles Scott Todd]. ALS incomplete. DLC. mDW 37212. Expresses mortification at the outcome of the Whig National Convention, and accuses the South of ingratitude; asks to be posted overseas.

July 10   To [Thatcher] Magoun & Son. Copy. DNA, RG 59. mDW 57025. Reports that a warship has been ordered to the Lobos Islands to protect American vessels loading guano.

July 10   To Harriette Story White Paige. ANS inscription. Facsimile of cover published in *W & S*, 13: at p. 463. mDWs.

July 11   From Charles Porter Wright. ALS. NhHi. mDW 37216. Reports a severe drought may affect the hay crop; reports on haying and the harvesting of turnips.

July 12[Aug 12?]   To Haley A. Barstow. LS. NOsU. mDW 37552. Regrets he has no position to offer Barstow.

July 12   To E[dward] C[odman] & Co. ALS. NhD. mDW 37220. Orders provisions sent to John Taylor at Franklin.

July 12   Millard Fillmore. LS. NBuHi. mDW 37221. Acknowledges two letters; has spent two days at Nahant.

July 12   From Edward Curtis.   336

[July 12]   From Daniel Fletcher Webster. ALS. NhHi. mDW 37235. Advises him to expect guests in a few days; will be sending the chairs and bookcase DW requested.

July 13   To Millard Fillmore. Printed. *PC*, 2: 535–536. Describes the scenery and the historical background of his farm in Franklin.

July 13   To Millard Fillmore. Printed. *Diplomatic Papers*, 2. Agrees with Fillmore that the Cuban and Sandwich Islands issues ought to be linked in the negiotiations with Britain; considers the question of Peru's rights to the Lobos Islands.

July 13   To Millard Fillmore. Printed. *PC*, 2: 537. Thinks Hilliard would be ideal to succeed Letcher in Mexico; hopes Letcher will be able to renegotiate Article 11 of the Treaty of Guadalupe Hidalgo.

July 13   To John Stimpson (with Stimpson to Edward Everett et al., Nov 17, 1852). Copy. NhHi. mDW 37239. Van Tyne, p. 534. Thanks him for a cane made from the U.S.S. *Constitution*.

July 13   From Daniel Dewey Barnard. ALS. CtY. mDW 37241. Expresses disappointment at DW's failure of nomination; thinks Scott has come under the influence of shady politicians.

July 13   From Henry Willis Kinsman. ALS. NhHi. mDW 37245. Asks DW to meet with Newburyport fishermen relative to the negotiations with Britain over fishing rights.

July 13   From T[homas] Loring. ALS. DNA, RG 59. mDW 54318. Reports he has received just one issue of the *Republic* since his appointment to publish the laws.

[July 13]   From Caroline Le Roy Webster. ALS. NhHi. mDW 37231. Reports finding the Marshfield house in chaos; advises him to remain in Franklin until it can be made habitable.

July 14   To James William Paige.   337

July 15   To Daniel Fletcher Webster. LS. NhHi. mDW 37248. *PC*, 2: 537–538. Asks Fletcher to bring lemons, chickens, and anything else which might appeal to "a man of little appetite."

July 14   From [Anonymous].   338

July 14   From Richard H. Bayard. ALS draft. DLC. mDW 37254. Reports on the June elections in Belgium.

July 15   From Ambrose Dudley Mann. LS. DNA, RG 59. mDW 56073. Comments on modifications of the convention being demanded by the Swiss Federal Council.

July 14[15]   From Daniel Fletcher Webster. ALS. NhHi. mDW 37258. Is coming to Franklin tomorrow; comments on John Taylor's goring by the bull.

Juy 16   To Edward Curtis. Printed. *PC*, 2: 538. Reports Taylor has recovered from injuries caused by the Hungarian bull.

July 16   To Franklin Haven. LS. MH–H. mDW 37262. Encloses letters of introduction for "Mr. Andensied."

July 16   To Charles B. Norton. LS. NHC. mDW 37263. Thanks him for Charles B. Stuart's *The Naval Drydocks of the United States.*

July 16   To Nelson Robinson. LS. MB. mDW 37265. Thinks it would be more convenient if "Mr. Elliot" were to visit him here in Franklin.

July 16   From Roswell L. Colt. Printed. Curtis, 2: 675. Apologizes for the Hungarian bull's unruly behavior, and suggests ways of controlling him; fears Scott's nomination will mean the destruction of the Whig Party.

July 16   From Millard Fillmore. LS. NhHi. mDW 37266. Severance, *Fillmore Papers*, 1: 371–372. Thinks of recognizing the independence of Haiti, the Dominican Republic, and Liberia; reports British views of Peru's rights to Lobos Islands.

July 17   To Sir John Fiennes Crampton (with DW to Fillmore, July 17, 1852). Copy. NBuHi. mDW 37275. *Diplomatic Papers*, 2. Comments on the threats of Provincial authorities against American fishing vessels; urges that something be done immediately to forestall any hostile proceeding, and wishes to see him as soon as possible about the matter.

July 17   To Millard Fillmore (enclosure: DW to Crampton, July 17, 1852). LS. NBuHi. mDW 37272. *Diplomatic Papers*, 2. Considers the fisheries problem very serious and fears much difficulty may come of it.

July 17   To Franklin Haven. Telegram. MH–H. mDW 37279. Has been called to Boston and asks Haven to inform "the Gentlemen."

July 18   From Charles Porter Wright. ALS. NhHi. mDW 37280. Reports on farm work at Marshfield.

July 19   To Baker & Morrill (with Fillmore from Daniel Fletcher Webster, July 19, 1852). Copy. NBuHi. mDW 37284. Advises them the president is deferring comment on the Lobos Islands; suggests it might be unwise to send ships there under present circumstances.

July 19 Millard Fillmore from Daniel Fletcher Webster (enclosure: DW to Baker & Morrill, July 19, 1852). AL. NBuHi. mDW 38283. Encloses the copy of a letter from DW to Baker & Morrill regarding the Lobos Islands.

July 19 To [Charles Chauncey Sewall]. LS. CSmII. mDW 37287. *PC*, 2: 540. Expresses high regard for Sewall's late father, Samuel Sewall, former chief justice of Massachusetts.

July 19 From Edward Everett. ALS. MHi. mDW 37290. Writes regarding his official correspondence on American fishing rights in the Bay of Fundy.

July 19 From Edward Everett. ALS. MHi. mDW 37296. Refers to his correspondence with Lord Aberdeen on American fishing rights in the Bay of Fundy.

July 19 From Edward Everett. LC. MHi. mDW 37299. Invites DW to an alumni festival at Harvard University.

July 19 From Newob-Amanuensis. 339

July 20 To Edward Everett. LS. MHi. mDW 37303. Thanks him for recent favors; will call this evening at eight.

July 20 To James Tappan. ALS. MGlHi. mDW 37305. Lyman, *Life and Memorials of DW* (New York, 1853), 2: 261–262. Pays tribute to his old schoolmaster.

July 20 From Atwood, Wymans & Buck. LS, DNA, RG 59. mDW 54120. Accept appointment of the Madison *Wisconsin State Palladium* to publish the laws.

July 20 From Edward Curtis. ALS. DNA, RG 76. mDWs. Writes regarding the *Volusia* claims against Great Britain.

July 20 From Edward Everett. ALS. MHi. mDW 37307. Is too busy with callers to leave; will be at home this evening.

July 20 From Edward Everett. ALS. MHi. mDW 37309. Again invites DW to the Harvard alumni festival.

July 20 From Millard Fillmore. LS. NhHi. mDW 37311. *Diplomatic Papers*, 2. Discusses the fisheries crisis and suggests a course of action.

July 21 To Caleb Cushing. Printed extract. Fuess, *Cushing*, 2: 89. Agrees to fix date when they can meet; doubts Cushing is in greater difficulty than himself.

July 21 To Edward Everett. Printed, *PC*, 2: 542. Agrees to attend the Cambridge dinner if the weather is not too hot; speaks affectionately of their long relationship.

July 21 To Millard Fillmore. LS. NBuHi. mDW 37319. *PC*, 2: 541–542. Discusses past diplomacy relative to the Newfoundland fisheries; is expecting to meet Crampton.

[July 21] To James William Paige. ALS. MH–H. mDW 37405. Thinks of coming to Nahant this morning.

July 21 From Moore & Harrison. LS. DNA, RG 59. mDW 54122. Accept appointment of the *Nacogdoches* (Tx.) *Chronicle* to publish the laws.

July 21 From John Taylor. ALS. NhHi. mDW 37323. Reports his purchase of 12 tons of good English hay.

July 22 To Millard Fillmore. Dictated letter. NBuHi. mDW 37327. Has heard nothing from the U.S. attorney relative to Samuel Johns's application for pardon.

July 23   To Benjamin C. Clark, Jr. Printed. Van Tyne, p. 717. Discusses
fishing for tautog.

July 23   To John Taylor. LS. NhHi. mDW 37329. Encloses a check for
hay; suggests he get to work on "the great field."

[July 23]   From Sir John Fiennes Crampton. ALS. DLC. mDW 37472.
Reports his arrival at the Revere House; asks where they should
meet.

July 23   From Amory Holbrook. Copy. UkLPR. mDWs. Reports that
Americans seeking gold at Queen Charlotte's Island returned empty-
handed, and that the excitement has quieted down.

July 24   To Millard Fillmore. LS. NBuHi. mDW 37331. *Diplomatic Papers*, 2. Reports Crampton has reached Boston fully disposed to
keep the peace.

July 24   From Israel D. Andrews. Telegram. NBuHi. mDW 37333. Reports British "devastation" of American fishermen in the Bay of
Fundy; warns of great loss unless things are settled quickly.

July 24   From J. R. Chadbourne. ALS. DLC. mDW 37334. Reports intense excitement among fishermen of the Passamoquody District
of Maine; says they are counting on DW to resolve the fisheries
crisis.

July 24   From Edward Everett. ALS. MHi. mDW 37339. Acknowledges
DW's kind expressions; thinks it is just as well that DW did not attend the Harvard alumni festival.

July 24   From Millard Fillmore.   340

July 24   From Charles E. Marsh. ALS. DLC. mDW 37347. Praises DW's
public service and oratorical skill.

July 24   From D[avid] C. Van Derlip. ALS. DNA, RG 59. mDW 54124.
Accepts appointment of the *San Antonio Ledger* to publish the laws.

July 25   To Millard Fillmore. LS. NBuHi. mDW 37349. *Diplomatic Papers*, 2. Reports Crampton has asked the Provincial authorities to
cease their harrassment of American fishermen; sees little else that
can be done at present.

July 25   To Millard Fillmore. ALS. NBuHi. mDW 37352. *Diplomatic
Papers*, 2. Explains why he cannot accept appointment as U.S. minister to England; does not like "Hilliard's letter"; considers resigning as secretary of state.

July 25   From Millard Fillmore. ALS. NhHi. mDW 37356. *Diplomatic
Papers*, 2. Discusses the fisheries controversy.

July 26   To Millard Fillmore. ALS. NBuHi. mDW 37360. Discusses the
fisheries controversy.

July 26   To Millard Fillmore. ALS. NBuHi. mDW 37362. *Diplomatic
Papers*, 2. Fears bad health will prevent his working in August and
September; wonders if it would not be best for him to resign.

July 26   To Millard Fillmore (with ANS by Fillmore). LS. NBuHi. mDW
37366. Again recommends that Samuel F. Train be appointed to a
vacant pursership.

July 26   To Samuel Jaudon. ALS. NHi. mDW 37368. Offers to appoint
him bearer of despatches, and asks by which ship he is sailing.

July 26   To A. C. Kingsland. Copy. NhHi. mDW 37369. Van Tyne, p.
637. Asks Kingsland to do what he can for the destitute family of
the late adjutant general, Roger Jones.

July 26   To John Taylor. LS. MBBS. mDW 37371. Explains arrangements he has made for the sale of cattle to Tilden Ames.

July 26   To Caroline Story White Webster. ALS. NhHi. mDW 37374. PC, 2: 544. Offers to exchange a "Green goose" for a pair of "your Boston chickens."

July 26   From S[olomon] D. Jacobs. ALS. DNA, RG 59. mDW 54971. Orders a commission for William H. Chandler, recently appointed postmaster at Evansville, Ind.

July 28   From George Ticknor Curtis. ALS. CtY. mDW 37376. Asks about a copy of the Constitution he sent to the State Department to have compared with the original document.

July 29   From Millard Fillmore. LS. NhHi. mDW 37378. *Diplomatic Papers*, 2. Has ordered the U.S.S. *Mississippi* to the Newfoundland fishing grounds; asks for DW's report about reasons the U.S. entered into the 1818 agreement on fishing rights.

July 29   From Benjamin C. Foster. LS. UkLPR. mDWs. Has received Schenck at Buenos Ayres; stresses the importance of maintaining the unity of the Republics of the La Plata.

July 30   To Millard Fillmore. LS. NBuHi. mDW 37381. PC, 2: 545. Reports Israel D. Andrews has just arrived from St. John's with his report.

July 30   To Millard Fillmore. LS. NBuHi. mDW 37383. *Diplomatic Papers*, 2. Discussses reciprocal trade, and provisions of the treaty of 1818 relative to the fisheries.

July 31   To Caroline Le Roy Appleton. Copy. MHi. mDW 37393. Presents her with a portrait of himself lately painted by Healy.

July 31   To Millard Fillmore. LS. NBuHi. mDW 37396. PC, 2: 546. Describes Israel D. Andrews as a man of great ability; states that Andrews is just finishing his report.

July 31   To Franklin Haven. LS. MH–H. mDW 37400. PC, 2: 546–547. Gives specifications for a fishing boat he wants built and asks that Train give them to a suitable builder.

July   From James Watson Webb (enclosure: Louis Kossuth, letter of authorization, July 13, 1852). Printed. *MHi Proc.*, 44 (1910–1911): 213. Reports Kossuth has sailed from New York under a false identity; encloses evidence of Kossuth's connection with a movement against Haiti.

[July]   Paper on the fisheries (with note by Daniel Fletcher Webster). Draft. NhHi. mDW 37407.

[July/Aug]   To [Israel D.] Andrews. ALS. CtY. mDW 38194. Invites Andrews to dinner with Crampton, and requests him to invite "Mr. Perley" to Marshfield.

Aug 1   To Millard Fillmore. LS. NBuHi. mDW 37474. *Diplomatic Papers*, 2. Agrees with the decision to order Commodore Perry to the fishing grounds: states his remarks on the fisheries have been misreported by the press.

Aug 1   To Millard Fillmore. LS. NBuHi. mDW 37478. Discusses the preparation of a report on "the business of Nicaragua."

Aug 1   To John Taylor. LS. NhHi. mDW 37481. Gives instructions for farm work to be done at The Elms.

Aug 1   To Daniel Fletcher Webster. ALS. CtY. mDW 37483. Has decided not to go to Salem; is expecting Fletcher and others at Marshfield on Tuesday (Aug. 3).

Aug 2   From Cornelius Conway Felton. ALS. NhHi. mDW 37484. Van Tyne, pp. 637–638. Will visit Marshfield, if convenient, once the Cambridge school exams are over; thanks DW for a set of his *Works*.

Aug 2   From C. Cather Flint. ALS. DLC. mDW 37487. Advocates war with England or some other great power.

Aug 3   To Millard Fillmore. LS. NBuHi. mDW 37489. *Dipomatic Papers*, 2. Is prepared to do everything possible to help Fillmore through the remainder of his administration.

Aug 3   From John L. Stephens.   341

Aug 3   Recommendation from Peter B. Mead, for James Hogg—"decorating the public grounds at Washington" (ALS. DNA, RG 48. mDWs).

Aug 4   To Timothy Childs. LS. NN. mDW 37493. Encloses a letter of introduction to the U.S. consul at Paris.

Aug 4   To Millard Fillmore. LS. NBuHi. mDW 37494. *Diplomatic Papers*, 2. Encloses drafts of treaties prepared by himself and Crampton on Oregon and on copyright; expresses alarm over the fisheries crisis, and sees a reverse parallel to the McLeod case.

Aug 4   To Jared Sparks. LS. MH–H. mDW 37498. Thanks him for his note recommending Lorenzo Sabine, an authority on the fisheries whose assistance may be required.

Aug 4   From William Cabell Rives. ALS draft. DLC. mDW 37500. Reports on the massacre of the crew of an American schooner on Madagascar; reports also on political developments in France.

Aug 5   To Franklin Haven. LS. MH–H. mDW 37504. Has been called suddenly to Washington; asks him to discount a note; will return once Congress adjourns.

Aug 5   To Harriette Story White Paige. ALS. MH–H. mDW 37506. States: "For Mrs. Paige; from her affectionate brother."

Aug 5   From S[olomon] D. Jacobs. ALS. DNA, RG 59. mDW 54923. Orders commissions for two recently appointed postmasters.

Aug 5   From [?] Zermar. ALS. DLC. mDW 37511. Asks DW to help "Captain Furber" obtain command of a Collins Line steamer.

Aug 5   Application from Anthony Southall—an army commission (ALS. DLC. mDW 37509).

Aug 6   To Caleb Cushing. ALS. NN. mDW 37513. Fuess, *Cushing*, 2: 89. Has been summoned to Washington; will see Cushing about "our business" after his return.

Aug 6   From George Ticknor Curtis. ALS. CtY. mDWs. Wants DW to find out if the *Intelligencer* will admit Gen. Scott's authorship of article on nationalization laws; asks DW to return a copy of the Constitution along with his signature verifying its authenticity before he leaves office; states "our eager friend Mr. White is pushing ahead with his paper," though Ticknor has persuaded him not to use it yet, to avoid embarrassing DW with the administration.

Aug 6   From W. H. Merriam. ALS. DLC. mDW 37515. Requests a copy of DW's address at the cornerstone-laying ceremony of "the Washington National Monument."

Aug 6   From Joseph C. Morton. ALS. DLC. mDW 37517. Invites DW's response to "the authors of the accompanying communication, and their fellow citizens."

Aug 7   To Edward Codman & Co. ALS. MWalB. mDW 37519. Orders two or three dozen bottles of claret sent to Marshfield.

Aug 8   To Millard Fillmore. Telegram. NBuHi. mDW 37520. Is leaving today for Washington.

Aug 9   From Lorenzo Sabine. ALS. NhD. mDW 37522. Will make every effort to come to Washington for consultations on the fisheries controversy.

Aug 10   To Millard Fillmore. LS. NBuHi. mDW 37524. Discusses the proposed message on Nicaragua.

Aug 10   To Samuel Jaudon. LS. NHi. mDW 37527. Reports his health is better; asks Jaudon and Blatchford to come for a short visit.

Aug 10   To John Taylor. ALS. Fiske Free Library, Claremont, N.H. mDW 37528. Makes various inquiries about the work at Elms Farm.

Aug 10   To Daniel Fletcher Webster. LS. NhHi. mDW 37532. Van Tyne, p. 536. Reports his arrival in Washington last night; finds the president quite cordial.

Aug 10   To Charles Porter Wright. ALS. NhHi. mDW 37533. PC, 2: 548–549. Discusses guano and lime fertilizers.

Aug 10   From William Cabell Rives. ALS draft. DLC. mDW 37537. ALS revised draft. DLC. mDW 37541. Reports the rescue and care of American seamen shipwrecked on Madagascar; reports also on elections in several departments in France.

Aug 10–11   From James Watson Webb.   342

Aug 11   To Sir John Fiennes Crampton. LS. UkLPR. mDW 37549. Will inform the secretary of the navy of alterations in the Admiralty's regulations governing the running lights carried on British ships.

Aug 11   To Daniel Fletcher Webster. LS. NhHi. mDW 37550. W & S, 16: 662. Reports his health is "uncommonly good."

Aug 11   From Nathan G. King. ALS. DNA, RG 59. mDW 55037. Requests commissions for Caleb Hersey and William S. Gibson, recently appointed postmasters.

Aug 12   To [James] Cooper. AL draft. CtY. mDW 37555. Invites him to "a kind of bachelor's dinner."

Aug 12   To Millard Fillmore. LS. NBuHi. mDW 37556. *Diplomatic Papers*, 2. Asks what should be done about the Lobos Islands.

Aug 12   To Millard Fillmore. LS. NBuHi. mDW 37560. Asks which of them should write Barnard concerning the outfit recommended to Congress for the Berlin mission.

Aug 12   To Alexander Hugh Holmes Stuart. Draft. CtY. mDW 37562. Asks him to look over something and then transmit it to the President.

Aug 12   To Charles Henry Thomas. LS. MHi. mDW 37563. Gives instructions about the cattle recently driven to Marshfield by Tilden Ames; is grieved to hear that Thomas's son is near death.

Aug 12   From Nathan G. King. ALS. DNA, RG 59. mDW 54919. Orders a commission for Goldsmith F. Bailey, newly-appointed postmaster for Fitchburg, Mass.

Aug 12   From William Henry Seward. ALS. John R. Morison, Peterborough, N.H. mDW 37565. Asks for a copy of DW's "letter to the Fishermen."

Aug 12   Recommendation from John G. Miller, for the St. Louis *Missouri Republican*—public printer (ALS. DNA, RG 59. mDW 54240).

Aug 13   To Millard Fillmore. LS. NBuHi. mDW 37566. Does not object if Fillmore sees "this Gentleman," but complains that confidential conversations and letters are being reported in the press.

Aug 13   To William Henry Seward. LS. NRU. mDW 37567. Sends him documents relative to the 1818 treaty with Great Britain, with comments; asks him to look over the Nicaragua message "before you speak."

Aug 13   To Daniel Fletcher Webster. ALS. NhHi. mDW 37569. Asks him to recommend someone qualified to be judge in Oregon.

Aug 14   To Edward Everett.   343

Aug 14   To Millard Fillmore. LS. NBuHi. mDW 37573. Thinks Fillmore might be interested in "some portions of this despatch."

[Aug 14]   To [Millard Fillmore]. AL. NBuHi. mDW 37575. Reports Soulé's assessment of three candidates for the Supreme Court.

Aug 14   To John Kintzing Kane. LS. PPAmP. mDW 37579. Requests a statement of the facts in the conviction and jailing of Thomas Powell.

Aug 14   To Hiram Ketchum. ALS. NhD. mDW 37581. *Diplomatic Papers*, 2. Asks for proof that American citizens have occupied the Lobos Islands for many years.

Aug 14   To Hiram Ketchum. ALS. NhD. mDW 37583. Calls for information on the Lobos Islands.

Aug 15   To Millard Fillmore. Unfinished draft. CtY. mDW 37585. Encloses a letter from "our mutual friend Barnard" thinks "all sensible Americans abroad" are disgusted by recent Whig Party proceedings.

Aug 15   To James Louis Petigru.   344

Aug 15   To William Henry Seward. LS. NRU. mDW 37593. Compliments Seward for his "successful" speech in the Senate yesterday on the fisheries.

Aug 15   To James Watson Webb. LS. CtY. mDW 37595. *Diplomatic Papers*, 2. Predicts the Lobos Islands and fisheries controversies will soon be resolved; is disgusted by calumnious "letter writers."

Aug 15   From Robert M. Walsh. ALS. DNA, RG 59. mDW 56335. Reports his arrival at New York from Nicaragua.

Aug 16   To Mrs. [Meredith Poindexter?] Gentry. Draft. CtY. mDW 37597. Presents a set of his *Works*.

Aug 16   Testimonial letter for Henry C. Yeatman. ALS. T. mDWs.

Aug 16   From Joseph Reed Ingersoll. ALS. NhD. mDW 37598. Is awaiting Senate action on his nomination as U.S. minister to Great Britain; invites DW to visit him in Philadelphia.

Aug 16   From James C. Jewett (with six attachments). ALS. DNA, RG 59. mDW 56961. Encloses papers relating to his guano operations in the Lobos Islands.

Aug 16   From Samuel Robinson. ALS. DNA, RG 59. mDW 56960. States that he fitted out vessels for the Lobos Islands from 1827 to 1832 "without asking Permission of anybody."

Aug 17   To George E. Badger. LS. CoHi. mDWs. Transmits the draft of an amendment to the Act of 1848 which would confer civil and criminal powers upon the U.S. minister and consuls in Turkey.

Aug 17   To Sir John Fiennes Crampton. LS. UkLPR. mDW 37601.

Transmits a presidential exequator for H.M. government's newly-appointed consul at Cincinnati, Charles Rowcraft.

[Aug 17]   To Millard Fillmore. ALS. NBuHi. mDW 37271. Decides to stay in because of the bad weather; will examine the consular papers at home.

Aug 17   To Millard Fillmore. LS. NBuHi. mDW 37602. Submits the cases of seventeen consulships, and asks Fillmore to indicate his wishes in each one.

[c. Aug 17]   From Sir John Fiennes Crampton. Invitation. CtY. mDW 37604.

Aug 17   From Millard Fillmore. Invitation. CtY. mDW 37606.

Aug 17   From C[harles?] Fletcher.   344

Aug 17   From Mrs. [Meredith Poindexter?] Gentry. AL. NhHi. mDW 37615. Thanks DW for the endorsed set of his *Works*.

Aug 17   From John S. Gilmer. Copy. UkLPR. mDWs. Transmits a letter relative to the attack on the brig *Mary Adeline* in the Zaire River.

Aug 17   From Nathan G. King. ALS. DNA, RG 59. mDW 54977. Orders commissions for John H. Denio and Benjamin M. Flint, recently appointed postmasters.

Aug 17   Recommendation from C[harles] P. Bertrand, for the Little Rock *Arkansas Whig*—public printer (ALS. DNA, RG 59. mDW 54246).

Aug 18   To Sir John Fiennes Crampton. LS. UkLPR. mDW 37619. Acknowledges Crampton's report of irregularities committed by an American in conveying coolies to Peru aboard a British vessel.

Aug 18   To Millard Fillmore. LS. NBuHi. mDW 37620. Reports the U.S. consulate at Bremen is being competently filled by Ralph King.

Aug 18   To John Taylor. LS with PS in DW's hand. MWalB. mDW 37622. Harvey, *Reminiscences of DW*, p. 307. Discusses farm business.

Aug 18   From John Salmon. ALS. DNA, RG 59. mDW 56986. Reports he has the log of a ship which visited the Lobos Islands in April, 1803.

Aug 19   To Millard Fillmore. LS. NBuHi. mDW 37624. Is sending Abbot with letters on the Lobos Islands question.

Aug 19   To John McLean. LS. DLC. mDW 37626. Reports [E. A.] Bradford has consented to be nominated to the Supreme Court.

Aug 19   From George Chipman. ALS. DNA, RG 59. mDW 56989. Comments in geological criteria which might be used in determining the ownership of islands.

Aug 19   From William Miles. ALS. DNA, RG 59. mDW 56987. Discusses the history of U.S. commerce with Peru and the Lobos Islands.

Aug 20   To Daniel Dewey Barnard. Unfinished draft. CtY. mDW 37629. Introduces Samuel Frothingham and his son-in-law.

Aug 20   Testimonial letter for Charles S. Horner. Draft. CtY. mDW 37630.

Aug 20   To Seth Weston. LS. NhHi. mDW 37631. Discusses plans for the construction of a house.

Aug 20   To Charles Porter Wright. Printed. PC, 2: 549. Gives instructions for spreading lime fertilizer.

Aug 20   From Sir John Fiennes Crampton. Copy. UkLPR. mDWs. Transmits a telescope to be given to an American captain who assisted a wrecked British ship.

Aug 20　From Hiram Ketchum (enclosures: press clippings; Ketchum to the editors of the *Journal of Commerce*). ALS. DNA, RG 59. mDW 57000. Calls attention to a news article on the Lobos Islands; comments on his own letter to the *Journal of Commerce* concerning the discovery of the islands.

Aug 20　From S[amuel] H. Walley. ALS. DLC. mDW 37633. Conveys a suggestion that DW recommend a consul for Aix-la-Chapelle.

Aug 20　From Daniel Fletcher Webster. ALS. NhHi. mDW 37635. Makes a suggestion regarding the present negotiations with Britain; reports a fair at Duxbury and a fishing party.

Aug 20　From J. Howard Williams. ALS. DNA, RG 59. mDW 56998. Comments on the Lobos Islands problem.

Aug 21　To Millard Fillmore. LS. NBuHi. mDW 37640. *Diplomatic Papers*, 2. Transmits despatches received from Letcher; thinks the situation in Mexico is "horrid" and predicts the U.S. will have trouble because of its "obligations about the Indians."

Aug 21　To Hiram Ketchum. LS. NhD. mDW 37644. *Diplomatic Papers*, 2. Is much disturbed by the Lobos Islands problem; sharply criticizes Jewett for preparing to arm vessels and wage a private war.

Aug 21　To Don Juan Y. de Osma. Typed copy. DNA, RG 59. mDW 57004. Discusses the ownership of the Lobos Islands.

Aug 21　From B. L. Stinky. ALS. DLC. mDW 37647. Discusses the presidential election; urges DW to run.

Aug 21　Recommendation from Daniel Fletcher Webster, for George R. Lord—a clerkship (ALS. NhHi. mDW 37651).

Aug 21　Receipt for $150 paid R[euben] Burdine for rent. ADS. NhHi. mDW 40637.

Aug 22　To Millard Fillmore. LS. NBuHi. mDW 37654. *Diplomatic Papers*, 2. Reports a conversation with Crampton on the fisheries question.

Aug 22　To Daniel Fletcher Webster. ALS. NhHi. mDW 37657. *Diplomatic Papers*, 2. Is winding up his official business; thinks the (Boston) port inspectors would be ill-advised to pay Greely anything

Aug 22　From Charles M[ynn] Conrad. ALS. CtY. mDW 37660. Accepts an invitation to dine.

Aug 22　From William Winston Seaton. Copy. DLC. mDW 37661. Writes regarding the house DW is renting from R[euben] Burdine

Aug 23　To Richard Milford Blatchford. ALS. NhD. mDWs. *PC*, 2: 550. Will remain until Congress adjourns unless his catarrh returns.

Apg 23　To Millard Fillmore. LS wth PS in DW's hand. NBuHi. mDW 37666. Reports his catarrh has not yet returned; is working on the fisheries problem; wants to clear up as much business as possible.

Aug 23　To Millard Fillmore. LS. NBuHi. mDW 37669. Encloses the draft of a response to Corcoran's application relative to "the Ogle money."

Aug 23　To Francis Markoe. AL. DLC. mDW 37672. Invites him to dinner.

Aug 23　To [?]. LS draft. CtY. mDW 37663. Wishes to purchase a pair of Newfoundland dogs.

Aug 23　From Millard Fillmore. LS. DLC. mDW 37674. Severance, *Fillmore Papers*, 1: 382–383. Blames Marcoleta and the canal agents for frustrating a settlement of the Nicaraguan problem; suggests that Marcoleta's recall should be requested.

Aug 24   To Richard Milford Blatchford. *Printed. Diplomatic Papers*, 2. Asks whether the Lobos Islands affair or "an elaborate article on the fisheries" ought to be his finale.

Aug 24   From George Thomas Davis. ALS. CtY. mDW 37677. Encloses a letter from N. A. Chapman on the subject of the China mission.

Aug 24   From Seth Weston. ALS. NhHi. mDW 37678. Discusses the construction of a house on "the Island."

Aug 24   Receipt for $100 paid R[euben] Burdine in full for rent. ADS. NhHi. mDW 40639.

Aug 25   To Rev. Mr. [?] Sanford. Copy. NhHi. mDW 37681. *PC*, 2: 551. Is glad that Sanford is to take charge of the education of Fletcher's son, Daniel; recalls Sanford's mother-in-law.

Aug 25   From Sir John Fiennes Crampton. Copy. UkLPR. mDWs. Requests the U.S. government to change the designation of trade between California and the west coast of the U.S.

Aug 25   From Edward Everett. LC. MHi. mDW 37684. Comments on the appointment of a U.S. minister to England, and also on correspondence pertaining to the fisheries.

Aug 25   From Daniel Fletcher Webster. ALS. NhHi. mDW 37687. Reports on "the Webster meetings"; reports also that "Mother and friends are still here."

Aug 25   From Charles Porter Wright. ALS. NhHi. mDW 37690. Discusses farm business.

Aug 26   To [Angela Georgina] Burdett-Coutts. ALS. NhD. mDWs. Introduces Joseph Reed Ingersoll, the new U.S. minister to Great Britain.

Aug 26   To Millard Fillmore. ALS. NBuHi. mDW 37693. Discusses various appointments and nominees for office.

Aug 26   To Franklin Haven. Telegram. MH–H. mDW 37697. Asks Haven to open and read the letter he has written Fletcher today.

Aug 26   To J. H. Mey. Draft. CtY. mDW 37698. Replies to Mey's suggestions about the U.S. consular system; asks for copies of a bust of Fulton and for a work on trees by Micheux.

Aug 26   To John R. Thompson. Recipient's copy. DLC. mDW 37701. Refuses to authorize the publication now of "the letter to my farmer."

Aug 26   To Daniel Fletcher Webster. LS. MH–H. mDW 37702. Declares again he will not advise his friends how to act regarding the presidential election.

Aug 26   From James Cooper. ALS. DLC. mDW 37704. Reports Mangum's explanation for comments reported in today's *Baltimore Sun* concerning the distribution of public printing in North Carolina and Tennessee.

Aug 26   From Millard Fillmore. LS. John M. Taylor, San Francisco, Calif. mDW 37706. Reports the acting U.S. consul at Vienna may be an Austrian spy, and thinks he should be replaced at once.

Aug 26   From Hamilton Fish. ALS. DLC. mDWs. Encloses a letter from Charles Callaghan requesting information from the State Department.

Aug 26   From S[amuel] Nelson. Copy. UkLPR. mDWs. Writes regarding the case of Thomas Kaine (or Cain), whose extradition has been requested by Britain.

Aug 26   From Benjamin Patterson. ALS. DNA, RG 59. mDW 55047. Accepts appointment as U.S. marshal for northern Alabama.

Aug 26   From William Cabell Rives. ALS draft. DLC. mDW 37707. Reports informing the French government of the proposed modification in the projected postal convention.

Aug 27   To the respective diplomatic and consular agents of the United States in Europe. LS. DNA, RG 45. mDWs. Introduces Charlotte E. Wise.

Aug 27   To Millard Fillmore (with AN by Fillmore). LS. MHi. mDW 37710. Stresses the need to fill the Supreme Court vacancy; suggests withdrawing the [E. A.] Bradford nomination.

[Aug 27]   To Millard Fillmore. ALS. NBuHi. mDW 37711. Reports discussing the [E. A.] Bradford nomination with Henry Sheffie Geyer; mentions miscellaneous Senate proceedings.

Aug 27   To Millard Fillmore. LS. NBuHi. mDW 37715. Reports receiving "a very amiable answer from Mr. [Juan Y. de] Osma."

Aug 27   To Thomas Nelson. LS. CtY. mDW 37717. Requests his opinion on claims of the Hudson's Bay and Puget Sound companies for compensation for the loss of various rights in Oregon.

Aug 27   To Charles Porter Wright. ALS. NhHi. mDW 37719. Encloses money for Seth Weston.

Aug 27   From John D. Elliott. ALS. DLC. mDW 37720. Requests a copy of DW's opinion in the Planter's Bank case to publish for political purposes in the Jackson, Mississippi *Southern Star*.

Aug 27   From Millard Fillmore. LS. DLC. mDW 37722. Severance, *Fillmore Papers*, 1: 383–384. Writes regarding appointments in Oregon and Acapulco; asks if the Peruvian government might be asked to grant permission to take guano from the Lobos Islands to American ships which set sail under the misapprehension that the U.S. will protect them.

Aug 27   Recommendations from Alexander Hamilton Stephens, for the *Augusta* (Ga.) *Chronicle and Sentinel*, the Milledgeville, Georgia *Southern Recorder*, the *Columbus* (Ga.) *Enquirer*, and the Macon *Georgia Journal and Messenger*—public printers, ALS. DNA, RG 59. mDW 54242).

Aug 27   Passport for Charlotte B. [E.?] Wise, her child and nurses. Printed DS with MS insertions. DNA, RG 45. mDWs.

Aug 28   To Thomas Corwin. LS. DLC. mDW 37725. Introduces marine architect William H. Webb of New York.

Aug 28   To Sir John Fiennes Crampton. LS. UkLPR. mDW 37727. Has requested a report from Justice Samuel Nelson about extradition proceedings against Thomas Kaine (or Cain).

Aug 28   From David Outlaw. ALS. NhD. mDW 37729. Describes the Wilmington, North Carolina *Advertiser* as an entiirely respectable Whig newspaper.

Aug 28   John Thomas [of New Jersey] to Caroline Le Roy Webster. ALS. DLC. mDW 37731. Sends something designed to reduce the danger of steamer travel, and asks that it be shown to DW and, if possible, to the president.

Aug 29   From John Grenier. ALS. DNA, RG 59. mDW 55008. Accepts appointment as territorial secretary of New Mexico.

[Aug 30]   To Joseph Reed Ingersoll. LS. NhD. mDW 38124. Makes arrangements for meeting or writing to Ingersoll according to circumstances.

Aug 30   To Franck Taylor. LS. DLC. mDW 37732. Asks for eleven volumes of state papers pertaining to the French Revolution.

Aug 30   To Charles Porter Wright. ALS. NhHi. mDW 37734. Discusses farm business.

Aug 30   From Joseph Pearson Caldwell. ALS. DLC. mDW 37736. Is gratified by the selection of the Wilmington, North Carolina *Weekly Commercial* to publish the laws; alludes to Mangum's "unprovoked attack, upon Mr. Webster."

[Aug 30]   From William Henry Seward. ALS. CtY. mDW 37739. States that the Lobos Islands message was printed without being read; asks that Webb be sent a copy.

Aug 31   To William A. Kobbé. LS. NN mDW 37741. Answers a passport request by stating a five years' residency is required of aliens desiring U.S. citizenship.

Aug 31   From Alexander Hugh Holmes Stuart. LS. DNA, RG 59. mDW 55006. Orders a commission for Robert Greenhow, newly-appointed associate land agent for California.

Sept 1   To Millard Fillmore. LS. NBuHi. mDW 37742. Asks him to read over a paper.

Sept 1   To Thomas M. Rodney. LS. NhExP. mDWs. Sends him a letter in relation to the U.S. consular agent at Cardenas, Mexico. and urges him to use caution in choosing consular agents.

Sept 1   From S[olomon] D. Jacobs. ALS. DNA, RG 59. mDW 55027. Orders commissions for postmasters recently appointed in Alabama and South Carolina.

Sept 2   To [Samuel] Rogers. Printed. *PC*, 2: 551–552. Introduces Joseph Reed Ingersoll.

Sept 2   From Ambrose Dudley Mann. ALS. DNA, RG 59. mDW 56077. Calls the refusal of the Russian consul at Paris to grant him a visa a "palpable violation" of the convention between Russia and the U.S.

Sept 3   From Leonidas Shaver. ALS. DNA, RG 59. mDW 55093. Agrees to be appointed associate justice of the Utah territorial supreme court.

Sept 4   From H[enry] Z. Hayner. ALS. DNA, RG 59. mDW 55041. Accepts appointment as chief justice of the Minnesota territorial supreme court.

Sept 4   From Samuel D. Hubbard. ALS. DNA, RG 59. mDW 55031. Accepts appointment as postmaster general.

Sept 4   From L[azarus] H. Read. ALS. DNA, RG 59. mDW 55082. Accepts appointment as chief justice of Utah, and asks for directions how to get there.

Sept 4   Applications from John H. Christy, for the Athens, Georgia *Southern Herald*—public printer, ALS. DNA, RG 59. mDW 54237); from Joseph L. Locke & Co., for the *Savannah* (Ga.) *Republican*— public printer (LS. DNA, RG 59. mDW 54234).

Sept 5   To John Taylor. LS. Robert and Richard Upton, Concord, N.H.
mDW 37743. Asks him to come to Marshfield.

Sept 7   Promissory note for $2000 payable to George S. Gideon & Co.
ADS. NhD. mDW 40641.

Sept 8   From S[olomon] D. Jacobs. ALS. DNA, RG 59. mDW 54941.
Orders a commission for Dexter C. Bloomer, newly-appointed postmaster for Seneca Falls, N.Y.

Sept 10   From Millard Fillmore. LS. NhHi. mDW 37748. Severance,
Fillmore Papers, 1: 385–386. Discusses a matter relating to the
Lobos Islands.

Sept 11   From H[iram] Becker. ALS. DNA, RG 59. mDW 54929. Accepts
appointment as U.S. marshal for Michigan.

Sept 11   From Caleb Cushing.   348

Sept 11   From Joseph L. Locke & Co. LS. DNA, RG 59. mDW 54116.
Accept appointment of the *Savannah* (Ga.) *Republican* to publish
the laws.

Sept 12   To Millard Fillmore   349

Sept 12   To Franklin Haven. ALS. M–HH. mDW 37754. Asks him to
discount an acceptance; reports the return of his catarrh.

Sept 13   To John Taylor. ALS. MHi. mDWs. Harvey, *Reminiscences of
DW*, pp. 307–308. Discusses farm business.

Sept 13   W. S. Jones to Charles M[ynn] Conrad for DW. Accepts appointment of the *Augusta* (Ga.) *Chronicle and Sentinel* to publish
the laws.

Sept 14   To [Franklin Haven]. ALS. MH–H. mDW 36531. Expects to see
the Havens in Marshfield next week if the weather is fair.

Sept 14   From Charles Edwards Lester. ALS. MHi. mDW 37756. Thanks
DW for [Charles S. J.] Goodrich's appointment to the Lyons consulate; sends a book on the "Napoleon Dynasty."

Sept 14   From Horace Noyes. ALS. NhHi. mDW 37758. Sends pears
grown at the site of DW's birth in West Franklin, N.H.

Sept 14   From Thomas Handasyd Perkins. ALS. NhHi. mDW 37760.
States that Gardiner will be in touch to arrange a meeting; presumes DW has all the necessary papers with him.

Sept 15   To Julia Maria Blatchford (enclosure: autograph of George
Washington). ALS. Mrs. J. H. N. Potter, Jamestown, R.I. mDW
37763. Presents her with autographs of George and Martha
Washington.

Sept 15   To Millard Fillmore. ALS. NBuHi. mDW 37764. *Diplomatic
Papers*, 2. Assumes full responsibility for the letter to Jewett regarding the Lobos Islands, and thinks it may have been a mistake.

Sept 15   From Millard L. Fell. ALS. NhHi. mDW 37769. Writes on the
presumption DW has agreed to lecture "before our association
[New York Mercantile Library Association?] upon the terms proposed."

Sept 15   From G. E. Waterton. ALS. DLC. mDW 37771. Asks him to peruse a pamphlet.

Sept 16   To [Caleb Cushing]. LS by proxy. NN. mDW 37775. Fuess,
Cushing, 2: 91. Promises to see Cushing and arrange their business
"if life lasts."

Sept 16   To Millard Fillmore. LS. NBuHi. mDW 37778. *PC*, 2: 553. Reports he is suffering from catarrh and severe diarrhea; is on a liquid diet.

Sept 16   To Millard Fillmore. Draft. CtY. mDW 37767. LS. NBuHi. mDW 37781. Suggests that new despatches be sent in hopes of preventing a possible conflict with Peru over the Lobos Islands.

Sept 16   To Joseph Reed Ingersoll. LS. NhD. mDW 37783. Reports someone is under consideration in case of [John C. B.] Davis' resignation (secretary to the U.S. legation at London).

Sept 16   From Henry K. Elkins. ALS. DNA, RG 59. mDW 54985. Accepts appointment as U.S. marshal for Wisconsin.

Sept 16   From Thomas Otis Le Roy & Co. LS. NhHi. mDW 37785. Solicit DW's professional services in the trial of a patent suit with the Tathems.

Sept 16   From John Taylor. ALS. NhHi. mDW 37787. Van Tyne, p. 686. Reports arriving home to find his wife thinking he had been killed.

Sept 16   From Thomas Wren Ward. ALS. NhHi. mDW 37790. *PC*, 2: 553. Invites DW to dine with Thomas Baring.

[Sept 17]   To Richard Milford Blatchford. ALS. NhD. mDW 37792. Reports feeling "rather well & strong today."

[Sept 17]   To Richard Milford Blatchford. LS by proxy. DLC. mDW 37793. Has written "Mrs. Duncan about the testimony."

Sept 17   To [Horace Noyes]. Copy. NhHi. mDW 37795. Van Tyne, pp. 638–639. Acknowledges a gift of pears from his New Hampshire birthsite; recollects that the tree was planted by his maternal grandfather.

Sept 17   To Thomas Wren Ward. Printed. *PC*, 2: 554. Excuses himself from a dinner invitation on doctor's orders.

Sept 17   Porter & Eckel to Charles M[ynn] Conrad, for DW. LS. DNA, RG 59. mDW 54118. Accept appointment of the Wilmington *Delaware State Journal* to publish the laws.

Sept 17   From J[oseph] Stillwell. ALS. DNA, RG 59. mDW 55101. Accepts appointment as U.S. attorney for eastern Arkansas.

Sept 17–Nov 10   Reports of William Miles, Special Agent in Peru, to DW (with Miles' journal). ALS. DNA, RG 59. mDW 56384.

Sept 18   To [Edward Codman & Co.?]. ALS. NhD. mDW 37797. Orders champagne.

Sept 18   From Samuel Appleton Appleton. ALS. MHi. mDW 37798. Has paid the freight, etc. on DW's furniture; reports family and society news.

Sept 18   From John Wilson. ALS. DNA, RG 59. mDW 55137. Accepts appointment as commissioner of the General Land Office.

[Sept 19]   To Charles H. Warren. AL incomplete. NN. mDW 37800. *MHi Proc.*, 2nd series, 15(1901, 1902), 280. Recollects his maternal grandfather, Roger Eastman; sends pears from a tree planted by Eastman near the site of DW's birth in West Franklin, N.H.

Sept 19   From Millard Fillmore. ALS. MeHi. mDW 37804. *Diplomatic Papers*, 2. Discusses DW's letter to Jewett and a more recent despatch from J. R. Clay on Peruvian rights to the Lobos Islands.

Sept 20   Note for $2000 drawn on G[eorge] S. Gideon & Co. ADS. MHi. mDWs.

Sept 21   From Cornelius Conway Felton. Copy. NhD. mDW 37842.

Sends two volumes for Mrs. Webster; comments on his recent stay at Marshfield, and urges DW to write an autobiography.

Sept 21   From Edward P. Little. LS. NhHi. mDW 37846. Asks DW to help him sell his farm.

[c. Sept 21]   From Daniel Fletcher Webster (enclosure: press clippings). ALS. NhHi. mDW 37848. Encloses articles discussing the question of Whig support for Scott.

Sept 22   To Millard Fillmore.   350

Sept 22   From Richard H. Bayard. ALS draft. DLC. mDW 37865. Reports on Belgian affairs.

Sept 22   From Alexander Hugh Holmes Stuart. ALS. DNA, RG 59. mDW 54959. Orders a commission for E. A. Cabell, newly-appointed principal clerk of the public lands.

Sept 22   Memorandum for Mr. Gardiner (on claim against Chilean government in the case of the brig *Macedonian*). DS. NhD. mDW 37861.

Sept 23   Application from John M. Butler, for the Little Rock *Arkansas Whig*—public printer (ALS. DNA, RG 59. mDW 54232).

Sept 24   From J[ohn] B[utler] Chapman. ALS. CtY. mDW 37874. Extract. DLC. mDW 37867. Discusses problems connected with the survey of public lands and land claimed by the Hudson's Bay and Puget Sound Agricultural Company in Oregon.

Sept 24   From Moses Hicks Grinnell et al. (with Grinnell to DW, Oct 9, 1852).   356

Sept 25   To John E. Addicks. LS. PHi. mDW 37884. Declines an invitation to address the Franklin Institute at Philadelphia.

Sept 25   To Edward P. Little. Draft. NhHi. mDW 37886. Van Tyne, p. 638. Speaks sympathetically of the recent death of Little's wife; promises to speak highly of his farm to prospective buyers.

[Sept 26]   To Richard Milford Blatchford. ALS. MHi. mDW 37888. *W & S*, 16: 681. Describes the consequences of a violent ocean storm; expects to see Blatchford here soon.

Sept 27   From Millard Fillmore. LS. DLC. mDW 37892. Severance, *Fillmore Papers*, 1: 389–390. Is distressed to hear of DW's poor health; is expecting a new minister from Peru; regrets being unable to give "our friend [Theodore S.] Fay" a diplomatic post.

Sept 28   To Millard Fillmore.   351

Sept 28   To Le Roy Pope et al. LS. NhHi. mDW 37897. Declines an invitation to speak at Memphis.

Sept 29   To Richard Milford Blatchford. Printed. *PC*, 2: 555. Has just gotten over "a bad turn"; reports the fish are arriving "in multitudes."

Sept 29   To Franklin Haven. Printed. *W & S*, 16: 665. Reports purchasing land for $1000; asks to draw on Haven in anticipation of his "India rubber fees."

Sept 29   To John Taylor. ALS. CSmH. mDW 37901. Directs Taylor to bring seven cattle to Brighton, and to come on to Marshfield with his accounts.

Sept 30   To Caleb Cushing.   352
Sept 30   To Millard Fillmore.   352

Sept 30   From William Hunter. ALS. DLC. mDW 37906. Writes regarding the consular convention with the Hanse towns in Germany.

Sept 30   From [Abbott Lawrence]. Draft. DLC. mDW 37910. Hamilton

Andrews Hill, *Memoir of Abbott Lawrence* (Boston, 1883), pp. 228–
232. Reviews his record as U.S. minister to Great Britain.

Sept 30 From Leonidas Shaver. ALS. DNA, RG 59. mDW 55091. Accepts appointment as territorial justice for Utah.

Oct 1 To Henry Fairbanks. LS.: Nh.. mDW 37937. Declines an invitation to address the United Literary Societies of Dartmouth College.

Oct 1 To J. J[ames] May. LS. NhD. mDW 37939. Encloses a draft for
$500 to be credited to his account.

Oct. 1 To John Taylor. Telegram. MBBS. mDW 37940. Tells him to look
out for "a verry handsome pair of oxen."

Oct 1 From [John C. Bancroft Davis]. AL draft. DLC. mDW 37941.
Asks to be recalled as secretary to the U.S. legation at London.

Oct 1 From Millard Fillmore. LS. NhHi. mDW 37942. *PC*, 2: 555–556.
Expresses concern over DW's health; has been unable to get a new
proposition from Osma on the Lobos Islands.

Oct. 2 Receipt for $8.69 paid Aaron Livermore for groceries. ADS.
NhHi. mDW 40644.

Oct 4 From George Perkins Marsh. ALS draft. VtU. mDW 37950. Writes
regarding Dr. Jonas King's conviction by a Greek court.

Oct 4 Application from Ryan & Co., for the *Green Bay* (Wisc.) *Spectator*—public printer (LS. DNA, RG 59. mDW 54229).

Oct 7 From Richard H. Bayard. ALS. draft. DLC. mDW 37953. Reports on Belgian politics.

Oct 8 To Millard Fillmore. Draft. DLC. mDW 37957. LS. NBuHi. mDW
37959. Suggests that [Theodore S.] Fay be transferred from Berlin
to London to succeed Davis as secretary to that legation.

Oct 8 To George Griswold. Copy. NhHi. mDW 37967. Van Tyne, pp.
732–733. Reminds Griswold of the $1000 fee promised in the event
of a favorable ruling in *Goodyear* v. *Day*.

Oct 8 To Charles H. Peirce. LS. NhD. mDWs. Declines an invitation to
lecture before the Rochester Athaeneum and Mechanics Association.

Oct 9 From J[ames] W. Boyden. ALS. DLC. mDW 37970. Invites DW to
give an address at the Amherst cattle show and agricultural fair.

Oct 9 From George Perkins Marsh. ALS copy. VtU. mDW 37979. Encloses his report regarding Dr. Jonas King's conviction by a Greek
court, and apologizes that the copy is not better.

Oct 9 From Alfred Pell. ALS. DLC. mDW 37981. Supports DW's position on the Lobos Islands question; insists the islands should not be
subject to Peru.

Oct 9 Recommendation from Isaac Scholfield, for C. Scholfield and
Selim E. Woodworth (with William Hayden to DW, Oct 13, 1852)—
claims commissioners in California (ALS. DLC. mDW 38030).

Oct 10 To William T. Savage (with Savage to George Ticknor, Jan 23,
1853). Copy. NhHi. mDW 37985. *Granite Monthly*, 8 (March,
1885): 81. Calls for "Christian intercession" in the dispute between
Horace Noyes and his mother over the will of Parker Noyes.

Oct 10 From John Barney. ALS. DLC. mDW 37989. Finds apathy prevailing among rank-and-file Whigs, and predicts Scott will be defeated; asks if DW wants anything done about a Webster ticket in Maryland.

Oct 10   From R[ichard] J. Mapes (enclosure: press clippings). ALS. NhHi. mDW 37993. Van Tyne, pp. 539–540. Asks if DW will accept nomination for president by the American Party.

Oct 11   From H[enry] Long & Brother. LS. DLC. mDW 37998. Presents the novel *Northwood* by Sarah J. Hale, written in response to the "prejudicial and unfair view of Southern institution's" portrayed in *Uncle Tom's Cabin.*

Oct 11   Recommendations from H. S. [Gregg?] to Charles M[ynn] Conrad, for DW, for the *Daily St. Louis Intelligencer,* and the *Lexington* (Mo.) *Weekly Express*—public printers (ALS. DNA, RG 59. mDW 54254).

Oct 12   *To Moses Hicks Grinnell* (enclosure: DW to Grinnell et al., Oct 12, 1852).   357

Oct 12   *To Moses Hicks Grinnell et al.* (with DW to Grinnell, Oct 12, 1852).   357

Oct 12   To Franklin Haven. LS. MH–H. mDW 38004. Discusses a bank note.

Oct 12   To Joseph Reed Ingersoll. Copy. MHi. mDW 38007. Supports plans for a World's Fair in New York next year and asks Ingersoll for his support of the enterprise.

Oct 12   To Theodore Sedgewick. LS. NjP. mDW 38011. Supports plans for a bonded warehouse for the purpose of a World's Fair at New York next year; will write unofficialy to U.S. diplomatic representatives and ask their support for it also.

Oct 12   From [Anonymous]. AL. NhHi. mDW 38015. Warns DW he must disclaim his supporters and declare for Scott or suffer public disgrace.

Oct 13   *To Moses Hicks Grinnell et al.*   358

Oct 13   From John B. Cross. ALS. DLC. mDW 38026. Offers to attempt to cure DW's diarrhea with "my electrical instruments."

Oct 13   From Millard Fillmore. LS. NhHi. mDW 38027. *PC,* 2: 558. Is relieved to hear of the favorable report from DW's physicians; doubts the threatened expedition against Cuba will materialize; reports the Lobos Islands controversy is yet unsettled.

Oct 13   From Mrs. A. P. S. Putnam. ALS. DLC. mDW 38032. Asks for a lock of DW's hair.

Oct 13   Recommendations from William Hayden, for Charles Scholfield and Selim E. Woodworth (enclosure: Isaac Scholfield to DW, Oct 9, 1852)—commissioners of claims in California (ALS. DLC. mDW 38031).

Oct 14   To John Taylor. ALS. NhD. mDWs. "All well; Mr. Noyes money goes with this."

Oct 14   To Diplomatic Agents and Consuls of the United States in Great Britain. LS. Mrs. James A. Shanahan, Jr., Manchester, N.H. mDWs. Asks them to assist John R. Tracy, who goes to Europe to dispose of the patent rights for a peculiar method of manufacturing shot.

Oct 14   *From William A. Bradley.*   359

Oct 14   *From James Dwight.*   360

Oct 14   From Edward A. Hopkins. ALS. DLC. mDW 38037. Offers to

come to Marshfield with the latest news from South America whenever DW feels well enough to see him.

Oct 14   From C[yrus] Huntington. ALS. DLC. mDW 38039. Asks for a
few lines in DW's hand.

Oct 15   *To Millard Fillmore.*   360

Oct 15   To Charles Augustus Stetson. LS. Private owner, Massachusetts.
mDWs. Accepts the offer of one of Roswell L. Colt's bulls.

Oct 15   *From Franklin Haven.*   361

Oct 15   From George C. Bates (with ANS by Fillmore). Copy. DNA, RG
206. mDWs. Writes regarding his compensation for assisting in the
prosecution of three steamships for violating Federal law regulating
the carriage of passengers.

Oct. 15   From Calhoun Benham. Copy. DNA, RG 206. mDWs. Writes regarding the petition for remission of fine by three steamships convicted for flagrantly violating the Federal law regulating the carriage of passengers; urges that the companies be forced to pay his
assistant prosecutor, George C. Bates, a liberal fee should be remission be granted.

Oct 15   *Inscription for DW's grave.*   361

Oct 15   From Matthew W. Haskell. ALS. DLC. mDW 38051. Invites DW
to address the Literary Societies of Amherst College.

Oct 15   *George Jacob Abbot to Anna Taylor Gilman Emery Abbot.*   362

Oct 16   From Hubert F. Peebles. ALS. DLC. mDW 38052. Is seeking a
"situation" in which he can pursue the study of law.

Oct 16   From Caleb Pratt (enclosure: plan of Webster family cemetery
plot). ALS. DLC. mDW 38054. Encloses a plan of the Webster
family cematary plot in the Winslow Burying Ground, Marshfield.

Oct 17   To Mrs. Edward Curtis. Copy in Edward Curtis' hand. NN.
mDW 38056. Is unwell but "growing better"; apologizes for detain-
ing her husband and wishes she were here also.

Oct 17   *To [Millard Fillmore].*   364

Oct 17   To Millard Fillmore. Draft. CtY. mDW 38060. LS. NBuHi.
mDW 38062. *Diplomatic Papers*, 2. Expresses gratitude for Conrad's
acting as secretary of state, and suggests inviting him to sign the
copyright treaty.

Oct 18   *To Millard Fillmore.*   364

[Oct 18]   To J. J[ames] May. Draft. NhHi. mDW 38068. Encloses a
check to be credited to his account at Merchants' Bank.

Oct 18   From Thomas L. Noyes. ALS. DLC. mDW 38070. Fears he will
be turned out of office should the Democrats win, and begs DW to
divert "your misguided friends in Boston and elsewhere . . . from
their course."

Oct 18   Warranty deed transferring poperty in Marshfield, Mass. from
DW to Charles Porter Wright, Jr. Registry of Deeds, Plymouth
County, Plymouth Mass. Book 249, p. 67.

Oct 19   To Millard Fillmore. Draft. CtY. mDW 38072. Again recommends that Samuel F. Train be appointed to a Navy pursership.

Oct 19   To Samuel F. Train. Draft. CtY. mDW 38073. Has written to
the president on the subject of Train's recent letter to Fletcher
Webster.

Oct 19   From Richard Milford Blatchford. ALS. DLC. mDW 38074. Is
relieved to hear that DW is much better.

Oct 19   From J[ohn] C. Brigham. LS. DLC. mDW 38075. Asks for a
statement of DW's view on the influence of the Bible, to be published in a pamphlet by the American Bible Society.

Oct 19   From Edward Burchell.   365

Oct 19   From Edwin J. Fairbank. ALS. DLC. mDW 38079. Offers to sell
fancy geese at $6 per pair; asks for "Whig documents."

Oct 19   From Charles Augustus Stetson. Telegram. DLC. mDW 38080.
"The Bull is at Lynn."

Oct 20   To Corcoran & Riggs. LS with PS in DW's hand. DLC. mDW
38081. Asks them to discount a note and remit the proceeds to Merchants' Bank in Boston.

Oct 21   *Notes by George Jacob Abbot Describing the Signing of
Webster's Will*   365

[Oct 21]   *DW's Last Will and Testament.*   367

[Oct 21]   Memorandum on Island Farm. Copy. NhHi. mDW 38083. Van
Tyne, p. 542.

Oct 22   From Charles Augustus Stetson. ALS. DLC. mDW 38085. States
that "the Alderney" will be driven from Lynn to Marshfield.

Oct 22   From J[ohn] B. Sturtevant. ALS. DLC. mDW 38086. Invites DW
to lecture before the Young Men's Association of Albany.

Oct 23   To Daniel Fletcher Webster. Printed. Evert A. and George L. Duy-
ckinck, *Cyclopedia of American Literature* (N.Y., 1856), 2: 31n. Asks
him to have a piece of silver inscribed and presented to Peter Harvey.

Oct 23   Millard Fillmore from George Jacob Abbot.   372

Oct 25   To Millard Fillmore from George Jacob Abbot. Printed. *PC,* 2:
561–562. Reports the death of Daniel Webster.

Oct 25   Millard Fillmore to Members of the Cabinet.   372

Oct 25   Protest for non-payment of a check for $124. Printed DS with
MS insertions. DLC. mDW 40646.

Oct 25   Autopsy on DW. Extract.   373

Oct 27   From Jose Manuel Tirado. ALS. MHi. mDW 38089. Speaks
highly of William Miles, a bearer of despatches to Peru.

Oct 30   From George Perkins Marsh. ALS draft. VtU. mDW 38091.
Comments on the case of Dr. Jonas King.

[Oct]   To [Franklin Haven]. Typed copy, "Reminiscences of Franklin
[1852]   Haven"; New England Merchants National Bank, Boston, Mass.
mDWs. Writes "I am better."

[Oct]   To [?]. Draft. CtY. mDW 38095. Fears the independent movement for his election as president will only help the opposition;
insists he has no desire to harm Scott.

Oct   From Hiram Ayres et al. LS. DLC. mDW 38098. Invite DW to lecture at the Spring Garden Institute of Philadelphia.

[Oct]   From Joseph Cook et al. LS. DLC. mDW 38100. Warn DW's
present position may prove disastrous to the Whig Party and urge
him to support Scott.

Nov 1   From George Perkins Marsh. ALS draft. VtU. mDW 38104. Has
come to Vienna to seek medical care for his wife; reports complications arising from the Jonas King case in Greece.

Nov 3   From Richard H. Bayard. ALS draft. DLC. mDW 38108. Reports
on Belgian politics.

Nov 10   Protest on Sept 7 note to George S. Gideon & Co. Printed D
with MS insertions. NhD. mDW 40643.

Nov 17   From John Stimpson to Edward Everett et al. (enclosure: DW
to Stimpson, July 13, 1852). ALS. NhHi. mDW 37239. Encloses the
copy of a letter written to him by DW during the previous summer.
Dec 14   Appraisal of DW's Marshfield estate by Charles Henry Thomas.
AD (notebook). MBAt. mDWs.
Dec 31   *Memorandum of Account with Caleb Cushing.*   373
[Dec]   *Schedule of Livestock and Property at Elms Farm.*   374
[1852]   Bill from Richard M. Blatchford to DW's Estate for notes due
in Dec 1852, plus balances on earlier notes for which he has "a new
acknowledgment from Mr. Webster of Jan. 1, 1849"—$9,210.71.
AD. NhD (Claims on DW's Estate). mDWs.
[1852]   Bill from Sturtevant & Marsh to DW's Estate, for fee and costs
in suits against DW brought by: D. E. Wheeler; George W. Niles;
Francis Price; Henry Randall—$1267.75 less credits of $115. AD
NhD (Claims on DW's Estate). mDWs.
[1852]   Statement by Charles Porter Wright of amounts totalling
$926.76 paid by him to laborers, etc. at Marshfield, "being the sums
due to them respectively by Mr. Webster at the time of his death."
NhD (Claims on DW's Estate). mDWs.
1852 et seq.   "Claims on the Estate of the Late Honorable Daniel Webster." AD's and ALS's bound in a notebook. NhD. mDWs. Collection
of approximately 150 pieces, with a list of contents and an index,
organized by Fletcher Webster.

1853

Jan 1   Inventory of DW's estate.   376
Jan 3   Quitclaim deed transferring property in Marshfield, Mass. from
Caroline Le Roy Webster to James William Paige et al., trustees.
Registry of Deeds, Plymouth County, Mass. Deed Book 251, p. 10.
Jan 8   From Samuel Smith to Daniel Fletcher Webster. ALS. NhD
(Claims on DW's Estate). Encloses statement of amounts due to Dr.
John C. Warren (whose clerk he is) for medical attendance on DW
and family from 1836 to 1849; states he saw DW many times on
the subject of payment, "but he said it had not been convenient to
make said payment."
Jan 25   From William T. Savage to George Ticknor (enclosure: DW to
Savage, Oct 10, 1852). ALS. NhHi. mDW 37987. Encloses a copy of a
letter to him by DW, since Ticknor is one of DW's literary executors.
June 21   From Samuel T. Tisdale to Daniel Fletcher Webster (en-
closure: DW to Tisdale, Aug 2, 1851). ALS. NhHi. mDW 34540.
PC, 2: 457–458. Reports on the Alderney heifer DW gave him two
years ago.
June 25   From Daniel Fletcher Webster to Samuel Bulkley Ruggles.
ALS. NhExP. mDWS. Requests that Ruggles, along with Richard M.
Blatchford, settle part of DW's estate for land in Illinois with Tilden
Ames of Marshfield.

1855

Feb 28   From Enoch Train & Co. to Executors of DW's Estate. DS. NhD
(Claims on DW's Estate). State they hold DW's notes for loans June

2 ($1000) and Sept 8, 1849 ($500), the latter "in form of a receipt on account of moneys that might become due him, on account of his Interest in the suits for alien Passenger Tax."

Supplemental Calendar

1802

[1802–1808?]   To [Nathaniel Webster (1781–1828)]. Typed copy. NhD. mDW 38832. Not to Nathaniel Sawyer as in *Correspondence*, 1, Calendar: 387.

1804

Sept 14   To James Hervey Bingham. ALS. CLU–C. mDWs. Published in *Correspondence*, 1: 58–59 from expurgated printed text.

Nov 5   Receipt to Rufus Greene Amory for $400 received "on account of a Journey with Joseph Taylor." ADS. DLC. mDWs.

1805

April 8   To Samuel Fessenden. Typed extract. NhD. mDWs. Misses his companionship in Boston.

May 10   To Samuel Ayer Bradley. ALS. Mrs. Francis Van Dusen, Wynnewood, Pa. mDWs. Writes about his state of being after "just 27 days" in Boscawen; gossips about mutual friends; comments on the undignified behavior of Judge [Jeremiah] Smith on the bench—"what a falling off!" when compared with certain Massachusetts judges.

Dec 7   To Samuel Ayer Bradley. Typed extract. NhD. mDWs. Praises Samuel Fessenden, who "keeps the school in our district."

1807

[Sept 1807?]   To Grace Fletcher. AD. Mrs. Irvin McD. Garfield, Southboro, Mass. mDWs. Love poem.

1808

[1808–1813]   Accounts with Timothy Gerrish, prisonkeeper of Rockingham County, New Hampshire, for service of writs. AD. NhD: Gerrish Account Books. mDWs.

1809

Dec 6   From Joseph Warren Backett. ALS. NhExP. mDWs. Thanks DW for his attention to some receipts; sends greetings from [Benjamin] Clark and inviites DW to their fireside in New York.

1810

March 20   To Moses Dow. ALS. NhD. mDWs. Sends him "the amount of

your debt against Peirce, & all his colleagues, companions & confed-
erates"; discusses a case he helped [Daniel] French argue in Portsmouth.

1812

Jan 29   To [Jonathan Warner]. ALS. NhHi. mDWS. Will take care of the
Frost debt "& see that there is no judgment agt. you."

Aug 14   From [William Sullivan]. AL draft. CSmH. mDWs. Wants to
know whether the presidential electors in New Hampshire "will be
men who will vote for a peace and commerce man without regard
to party distinctions," and whether "your leading men will be disposed to send delegates to New York" to meet those from other states
on Sept 15.

[1812]   To Jonathan Warner. ALS. NhHi. mDWs. Cannot accomodate
Warner today.

1813

Sept 14 [1813]   To Noah Emery. ALS. MB. mDWs. Reports that actions
in a certain case (*Seavey* v. *Pendleton?*) were not continued, and
asks for "the Exe[cuti]ons, for the amounts severally marked on
the writ."

1814

June 18   To Alexander Ladd, Samuel Lord, and Robert Rice from DW et
al. LS. NhHi. Write as members of the standing committee of the
Washington Benevolent Society of New Hampshire, appointing the
addressees a committee to raise funds for an Independence Day
celebration in Portsmouth.

June   Report by Judge Isaac Parker in *Webster* v. *Inhabitants of Orono*.
True copy. DLC. mDW 1670a. Suit by DW to recover a sum paid by
the town to a schoolmaster in settlement of his claim for wages, contrary to an order directing that it be paid to DW, to whom the
schoolmaster was indebted in an equal amount.

1815

Sept 5   Bill to J. Daniels for $9.00, to cash for fees in "the Bickford
act[io]n" on Sept 5 and Nov 20.

1816

July 30   To Joseph Story. ALS. MHi. mDWs. Published in *Correspondence*, 1: 201–202 from printed text.

1817

April 2   To Richard Rush. ALS. DNA, RG 59. mDWs. Introduces Nathaniel Goddard, who "thinks of applying to the President to remit

that part of the property of the vessel & cargo condemned, which will
accrue to the U.S." in the *Ariadne* case.

June 6   To [?]. ALS. NhD. mDWs. Gives thanks for the honor conferred
upon him by "the Society" in appointing him to deliver an oration on
"the Anniversary"; regrets he cannot comply.

Sept 21 [1817?]   To Ezekiel Webster. ALS. NhD. mDW 3593. *Correspondence*, 1, Calendar: 451 as Sept 21, 1823.

1818

[c. April 22]   To [John Marshall]. AN. MSaE. mDWs. Inscription: "Mr
Webster begs the Chief Justice's acceptance of this [argument in the
Dartmouth College case]. It is not *published*; but printed only."

May 14   To Joseph Story. ALS. MHi. mDWs. Calendared in *Correspondence* 1: 425 from printed text.

May 16   To Upton & Adams. ALS. NhD. mDWs. Informs them that their
cause is continued in Boston, and not removed to Washington.

June 29   To Joseph Story. ALS. MHi. mDWs. Reports that he has
brought an action for the next term of the circuit court, "John W.
Telford v. William B. Sweat et al.," and asks who should execute
commissions in Philadelphia and Nashville; cites and quotes from
two cases relevant to the Dartmouth College cause.

July 25   To Joseph Story. ALS. MHi. mDWs. Draws attention to the
opinion by James Kent in *Frost* v. *Carter*, I Johnson's Cases 73
1799, that goes "directly agt. my opinion;—but it has not satisfied
me." (Kent's opinion: If the indorser of a note pay it after the maker
has been discharged under the insolvent law, such discharge is no
bar to a suit on the note brought by the indorser against the maker.)

July 25   Power of attorney to Martin Whiting. LS. Arthur E. Nissen,
Damariscotta, Me. mDWs.

Aug 16 [1818]   To Joseph Story. ALS. MHi. mDWS. Calendared in *Correspondence*, 1: 426 from printed text.

Sept 9   To Joseph Story. ALS. MHi. mDWs. Published in *Correspondence*, 1: 227–228 from printed text.

1819

April 26   To Jeremiah Mason. ALS. NhExP. mDWs. Reports on [Nathaniel P.] Russell's advice to [Robert] Elwell in the *Volant* case.

Aug 9   to Joseph Storey. ALS. MHi. mDWs. Has just returned from a
"long & very pleasant tour," and encloses a letter to Story from
James Kent; plans to attend the Dartmouth College commencement.

Aug 14   To [John Thornton Kirkland]. ALS. MH–Ar. mDWs. Is honored
to take part in "adjudging the Boylston prizes," and will attend the
service with pleasure.

Sept 21   To [Jeremiah Mason?]. ALS. NhD. mDWs. Discusses the defense of a case and the timing of an appearance in court for [Nathaniel P.?] Russell.

Oct 26   From Joseph Story. ALS. MHi. mDWs. Has not yet had an opportunity to examine the cases applicable to replevin; cites his "Selection of Pleadings."

Dec 4   To Joseph Story. ALS. MHi. mDWs. Regrets not having seen more of him yesterday; explains that in the "previous arrangements for the meeting [at the State House, Boston] we had, at one time, agreed to request the favor of yourself & the Chief Justice [Isaac Parker] to be on the Comee," but "on further consideration thought it possible both of you would be as well satisfied not to be called to take an active part. We must now have a *Memorial . . . that* shall present the *Law Argument,*" and asks Story if he will write it. See *Correspondence, 1: 267–268,* re *Memorial to the Congress of the United States, on the Subject of Restraining the Increase of Slavery in the New States to be Admitted into the Union* (Boston, 1819). See also *Speechs and Formal Writings, 1.*

Dec 13   From Thomas Gibbons. LC. NjMD. mDWs. Asks if DW can help represent him if he takes his case against Aaron Ogden to the U.S. Supreme Court.

[1819–1821]   To Joseph Story. ALS. MHi. mDWs. Proposes rounding up support in Salem for the appointment of "our friend Mr L[?]" to the Spanish Claims commission.

1820

March 12   To Nathaniel F. Hoar. ALS. Arthur E. Nissen, Damariscotta, Me. mDWs. Regrets to hear of Hoar's "continued indisposition," and offers him a loan.

[June 22, 1820?]   To Joseph Story. ALS. MHi. mDWs. Inquires whether "the 40th printed rule [of the Circuit Court for the U.S. First Circuit] is now in force"; expects to see Story on Saturday at Nahant; comments on cases he has been reading in the English Chancery Reports.

June 23   To William Chamberlain. ALS. ViU. mDWs. Agrees to receive Chamberlain into his Boston office.

July 6   From Samuel Davis. ALS. copy. MPIPS. mDWs. Invites DW to give a speech in Dec before the Pilgrim Society, to commemorate the bicentennial of the first permanent settlement in New England.

July 8   To [Samuel Davis]. ALS. MPIPS. mDWs. Agrees to deliver an address before the Pilgrim Society in December.

Oct 23   To [Nathaniel] M. Davis. ALS. MHi. mDW 2914. Not "William" as in *Correspondence, 1: Calendar: 434–435* (misaddressed by DW).

[Nov]   To Dudley Atkins Tyng. ALS. NhD. mDWs. *Correspondence, 1, Calendar: 432* as Nov 1819 (with middle name as misspelled by DW).

Dec 23   From Samuel Davis. LC MPIPS. mDWs. Calendared in *Correspondence, 1: 435* from printed text.

1821

Feb 14 [1821]   To Alexander Bliss. ALS. DLC. mDW 2825. *Correspondence, 1, Calendar: 432* as Feb 14, 1820.

March 10   To S. Crembling. ALS. MiU–C. mDWs. Writes respecting the cause of Mr. Inglee against Mr. Robinson, "now in your care & management."

April 28 [1821]   To George Bliss. ALS. DLC. mDWs. Has received his

letter, and one from [William] Ely; thinks "a case exists, which has
not yet been decided, & that the Insolvent Law of N York ought
now . . . to be pleaded"; [Alexander] Bliss will forward to Springfield
a copy of the pleas in the case against [Richard Crownenshield] in
circut court, to use as a guide: "I suppose Mr Ely's discharge was
under the same law, viz the law of 1811"; hopes arrangments can be
made to dispense with his presence in Springfield, where he will
otherwise go by stage on Tuesday (May) 8.

May 9   To Thomas Gibbons. ALS. NjMD. mDWs. Gives advice on "the
Steamboat controversy," in response to Gibbons's letter of April 2; refers him to his earlier letter to David Bayard Ogden on the subject.

July 15   To Joseph Story. ALS. MHi. mDWs. Postpones a visit to Portsmouth on account of the death of Mrs. Webster's mother; adds:
"Thou hast seen the Nat. Intelligencer: —& some good matter in it."

Sept 20 [1821]   To A[ugustus] Peabody and J[osiah] P. Cook. ALS. Vincent E. Edmunds, Staten Island, N.Y. mDWs. Gives advice in a
case: "An instrument might be drawn, relinquishing a right to pursue particular remedies, or to abstain from all suits for a limited
time, without amounting to a release . . . [but] I think . . . I should
advise my client to give me a letter of instructions . . . to execute
the judgment on the party wished to be charged, & on no other."

Sept 24   To Joseph Story. ALS. MHi. mDWs. Calendared in *Correspondence,* 1: 439 from printed text.

Oct 2   To Joseph Story. ALS. MHi. mDWs. Hopes that he and Mrs. Story
will come for a visit this week; transmits a dinner invitation from
Col. [Thomas H.] Perkins.

Nov 7   To Joseph Story. ALS. MHi. mDWs. Calendared in *Correspondence,* 1: 440 fom printed text.

Nov 12   To Joseph Story. ALS. MHi. mDWs. Intends to go to Providence,
to be there by Thursday noon (Nov 15), where he is "desired to appeal a Chancery suit, decided by you." *Barker* v. *Marine Ins. Co.,* 2
Mason 369 (1821).

Dec 1   To Joseph Story. ALS. MHi. mDWs. Hopes to see Story and his
wife "under one roof" next Friday; states *"By what I learn, there
will be no avoiding the main question in the Young Eugenie";* informs him that "the Patent causes will not be pressed, at this time";
has left him "something like an argument" in the case *Barker* v.
Newport Ins. Co.

Dec 21   From Wells & Lilly. Copy. MPlPS. mDWs. Send DW copies of his
speech before the Pilgrim Society in December of last year.

[Dec? 1821]   To [John] Sarge[a]nt. ALS. NhD. mDW 38830. Prays him
to "say something of this miserable Vermont Law [act of 1821,
granting a new trial in *Herman Allen* v. *Silas Hathaway and Uzal
Pierson*]. I understand all the members from that State reprobate";
adds: "The Vermont Law is clearly unconstitutional." (See "Opinion on the Validity of a Vermont Statute," December 1821, *W & S,*
15: 275, in which DW writes: "I have had occasion to state this case
to a gentleman of the first eminence in the middle States, in whom
it excited great surprise.")

[1821–1824?]   Remarks by DW on the power of attention, and on pursuit of eminence in law. In Josiah Quincy to Josiah Quincy, Jr., Feb
4, 1827. ALS. MHi. mDWs.

1822

Jan 3 [1822]   To Joseph Story. ALS. MHi. mDWs. Published in *Correspondence*, 1: 299–300 from printed text.

Jan 14   To Joseph Story. ALS. MHi. mDWs. Published in *Correspondence*, 1: 302 from printed text.

Jan 21   To William Davis (1758–1826). ALS. MPlPS. mDWs. Reports that the Spanish Claims commissioners find Davis "entitled to *some* compensation" in the case of the *Governor Carver*; but as to "Capt. Spooner's case," they "seem to think personal injuries not within the Treaty."

Jan 28   From J[ames] & T[homas] H[andasyd] Perkins & Sons. Printed. L. Vernon Briggs, *History and Genealogy of the Cabot Family, 1475–1927* (2 vols., Boston, 1927), 2: 567. Discuss claim in the case of the *Betsy*.

Feb 20   To [William Davis]. ALS. CCC. mDW 3216. Not to Samuel Davis as in *Correspondence*, 1, Calendar: 442.

Feb 21   To Thomas Gibbons. AL, signature removed. NjMD. mDWs. Thinks Gibbons's cause cannot be tried this term, and that William Wirt and David Bayard Ogden should argue it, unless Gibbons specifically request's DW's aid; adds: "God grant we may live long enough to try the Constitutional character of this cause."

Feb 25   To Joseph Waters and Jonathan Hodges. ALS MSaE. mDWs. Informs them that their memorial in the case of the *Swallow* "was this day rec'd, in pursuance to the Resolution to which the Commissioners have come, in relation to cases of that class."

March 12   To [William Eustis]. ALS. CU–BANC. mDWs. Introduces Allen Melville of Boston, who desires "to be made known to the President, thro some gentleman of weight and influence."

[March 31, 1822]   To Joseph Story. ALS. MHi. mDWs. Rejoices to learn that Story has recovered from his accident; comments on the late election in New Hampshire, "the *worst*, I think, which I have ever *known*. I am afraid some new spirit of mischief is at work there, respecting their *Judiciary*."

April 7   To [Joseph Waters and/or Jonathan Hodges]. ALS. MSaE. mDWs. Discusses the facts in the *Swallow* case; gives directions for taking depositions.

April 25   To Joseph Story. ALS. MHi. mDWs. Advises Story not to attend to court business in Portsmouth and Portland until he has got rid of his rheumatism, but hopes Story and his wife will be able to join DW and Mrs. Webster in a visit to Maine early in May.

July 18   To Joseph Story. ALS. MHi. mDWs. Hopes the Storys are planning to go to Dorchester tomorrow, to meet the Jeremiah Masons "at our house," and perhaps also "the good creature" David Bayard Ogden.

Aug 6   To Joseph Story. ALS. MHi. mDWs. Published in *Correspondence*, 1: 313 from printed text.

Aug 6   From Joseph Story. ALS. MHi. mDWs. Published in *Correspondence*, 1: 313–314 from printed text.

Sept 7   To George Bliss. ALS. Dr. Williams's Library, London. mDWs. Proposes that they present their arguments in [William] Ely's case "*in writing*."

[Oct 1822]   To Joseph Story. ALS. MHi. mDWs. Is delayed by an important case at Cambridge, but does not want to ask him to change his arrangements for the circuit court: "Mr [Alexander] Bliss will cite the authorities in Barrett v Goddard, & if the case of the *Friendship* should come on today, Mr Nichols must take care of it."

[Nov 7, 1822]   To Joseph Story. ALS. MHi. mDWs. Would like to "make an arrangement to try the *Gold* cause" on Monday (Nov 18)—*Tracy et al.* v. *Wood*, 3 Mason 132 (1822); adds "You learn I suppose that I am not an inhabitant of Boston."

1823

Feb 6   To Samuel Upton. ALS. NhD. mDWs. Discusses some notes which "should entirely be sued, if sued they must be, in the name of the real proprietor, Mr Lyman."

March 14   To William Davis. ALS. MHi. mDW 3449. Not to William "M." as in *Correspondence*, 1, Calendar: 447.

March 25, [1825?]   To [Joseph Waters]. ALS. MSaE. mDWs. Based on decisions the commissioners have made in other cases, he begins "to fear for the fate of the *Swallow*," but is inclined to let it continue.

April 26   From Nathaniel Hazeltine Carter. ALS. ViU. mDWs. Reports the contents of a letter from former chief justice Ambrose Spencer; supports Spencer as a candiidate for appointment to the New York bench.

May 12   To Joseph Story. ALS. MHi. mDWs. published in *Correspondence*, 1: 327–328 from printed text.

June 26 [1823]   To John Adams. ALS. MHi. mDW 3545. Not to John "Quincy" as in *Correspondence*, 1: Calendar: 450.

Nov 8   To Joseph Story. ALS. MHi. mDWs. Bids him farewell and asks to hear from him often; remarks that "W" [Henry Wheaton] is elected to the New York legislature, and that a substitute will be needed to report Supreme Court cases during his absence.

Dec 20   To [Isaac P. Davis]. ALS. NhD. mDWs. Sends ducks with instructions for their distribution; chats about his family.

Dec 23   To James William Paige from Grace Fletcher Webster. ALS. with ANS by DW. MHi. mDWs. Relates news of friends and acquaintances.

Dec 26 [1823]   To Joseph Story. ALS. MHi. mDWs. Calendared in *Correspondence*, 1: 455 from printed text.

1824

Jan 4   To Joseph Story. ALS. MHi. mDWs. Calendared in *Correspondence*, 1: 457 from printed text.

Jan 4   From Joseph Story. ALS. MHi. mDWs. Calendared in *Correspondence*, 1: 457 from printed text.

Jan 10   From Joseph Story. ALS. MHi. mDWs. Calendared in *Correspondence*, 1: 457–458 from printed text.

[Feb 28? 1824]   To John C. Calhoun. ALS. MHi. mDW 4020. *Correspondence*, 1: Calendar: 462 as Feb 28, 1824, but appears as c. Jan 10 in Edwin Hemphill, ed., *The Papers of John C. Calhoun*, 8: 470–471.

April 10   To Joseph Story. ALS. MHi. mDWs. Published in *Correspondence*, 1: 356–357 from printed text.

May 4   To Joseph Story. ALS. MHi. mDWs. Calendared in *Correspondence* 1: 467 from printed text.

July 23   To Henry Clark. ALS. MBAt. mDWs. Refers him to Tobias Watkins, late secretary to the board of the Spanish Claims commission, who "probably wd furnish you copies of the invoice."

[May 9, 1824]   To [Alexander Bliss]. AN. DLC. mDW 4205. *Correspondence*, 1, Calendar: 468 as May 1824—belongs with DW to Bliss, May 9, mDW 4162 (see *Legal Papers*, 2: 22).

May 20   To Samuel Lewis Southard. ALS. DLC. mDWs. Recommends William Coolidge for a clerkship in the navy.

June 1 [1824]   To James William Paige. ALS. Mrs. Irvin McD. Garfield, Southboro, Mass. mDWs. Notes his itinerary.

June 8   From John C. Calhoun. LC. DNA, RG 77. mDWs. Reports that the country between Barnstable Bay and Buzzard Bay will be surveyed for a canal.

June 12   To John Glenn King. AL, signature removed. MSaE. mDWs. Discusses the award in the case of the brig *Patty*.

July 12   To Ebenezer Gay. ALS. TNJ. mDWs. Sends Gay the balance due him as a claimant under the Spanish treaty in behalf of Thomas English; needs Gay's power of attorney to recover the sum awarded him in behalf of Samuel Soley.

July 13   To [Charles Morris]. ALS. NhD. mDWs. Recommends C. B. Jaudon for a navy appointment.

Aug 19   From Robert Walsh, Jr. ALS. NhD. mDWs. Replies to DW's "kind letter on the subject of the History" (of the Federal Government from its commencement to the end of Mr. Madison's Administration—see *Correspondence*, 2: 46–48); finds the "pecuniary plan" acceptable if DW thinks "the whole project of the work worth pursuing."

[Dec 1824]   Memorandum of visit to Thomas Jefferson at Monticello. AD in unidentified hand. ViU. mDWs. Includes a ground plan of the house, not present in the variant published in *Correspondence*, 1: 370–377.

1825

Jan 8   From George Blake. ALS. NhD. mDWs. Thanks DW for his letter from Monticello; asks if he will allow a part of it to be printed "in one of our public gazettes"; notes a legal engagement he has undertaken.

Feb 16   To Felix Huston. LS. CSmH. mDWs. Open letter of introduction for Huston, who is on his way to Europe and Greece.

[Feb 22, 1825]   To James William Paige. ALS. Mrs. Irvin McD. Garfield. Southboro, Mass. mDWs. Asks him to watch out for rumors of a challenge issued to DW by John Randolph of Virginia, and to prevent Grace from becoming alarmed.

[Feb 22, 1825]   Report of DW's remarks in the House of Representatives on the subject of Massachusetts claims for services rendered by the militia in the war of 1812. AD. CSmH. mDWs.

March 23 [1825]   To Julius von Wallenstein. ALS. Br. mDWs. Reports "I have written as much, to Princeton, as I could do, without making it suspected I knew secrets" (about Wallenstein's attachment to Julia Stockton).

April 8   From Julius von Wallenstein. ALS. NhD. mDWs. Praises DW's April 3 speech on the Massachusetts general election, and would like "an account of the evening"; relates Washington news.

April 10   To Julius von Wallenstein. ALS. Br (first part of letter). Samuel J. Feigus, Uniontown, Pa. (concluding part). mDWs. *Correspondence*, 2, Calendar: 447 (concluding part only). Reports his activities since his return home; sets forth summer plans "so that you may not disappoint us, as to your visit here, by coming at a time when I shall be absent."

April 12   To Julius von Wallenstein. ALS. Br. mDWs. Comments on their friendship; asks for suggestions about the shape of the Bunker Hill Monument.

April 21   Interrogatories on plaintiff's part in *Bryant et al.* v. *General Interest Assurance Co.* True copy. NhD. mDW 4956.

April 24   To Julius von Wallenstein. ALS. Br. mDWs. Reports he has been busy in court; mentions various friends; suggests that Wallenstein read William Huskisson's speech "introducing his resolutions relative to the Colonial trade, &c."; describes difficulties in preparing his Bunker Hill Monument speech.

May 7   To Julius von Wallenstein. ALS. Br. mDWs. Has read "Lord John Russell's Memoires of the Affairs of Europe, from the Peace of Utrecht" and also "a little French"; chats about various people.

May 23   To James Kent. ALS. DLC. mDWs. Published in *Correspondence*, 2: 49 from printed text.

May 25   From Alexander Hill Everett. ALS. NhD. mDW 12534. Comments on an article he intends to write for the *Patriot* "on the subject we spoke of"; discusses the newspaper he plans to establish with his brothers, and trusts that DW and Judge Story will aid in contributing materials. (See *Correspondence*, 2: 69–70 re the *Massachusetts Journal.*)

June 4   To Julius von Wallenstein. ALS. Br. mDWs. Has made "little or no progress" in preparing for "the 17th of June" (laying of the cornerstone of the Bunker Hill Monument)—"When you come, I hope you will give me some ideas."

[June 18, 1825?]   From Marquis de Lafayette. ALS. NhD. mDWs. Has made arrangements for DW to go up to his room at "Mr Lloyd's" in the afternoon, where he will join him as soon as he is back from Quincy.

June 20   From Joseph Story. ALS. NhD. mDWs. Is grateful for the postponement of their trip until Friday, allowing for Mrs. Story's recovery from influenza; compliments DW's Bunker Hill oration; instructs him to "talk a little in favour of Govr. Lincoln."

[June 25, 1825]   To James William Paige. ALS. Mrs. Irvin McD. Garfield, Southboro, Mass. mDWs. Informs him of the safe arrival of "our party" at Worcester.

[Aug 3] [1825?]   To Joseph Story. ALS. MHi. mDWs. Thinks it unnecessary to "insert the paragraph in the Courier at present," since Story's denial "has been noticed in some of the [Boston] papers"; reports that "Col. [Alexander Hill] Everett is in much trouble on the occasion" and that "the idea of a paper, under his management, is *wholly given up.*"

Aug 4 From William Plumer, Jr. ALS draft. Nh. mDWs. Compliments DW on the Bunker Hill oration; discusses the recent senatorial election in New Hampshire.

Sept 12 To Julius von Wallenstein. ALS. Br. mDWs. Talks of stay at Sandwich; will give him a letter to [Richard] Stockton; reports general satisfaction with the result of Captain [Charles] Stewart's court-martial trial.

Sept 17 [1825] To Joseph Story. ALS. MiU–C. mDW 2777. *Correspondence*, 1, Calendar, 431 as Sept 17, 1819.

Sept 21 To Edward Livingston. Printed. Charles Havens Hunt, *Life of Edward Livingston* (New York, 1864), p. 298. Hopes that Livingston will visit Boston before he goes South.

Sept 28 To Julius von Wallenstein. ALS. Br. mDWs. Complains of not hearing from Wallenstein and admits his own poor correspondence habits; reports he is "oppressed—overwhelmed with a variety of little things."

Dec 31 To Joseph Story. ALS. MHi. mDWs. Calendared in *Corrrespondence*, 2: 454 from printed text.

1826

Jan 14 From William Plumer, Jr. ALS. Nh. mDWs. Asks if anything is likely to be done "on the subject of manufactures" and on the bankrupt law, asks other questions about affairs in Washington.

Jan 27 From Charles Jackson. ALS. NhD. mDWs. Thanks DW for sending him a copy of an act of Parliament.

Feb 2 From George Ticknor. Printed. G. S. Hillard, ed., *Life, Letters, and Journals of George Ticknor* (2 vols., Boston, 1876), 1: 370–372. Tells of his ideas to combine all the libraries of Boston with the Athenaeum.

April 8 [1826] To Joseph Story. ALS. MHi. mDWs. Calendared in *Correspondence*, 2: 456 from printed text and misdated April 16.

[April, 1826?] To [Edward Everett]. Copy. NhHi. mDW 38366. Makes an inquiry regarding the president's sanction of "the principle of our interest bill" in the case of South Carolina's militia claim.

May 8 To Joseph Story. ALS. MHi. mDWs. Published in *Correspondence*, 2: 113–114 from printed text.

May 13 To Joseph Story. ALS. MHi. mDWs. Notes "We are in a great *quandary* about the Judiciary," and that the end of the session is hectic; closes "Yrs, in midst of a thousand vexations."

July 1 To William Sturgis et al. ALS. OClW. mDWs. Will arrive late to their 4th of July celebration at the Exchange Coffee House (Boston).

Sept 18 To Samuel Larkin. ALS. IGK. mDWs. Does not recall the case of "Genl. Eaton," and suggests Larkin write to the state department to ask if the papers are on file.

Sept 29 To George C. Shattuck. ALS. MHi. mDWs. Describes the extreme misfortunes of Thomas Rich, a contemporary of theirs at Dartmouth, and asks if Shattuck can render assistance.

Nov 2 From DeWitt Clinton. ALS. NhHi. mDW 5696. Not "Daniel Clark as misread in *Correspondence*, 2, Calendar: 469.

Dec 6 [1826]   From Gertrude G. Meredith. ALS. NhD. mDWs. Asks assistance in obtaining a navy warrant for her son.

[1826]   From Jeremiah Smith. Printed. John Hopkins Morrison. *Life of the Hon. Jeremiah Smith, LL.D* (Boston, 1845), p. 304. Praises Edward Livingston's system of penal law for Louisiana and asks DW to get him a copy of Livingston's writings.

1827

[Feb 8, 1827?]   To John Quincy Adams. ALS. MHi. mDW 5883. *Correspondence*, 2, Calendar: 460 (as Feb 28, 1826), 476 (as Feb 8, 1827). Concerns the appointment of "Mr. Seawell" (Henry Seawell of North Carolina, as a commissioner of claims under the convention with Great Britain of Nov 13, 1826), as favored by [Lewis] Williams.

March 6 [1827]   To James William Paige. ALS. Mrs. Irvin McD. Garfield, Southboro, Mass. mDWs. Asks him to attend to some financial matters.

March 6   From William Plumer, Jr. ALS. Nh. mDWs. Discusses politics in Washington, agreeing with DW that the northern character of the Adams administration is the real source of Congressional opposition; thinks the next presidential election will hinge on New York and Pennsylvania.

April 16   From Daniel W. Coxe. ALS. PHi. mDWs. Requests DW's legal services in a case before the Supreme Court involving the Spanish land grants of 1803–1804—*Foster & Elam* v. *Neilson.*

May 19   From Daniel W. Coxe. ALS. PHi. mDWs. Discusses *Foster & Elam* v. *Neilson.*

Oct 11   From Daniel W. Coxe. ALS draft. PHi. mDWs. Reports on the progress of *Foster & Elam* v. *Neilson* and asks if DW will accept the case.

Oct 15   To Daniel W. Coxe. ALS. PHi. mDWs. Agrees to undertake the case of *Foster & Elam* v. *Neilson.*

[Oct 1827?]   From Daniel W. Coxe. AN. PHi. mDWs. Notes for DW on *Foster & Elam* v. *Neilson.*

Nov 25 [1827]   To James William Paige. ALS. Mrs. Irvin McD. Garfield, Southboro, Mass. mDWs. Describes in detail the bad weather he and Mrs. Webster and the children have encountered on their way to New York.

Nov 28 [1827]   To James William Paige. ALS (incomplete). Mrs. Irvin McD. Garfield, Southboro, Mass. mDWs. Continues the saga of their difficult journey to New York.

Nov 29 [1827]   To James William Paige. ALS. Mrs. Irvin McD. Garfield, Southboro, Mass. mDWs. Notes their arrival at New York.

Nov 30   To James William Paige. ALS. Mrs. Irvin McD. Garfield, Southboro, Mass. mDWs. Tells how a wrong kind of plaster was applied to Mrs. Webster's side by accident, with distressing results.

Dec 13   From Joseph Story. ALS. MHi. mDWs. Expresses his sympathy for the Websters in the troubles they are experiencing in New York and advises DW not to go to Washington until after Christmas; comments on the verdict obtained by [Willard] Peale in the case of the

Argonaut; notes praise for the president's recent message but despondency in Salem about the upcoming election.

Dec 18   To Joseph Story. ALS. MHi. mDWs. Calendared in *Correspondence*, 2: 489 from printed text.

[Dec 26, 1827]   To Nicholas Biddle. ALS. DLC. mDW 38255. Notes the appointment of Biddle and four others as directors of the Bank of the U.S.

Dec 27   To Daniel W. Coxe (with Coxe to DW, Dec 31, 1827). ALS. PHi. mDWs. Will use his "earliest health & leisure to study & understand the case" (*Foster & Elam* v. *Neilson*); asks for his fees.

Dec 31   From Daniel W. Coxe (with DW to Coxe, Dec 27, 1827). ALS draft. PHi. mDWs. Sends DW a draft for "the moiety of your fee" in *Foster & Elam* v. *Neilson*.

1828

Jan 8   Receipt for retainer in *Foster & Elam* v. *Neilson*. ADS. PHi. mDWs.

Jan 10   To Sarah Preston Everett Hale. ALS. MNS–S. mDWs. Describes Grace's illness asks Mrs. Hale to continue writing to her.

Jan 14   From Joseph Story. ALS. MHi. mDWs. Expresses the "intense anxiety" he and his wife feel about Grace's health; will take care of DW's business for a bit, but repeats that DW's "public & professional duties" in Washington are pressing; appends a steamboat schedule.

Feb 20   To David Sears et al. from DW and Nathaniel Silsbee. LS. MHi. mDWs. Acknowledges with gratitude their expressions of confidence.

March 8   To James William Paige. ALS. Mrs. Irvin McD. Garfield, Southboro, Mass. mDWs. Writes he is not now inclined to go to Europe, having "lost one half of my interest, & motives, in all the pursuits of life"; hopes to be able to send money to "Mr. Pratt" shortly.

March 18   From Joseph Story. ALS, signature removed. MHi. mDWs. Comments on the "glorious" news from New Hampshire; encloses a letter for Chief Justice Marshall about a lost coat.

April 18   From Redwood Fisher. ALS. ViU. mDWs. Writes in support of the tariff bill.

April 29   From Nathan Hale. ALS. NhD. mDWs. Writes in support of a bill to allow the importation of iron for railroads free of duty; discusses a note.

April 30   From [illegible]. ALS. MCo. mDWs. Write in favor of the tariff provisions for woollens.

[c. May 10, 1828?]   To Dutee Jerauld Pearce. ALS. NIC. mDW 38795. Will send him some speeches, but doubts whether the one on the tariff will be published "until I get home."

May 11   To James William Paige. ALS. Mrs. Irvin McD. Garfield, Southboro, Mass. mDWs. Advises him to "calculate on the idea" that the tariff bill will pass.

[May 30, 1828]   To James William Paige. ALS. NhD. mDWs. Hopes to leave for Boston tomorrow.

June 12   To Robert F. Stockton. ALS. GEU. mDWs. Sends George Blake's regards; is sorry not to have seen more of Stockton's family; reports nothing new in the political world.

Aug 12   Application to Merchants' Insurance Company for renewal of policy on house, outhouses and stable in Summer Street, Boston. DS. MHi. mDWs.

Sept 27   To [?]. ALS. CU–BANC. mDWs. Reports he has today written to [John E.] Frost.

Oct 7   From Aaron Ogden. ALS. NjR. mDWs. Thinks the "administration ticket" will prevail in the choice of presidential electors.

Nov 27   Resolutions adopted at a meeting held in Boston to discuss the American Lyceum, signed by DW, Chairman and G. B. Emerson, Secretary. Printed. *American Journal of Education*, 3 (December, 1828): 753–754.

Dec 11 [1828]   To [William] Sullivan. Copied in George Brinley to Samuel H. Huntington, Dec 12, 1828. CtHi. mDWs. Denies he recommended anyone for a local office in Connecticut, and cannot with propriety support Huntington, whom he does not even know.

[1828?]   To Samuel Lewis Southard. ALS. NjP. mDW 38862. Announces that George Ticknor and [William Hickling] Prescott would like to see him.

[1828?]   To [Ann] Thomas. ANS. Mrs. T. G. O'Brien, Jr., New York, N.Y. Will call for her this afternoon if she would find it agreable to go with him to Cambridge and return through Brighton.

1829

Jan 15   To Josiah Quincy. ALS. MHi. mDWs. Praises Quincy's address, delivered at the end of his last term as mayor of Boston.

Feb 15   To Henry Willis Kinsman. ALS. NhD. mDWs. Asks him to take care of sundry financial matters.

Feb 21   Order to Daniel W. Coxe to pay $500 to DW. ADS. PHi. mDWs.

Feb 21   Receipt for $500 paid to DW by Daniel W. Coxe for balance of fees in *Foster & Elam* v. *Neilson*. ADS. PHi. mDWs.

March 12   To Daniel W. Coxe. ALS. PHi. mDWs. Reports their defeat in *Foster & Elam* v. *Neilson* and explains the Court's logic.

[March, 1829?]   Memorandum re *Foster & Elam* v. *Neilson*. AN. PHi. mDWs.

[April 12]   To James William Paige. ALS. Mrs. Irvin McD. Garfield, Southboro, Mass. mDWs. Reports "We have got thro the solemn duties of this most melancholy occasion" (Ezekiel Webster's funeral).

May 11   To George C. Shattuck. ALS. MHi. mDWs. Wants "a little of this world's needful," and asks to borrow $1000.

[May]   From [a private citizen of Washington]. Printed extract. Curtis, 1 : 348n. Writes that loss of confidence in the stability of office has stopped all investment in Washington real estate.

May   Account with Abraham G. Stevens for labor and supplies at Elms Farm, through March, 1830. AD. Allen G. Wright, San Anslemo, Calif. mDWs.

Nov 19   To James Barbour. ALS. ViU. mDWs. Explains his attendance at the New York Bar Association dinner for James Brown, despite his original intention not to go.

[Nov 23, 1829] To [Henry Willis Kinsman?]. ANS. NhD. mDWs. Advises him that "Mr [Jeremiah] Mason of Portsmo." has asked for printed forms of proxy, which DW will send as soon as they are ready, and asks "Is the *form* finally settled?"

Dec 5 To James William Paige. ALS. Mrs. Irvin McD. Garfield, Southboro, Mass. mDWs. Advises Paige how best to reach New York on Sunday the 12th (to be present at DW's marriage to Caroline Bayard Le Roy), and that he will keep the date and time open until he knows when Paige can arrive; mention's Caroline's desire to take Julia to Washington.

Dec 23 From Joseph H. Dorr to DW and Nathaniel Silsbee. ALS. DNA, RG 46. mDW 50101. Remonstrates against the confirmation of David Henshaw as collector of customs for Boston.

[1829?] From Abiel Holmes. ANS inscription. CtWat. mDW 38652. Presents his *Annals of America*.

1830

Jan 4 To Theodore Dwight, Jr. ALS. RPB–JH. mDWs. Thanks him "sincerely & fervently" for his interesting letter of Dec 30 concerning what is now passing "between certain cabinets"; assuring him "I shall not expose you, nor bring you into any difficulty," asks him to continue his inquiries; states "I lost all faith in Bolivar, years ago."

Jan 6 To [Henry Willis Kinsman]. AL fragment. NhD. mDWs. Discusses a financial matter, and a case that is coming on.

Jan 6 From Henry Clay. ALS. MBAt. mDWs. Congratulates DW on his recent marriage; has heard a rumor that he is moving to New York; is curious about political appointments.

[Jan, 1830] To Edward Everett. ALS. MHi. mDWs. Asks another favor—"I want the shape, as definitely as may be, in which he puts his right of State interference."

Feb 8 To William Sullivan. ALS. DLC. mDWs. In response to Sullivan's letter, says there is no danger of "any attempts to put me down, in that way . . . *it is too late*"; asserts "everything but *power*, and numbers, is on our side here"; describes the development of his debate with Hayne.

Feb 16 [1830] To [Henry Willis Kinsman]. ALS. NhD. mDWs. Asks him to attend to a financial matter involving "Messrs Peters & Pond"—"I cannot give ten days to the trial of a cause, without being paid for it."

March 3 To A. Wickham. ALS photocopy. NhD. mDWs. Complies with the request made in Wickham's letter of Feb 12 and sends good wishes to "the members of your Society."

April 15 To William Leete Stone. ALS. NHi. mDWs. Will answer Stone's "various, & interesting questions" when he sees him.

April 24 [1830] To Nathan Hale. ALS. MNS-S. mDWs. "The House is trying to impeach a judge. We are dreading it, as the trial may prolong the session."

[April 30] [1830?] To [Jabez Williams?] Huntington. ALS. NhD. mDWs. Invites him to go riding.

May 22 To [William Sullivan]. ALS. MHi. mDW 8829. Not to Amos Lawrence as published in *Correspondence*, 3: 72–73.

June 27   To Samuel Jones. ALS. Scottish Record Office. mDWs. Letter
    of introduction for Edward B. Emerson, who read law in DW's
    office.
July 31 [1830?]   To Samuel B. Walcott. ALS. MeHi. mDW 39284. Noti-
    fies Walcott that Fletcher will return to Harvard the first of the
    week, DW having sent him to Marshfield with his mother.
[Aug 11, 1830]   To Joseph Story. ALS. MHi. mDWs. Calendared in *Cor-
    respondence*, 3: 409 from printed text.
Aug 23   From Lemuel Shaw. ALS. NhExP. mDWs. Does not accede to
    the proposal DW made last evening.
Sept 1 [1830]   From John G. Palfrey. ALS. OClW. mDWs. Sends a pam-
    plet, and thanks DW for allowing him "to witness, under such fa-
    vourable circumstances, your management of the cause at Salem."
    Commonwealth v. *Knapp*, 10 Pickering 477.
Sept 27   To Jeremiah Smith. Abstract. NhExP. mDWs. Will send him
    the work done by his clerk on questions relevant to *Phillips Exeter
    Academy* v. *Exrs. of J. T. Gilman* as soon as the franking privilege
    recommences on Oct 5; his opinion (that the executors are liable)
    remains unchanged.
Sept   Opinions by DW on John Taylor Gilman's bond in *Phillips Exeter
    Academy* v. *Exrs. of J. T. Gilman*, copies recorded in Jeremiah
    Smith's notebook at p. 31 and pp. 41–48. NhExP. mDWs.
Oct 4   From William Plumer, Jr. ALS. Nh. mDWs. Asks to have books
    sent to him at Portsmouth; thinks things are "at the very worst" in
    New Hampshire and sees signs of a change for the better.
Nov 14   To Joseph Story. ALS. MHi. mDWs. Is worn down from "the
    toil & fatigue of New Bedford Court"; has written to "Mr Greene
    and "Mr Tillinghast" to ask to be excused from going to Providence,
    but names day later in the week when he could go if needed.
Dec 24   To Thomas Treadwell Davis. ALS. NCH. mDWs. Deems it an
    honor to have been elected to the Phoenix Society of Hamilton
    College.
[1830]   Notes by Justice John McLean on DW's arguments in five cases
    argued before the Supreme Court in the January term. AD. DLC.
    mDW 39398.
[1830?]   To Nathan Hale. ALS. NhD. mDWs. Writes Dorchester, en-
    closing something he has written that he would like to see published
    in the *Boston Patriot and Mercantile Advertiser*, or the *Daily Centinel
    and Gazette*; is leaving for Salem tomorrow.

1831

Jan 1   From William Jarvis. AL (incomplete). DNA, RG 76. mDWs.
    Discusses his claim against the Danish government for capture and
    detention in Norway in 1809; would like DW to be his agent and
    attorney.
Jan 3 [1831?]   To Nicholas Biddle. ALS. Biddle Family Papers, Anda-
    lusia. mDWs. Writes that "everyone approves the prudence & pro-
    priety" of Commodore James Biddle's conduct, but that "for the rest,
    time must show."
Jan 7   To Josiah Quincy. ALS. MHi. mDWs. Will comply with Quincy's
    suggestions; wants to keep Fletcher at Harvard "just so long, & no

longer, as he does his best"; encloses a letter; would like to distribute copies of Quincy's discourse in the west and south.

Jan 13   From Josiah Quincy. ALS. MHi. mDW 9130A. *Correspondence*, 3, Calendar: 414 as Jan 12.

Feb 18, 183[1]   From James McFarlane Mathews. ALS. DLC. mDW 16365 (as 1840). Invites DW to lecture at "the new University in this City" (New York University).

[March 8?, 1831]   To Richard Smith. ALS. NhD. mDWs. Sends him some papers and will see him later this morning "on the subject of the other little note."

April 20   Account with Abraham G. Stevens for expenses connected with Elms Farm, through Nov 4, 1831. AD (in Stevens's hand with added notes by DW). NhD. mDWs.

May 7   From Charles Otis. ALS. DNA, RG 76. mDWs. Inquires about his claim against the Danish government.

June 8 [1831?]   To Edward Everett. AD. MHi. mDWs. Invitation to dine.

Aug 25   To Robert Field Stockton. ALS. NjPHi. mDWs. Explains his position on the tariff; affirms the importance of the judiciary; does not see the dangers many see in the Federal government undertaking internal improvements; believes the country is in a crisis, but that he has no claim to be its savior. (See *Correspondence*, 3: 118–119 for DW's summary of this reply to Stockton's letter of August 19.)

Oct 26   From William Patterson. ALS. NhD. mDWs. Sends a retaining fee in case DW's services should be found necessary on behalf of the plaintiff in the case of *Baltimore & Ohio Railroad Company* v. *Chesapeake & Ohio Canal Company*.

[Dec 21, 1831]   To John L. Lawrence. AN. NHi. mDWs. Sends under cover a printed roll of the National Republican Convention at Baltimore Dec 12, 1831—"Consider the enclosed a Corresponding Committee."

Dec 23   To James William Paige. ALS. Mrs. Irvin McD. Garfield, Southboro, Mass. mDWs. Calendared in *Correspondence*, 3: 427 from printed text.

[c. Dec, 1831]   From John Marshall. ALS. MHi. mDWs. *Correspondence*, 1, Calendar: 416 as 1814–1835. Introduces Major [William] Duval, who attends Congress to represent the revolutionary claims of Virginia.

1832

Jan 20 [1832]   To Stephen White. ALS. Private owner, Massachusetts. mDWs. Published in *Correspondence*, 3: 142–143 from a typed copy with erroneous assumption about the final sentence, which correctly reads: "They are of no in[teres]t! except the report on the Mint." (President Jackson, Message on the Mint, January 16, 1832, *House Documents*, 22d Cong., 1st sess., Serial 217, No. 57.)

[Jan 22, 1832]   To James William Paige. ALS. Mrs. Irvin McD. Garfield, Southboro, Mass. mDWs. Asks him to send a pamphlet on Federal lands that DW needs for a case in which he is representing the city of Cincinnati; remarks on Nathan Appleton's speech in the House on [Thomas] Bouldin's tariff resolution.

Feb 22 Notes for a speech at a public dinner in honor of the centennial birthday of Washington. AD. COMC. mDWs.

March 10 To James William Paige. ALS. NhD. mDWs. Calendared in *Correspondence*, 3: 435 from printed text.

April 10 To Theodore Dwight. ALS. RPB–JH. mDWs. Responds to Dwight's letter of Apr 5, concurring with his general views of the Georgia case—*Worcester* v. *Georgia*, 6 Peters 515 (1832); states he is not "very sanguine, that, on a direct issue between Genl Jackson & the Constitution, the former would not carry the point."

May 10 From Salmon Portland Chase. ALS. NNC. mDWs. Asks DW to write an article to help get the new *Western Review* established; remarks on political and commercial sentiment in Cincinnati.

May 16 From Joseph Gales, Jr. (with DW's reply, May 16). ALS. NhD. mDWs. Asks for DW's opinion on printing "the great Edition of State Papers."

May 16 To Joseph Gales, Jr. (with Gales to DW, May 16). ALS. NhD. mDWs. Approves the printing of the state papers and recommends a large number of extra copies.

June 30 To James William Paige. ALS. Mrs. Irvin McD. Garfield, Southboro, Mass. mDWs. Speculates on Mrs. Webster's whereabouts; comments on the tariff and bank bills.

July 1 From Harrison Gray Otis. ALS. NhD. mDWs. Expresses a mostly favorable opinion of the tariff bill, and hopes DW will aid in its passage without further amendments.

Sept 12 To [Simon] Greenleaf. ALS. NhD. mDWs. Discusses "Mr. Allen's suit . . . agt. the Treasurer," and notes it might not be worth Allen's expense to retain him, since he has "no other call, this fall, to Maine."

[Sept 13, 1832?] To Harriette Story White Paige. ALS. MH–H. mDW 28091 (as 1847). Writes that Mrs. Webster's health is improving, and when she is strong enough they will set out for Cherry Hill; sends "all love to Miss P."

Sept 17 Promissory note to William Appleton for $1500. DS. NHi. mDWs.

Dec 18 To Nathaniel F. Williams from Henry Willis Kinsman, for DW. ALS. NhD. mDWs. Encloses draft for $1000.

[1832?] To Jared Sparks. ALS. MH–H. mDW 38869. Invites him to dinner with some other friends.

[1832?] To Abraham G. Stevens. ALS. NhD. mDWs. Calendared in *Correspondence*, 3: 449 from printed text.

1833

Jan 2 To William Cushing Aylwin. ALS. MHi. mDWs. Has heard nothing about "Mr Alsop's case"—*Alsop* v. *Commercial Insurance Company*, 1 Sumner 451 (1833)—since he left Boston.

Jan 5 From William Sullivan. ALS. NhD. mDWs. Since he supposes that "the Legis. of Mass. must express some opinion on National affairs," asks DW if he would "communicate the leading tenor" of such an address, or even the whole address.

Feb 27 [1833] To Richard Smith. ALS. NhD. mDWs. Sends three checks, and draws one.

Feb 28   From Nicholas Fish. AL copy. NNC. mDWs. Asks DW's help in obtaining a midshipman's warrant for his son, Petrus Stuyvesant Fish.

March 15   To Henry Willis Kinsman. ALS. NhD. mDWs. Asks Kinsman to distribute his speech on nullification.

March 27   To Louise D'Avezac Livingston. Printed. Louise Livingston Hunt, *Memoir of Mrs. Edward Livingston* (New York, 1886), pp. 104–105. Praises her brother's speech, and sends two of his own.

March 28 [1833]   To [Henry Willis Kinsman]. AL. NhD. mDWs. Is attending to professional business in New York; asks him to get in touch with a carpenter who is to put up certain buildings for DW; is sending an order on Kinsman "for some money, to Chs H. Thomas, of Marshfield," and if Thomas should present it, "I wish you to get the money, *in bills*, & pay it to him . . . & *say nothing about it, to any body*."

April 27   To Benjamin Franklin Perry. LS. A–Ar. mDWs. Published in *Correspondence*, 3: 246–247 from a typed copy.

May 30   To Joseph Story. ALS. MHi. mDWs. Writes from LeRoy, N.Y. "We have loitered along, until this present; but now, if I go further, I must spur up. I think I shall go to Ohio," but Stephen White will return from "the Falls" to look after his ships and goods.

June 10   From Lyne Sterling et al. Printed. *Ohio State Journal and Columbus Gazette*, June 15, 1833. mDWs. Invite DW to a public dinner at Columbus.

June 10   To Lyne Sterling et al. Printed. *Ohio Journal and Columbus Gazette*, June 15, 1833. mDWs. Declines their invitation.

[Aug 16, 1833?]   To Charles Henry Thomas. ALS. MHi. mDW 39037. Thinks of going to Marshfield on Sunday; plans to spend the next week in a "little lonely tour down the Cape."

Dec 14, [13, 1833]   To Robert Todd Lytle. LS. OCHP. mDWs. Has mistakenly asked Lytle to dine on Tuesday instead of Wednesday (see DW's invitation to Edward Everett, Dec [13], mDW 11220).

Dec 14   To [Henry Willis Kinsman]. ALS. NhD. mDWs. Comments on the French Claims commission; describes a difficulty in the case of the *Franklin*.

Dec 25   From Joseph Story. ALS. MHi. mDWs. Published in *Correspondence*, 3: 292–294 from printed text.

Dec 28   To Thomas Lyon Hamer. AN. CSmH. mDWs. Invites him to dinner on Tuesday.

Dec 30   From Thomas Lyon Hamer. AN. CSmH. Accepts DW's dinner invitation.

1834

Jan 15   To Henry Willis Kinsman. ALS. NhD. mDWs. Reports he is sending $1000 to Samuel Frothingham; also that "the Treasury has interfered, & corrected the instruction & construction respecting the *Cotton*," and that Virginia "is going for a restoration of the Deposits."

March 8   To James William Paige. ALS. Mrs. Irvin McD. Garfield, Southboro, Mass. mDWs. In response to Paige's letter of March 2, writes that he may give notice of "such a measure as you describe" when presenting the Massachusetts resolutions on Monday.

[March 21, 1834]   To Samuel Jaudon. ALS. NHi. mDW 14170. Reports that Calhoun has delivered his speech, and that he is against DW's bill to renew the charter of the Bank of the U.S. for six years, preferring twelve.

April 6 [1834]   To Sarah Goodridge. ALS. NhD. mDW 38390. Will call "to say something abt. your Masi debt."

April 24   From Thomas Brothers. Printed. *The Senator Unmasked . . .* (Philadelphia, 1834). mDWs. On DW's speech in the Senate asking leave to bring in a bill to continue for six years the charter of the Bank of the U.S.

[May 2, 1834]   To John Frazee (with Thomas Handasyd Perkins to Frazee, Apr 30, 1834). ANS. DSI. mDWs. Mabel Munson Swan, *The Athenaeum Gallery,* 1827–1873 (Boston Athenaeum, 1940), p. 146. Transmits Frazee's commission to sculpt a bust of John Marshall.

June 9   From James Kent. ALS. NhD. mDWs. Praises DW's speech on the president's protests of the Senate resolution censuring him for his actions in the Bank controversy.

June 16   To Benjamin Troppan Pickman. ALS. MHi. mDWs. Reports that "the silver coin bill" has been engrossed in the Senate and will be read a third time tomorrow; the bill on gold coins is in process in the House.

Aug 6 [1834]   To [Tristan] Burges. ALS. UkENL. mDW 38289 and mDWs. *Correspondence,* 5, Calendar as 1835–1843.

Aug 22   Opinion on an act by the Territory of Florida "to incorporate the subscribers to the Union Bank of Florida." Printed. *Executive Documents,* 26th Cong., 2d sess., Serial No. 385, Doc. No. 111, p. 277. mDWs.

[Dec 12, 1834?]   Opinion of James Kent, endorsed by DW, "that the Trenton and New Brunswick Turnpike Company may . . . lawfully construct and use a railway . . . upon their Turnpike Road." Reprint from the *New York Journal of Commerce* in an unidentified publication, without date. NhD. mDWs.

[Dec]   Declaration for the *Temperance Recorder.* DS. NjR. mDWs. Flyer bearing the printed signatures of James Madison, Andrew Jackson, and John Quincy Adams, with appended manuscript signatures of DW et al. (circulated from Albany, Nov 20, 1834).

1835

July 1   To [Joseph] Duncan. ALS. NhD. mDWS. Introduces Fisher Ames Harding, who is moving to Illinois.

Aug 5   To George Grennell, Jr. et al. LS. MDeeP. mDWs. Regrets he cannot give an address at a ceremony erecting a monument at the site of the massacre of Lathrop's Company by Indians under King Philip in 1675.

Sept 14   Bill of sale for stock and produce transferred to DW by Abraham G. Stevens, with DW's added memorandum of sale of same to John Taylor, Jr. AD (in DW's hand). NhD. mDWs.

Oct 14   From Edward Walcott. ALS. RPB–JH. mDWs. Asks DW to be attorney for the mill owners in their case against the Blackstone Canal Corporation—*Farnum* v. *Blackstone Canal Corporation,* U.S. Circuit Court, Rhode Island, November 1835.

Oct 16 [1835]   Opinion in *Farnum* v. *Blackstone Canal Corporation*. DS
(with corrections in DW's hand). RPB–JH. mDWs.

[Oct 26 1835?]   To Samuel Turell Armstrong. ALS. MHi. mDW 38199.
Hopes he has "no thought of declining your place at the head of our
Representative ticket."

[Oct 1835?]   To Donald Macleod. Printed. DLC. mDW 38708. Thanks
him for a copy of his discourse on elocution (delivered in Cincinnati
in Oct 1835).

[1835?]   To [Henry Willis Kinsman?]. ALS. NhD. mDWs. Instructs him
to have a confidential conversation with Abbott Lawrence, who is
"possessed of the pros and cons" of a land speculation, with view to
getting three or four friends to subscribe to shares.

[1835?]   Blank certificate for shares in the Massabesick Canal Company. DS. NhD. mDWs. Signed by DW as president.

1836

Jan 18   To David A. Hall. ALS. NHi. mDWs. Sends a copy of an acceptance by John Randall, Jr. of New Castle, Delaware of an order for
$1500 signed by Hall, which he asks Hall to cash, stating that he
will hold himself responsible for it.

[Feb 18, 1836?]   To Willie Person Mangum. ALS. NcD. mDW 38712.
Mangum Papers, 5: 454–455. Hopes to be able to go to the Senate
at one o'clock to hear the remainder of Mangum's speech (on the national debt?).

May 16   To George Blake. LS. OCHP. mDWs. Introduces General [Robert
T.] Lytle of Cincinnati, surveyor general of the U.S. for Ohio, who
is visiting Boston.

June 8 [1836]   To Samuel Upton. ALS. NhD. mDWs. Advises him to buy
federal lands in the West, especially in Wisconsin.

June 12   From John Catron. ALS. NhD. mDWs. Published in *Correspondence*, 4: 131–133 from printed text.

July 21   Opinion on an act concerning banks passed at the June session
of the Rhode Island General Assembly. DS. RPB–JCB. mDWs. Finds
"that several sections of the Act are inconsistent with the Constitution of the United States."

Aug 11   Opinion on the title of James Temple Bowdoin and his son to
certain estates in Massachusetts. ADS. NhD. mDW 13516.

Sept 9   Assignment to Merchants' Bank, Boston of his interest in "the
Land Company, of which Lewis Cass is, or was, President, & Henry
Hubbard is Treasurer," to secure to the bank the payment of two
bills of exchange, for $5000 each, dated in August, 1836 and ac-
cepted by William A. Bradley.

Sept 28   Agreement by DW to take stock in the Bank of the Metropolis
to the amount of $15,000; with endorsement dated Dec 28, 1836 re-
cording DW's payments and agreement by J. P. Van Ness to transfer
the stock to DW. AD. NHi. mDWs.

Dec 29   To John Peter Van Ness. ALS. NHi. mDWs. "If these papers are
found to be right, please sign what I have written on the original
agreement, & return that paper to me."

[1836]   From Peter Wilkins. Printed. *A Letter to Daniel Webster* (Boston, 1836). mDWs. Writes on DW's "pretensions to the presidency,"

finding nothing "in your private character, your public conduct, or your political associations . . . to entitle you to the vote of a democratic citizen."

1837

Jan 10   From James Kent. ALS. NhD. mDWs. Commends DW's speech on the Treasury circular.

[Feb 12? 1837]   To Joseph Story. Printed. William W. Story, ed., *Life and Letters of Joseph Story* (2 vols., Boston, 1851), 2: 269. Refers not to the Charles River Bridge case, but to Story's opinion in *Briscoe* v. *Bank of the Commonwealth of Kentucky.* In *Correspondence,* 4, Calendar: 459 as Feb 19.

Feb 27   To Albion K. Parris. Printed. *The Madisonian,* Washington, D.C., Jan 31, 1843. mDWs. Clarifies the matter of a bill passed last session for the relief of C. J. Catlett.

[Feb 1837]   To John Plummer Healy. AN. MHi. mDW 38631. Memorandum instructing Healy to tell [Ira] Wadleigh that his acceptance must be paid *"or else I shall withdraw my connexion with the controversy between him & S[amuel] Veazie."*

March 6   Note re "Col. Ebenr Webster's Bond" (bond not found). AN, with added ANS. MWalB. mDW 39835-129. See *Correspondence,* 6: 139, n.2.

March 13   To John Peter Van Ness. ALS. NHi. mDWs. Encloses papers which will "suffice to put our arrangement [transferring stock in the Bank of the Metropolis] into proper form."

March 23   From John Peter Van Ness (inscribed on DW to Van Ness, March 13). ANS. NHi. mDWs. Notes that he wrote informing DW "that our business was put in proper form as desired, and that Mr. [George] Thomas would promptly so advise him."

March 31   To George Thomas. ALS. American Security Bank, Washington, D.C. mDWs. Writes he has arrived in Boston to find that his acceptance of C[harles] S. Fowler's draft was not paid quite on time—"I never, in my life, met with such an *accident* before." See *Correspondence,* 4: 197n.

April 14   To Edward Augustus Le Roy. ALS. NHi. mDWs. Is "thunderstruck" by Levi C. Turner's failure to deposit the money; the failures in New York "have distressed us all here" (in Boston); has received three protests on notes and bills that were esteemed good a short time ago.

May 24   From Charles M. Thruston et al. Printed. *Louisville* (Ky.) *Daily Journal,* June 2, 1837. Invite DW to Louisville for a public barbecue in his honor.

May 27   To Charles M. Thruston et al. Printed. *Louisville Daily Journal,* June 2, 1837. Accepts their invitation to meet them in Louisville.

[Sep 26 1837?]   To Nathan Hale. ALS. MNS–S. mDWs. Thinks it time to "come out, with spirited & steady efforts, against the Van Buren policy [with respect to the currency]. This paper of the President's ought to be ably examined, & its weakness exposed."

Dec 12   Agreement with Roswell L. Colt for a $5000 loan in exchange for ten shares of DW's Clamorgan scrip as security. ADS. PHi. mDWs.

Dec 13   Check for $20 payable to George Thomas. DS. Mrs. Phyllis
Weiss, Oneida, N.Y. mDWs.

1838

Jan 3   To Robert Greenhow. ALS. Ronald von Klaussen, Dade County,
Florida. mDWs. Thanks him for a copy of his book (on the history
of Tripoli).

Jan 31   From John Davis (1787–1854). ALS. PHi. mDWs. Discusses the
impact of improvements in machinery upon cotton manufacturers
in the U.S., concluding that they must mechanize in order to com-
pete with the Europeans—"The more extensively *machinery* is made
by *machinery* the better."

Feb 12 [1838]   To Hiram Ketcham (with enclosures: Minutes from the
Journal of the House of Representatives on the compromise tariff
bill of 1833, mDW 14643; from the *Journal of the Senate* on same,
mDWs). ALS. CSmH. mDW 14640. Partially calendared in *Correspondence*, 4: 483 as Feb 12?.

[c. Feb 15, 1838]   To Hiram Ketchum. ALS. NhD. mDW 38668. Sends a
copy of a letter he has written to Richard Haughton "in answer to
one from him, which enclosed a letter from you," and asks Ketchum
to write Haugton with his suggestions.

Feb 24   To [Ruel] Williams. ALS. Biddle Family Papers, Andalusia, Pa.
mDWs. Reports that General [Winfield] Scott is about to depart for
the northeast frontier, and probably it is hoped that his "pacific
interposition . . . together with the *Boom* &c" may preserve the
peace.

May 11 [1838]   To Caleb Cushing from DW and Edward Curtis. Invitation in Caroline Le Roy's Webster hand. DLC. mDWs.

May 12   To [?] Blunt. ALS. William W. Layton Collection, Millwood, Va.
mDWs. States "this Memorial appears to be well hewn, & sufficient,"
and recommends omission of parts which might be thought "not
entirely respectful, in language."

June 4   To William Kelly et al. Printed. *Army and Navy Chronicle*, July
12, 1838, p. 30. mDWs. Thanks them for a cane carved from wood
taken from Commodore Perry's flagship, the *Lawrence*.

[c. June, 1838?]   To James Buchanan. ALS. NNC. mDW 38286. Introduces Charles S. Daveis, agent of the state of Maine.

Nov 15   From George Combe to Isaac P. Davis (with enclosure: Dr.
Combe's notes of DW's cerebral development, Nov 14, 1838). ALS
with ADS. MHi. mDWs (with ANS by Harriette Story White Paige,
Nov 20, 1854).

Dec 17   To James Thatcher. LS. MBCo. mDWs. Calendared in *Correspondence*, 4: 500 from a photocopy.

[Dec 26, 1838]   To John Forsyth. LS. DNA, RG 59. mDWs. Transmits a
letter from John Codman to Forsyth, concerning Francis Coffin's
claim against Spain for spoliations committed on the brig *Canton*.

1839

March 26 [1839?]   To Francis Calley Gray. ALS. OClWHi. mDW 38410.
Accepts a dinner invitation.

April 24 [1839]   To David Sears. ALS. MHi. mDWs. Thanks him for his
kind letter to Mr. Clay (Sir William Clay); intends to embark about
May 15.

April 27, [1839?]   To Charles Henry Thomas. ALS. MHi. mDW 39001.
Wants Seth Weston to build a root cutter and a potato splitter to
present to John Perkins Cushing, who has offered to breed some
of DW's cows to his bull; plans making a pit to force vegetables,
and a greenhouse—"All this is only to think about, if we ever get
over these hard times, and if I should not *settle* in Illinois."

May 6   From Milton & Slocomb. Printed. *Niles' National Register*, June
1, 1839, p. 211. mDWs. Present DW with a suit of clothes for his
trip to Europe.

May 6   Deed transferring DW's Summer Street property in Boston to
Peter Chardon Brooks for $32,500. Copy. Registry of Deeds, Suffolk
County, Massachusetts. mDWs.

May 7   To Milton & Slocomb. Printed. *Niles National Register*, June 1,
1839, p. 211. mDWs. Thanks them for their present of a suit of
clothes.

May 28   To James William Paige from Harriette Story White Paige,
with postscript by DW. ALS with ANS. MHi. mDWs. Their ocean
voyage fully described by Harriette, with "a word of love & remembrance" by DW—"We are . . . expecting to debark tomorrow
morning."

June 3   To John Pollock. Printed. *Niles' National Register*, July 6, 1839,
p. 294. mDWs. Commends the Liverpool Steam Ship Company for
the quality of its transatlantic service.

June 26   From [Angelina Georgina Burdett-] Coutts. AD. NNC. mDWs.
Invitation.

[July 8]   From John Kenyon. ALS. NNC. mDWs. Asks DW to go with
him to look at a carriage, and discusses their itinerary.

[July 11]   To Samuel Starkweather. ALS. NHi. mDWs. Makes arrangements to meet him in London.

July 27   To John H. Tredgold. ALS. NBu. mDWs. Acknowledges Tredgold's communications; will see him at the end of August when he
returns to London.

Oct 13/16   To [James William Paige]. ALS. Mrs. Irvin McD. Garfield,
Southboro, Mass. mDWs. Gives itinerary of Mrs. Webster and Mrs.
Paige in their travels on the continent; reports Jaudon's efforts in
London on behalf of the Bank of the United States and comments on
financial relations between the two countries.

Nov 8   Transfer of stock worth $15,000 by John P. Van Ness to Richard
Smith in trust for DW. Copy. NHi. mDWs.

Nov 18   To [Virgil Maxcy]. ALS. MHi. mDWs. Has arranged for Maxcy
to receive scrip to sell if he can find a purchaser.

[1839]   To Nicholas Biddle. AN (probably separated from an ALS).
DLC. mDWs. *Correspondence*, 5, Calendar: 348 as 1840?.

[1839–1841?]   To [Moses Hicks?] Grinnell. ALS. DLC. mDWs. "I have
quite an occasion to see you, this morning."

1840

March 4 [1840]   To John Plummer Healy (enclosed with DW to Sarah

Goodridge, Mar 4 [1840]. ALS. MHi. mDW 38554. Asks him to attend to "some troublesome law business" for Sarah Goodridge.

March 24   To Sir Henry Halford. ALS. Mr. and Mrs. T.G.M. Brooks,
Wistow Hall, Leicestershire, England. mDWs. Renews his expressions of sympathy over the death of Sir Henry's brother, Sir
John Vaughan, and sends Judge Story's condolences; tells of his return voyage; notes that Congress is in session and that "our financial affairs are dreadfully deranged."

[c. April 1, 1840]   To [Emeline C. Webster Lindsly]. ALS. DLC. mDW
39187. Is grateful to hear that her daughter Harriet is recovering
from an illness.

[April 17, 1840?]   To Charles Henry Thomas. ALS. MHi. mDW 39016.
Gives directions for fixing a boat.

May 10   From Jospeh Story. ALS. MHi. mDWs. Calendared in Correspondence, 5: 336 and published in Legal Papers, 2: 300–301 from
printed text.

June 20   To N. Quincy Tirrell. ALS. ViW. mDWs. Complies with Tirrell's wishes expressed in his letter of June 14, "not having made
any selections on the subject"; will send Tirrell's letter to Dr.
[Thomas] Sewall.

July 16   To David Sears. ALS. MHi. mDWs. Cannot now go to Philadelphia, but will go on the shortest notice "if there is to be a serious
trial there."

Nov 6   To [Samuel Bulkley] Ruggles. ALS. NhD. mDWs. Asks him to
send a fee; is "half frighted, abt. N. York; two thirds ditto, abt. Va."

1841

Feb. 3   To Issac P. Davis. ALS. CSmH. mDWs. Suggests names of a
few prominent persons who should sign a paper "expressing their
opinion of your fitness for the office of Naval officer."

March 11   From William Cabell Rives. ALS. NHi. mDWs. Letter of
recommendation for Samuel Starkweather of New York, who seeks
a diplomatic appointment.

[March 12, 1841]   To [Solomon Lincoln]. ALS. NhHi. mDW 39303. Informs him that he will receive his commission by this mail or the
next, and will immediately enter into the duties of his office—"A
Collector [Levi Lincoln] will be appointed by the 1st of April."

March 12   From James Turner Morehead. ALS. NHi. mDWs. Letter of
of recommendation for Samuel Starkweather.

March 13   To Solomon Lincoln. ALS. New England Merchants National
Bank, Boston. mDWs. Sends Lincoln his commission as a U.S.
marshal.

April 2   To [Hugh Swinton Legaré]. LS. Private owner, Massachusetts.
mDWs. Asks for lists of persons employed in his department for
publication in the Biennial Register.

April 8   From John Woodworth. ALS. NHi. mDWs. Letter of recommendation for Samuel Starkweather.

May 19   from James N. Reynolds. ALS. ViU. mDWs. Letter of recommendation for Aaron B. Quinby of New York who seeks appointment
as an examiner in the patent office.

May 26   To Benjamin Chew. LS. PHi. mDWs. Reports that the state department has accepted the request of Chew's son, William W. Chew, to be recalled as secretary of the legation at St. Petersburg.

May 31 [1841]   From Francis Ormand Jonathan Smith. ALS copy. MeHi. mDW 38847. Declines DW's proposal that he join the northeast boundary investigating committee at New York; has devoted much time to national affairs in the past three years and wants now to give precedence to his private and personal engagements.

June 15   To Thomas Walker Gilmer. ALS. ViU. mDWs. Believes he will be able to "funish the information required in your friend's letter by Saturday."

June 18   To Thomas Walker Gilmer. LS. ViU. mDWs. Encloses a statement from the census returns, as requested by Gilmer on behalf of a friend.

June 14   From John J. Abert and Peter Force. LS. DSI. mDWs. In reply to DW's letter of June 14, submit statements and remarks on the scientific collections under the care of the National (Smithsonian) Institution.

June 26   From Nicholas Biddle. ALS. Biddle Family Papers, Andalusia, Pa. mDWs. Asks for consideration of Thomas Willing's application (to be consul in Paris), since the "Citizen King . . . declines receiving Mr [Lorenzo] Draper"; asks "What is the matter at Washington?"

June 30   To John Tyler. LS. CSmH. mDWs. Recommends appointment of Demas Adams as marshal for Ohio and states his reasons.

July 14   From Isaac Dashiel Jones. ALS. ViU. mDWs. Letter of recommendation for Aaron B. Quinby.

Aug 27 [1841]   To [Samuel Bulkley] Ruggles. AD (in another hand). NhD. mDW 38820. Invitation

[Sept 13, 1841]   To Willie Person Mangum. ALS. NcD. mDW 38710. Shanks. *Mangum Papers*, 5: 452. "No man could be more unjustly attacked—no man could repel an attack better" (in reference to remarks by Calhoun).

Sept 20   To Thurlow Weed. AL. NhD. mDW 39286. Thurlow Weed Barnes, *Memoir of Thurlow Weed* (Boston, 1884), pp. 95–96. Writes "These violent proceedings will ruin us, most unnecessarily"; discusses appointments; asks "Pray, have people lost all their senses?" The signed note to [?] published in *Correspondence*, 5: 158 is possibly an addendum to this letter.

Sept 22 [1841?]   To [Edward Curtis?]. ALS. NN. mDW 39290. "Appointments will be immediately made for Utica & Oswego"; will be "in N.Y. 28th inst.—of which say nothing."

Oct 29   To [Robert] Wash. ALS. NhD. mDWs. Introduces Theodore B. Cunningham of Massachusetts, who proposes to visit St. Louis.

Nov 19   Order to pay $1000 to Henry Hubbard on Jan 1, 1842. DS. New England Merchants National Bank, Boston. mDWs.

[1841]   To Sarah Goodridge. ALS. MHi. mDW 38398. Asks if he can be of help in finding suitable rooms for her in Washington, since Mr. Masi is unable to accommodate her.

[1841?]   To [?]. ALS. NhD. mDW 39307. Notes that "Mr [Levi] Lincoln has consented to provide some little thing for Mr [Timonthy] Fletcher," and asks if he can give "a clerkship of a thousand Dollars."

[1841]   Memoranda of testimonials in favor of John A. Tardy of New

York for office of consul at Havre. AD. DNA, RG 59. mDWs. List includes letters (not found) to DW from: Luther Bradish, John C. Spencer, Simeon Draper, Mordecai M. Noah, Christopher Morgan, P. R. Shelton, John S. Ellery, Thomas Handasyd Perkins, William Cost Johnson, and Lewis Cass.

[1841 1842?] From John Jordan Crittenden. ALS. RP. mDW 38310. Forwards a recommendation of "Mr Green" for an appointment "belonging to your Department."

1842

Feb 1 [1842] From Harrison Gray Otis. ALS. DLC. mDW 17399. Not Feb 1, 1841 as in *Correspondence*, 5, Calendar: 351.

March 10 To Jabez Williams Huntington. LS. NCH. mDWs. Sends the recommendations upon which Thomas Carlile, Samuel Haight, and John F. Mullowny were nominated to the Senate.

Apri 12 From David Sears. ALS. MHi. mDWs. Proposes preliminary actions that can be taken to head off the brewing Dorr rebellion in Rhode Island.

April 16 To David Sears. ALS. MHi. mDWs. Calendared in *Correspondence*, 5: 459 from printed text.

April 27 To David Lowry Swain. LS. Nc–Ar. mDWs. *Correspondence*, 5, Calendar: 523 as April 27, 1843 to D. "S." Swain.

April 29 To Isaac Chapman Bates. LS. NjMD. mDWs. Sends a passport for "Mr Salisbury."

April 30 [1842?] To Roswell L. Colt. AN. PHi. mDWs. Dinner invitation.

May 7 To John Quincy Adams. LS. MHi. mDW 22406. Not from him as in *Correspondence*, 5, Calendar: 463.

[May 10, 1842?] To Harrison Gray Otis. ALS. MHi. mDW 21012. Not Feb 2, 1841 as in *Correspondence*, 5, Calendar: 351.

Aug 23 To Peter Hotz. LS. NhExP. mDWs. Asks him to draw up and submit a memorial to press his claim against the Mexican government.

Nov 5 Declaration re land in Lincoln County, Missouri conveyed by Charles Collins to Edward H. Nichols in trust for DW. Copy. Nhi. mDWs.

Nov 10 To Mrs. Jeremiah Smith. ALS. NhD. mDWs. Is flattered at her request to write an inscription for Judge Smith—"Would that an impression of his virtues & talents, fresh & deep as that which exists in my own heart, could be made immortal in stone!"

[c. Dec 5, 1842?] To [Harriette Story White Paige.] ALS (incomplete). Mrs. Irvin McD. Garfield, Southboro, Mass. mDWs. Will do all he can for George Paige, including going to the secretary of war if "the Bill now pending should pass."

Dec 9 [1842?] To [Seth Weston]. ALS. NhHi. mDW 39208. Writes of farming matters: apples, oxen, kelp.

Dec 31 To John Lorimer Graham. AN. CSmH. mDWs. Dinner invitation.

1843

Jan 11 To Francis Ormand Jonathan Smith. Printed. *Reports of Committees*, 28th Cong., 1st sess., Serial 446, No. 474, May 15, 1844,

p. 52. mDWs. Recalls cases mentioned by Smith and states that when Congress "remits forfeitures by *special laws*, it has always appeared to me to be just that the rights of individuals, as informers, having already attached, should be protected."

Jan 16 [1843?]   To William Winston Seaton. ALS. DLC. mDWs. An unexpected call of public business has compelled him to postpone for a day or two "what I intended to have sent you this morning."

March 27 [1843?]   To Elisha Whittlesey. ALS. OClWHi. mDW 39228. Invites him to dine on Wednesday.

April 5 [1843?]   To [Seth Weston]. ALS. NhHi. mDW 39219. Writes that a storm may keep him in New York a day or two longer.

April 9 [1843?]   To [Edward Curtis?] ALS. NN. mDW 39280. Is glad "the Genl. [Samuel P. Lyman?] is so gracious"; thinks the despatch "will stand" and wants it to circulate.

May 3   To David Sears et al. LS. MHi. mDWs. Published in *Correspondence*, 5: 301–302 from printed text.

May 6   To Henry Ledyard. LS. RPB-JH. mDWs. Introduces James H. Behan of Norfolk, Va. who is about to visit Europe.

Oct 2   To John Peter Van Ness from Richard Smith. ALS. NHi. mDWs. Informs him that he, Lewis Johnson, and John F. Maury were appointed a committee to confer with DW about his debt and that DW will visit the bank (Bank of the Metropolis) tomorrow morning.

[Nov–Dec, 1843?]   To Moses Stuart. Printed. *PC*, 2: 111. Expresses warm thanks for Stuart's defense of his speeches; is gratified that Stuart "comprehends perfectly my opinion of what oratory should be, and the purpose by which I am governed in making public addresses."

Dec 4   Promissory note from Rufus Choate for $500. DS. New England Merchants National Bank, Boston. mDWs.

Dec 18   To David Sears. ALS. MHi. mDWs. Calendared in *Correspondence*, 5: 533 from printed text.

1844

Jan 1   From Joseph A. S. Ackeen, addressed to DW as secretary of state (enclosure: presentment of the Grand Jury of the Middle District of Alabama, Fall Term, 1843). ALS. DNA, RG 59. mDWs. Sends the request of the grand jurors of the middle district of Alabama for money to build a courthouse.

Feb 19 [1844]   To Samuel Finley Vinton. ALS. DNA, RG 233. mDWs Carl B. Swisher, *History of the Supreme Court of the United States: The Taney Period 1836–64* (New York and London, 1974), p. 431 extract). Discusses a bill (reported by the Committee on the Judiciary on May 24, 1844) extending the jurisdiction of the district courts to certain admiralty cases; supposes the provision for trial by jury "may save this Bill from Constitutional objection."

1845

Aug 13   To Edward Curtis. Printed. *PC*, 2: 210–212. Not from him as in *Correspondence*, 6, Calendar: 383.

[1845–1847]   To George Ticknor. ALS. CU–S. mDWs. Wants to introduce Ticknor to George Hooker Colton, editor of the *American Whig*

Review, who "wishes some advice &c—about pictures, &c—for a print of me."

1846

Jan 16 [1846]   To Franklin Haven. ALS. MH H. mDW 26071. *Correspondence,* 6, Calendar: 375 as Jan 16, 1845 (DW's error).

Feb 14   To [?]. ALS. CSmH. Discusses a mortgage for "Mr Taylor"; is inclined to have the two oxen disposed of; wants salt beef and salt pork sent to him—"Speak to Porter [Charles Porter Wright] and Henry [Charles Henry Thomas] about these matters"; concludes "I cannot well go home till the Court rises; & till we know how the Oregon business is coming out."

Feb 20 [1846]   To William Winston Seaton. Copy. DLC. mDWs. States that the leading paragraph in this morning's *National Intelligencer* (on the Oregon debate) is "indicative of the general sentiment of the Senate" but that no final measure on the subject of notice will be adopted "till the course which England may adopt . . . shall be fully known here."

July 18   Deed to Richard Smith, in trust for the Bank of the Metropolis, of lands in Missouri and Arkansas previously conveyed to Smith by Edward H. Nichols and by John Wilson and his wife. DS. American Security Bank, Washington. mDWs.

Nov 16   To Roswell L. Colt. ALS. Phi. mDWs. Informs him he will give a speech in Philadelphia on Dec 3; asks Colt for his thoughts on how "the present Tariff, or the late reduction of Duties, acts injuriously on the labor & industry of the Country."

[1846?]   Inscription for Aaron Foster's "Book of Peace." Printed. Undated clipping (1852) from the *Congregational Journal,* Concord, N.H. NhD. mDWs. Supports the goals of the American Peace Society.

1847

Feb 10   Circular letter (to mayors and other personages of Boston, New York, Philadelphia, and New Orleans) regarding relief of the poor in Ireland. AD draft. NhD. mDWs. See *Correspondence,* 6: 415 for Feb 10, 1847 to Moses Hicks Grinnell et al. calendared from printed text.

March 6 [1847]   From John Mandeville Carlisle. LS. DLC. mDW 36162. Discusses his interest in the case of the *Macedonian.*

March 19   Agreement with Paul Jennings regarding DW's purchase of Jennings's freedom. ADS photocopy. DHU. mDWs.

April 5   To [Aaron Fyfe] Perry. Copy. NhHi. mDW 27800. Not to Benjamin Franklin Perry as in *Correspondence,* 6, Calendar: 420 and Van Tyne, p. 356.

Dec 14   To George Nixon Briggs. ALS. WMUW. mDWs. Asks Briggs to appoint Henry Willis Kinsman adjutant general of Massachusetts.

1848

Feb 16 [1848]   To [Benjamin Smith?] Rotch. LS. MHi. mDWs. Invites him for dinner tomorrow.

Feb 19 [1848]   To [Benjamin Smith?] Rotch. LS. MHi. mDWs. Invites
    him to "take a chance with us" fishing.
June 10   To [Aaron Fyfe] Perry. Printed. *PC*, 2: 279. mDWs. Not to
    "Benjamin Franklin" Perry as in *Correspondence*, 6, Calendar: 440.
Oct 29 [1848?]   To James Savage (under cover to Jonathan Mason War-
    ren). LS. MHi. mDW 28879. Asks the librarian of the Massachusetts
    Historical Society to make books available to Dr. Warren. *Corre-
    spondence*, 5, Calendar 445 as to Joseph B. Felt.
[June, 1848?]   To John Fiennes Crampton (enclosed with Crampton to
    Abbott Lawrence, same day). ALS. MHi. mDWs. Asks to borrow a
    copy of the London *Times* so he can follow the debate on the resolu-
    tion by Henry Labouchere (president of the Board of Trade) to re-
    move the restrictions on free trade with England and her colonies.

1849

Feb 22   To [Aaron Fyfe] Perry. Copy. NhHi. mDW 29094. Not to Ben-
    jamin Franklin Perry as in *Correspondence*, 6, Calendar: 453.
[Feb 23, 1849?]   To Mr. and Mrs. Edward Curtis. Printed. *PC*, 2: 311.
    Correspondence, 6, Calendar: 456 as March 24.

Undated

To [?] Washington, July 8. ALS. Private owner, Massachusetts. mDWs.
    Warns that the party of the administration "will make a desperate
    attempt in *Maine* . . . I hope your Press will do its duty, with *judg-
    ment* as well as *spirit*."
To Col. Davis. Thursday morning, September 20. ALS. MPlPS. mDWs.
    Would be glad to have him "& the Ladies" pay a visit to Marshfield
    over the weekend.
To Edward Everett. Copy. NhHi. mDW 38366. Asks if Everett can re-
    mind him of an incident where he was handed a note while speak-
    ing in Washington on the subject of the Massachusetts (militia)
    claim, the import of which was "that in the case of South Carolina,
    the President had sanctioned the principle of our interest bill"; con-
    gratulates him on his address—"I think it your best political paper.."
To [?]   Gray. Wednesday morning. ALS. MBAt. mDWs. Will see him "if
    agreeable to you, at my office, at 11 oclock, today."
To Publishers of the (New York) *Commercial Advertiser*. May 16
    [1832?]. AL. MHi. mDW 26360. Desires his paper "now to be sent
    to *Marshfield*, Mass instead of Boston"; sends "friendly remem-
    brances to Mr [Francis] Hall." In *Correspondence*, 6, Calendar: 382
    as May 16, 1845 in error as to addressee and identification of news-
    paper.
To Josiah Quincy. Wednesday morning. ALS. MHi. mDWs. Has not yet
    spoken to "Mr Johnstone on the subject of your letter of yesterday";
    will not be able to visit him on Saturday because he will be on his
    way to a court engagement in Plymouth.
To William Winston Seaton. ALS. DLC. mDWs. Thanks him for sum-
    mer ducks and a woodcock. Calendared in *Correspondence*, 6: 485
    from printed text, mistakenly combined with a separate note to
    Seaton.

To William Winston Seaton. Printed. Josephine Seaton, *William Winston Seaton: A Biographical Sketch* (Boston, 1871), p. 303. Describes how Monica cooks Tautog fish. Mistakenly combined with above note in *Correspondence* 6, Calendar: 485.

To Joseph Story. Tuesday [1816–1829]. ALS. MHi. mDWs. Writes to him at Salem: "We have obtained very good seats [for the play], & expect you and Mrs. S. tomorrow."

To Joseph Story. Wednesday, 1 oclock. ALS. MHi. mDWs. Is about to depart for the south, and writes to say good-bye; "If you have time I hope you will call on my wife as you come along. God bless you."

To Joseph Story. ANS. MHi. mDWs. "Good bye, my Dear Judge—I beg of you to call & see my wife & children & tell them I am well & flourishing. God preserve you."

To Joseph Story. [1829–1845]. ANS. MHi. mDWs. Points out two inaccuracies of expression on a page of Story's *Commentaries*.

To Joseph Story. Nov 27. ALS. MHi. mDWs. Begs for loan of as many volumes as Story has of Barnewell & Alderson's (English King's Bench) reports: "I want to prepare myself for the battle tomorrow."

To Joseph Story. ALS. MHi. mDWs. "If Congress shall pass no law for Hogan's case, & like cases, what do you say to providing for such cases by Treaty?. . . . Suppose you draw a short Act."

To Joseph Story. p/m Aug 23 [1843?]. ANS MHi. mDWs. Asks Story to call on him at Summer Street if he comes to town "today (Wednesday) or tomorrow, or next day"; adds: "I have no letters of Mr Wirts."

To Joseph Story. Friday, 4 oclock. ALS. MHi. mDWs. Wants to see him tonight or early tomorrow on an important matter.

To Joseph Story. Tuesday morning. ALS. MHi. mDWs. Has come up from Marshfield and expects "Mr Goldsboro's company, at dinner, today" with others: "You will do me a *particular* favor, not to be forgotten, if you will join us."

To Joseph Story. Wednesday 11 oclock. ALS. MHi. mDWs. Has made arrangements "to go off on *friday*—via Northhampton"; adds "I am in the Printer's hands."

To [Stephen White]. [1832?] Monday mornnig. ALS. NhD. mDWs. Calendared in *Correspondence*, 6: 492 from a typed copy.

Bill from Abraham G. Stevens—$2.50 for 1000 bricks delivered to Samuel George. ADS. NhD. mDW 40556, 40558.

Index

The following abbreviations are used: DW, Daniel Webster; DFW, Daniel Fletcher Webster. Page-entry numbers between 379 and 627 refer to material in the Calendar. Numbers set in boldface type indicate pages where individuals are identified. Individuals identified in the *Dictionary of American Biography* are denoted by an asterisk immediately following the name. Those identified in the *Biographical Directory of the American Congress* are denoted by a dagger.

LIBRARY OF CONGRESS CATALOGING IN PUBLICATION DATA

(Revised for vol. 7)

Webster, Daniel, 1782–1852.
  The papers of Daniel Webster.
  Includes indexes.
  Contents: ser. 1. Correspondence: v. 1, 1798–1824.—
v. 2, 1825–1829. [etc.] v. 7, 1850–1852.
  1. United States—History—1801–1809; Collected
works. 2. United States—History—1809–1817—Collected
works. 3. United States—History—1815–1861—Collected
works. 4. Webster, Daniel, 1782–1852. I. Wiltse,
Charles Maurice, 1907–   . II. Moser, Harold D.
III. Dartmouth College. IV. Title. V. Series.

E337.8.W373   973.5′092′4   73-92705
ISBN 0–87451–096–1 (ser. 1, v. 1)